D1733116

INTERNATIONAL SERIES OF MONOGRAPHS IN

ELECTRICAL ENGINEERING

GENERAL EDITOR: D. J. SILVERLEAF

EXECUTIVE EDITOR: W. T. NORRIS

VOLUME 7

COMPUTER TECHNIQUES FOR ELECTROMAGNETICS

OTHER TITLES IN THE SERIES IN ELECTRICAL ENGINEERING

COMPUTER TECHNIQUES
FOR
ELECTROMAGNETICS

EDITED BY

R. MITTRA
University of Illinois, Urbana, Illinois

1973

PERGAMON PRESS
OXFORD · NEW YORK · TORONTO
SYDNEY · BRAUNSCHWEIG

Pergamon Press Ltd., Headington Hill Hall, Oxford

Pergamon Press Inc., Maxwell House, Fairview Park, Elmsford, New York 10523

Pergamon of Canada Ltd., 207 Queen's Quay West, Toronto 1

Pergamon Press (Aust.) Pty. Ltd., 19a Boundary Street, Rushcutters Bay, N.S.W. 2011, Australia

Vieweg & Sohn GmbH, Burgplatz 1, Braunschweig

First edition 1973

Library of Congress Cataloging in Publication Data

Mittra, Raj.
Computer techniques for electromagnetics.

(International series of monographs in electrical engineering, v. 7)

Bibliography: p.
1. Electronic data processing—Antennas (Electronics)
2. Electronic data processing—Wave guides
3. Electronic data processing—Electromagnetic field.

I. Title.

TK 7871.6.M58   1973   621.381′028′54   72–10079
ISBN 0–08–016888–4

Printed in Germany

Contents

4. INTEGRAL EQUATION SOLUTIONS OF THREE-DIMENSIONAL SCATTERING PROBLEMS *by* A. J. POGGIO *and* E. K. MILLER

5. VARIATIONAL AND ITERATIVE METHODS FOR WAVEGUIDES AND ARRAYS *by* C. P. WU

Preface

COMPUTER Electromagnetics is a relatively new and rapidly growing field. Yet, to date most of the publications on the subject have appeared only in technical journals or reports, some of which are not readily accessible. It is hoped that this book will serve to fill the existing need for a comprehensive text on the subject of computer techniques for solving a wide class of practical problems in applied electromagnetics, e.g. calculation of current distribution on antennas; computation of radar scattering from conducting or dielectric bodies; evaluation of discontinuity effects in waveguides and arrays; numerical reconstruction of wavefronts and aperture fields; and so on.

The manuscript is an outgrowth of a text originally prepared for a seminar series on the same topic offered at the University of Illinois on October 1970. Each of the seminar speakers for the course was asked to provide written notes describing the content of his lecture. These were later edited and put together in the form of the present text. The short course was repeated in 1971, with only a slight change in the contents, at Copenhagen under the auspices of the Technical University of Denmark and the Danish Engineering Society. The notes were well received on both of these occasions and provided encouragement to the authors for completing the monumental task of revising, proofing and editing their contributions.

During the course of the preparation of the manuscript the authors have received encouragement and moral support from many individuals and organizations, too numerous to list here on individual basis. Nevertheless, the authors would like to take this opportunity to thank their colleagues for the generous help and suggestions they have received that have undoubtedly left indelible marks on the text and have served to improve it.

The editor (R. M.) would like gratefully to acknowledge collaboration he has received from his co-authors, even through the periods of disappointing delays that severely taxed their patience.

The manuscript was very ably reviewed for the publisher by Professor Alex Cullen of University College, London. His comments and criticisms on the script were most welcome and have helped to unify the presentation and to improve the contents of the book.

The final editing of the book was carried out during a sabbatical leave of absence from the University of Illinois when the editor (R. M.) was at the Technical University of Denmark, Lyngby, Denmark. He is particularly grateful to Professor H. L. Knudsen, Head of Laboratory for Electromagnetic Theory, for the facilities and support provided him during the six-month period of 1971–2. Needless to say, the bulk of the editing work and the writing of Chapters 6 and 7 of the book were carried out at the University of Illinois and it is a pleasure to acknowledge the support of the Electrical Engineering Department received during the years 1970–2.

University of Illinois   RAJ MITTRA
Urbana, Illinois

CHAPTER 1

A Brief Preview

R. MITTRA

CLASSICALLY, the solutions of boundary value problems associated with electromagnetic radiation and scattering phenomena were based upon analytical techniques that attempted to generate closed-form solutions expressible in terms of known functions. Since such solutions were possible only for a limited class of problems, one often aimed at what was regarded as the next best thing—finding approximate solutions, typically in series forms, that required a minimum amount of numerical computation. However, the advent of high-speed computers has opened up new vistas in the study of electromagnetics and has made it practicable successfully to attack a wide variety of problems which were previously considered to be totally beyond the scope of analytical techniques.

Of the many approaches available for the formulation of the electromagnetic radiation and scattering problems, the integral equation method appears to be the one most conveniently adaptable to computer solution. We mention here for the sake of historical interest that Maxwell (1879) himself attempted to solve the problem of computing the capacitance of a rectangular plate by using an approximate technique, known as the method of subareas, to derive a numerical solution of the associated integral equation.

Needless to say, a large number of mathematical analysts have devoted their attention to the general topic of integral equation techniques. The reader is referred to excellent works by Lovitt (1950), Kellog (1953), Morse and Feshbach (1953), Mikhlin (1957), Tricomi (1957), Smithies (1958) and several recent works on the exposition on integral equations. Discussion of numerical solution of integral equations may be found in Hildebrand and Crout (1941), Crout (1946), Young (1954), Kantorovich and Krylov (1964), Noble (1966) and in the work by Walther and Dejon (1960), where an excellent bibliography is given pertaining to the numerical aspects of solution of integral equations. The list presented above is rather sketchy since no attempt is being made here to include a compendium of references on the subject of integral equations. Nevertheless, we would be totally remiss if we were to omit a reference to the work by Harrington (1968), who was the first to publish the now classic text on the moment method of solution of integral equations arising in electromagnetic theory.

Most of the discussions of computer solution of radiation and scattering problems presented in this text is based upon the integral equation formulation. This includes Chapter 2

1

on wire antennas, Chapter 3 and Chapter 4 on scattering, Chapter 5 on waveguide discontinuities and portions of Chapter 7 on inverse scattering. For the methods discussed in Chapter 6 it is convenient to work directly with the mode-matching approach, which represents an alternative to the integral equation formulation. Finally, several of the inverse problems dealt with in Chapter 7 do not lend themselves to integral equation formulation and special steps are required to handle them. Nevertheless, the formulation of an overwhelming number of problems dealt with in this text is based on the integral equation approach.

Consider, for instance, the problem of determining the current distribution in an antenna which is energized by a specified source. This problem can be readily formulated in terms of an inhomogeneous integral equation. Until the advent of the computers such a formulation was often academic, but now the integral equation can be solved using the computer by first transforming it into a matrix equation. The solution for the current distribution on the antenna, the input impedance and the radiation pattern, etc., may all be computed from the knowledge of the numerical solution of the integral equation. In contrast to this approach, the techniques for solution of the same problem in the pre-computer era depended mainly on manipulations based upon the variational methods, perturbation techniques, asymptotic and approximate methods and so on. Though these techniques are often very efficient in generating good approximate solutions for the single, straight-wire antenna problem, they are seldom capable of yielding results that have the desired accuracy when applied to curved-wire antennas, antennas mounted in the vicinity of other structures, or when one is dealing with an array type of configuration. In contrast, the computer techniques can, in principle, extract a solution with an arbitrary degree of accuracy for all of the problems mentioned above.

Let us turn now to the scattering problems. The general remarks made above in connection with the wire antenna problem applies equally well to the scattering problems dealt with in this text with one important exception. Even with today's large computers, it is not possible to handle matrix sizes much beyond 200 × 200. This in turn limits the size of the scatterer in terms of the wavelength of the illuminating field that can be solved on the computer. The current approach to the solution of scattering by electrically large scatterers is based upon asymptotic techniques such as ray optical or physical optics methods. However, some progress has recently been reported toward computer solution of integral equations for a class of large scatterers (see Mittra and Li, 1972) though much work still remains to be done in this direction.

There are a number of approaches available to the numerical analyst for reducing the integral equation to a matrix equation for computer processing. Many of these may be grouped under the title of the "moment method". There are a number of variants of the technique that differ in numerical detail, as illustrated in the Chapters 2, 4 and 5.

An integral equation may be written symbolically as

$$Lf = g$$

where L is an integral operator, g the known function and f the unknown. This equation may be transformed into a matrix equation by expanding the unknown in terms of a set of basis functions ϕ_n, e.g.

$$f = \sum_{n=1}^{N} C_n \phi_n$$

where C_n are the unknown expansion coefficients. The matrix equation in the moment method of solution has the general form

$$\sum_{m=1}^{N} C_m \langle \chi_m, L\phi_n \rangle = \langle g, \chi_m \rangle$$

where $\langle \ \rangle$ indicates a suitably defined scalar product and χ_m are the so-called testing functions. Examples of different choices for the functions ϕ_n and χ_m are illustrated in Chapters 2, 4 and 5. Relative advantages and disadvantages of various choices for ϕ_n and χ_m may be ascertained from a numerical point of view by comparing the pre-processing complexities, and numerical size and nature of the final matrix that results for the different choices of basis functions.

The solution of the matrix equations is typically carried out in the computer via inversion or elimination, and sometimes by iterative techniques. The relative merits of these approaches may be found in the discussions appearing in the text, primarily in Chapters 4 and 5. It is well known that standard library routines are available on the computer for the matrix inversion or elimination.

Though the thread of continuity indicated above exists in the three Chapters 2, 4 and 5, they nevertheless differ substantially in the types of problems they consider, and consequently, in the specialized numerical techniques they utilize. The wire antenna or scattering problem allows one to deal with the one-dimensional version of the general surface current integral equation which is considerably simpler. It should be pointed out, however, that the conventional magnetic field integral equation (MFIE), which is found to be very suitable (and in fact preferable) for solid surface scatterers, is not convenient for electrically thin antennas or scatterers, e.g. wires of various shapes. One therefore uses an alternative form of the integral equation, viz. the electric field integral equation (EFIE) for such geometries. The above difference in the use of the type of integral equation is an important feature that distinguishes the treatment of thin and solid surface structures. Differences also arise in these two cases in the use of the type of basis functions ϕ_n employed for the expansion of the unknown current distribution on the antenna (or scatterer). This is because for the one-dimensional case it is often possible analytically to evaluate certain integrations that arise in the process of using more elaborate basis functions than, say, simple pulse functions. The use of more elaborate basis functions is prompted by the fact that these can significantly increase the efficiency of computation. This is because using these functions one can better represent the integral associated with the equation for the unknown current in the form of a summation, and hence obtain more accurate results for the same number of unknowns representing the current. These points are discussed in considerable detail in Chapter 4.

For the waveguide-type problems dealt with in Chapter 5, the natural choice for the basis function is often the modal fields of the associated waveguides, since the integrations required to be performed for reducing the integral equation into a matrix equation can then be carried out in a closed form. This particular feature is often the most important consideration in the choice of the type of basis functions in transforming an integral equation into a matrix equation. For the cases where the integrations for the scalar products that lead to the matrix elements have to be carried out numerically, it is often more efficient in terms of total computer time to abandon this choice of basis and testing functions and to work instead with simpler functions, e.g. pulse and δ-functions for which closed form evaluation of integrals becomes possible. This is true even though the latter choice almost always requires the solution of a larger size matrix equation to achieve comparable accuracy.

Let us now turn briefly to the method employed in the derivation of the matrix equation in Chapter 3. It is based on the so-called extended boundary condition or analytic continuation method and is found to be totally different in its approach of transforming the integral equation into a matrix equation when compared to the methods employed in Chapters 2, 4 and 5. This radically different technique naturally leads to expressions for the matrix elements that are also different in character than those appearing in other methods. Special techniques required to generate numerically the matrix elements and solving the associated matrix equations are discussed in Chapter 3. Numerous applications of the extended boundary condition method, which is in fact equivalent (see Burrows, 1969) to the Rayleigh-hypothesis technique (Rayleigh, 1945), have recently appeared in the literature in connection with the solution of scattering problems from gratings, solid scatterers and even waveguide problems. In view of this, Chapter 3 has been included in this text to cover this alternate approach for solving scattering problems.

Chapter 6 dealing with some efficient numerical techniques can perhaps be described as one concerned with a hybrid approach. The methods discussed there require analytical preprocessing before the problem is entered into the computer. Efficiency and accuracy of computation is thus gained at the cost of some analytical work that requires a certain amount of sophisticated mathematical background. As is the common feature of analytically oriented computer techniques, these methods cannot be applied to arbitrary configurations. However, when applicable, they are usually capable of generating accurate and reliable numerical results with a fraction of computer time. It is interesting to note that in contrast to the Western researchers, Soviet scientists have concentrated largely on the quasi-analytic techniques for electromagnetic boundary-value problems that lead to representations requiring a minimal amount of computer work. This is perhaps due to the fact that in the earlier years the development of high-speed computers had lagged behind in Soviet Russia. Of course, there is much to be said in favor for concomitant development of quasi-analytical numerical techniques, since as has already been brought out earlier in this chapter, even the large computers have their limitations and the "brute force" use of the computer is seldom economical or practical except in trivial cases.

Finally, as alluded to earlier, many of the inverse scattering problems dealt with in Chapter 7 require techniques of formulation and solution that can be quite different from the integral equation methods. Workers in the area of electromagnetics have only recently devoted their attention to the computer aspects of inversion problems. This is due perhaps to a recent surge of interest in the areas of remote sensing and the development of techniques for wavefront reconstruction for which the analytical techniques are often severely limited in scope. This has prompted the development of special techniques, e.g. those dealing with the processing of measured data corrupted by noise, to extract certain pertinent information about a medium or a scatterer that is being probed. The numerical considerations associated with such problems are distinctly different in character from those arising in the forward scattering problems considered in Chapters 2 through 6. The inverse problems represent one important future area of research to which increasing attention is being focused by analysts interested in the numerical aspects of remote sensing.

We have attempted in the above to give a brief overview of the computer aspects of electromagnetics. It is hoped that this cursory introduction, though quite sketchy, will nevertheless arouse enough curiosity in the reader's mind so that he will now continue on to the following chapters that unfold the details of numerous approaches to "computer electromagnetics".

REFERENCES

BURROWS, M.L. (1969) Equivalence of the Rayleigh solution and the extended-boundary-condition solution for scattering problems, *Electron. Lett. 5*, 277.

CROUT, P.D. (1946) An application of polynomial approximation to the solution of integral equations arising in physical problems, *J. Math. Phys. 19*, 34–92.

HARRINGTON, R.F. (1968) *Field Computation by Moment Methods*, MacMillan, New York.

HILDEBRAND, F.B. and CROUT, P.D. (1941) A least squares procedure for solving integral equations by polynomial approximation, *J. Math. Phys. 20*, 310–35.

KANTOROVICH, L.V. and KRYLOV, V.F. (1946) *Approximate Methods of Higher Analysis*, Interscience, New York.

KELLOGG, O.D. (1953) *Foundations of Potential Theory*, Dover Publications, New York.

LOVITT, W.V. (1950) *Linear Integral Equations*, Dover, New York.

MAXWELL, J.C. Ed. (1879) *Electrical Researches of the Hon. Henry Cavendish, F.R.S.* (1771–81), Cambridge Univ. Press, London.

MIKHLIN, S.G. (1957) *Integral Equations*, Pergamon Press, London.

MITTRA, R. and LI, T.S. (1972) *Spectral Domain Approach for the Solution of a Class of Scattering Problems Involving Electrically Large Bodies* (to appear).

MORSE, P.M. and FESHBACK, H. (1953) *Methods of Theoretical Physics*, Part I, McGraw-Hill, New York.

NOBLE, B. (1966) The Numerical Solution of Singular Integral Equations, MRC Technical Rept. No. 730, Mathematics Research Center, U.S. Army, Univ. of Wis., Madison, Wisconsin.

RAYLEIGH, Lord (1945) *The Theory of Sound 2*, Dover, New York.

SMITHIES, F. (1958) *Integral Equations*, Cambridge University Press, London.

TRICOMI, F.G. (1957) *Integral Equations*, Interscience, New York.

WALTHER, A. and DEJON, B. (1960) General report on the numerical treatment of integral and integro-differential equations, *Symposium Proceedings, Provisional International Computation Center, Rome* (Birkhäuser, Verlag).

YOUNG, A. (1954) The application of approximate product-integration to the numerical solution of integral equations, *Proc. Roy Soc. (London)*, A, *224*, 561.

CHAPTER 2

Wire Antennas

G. A. THIELE

Assistant Professor of Electrical Engineering,
The Ohio State University

2.1. INTRODUCTION

It is the purpose of this chapter on wire antennas to present basic principles and techniques associated with the numerical solutions of wire antenna problems and then to illustrate the application of these principles and techniques with several examples. Although there are many different sound ways of formulating a given problem, particularly with respect to the choice of expansion or basis functions, substantial use in the examples of pulse functions as basis functions and point-matching is made for ease of illustration of the principles and techniques. More complex formulations are either discussed or referenced throughout this chapter.

Included at the beginning of the chapter is a discussion of the two basic integral equations used in treating wire antenna problems and a comparison of their merits. Following this section, the method of moments is discussed in Section 2.3. Here the integral equation is reduced to a system of linear equations and hence to a matrix formulation. Since the choice of basis functions plays an important part in this process, Section 2.4 is devoted to a discussion of the two basic philosophies pertaining to expansion functions and also to the merits of various choices of bases. Following this are Sections 2.6 through 2.8 which illustrate some of the topics discussed in the preceding sections.

Included at the end of the chapter are exercises designed to aid the reader in gaining experience and confidence in the numerical solution of wire antenna problems. For those already proficient in this area, certain selected computer programs have been included in the appendices to help the reader in his work with wire radiator problems. A fairly extensive list of references to other related works, by no means complete, is also included.

2.2. INTEGRAL EQUATIONS FOR WIRE ANTENNAS

In attacking thin wire antenna problems there are at least three popular integral equations, two distinct philosophies as to the expansion of the unknown and a variety of choices for expansion functions or interpolating in the use of these functions. It is the purpose of this section to look at two of these three integral equations in some detail. Subsequent sections will consider the merits of different schemes for expanding or interpolating the unknown in the solution of the integral equation. However, before investigating these integral equations, let us first examine a volume equivalence theorem which will help us visualize the nature of the fields and currents related by the integral equations.

2.2.1. A Volume Equivalence Theorem

The volume equivalence theorem presented here is really a special case of the compensation theorem. Let $(\mathbf{E}, \mathbf{H})$ represent the field generated by a harmonic electric current in a linear, isotropic medium (μ, ε). Such a field will satisfy Maxwell's equations:

$$\nabla \times \mathbf{E} = -j\omega\mu\mathbf{H} \tag{2.1}$$

and

$$\nabla \times \mathbf{H} = \mathbf{J} + j\omega\varepsilon\mathbf{E} \tag{2.2}$$

where $\mathbf{J}$ is the harmonic source current density. When the same current density $\mathbf{J}$ radiates in a different mediun, say free space, it sets up a different field $(\mathbf{E}_0, \mathbf{H}_0)$ which also satisfies Maxwell's equations:

$$\nabla \times \mathbf{E}_0 = -j\omega\mu_0\mathbf{H}_0 \tag{2.3}$$

and

$$\nabla \times \mathbf{H}_0 = \mathbf{J} + j\omega\varepsilon_0\mathbf{E}_0. \tag{2.4}$$

By definition, the difference between these fields is denoted the "scattered field", $\mathbf{E}^s$. That is,

$$\mathbf{E}^s = \mathbf{E} - \mathbf{E}_0 \tag{2.5}$$

and

$$\mathbf{H}^s = \mathbf{H} - \mathbf{H}_0. \tag{2.6}$$

When the above curl equations for the two sets of fields are subtracted, we obtain Maxwell's curl equations for the scattered fields:

$$\nabla \times \mathbf{E}^s = -j\omega(\mu - \mu_0)\mathbf{H} - j\omega\mu_0\mathbf{H}^s \tag{2.7}$$

and

$$\nabla \times \mathbf{H}^s = j\omega(\varepsilon - \varepsilon_0)\mathbf{E} + j\omega\varepsilon_0\mathbf{E}^s. \tag{2.8}$$

These equations can be rewritten in the form

$$\nabla \times \mathbf{E}^s = -\mathbf{K}_{eq} - j\omega\mu_0\mathbf{H}^s \tag{2.9}$$

and

$$\nabla \times \mathbf{H}^s = \mathbf{J}_{eq} + j\omega\varepsilon_0\mathbf{E}^s \tag{2.10}$$

where

$$\mathbf{K}_{eq} = j\omega(\mu - \mu_0)\mathbf{H} \tag{2.11}$$

and

$$\mathbf{J}_{eq} = j\omega \left(\varepsilon - \varepsilon_0\right) \mathbf{E}. \qquad\qquad (2.12)$$

Thus, these equations show that the field scattered by a material body may be generated by equivalent electric and magnetic currents $\mathbf{K}_{eq}$ and $\mathbf{J}_{eq}$ *radiating in free space*. These equivalent currents are sometimes referred to as "polarization currents".

It should be noted in eqns. (2.9) and (2.10) that the equivalent currents exist only in the region of space occupied by the material body, since the factors $(\mu - \mu_0)$ and $(\varepsilon - \varepsilon_0)$ vanish elsewhere.

It is not difficult to calculate the fields of a known current radiating in free space, but the equivalent currents in eqns. (2.11) and (2.12) are really unknown functions of space since the field quantities $\mathbf{E}$ and $\mathbf{H}$ are unknown. Therefore, while the volume equivalence theorem does not offer a direct solution for radiation problems, it is useful in helping us visualize the nature of the scattered field and also in developing integral equations for $\mathbf{E}$ and $\mathbf{H}$. In this regard one further point is quite useful. Let the complex permittivity in eqn. (2.12) be written as

$$\varepsilon = \varepsilon' - j\sigma/\omega. \qquad\qquad (2.13)$$

Thus, eqn. (2.12) becomes

$$\mathbf{J}_{eq} = \left[\sigma + j\omega \left(\varepsilon' - \varepsilon_0\right)\right] \mathbf{E}. \qquad\qquad (2.14)$$

The first term on the right side of eqn. (2.14) is simply the conduction current density. In a good conductor, this term is much greater than the other terms. Thus, our expression for $\mathbf{J}_{eq}$ reduces to

$$\mathbf{J}_{eq} = \sigma\mathbf{E}. \qquad\qquad (2.15)$$

Furthermore, in most good conductors the permeability is the same as that of free space causing $\mathbf{K}_{eq}$ to vanish.

Thus, for a highly conducting body the equivalent current is essentially the same as the conduction current and the field scattered by such a body may be generated by this conduction current radiating in free space. In general, the equivalent current is a volume current density. However, in this chapter we will only be considering perfect conductors since, for our purposes, they will approximate good conductors. Hence, in the limit of perfect conductivity the equivalent volume current density reduces to an equivalent surface current density.

2.2.2. Pocklington's Integral Equation

In regions having electric and magnetic sources, Maxwell's equations are given by

$$\nabla \times \mathbf{E} = -j\omega\mu\mathbf{H} - \mathbf{K} \qquad\qquad (2.16)$$

and

$$\nabla \times \mathbf{H} = j\omega\varepsilon\mathbf{E} + \mathbf{J}. \qquad\qquad (2.17)$$

The field intensities may be expressed in terms of $\mathbf{J}$ and $\mathbf{K}$ as

$$\mathbf{E} = -j\omega\mathbf{A} - \nabla V - \frac{1}{\varepsilon} \nabla \times \mathbf{F} \qquad\qquad (2.18)$$

and

$$\mathbf{H} = \frac{1}{\mu} \nabla \times \mathbf{A} - \nabla U - j\omega\mathbf{F} \tag{2.19}$$

where

$$\mathbf{A} = \mu \iiint \frac{\mathbf{J} e^{-jkr}}{4\pi r} \, dv', \tag{2.20}$$

$$\mathbf{F} = \varepsilon \iiint \frac{\mathbf{M} e^{-jkr}}{4\pi r} \, dv', \tag{2.21}$$

$$V = \iiint \frac{\varrho \, e^{-jkr}}{4\pi\varepsilon r} \, dv', \tag{2.22}$$

$$U = \iiint \frac{m \, e^{-jkr}}{4\pi\mu r} \, dv', \tag{2.23}$$

where r is the distance between the observation point (x, y, z) and the source point (x', y', z'), or

$$r = \sqrt{\{(x - x')^2 + (y - y')^2 + (z - z')^2\}}, \tag{2.24}$$

and where ϱ and m are the volume densities of electric and magnetic charge. Due to the fact that the current passing out of a given volume must equal the rate of decrease of the charge in the volume, the charge densities are not independent of the current densities. Thus, the scalar potentials V and U may be related to the vector potentials $\mathbf{A}$ and $\mathbf{F}$ by using the Lorentz gauges,

$$\nabla \cdot \mathbf{A} = -j\omega\mu\varepsilon V, \tag{2.25}$$

$$\nabla \cdot \mathbf{F} = -j\omega\mu\varepsilon U. \tag{2.26}$$

In the sections that follow, we will only consider situations where the permeability is that of free space. That is, $\mu = \mu_0$, $m = 0$ and $\mathbf{K} = 0$. Thus, if there are no magnetic currents and if all electric currents are parallel to the z-axis, the magnetic vector potential $\mathbf{A}$ is also parallel to the z-axis. The electric vector potential, of course, vanishes. From eqn. (2.25) we have

$$\frac{\partial A_z}{\partial z} = -j\omega\mu\varepsilon V. \tag{2.27}$$

From eqn. (2.18) we have

$$E_z = -j\omega A_z - \frac{\partial V}{\partial z}. \tag{2.28}$$

Employing eqn. (2.27) in (2.28),

$$E_z = \frac{1}{j\omega\varepsilon\mu} \left(\frac{\partial^2 A_z}{\partial z^2} + k^2 A_z \right), \tag{2.29}$$

where $k^2 = \omega^2\mu\varepsilon$. If one considers a current element $J \, dv'$, then

$$dE_z = \frac{1}{j\omega\varepsilon} \left[\frac{\partial^2 G(z, z')}{\partial z^2} + k^2 G(z, z') \right] J \, dv' \tag{2.30}$$

where

$$G\left(z, z'\right) = \frac{\exp\left(-jkr\right)}{4\pi r}.$$ (2.31)

Hence, for a current density J parallel to the z-axis,

$$E_z = \frac{1}{j\omega\varepsilon} \iiint \left[\frac{\partial^2 G\left(z, z'\right)}{\partial z^2} + k^2 G\left(z, z'\right)\right] J \, dv'.$$ (2.32)

If we consider the situation where the current density J is restricted to the surface of a circular cylinder whose axis coincides with the z-axis, then eqn. (2.32) reduces to a surface integral. Further, if the cylinder is of radius a, where $a \ll \lambda$, the current may be assumed to be distributed uniformly around the cylinder. If one observes the current distribution from an observation point on the cylinder axis, eqn. (2.24) reduces to

$$r = \sqrt{\{(z - z')^2 + a^2\}}$$ (2.33)

and the surface current distribution may thus be represented by an equivalent filamentary line source located a radial distance a away from the observation point. Thus, if we denote the quantity E_z in eqn. (2.32) as the scattered field and reduce the equivalent volume current density to an equivalent surface current density as discussed in Section 2.2.1 we obtain

$$\int_{-L/2}^{L/2} I(z') \left[\frac{\partial^2 G\left(z, z'\right)}{\partial z^2} + k^2 G\left(z, z'\right)\right] dz' = -j\omega\varepsilon E_z^i\left(z\right)$$ (2.34)

where $E_z^i(z)$ is the incident or impressed field and is assumed to be distributed uniformly around the cylinder since the wire is thin. The limits of integration are the result of the dipole extending from $z = -L/2$ to $z = L/2$ as shown in Fig. 2.1. Equation (2.34) is the type used by Pocklington (1897) to show that on thin wires the current distribution is approximately sinusoidal and propagates with the velocity of light. Equation (2.34) is an integral equation of the first kind. It is to be emphasized that the dipole or wire cylinder is *not* assumed to be

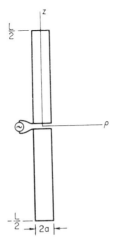

FIG. 2.1. Dipole of length L, radius a centered about z-axis.

infinitesimally thin. Rather, the so-called thin wire approximations have been employed whereby the radius is considered to be much less than the wavelength but finite nevertheless.

Pocklington's form of the integral equation for thin wire antennas is essentially that used by Richmond (1965) although the equations used by Richmond are derived in a somewhat different manner. Let us for the present consider a more general case than simply that of a dipole. That is, consider an arbitrary source with coordinates (x', y', z') as shown in Fig. 2.2.

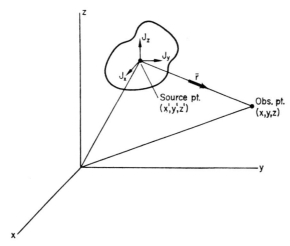

FIG. 2.2. Coordinate system for a general radiating body with components of current density J_x, J_y and J_z.

Starting with the vector potential

$$\mathbf{H} = \frac{1}{\mu} \nabla \times \mathbf{A} \tag{2.35}$$

then

$$\mathbf{H} = \frac{1}{4\pi} \iiint_{v'} \nabla \times \frac{[\mathbf{J} \exp(-jkr)]}{r} \, dv'. \tag{2.36}$$

Using the vector identity

$$\nabla \times (f\mathbf{G}) = (\nabla f) \times \mathbf{G} + f(\nabla \times \mathbf{G}), \tag{2.37}$$

we obtain

$$\mathbf{H} = \frac{1}{4\pi} \iiint_{v'} \left[\nabla \frac{\exp(-jkr)}{r} \right] \times \mathbf{J} \, dv' \tag{2.38}$$

because $\nabla \times \mathbf{J} = 0$ due to $\mathbf{J}$ being a function of the source coordinates (x', y', z') and not of the observation coordinates. It can be shown that

$$\nabla \left[\frac{\exp(-jkr)}{r} \right] = -\hat{r} \, \frac{1 + jkr}{r^2} \exp(-jkr) \tag{2.39}$$

where $\hat{r}$ is the unit vector directed from the source point to the observation point. Thus, our expression for **H** becomes

$$\mathbf{H}(x, y, z) = \frac{-1}{4\pi} \iiint (\hat{r} \times \mathbf{J}) \frac{1 + jkr}{r^2} \exp(-jkr) \, dv'. \qquad (2.40)$$

Taking the curl of both sides of the last equation we can obtain the following expressions for the three rectangular components of the electric field intensity due to an electric current source in unbounded free space:

$$E_x = \frac{\sqrt{(\mu/\varepsilon)}}{4\pi jk} \iiint [F_1(r) J_x + (x - x') F_2(r)$$

$$\times \, [(x - x') J_x + (y - y') J_y + (z - z') J_z]] \, dv', \qquad (2.41)$$

$$E_y = \frac{\sqrt{(\mu/\varepsilon)}}{4\pi jk} \iiint [F_1(r) J_y + (y - y') F_2(r)$$

$$\times \, [(x - x') J_x + (y - y') J_y + (z - z') J_z]] \, dv', \qquad (2.42)$$

$$E_z = \frac{\sqrt{(\mu/\varepsilon)}}{4\pi jk} \iiint [F_1(r) J_z + (z - z') F_2(r)$$

$$\times \, [(x - x') J_x + (y - y') J_y + (z - z') J_z]] \, dv' \qquad (2.43)$$

where

$$F_1(r) = \frac{-1 - jkr + k^2 r^2}{r^3} \exp(-jkr), \qquad (2.44)$$

$$F_2(r) = \frac{3 + 3jkr - k^2 r^2}{r^5} \exp(-jkr). \qquad (2.45)$$

For a dipole about the z-axis, eqn. (2.43) for the scattered field reduces to

$$E_z^s(0, z) = \frac{1}{4\pi j\omega\varepsilon} \int_{-L/2}^{L/2} I(z') \, [\exp(-jkr)] \, r^{-5} \cdot [(1 + jkr)(2r^2 - 3a^2) + k^2 a^2 r^2] \, dz'. \qquad (2.46)$$

This equation could also be deduced from eqn. (2.34). In any event eqn. (2.46) is the equation used by Richmond (1965) in his work with wire scatterers.

On the other hand eqns. (2.18), (2.20) and (2.22) serve as the starting point for Harrington in his work with thin wire radiators. These relationships may be written in the form of a single integral equation (Kyle, 1968) as

$$E_z^i(0, z) = \int_{-L/2}^{L/2} \left[j\omega\mu \, I(z') - \frac{1}{j\omega\varepsilon} \frac{\partial I(z')}{\partial z'} \frac{\partial}{\partial z} \right] \frac{\exp(-jkr)}{4\pi r} \, dz' \qquad (2.47)$$

which is equivalent to eqn. (2.46).

2.2.3. Hallen's Integral Equation

In the integral equation approach to the antenna boundary value problem of the previous section, the independent variable ranged over the antenna surface (boundary) with the result that the actual boundary conditions were incorporated in the integral equation itself. In deriving Hallen's equation, the usual differential equation approach will be used. That is, the independent variable ranges over all space with a solution being sought to the differential equation that satisfies the boundary conditions.

To start, consider the vector potential which must satisfy the wave equation,

$$\left(\frac{d^2}{dz^2} + k^2 \right) A_z(z) = 0. \tag{2.48}$$

If one considers the symmetry conditions on a dipole $I_z(-z) = I_z(z)$ and $A_z(-z) = A_z(z)$, then a solution to eqn. (2.48) is

$$A_z(z) = -j \sqrt{(\mu \varepsilon)} (C_1 \cos kz + C_2 \sin k |z|) \tag{2.49}$$

where C_1 and C_2 are arbitrary constants. For our perfectly conducting thin wire antenna,

$$A_z(z) = \mu_0 \int_{-L/2}^{L/2} I_z(z') G(z, z') \, dz' \tag{2.50}$$

where $G(z, z')$ is given by eqn. (2.31) and r by eqn. (2.33). Equating eqns. (2.49) and (2.50), one obtains

$$\int_{-L/2}^{L/2} I_z(z') G(z, z') \, dz' = -\frac{j}{\eta} (C_1 \cos kz + C_2 \sin k |z|) \tag{2.51}$$

where η is the intrinsic impedance of free space. This is Hallen's (1938) integral equation for the perfectly conducting dipole antenna of Fig. 2.1. The constant C_2 may be evaluated as $C_2 = V_T/2$ where V_T is the terminal voltage of the antenna. The constant C_1 must be evaluated from the conditions that the current goes to zero at the ends of the antenna.

Many workers have advanced various solutions to Hallen's integral equation. Particularly significant is the work of Mei (1965) which extended Hallen's equation to antennas of arbitrary geometry. An excellent summary of various works related to Hallen's integral equation has been given by King (1967).

The third popular integral equation mentioned at the beginning of Section 2.2 is a form of Hallen's integral equation used and well documented by King (1956). Hence, for this reason and also for the reasons in the following paragraph, it will not be discussed here.

Although both Pocklington's and Hallen's integral equations can be used to treat wire antennas, most of the remainder of this chapter will use the Pocklington form since it is, in a sense, more general for our purposes. That is, Pocklington's integral equation has E^i on the right-hand side where E^i represents the field from a source. For example, the source might be the aperture created by a coaxial feed terminating at the surface of a ground plane. Or, for example, in the case of an antenna such as a slot on a metallic body, the source of E^i is the slot while the metallic surface is represented or modeled by parasitic antenna elements or wire segments. Hallen's integral equation, on the other hand, exclusively uses a delta-gap voltage generator and therefore does not afford us the flexibility of using different sources of excitation. Furthermore, although the delta-gap is a useful tool, it is a rather poor model of actual physical situations when compared to finite models and can present difficulties in calculating accurately the imaginary part of the input impedance.

Thus, with a suitable integral equation in hand, there remains the task of finding solutions for a variety of wire antenna problems. Solutions may be obtained by reducing the integral equations to a set of simultaneous linear algebraic equations and it is to this end that we proceed on to the following section.

2.3. METHOD OF MOMENTS

The unifying concept in the numerical treatment of radiation problems is the method of moments (Harrington, 1968). This general approach to radiation problems is essentially a reduction of the associated integral equation to a system of linear algebraic equations in, say, N unknowns where the N unknowns are usually coefficients in some appropriate expansion of the current. Let us see how this comes about in a general sort of electromagnetics problem.

Consider a general metallic body with a current density $\mathbf{J}$ on it. We require that the total tangential electric field be zero everywhere on the surface of the body, or that

$$0 = \mathbf{E}^s_{\text{tan}} + \mathbf{E}^i_{\text{tan}} \tag{2.52}$$

where $\mathbf{E}^s_{\text{tan}}$ is the scattered electric field radiated by the current density $\mathbf{J}$ as defined in Section 2.2.1. $\mathbf{E}^i_{\text{tan}}$ is the tangential component of the incident electric field due to a source located anywhere on or outside the body. Hereafter we will drop the subscript tan since it will be understood that the tangential electric field boundary condition is being used.

Rewriting eqn. (2.52) in the form

$$-\mathbf{E}^s = \mathbf{E}^i \tag{2.53}$$

and defining the operator

$$L_{\text{op}}(\mathbf{J}) \equiv -(\mathbf{E}^s) \tag{2.54}$$

we can use the concept of linear vector spaces and operators to write the operator equation

$$L_{\text{op}}(\mathbf{J}) = (\mathbf{E}^i) \tag{2.55}$$

where L_{op} is an operator that must be determined for the problem of interest, $(\mathbf{E}^i)$ is a known excitation function or source, and $\mathbf{J}$ is the unknown response function to be determined. In the problems that will be considered in this chapter, L_{op} is an integral operator operating on the current $\mathbf{J}$. We assume that for a given source there exists one and only one $\mathbf{J}$. That is L_{op}^{-1} exists such that

$$\mathbf{J} = L_{\text{op}}^{-1}(\mathbf{E}^i). \tag{2.56}$$

For a given problem we must determine the domain of definition of the operator or, in other words, the space of functions on which it operates and also the range of the operator or the functions resulting from the operation. In reality, the operator performs a mapping from some subset containing **J** to one containing (**E**^{i}). If the solution is to be unique, this mapping must be one to one.

In addition to determining the domain and range of the operator, it is often necessary to formulate an inner product $\langle \mathbf{J}, \mathbf{E} \rangle$ which is a scalar quantity obtained by integrating $\mathbf{J} \cdot \mathbf{E}$ over the surface under consideration. This particular inner product is called reaction (Rumsey, 1954). Reaction, like momentum or energy, is a physical observable. We will define the inner product such that the following conditions are satisfied:

$$\langle \mathbf{J}, \mathbf{E} \rangle = \langle \mathbf{E}, \mathbf{J} \rangle \qquad (2.57)$$

$$\langle \alpha \mathbf{J} + \beta \mathbf{J}, \mathbf{E} \rangle = \alpha \langle \mathbf{J}, \mathbf{E} \rangle + \beta \langle \mathbf{J}, \mathbf{E} \rangle \qquad (2.58)$$

if

$$\langle \mathbf{J}^*, \mathbf{J} \rangle > 0, \quad \text{then } \mathbf{J} \neq 0 \qquad (2.59)$$

if

$$\langle \mathbf{J}^*, \mathbf{J} \rangle = 0, \quad \text{then } \mathbf{J} = 0 \qquad (2.60)$$

where α and β are scalars and * denotes complex conjugation.

The procedure for obtaining a solution, such as in eqn. (2.56), can be divided into four steps:

1. Expand the unknown in a series of basis functions, J_n, spanning **J** in the domain of L_{op}.
2. Determine a suitable inner product and define a set of weighting functions.
3. Take the inner products and thereby form the matrix equation.
4. Solve the matrix equation for the unknown.

Once the unknown (i.e. the current) is obtained, quantities such as far-field patterns and impedance are easily calculated.

Let us consider the above four steps in some detail in the next section where the choice of weighting functions is restricted to a particularly appropriate set of functions, namely the response functions themselves.

2.3.1. Galerkin's Method

For electromagnetic radiation problems a specialization of the general method of moments is particularly convenient. Considering the first of the four steps above, expand the response function **J** in eqn. (2.55) in a series of basis functions $\mathbf{J}_1, \mathbf{J}_2, \mathbf{J}_3, \ldots$ on a surface S and defined in the domain of L_{op}. That is,

$$\mathbf{J} = \sum_n I_n \mathbf{J}_n \qquad (2.61)$$

where the coefficients I_n are in general complex. The I_n's are the unknown coefficients that we wish to determine. Once they are found we will then know the amplitude and phase of the current on the radiator. When substituting eqn. (2.61) into eqn. (2.55) we obtain

$$L_{op} \left(\sum_n I_n \mathbf{J}_n \right) = (\mathbf{E}^i) \qquad (2.62)$$

or, using the linearity of L_{op},

$$\sum_n I_n L_{op} (\mathbf{J}_n) = (\mathbf{E}^i). \qquad (2.63)$$

The second step in the solution outlined above is to define a set of weighting functions $\mathbf{W}_1, \mathbf{W}_2, \ldots$ in the domain of L_{op} and then form the inner product

$$\sum_n I_n \langle \mathbf{W}_m, L_{\mathrm{op}} \mathbf{J}_n \rangle = \langle \mathbf{W}_m, \mathbf{E}^i \rangle. \tag{2.64}$$

However, if we require that $\mathbf{W}_m = \mathbf{J}_m$ then the formulation of the problem is known as Galerkin's method. Thus, eqn. (2.64) becomes

$$\sum_n I_n \langle \mathbf{J}_m, L_{\mathrm{op}} \mathbf{J}_n \rangle = \langle \mathbf{J}_m, \mathbf{E}^i \rangle \tag{2.65}$$

and the inner products appear as the reaction quantity mentioned earlier. It is interesting to note that Galerkin's method possesses stationary properties and is equivalent to the Rayleigh–Ritz variational method discussed by Dr. Wu in Chapter 5.

The third step is to calculate the various inner products given in eqn. (2.65) and thereby form the matrix equation

$$\begin{bmatrix} \langle \mathbf{J}_1, L_{\mathrm{op}} \mathbf{J}_1 \rangle & \langle \mathbf{J}_1, L_{\mathrm{op}} \mathbf{J}_2 \rangle \cdots \\ \langle \mathbf{J}_2, L_{\mathrm{op}} \mathbf{J}_1 \rangle & \ddots \\ \vdots & \ddots \\ \vdots & \ddots \\ \vdots & \ddots \end{bmatrix} \begin{bmatrix} I_1 \\ I_2 \\ \vdots \\ \vdots \\ I_n \end{bmatrix} = \begin{bmatrix} \langle \mathbf{J}_1, \mathbf{E}^i \rangle \\ \langle \mathbf{J}_2, \mathbf{E}^i \rangle \\ \vdots \\ \vdots \\ \langle \mathbf{J}_n, \mathbf{E}^i \rangle \end{bmatrix} \tag{2.66}$$

or, in more compact notation,

$$[Z](I) = (V) \tag{2.67}$$

where the elements of $[Z]$ may be thought of as generalized impedances, those of (I) as generalized currents and those of (V) as generalized voltages. Equation (2.67) may be solved by standard matrix inversion techniques for the current column vector (I),

$$(I) = [Z]^{-1} (V) \tag{2.68}$$

where

$$\mathbf{J} = \sum_n I_n \mathbf{J}_n. \tag{2.69}$$

In practice, the evaluation of the N^2 impedance elements suggested by eqn. (2.66) may be very laborious even on a high-speed computer since at least two integrations may have to be done numerically. That is, if L_{op} is an integral operator, one must compute $L_{\mathrm{op}}(\mathbf{J}_n)$ via integration and then perform the integration dictated by the inner product. However, one of these integrations may be avoided as discussed in the following section.

2.3.2. Point-matching

In Galerkin's method we are required to evaluate the generalized impedance elements

$$Z_{mn} = \langle \mathbf{J}_m, L_{\mathrm{op}}(\mathbf{J}_n) \rangle \tag{2.70}$$

where L_{op} itself is an integral operator. Therefore the evaluation of Z_{mn} may be tedious and computationally expensive if all the integrations are to be done largely using numerical procedures. This difficulty can be minimized if one uses Dirac delta functions as weighting functions in eqn. (2.66). Thus,

$$
\begin{bmatrix}
\langle \delta(\mathbf{S}-\mathbf{S}_1), L_{op}(\mathbf{J}_1) \rangle & \langle \delta(\mathbf{S}-\mathbf{S}_1), L_{op}(\mathbf{J}_2) \rangle & \cdots \\
\langle \delta(\mathbf{S}-\mathbf{S}_2), L_{op}(\mathbf{J}_1) \rangle & & \\
\vdots & & \ddots \\
\vdots & & & \ddots \\
\vdots & & & & \ddots
\end{bmatrix}
\begin{bmatrix}
I_1 \\
I_2 \\
\vdots \\
\vdots \\
I_N
\end{bmatrix}
=
\begin{bmatrix}
\langle \delta(\mathbf{S}-\mathbf{S}_1), \mathbf{E}_1^i \rangle \\
\langle \delta(\mathbf{S}-\mathbf{S}_2), \mathbf{E}_2^i \rangle \\
\vdots \\
\langle \delta(\mathbf{S}-\mathbf{S}_N), \mathbf{E}_N^i \rangle
\end{bmatrix}
\qquad (2.71)
$$

where $\mathbf{S}$ is the distance from some reference point and $\mathbf{S}_m$ represents the distance to the point where the boundary condition is being applied. Here, $\mathbf{E}_1^i$ indicates that matching is being done at point 1, $\mathbf{E}_2^i$ indicates that matching is being done at point 2, etc. Any integrations that are required are limited to those defined by L_{op}.

This use of Dirac delta functions is recognized in the physical problem as a relaxation of the electric field boundary condition such that it is enforced only at discrete points on the surface S rather than continuously over the surface. Hence the term point-matching has come into use. Experience has shown that if one chooses a sufficient number of points at which to match boundary conditions, then accurate solutions can be obtained. However, the accuracy of the solutions may depend not only on the number of points, but also on their locations. Often the use of equispaced points will give good results. This is especially true in the radar scattering problem or in the calculation of far-field patterns where the observation point is far-removed from the radiator. But, as one might expect, the calculation of near-field data such as impedance is more sensitive to the number and location of the match points. Nevertheless, point-matching is a relatively simple and sufficiently accurate technique for many problems.

2.4. BASES

One of the fundamental decisions to be made in numerically attacking a given radiation problem concerns the choice of basis functions $\mathbf{J}_n$. In theory there are infinitely many sets of basis functions. In practice there are often only a small number well suited to a given problem. It is inevitable that certain basis functions give faster convergence than others which means less computational effort for a given accuracy since one has a smaller impedance matrix to calculate and invert. It appears generally true that the closer the basis functions $\mathbf{J}_n$ resemble the actual current distribution on the radiator, the better the convergence and, in some cases, the better the conditioning (stability) of the impedance matrix.

In this section we will discuss some possible choices of basis functions. Further, we will divide our discussion into two classes of bases. The first class will be basis functions defined and non-zero over the entire domain of L_{op} except possibly for a set of measure zero. This class of basis functions will be denoted entire-domain bases. Contrasted with this class is the second class whereby the basis functions are defined in the domain of L_{op} but are zero over part of the domain. This class will be denoted sub-domain bases. In the case of wire radiators this constitutes dividing the antenna into sections. Hence, the terms segmentation and subsectional bases are sometimes used in connection with this second class. It appears that most recent work utilizes the sub-domain approach for reasons which will be discussed later. However, the full-domain approach has its advantages in certain problems.

Also, in this section we will discuss a basis transformation method that can be used when a problem is set up using one set of basis and one desires to obtain a solution in terms of a different set of basis. The choice of basis can have a marked effect on the stability of the impedance matrix. This section on bases will conclude with a discussion of the stability problem.

2.4.1. Entire-domain Bases

In this section we wish to consider basis functions $\mathbf{J}_n$ defined and non-zero over the entire domain spanned by $\mathbf{J}$ where

$$\mathbf{J} = \sum_{n=1} I_n \mathbf{J}_n. \tag{2.72}$$

To illustrate, let us use a dipole antenna as an example radiator and employ the point-matching technique of Section 2.3.2. Figure 2.3 defines the parameters associated with the dipole antenna. Let the unprimed coordinate z denote a point at which we wish to enforce boundary conditions (observation point) and the primed coordinate denote the source region. Since the wire antenna is assumed perfectly conducting

$$-\mathbf{E}_z^s(0, z) = \mathbf{E}_z^i(0, z) \tag{2.73}$$

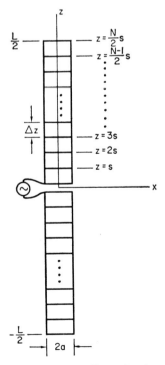

FIG. 2.3. Dipole of length L, radius a showing subsections.

or

$$L_{\text{op}}(\mathbf{J}) = E_z^i(0, z). \tag{2.74}$$

A suitable expression for L_{op}, given previously in eqn. (2.46), is

$$L_{\text{op}} = \frac{-\lambda \sqrt{(\mu/\varepsilon)}}{8\pi^2 \mathrm{j}} \int_{-L/2}^{L/2} G(r, r')\, \mathrm{d}z' \tag{2.75}$$

where here

$$r = \sqrt{\{a^2 + (z - z')^2\}} \tag{2.76}$$

and

$$G(r, r') = \frac{\exp(-\mathrm{j}kr)}{r^5} [(1 + \mathrm{j}kr)(2r^2 - 3a^2) + k^2 a^2 r^2]. \tag{2.77}$$

Note that the limits of integration for L_{op} are in general the extreme upper and lower ends of the dipole. Now if we choose basis functions such as

$$J(z) = \sum_{n=1}^{N} I_n \cos(2n - 1)\frac{\pi z}{L}, \quad -L/2 \le z \le L/2 \tag{2.78}$$

where

$$\mathbf{J} = \hat{z} J(z) \tag{2.79}$$

then we have basis functions $\cos(2n - 1)\pi z/L$ which are defined over the entire domain spanned by $\mathbf{J}$. Equation (2.78) is a finite Fourier series of odd ordered even modes chosen such that the current goes to zero at the ends of the antenna.

As an example of the rate of convergence one might obtain using the point-matching technique in conjunction with the entire-domain basis functions given in eqn. (2.78), Figs. 2.4a and 2.4b show the calculated values for the real and imaginary parts of the impedance for a given dipole. The convergence is fairly rapid which is important since the computer time is essentially proportional to N^3.

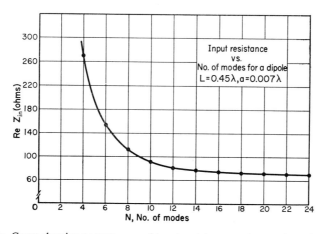

FIG. 2.4a. Curve showing convergence of input resistance as the number of cosine modes is increased.

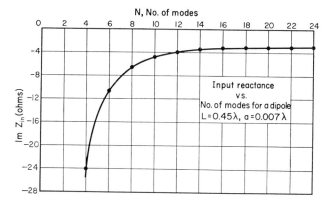

FIG. 2.4b. Curve showing convergence of input reactance as the number of cosine modes is increased.

2.4.2. Sub-domain Bases

In contrast with the entire-domain bases of the previous section, it is sometimes more convenient to employ basis functions that exist in the domain of L_{op} but are zero over part of that domain. This approach lends itself quite well to the process of segmentation whereby an arbitrarily shaped radiator is geometrically approximated by N wire segments. Usually the segments are chosen to be straight although this need not be the case (Mei, 1965).

To illustrate this approach, let us again use the dipole as an example and the integral operator given in eq. (2.75). Now define the basis functions

$$J(z) = \begin{cases} I_j & \text{for } z' \text{ in } \Delta z_j, \\ 0 & \text{for } z' \text{ not in } \Delta z_j \end{cases} \tag{2.80}$$

That is, we have approximated the current by a staircase function composed of piecewise-uniform current segments. While this is a crude representation for the actual current on the dipole, it is the simplest current function to use in the segmentation approach. Other possible basis functions well suited to the segmentation approach will be given in a following section.

As an example of the rate of convergence one might obtain using the point-matching technique in conjunction with the sub-domain basis functions in eqn. (2.80), Figs. 2.5a and 2.5b show the calculated impedance values for a dipole similar to that used for Figs. 2.4a and 2.4b. Note the slower rate of convergence for the simple basis functions used here compared with the entire-domain basis functions in the previous section. However, due to the considerable symmetry that exists if the segments representing the dipole are of the same length, the computer time for this special radiator is better than for the entire-domain case in the previous section. That is, for certain geometries (i.e. linear dipole, open or closed circular loop and the helix) there are only N *independent* elements in the segmental impedance matrix of N^2 elements that need be calculated.

To further illustrate the accuracy that may be obtained using the point-matching technique with either the entire-domain basis functions of Section 2.4.1 or the sub-domain

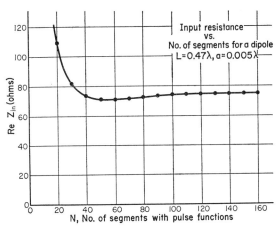

FIG. 2.5a. Curve showing convergence of input resistance as the number of pulse functions is increased.

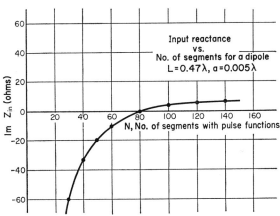

FIG. 2.5b. Curve showing convergence of input reactance as the number of pulse functions is increased.

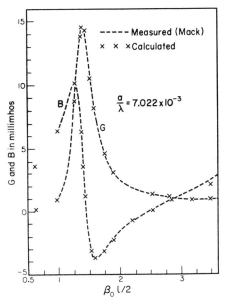

FIG. 2.6. Comparison of measured dipole and admittance with data calculated by both entire-domain and sub-domain methods.

uniform basis just mentioned, consider Fig. 2.6. Here the admittance of a dipole calculated by both methods is compared with data measured by Mack (1963). Note that the results are excellent for both the real and imaginary parts. This is partly due to the accurate modeling of the feed point which will be discussed further in following sections and in Appendix I.

2.4.3. Some Common Basis Functions

As mentioned previously, the choice of basis functions is determined by many factors dictated by the problem under consideration. As illustrative examples of basis functions that can be used, consider the following entire-domain functions that could be used to investigate a dipole type wire antenna:

Fourier: $\quad I(z) = I_1 \cos \pi x/2 + I_2 \cos 3\pi x/2 + I_3 \cos 5\pi x/2 + \cdots$ (2.81)

Chebyshev: $\quad I(z) = I_1 T_0(x) + I_2 T_2(x) + I_3 T_4(x) + \cdots$ (2.82)

Maclaurin: $\quad I(z) = I_1 + I_2 x^2 + I_3 x^4 + \cdots$ (2.83)

Legendre: $\quad I(z) = I_1 P_0(x) + I_2 P_2(x) + I_3 P_4(x) + \cdots$ (2.84)

where

$$x = 2z/L.$$

There are others that could, of course, also be used.

As examples of sub-domain bases consider the following:

Piecewise uniform (pulse function):

$$J(z) = \begin{cases} I_j & \text{for } z \text{ in } \Delta z_j, \\ 0 & \text{otherwise.} \end{cases}$$ (2.85)

Triangle functions (piecewise linear):

$$J(z) = \begin{cases} \dfrac{I_j(z_{j+1} - z) + I_{j+1}(z - z_j)}{\Delta z_j} & \text{for } z \text{ in } \Delta z_j, \\ 0 \quad \text{otherwise.} \end{cases}$$ (2.86)

Piecewise sinusoidal:

$$J(z) = \begin{cases} \dfrac{I_j \sin k(z_{j+1} - z) + I_{j+1} \sin k(z - z_j)}{\sin k \Delta z_j} & \text{for } z \text{ in } \Delta z_j, \\ 0 \quad \text{otherwise.} \end{cases}$$ (2.87)

Quadratic interpolation:

$$J(z) = \begin{cases} A_j + B_j(z - z_j) + C_j(z - z_j)^2 & \text{for } z \text{ in } \Delta z_j, \\ 0 & \text{otherwise.} \end{cases}$$ (2.88)

Sinusoidal interpolation:

$$J(z) = \begin{cases} A_j + B_j \sin k\,(z - z_j) + C_j \cos k\,(z - z_j) & \text{for } z \text{ in } \varDelta z_j, \\ 0 & \text{otherwise.} \end{cases} \tag{2.89}$$

Of these, the constant or piecewise uniform function in conjunction with the point-matching approach is probably the simplest. The two interpolation schemes, while affording faster convergence, require the evaluation of rather complex integrals.

An interesting comparison of several current functions has been made by Neureuther (1968), primarily using Hallen's integral equation.

Neureuther used a delta-gap voltage generator in both Pocklington's and Hallen's integral equations and his results tended to indicate a somewhat more rapid rate of convergence could be obtained with Hallen's integral equation. However, Fig. 2.7 shows a rate of con-

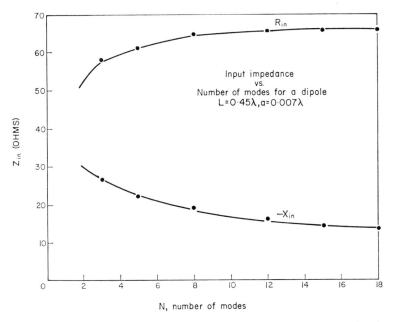

FIG. 2.7. Curves showing convergence of the input impedance as the number of cosine modes is increased using Hallen's integral equation.

vergence for Hallen's equation similar to that of Fig. 2.4 for the same basis functions on the same dipole. The sources are, however, different in the two situations in that a magnetic frill current was employed as the source in Fig. 2.4.

2.4.4. A Basis Transformation Method

Upon comparing in practice the two types of basis functions described in Sections 2.4.1 and 2.4.2, we can make several observations. First, while the use of bases spanning the whole domain can result in rapid convergence, the derivation of the generalized impedance matrix is usually not efficient in terms of computer time. On the other hand, the subspace basis functions of Section 2.4.2 usually afford efficient derivation of the generalized impedance matrix but can require a large number of equations to describe the problem. This is especially true if the geometry of the problem is such that there is considerable curvature of the radiator and many short segments are needed adequately to approximate the radiator geometrically. One might conclude, then, that it would be desirable to have an alternative approach that would have some of the advantages of both the entire-domain and sub-domain approaches. In this section we discuss such a method and apply it to a wire antenna although its original development by Turpin (1969) was for wire scatterers.

Consider solutions to thin wire radiation problems composed of either straight or continuously curved perfect conductors that can be approached using the point-matching technique. That is, the problem is represented by a set of N linear equations expressed in matrix notation as

$$(V) = [Z] (I) \qquad (2.90)$$

where the components I_n of the current vector (I) are coefficients of an expansion of the current induced on the wire in terms of a set of orthogonal basis functions $i_1, i_2, \ldots, i_N$. The mnth element of the $N \times N$ impedance matrix $[Z]$ gives the tangential component of the electric field at the mth point on the wire due to the nth basis function of current (represented by the vector (i_n)) distributed over the wire length. For a piecewise uniform formulation, the basis functions are unit pulses of width L/N, i.e.

$$(i_1) = \begin{bmatrix} 1 \\ 0 \\ 0 \\ \vdots \\ 0 \\ 0 \end{bmatrix}, \quad (i_2) = \begin{bmatrix} 0 \\ 1 \\ 0 \\ \vdots \\ 0 \\ 0 \end{bmatrix}, \quad \ldots, \quad (i_N) = \begin{bmatrix} 0 \\ 0 \\ 0 \\ \vdots \\ 0 \\ 1 \end{bmatrix}. \qquad (2.91)$$

We now wish to transform our basis to a new basis.

Assume that the set of linear equations, eqn. (2.91), has as basis the set of orthogonal functions $i_1, i_2, \ldots, i_N$. We can, if we choose, refer eqn. (2.91) to a new basis $i'_1, i'_2, \ldots, i'_N$, by means of a linear transformation

$$(I) = [T] (I'), \qquad (2.92)$$

where $[T]$ is the transformation matrix and (I') is a column vector representing the current on the wire relative to the new basis functions, i.e. with the vector (i'_n) representing the function i'_n,

$$(I') = I'_1(i'_1) + I'_2(i'_2) + \cdots + I'_N(i'_N), \qquad (2.93)$$

where the $I'_n, n = 1, 2, \ldots, N$, are the components of the vector (I'). Substituting eqn. (2.92) into eqn. (2.90),

$$[Z] [T] (I') - (V) = (0). \qquad (2.94)$$

Letting

$$[Z'] = [Z] [T], \qquad (2.95)$$

we write

$$[Z'](I') - (V) = (0). \tag{2.96}$$

Equation (2.96) is equivalent to eqn. (2.90), referred to the new basis.

Consider, for example, the transformation from the pulse function basis set to a basis of modal orthonormal functions, such as the cosine and sine functions. In this application we find that the matrix $[T]$ of eqn. (2.92) is simply defined. In fact, inspection of eqn. (2.92) reveals that each member of the new set of basis functions forms a column of the matrix $[T]$. If, for example, the cosine functions $\cos(n\pi l)/L$, $n = 1, 2, \ldots, N$, form the new basis, then the nth column of $[T]$ represents an nth order cosine function distributed over the wire, i.e. the mnth element of $[T]$ is $\cos(n\pi l_m)/L$, where l_m is the location of the mth match point on the center-line of the wire. Thus, eqn. (2.92) would be

$$\begin{bmatrix} I_1 \\ I_2 \\ \vdots \\ I_N \end{bmatrix} = \begin{bmatrix} \cos\dfrac{\pi l_1}{L} & \cos\dfrac{2\pi l_1}{L} & \cdots & \cos\dfrac{N\pi l_1}{L} \\ \cos\dfrac{\pi l_2}{L} & \cos\dfrac{2\pi l_2}{L} & \cdots & \cos\dfrac{N\pi l_2}{L} \\ \vdots & \vdots & \vdots & \vdots \\ \cos\dfrac{\pi l_N}{L} & \cos\dfrac{2\pi l_N}{L} & \cdots & \cos\dfrac{N\pi l_N}{L} \end{bmatrix} \begin{bmatrix} I'_1 \\ I'_2 \\ \vdots \\ I'_N \end{bmatrix} \tag{2.97}$$

The simple definition of the transformation matrix in this example is a consequence of the fact that each component I_n of the current vector (I) in the piecewise uniform basis system equals the current at l_n, $(-L/2 \leq l_n \leq L/2)$, on the wire. This is true since only the nth basis function is nonzero at l_n. It is not true in general, however. For example, it is not true of the new current vector (I').

Once we have determined the desired basis and have thus specified the transformation matrix $[T]$, the impedance matrix $[Z]$ is transformed as in eqn. (2.95), and the new set of equations, eqn. (2.96), is obtained with reference to the new basis.

Usually one finds that the components I'_m of the current solution vector (I') of eqn. (2.96) are negligible for $m > M$, $(M < N)$. That is the solution

$$(I') = I'_1(i'_1) + I'_2(i'_2) + \cdots + I'_M(i'_M) + \cdots I'_N(i'_N) \tag{2.98}$$

is quite well approximated by retaining only the first M terms (assuming proper ordering of the I'_m). In fact, it is not unusual to obtain sufficient accuracy with $M < N/10$. Recalling that the computer solution time for N linear equations is approximately proportional to N^3, one of the advantages afforded by such a basis transformation is evident.

Thus, when this approximation can be made we need only to solve eqn. (2.96) for M of the N unknowns. The $N \times N$ impedance matrix $[Z']$ may be replaced by an $N \times M$ rectangular matrix $[Z'_a]$ formed by taking the first M columns of $[Z']$, and the column vector (I') is replaced by an M-dimensional column vector (I'_a) whose components are the first M components of (I'). The excitation vector (V) remains unchanged. The result is the overdetermined set of N equations in M unknowns,

$$
\begin{bmatrix}
Z'_{a_{11}} & Z'_{a_{12}} & \cdots & Z'_{a_{1M}} \\
Z'_{a_{21}} & Z'_{a_{22}} & \cdots & Z'_{a_{2M}} \\
\vdots & \vdots & & \vdots \\
Z'_{a_{N1}} & Z'_{a_{N2}} & \cdots & Z'_{a_{NM}}
\end{bmatrix}
\begin{bmatrix} I'_{a_1} \\ I'_{a_2} \\ \vdots \\ I'_{a_M} \end{bmatrix}
-
\begin{bmatrix} V_1 \\ V_2 \\ \vdots \\ V_N \end{bmatrix}
=
\begin{bmatrix} 0 \\ 0 \\ \vdots \\ 0 \end{bmatrix}
\tag{2.99}
$$

for which many solutions exist, depending upon which subset of M equations is chosen. To avoid this non-uniqueness, we multiply by the complex conjugate transpose of $[Z'_a]$ to obtain

$$
\begin{bmatrix}
Z'^*_{a_{11}} & Z'^*_{a_{21}} & \cdots & Z'^*_{a_{N1}} \\
Z'^*_{a_{12}} & Z'^*_{a_{22}} & \cdots & Z'^*_{a_{N2}} \\
\vdots & \vdots & & \vdots \\
Z'^*_{a_{1M}} & Z'^*_{a_{2M}} & \cdots & Z'^*_{a_{NM}}
\end{bmatrix}
\begin{bmatrix}
Z'_{a_{11}} & Z'_{a_{12}} & \cdots & Z'_{a_{1M}} \\
Z'_{a_{21}} & Z'_{a_{22}} & \cdots & Z'_{a_{2M}} \\
\vdots & \vdots & & \vdots \\
Z'_{a_{N1}} & Z'_{a_{N2}} & \cdots & Z'_{a_{NM}}
\end{bmatrix}
\begin{bmatrix} I'_{a_1} \\ I'_{a_2} \\ \vdots \\ I'_{a_M} \end{bmatrix}
$$

$$
-
\begin{bmatrix}
Z'^*_{a_{11}} & Z'^*_{a_{21}} & \cdots & Z'^*_{a_{N1}} \\
Z'^*_{a_{12}} & Z'^*_{a_{22}} & \cdots & Z'^*_{a_{N2}} \\
\vdots & \vdots & & \vdots \\
Z'^*_{a_{1M}} & Z'^*_{a_{2M}} & \cdots & Z'^*_{NM}
\end{bmatrix}
\begin{bmatrix} V_1 \\ V_2 \\ \vdots \\ V_N \end{bmatrix}
=
\begin{bmatrix} 0 \\ 0 \\ \vdots \\ 0 \end{bmatrix}
\tag{2.100}
$$

where the superscript * denotes the complex conjugate. The product $[\widetilde{Z'_a}]^* [Z'_a]$, where $\sim$ denotes the matrix transpose, yields an $M \times M$ complex symmetric matrix. The solution of eqn. (2.100) provides a least mean square "match" by M modes of the boundary conditions at N points on the wire. Only M simultaneous equations need be solved, where M, the number of modes, may be less than 10, while the number of match points, N, may be greater than 100, for example. There can be substantial savings in computer time and storage requirements when this technique is used, as is demonstrated by the example given later.

The least square solution of problems associated with wires of closed configuration, such as a loop, causes no problems, but the application of least square methods to wires of open configuration, such as a dipole, requires special consideration.

The field in the vicinity of the end of a wire of open configuration exhibits certain discontinuities depending on the geometry of the wire termination. In the case where flat ends are assumed, an edge-type singularity results. In numerical calculations this singularity induces erroneous values for the scattered field on the wire in the vicinity of the ends. Consequently, any solution which satisfies the boundary conditions on the wire in a least square sense must account for this effect.

To clarify the effect which the field near the wire ends will have on a least square solution, consider a straight wire scatterer with a plane wave incident from the broadside aspect. The incident electric field is assumed to have unit magnitude and zero phase on the wire axis. Ideally the induced current would produce the scattered field shown in Fig. 2.8a, so that the total tangential field ($E^i + E^s$) on the wire is zero. Numerical solutions, however, provide only an approximation (Fig. 2.8b) to that field. In deriving a least square solution it is seen that, roughly speaking, the scaling coefficient A in Fig. 2.8b will be adjusted to produce a least mean squared error in the total field. The large error in the approximate fields near the wire ends forces A to be less than unity. The associated current is thus reduced in magnitude and is in error. If, however, in obtaining a least square solution, the match points within a

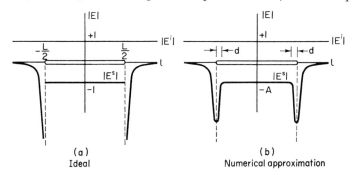

FIG. 2.8. Incident and scattered fields on axis for a plane wave incident on a straight wire (courtesy of R. Turpin).

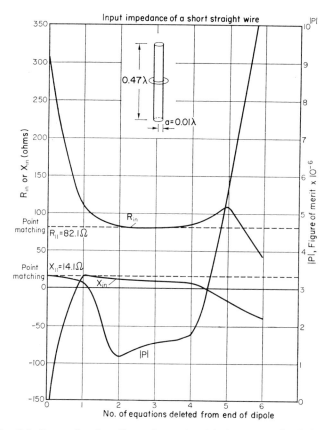

FIG. 2.9. Curves showing effects of equation deletion near ends of dipole.

certain distance, d (Fig. 2.8b), from the wire ends are ignored (i.e. the equations correspond-ing to these points are deleted from the set of equations) a better solution results as has been shown by Turpin (1969).

The need for these special considerations is not unusual. Other numerical solution methods (Ott *et al.*, 1967) have shown a critical dependence on the choice of match points.

There is a need, then, for some measure of the error in the field matching achieved by a given solution both for the purpose of optimizing the solution conditions just discussed and to serve as an estimate of the accuracy of the final solution. A useful figure of merit is

$$P = -\tfrac{1}{2} \operatorname{Re} \left\{ \int_L \mathbf{J}^* \cdot \mathbf{E}^T \, dl \right\}, \tag{2.101}$$

where $\mathbf{J}^*$ is the complex conjugate of the current density and $\mathbf{E}^T$ is the total electric field (i.e. the error field) on the wire. P is the average power radiated, in the absence of the scat-terer, by an equivalent source current $\mathbf{J}$ which generates an electric field intensity $\mathbf{E}^T$. A nega-tive value for P corresponds to the absorption of power while a positive value corresponds to radiation. Because the wire is a perfectly conducting scatterer it can neither absorb nor generate power. In this case the condition $P = 0$ corresponds to satisfying the condition of conservation of power. It is desirable, then, to minimize the magnitude of P.

It must be pointed out, however, that to obtain $|P| = 0$ in a numerical solution such as that being discussed here does not necessarily imply that the solution is exact, for the figure of merit is itself computed by approximate methods. Equation (2.101) is, in this work, approximated by

$$P \approx -\tfrac{1}{2} \operatorname{Re} \left\{ \sum_{n=1}^N I_n^* \cdot E_n^T \right\}, \tag{2.102}$$

where I_n and E_n^T are the current and the total electric field intensity at the N match points.

Figure 2.9 shows the figure of merit and impedance for a dipole of length $L = 0.47\lambda$ with radius $a = 0.01\lambda$. Note that a very significant improvement is obtained by simply deleting the point nearest each end. This is usually true for most situations. Note further that this is not the optimum for the dipole being considered. The optimum distance depends on the wire radius and on the accuracy of the numerical impedance matrix. The impedance matrix $[Z_a']$ used to obtain these solutions was derived by a transformation from a piecewise uniform basis of dimension $N = 80$ to a cosine basis where $M = 20$.

As an example of the possible improvement afforded by the basis transformation method given here, consider Fig. 2.10 which applies to a half-wave long wire radiator. Notice for, say, 100 match points the substantially shorter running time. Note also, the potential for obtaining more match points (in a least square sense) than might be conveniently done using just the piecewise uniform method.

2.4.5. Piecewise-sinusoidal Basis: Reaction-matching

In the previous section we considered a method of transforming from one basis requiring a large system of equations to a basis that resulted in a smaller system of equations to describe the problem. A motivation for performing such a transformation is to reduce the required amount of computation time.

2a M.-CTE

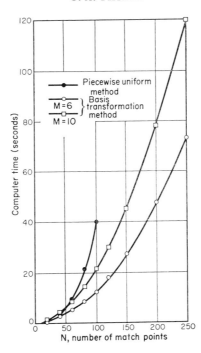

Fig. 2.10. Computation times for a piecewise uniform method and for the basis transformation
method with cosine modes (courtesy of R. Turpin).

In solving problems using the method of moments, computation time depends mainly on two factors. The first factor is the amount of computational effort needed to obtain the elements in the generalized impedance matrix $[Z]$. Usually this relates to the amount of numerical integration required to calculate the Z_{mn}'s. The second factor is the size of the matrix $[Z]$ and hence the computational time required to obtain $[Z]^{-1}$.

In this section a method developed by Richmond (1969) will be discussed whereby the piecewise-sinusoidal basis functions previously mentioned are used to obtain the elements in the impedance matrix $[Z]$ using the reaction concept. The advantages of the method are twofold. First, the amount of computational effort required to obtain the elements of $[Z]$ is relatively low because closed form expressions can be obtained for many of the required integrations. In fact, for coplanar antenna elements all integrations are in closed form involving sine and cosine integrals which simply need to be evaluated on the computer (Richmond and Geary, 1970). Secondly, the method converges very quickly and therefore the size of the $[Z]$ matrix for a given problem is relatively small when compared to the use of other basis and weighting functions.

Since the reaction concept is important in the method to be presented in this section, it is sometimes called reaction-matching. The technique of reaction-matching is really an extension of the induced e.m.f. technique (Jordan, 1950). To illustrate, consider a dipole antenna with source at the center. The dipole, then, is made up of two pieces or segments, one on either side of the source. Reaction-matching employs two or more such segments in representing an antenna such as a dipole.

The reaction-matching or N-segment induced e.m.f. technique can be shown to be equivalent to Galerkin's method. The proof is somewhat lengthy and will not be presented here. Instead, the implementation of the technique will be demonstrated starting with the two segment solution.

For a linear antenna, we replace the original source (i.e. $\mathbf{J}_i$ and $\mathbf{K}_i$ on the dipole) with

$$\mathbf{J} = \hat{n} \times \mathbf{H}, \qquad (2.103)$$

$$\mathbf{K} = \mathbf{E} \times \hat{n} \qquad (2.104)$$

on the closed surface S of the antenna. The outward unit normal vector on S is denoted $\hat{n}$ and the electric and magnetic current densities $\mathbf{J}$ and $\mathbf{K}$ are called the "true sources". From the equivalence principle of Schelkunoff, $\mathbf{J}$ and $\mathbf{K}$ generate the true field outside S and a null field in the interior region. For perfectly conducting antennas, such as we will consider here, $\mathbf{K}$ vanishes except in the gap region.

The next step is to place a filamentary electric line source on the axis of the antenna and "react" this "test source" with the true source. By react we mean apply the reciprocity theorem. That is, if source distributions $\mathbf{J}(a)$ and $\mathbf{K}(a)$ generate fields $\mathbf{E}(a)$ and $\mathbf{K}(a)$ in the presence of source b acting as a receiver (and vice versa), then a complex number defined as the reaction between sources a and b is given by

$$\langle a, b \rangle = \iiint_{V_a} [\mathbf{J}(a) \cdot \mathbf{E}(b) - \mathbf{K}(a) \cdot \mathbf{H}(b)] \, dV_a. \qquad (2.105)$$

Thus, reaction is a measure of the coupling between the two sources a and b. If the physical situation satisfies the conditions for reciprocity, then

$$\langle a, b \rangle = \langle b, a \rangle. \qquad (2.106)$$

In our situation here, the electric surface current density $\mathbf{J}$ on the cylindrical surface of the dipole can usually be replaced by an equivalent filamentary source parallel with the test source. Thus, we react two line sources that are displaced from each other by the dipole radius.

Let us assume the current distribution on the test dipole is given by

$$I_t(z) = \frac{\sin k \, (h - |z|)}{\sin kh} \qquad (2.107)$$

where h is the arm length, z is measured from the center and $k = 2\pi/\lambda$. Thus, in a two-segment solution, the current on the true source (or actual dipole current distribution) is expressed by

$$I(z) = I_1 \frac{\sin k \, (h - |z|)}{\sin kh} \qquad (2.108)$$

and the objective is to determine the terminal current I_1 excited by a given voltage generator V_1. From the reciprocity theorem, the solution is found from $I_1 Z = V_1$ where Z is the reaction between the test source having fields $\mathbf{E}_t$ and $\mathbf{H}_t$ and the true source J of eqn. (2.103):

$$Z = -\frac{1}{I_1} \int \mathbf{J} \cdot \mathbf{E}_t \, dl. \qquad (2.109)$$

Note that this two-segment solution for the linear antenna coincides with the well-known induced e.m.f. theory presented in many textbooks.

The two-segment solution is, of course, useful only for a limited range of antenna lengths and radii. Therefore, let us consider next the four-segment solution for a single linear antenna. The extension to the N-segment solution for single and coupled antennas will then be obvious.

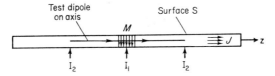

FIG. 2.11. In the four-segment solution, the antenna is divided into four segments for a piecewise-sinusoidal current expansion (courtesy of J. H. Richmond).

Consider the symmetrical dipole of Fig. 2.11 divided into four segments. The complex I_1 and I_2 represent samples of the current function $I(z)$ at the junctions of the various segments:

$$I_1 = I(0), \tag{2.110}$$

$$I_2 = I(h/2) \tag{2.111}$$

and the current is assumed to vanish at the ends of the antenna. Thus, extending the current expression of eqn. (2.107) to a piecewise sinusoidal expansion,

$$I(z) = I_1 \frac{\sin k(h/2 - z)}{\sin kh/2} + I_2 \frac{\sin kz}{\sin kh/2} \quad \text{for} \quad 0 \le z \le h/2, \tag{2.112}$$

$$I(z) = I_2 \frac{\sin k(h - z)}{\sin kh/2} \quad \text{for } h/2 \le z \le h. \tag{2.113}$$

The objective is to determine I_1 and I_2. This is accomplished by applying two reaction tests on the true current $I(z)$. One equation is obtained by reacting $I(z)$ with a test dipole centered on the antenna axis as in Fig. 2.11. This test dipole has arm length $h/2$. The dipole is then moved to the right a distance $h/2$ and reacted with $I(z)$. This yields a pair of simultaneous linear equations.

$$I_1 Z_{11} + I_2 Z_{12} = V_1, \tag{2.114}$$

$$I_1 Z_{21} + I_2 Z_{22} = 0. \tag{2.115}$$

Z_{11} and Z_{22} represent the mutual impedance between parallel filamentary dipoles with sideways displacement a and no stagger. In Z_{12} and Z_{21} the dipoles are in echelon with displacement a and stagger $h/2$. Due to the symmetry of the dipole, the impedance matrix is made symmetric by doubling Z_{21} and Z_{22} in eqn. (2.115).

If the piecewise-sinusoidal current distribution is employed for each segment as above, then the current on any given segment can be considered as the sum of two sinusoidal currents, each of which vanishes at one or the other end of the segment. For this reason the equivalent surface distribution is treated as a collection of, say, N overlapping tubular dipole current densities. The nth dipole has terminal current I_n at the nth junction with the current vanishing at the far ends of the two segments forming the nth junction.

The solution for the unknown complex junction currents I_n proceeds by introducing a set of N filamentary test dipoles each having sinusoidal currents and each being located along the axis of the original wire antenna. Reciprocity is enforced successively between each test dipole and all the tubular surface true dipoles in turn (Richards, 1970). This yields the following relationship between the nth test dipole and the nth true dipole:

$$V_m \delta_{mn} = - \int \mathbf{I}_n(\tau_n) \cdot \mathbf{E}_m \, d\tau_n. \tag{2.116}$$

The integration is carried out on τ_n the coordinate along the arms of the nth true dipole filaments. The symbol δ_{mn} is the standard Kronecker delta. Let the assumed form of $\mathbf{I}_n(\tau_n)$ for the true dipole be inserted into eqn. (2.116) and define a mutual impedance term as

$$Z_{mn} = - \int_{l_{n-1}}^{l_n} \frac{\sin k \, (l_n - l)}{\sin k d_{n-1}} \hat{\tau}_{n-1} \cdot \mathbf{E}_m \, dl - \int_{l_n}^{l_{n+1}} \frac{\sin k \, (l - l_n)}{\sin k d_n} \hat{\tau}_n \cdot \mathbf{E}_m \, dl. \tag{2.117}$$

The dummy variable l is the coordinate along a particular segment where d_{n-1} and d_n are the lengths of the $(n-1)$th and nth segments, respectively. The unit vectors $\hat{\tau}_{n-1}$ and $\hat{\tau}_n$ are in the direction of positive current for the $(n-1)$th and nth segments, respectively while $\mathbf{E}_m$, as before, is the free-space electric field intensity radiated by the mth test dipole with piecewise-sinusoidal current. Thus the mutual impedance terms Z_{mn} are given by the classical induced-e.m.f. formula. As mentioned previously, these integrals can be obtained in closed form for coplanar segments. In the case of non-coplanar segments, the integrals in eq. (2.117) may be calculated numerically using one of the standard numerical integration formulas.

Equation (2.116) may now be written

$$V_m \delta_{mn} = Z_{mn} I_n, \tag{2.118}$$

where I_n is the complex terminal current at the nth junction. The calculation of the reaction between the mth test dipole and the entire true surface current density, consisting of the N overlapping surface dipoles, yields the following relations:

$$V_m = \sum_{n=1}^{N} Z_{mn} I_n. \tag{2.119}$$

Equation (2.119) represents one linear equation out of a system of N equations that are obtained by successively enforcing reciprocity (or calculating the reaction) between the N surface dipoles and each of the N axial test dipoles in turn. This set of equations can be written in matrix form as

$$[V] = [Z] [I] \tag{2.120}$$

and solved by standard techniques for the unknown current vector $[I]$. Since a unit voltage source is usually assumed, the current coefficient at the feed junction represents the input admittance for the antenna.

By now certain similarities to Galerkin's method are apparent. In fact, reaction-matching could be derived by starting with the method of moments. Its original derivation, however, was from the fundamental principles of reaction and reciprocity (Richmond, 1969).

In our discussion of reaction-matching, we have stated that $\mathbf{E}_m$ in eqn. (2.117), for example, is the free-space electric field intensity radiated by a test dipole having a piecewise, sinusoidal current. We associate, of course, the current on the test source with the weighting function discussed earlier. Let us now obtain expressions for the fields radiated by a test dipole having a piecewise-sinusoidal current (Otto and Richmond, 1969).

Schelkunoff and Friis (1952) have presented in a very useable form the exact fields of a time-harmonic electric line source with sinusoidal current distribution

$$I(z) = A \cos kz + B \sin kz. \tag{2.121}$$

The z-component of this field is

$$E_z(\varrho, z) = \frac{j}{4\pi\omega\varepsilon} \left[I'(z') \frac{\exp(-jkr)}{r} + I(z') \frac{\partial}{\partial z} \frac{\exp(-jkr)}{r} \right]_{z'=z_1}^{z'=z_2} \tag{2.122}$$

where

$$r = \sqrt{\{\varrho^2 + (z - z')^2\}}. \tag{2.123}$$

As indicated in Fig. 2.12, the line source extends from z_1 to z_2 on the z-axis. $I'(z)$ denotes the first derivative of $I(z)$ and $k = \omega \sqrt{(\mu\varepsilon)}$.

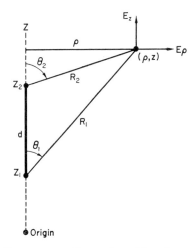

FIG. 2.12. An electric line source on the z-axis and the observation point at (ϱ, z)
(courtesy of G.A.Richards).

By superposition, the field of a line source with piecewise-sinusoidal current distribution is

$$E_z(\varrho, z) = \frac{j}{4\pi\omega\varepsilon} \sum_{i=1}^{n-1} \left[I'(z') \frac{\exp(-jkr)}{r} + I(z') \frac{\partial}{\partial z} \frac{\exp(-jkr)}{r} \right]_{z'=z_i}^{z'=z_{i+1}}. \tag{2.124}$$

The current $I(z)$ is assumed to have the form of eq. (2.121) between each neighboring pair of points z_i and z_{i+1}.

If the current $I(z)$ is continuous across the junctions z_i and vanishes at the endpoints z_1 and z_n, eqn. (2.124) reduces to

$$E_z(\varrho, z) = \frac{j}{4\pi\omega\varepsilon} \sum_{i=1}^{n} \Delta I_i' \frac{e^{-jkr_i}}{r_i} \tag{2.125}$$

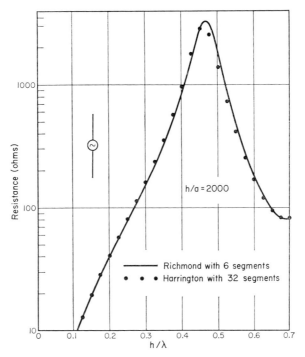

FIG. 2.13. Input resistance versus h/λ for cylindrical-wire antenna with radius a and total length $L = 2h$ (courtesy of J.H. Richmond).

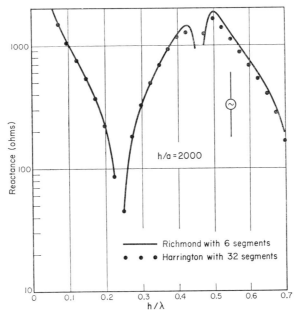

FIG. 2.14. Input reactance versus h/λ for cylindrical-wire antenna with radius a and total length $L = 2h$ (courtesy of J.H. Richmond).

where

$$\Delta I_i' = \lim_{\varepsilon \to 0} [I'(z_i - \varepsilon) - I'(z_i + \varepsilon)]. \tag{2.126}$$

The constants $\Delta I_i'$ represent the slope discontinuities in the current function at the points z_i. Of course, $I'(z_1 - \varepsilon) = I'(z_n + \varepsilon) = 0$.

In a similar manner, it is found that the radial field is

$$E_\varrho(\varrho, z) = \frac{-j}{4\pi\omega\varepsilon\varrho} \sum_{i=1}^{n} \Delta I_i' \, \mathrm{e}^{-jkr_i} \cos\theta_i. \tag{2.127}$$

Despite their apparent simplicity, these field expressions for E_z and E_ϱ are rigorous even in the near-zone.

As an example of the accuracy and rate of convergence afforded by reaction-matching, consider Figs. 2.13 and 2.14. Note that reaction-matching required only six segments while for the same accuracy point-matching with triangle functions (i.e. piecewise linear) required about five times as many segments.

2.4.6. Characteristic Mode Currents: An Eigenvalue Problem

In considering the advantages and disadvantages of the various basis functions discussed earlier in this section on bases, one might be led to the question of whether or not there exists a particular set of surface currents and their corresponding radiated fields which characterize the antenna size and shape independent of any specific excitation. Indeed there is such a basis set and they are called "characteristic modes". These modes have many interesting mathematical properties, the most notable of which is that they are orthogonal. Thus, the power radiated by each mode may be considered independently of any other modes which may exist.

The concept of characteristic modes is not new for they have long been used in radiation analysis of conducting bodies whose surfaces coincide with one of the coordinate systems in which the wave equation is separable (e.g. the sphere). Garbacz (1965) proposed that such modes exist for perfectly conducting radiators of arbitrary shape. In 1968 he succeeded in finding the characteristic modes for several simple cases (Garbacz, 1968). The procedure was essentially to diagonalize the scattering matrix. However, the calculation of the modes was generally quite tedious. Turpin (1969) was successful in calculating characteristic modes for several somewhat more difficult problems (e.g. scattering by a circular wire arc) but the computational problems inherent in calculating the modes remained (Garbacz and Turpin, 1971). Recently, Harrington and Mautz (1971a, b) approached the characteristic mode problem from the alternative viewpoint of diagonalizing the impedance matrix formed by the operations indicated in eqns. (2.66) and (2.67). They cast the work of Garbacz into the notation of the method of moments with the important result that general formulas were derived which permit the calculation of characteristic modes of arbitrary bodies in a relatively straightforward manner.

At the time of the initial preparation of this chapter the usefulness of characteristic modes was in considerable doubt. However, due to the aforementioned computational advances they will undoubtedly find increasing utilization in certain radiation problems in the near future (e.g. maximizing the directivity of an N-port array). Thus, this introduction to characteristic modes is being included in the section on bases while in Appendix II, at the end of the chapter, we briefly consider some of the mathematical details of characteristic mode theory.

2.4.7. The Stability Problem

One very important problem that is seldom discussed in the literature is that of obtaining a stable numerical solution and recognizing an unstable one. Obviously, if the impedance matrix $[Z]$ is singular, then its inverse does not exist and we cannot write

$$[I] = [Z]^{-1} [V]. \tag{2.128}$$

Thus, a unique solution does not exist. However, if the impedance matrix is "almost singular", then it is possible to obtain a solution under certain conditions and an unstable solution under other conditions as we shall presently see. A system of simultaneous equations having an "almost singular" coefficient matrix is said to be ill-conditioned. An ill-conditioned system can give rise to unstable solutions, In the two-dimensional case, singularity of the coefficient (impedance) matrix means that two lines (solutions) are parallel. Since they cannot intersect, no solution exists. A similar situation occurs with parallel planes or hyperplanes when the order of the system is greater than two. A well-conditioned system describes hyperplanes that intersect at nearly 90° (Wexler, 1969). The intersection (solution) is relatively insensitive to roundoff error as a consequence. As the intersection angle of the hyperplanes tends toward zero, roundoff error tends to cause appreciable motion of the intersection resulting in an unstable solution that one cannot trust.

As an example consider first the following well-condititioned system

$$300x + 400y = 700, \tag{2.129a}$$
$$100x + 100y = 200, \tag{2.129b}$$

for which the values $x = 1$ and $y = 1$ form a unique solution. If the equations are changed to

$$303x + 400y = 700, \tag{2.130a}$$
$$101x + 100y = 200, \tag{2.130b}$$

the solution only changes to $x = 100/101 \cong 0.99$ and $y = 1$. Thus a change of 1 per cent in coefficients produces a change of 1 per cent in the solution. In contrast, consider the following ill-conditioned system

$$300x + 400y = 700, \tag{2.131a}$$
$$100x + 133y = 233, \tag{2.131b}$$

which also has the solution $x = 1$ and $y = 1$. If we change the coefficients in various small ways such that

$$300x + 400y = 700, \tag{2.132a}$$
$$100x + 133y = 232 \tag{2.132b}$$

and

$$300x + 400y = 700, \tag{2.133a}$$

$$100x + 132y = 233 \tag{2.133b}$$

and

$$300x + 400y = 700, \tag{2.134a}$$

$$100x + 132y = 234, \tag{2.134b}$$

then the solutions for these systems are respectively ($x = -3$, $y = 4$), ($x = 2$, $y = \frac{1}{4}$) and $x = 3$, $y = -\frac{1}{2}$). Here we see that the relative changes in the solutions are of the order of hundreds of per cent while the coefficient changes were only a fraction of 1 per cent.

Each of these three ill-conditioned systems of equations has a nearly singular coefficient matrix which is the reason for the sensitivity of the solutions to the coefficient values. If one normalizes the coefficients in each equation, it will become obvious that the value of the coefficient determinant is nearly zero, being much less than unity in each case. For example, the normalizing factors for eqns. (2.131) are 500.0 and 166.4, respectively. The resulting magnitude of the coefficient determinant is but 0.0012. In contrast, the value of the first set of well-conditioned equations (eqns. (2.129)) has a coefficient determinant whose value is 0.1414.

It is worthwhile to be aware of the type of solution behavior that an ill-conditioned system of equations can produce for the user of numerical methods in the pursuit of radiation problems is very likely to encounter such a situation sooner or later. The rapid variation of a problem solution with certain parameters may well not be due to an actual error in the problem formulation or in the writing of a computer program, but rather due to the degree of conditioning of the system of equations. While accurate solutions can sometimes be obtained from poorly conditioned systems of equations if one pays close attention to sources of numerical error in calculating the coefficients, often a change in basis or weighting functions is required to alleviate the situation.

2.5. CALCULATION OF ANTENNA CHARACTERISTICS

Before proceeding on to the sections containing examples, it is perhaps beneficial to discuss the basic procedures for the calculation of such antenna characteristics as impedance, patterns, gain and so forth. Specific examples of such calculations are given in Solution 2.6–2.8. Thus, in Section 2.5.1 we will discuss the calculation of current distributions, impedance and the inclusion of lumped loading. In Section 2.5.2 we will deal with the calculation of the far-zone quantities such as radiation patterns, gain and radiation efficiency.

2.5.1. Current Distribution, Impedance and Lumped Loading

As we have already stated, once the current on a radiator or radiator and metallic body combination is known, calculation of other antenna characteristics follows quickly. First, let us consider the current distribution. If one is using pulse functions as basis functions in the point-matching technique, then once the current coefficients I_n are known, the current is known precisely at the match points assuming, of course, that the solution has converged. Since the distance between match points is small in terms of the wavelength, one can simply fit a curve through the current values at the match points to obtain a good approximation to the current distribution along the radiator. In the case of quadratic or sinusoidal interpolation, the interpolation formula gives the distribution between match points. In the case of the piecewise-sinusoidal functions the current distribution is obtained in a similar manner. That is, the two currents shown in Fig. 2.15 are added at various points along the wire antenna to obtain the distribution.

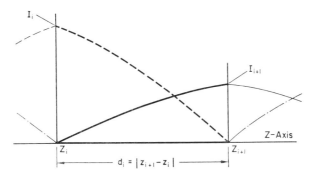

FIG. 2.15. Piecewise-sinusoidal currents on a wire segment (courtesy of G. A. Richards).

In the case of entire-domain basis functions such as the Fourier series in eqn. (2.78) the current distribution is obtained by summing the series at as many points as are deemed necessary and a smooth curve drawn through the points to give the current distribution along the radiator. The summation process is, of course, easily done on a computer.

Once the current I_t at the antenna terminals is known due to a given antenna terminal voltage V_t, then Z_t may be obtained as

$$Z_t = V_t/I_t. \tag{2.135}$$

The calculation of accurate impedance data is a task that is sensitive to the model used for the feed point. Some examples (e.g. Section 2.7.2) that follow will use the delta-gap representation mentioned in Section 2.2.2. Other examples will use a magnetic frill current which accurately models the coaxial feed point of a ground plane mounted monopole as indicated in Fig. 2.16. Since the magnetic frill current provides a model of the feed point in a one to one correspondence with the real feed point, it provides a means of calculating the input impedance with excellent accuracy. A computer program for the fields of a magnetic frill current is given in Appendix I.

Next, let us see how lumped loading may be included in a problem formulation. If a load Z_m is inserted into a wire antenna at a match-point or sample-point m having a current I_m, then the total voltage acting at that point is

$$V_m = V_m^g - I_m Z_m \tag{2.136}$$

where V_m^g represents a voltage generator that may be located at point m in series with Z_m. In many cases V_m^g will be zero.

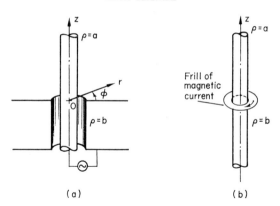

FIG. 2.16. (a) Coaxial line feeding a monopole through a ground plane. (b) Mathematical model of the antenna (courtesy of D. V. Otto).

Considering the mth equation in a system of N linear equations, we can write

$$\sum_{n=1}^{N} Z_{mn} I_n = V_m^g - I_m Z_m \qquad (2.137)$$

or

$$\sum_{n=1}^{N} Z'_{mn} I_n = V_m^g \qquad (2.138)$$

where

$$Z'_{mm} = Z_{mm} + Z_m. \qquad (2.139)$$

Thus, except for the diagonal elements, the new impedance matrix is the same as the original, or $Z'_{mn} = Z_{mn}$, $m \neq n$. Thus, the effect of lumped loading may be accounted for by simply adding the load impedances Z_m to the corresponding diagonal elements in the impedance matrix (Richmond, 1969). This will be demonstrated by the example in Section 2.7.2.

2.5.2. Radiation Patterns, Gain and Efficiency

It is a straightforward task to calculate the far-fields anywhere in space due to a known current. In the far-zone $\mathbf{E} = -j\omega \mathbf{A}$. Thus, for a filamentary source

$$\mathbf{E}(r, \theta, \phi) = -j\omega\mu \frac{e^{-jkr_0}}{4\pi r_0} \int_{\substack{\text{along} \\ \text{wire} \\ \text{antenna}}} \mathbf{I}(\xi)\, F(\theta, \phi)\, d\xi. \qquad (2.140)$$

where

$$F(\theta, \phi) = \exp jk\,[x' \sin\theta \cos\phi + y' \sin\theta \sin\phi + z' \cos\theta] \qquad (2.141)$$

and (x', y', z') denotes the source coordinates while (θ, ϕ) denotes the angular position of the observation point in space. After performing the above integration over all parts or elements of the antenna, one obtains the orthogonal components of the far-field $E_\theta (r, \theta, \phi)$

and $E_\phi(r, \theta, \phi)$. The power gain may then be determined as

$$G(\theta, \phi) = \frac{[|E_\theta|^2 + |E_\phi|^2] r_0^2}{30 |I_t|^2 R_t} \tag{2.142}$$

where R_t is the real part of the antenna input impedance. The directivity may be obtained by replacing R_t with R_r, the radiation resistance since in a lossless case $R_t = R_r$ and thus the directivity and gain are equal.

To calculate the radiation efficiency consider

$$P_{in} = |I_t|^2 R_t \tag{2.143}$$

which is the time average power input to the antenna. The radiated power is

$$P_r = |I_t|^2 R_r \tag{2.144}$$

and the power loss is

$$P_l = |I_t|^2 R_l \tag{2.145}$$

where R_l is the loss resistance. We can define the radiation efficiency as

$$\frac{P_r}{P_{in}} = \frac{|I_t|^2 R_r}{|I_t|^2 R_t} = \frac{R_r}{R_r + R_l}. \tag{2.146}$$

Alternatively, we could determine the radiated power by integrating the power density in the far-field. However, the above method is computationally more efficient.

With these antenna characteristics computationally in hand, let us now investigate several example wire antennas in the following three sections.

2.6. THE YAGI–UDA ARRAY

In this section we wish to demonstrate the use of entire-domain basis functions in conjunction with a point-matching solution of Pocklington's integral equation. Both will be used to formulate a solution to the classical problem of the Yagi–Uda array. This wire antenna, although well-known for many years (Uda, 1926; and Yagi, 1928), had not been accurately analysed in general until the advent of the modern-day digital computer (Thiele, 1969a).

Two somewhat different formulations to the problem will be offered. The first solution will use a current generator as a source on the driven element (Thiele, 1969a). This formulation provides for rapid convergence of results for the far-field patterns, phase velocity and current distributions but does not easily provide a means of determining the input impedance of the array. The second formulation offers less rapid convergence but does provide for very accurate impedance data (Thiele, 1969b). These two formulations are simply intended as illustrative examples of how a wire antenna problem, such as the Yagi–Uda array, could be formulated. There are of course, other formulations that one could conceive of.

2.6.1. The Integral Operator

In determining the integral operator for this problem, we wish to determine L_{op} where

$$L_{op}(\mathbf{J}) = (\mathbf{E}^i) \tag{2.147}$$

and $\mathbf{J}$ is the current density on the various elements in the array as depicted in Fig. 2.17. Viewing each element in the array as an individual wire antenna, we then have a suitable expression for L_{op} given by a simple extension of eqn. (2.75). That is, L_{op} for the pth element in the array is given by

$$L_{op} = \frac{-\lambda\sqrt{(\mu/\varepsilon)}}{8\pi^2 j}\int_{-L_p/2}^{L_p/2} G(r, r')\, dz' \tag{2.148}$$

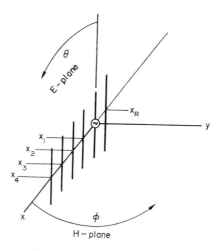

FIG. 2.17. Coordinate system used to analyze Yagi–Uda array.

where $G(r, r')$ is given by eqn. (2.77) and where now

$$r = \sqrt{\{(x' - x)^2 + (y' - y)^2 + (z' - z)^2 + a^2\}}. \tag{2.149}$$

Since we are considering each element in the array to be an individual wire antenna, let us use the entire-domain basis functions

$$I_p(z) = \sum_{n=1}^{N} I_{n_p}\cos(2n-1)\frac{\pi z}{L_p}, \quad -L_{p/2} \le z \le L_{p/2} \tag{2.150}$$

where

$$I_p(z) = \frac{J_p(z)}{2\pi a}. \tag{2.151}$$

The operator $L_{op}(J)$ must be evaluated not only when the observation point is on element p, but also when it is on the other elements as well, as indicated in Fig. 2.18. Thus, one can write

$$L_{op}(J) = \frac{-\lambda\sqrt{(\mu/\varepsilon)}}{8\pi^2 j}\sum_{p=1}^{D+2}\sum_{n=1}^{N} I_{n_p}\int_{-L_p/2}^{L_p/2} G(r, r')\cos(2n-1)\frac{\pi z'}{L_p}\, dz' \tag{2.152}$$

where $D + 2$ represents the total number of elements in the Yagi–Uda array (D being the number of director elements) and N is the number of entire domain basis functions retained on each element in the array. Equation (2.152) represents the total field E_z^s radiated by the array.

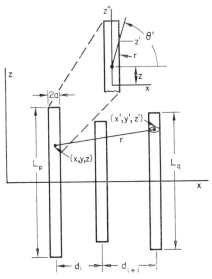

Fig. 2.18. Diagram showing distance from a matching point (observation point) on pth element to source region on qth element. Insert shows relationship between z' and θ' when observation point and source region are on the same element.

It has been found that z' is an efficient variable of integration for numerical integration purposes when the current on wire p is observed at a matching point on element q, $p \neq q$. However, when $p = q$, it is more efficient to use θ' as the variable of integration since the integrand varies rapidly when $z' \approx z$. Details of this change of variables are given by Richmond (1965). However, an even better way of handling the above situation when $p = q$ is to express the integration in terms of sine and cosine integrals which need only be evaluated on the computer (Richmond, 1966). Thus, the most sensitive and expensive numerical integration is removed from the problem.

To examine further the above formulation of the Yagi–Uda antenna problem and to investigate some further short cuts that one can take when programming such a solution, let us look at the matrix formulation of the problem in some detail.

2.6.2. Matrix Formulation

Considerable insight into the point-matching technique, when applied to a problem as complex as the Yagi–Uda array, can be obtained by looking at the system of linear equations and the resulting matrix representation. For the moment, let us consider an array composed of D directors, a reflector, and a driven element. Let us have N modes on each element, but let each element be of different length. Using (2.152), the first part of the system of equations is then of the form

$$\sum_{p=1}^{D+2} \sum_{n=1}^{N} Z_{m,n_p} I_{n_p} = 0, \quad m = 1, 2, \dots, N \times D. \tag{2.153}$$

These equations are generated by requiring that tangential E be zero at N points on each director. That is to say, tangential E is zero at a total of $N \times D$ points on the directors. The matching points on any one director are illustrated in Fig. 2.19.

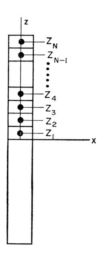

FIG. 2.19. Parasitic element with N matching points along its axis.

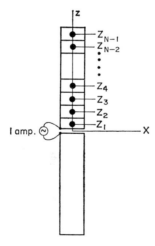

FIG. 2.20. Driven element with $N - 1$ matching points along its axis.

The next N equations are similar to the previous $N \times D$ equations since tangential E vanishes at N points on the reflector element, as shown in Fig. 2.19. Thus

$$\sum_{p=1}^{D+2} \sum_{n=1}^{N} Z_{m,n_p} I_{n_p} = 0, \quad m = (N \times D) + 1, \dots, N \times (D + 1) \tag{2.154}$$

The last N equations are generated by using the boundary condition on the driven element, as shown in Fig. 2.20. That is,

$$\sum_{p=1}^{D+2} \sum_{n=1}^{N} Z_{m,n_p} I_{n_p} = 0, \quad m = N \times (D+1) + 1, \ldots, N \times (D+2) - 1 \quad (2.155)$$

and

$$\sum_{n=1}^{N} I_{n_e} = 1, \quad e = D+2, \quad m = N \times (D+2) \quad (2.156)$$

On the driven element the tangential E boundary condition is only enforced at $N - 1$ points even though there are N modes. The Nth equation on the exciter arises from the constraint on the terminal current value (Thiele, 1965).

Note that in the general formulation

$$L_{op}(\mathbf{J}) = (\mathbf{E}^i) \quad (2.157)$$

we have set $(\mathbf{E}^i)$ to zero. That is to say, there is no incident field in this formulation.

To examine the matrix formulation further, let us examine a simple example. Consider an array composed of a director, a reflector, and a driven element. Further, assume only two modes on each element. Thus the complete system for this example would be similar to

$$\begin{bmatrix} Z_{11} & Z_{12} & Z_{13} & Z_{14} & Z_{15} & Z_{16} \\ Z_{21} & Z_{22} & Z_{23} & Z_{24} & Z_{25} & Z_{26} \\ Z_{31} & Z_{32} & Z_{33} & Z_{34} & Z_{35} & Z_{36} \\ Z_{41} & Z_{42} & Z_{43} & Z_{44} & Z_{45} & Z_{46} \\ Z_{51} & Z_{52} & Z_{53} & Z_{54} & Z_{55} & Z_{56} \\ 0 & 0 & 0 & 0 & 1 & 1 \end{bmatrix} \cdot \begin{bmatrix} I_1 \\ I_2 \\ I_3 \\ I_4 \\ I_5 \\ I_6 \end{bmatrix} = \begin{bmatrix} 0 \\ 0 \\ 0 \\ 0 \\ 0 \\ 1 \end{bmatrix} \cdot \quad (2.158)$$

The physical interpretation of the matrix elements is as follows: at point z_1 on element 1 (the director), Z_{11} is the "field" generated by mode 1, and Z_{12} is the field generated at the same point by mode 2. Z_{21} is the field generated by mode 1 at point z_2 on the director, and Z_{22} is that of mode 2. In a similar manner we can interpret Z_{33}, Z_{34}, Z_{43}, and Z_{44}.

If we write the above matrix in a submatrix representation,

$$\begin{bmatrix} S_{11} & S_{12} & S_{13} \\ S_{21} & S_{22} & S_{23} \\ S_{31} & S_{32} & S_{33} \end{bmatrix} \cdot \begin{bmatrix} I_1 \\ I_2 \\ I_3 \\ I_4 \\ I_5 \\ I_6 \end{bmatrix} = \begin{bmatrix} 0 \\ 0 \\ 0 \\ 0 \\ 0 \\ 1 \end{bmatrix} \quad (2.159)$$

then it is apparent that, regardless of the number of submatrices, those on the main diagonal of submatrices will represent the field generated by the current on the element at which the tangential E boundary condition is being enforced. Hence if there are D identical directors, the first D submatrices on the main diagonal will all be identical. This fact is utilized to shorten the running time of the program but is no restriction on the method itself which could be used on tapered or modulated structures.

For elements off the main diagonal of submatrices the following reasoning applies. The quantity Z_{35} represents the field at point 1 on element 2 (the reflector) due to the first mode (mode 5) on the driven element (element 3). A similar interpretation applies to Z_{36}, Z_{45}, and Z_{46}. Thus submatrices $S_{qr}, q \neq r$, represent the interaction between elements q and r. If all the directors are of the same length, then $S_{qr} = S_{rq}$ for director submatrices. Further, for uniform director spacing there will be several interdirector spacings or distances that will be the same. Consider the four-director Yagi in Fig. 2.17. The distance between directors 1 and 3 is the same as that between 2 and 4, for instance. Hence $S_{13} = S_{24}$, assuming the directors are of the same length.

Thus we see that it may not be necessary to calculate all the submatrices individually, and, consequently, a significant saving in computer time is realized when working with long and complex problems that require large amounts of numerical integration.

2.6.3. Far-zone Radiation

The far-field pattern of a single element of the Yagi antenna in Fig. 2.17 is given by

$$E_\theta(\theta) = \frac{j\omega\mu}{4\pi r_0} \exp\left[-jkr_0\right] \sin\theta \int_{-L/2}^{L/2} I(z') \cdot \exp\left[jkz\cos\theta\right] dz'. \tag{2.160}$$

Since the current is expressed as a Fourier series, we obtain

$$E_\theta(\theta) = \frac{-jL\sqrt{(\mu/\varepsilon)}}{\pi r_0} \exp\left[-jkr_0\right] \sin\theta \cdot \sum_{n=1}^{N} (-1)^n \frac{(2n-1) I_n \cos(\pi L' \cos\theta)}{(2n-1)^2 - (2L'\cos\theta)^2} \tag{2.161}$$

where $L' = L/\lambda$. Since

$$r_0 \approx r - (x\sin\theta\cos\phi + y\sin\theta\sin\phi + z\cos\theta) \tag{2.162}$$

we can define a pattern factor

$$F(\theta, \phi) = L_p \sin\theta \exp\left[+jk(x_p\sin\theta\cos\phi + y_p\sin\theta\sin\phi + z_p\cos\theta)\right] \sum_{n=1}^{N} (-1)^n$$

$$\times \frac{(2n-1) I_{n_p} \cos(\pi L'\cos\theta)}{(2n-1)^2 - (2L'\cos\theta)^2}. \tag{2.163}$$

Thus if we have W elements each with N modes, we may write for the total pattern factor $F_T(\theta, \phi)$,

$$F_T(\theta, \phi) = \sin\theta \cdot \sum_{p=1}^{W} L_p \exp\left[+jk(x_p\sin\theta\cos\phi + y_p\sin\theta\sin\phi + z_p\cos\theta)\right] \sum_{n=1}^{N} (-1)^n$$

$$\times \frac{(2n-1) I_{n_p} \cos(\pi L'\cos\theta)}{(2n-1)^2 - (2L'\cos\theta)^2}, \quad W = D + 2. \tag{2.164}$$

If the number of modes on each element is not the same, then the above expression is necessarily more complicated. In practice it has been found desirable to retain more modes on the driven element than are required for the parasitic elements. For example, as a minimum, it has been observed that as few as three modes on the parasitic elements are sufficient while at the same time at least five modes must be retained on the driven element.

Excellent results were obtained with the point-matching method applied to the Yagi–Uda antenna problem. The patterns calculated by this method agree quite well with experimental patterns published in the literature. For example, Fig. 2.21 shows a calculated E-plane pattern for a fifteen-element Yagi–Uda array. The pattern agrees so well with an experimental one published by Fishenden and Wiblin (1949) that there is no reason to attempt to distinguish between them in the figure. In this and subsequent figures L_D, L_E, and L_R are, respectively, the director length, exciter length, and reflector length. As implied by Fig. 2.17, X_R is the x-coordinate of the reflector, and X_D indicates the uniform director spacing.

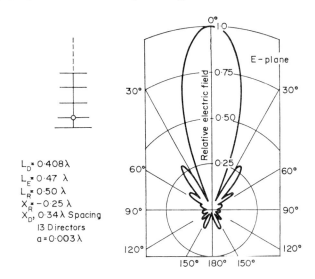

FIG. 2.21. E-plane pattern of fifteen-element Yagi–Uda array.

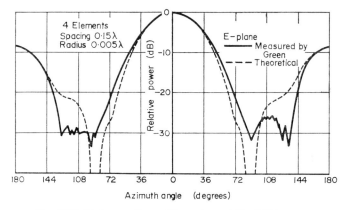

FIG. 2.22. E-plane pattern of four-element Yagi–Uda array.

Figure 2.22 shows an experimental power plot of a four-element array published by Green (1966). Good agreement is seen to exist between the experimental pattern and the theoretical one obtained with the point-matching method. In fact, the front-to-back ratio is precisely the same.

Figures 2.23 and 2.24 show calculated *E*-plane and *H*-plane patterns, respectively, for a twenty-seven-element array. This was the largest number of elements that could be handled conveniently by the computer program on the IBM 7094. With a computer of larger memory, such as the IBM 360-75 or CDC 6600, more elements could be accommodated.

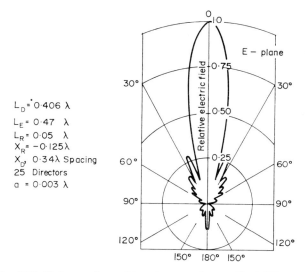

$L_D = 0.406 \, \lambda$
$L_E = 0.47 \, \lambda$
$L_R = 0.05 \, \lambda$
$X_R = -0.125 \lambda$
X_D, 0.34λ Spacing
25 Directors
$a = 0.003 \, \lambda$

FIG. 2.23. *E*-plane pattern of twenty-seven-element Yagi–Uda array.

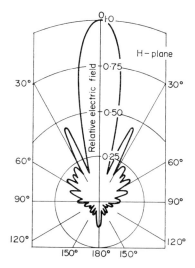

FIG. 2.24. *H*-plane pattern for array of Fig. 2.23.

2.6.4. Current Distributions

After the matrix equation has been solved for the current expansion coefficients I_{n_p}, one not only is able to compute easily the far-field patterns as in the previous section, but one is also in a position to examine the current distributions on the various elements in the array. That is, one evaluates eqn. (2.150) for various values of z. To obtain the relative current amplitudes at the center of the elements, it is simply necessary to sum the coefficients I_{n_p} for a fixed p. Doing so for the array of Fig. 2.23 gives the results of Fig. 2.25. The actual distribution on any given element in the array is nearly sinusoidal.

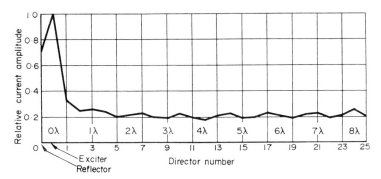

FIG. 2.25. Relative current amplitudes for array of Fig. 2.23.

Of course, knowing the terminal current value on the driven element yields the array input impedance if the terminal voltage is known. It is to this last task that we now turn our attention.

2.6.5. Array Input Impedance

In the above sections the Yagi–Uda antenna was analyzed using the general operator formulation

$$L_{op}(\mathbf{J}) = (\mathbf{E}^i) \tag{2.165}$$

where $(\mathbf{E}^i)$ was zero and the inhomogeneity of the system was preserved by the constraint on the terminal current value of the driven element. However, since the terminal voltage was unknown and not easily determined, the array input impedance could not readily be calculated.

If instead we formulate the Yagi–Uda problem with $(\mathbf{E}^i)$ being the fields from some source of known voltage at the terminals of the driven element, then solution for the current expansion coefficients provides for easy calculation of the array input impedance.

A particularly appropriate source to use in this problem is a frill of magnetic current which represents the electric field distribution in the aperture of a coaxial fed monopole mounted on a ground plane as depicted in Fig. 2.16. That is, a pure dominant mode of the form

$$\mathbf{E}_\varrho = \frac{V}{2\varrho \ln (b/a)} \tag{2.166}$$

is assumed to exist in the aperture where V is the applied voltage, a is the inner radius and b the outer radius as shown in Fig. 2.26. The advantage of using a source such as this lies in the fact that one has an exact (or nearly so) model of the physical gap at the feed point. A delta gap is not used. Thus, the feed point geometry is modeled as it is in practice and one can expect to predict accurate values for both real and imaginary parts of the impedance of the antenna on a ground plane as illustrated in Fig. 2.27. The impedance of the corresponding antenna in free space is, of course, simply double that of the ground plane case.

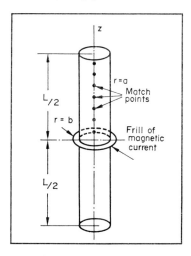

FIG. 2.26. Free space equivalent of ground plane mounted driven element
showing match points.

By calculating the tangential electric field at the various match points (in the absence of the actual metal conductor) due to the magnetic frill current (see Appendix I), values for $(\mathbf{E}^i)$ in the matrix equation may be obtained for a given value of voltage V in eqn. (2.166). For our problem here, we only need the z-component of the electric field due to the frill. If we assume V to be 1 volt, then

$$E_z = \frac{(b^2 - a^2)}{8 \ln (b/a)} \frac{k\, e^{-jkR_0}}{R_0^2} \left\{ 2 \left(\frac{1}{kR_0} + j - j\frac{(b^2 + a^2)}{2R_0^2} \right) \right.$$

$$\left. + \frac{\varrho^2}{R_0} \left[\left(\frac{1}{kR_0} + j - j\frac{(b^2 + a^2)}{2R_0^2} \right) \left(-jk - \frac{2}{R_0} \right) + \left(\frac{-1}{kR_0^2} + j\frac{(b^2 + a^2)}{R_0^3} \right) \right] \right\}$$

$$\tag{2.167}$$

where

$$R_0 = \sqrt{\{(z - z')^2 + \varrho^2\}} \tag{2.168}$$

and the various coordinates are defined by Fig. 2.28.

Having solved the equation $[Z](I) = (V)$ for (I) and denoting the resulting terminal current value on the driven element as I_0, then the input impedance to the array is simply given by

$$Z_{\text{in}} = \frac{1}{I_0} \tag{2.169}$$

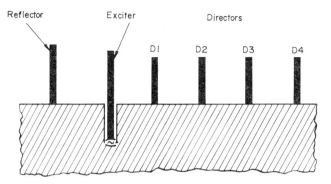

FIG. 2.27. Ground plane mounted Yagi–Uda antenna.

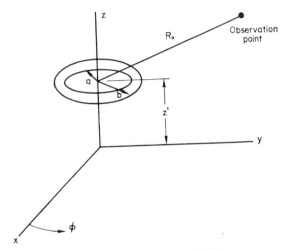

FIG. 2.28. Geometry for magnetic frill source.

when the voltage generator has been given unity voltage. As in the previous formulation, all interactions in the array have been taken into account. The only significant difference in the two formulations is the use of a current generator in the former and a voltage generator in this section.

Due in large measure to the modeling of the finite source, Fig. 2.29 depicts an excellent comparison between theory and experiment for a four-element Yagi over a ground plane similar to that shown in Fig. 2.27. The method is not without its limitations, however. The number of modes required on the driven and parasitic elements is about four times the minimum number needed for the current generator formulation as stated in Section 2.6.3. Further, the number of modes cannot be increased without limit since the impedance matrix will tend toward instability if N becomes too large. This is due to the rapid variation of the higher ordered cosine modes in the point-matching technique. The use of pulse weighting functions would tend to overcome this.

It is interesting to note the difference in the rates of convergence for the two formulations and to observe that while the current is fixed at the ends of the element the use of a current generator fixes the current value at the center of the driven element as well. Thus, a sufficient number of modes are required only to represent the current distribution and not its amplitude at the center, whereas the use of a voltage generator allows the current amplitude and phase to be without constraint at the center. Hence, it is not surprising that the rate of convergence in the latter case would tend to be slower than in the former.

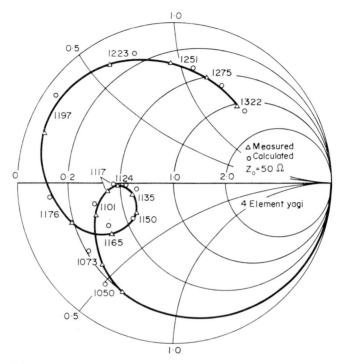

FIG. 2.29. Calculated and measured input impedances for a four-element Yagi–Uda array.

In Section 2.6 two formulations for the Yagi–Uda antenna have been presented. The first method used a curent generator and provided a rapidly converging means of studying the array pattern, current distributions and phase velocity, but did not readily provide for determining the array input impedance. The second method used a voltage generator and did furnish an accurate way of investigating the input impedance. However, the convergence was about only one-fourth as rapid. Both methods used entire-domain basis functions. In the next section we turn our attention to electrically small antennas and the use of sub-domain basis functions.

2.7. ELECTRICALLY SMALL ANTENNAS

In contrast to the use of entire-domain basis functions in the previous section, we wish now to demonstrate the application of sub-domain basis functions in solving Pocklington's integral equation. As an example antenna, we will investigate the multiturn loop antenna. As a further example, we will apply the reaction-matching technique of Section 2.4.5 to the TEM-line antenna. The TEM-line antenna, like the multiturn loop antenna, is generally an electrically small wire radiator.

2.7.1. Multiturn Loop Antenna

The multiturn loop antenna is a recent development of the Ohio State University Electro-Science Laboratory. In its most common configuration it consists of a quarter wavelength of conductor coiled into several turns and mounted over a ground plane (Shreve, 1970) as illustrated in Fig. 2.30. The antenna is fed with an unbalanced line and together with its image forms a half wavelength of conductor at its lowest anti-resonant frequency (Shreve and Thiele, 1970). The second most common configuration consists of the antenna in free space fed with a balanced line (Richards, 1970). However, we will only consider the unbalanced case here.

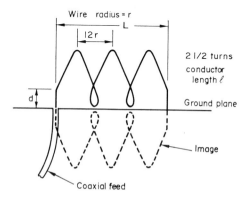

FIG. 2.30. A $2\frac{1}{2}$-turn multiturn loop antenna over a ground plane.

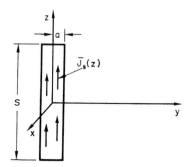

FIG. 2.31. A wire segment of length "s" and radius "a" has uniform current density on its surface.

For simplicity, we will use the constant basis function given in eqn. (2.85) to analyse the multiturn loop. Each turn in the antenna will be geometrically approximated by many short, straight segments. Since the segments are not all parallel to each other, the integral operator for this problem is more complicated than in our previous examples. Here we must consider both the axial and radial components of the electric field from each segment. That is, for the segment of Fig. 2.31,

$$-L_{\text{op}}\left(\mathbf{J}(z)\right) = \hat{z}E_z^s + \varrho E_\varrho^s \tag{2.170}$$

where

$$E_z^s = \frac{I\sqrt{(\mu/\varepsilon)}}{4\pi jk} \int_{-s/2}^{s/2} [(1 + jkr)(2r^2 - 3a^2) + k^2a^2r^2] \frac{\exp(-jkr)}{r^5} \, dt, \quad (2.171)$$

$$E_\varrho^s = \frac{I\varrho\sqrt{(\mu/\varepsilon)}}{4\pi jk} \int_{-s/2}^{s/2} (z - t)(3 + 3jkr - k^2r^2) \frac{\exp(-jkr)}{r^5} \, dt \quad (2.172)$$

and

$$r = \sqrt{\{\varrho^2 + a^2 + (z - t)^2\}}. \quad (2.173)$$

The integration for E_ϱ^s may be carried out in closed form giving

$$E_\varrho^s = \frac{\varrho I\sqrt{(\mu/\varepsilon)}}{4\pi jk} (1 + jkr) \frac{\exp(-jkr)}{r^3} \bigg|_{r_1}^{r_2} \quad (2.174)$$

where

$$r_1 = \sqrt{\{\varrho^2 + a^2 + (z + s/2)^2\}}, \quad (2.175)$$

$$r_2 = \sqrt{\{\varrho^2 + a^2 + (z - s/2)^2\}}. \quad (2.176)$$

These expressions are accurate if $\varrho = 0$ or r_1^2 and r_2^2 are large in comparison with the quantity $a\varrho$ (Richmond, 1966b). For the segmentation problem of interest here, these conditions will hold true.

To calculate the elements in the impedance matrix, we must in effect calculate the tangential component of the electric field radiated by segment j when the observation point is at the center of segment i. Details of this calculation may be found in Appendix III. The number of equations N is, of course, equal to the total number of segments. Thus, the ith equation may be written as

$$\sum_{j=1}^{N} Z_{ij}I_j = E_i^i. \quad (2.177)$$

However, in this problem there exists a two-fold symmetry between the multiturn loop antenna and its image. Thus the number of unknowns can be reduced by a factor of two and the ith equation may be written as

$$\sum_{j=1}^{N/2} (Z_{ij} + Z_{i,N/2+j}) I_j = E_i^i \quad (2.178)$$

where $I_j = I_{N/2+j}$.

The quantity E^i represents the field due to the source. As in Section 2.6.5 it is advantageous to use the magnetic frill current to represent the aperture where the coaxial cable joins the ground plane. Thus, an accurate modeling of an actual source aids in computing accurate impedance data that can be confirmed experimentally. For example, Figs. 2.32 and 2.33 show both calculated and experimental values for the input impedance of a $2\frac{1}{2}$-turn version of the multiturn loop antenna. The agreement between theory and experiment for the reactance as well as the resistance is seen to be excellent. In the calculations, 126 segments were used.

The rate of convergence, even using pulse basis functions, is not particularly bad. For a total wire length (antenna plus image) of 0.4λ, the impedance has converged for about

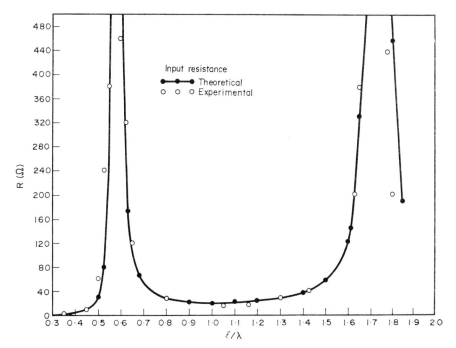

FIG. 2.32. Input resistance of the $2\frac{1}{2}$-turn loop (courtesy of D. Shreve).

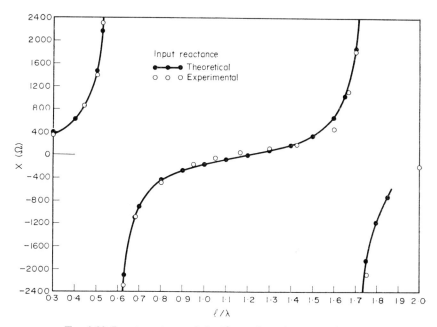

FIG. 2.33. Input reactance of the $2\frac{1}{2}$-turn loop (courtesy of D. Shreve).

100 segments as shown in Fig. 2.34. For longer lengths of wire more segments are required. For instance, Fig. 2.35 shows the convergence for a total wire length of one wavelength and the results indicate that at least 126 segments are required.

In brief, Shreve (1970) has shown the effects of adding more turns to the multiturn loop antenna while keeping the physical length of conductor constant and the same turn to turn spacing are three-fold. That is to say, the bandwidth decreases, the first antiresonant frequency is lowered somewhat, and the radiation resistance at non-antiresonant frequencies is reduced.

In summary, the segmentation procedure and point-matching have been employed to obtain a solution to the multiturn loop antenna problem. Certainly more sophisticated basis

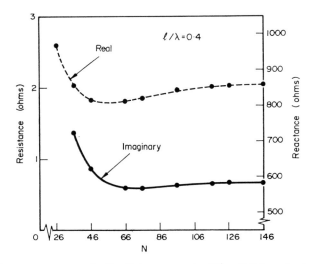

FIG. 2.34. Convergence curves for the $2\frac{1}{2}$-turn geometry ($l/\lambda = 0.4$) (courtesy of D.Shreve).

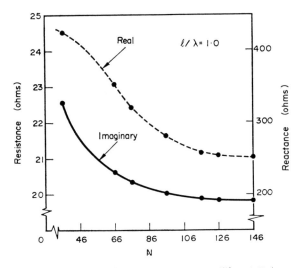

FIG. 2.35. Convergence curves for the $2\frac{1}{2}$-turn loop geometry ($l/\lambda = 1.0$) (courtesy of D.Shreve).

functions could have been used and the reader is encouraged to consider this in his work. Indeed, in the following section we will employ the piecewise-sinusoidal functions and reaction-matching to study the TEM-line antenna.

2.7.2. TEM-line Antenna with Loading

A TEM-line antenna consists of TEM transmission lines with radiating discontinuities. Three basic configurations of the TEM-line are shown in Fig. 2.36. As can be seen, the TEM-line is essentially low-profile and can be made quite rugged and hence is well suited for many applications demanding these characteristics. Further, its electrical properties allow the designer a wide latitude in choosing configurations meeting given electrical requirements.

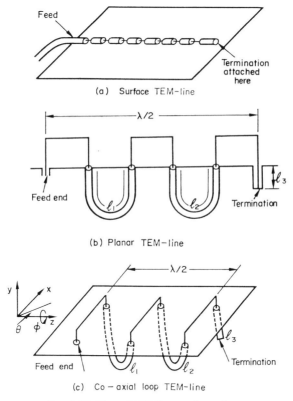

FIG. 2.36. Three TEM-line configurations.

The first version of the TEM-line antenna shown in Fig. 2.36(a) is a surface mounted version suited for array applications in which the array may be quite long and composed of many elements. This TEM-line, as well as the others, is usually terminated in an adjustable coaxial-line short circuit for turning purposes. For this configuration, lengths on the order of two wavelengths or longer usually are necessary in order to achieve satisfactory radiation resistance because the radiation resistance of each radiating gap is small. However, when properly designed, moderate directivity and a VSWR of less than 2 : 1 can be obtained.

Figure 2.36(b) shows a smaller version of the TEM-line antenna. This configuration permits more flexible designs than the antenna shown previously because the cable is behind the ground plane which gives the designer greater freedom in choosing cable characteristics and loop geometry. This version is well suited for low scan angles although satisfactory broadside operation is possible. The best configuration for broadside radiation is that in Fig. 2.36(c).

Suppose we wish to analyze the configuration in Fig. 2.36(b) having three radiating elements. These elements are coupled in two ways; that is, through electromagnetic field coupling between every pair of elements and through the interconnecting transmission lines. We will apply the reaction-matching of Section 2.4.5 to account for the field coupling between elements and use transmission line relationships to account for the second kind of coupling as done by Agrawal (1969).

To facilitate the application of reaction-matching, we assume that the antenna is perfectly conducting and that each loop, including its image, is divided into eight segments as shown in Fig. 2.37. The currents at the junctions are denoted by $I_{01}, I_{02}, \ldots, I_{024}$. In

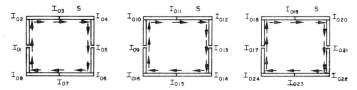

FIG. 2.37. Junction currents and their reference directions for three-element TEM-line antenna (courtesy of P. Agrawal).

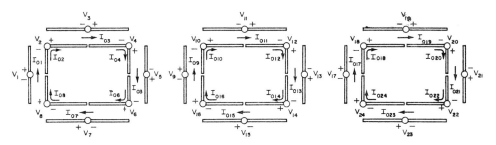

FIG. 2.38. Eight overlapping dipoles represent each loop (courtesy of P. Agrawal).

applying reaction-matching, each loop is represented by a collection of eight overlapping dipoles and thus each of the segments belongs to two adjacent (linear and/or vee) dipoles as shown in Fig. 2.38. Of course, along each of the twenty-four dipoles, the current is assumed to be piecewise sinusoidal as in Section 2.4.5.

Using a delta-gap voltage generator, ignoring displacement currents in the gap and enforcing reciprocity between the true dipoles or segments and a test dipole, we can write

$$\sum_{n=1}^{24} \left[\frac{-1}{I'_{om}I_{on}} \int_{\substack{n\text{th} \\ \text{"true"} \\ \text{dipole}}} \mathbf{I}_n(l) \cdot \mathbf{E}'_m(l) \, dl \right] I_{on} = V_m \qquad (2.179)$$

where $I_n(l)$ is the piecewise sinusoidal current along the nth "true" dipole which is I_{on} at the terminals and goes to zero at the ends, $E'_m(l)$ is the free space electric field of the mth "test" dipole having a piecewise-sinusoidal current that goes to zero at the ends, and V_m is the applied voltage across the mth "true" dipole.

Recognizing the term in the square brackets of eqn. (2.179) as the mutual impedance (or self-impedance when $n = m$) between the mth "test" dipole and nth "true" dipole, a set of twenty-four simultaneous linear equations is obtained:

$$\sum_{n=1}^{24} I_{on} Z_{mn} = V_m, \quad m = 1, 2, \ldots, 24. \tag{2.180}$$

Thus the problem is reduced to a twenty-four port linear, lumped, finite, passive, and bilateral network with transmission-line interconnections and loading effects yet to be included. The V_m's are the voltages that appear at the terminals of each "true" dipole, and except for V_1 they are either zero or related to terminal currents through transmission line or load constraints.

To introduce the effects of the transmission lines into the analysis, we can start with the voltage and current relations for a section of transmission line

$$V = A\,e^{-j\gamma x} + B\,e^{+j\gamma x} \tag{2.181}$$

and

$$I = \frac{1}{Z_0}[A\,e^{-j\gamma x} - B\,e^{+j\gamma x}] \tag{2.182}$$

where A and B are constants to be determined by boundary conditions, and γ and Z_0 are the propagation constant and the characteristic impedance of the line, respectively.

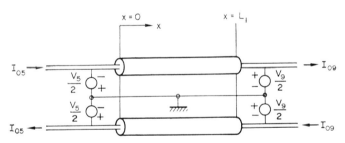

FIG. 2.39. Transmission line connections between 5th and 9th ports (courtesy of P. Agrawal).

For the upper line in Fig. 2.39, at $x = 0$, $V = V_5/2$ and $I = I_{05}$, and at $x = L_1$, $V = V_9/2$ and $I = I_{09}$, L_1 being the length of the transmission-line section between first and second radiating elements. Use of these boundary conditions yields:

$$\begin{bmatrix} V_5 \\ V_9 \end{bmatrix} = 2Z_0 \begin{bmatrix} -\coth \gamma L_1 & \operatorname{cosech} \gamma L_1 \\ \operatorname{cosech} \gamma L_1 & -\coth \gamma L_1 \end{bmatrix} \begin{bmatrix} I_{05} \\ I_{09} \end{bmatrix}. \tag{2.183}$$

However, for the lossless transmission line $\gamma = j\beta_0$ where β_0 is the phase constant. Thus

$$\begin{bmatrix} V_5 \\ V_9 \end{bmatrix} = j2Z_0 \begin{bmatrix} \cot \beta_0 L_1 & -\operatorname{cosec} \beta_0 L_1 \\ -\operatorname{cosec} \beta_0 L_1 & \cot \beta_0 L_1 \end{bmatrix} \begin{bmatrix} I_{05} \\ I_{09} \end{bmatrix}. \tag{2.184}$$

Similarly

$$\begin{bmatrix} V_{13} \\ V_{17} \end{bmatrix} = j2Z_0 \begin{bmatrix} \cot \beta_0 L_2 & -\operatorname{cosec} \beta_0 L_2 \\ -\operatorname{cosec} \beta_0 L_2 & \cot \beta_0 L_2 \end{bmatrix} \begin{bmatrix} I_{013} \\ I_{017} \end{bmatrix} \tag{2.185}$$

where L_2 is the length of the transmission line section between the second and the third radiating elements, i.e. between the 13th and 17th ports.

The value of V_{21} may be related to I_{021} by a factor of $2Z_L$ since the load at the end of the actual antenna appears as $2Z_L$ due to image theory. Therefore, use of the reference current directions in Fig. 2.35 dictates that

$$V_{21} = -2Z_L I_{021}. \tag{2.186}$$

Substituting eqns. (2.184), (2.185), and (2.186) in eq. (2.180) and recognizing that all voltages are zero except for the applied voltage, load voltage, and voltages at the ends of the transmission lines, the following is obtained:

$$\begin{bmatrix} V_1 \\ 0 \\ 0 \\ \vdots \\ 0 \end{bmatrix} = [Z'] \begin{bmatrix} I_{01} \\ I_{02} \\ \vdots \\ I_{024} \end{bmatrix} \tag{2.187}$$

The elements of $[Z']$ are the same as the elements of $[Z]$ in eqn. (2.167) except for $Z_{5,5'}$, $Z_{5,9'}$, $Z_{9,5'}$, $Z_{9,9'}$, $Z_{13,17'}$, $Z_{17,13'}$, $Z_{17,17'}$, and $Z_{21,21'}$ which are:

$$Z_{5,5'} = Z_{5,5} - j2Z_0 \cot \beta_0 L_1, \tag{2.188}$$

$$Z_{5,9'} = Z_{5,9} - (-j2Z_0 \operatorname{cosec} \beta_0 L_1), \tag{2.189}$$

$$Z_{9,5'} = Z_{9,5} - (-j2Z_0 \operatorname{cosec} \beta_0 L_1), \tag{2.190}$$

$$Z_{9,9'} = Z_{9,9} - j2Z_0 \cot \beta_0 L_1, \tag{2.191}$$

$$Z_{13,13'} = Z_{13,13} - j2Z_0 \cot \beta_0 L_2, \tag{2.192}$$

$$Z_{13,17'} = Z_{13,17} - (-j2Z_0 \operatorname{cosec} \beta_0 L_2), \tag{2.193}$$

$$Z_{17,13'} = Z_{17,13} - (-j2Z_0 \operatorname{cosec} \beta_0 L_2), \tag{2.194}$$

$$Z_{17,17'} = Z_{17,17} - j2Z_0 \cot \beta_0 L_2 \tag{2.195}$$

and

$$Z_{21,21'} = Z_{21,21} + 2Z_L. \tag{2.196}$$

If V_1 is assumed to be 1 volt in eqn. (2.187), then the input impedance of the antenna structure shown in Fig. 2.36(b) is numerically given by

$$Z_{\text{IN}} = \frac{0.5}{I_{01}}. \tag{2.197}$$

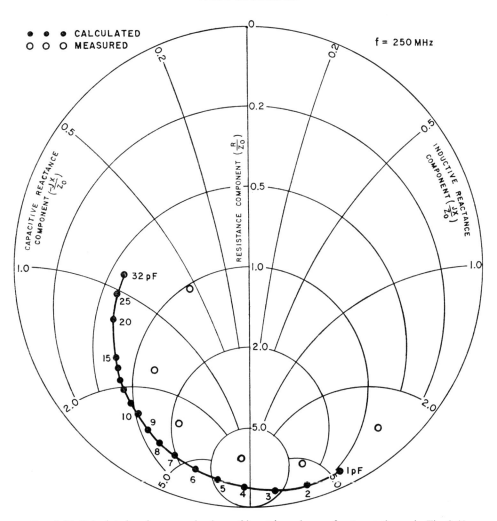

FIG. 2.40. Calculated and measured values of input impedance of antenna shown in Fig. 2.41
with various values of load capacitance (courtesy of P. Agrawal).

To illustrate the accuracy of the analysis, some typical impedance results are shown in
Fig. 2.40 for various values of load capacitance. All things considered, especially the many
possible sources of experimental error, the results are quite good. Pattern results are not
shown, but knowing the currents on the antenna, the radiation patterns may be easily
calculated.

2.8. MODELING OF WIRE ANTENNAS ON METALLIC BODIES

The purpose of this section is to demonstrate the application of the segmentation procedure to model not only an antenna such as was done in the previous section, but also to
model the metallic environment of the antenna. Specifically, two examples will be considered.

3a M.-CTE

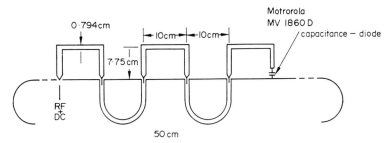

FIG. 2.41. Three-element coplanar TEM-line antenna used for comparing calculated and measured input impedance.

The first is a cone and the second an F4 Naval aircraft. The surfaces of these two bodies are modeled by a system or grid of wire segments. Consequently, such a modeling procedure essentially has the capability of representing a surface of arbitrary shape (Richmond, 1966b). The only real practical limitation of the wire-grid modeling approach is the size of the matrix [Z] that one is willing to calculate and invert. The matrix size is, of course, proportional to the surface area that is to be modeled.

2.8.1. Monopole or Circular Slot in the Base of a Cone

Let us first consider the situation where a monopole is axially mounted on the base of a cone as shown in Fig. 2.42 (Thiele et al., 1969). A wire-grid representation can be used in which the cone or frustum is represented by a number of "generating lines" consisting of a number of wires joined end to end, as shown in Fig. 2.43(a). No wires need to be provided in planes normal to the z-axis because of the symmetry of the structure. The length of the antenna and the dimensions for the cone, frustum, or frustum and spherical cap can be arbitrarily specified.

An interesting simplification can be obtained from the symmetry of the configuration in the case where all generating lines have the same number of segments, each segment being identical (except for the orientation on the ϕ-coordinate) to the corresponding one on each other generating line.

The currents on such corresponding segments should be equal in magnitude and phase, since $I(z)$ is independent of ϕ. Let the segments be numbered in a consecutive way, starting with the line at $\phi = 0$ and proceeding in a counterclockwise direction along the other lines. Let M be the number of segments on each line, and L the number of generating lines. Thus, one can write

$$\sum_{j=1}^{L \cdot M} Z_{kj} I_j = -E_k^i, \quad k = 1, 2, \dots, L \cdot M. \tag{2.198}$$

Since the currents on corresponding segments are equal,

$$I_j = I_{(j+M)} = I_{(j+2M)} = I_{(j+(L-1)\cdot M)} \tag{2.199}$$

λ = 29.52 "

λ/4 = 7.38 "

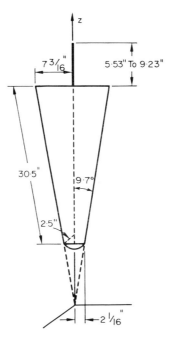

FIG. 2.42. Dimensions of experimental models. A 7.38-in. monopole is a quarter wave long at 400 MHz.

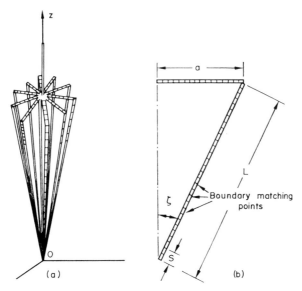

FIG. 2.43. (a) Wire-grid model of the monopole and cone; (b) cone generating line showing distribution of segments and boundary matching points.

and eqn. (2.198) can be written as

$$\sum_{j=1}^{M} I_j \left(\sum_{n=0}^{L-1} Z_{k(j+nM)} \right) = -E_k^i, \quad k = 1, 2, \ldots, M.$$ (2.200)

The advantage of eqn. (2.200) is that it permits us to reduce the number of unknown currents to M, while the actual number of wire segments is $L \cdot M$, where L is arbitrary. As a result, there is no limitation other than computer running time to the number of generating lines (and thus to the total number of segments represented). The number of segments M in a generating line is, however, limited because of computer memory size. When using the IBM 7094, for instance, M cannot exceed about 100; with the IBM 360-75, the maximum number is about 300. For the patterns calculated here L was chosen to be ten.

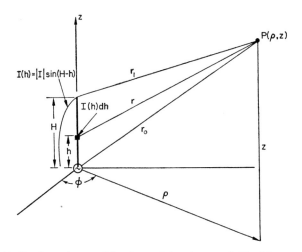

FIG. 2.44. Configuration used for determining the near field of the monopole.

The left-hand side of eqn. (2.200) represents $L_{op}(\mathbf{J})$ for the cone problem under consideration here. It remains to determine $\mathbf{E}^i$. For the monopole consider the geometry depicted in Fig. 2.44. Starting with the vector potential, the following expressions for the monopole configuration of Fig. 2.44 may be derived as

$$E_z = -j29.975\,|I| \left[\frac{e^{-j\beta r_1}}{r_1} - \frac{e^{-j\beta r_0}}{r_0} \cos \beta H - j\frac{z}{r_0^2} e^{-j\beta r_0} \sin \beta H - \frac{z}{\beta r_0^3} e^{-j\beta r_0} \sin \beta H \right]$$ (2.201)

and

$$E_\varrho = \frac{j29.975\,|I|}{\varrho}$$

$$\times \left[(z-H)\frac{e^{-j\beta r_1}}{r_1} - \frac{z}{r_0} e^{-j\beta r_0} \cos \beta H - \frac{jz^2}{r_0^2} e^{-j\beta r_0} \sin \beta H + \frac{\varrho^2}{\beta r_0^3} e^{-j\beta r_0} \sin \beta H \right].$$ (2.202)

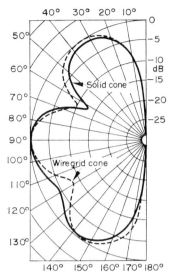

(a) Experimental comparison at 400 MHz with a λ/4 monopole

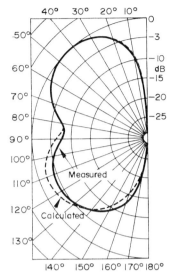

(b) Patterns at 300 MHz using a λ/4 monopole

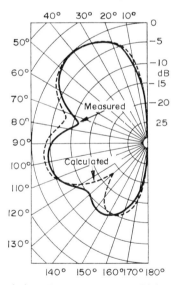

(c) Patterns at 350 MHz using a λ/4 monopole

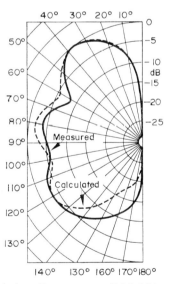

(d) Patterns at 500 MHz using a 0·312λ monopole

Fig. 2.45

66   G. A. THIELE

Solving for the current on the cone makes it possible to calculate the far-field pattern of the cone-monopole structure by superimposing the fields of the cone and those of the monopole. The far-field E_θ of the cone is given in Appendix III while E_θ for the monopole may be derived from the above equation for E_z as

$$E_\theta = \frac{29.975\,|I|}{\sin\theta}\{\cos\theta\sin\beta H - \sin(\beta H\cos\theta) + j[\cos(\beta H\cos\theta) - \cos\beta H]\} \quad (2.203)$$

where the $e^{-j\beta r}/r$ factor has been suppressed in order to refer the phase of the field to the origin of the coordinate system. The component E_ϱ is negligible due to $1/r^2$ dependence.

To test experimentally the validity of the wire grid representation of a metallic surface, an actual wire-grid cone was built around a styrofoam core in a configuration similar to that shown in Fig. 2.43(a). A typical experimental comparison of the solid cone and its wire-grid counterpart is shown in Fig. 2.45(a). Some representative results showing both the results calculated for the wire-grid cone and measurements for the solid surface cone are shown in Figs. 2.45(b), (c) and (d). The results in all four cases are generally quite good. The difference between the two patterns in Fig. 2.45(d) for large angular values is thought to be due to the coaxial cable used on the experimental cone for measurement purposes.

Other variations of the formulation given here are possible, of course. For example, instead of assuming the current distribution on the monopole, it may be treated as an unknown as are the currents on the metallic body. This could be done in a number of ways. The monopole terminal current value could be constrained to a particular value as was done in Section 2.6.2. This would take into account the interaction between the cone and monopole but would not conveniently provide for the calculation of impedance. Alternatively one could use a voltage generator at the base of the monopole such as the magnetic frill current discussed previously. Calculation of the currents on the cone and monopole would account for the cone–monopole interaction and also yield directly the monopole impedance. Note that in either case the previously described symmetry for the cone due to the symmetrical excitation could still be used to advantage.

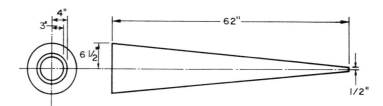

FIG. 2.46a. Cone with single circular slot.

Once a particular problem, such as the cone, is programmed for the computer it is easy to examine and compare the results for other sources of excitation since one has only to determine $(\mathbf{E}^i)$ in the operator equation $L_{op}(\mathbf{J}) = (\mathbf{E}^i)$. For example, consider the circular slot on the cone base as shown in Fig. 2.46(a). The same wire-grid representation applies to this problem except that no segments are allowed to cross the slot or to protrude into it. The

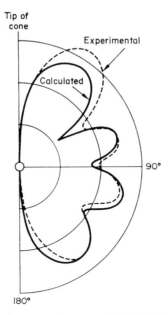

FIG. 2.46b. Calculated and measured patterns at 300 MHz for single slot excitation.

slot may be represented by the magnetic frill current discussed previously and given in Appendix I. A typical result for the far-field pattern is shown in Fig. 2.46(b).

As one last example of the modeling technique, we will next consider modeling of an aircraft.

2.8.2. Small Loops of TEM Line on an Aircraft

In the HF band of frequencies (i.e. 2–30 MHz) aircraft lend themselves quite well to the wire-grid modeling techniques since at these frequencies an aircraft is not electrically large. Consider the simulation of the F4 Naval aircraft shown in Fig. 2.47. Some of the electrical dimensions at 10 MHz are also shown. The placement of the wire segments is such that the fuselage is three-dimensional while the wings and tail sections are planar. However, each straight line in the model may be represented by more than a single segment depending upon the length to be spanned. The same basic wire grid program is used that was employed for the cone. The source, ($\mathbf{E}^i$), is obtained by assuming a constant current on the loops since they are electrically quite small. Thus, in the computer program, the currents on the segments representing the loops are assumed to be known and hence do not appear in the current column matrix. Instead the fields from these segments are appropriately superimposed to obtain ($\mathbf{E}^i$).

As sources of excitation for the aircraft, TEM-lines of one element (i.e. small single loops; see Section 2.7.2) are employed. One good reason for using such elements is that they are magnetic in character and therefore tend to excite the structure on which they are mounted. The structure may then be used to advantage as part of the radiating mechanism rather than using an electric or dipole-type element and attempting electrically to isolate the antenna

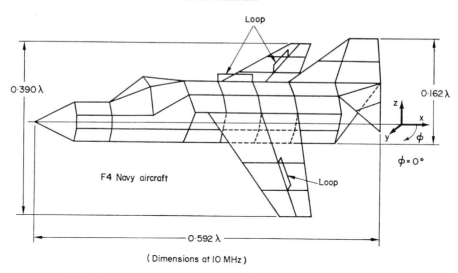

(Dimensions at 10 MHz)

FIG. 2.47. Mathematical computer model of F4 aircraft (courtesy of M. Diaz).

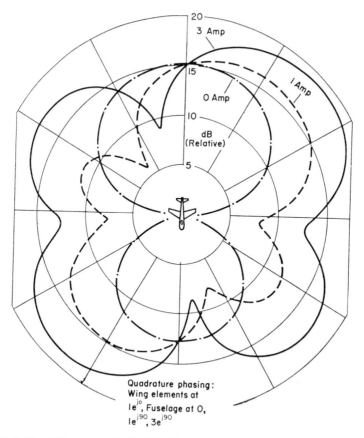

FIG. 2.48. Far-field patterns for the F4 with quadrature phasing (courtesy of M. Diaz).

from the vehicle. To demonstrate, suppose we wish to obtain nearly omni-directional coverage in azimuth. If the wings and fuselage are thought of as crossed dipoles, then phasing them in quadrature will tend to give good azimuthal coverage. Figure 2.48 tends to show these effects. Excitation of just the wings produces a dipole-type pattern radiating fore and aft while additional quadrature excitation of the fuselage tends to give increasingly better coverage in azimuth as the magnitude of fuselage excitation is increased.

2.9. CONCLUSIONS

This chapter has presented those principles and techniques necessary for the numerical solution of wire antenna electromagnetic boundary-value problems. First, in Section 2.2 were discussed the two basic integral equations used in wire antenna investigations. Although Hallen's integral equation is favored by some researchers for wire antenna problems, it was pointed out in Section 2.2 that, in a sense, Pocklington's integral equation is more general and therefore more flexible. This is because Hallen's equation exclusively uses a fictitious delta-gap to represent the feed-point whereas Pocklington's equation permits one to use a wider range of sources such as the magnetic frill current model of a true physical feed-point configuration. Thus, most of this chapter used Pocklington's integral equation in formulating solutions to various wire antenna problems.

In Section 2.3 was discussed the general method of moments which is the unifying concept in the numerical solution of certain electromagnetic field problems. In essence, the method of moments provides a means of accurately approximating an integral equation with a system of simultaneous linear algebraic equations. Although the general method of moments itself was not treated mathematically, two special cases were. Both special cases resulted from a particular choice of weighting or testing functions. The first special case treated was Galerkin's method which uses weighting functions that are the same as the expansion or basis functions. Galerkin's method, however, generally requires that two integrations be performed in order to obtain the elements of the impedance matrix $[Z]$. Thus, if both integrations must be done using largely numerical integration techniques, the calculation of $[Z]$ can be computationally rather lengthy. Bearing in mind that in Galerkin's method one is satisfying an integral relationship over some surface, one can reduce the number of integrations required in the calculation of $[Z]$ by choosing as weighting functions Dirac-delta functions. This second special case of the method of moments is usually referred to as point-matching. That is, a boundary condition is satisfied at a discrete number of points rather than continuously over some surface. Point-matching is a more straightforward approach than Galerkin's method and is sufficiently adequate for many problems. It tends, however, to be a slower converging method.

A very important choice to be made in formulating a problem is in choosing the basis functions or expansion functions of the current. Thus, considerable discussion was devoted in Section 2.4 to bases. Two basic philosophies as to the choice of basis functions were presented. That is, entire-domain bases and sub-domain bases with the latter being used in the segmentation process. Examples of the segmentation process were given in Sections 2.7 and 2.8 while entire-domain basis functions were used in the Yagi–Uda example of Section 2.6.

Also in Section 2.4 a basis transformation method was discussed. This transformation method in conjunction with point-matching provides a means of formulating a problem in terms of one basis and then transforming to another basis having a smaller [Z] matrix to invert.

A particularly useful set of basis functions, the piecewise-sinusoidal functions, were discussed in Section 2.4.5. The calculation of [Z] is considerably aided by the use of these functions since many of the integrals can be obtained in closed form thereby eliminating the use of numerical integration to a significant extent. This technique, called reaction-matching, is an extension of the induced e.m.f. technique and is an equivalent of Galerkin's method. It possesses the property of rapid convergence. Reaction-matching represents, perhaps, a computationally ultimate approach to wire antenna problems since it is accurate, rapidly converging and offers very efficient computer running times. Currently, the reaction-matching technique is being extended to permit its use in modeling metallic surfaces (e.g. Section 2.8).

With attractive and efficient methods now available to solve wire antenna problems, the future will no doubt see an ever increasing application of these techniques. Nevertheless much remains to be done, particularly with respect to antennas in various environments.

ACKNOWLEDGMENTS

The author would like to acknowledge the various forms of generous assistance given by his colleagues at The Ohio State University Electroscience Laboratory and Department of Electrical Engineering. In particular, appreciation is extended to his former advisor and teacher, Professor J. H. Richmond, for permission to draw upon his teachings, particularly Section 2.2.2 and the equations from (2.35) to (2.45). Appreciation is also expressed to Professors C. H. Walter and R. J. Garbacz for their reading of the manuscript and constructive suggestions.

2.10. EXERCISES

1. Show that eqn. (2.39) is valid.
2. Derive eqn. (2.46) from eqn. (2.43).
3. Show that eqn. (2.47) reduces to eqn. (2.46). You may wish to consider the equation of continuity.
4. Show that $C_2 = V_T/2$ in Hallen's integral equation.
5. Following eqn. (2.67), [Z], (I) and (V) are referred to as "generalized" impedance, current and voltage matrices respectively. Why is the term "generalized" used here?
6. Write a computer program using the entire-domain basis functions of eqn. (2.78) and Pocklington's integral eqn. (2.46) to obtain a point-matching solution for a half wavelength dipole. (This is easily done in less than 150 FORTRAN IV statements). Use the subroutine in Appendix I for the source and compare your results to Fig. 2.6.
7. Repeat exercise 6 but use instead the pulse basis functions of eqn. (2.85).
8. Repeat exercise 6 using Hallen's integral equation and a delta-gap with one volt excitation.
9. Determine whether or not the following set of equations is ill-conditioned.

$$5w + 7x + 6y + 5z = 23$$
$$7w + 10x + 8y + 7z = 32$$
$$6w + 8x + 10y + 9z = 33$$
$$5w + 7x + 9y + 10z = 31$$

10. Derive eqn. (2.125).
11. Use eqn. (2.140) to derive eqn. (2.161).
12. Verify eqn. (2.183).
13. Derive eqn. (2.201) and hence show that eqn. (2.203) follows.
14. Derive eqn. (2.227) from eqn. (2.221).
15. Show that reaction-matching is related to Galerkin's method.

Appendix I

FIELDS OF A MAGNETIC FRILL CURRENT

For a coaxial aperture terminated in an infinite ground plane, the field quantities of interest can be obtained from a frill (or annular ring) of magnetic current. Tsai (1970) has obtained accurate expressions for the near fields of such a frill and the following closely parallels his work.

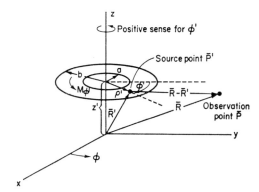

FIG. 2.49. Geometry of the magnetic frill (courtesy of L. Tsai).

Consider now the geometry of the frill as shown in Fig. 2.49, where the frill is assumed to have inner and outer coax radii, a and b, respectively, and centrally located along the z-axis at $z = z'$. Assuming dominant mode distributions (TEM) and rotational symmetry, the aperture distribution is

$$E_{\varrho'}(\varrho') = \frac{1}{2\varrho' \ln (b/a)} \frac{\text{volts}}{\text{meter}} \qquad (2.204)$$

for one volt excitation. Hence the corresponding magnetic current distribution by image theory is

$$K_{\phi'} = \frac{-1}{\varrho' \ln (b/a)}. \qquad (2.205)$$

With the aid of the electric vector potential $\mathbf{F}$, where

$$\mathbf{F}(\mathbf{P}) = \frac{\varepsilon_0}{4\pi} \iint\limits_{\substack{\text{frill} \\ \text{surface}}} \mathbf{K}'(\mathbf{P}') \frac{e^{-jk|\mathbf{R}-\mathbf{R}'|}}{|\mathbf{R} - \mathbf{R}'|} \, ds' \qquad (2.206)$$

and the prime denotes source coordinates, one can determine the E and H fields by

$$\mathbf{E} = \frac{1}{j\omega\varepsilon_0} \{\nabla \cdot \nabla + k^2\} \mathbf{A} + \frac{1}{\varepsilon_0} \nabla \times \mathbf{F} \qquad (2.207)$$

72

and

$$\mathbf{H} = \frac{1}{j\omega\mu} \{\nabla \cdot \nabla + k^2\} \mathbf{F} + \frac{1}{\mu_0} \nabla \times \mathbf{A}. \qquad (2.208)$$

Since only magnetic currents are used, $\mathbf{A} = 0$.

For the evaluation of $\mathbf{F}$ from eqn. (2.206), the incremental source area ds' on the frill is $\varrho' d\varrho' d\phi'$. If now integration is first performed on $d\phi'$ and then $d\varrho'$, the frill can be conveniently divided up into $d\varrho'$ wide magnetic ring currents. The contribution of each ring will be evaluated first before summation over all rings. Because of the rotational symmetry of the problem (ϕ independent) the observation point can further be located in the y–z plane with no loss of generality (hence $\varrho = y$ and $\mathbf{F}$ is ϕ polarized). This results in the following expression for $\mathbf{F}$ from eqns. (2.205) and (2.206)

$$F_\phi = \frac{-\varepsilon_0}{2\pi} \frac{1}{\ln(b/a)} \int_a^b \int_0^\pi \cos\phi' \frac{e^{-jkR'}}{R'} d\varphi' d\varrho' \qquad (2.209)$$

with the explanations for the individual terms in the integrand as follows:

(1) $|\mathbf{R} - \mathbf{R}'|$ from Fig. 2.49, denoted now simply as R', can be easily seen from the detailed geometry depicted in Fig. 2.50 as

$$R' = \sqrt{\{(z - z')^2 + \varrho^2 + \varrho'^2 - 2\varrho\varrho' \cos\phi'\}}. \qquad (2.210)$$

(2) Since the ring current is ϕ' polarized (i.e. in the source coordinates), its contribution to F_ϕ is such that there is a $2\cos\phi'$ factor and integration of ϕ' is only from 0 to π.

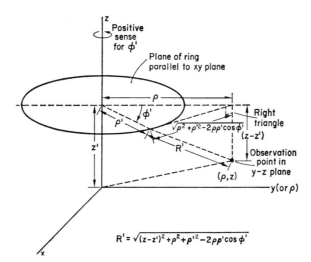

FIG. 2.50. Detailed geometry for source and observation coordinates for the ring
(courtesy of L. Tsai).

For the practical evaluation of eqn. (2.209) numerical integration techniques are used. For a particular frill size of $a = 0.002\lambda$ and $b/a = 2.23$ integration in $d\phi'$ can be done very accurately by summing over merely three equally divided segments. More segments can of course be added for wider frills.

Tsai (1970a) has shown that the electric vector potential of the frill is calculated by

$$F_\phi = \frac{-\varepsilon_0}{2\pi} \frac{1}{\ln(b/a)} \int_a^b \left[\frac{2}{R_1} K\left(\frac{\pi}{2}, p^2\right) + \int_0^\pi \left(\cos\phi' \frac{e^{-jkR'}}{R'} - \frac{1}{R'}\right) d\phi' \right] d\varrho \qquad (2.211)$$

with

$$R' = \sqrt{\{(z-z')^2 + \varrho^2 + \varrho'^2 - 2\varrho\varrho'\cos\phi'\}} \qquad (2.212)$$

$$R_1 = \sqrt{\{(z-z')^2 + (\varrho + \varrho')^2\}} \qquad (2.213)$$

$$p^2 = \frac{4\varrho\varrho'}{(z-z')^2 + (\varrho + \varrho')^2} \qquad (2.214)$$

$K(\pi/2, p^2)$ = complete elliptical integral of the first kind. Equation (2.211) is now useful for the accurate numerical determination of F_ϕ at any observation point not on the frill surface (even for $\varrho < a$). The computer subroutine to be given performs the prescribed integration on ϕ' by Simpson's rule. In general, a division of only five segments from 0 to π for ϕ' gives convergent results (as compared to more segments).

In the "near-zone" it is necessary to obtain E_z and E_ϱ by numerical integration where

$$E_z = -\frac{1}{\varepsilon_0} \frac{1}{\varrho} \frac{\partial}{\partial \varrho} (\varrho K_\phi) \qquad (2.215)$$

and

$$E_\varrho = \frac{1}{\varepsilon_0} \frac{\partial}{\partial z} (K_\phi). \qquad (2.216)$$

The partial differentiation processes indicated are performed numerically using Lagrange's three-point (equally spaced abscissas) formula which is

$$f_p' = f'(x_0 + ph) = \frac{1}{h}\{(p - \tfrac{1}{2})f_{-1} - 2pf_0 + (p + \tfrac{1}{2})f_1\} \qquad (2.217)$$

where x_0 is the center point in the range $\pm ph$ (here either ϱ or z) where the derivative is needed and $f_{\pm 1}$ is the value of the function at $x = x_0 \pm h$. The accuracy is checked using the corresponding four-point formula and in general, except at $z = 0$ for E_ϱ and $\varrho = 0$ for E_z, better than 1 per cent accuracy is achieved by the three-point formula.

Closed form expressions for $\mathbf{E}$ and $\mathbf{H}$ can be derived in order to simplify calculations when $\varrho \gg b$. The usual far-field approximations are not made here because $\lambda \gg \varrho \gg b$ hence this may be thought of as a "far near zone" form.

Proceeding directly from eqn. (2.210), let

$$R_0 = \sqrt{\{(z-z')^2 + \varrho^2\}}. \qquad (2.218)$$

Then

$$R' = R_0 \sqrt{\left(1 + \frac{\varrho'^2}{R_0^2} \frac{2\varrho\varrho'\cos\phi'}{R_0^2}\right)} \cong R_0 + \tfrac{1}{2} \frac{(\varrho'^2 - 2\varrho\varrho'\cos\phi')}{R_0}, \quad \text{for } \varrho \gg \varrho'. \qquad (2.219)$$

Hence, we can obtain

$$\frac{E_\varrho}{k} \cong -\frac{(b^2 - a^2)}{8 \ln (b/a)} \varrho \frac{(z - z')}{R_0} \frac{e^{-jkR_0}}{R_0^2}$$

$$\times \left\{ k - \left(\frac{3}{k} + \frac{k(b^2 + a^2)}{2} \right) \frac{1}{R_0^2} + j \left[\frac{2(b^2 + a^2)}{R_0^3} - \frac{3}{R_0} \right] \right\}, \qquad (2.220)$$

and

$$\frac{E_z}{k} \cong \frac{(b^2 - a^2)}{8 \ln (b/a)} \frac{e^{-jkR_0}}{R_0^2} \left\{ 2 \left(\frac{1}{kR_0} + j - \frac{j(b^2 + a^2)}{2R_0^2} \right) \right.$$

$$+ \frac{\varrho^2}{R_0} \left[\left(\frac{1}{kR_0} + j - \frac{j(b^2 + a^2)}{2R_0^2} \right) \left(-jk - \frac{2}{R_0} \right) + \left(\frac{-1}{kR_0^2} + j \frac{(b^2 + a^2)}{R_0^3} \right) \right] \right\}. \qquad (2.221)$$

The magnetic field is given by

$$\frac{H_\phi}{k} \cong \frac{j}{120\pi} \frac{(b^2 - a^2)}{8 \ln (b/a)} k \left[\varrho \frac{e^{-jkR_0}}{R_0^2} \left(\frac{1}{kR_0} + j - \frac{j(b^2 + a^2)}{2R_0^2} \right) \right]. \qquad (2.222)$$

Equations (2.220) to (2.222) have also been programmed into the computer subroutine *EB* for magnetic frill fields.

On the axis, at $\varrho = 0$, the ϕ symmetry of the problem dictates that $E_\varrho (0, z) \equiv 0$. Equations (2.220) to (2.222) are inaccurate when $\varrho \to 0$. Numerical differentiation, moreover, also becomes invalid due to singularity problems. Consequently a form for axial fields will now be derived. The z-component of the electric field can be written as

$$E_z = -\frac{1}{\varepsilon_0} \frac{F_\phi}{\varrho} - \frac{1}{\varepsilon_0} \frac{\partial}{\partial \varrho} F_\phi. \qquad (2.223)$$

At $\varrho = 0$, from eqn. (2.210),

$$R' = \sqrt{\{(z - z')^2 + \varrho'^2\}}. \qquad (2.224)$$

Performing the operations indicated in eqn. (2.223), we can obtain an axial form for E_z:

$$E_z (0, z) = \frac{1}{2 \ln (b/a)} \left[\frac{e^{-jk\sqrt{\{(z-z')^2 + a^2\}}}}{\sqrt{\{(z - z')^2 + a^2\}}} - \frac{e^{-jk\sqrt{\{(z-z')^2 + b^2\}}}}{\sqrt{\{(z - z')^2 + b^2\}}} \right] \qquad (2.225)$$

and $E_\varrho (0, z) \equiv H_\phi (0, z) \equiv 0$.

Equation (2.225) is rigorous with no approximations.

In summary, the near fields from the magnetic frill source can be calculated by a combination of the various methods just described. Figure 2.51 shows the frill and the regions of applicability for the respective methods. The following Fortran IV computer subroutine has the built-in decision logic for choosing when the various methods should be used and consequently can be regarded as the general functional for calculating the near fields of magnetic frills.

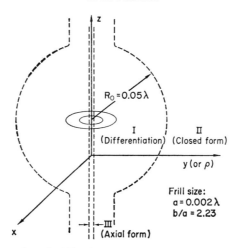

FIG. 2.51. The regions of applicability for the various methods of computing the near field of a magnetic frill (courtesy of L. Tsai).

Far-field expressions can be derived even for relatively large frills, i.e. $\lambda \simeq \varrho' \ll R_0$. They are

$$H_\phi \cong -\frac{\omega\varepsilon_0 (b^2 - a^2)}{8 \ln (b/a)} k \frac{e^{-jkR_0}}{R_0} \{\sin \theta - \tfrac{1}{6}\tfrac{3}{8} k^2 (b^2 + a^2) \sin^3 \theta\} \qquad (2.226)$$

and

$$E_\theta \cong -\frac{\pi^2}{2} \frac{(b^2/\lambda^2 - a^2/\lambda^2)}{\ln (b/a)} \left\{\sin \theta - \frac{\pi^2}{4} \left(\frac{b^2}{\lambda^2} + \frac{a^2}{\lambda^2}\right) \sin^3 \theta\right\} \frac{e^{-jkR_0}}{R_0} \qquad (2.227)$$

with the geometry as shown in Fig. 2.52.

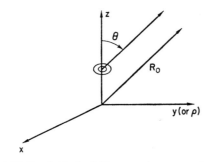

FIG. 2.52. Far-field of a frill source (courtesy of L. Tsai).

Equation (2.227) was found to give accurate far zone fields for frills as large as $\lambda/4$, ($b = \lambda/8$). It is quite similar but more general than the form given by Harrington (1961) for the small coax aperture opening into a ground plane whose far field is

$$H_\phi = \frac{\omega\varepsilon\pi V (b^2 - a^2)}{2\lambda r \ln (b/a)} e^{-jkr} \sin \theta. \qquad (2.228)$$

The author is grateful to Professor L. Tsai for making available the magnetic frill current computer program which follows. To use the program one needs to know the variables in the SUBROUTINE statement. Thus, EZB is the z-component of the electric field, ERB is the ϱ-component of the electric field and HPHB is the ϕ-component of the magnetic field. AB and BB are the inner and outer electrical radii of the frill respectively. ZB and RB denote the cylindrical coordinates in terms of the wavelength at which the field quantities are to be calculated. And finally, ZPB represents the distance from the origin along the z-axis to the center of the frill.

```
C
C
C      MAGNETIC FRILL CURRENT PROGRAM
       SUBROUTINE EB (EZB,ERB,HPHB,AB,BB,ZB,ZPB,RB)
       COMPLEX EZB,ERB,FINT,XMB(5),T1,T2,T3
       COMPLEX HPHB
       PI=3.1415927
       TPI=2.0*PI
       DAB=(BB—AB)/3.
       D=RB/50.
       BAL=ALOG(BB/AB)
       IF (RB.NE.0.) GO TO 10
       TO=SQRT((ZB—ZPB)**2+AB**2)
       TT=SQRT((ZB—ZPB)**2+BB**2)
       EZB=(CEXP(CMPLX(0.0,—TPI*TO))/TO—CEXP(CMPLX(0.0,—TPI*TT))/TT)/BAL
       EZB=EZB/(2.*TPI)
       ERB=(0.0,0.0)
       GO TO 200
10     H=PI/5.
       RO=SQRT((ZB—ZPB)**2+RB**2)
       IF (RO.LT.0.05.AND.RB.NE.0.0) GO TO 25
       BMA=BB**2—AB**2
       BPA=BB**2+AB**2
       RO2=RO**2
       RO3=RO**3
       T1=BMA/8./BAL/RO2*CEXP(CMPLX(0.0,—TPI*RO))
       ERB=—T1*RB/RO*(ZB—ZPB)*CMPLX(TPI—(3./TPI+0.5*TPI*BPA)/RO2,2.*BPA/
      2RO3—3./RO)
       T2=CMPLX(1./TPI/RO,1.—BPA/2./RO2)
       T3=CMPLX(—1./TPI/RO2,BPA/RO3)
       EZB=T1*(2.0*T2+(RB**2)/RO*(T2*CMPLX(—2./RO,—TPI)+T3))
       HPHB=CMPLX(0.,1./60.)*RB*T1*CMPLX(1./(TPI*RO),1.—BPA/2./RO2)
       GO TO 200
25     DO 150 J=1,5
       R=RB
       Z=ZB
       RP=AB+DAB/2.0
       IF (J.EQ.2) Z=ZB+D
       IF (J.EQ.3) Z=ZB—D
       IF (J.EQ.4) R=RB—D
       IF (J.EQ.5) R=RB+D
       XMB(J)=CMPLX(0.0,0.0)
       DO 100 I=1,3
       R1=SQRT((Z—ZPB)**2+(R+RP)**2)
       PP=4.0*R*RP/(R1**2)
       CALL ELPING (ELT,PP)
       TEMP=2.0/R1*ELT
       CON1=(Z—ZPB)**2+R**2+RP**2
       CON2=2.0*R*RP
       CALL FUNCT (FR1,FI1,CON1,CON2,0.0)
       CALL FUNCT (FR2,FI2,CON1,CON2,PI)
       FINT=CMPLX(FR1+FR2,FI1+FI2)
       U=H
       P=2.0
50     CALL FUNCT (FR3,FI3,CON1,CON2,U)
       FINT=FINT+P*CMPLX(FR3,FI3)
       U=U+H
       IF (U+H/4..LT.PI) GO TO 50
       U=H/2.
```

```
      P=P*2.
      IF (P.LT.5.) GO TO 50
      FINT=FINT*H/6.+TEMP
      RP=RP+DAB
      XMB(J)=XMB(J)+FINT*DAB
100   CONTINUE
      XMB(J)=XMB(J)/(TPI*BAL)
150   CONTINUE
      EZB=XMB(1)/RB/TPI+(XMB(5)-XMB(4))/D/2./TPI
      ERB=-(XMB(2)-XMB(3))/D/2./TPI
      HPHB=CMPLX(0.,1./(120.*PI))*XMB(1)
200   CONTINUE
      RETURN
      END
      SUBROUTINE FUNCT (FCR,FCI CONS1,CONS2,V)
      RR=SQRT(CONS1-CONS2*COS(V))
      RPI=6.283185*RR
      FCR=(COS(V)*COS(RPI)-1.)/RR
      FCI=-(COS(V)*SIN(RPI))/RR
      RETURN
      END
      SUBROUTINE ELPING (ELPO,ELPC)
C     COMPLETE ELLIPTICAL INTEGRAL OF THE FIRST KIND
      ELPI=1.0-ELPC
      A0=1.3862944
      A1=0.096663443
      A2=0.035900924
      A3=0.037425637
      A4=0.014511962
      B0=0.5
      B1=0.12498594
      B2=0.068802486
      B3=0.033283553
      B4=0.0044178701
      ELPO=(((((((A4*ELPI)+A3)*ELPI)+A2)*ELPI)+A1)*ELPI)+A0+ALOG(1.0/ELPI)
     2*(((((((B4*ELPI)+B3)*ELPI)+B2)*ELPI)+B1)*ELPI)+B0)
      RETURN
      END
```

Appendix II

CALCULATION OF CHARACTERISTIC MODE CURRENTS

Following the discussion of Section 2.4.6 let us consider the operator equation

$$L_{op}(\mathbf{J}) = Z(\mathbf{J}) \qquad (2.229)$$

where $Z = R + jX$. As in our previous examples, Z is symmetric. Hence, Z is a symmetric operator. Therefore, R and X are real symmetric operators and R must be positive semi-definite since the power radiated by a current $\mathbf{J}$ on a body must also be at least positive semidefinite.

The eigenvalue equation we seek a solution for is

$$Z(\mathbf{J}_n) = \nu_n R(\mathbf{J}_n) \qquad (2.230)$$

since it is only this eigenvalue equation that will result in orthogonal modes and hence orthogonal radiation patterns. If we let

$$\nu_n = 1 + j\lambda_n = -a_n^{-1} \qquad (2.231)$$

then we can obtain the following important relationship in matrix form (Garbacz, 1968; Harrington and Mautz, 1971a)

$$[X](I) = \lambda[R](I) \qquad (2.232)$$

where $\mathbf{J}$ has been expanded as in eq. (2.61). Thus, we seek the λ_n's such that

$$\det |[X] - \lambda[R]| = 0. \qquad (2.233)$$

This equation is efficiently solved by the method given in Harrington and Mautz (1971b). It should be noted that all the eigenvalues λ_n and all the eigenfunctions or characteristic currents $\mathbf{J}_n$ will be real quantities (Garbacz, 1968). Further, the tangential component of the electric field due to any characteristic mode current will be equiphase everywhere on the surface of the radiator (Garbacz, 1968; Turpin, 1969). Therefore, when we calculate a characteristic field (or voltage) it will be complex in general but of constant phase. To do this, it is convenient to use the normalized vector representation $(I_c)_n$ of the characteristic current $\mathbf{J}_n$ determined such that

$$(\tilde{I}_c)_m [Z] (I_c)_n = (1 + j\lambda_n) \delta_{mn}. \qquad (2.234)$$

That is, each normalized characteristic current radiates unit power. Hence, to obtain the nth characteristic field we perform the operation

$$(E_c)_n = [Z] (I_c)_n. \qquad (2.235)$$

In most antenna problems we know the applied voltage and wish to find the actual current distribution which can be obtained from the characteristic currents according to the relationship

$$(I) = \sum_n C_n (I_c)_n. \qquad (2.236)$$

80

To obtain the weighting coefficients C_n we write

$$(E) = \sum_n C_n (E_c)_n \tag{2.237}$$

where (E) is the tangential component of the total electric field everywhere on a surface. Consider as an example a dipole for which all the entries in (E) would be zero except at the feeding gap.

Multiplying eqn. (2.237) from the left by the transpose of $(I_c)_m$ we get

$$(\tilde{I}_c)_m (E) = \sum_n C_n (\tilde{I}_c)_m (E_c)_n \tag{2.238}$$

$$= C_n (1 + j\lambda_n)$$

by virtue of eqn. (2.234). Therefore,

$$C_n = \frac{(\tilde{I}_c)_n (E)}{1 + j\lambda_n} = -a_n (\tilde{I}_c)_n (E) \tag{2.239}$$

where the definition of a_n implied by eqn. (2.239) is given in eqn. (2.231) and conforms to the notation of Garbacz and Turpin. Substituting eqn. (2.239) into eqn. (2.236) we obtain

$$(I) = -\sum_n a_n (\tilde{I}_c)_n (E) (I_c)_n. \tag{2.240}$$

For an m-port antenna the entries in (E) will all be zero except those at the various ports. Hence, at any given port only the values of the characteristic modes at that port enter into the product of eqn. (2.240) with the result that we obtain the value of the actual terminal current, I_t, in terms of the excitation voltage, V_t. Hence,

$$I_t = -\sum_n a_n V_t I_{ctn}^2 \tag{2.241}$$

where I_{ctn} represents the value of the nth mode at a specified pair of terminals. Thus, for the self-admittance of a wire antenna we may write

$$Y_{11} = -\sum_n a_n I_{ctn}^2. \tag{2.242}$$

Similarly, the mutual admittance between two wire antennas can be expressed as

$$Y_{ij} = -\sum_n a_n I_{crn} I_{ctn} \tag{2.243}$$

where I_{csn} represents that component of the nth characteristic mode current at the terminals of the sth wire antenna.

Let us next consider a numerical example of an admittance calculation for a single dipole antenna. Figure 2.53 shows the first three characteristic mode currents normalized to unit amplitude for a half wavelength dipole of radius 0.0025λ. Of course, the odd-numbered modes are symmetric and the even modes are asymmetric. The respective eigenvalues were found to be

$$\lambda_1 = 0.5941$$
$$\lambda_2 = -98.48$$
$$\lambda_3 = -62.64 \times 10^2$$
$$\lambda_4 = -82.87 \times 10^4$$

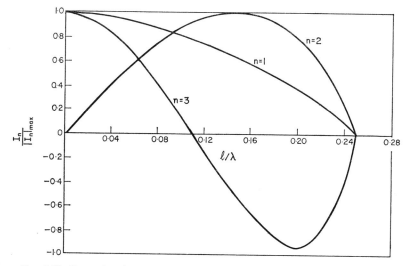

FIG. 2.53. Curve showing the first three unit normalized characteristic mode currents on a half-wave dipole.

The fourth eigencurrent is not plotted in Fig. 2.53 since the accuracy of the fourth eigenvalue is open to question. As a check on its accuracy, the fourth eigencurrent was found not to be orthogonal within numerical limits to the other three eigencurrents as is required by eqn. (2.234). To normalize the initial eigencurrents in the computer program [eqn. (27) of Harrington and Mautz (1971b)] such that they radiate unit power, the following normalization factors were obtained:

$$N_1 = 2.875$$
$$N_2 = 1.795$$
$$N_3 = 0.759$$
$$N_4 = 0.341$$

Since the respective eigencurrents had to be divided by the above values of N^2 it is clear that the first mode is the most efficiently excited as one would expect. Finally, the summation of eqn. (2.242) after the nth term was found to be (in millimhos)

$$Y_{11} = 9.492 - j5.640, \quad N = 1$$
$$Y_{11} = 9.492 - j5.640, \quad N = 2$$
$$Y_{11} = 9.493 - j5.161, \quad N = 3$$
$$Y_{11} = 9.493 - j5.130, \quad N = 4$$

It is apparent that the self-admittance is essentially determined by the first mode. The second mode, which is zero at the feed point, does not contribute to the admittance while the contribution of the third mode is primarily to the susceptance. The contribution by the fourth mode is inaccurate. Hence, the summation should be terminated at $N = 3$ even though the corresponding solution obtained employing Galerkin's method and the same triangle functions as basis functions was $Y_{11} = 9.49 - j4.35$ millimhos. For wire antennas further removed from a resonance than the case considered here, the higher-order modes would have more importance. For the case presented above we note that the real part of the input admittance is in excellent agreement while the imaginary part differs somewhat from that computed by Galerkin's method. However, this is not detrimental to characteristic mode theory for it is only the real part that has real meaning to us in a practical sense. The imaginary part, as we have discussed previously, will be intimately dependent upon the feed-point configuration.

Appendix III

FORTRAN IV PROGRAM FOR WIRE ANTENNAS
ON METALLIC BODIES

In this appendix, we will discuss the computer program that was used to calculate the results in Sections 2.7.1, 2.8.1, 2.8.2 as well as the dipole results discussed in Section 2.4.2. It was also used to derive the initial impedance matrix in Section 2.4.4. As an example, the program is set up to compute the radiation patterns of the body shown in Fig. 2.47.

Equations (2.170) to (2.176) are useful for calculating the impedance matrix coefficients z_{ij}. Before using these equations, however, we must calculate the cylindrical coordinates of the center of segment i in a system having its origin at the center of segment j and its z-axis parallel with the axis of segment j as discussed by Richmond (1966b).

Let the points at the centers of segments i and j have rectangular coordinates (x_i, y_i, z_i) and (x_j, y_j, z_j). The distance between these points is

$$r_{ij}^2 = \sqrt{(x_{ij}^2 + y_{ij}^2 + z_{ij}^2)}, \qquad (2.244)$$

where

$$x_{ij} = x_i - x_j, \quad y_{ij} = y_i - y_j, \quad \text{and} \quad z_{ij} = z_i - z_j. \qquad (2.245)$$

The radial vector extending from point j to point i is

$$\mathbf{r}_{ij} = \hat{x} x_{ij} + \hat{y} y_{ij} + \hat{z} z_{ij}. \qquad (2.246)$$

Let $\hat{i}$ and $\hat{j}$ denote unit vectors parallel with the axes of segments i and j respectively. The unit vector i can be specified by its angle α_i with respect to the xy plane and the angle β_i between the x-axis and the projection of $\hat{i}$ on the xy plane. Thus,

$$\hat{i} = \hat{x} \cos \alpha_i \cos \beta_i + \hat{y} \cos \alpha_i \sin \beta_i - \hat{z} \sin \alpha_i. \qquad (2.247)$$

The unit vector $\hat{j}$ is given by a similar expression in terms of α_j and β_j.

At this point, it is convenient to define a rotated cylindrical coordinate system (ϱ', ϕ', z') with an origin at (x_j, y_j, z_j) and with the z'-axis coinciding with the axis of segment j. The pertinent coordinates of the center of segment i in this system are given by

$$z' = x_{ij} \cos \alpha_j \cos \beta_j + y_{ij} \cos \alpha_j \sin \beta_j - z_{ij} \sin \alpha_j \qquad (2.248)$$

and

$$\varrho' = \sqrt{(r_{ij}^2 - z'^2)}. \qquad (2.249)$$

The field of segment j at an observation point at the center of segment i can be written as follows:

$$\mathbf{E}_{ij} = \hat{\varrho}' E_{\varrho}' + \hat{j} E_z', \qquad (2.250)$$

where

$$\hat{\varrho}' = (\mathbf{r}_{ij} - z'\hat{j})/\hat{\varrho}' \qquad (2.251)$$

and E_{ϱ}' and E_z' are given by eqns. (2.170) to (2.176), with ϱ and z replaced by ϱ' and z'.

Finally, the coefficient Z_{ij} is the component of $\mathbf{E}_{ij}$ which is tangential to segment i:

$$Z_{ij} = \hat{i} \cdot \mathbf{E}_{ij}. \tag{2.252}$$

From eqns. (2.247), (2.250), and (2.252),

$$Z_{ij} = (E'_z - z' E'_0/\varrho') (\cos \alpha_i \cos \beta_i \cos \alpha_j \cos \beta_j + \cos \alpha_i \sin \beta_i \cos \alpha_j \sin \beta_j$$
$$+ \sin \alpha_i \sin \alpha_j) + E'_0 (x_{ij} \cos \alpha_i \cos \beta_j + y_{ij} \cos \alpha_i \sin \beta_i - z_{ij} \sin \alpha_i)/\varrho'. \tag{2.253}$$

We will now discuss the computer program for the wire-grid body of arbitrary shape using the aircraft of Fig. 2.47 as an example. The program will handle a maximum of 169 wire segments arranged in any spatial configuration. The program may be dimensioned for more segments if desired. The symbols used for the input data are defined as follows:

NWIRE = number of segments in the wire-grid body

NEL = number of segments having a known (assumed) current, if any

IKM = number of positions of the antenna to be considered

IDM = number of pattern cuts to be computed for each position of the antenna

DPHI = increments in ϕ

DTHET = increments in θ

FREQ = frequency in MHz

LINSEG = subroutine for calculating segment locations

X(I) = x_i/λ coordinate of center of segment i

Y(I) = y_i/λ coordinate of center of segment i

Z(I) = z_i/λ coordinate of center of segment i

SI(I) = s_i/λ, the length of segment i

ALP = orientation angle α_i of segment i (degrees)

BET = orientation angle β_i of segment i (degrees).

The Symbol B is defined by $B = a/\lambda$ where "a" is the wire radius. In the program, B is set equal to 0.001.

Some of the other symbols used in the program are defined as follows:

SALP(I) = $\sin \alpha_i$

CAB(I) = $\cos \alpha_i \cos \beta_i$

SAB(I) = $\cos \alpha_i \sin \beta_i$

CTHET = $\cos \theta$

STHET = $\sin \theta$

CPHI = $\cos \phi$

SPHI = $\sin \phi$

STCP = $\sin \theta \cos \phi$

STSP = $\sin \theta \sin \phi$

CTCP = $\cos \theta \cos \phi$

CTSP = $\cos \theta \sin \phi$

XIJ = x_{ij}/λ

YIJ = y_{ij}/λ

ZIJ = z_{ij}/λ

$RS = (r_{ij}/\lambda)^2$

$ZP = z'/\lambda$

$RH2 = (\varrho'/\lambda)^2$

ERR = real part of $(1/\varrho') E'_\varrho$

ERI = imaginary part of $(1/\varrho') E'_\varrho$

EZR = real part of E'_z

EZI = imaginary part of E'_z

$CR(I,J)$ = real part of coefficient Z_{ij}

$CI(I,J)$ = imaginary part of Z_{ij}

$COSA(I) = \cos k\,(x_i \sin \theta \cos \phi + y_i \sin \theta \sin \phi + z_i \cos \theta)$

$SINA(I) = \sin k\,(x_i \sin \theta \cos \phi + y_i \sin \theta \sin \phi + z_i \cos \theta)$

$P(I) = \cos \phi \cos \alpha_i \sin \beta_i - \sin \phi \cos \alpha_i \cos \beta_i$

$Q(I) = \cos \theta \cos \phi \cos \alpha_i \cos \beta_i + \cos \theta \sin \phi \cos \alpha_i \sin \beta_i + \sin \theta \sin \alpha_i.$

The coefficients Z_{ij} are calculated in the part of the program between statements 101 and 300. The diagonal elements Z_{ii} are calculated between statements 42 and 45 with the aid of an expression obtained by making a change of variables in the integral in eqn. (2.171) and integrating term by term.

Equations (2.244), (2.245), (2.248), and (2.249) are programmed between statements 103 and 104.

The scattered fields E'_ϱ and E'_z of wire segment j are calculated between statements 103 and 50 via eqns. (2.171) and (2.174). The fifth-order Newton–Cotes formula is employed to carry out the integration in eqn. (2.171). The integrand is sampled at five equally spaced points along segment j if the observation point (at the center of segment i) is more than five segment lengths away from the center of wire j. Otherwise it is sampled at nine points.

Equation (2.253) for the coefficients Z_{ij} is programmed between statements 50 and 280.

Between statements 270 and 280, the quantity E^i is calculated. The real and imaginary parts of this quantity are denoted by $CR(I,NP)$ and $CI(I,NP)$, respectively. In this example, E^i is obtained from the currents that are assumed to exist on the three small loops of Fig. 2.47. Other sources could, of course, be substituted for E^i.

The system of simultaneous linear equations is solved between statements 300 and 122 by the method of Crout. The solution is then printed out in the form of a list of the currents induced on the various segments of the wire-grid body. In statement 160, the output data symbols are defined as follows:

FI = the index number i of the segment

$CURR(I)$ = real part of the current on segment i

$CURI(I)$ = imaginary part of the current on segment i

CMAG = absolute magnitude of the current on segment i

PH = phase angle (in degrees) of the current on segment i

Just before statement 441, the program writes out the following output:

THET = θ in degrees

PHI = ϕ in degrees

TB = E_θ^2

$TC = E_\phi^2$
$ETM = |E_\theta|$
$EPM = |E_\phi|$
GAINT = θ pattern function in dB
GAINP = ϕ pattern function in dB

The subroutine LINSEG at the end of the main program can be used to calculate the center of the segments and their angular orientations. The subroutine requires the following data:

X_1 and X_2 = x-coordinate end points of a straight line in the model
Y_1 and Y_2 = y coordinates of a straight line in the model
Z_1 and Z_2 = z coordinates of a straight line in the model
NINC = number of segments in a straight line

```
C
C
C          WIRE—GRID BODY PROGRAM
   1   FORMAT(1H, 1P8E15.7)
   2   FORMAT(1H ,8F15.8)
   7   FORMAT(7F10.5)
   8   FORMAT(14I5)
  11   FORMAT(1H1)
       DIMENSION D(10),X(180),Y(180),Z(180),SI(180),SALP(180),CURR(180),
      2CURI(180),CAB(180),SAB(180),
      3CR(168,169),CI(168,169)
       DOUBLE PRECISION S,CADR,CADI,SI,ST,B2,BK,BK2,BK4,R,SINB,COSB,TANB,
      2PI,TP,FPP,PSQ,ER,EI,ZZ,X,Y,Z,XI,YI,ZI,CABI,SABI,CABJ,SABJ,SS,XIJ,
      3ZIJ,YIJ,SALP,CALP,ZP,RS,RH2,RBRBK,EZR,EZI,ERR,ERI,T,SSS,DEL,RJ,
      4RK,RKCS,CRKS,TRBR,CRY,CCST,Q1,Q2,CSR,CSI,CR,CI,CURR,CURI,CRP,CLL,
      5TAD,ALP,BET,CBET,SBET,CAB,SAB,CMAG,PH,TD,RK2,CP1
       LOGICAL LND
       ZZ=376.72727
       READ(5,7)FREQ
       WAVE=299.776/FREQ
       WFT=1./WAVE/3.280833
       PI=3.141592653590
       P2=PI/2.
       TP=2.*PI
       FPP=TP*TP
       PSQ=PI*PI
       CRY=ZZ/8./PSQ
       CCST=ZZ/180./PSQ
       ZZ2=ZZ/2.
       D(1)=7.
       D(2)=32.
       D(3)=12.
       D(4)=32.
       D(5)=14.
       D(6)=32.
       D(7)=12.
       D(8)=32.
       D)9)=7.
       CNSNT=4.*PL
       TA=.01745329
       TD=57.29578
       TPS=TP
       TAD=TA
       READ(5,8) NWIRE,NEL,IKM,IDM
       READ(5,7) DPHI,DTHET
       B=.001
       B2=B*B
       TRD=10.*B
       BK=TP*B
       BK2=BK*BK
       BK4=BK2*BK2
       L=0
       CALL LINSEG(NWIRE,L,X,Y,Z,SI,SALP,CAP,SAB,WFT)
       N=L
       NN=N+1
       WRITE(6,11)
       IF(N−181)41,41,500
  41   CONTINUE
       J1=1
```

```
      J2=N
      LND=.FALSE.
C     NO2=N/2
      NO2=N
      NP=NN
      WRITE(6,8)N,NO2
  99  DO 300 I=1,NO2
      IF(LND) GOTO 45
      S=SI(I)
      IF(I—1) 101,42,101
 101  II=I—1
      CR(I,I)=CR(II,II)
      CI(I,I)=CI(II,II)
      SII=S—SI(II)
      SII=ABS(SII)
      IF(SII.LT..00001)GO TO 45
  42  ST=S/2.
      R=DSQRT(B2+ST*ST)
      SINB=ST/R
      COSB=B/R
      TANB=(1.+SINB+COSB)/(1.—SINB+COSB)
      RK=TP*R
      RK2=RK*RK
      ER=—PI/3.*S*(2.—BK2/3.+BK4/60.+RK2*(BK2—8.)/120.)
      EI=SINB*(1./RK2+.5+RK2*(1.—7./60.*BK2)/8.—RK2*RK2/240.)
    2—(1.—BK2/4.+7./480.*BK4)*DLOG (TANB)
      CR(I,I)=ZZ*ER
      CI(I,I)=ZZ*EI
  45  XI=X(I)
      YI=Y(I)
      ZI=Z(I)
      CABI=CAB(I)
      SABI=SAB(I)
      FI=I
      DO 280 J=J1,J2
      FJ=J
      IF(I—J) 103,280,103
 103  S=SI(J)
      ST=S/2.
      SS=S*S
      CABJ=CAB(J)
      SABJ=SAB(J)
      XIJ=XI—X(J)
      YIJ=YI—Y(J)
      ZIJ=ZI—Z(J)
      ZP=XIJ*CABJ+YIJ*SABJ—ZIJ*SALP(J)
      RS=XIJ*XIJ+YIJ*YIJ+ZIJ*ZIJ
      RCH=DSQRT(RS)
      RDSN=RCH/B
      IF(RCH.LT.TRD)WRITE(6,7)FI,FJ,RCH,RDSN
      RH2=RS—ZP*ZP
      RB=RH2+B2
      RBK=FPP*RB
      KK=8
      EZR=0.
      EZI=0.
      ERR=0.
      ERI=0.
      W=—1.
```

G. A. THIELE

```
        T=-ST
        SSS=25.*SS
        IF(RS.GT.SSS) KK=4
        KKK=KK+1
        D(5)=(7*KK)/4
        FKK=KK
        DEL=S/FKK
        DO 50 K=1,KKK
        R2=RB+(ZP-T)*(ZP-T)
        R=DSQRT(R2)
        RK=TP*R
        COSB=DCOS(RK)/R/R2
        SINB=DSIN(RK)/R/R2
        RKCS=RK*COSB-SINB
        CRKS=COSB+RK*SINB
        TRBR=2.-3.*RB/R2
        IF(D(K)-7.) 104,104,49
  104   ERR=ERR+W*CRY*RKCS
        ERI=ERI-W*CRY*CRKS
        W=1.
   49   EZR=EZR+D(K)*(TRBR*RKCS-RBK*SINB)
        EZI=EZI-D(K)*(RBK*COSB+TRBR*CRKS)
   50   T=T+DEL
        EZR=EZR*CCST*DEL
        EZI=EZI*CCST*DEL
        Q1=CABI*CABJ+SABI*SABJ+SALP(I)*SALP(J)
        Q2=XIJ*CABI+YIJ*SABI-ZIJ*SALP(I)
        IF(LND) GOTO 270
        CR(I,J)=(EZR-ZP*ERR)*Q1+ERR*Q2
        CI(I,J)=(EZI-ZP*ERI)*Q1+ERI*Q2
        GO TO 280
  270   CSR=(EZR-ZP*ERR)*Q1+ERR*Q2
        CSI=(EZI-ZP*ERI)*Q1+ERI*Q2
        CR(I,NP)=CR(I,NP)-CSR*CURR(J)+CSI*CURI(J)
        CI(I,NP)=CI(I,NP)-CSR*CURI(J)-CSI*CURR(J)
  280   CONTINUE
C       WRITE(6,1)FI,CR(I,NP),CI(I,NP)
  300   CONTINUE
        WRITE(6,11)
        IF(LND) GOTO 630
        DO 118 L=1,NO2
        LLL=L-1
        DO 118 I=L,NO2
        II=I+1
        IF(LLL) 105,106,105
  105   DO 117 K=1,LLL
        CP1=CR(I,K)*CR(K,L)-CI(I,K)*CI(K,L)
        CR(I,L)=CR(I,L)-CP1
        CP1=CI(I,K)*CR(K,L)+CR(I,K)*CI(K,L)
        CI(I,L)=CI(I,L)-CP1
        CP1=CR(L,K)*CR(K,II)-CI(L,K)*CI(K,II)
        CR(L,II)=CR(L,II)-CP1
        CP1=CI(L,K)*CR(K,II)+CR(L,K)*CI(K,II)
  117   CI(L,II)=CI(L,II)-CP1
  106   CRP=CR(L,II)
        CLL=CR(L,L)*CR(L,L)+CI(L,L)*CI(L, L)
        CR(L,II)=CRP*CR(L,L)/CLL+CI(L,II)*CI(L,L)/CLL
  118   CI(L,II)=CI(L,II)*CR(L,L)/CLL-CRP*CI(L,L)/CLL
        WRITE(6,2)WFT,WFT
```

```
         DO 450 MKI=1,IKM
         JJ=N+NEL
         DO 620 J=NN,JJ
         READ(5,7)X(J),Y(J),Z(J),SI(J),ALP,BET
         X(J)=X(J)*WFT
         Y(J)=Y(J)*WFT
         Z(J)=Z(J)*WFT
         SI(J)=SI(J)*WFT
         READ(5,7)CURR(J),CURI(J)
         WRITE(6,2)CURR(J),CURI(J)
         CALP=DCOS(TAD*ALP)
         SALP(J)=DSIN(TAD*ALP)
         CBET=DCOS(TAD*BET)
         SBET=DSIN(TAD*BET)
         CAB(J)=CALP*CBET
         SAB(J)=CALP*SBET
620      WRITE(6,2) X(J),Y(J),Z(J),SI(J),ALP,BET
         J1=NN
         J2=JJ
         DO 621 I=1,N
         CR(I,NP)=0.
621      CI(I,NP)=0.
         LND=.TRUE.
         GOTO 99
630      CONTINUE
         WRITE(6,2)WFT,WFT,WFT
         DO 120 L=1,NO2
         LLL=L-1
         IF(LLL) 205,206,205
205      DO 119 K=1,LLL
         CR(L,NP)=CR(L,NP)-CR(L,K)*CR(K,NP)+CI(L,K)*CI(K,NP)
119      CI(L,NP)=CI(L,NP)-CI(L,K)*CR(K,NP)-CR(L,K)*CI(K,NP)
206      CRP=CR(L,NP)
         CLL=CR(L,L)*CR(L,L)+CI(L,L)*CI(L,L)
         CR(L,NP)=(CRP*CR(L,L)+CI(L,NP)*CI(L,L))/CLL
120      CI(L,NP)=(CI(L,NP)*CR(L,L)-CRP*CI(L,L))/CLL
         DO 122 L=2,NO2
         I=NP-L
         II=I+1
         DO 122 K=II,NO2
         CR(I,NP)=CR(I,NP)-CR(I,K)*CR(K,NP)+CI(I,K)*CI(K,NP)
122      CI(I,NP)=CI(I,NP)-CI(I,K)*CR(K,NP)-CR(I,K)*CI(K,NP)
123      DO 160 I=1,NO2
         CURR(I)=CR(I,NP)
         CURI(I)=CI(I,NP)
         CMAG=DSQRT(CURR(I)*CURR(I)+CURI(I)*CURI(I))
         FI=I
         PH=TD*DATAN2(CURI(I),CURR(I))
160      WRITE(6,2) FI,CURR(I),CURI(I),CMAG,PH
162      WRITE(6,11)
         DO 443 IDEG=1,IDM
         IF(IDEG-1) 410,410,411
410      THET=90.
         STHET=SIN(TA*THET)
         CTHET=COS(TA*THET)
         LPH=360./DPHI
         PHI=0.
         CPHI=COS(TA*PHI)
         SPHI=SIN(TA*PHI)
```

```
        GO TO 412
411     FDEG=IDEG-2
        PHI=FDEG*90.
        SPHI=SIN(TA*PHI)
        CPHI=COS(TA*PHI)
        THET=0.
        STHET=SIN(TA*THET)
        CTHET=COS(TA*THET)
        LPH=360./DTHET
412     CONTINUE
        DO 443 L=1,LPH
        STCP=STHET*CPHI
        STSP=STHET*SPHI
        CTCP=CTHET*CPHI
        CTSP=CTHET*SPHI
        ETR=0.
        ETI=0.
        EPR=0.
        EPI=0.
        DO 400 I=1,JJ
        S=SI(I)*ZZ2
        ARG=X(I)*STCP+Y(I)*STSP+Z(I)*CTHET
        COSA=COS(TPS*ARG)
        SINA=SIN(TPS*ARG)
        CABI=CAB(I)
        SABI=SAB(I)
        P=CPHI*SABI-SPHI*CABI
        Q=CTCP*CABI+CTSP*SABI+STHET*SALP(I)
        FR=(SINA*CURR(I)+COSA*CURI(I))*S
        FI=(SINA*CURI(I)-COSA*CURR(I))*S
        ETR=ETR+FR*Q
        ETI=ETI+FI*Q
        EPR=EPR+FR*P
400     EPI=EPI+FI*P
        TB=ETR*ETR+ETI*ETI
        TC=EPR*EPR+EPI*EPI
        ETM=SQRT (TB)
        EPM=SQRT (TC)
        GAINT=20.*ALOG10(ETM)
        GAINP=20.*ALOG10(EPM)
        WRITE(6,2)THET,PHI,TB,TC,ETM,EPM,GAINT,GAINP
        IF(IDEG-1) 441,441,442
441     PHI=PHI+DPHI
        SPHI=SIN(TA*PHI)
        CPHI=COS(TA*PHI)
        GO TO 443
442     THET=THET+DTHET
        STHET=SIN(TA*THET)
        CTHET=COS(TA*THET)
443     CONTINUE
450     WRITE (6,11)
500     CONTINUE
        STOP
        END
        SUBROUTINE LINSEG (NW,M,X,Y,Z,SI,SAL,CCAB,CSAB,WFT)
        DOUBLE PRECISION X,Y,Z,SI,SAL,CCAB,CSAB
12      FORMAT(1H ,8F15.8)
13      FORMAT(6F10.5,I5)
        DIMENSION X(1),Y(1),Z(1),SI(1),SAL(1),CCAB(1),CSAB(1)
```

```
      WRITE(6,13)WFT
      DO16 I=1,NW
      READ(5,13)X1,Y1,Z1,X2,Y2,Z2,NINC
      WRITE(6,13)X1,Y1,Z1,X2,Y2,Z2,I
      X1=X1*WFT
      Y1=Y1*WFT
      Z1=Z1*WFT
      X2=X2*WFT
      Y2=Y2*WFT
      Z2=Z2*WFT
      S2=(X2—X1)*(X2—X1)+(Y2—Y1)*(Y2—Y1)
      ST2=S2+(Z2—Z1)*(Z2—Z1)
      S=SQRT(S2)
      ST=SQRT(ST2)
      FNI=NINC
      DX=.5*(X2—X1)/FNI
      DY=.5*(Y2—Y1)/FNI
      DZ=.5*(Z2—Z1)/FNI
      SL=ST/FNI
      CBET=1.
      SBET=0.
      IF(S.EQ.0.) GO TO 14
      CBET=(X2—X1)/S
      SBET=(Y2—Y1)/S
   14 SLP=(Z1—Z2)/ST
      CLP=S/ST
      CABL=CLP*CBET
      SABL=CLP*SBET
      DO15 J=1,NINC
      M=M+1
      SI(M)=SL
      SAL(M)=SLP
      CCAB(M)=CABL
      CSAB(M)=SABL
      FJ=2*J—1
      X(M)=X1+FJ*DX
      Y(M)=Y1+FJ*DY
      Z(M)=Z1+FJ*DZ
      FM=M
   15 WRITE(6,12) FM,X(M),Y(M),Z(M),SI(M),SAL(M),CCAB(M),CSAB(M)
   16 CONTINUE
      RETURN
      END
```

REFERENCES

AGRAWAL, P.K. (1969) Analysis of coplanar TEM line antenna using reaction technique, M.Sc. thesis, The Ohio State University, Columbus, Ohio.

FISHENDEN, R.M. and WIBLIN, E.R. (1949) Design of Yagi aerials, *Proc. IEEE (London)*, pt. 3, *96*, 5–13.

GREEN, H.E. (1966) Design data for short and medium length Yagi–Uda arrays, *Elec. Engrg. Trans. Inst. Engrs. (Australia)*, pp. 1–8 (March).

HALLEN, ERIK (1938) Theoretical investigations into the transmitting and receiving qualities of antennae, *Nova Acta Regiae Soc. Sci. Upsaliensis*, Ser. IV, *11*, 1–44.

HARRINGTON, R.F. (1961) *Time-harmonic Electromagnetic Fields*, McGraw-Hill, New York, pp. 108–12.

HARRINGTON, R.F. (1968) *Field Computation by Moment Methods*, The Macmillan Company, New York.

JORDAN, E.C. (1950) *Electromagnetic Waves and Radiating Systems*, Prentice-Hall, New York, pp. 342–5.

KING, R.W.P. (1956) *Theory of Linear Antennas*, Harvard University Press, Cambridge, Mass.

KING, R.W.P. (1967) The linear antenna—eighty years of progress, *Proc. IEEE 55*, 2–16.

KYLE, R.H. (1968) Mutual coupling between log-periodic dipole antennas, Ph.D. dissertation, Syracuse University, Syracuse, New York, p. 23.

MACK, R.B. (1963) A study of circular arrays, Cruft Lab., Harvard University, Cambridge, Mass., Tech. Repts. 381–6.

MEI, K.K. (1965) On the integral equations of thin wire antennas, *IEEE Trans. on Ant. and Prop. 13*, 374–8

NEUREUTHER, A.R. *et al.* (1968) A comparison of numerical methods for thin wire antennas, *Digest* of the 1968 URSI Fall Meeting.

OTT, R.H., KOUYOUMJIAN, R.G. and PETERS, L., Jr. (1967) Scattering by a two-dimensional periodic array of narrow plates, *Radio Science 2*, 1347–59.

OTTO, D.V. (1969) A note on the induced EMF method for antenna impedance, *IEEE Trans. on Ant. & Prop. 17*, 101–2.

OTTO, D.V. and RICHMOND, J.H. (1969) Rigorous field expressions for piecewise-sinusoidal line sources, *IEEE Trans. on Ant. & Prop. 17*, 98.

POCKLINGTON, H.C. (1897) Electrical oscillations in wire, *Camb. Phil. Soc. Proc. 9*, 324–32.

POGGIO, A.J. and MAYES, P.E. (1969) Numerical solution of integral equations of dipole and slot antennas including active and passive loading, Antenna Laboratory, University of Illinois, Urbana, Illinois, Tech. Rept. AFAL-TR-69-180.

RICHARDS, G.A. (1970) Reaction formulation and numerical results for multiturn loop antennas and arrays, Ph.D. dissertation, The Ohio State University, Columbus, Ohio.

RICHMOND, J.H. (1965) Digital solutions of the rigorous equations for scattering problems, *Proc. IEEE 53*, 796–804.

RICHMOND, J.H. (1966a) Scattering by imperfectly conducting wires, ElectroScience Laboratory, The Ohio State University, Tech. Rept. 2169-1.

RICHMOND, J.H. (1966b) A wire-grid model for scattering by conducting bodies, *IEEE Trans. on Ant. & Prop. 14*, 782–6.

RICHMOND, J.H. (1966c) Scattering by wire loops and square plates in the resonance region, ElectroScience Laboratory, Ohio State University, Columbus, Ohio, Tech. Rept. 2097-1.

RICHMOND, J.H. (1969) Computer analyis of three-dimensional wire antennas, ElectroScience Laboratory, Ohio State University, Columbus, Ohio, Tech. Rept. 2708-4.

RICHMOND, J.H. and GEARY, N.H. (1970) Mutual impedance between coplanar-skew dipoles, *IEEE Trans. on Ant. & Prop. 18*, 414–16.

RUMSEY, V.H. (1954) The reaction concept in electromagnetic theory, *Phys. Rev.*, Ser. 2, *94*, 1483–91.

SCHELKUNOFF, S.A. and FRIIS, H.T. (1952) *Antennas, Theory and Practice*, Wiley, New York.

SHREVE, D.H. (1970) Numerical and experimental investigation of impedance and matching techniques associated with multiturn loop antennas, M.Sc. thesis, The Ohio State University, Columbus, Ohio.

SHREVE, D.H. and THIELE, G.A. (1970) An electrically small antenna; the multiturn loop antenna, *Digest* of the 1970 IEEE G-AP International Symposium.

THIELE, G.A. (1965) Calculation of the current on a thin linear antenna, *IEEE Trans. on Ant. & Prop. 14*, 648–9.

THIELE, G.A. (1969a) Analysis of Yagi–Uda type antennas, *IEEE Trans. on Ant. & Prop. 17 pp.* 24–31.

THIELE, G.A. (1969b) Impedance analysis of Yagi–Uda type antennas, *Digest* of the 1969 URSI Fall Meeting.

THIELE, G.A., TRAVIESO-DIAZ, M. and JONES, H.S. (1969) Radiation of a monopole antenna on the base of a conical structure, *Proc. of Conf. on Environmental Effects on Antenna Performance*, vol. I, edited by J.R. Wait.

TSAI, L.L. (1970a) Analysis and measurement of a dipole antenna mounted symmetrically on a conducting sphere or cylinder, Ph.D. dissertation, The Ohio State University, Columbus, Ohio.

TSAI, L.L. (1970b) Near and far fields of a magnetic frill current, *Digest* of the 1970 URSI Spring Meeting.

TURPIN, R.H. (1969) Basis transformation, least square, and characteristic mode techniques for thin-wire scattering analysis; Ph.D. dissertation, The Ohio State University, Columbus, Ohio.

UDA, S. (1926) Wireless beam of short electric waves, *J. IEEE (Japan) 452*, 273–82, and also *472*, 1209–19.

WEXLER, A. (1969) Computation of electromagnetic fields, *IEEE Trans. on Microwave Theory and Techniques 17*, 416–39.

YAGI, H. (1928) Beam transmission of ultra short waves, *Proc. IRE 16*, 715–41.

ADDITIONAL REFERENCES

AGRAWAL, P.K., RICHARDS, G.A. and THIELE, G.A. (1972) Analysis and design of TEM-line antennas, *IEEE Trans. on Ant. & Prop. 20*, 561–8.

ALBERSTEN, N.C. *et al.* (1970) Methods of evaluating the influence of spacecraft structures on antenna radiation patterns, Part I: A literature survey, Laboratory of Electromagnetic Theory, The Technical University of Denmark.

GARBACZ, R.J. (1965) Modal expansions for resonance scattering phenomena, *Proc. IEEE 53*, 856–64.

GARBACZ, R.J. (1968) A generalized expansion for radiated and scattered fields, Ph.D. dissertation, The Ohio State University, Columbus, Ohio.

GARBACZ, R.J. and TURPIN, R.H. (1969) A generalized expansion for radiated and scattered fields with application to thin wire scatterers, 1969 G-AP/URSI International Symposium Record.

GARBACZ, R.J. and WICKLIFF, R. (1970) Introduction to characteristic modes for chaff applications, Ohio State University ElectroScience Laboratory, Tech. Rept. 2584-6.

GARBACZ, R.J. and TURPIN, R.H. (1971) A generalized expansion for radiated and scattered fields, *IEEE Trans. on Ant. & Prop. 19*, 348–58.

HARRINGTON, R.F. and MAUTZ, J.R. (1971a) Theory of characteristic modes for conducting bodies, *IEEE Trans. on Ant. and Prop. 19*, 622–8.

HARRINGTON, R.F. and MAUTZ, J.R. (1971b) Computation of characteristic modes for conducting bodies, *IEEE Trans. on Ant. & Prop. 19*, 629–39.

TRAVIESO-DIAZ, M.F. (1970) Wire-grid reaction solution of electromagnetic scattering and radiation problems, Ph.D. dissertation, The Ohio State University, Columbus, Ohio.

CHAPTER 3

Numerical Solution
of Electromagnetic Scattering Problems

P. C. WATERMAN

MITRE Corporation, Bedford, Massachusetts 01730

3.1. INTRODUCTION

3.1.1. General Discussion

In recent years work has begun to appear in the literature on the numerical solution of electromagnetic scattering problems by digital computer. For the most part these methods have involved numerical solution of a vector surface integral equation. An alternative theoretical approach, also leading to numerical results, has been given by Waterman (1965). The purpose of the present work is to document a computer program for the implementation of this method. Section 3.2 gives the theory, which has been modified considerably from that given earlier. Section 3.3 gives the analysis and logic which forms the basis for the various subroutines of the computer program. Appendix I gives the complete FORTRAN listing of the computer program.

3.1.2. Computational Aspects

In addition to their role in the present work, it should be noted that certain of the subroutines contained below may be of interest for other applications.

Principal among these are those routines for generating the spherical Bessel and Hankel functions by a combination of power series and recursion techniques, noting that both precision checks and alternative procedures are included for those cases where precision is difficult to maintain. The subroutine for generating associated Legendre functions, and their derivatives, by recursion is also essentially self-contained. Finally, certain of the matrix processing operations, e.g. orthogonalization, may prove of use elsewhere, perhaps with modifications.

3.2. THEORY

3.2.1. Matrix Formulation

Consider an incident electromagnetic wave $\mathbf{E}^i(\mathbf{r})$, $\mathbf{H}^i(\mathbf{r})$ impinging on the closed, perfectly conducting surface S of Fig. 3.1 in otherwise free space. It is assumed throughout that S is sufficiently regular that Green's theorem is applicable, but S need not possess a continuous

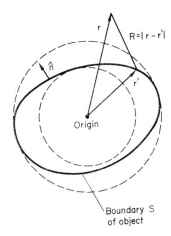

FIG. 3.1. Geometry of a scattering region bounded by the closed surface S.

single-valued normal $\hat{n}$ at each point. Only simple harmonic time dependence at angular frequency ω is considered; a factor $\exp(j\omega t)$ is suppressed in all field quantities. Field behavior is described by Maxwell's equations in the form

$$\mathbf{V} \times \mathbf{V} \times \mathbf{E} - k^2\mathbf{E} = 0, \tag{3.1}$$

with an identical equation governing $\mathbf{H}$. In these equations $k = \omega/c = 2\pi/\lambda$ is the free-space propagation constant.

Because the surface conductivity is infinite on S, no tangential components of electric field can be supported. Currents are induced in the surface, the electric field of which must precisely cancel the tangential components of $\mathbf{E}^i$ at each point on S. Hönl, Maue and West-pfahl have given a representation of the fields for this problem in terms of surface current. After minor modification their formulas may be written (Hönl et al., 1961)

$$\mathbf{E}(\mathbf{r}) = \mathbf{E}^i(\mathbf{r}) + \int ds' \, \mathbf{V} \times \mathbf{V} \times \mathbf{J}_s(\mathbf{r}') \, g_0 \, (k \, |\mathbf{r} - \mathbf{r}'|), \tag{3.2a}$$

$$\mathbf{H}(\mathbf{r}) = \mathbf{H}^i(\mathbf{r}) + jk \int ds' \, \mathbf{V} \times \mathbf{J}_s(\mathbf{r}') \, g_0 \, (k \, |\mathbf{r} - \mathbf{r}'|), \tag{3.2b}$$

where $\mathbf{E}$, $\mathbf{H}$ is the total field, $g_0 \, (kR) = (4\pi R)^{-1} \exp(-jkR)$ is the (scalar) free space Green's function appropriate to outgoing waves, and the curl operators are with respect to the unprimed (i.e. not the integration) variables. The integrals represent the $\mathbf{E}$ and $\mathbf{H}$ fields, respectively, due to a surface distribution of electric dipoles, as one would anticipate on physical grounds. The quantity $\mathbf{J}(\mathbf{r})$, which we identify with induced surface current, stands for the jump discontinuity in magnetic field encountered in crossing the surface, i.e.

$$\mathbf{J}_s = (1/jk)\,\hat{n} \times [\mathbf{H}_+ - \mathbf{H}_-]\quad \text{on}\quad S. \tag{3.2c}$$

In the course of obtaining eqns. (3.2), the boundary conditions appropriate to conducting surfaces were employed, namely, that $n \times \mathbf{E}_+ = n \times \mathbf{E}_- = 0$ on S.

The nature of jump discontinuities in the field vectors across S can be shown directly from eqns. (3.2) giving

$$\mathbf{E}_+ - \mathbf{E}_- = (\nabla_s \cdot \mathbf{J}_s)\,\hat{n} = -j\omega\varrho_s\hat{n}, \tag{3.3a}$$

$$\mathbf{H}_+ - \mathbf{H}_- = -jk\hat{n} \times \mathbf{J}_s. \tag{3.3b}$$

In the first of these equations, the surface divergence (Van Bladel, 1964) $\nabla_s \cdot \mathbf{J}_s$ of the current may be defined by the physical requirement that it equal the net flow of charge out of infinitesimal element of area (per unit area per unit time). The second equality, involving the surface charge density ϱ_s, follows from the continuity equation $\nabla_s \cdot \mathbf{J}_s = -\partial\varrho_s/\partial t$.

The extended boundary condition, requiring that the total electromagnetic field vanish identically in the interior (thus in particular $\mathbf{E}_- = 0$ on S), is from eqn. (3.3a) sufficient to guarantee the usual exterior boundary condition $\hat{n} \times \mathbf{E}_+ = 0$. Applying the extended boundary condition in eqn. (3.2a) gives

$$\int ds'\, \nabla \times \nabla \times \mathbf{J}_s\,(\mathbf{r}')\, g_0\,(k\,|\mathbf{r} - \mathbf{r}'|) = -\mathbf{E}^i(\mathbf{r}), \tag{3.4}$$

an "extended" integral equation that is to hold for all points $\mathbf{r}$ in the small dashed sphere in Fig. 3.1. By taking the curl of both sides of this equation, it follows that the total magnetic field $\mathbf{H}$ will also vanish in this region, once eqn. (3.4) is satisfied. Equation (3.4) is equivalent to three scalar equations for the two unknown tangential components of $\mathbf{J}_s$; only two of the equations are independent, however, in consequence of the fact that each side of eqn. (3.4) must have zero divergence.

Equation (3.4) may be satisfied by expanding both sides in regular vector eigenfunctions (Morse and Feshbach, 1953) $\mathbf{M}_{\sigma mn}$, $\mathbf{N}_{\sigma mn}$ of the vector Helmholtz eqn. (3.1). To treat the integral one writes $\mathbf{J}_s g_0 = \mathbf{J}_s \cdot \mathbf{1}g_0$; the expansion of the "free space Green's dyad" $\mathbf{1}g_0$ has been given by Morse and Feshbach (1953). Because of orthogonality over any spherical surface about the origin shown in Fig. 3.1, corresponding coefficients may be equated on both sides of eqn. (3.4) to give, for incident plane wave $\mathbf{E}^i(\mathbf{r}) = \hat{e}_0\,e^{-jk\cdot r}$,

$$\int ds\, \mathbf{J}_s(\mathbf{r}) \cdot \mathbf{M}^4_{\sigma mn}(\mathbf{r}) = +(4\pi/jk^3)\,(-j)^n\,[n\,(n+1)]^{1/2}\,\hat{e}_0 \cdot \mathbf{C}^{\sigma}_{mn}(\hat{k}), \tag{3.5a}$$

$$\int ds\, \mathbf{J}_s(\mathbf{r}) \cdot \mathbf{N}^4_{\sigma mn}(\mathbf{r}) = -(4\pi/jk^3)\,(-j)^n\,[n\,(n+1)]^{1/2}\,\hat{e}_0 \cdot (-j)\,\mathbf{B}^{\sigma}_{mn}(\hat{k}). \tag{3.5b}$$

The $\mathbf{M}^4$, $\mathbf{N}^4$ are the outgoing wave functions, and dependence on the direction of incidence $\hat{k}$ is contained in the vector spherical harmonics $\mathbf{C}^{\sigma}_{mn}$, $\mathbf{B}^{\sigma}_{mn}$ (Morse and Feshbach, 1953). These equations are to hold for each triplet of values (σ, m, n), with $\sigma = e, o$ (even, odd), $m = 0, 1, \ldots, n$, $n = 1, 2, \ldots$ These are the conditions under which the total $\mathbf{E}$, $\mathbf{H}$ field will vanish identically in that volume consisting of the largest sphere inscribable within S about the coordinate origin employed. As has been shown elsewhere (Waterman, 1965), because of analytic continuability this is adequate to guarantee that $\mathbf{E}$ and $\mathbf{H}$ will vanish identically throughout the *entire* interior volume.

The surface current is next approximated by expansion in the assumed complete set of tangential vector functions $\hat{n} \times \mathbf{M}$ and $\hat{n} \times \mathbf{N}$; one writes

$$\mathbf{J}_s(\mathbf{r}) = -(4/\mathrm{j}k) \sum_{\sigma'm'n'} [a_{\sigma'm'n'}\hat{n}(\mathbf{r}) \times \mathbf{M}_{\sigma'm'n'}(\mathbf{r}) + b_{\sigma'm'n'}\hat{n}(\mathbf{r}) \times \mathbf{N}_{\sigma'm'n'}(\mathbf{r})]; \quad \mathbf{r} \quad \text{on} \quad S \qquad (3.6)$$

where the expansion coefficients remain to be determined. At this point one can expedite the discussion by introducing a matrix notation. First, the triplet of indices appearing in eqns. (3.5) and (3.6) are regrouped into a single index ν by the ordering $(\sigma mn) = e01, o01, e11, o11, e02, \ldots$ The vector spherical harmonics may then be written as column matrices $\mathbf{C}$, $\mathbf{B}$, having as their νth elements $(-\mathrm{j})^n [n(n+1)]^{1/2} \mathbf{C}_{mn}^{\sigma}(\hat{k})$, and $(-\mathrm{j})^n [n(n+1)]^{1/2} \mathbf{B}_{mn}^{\sigma}(\hat{k})$, respectively. The undetermined expansion coefficients of Eqn. (3.6) are simply designated by the column matrices $\mathbf{a}$, $\mathbf{b}$.

In this notation, substitution of the expansion eqn. (3.6) into eqn. (3.5) yields a pair of coupled matrix equations

$$\begin{bmatrix} [I] & [J] \\ [K] & [L] \end{bmatrix} \begin{bmatrix} \mathbf{a} \\ \mathbf{b} \end{bmatrix} = \begin{bmatrix} \hat{e}_0 \cdot \mathbf{C} \\ \hat{e}_0 \cdot \mathrm{j}\mathbf{B} \end{bmatrix} \qquad (3.7)$$

for the determination of $\mathbf{a}$ and $\mathbf{b}$. The matrix elements of $[I]$ are given, after rewriting the triple scalar product that appears, by

$$I_{\nu\nu'} = (k^2/\pi) \int \mathrm{d}s\hat{n}(\mathbf{r}) \cdot \mathbf{M}_{\sigma mn}^4(\mathbf{r}) \times \mathbf{M}_{\sigma'm'n'}(\mathbf{r}), \qquad (3.8a)$$

and the four matrices $[I]$, $[J]$, $[K]$, $[L]$ differ from each other only in the vector products appearing in the integrand of eqn. (3.8a) which are, respectively, $\mathbf{M}_{\nu}^4 \times \mathbf{M}_{\nu'}$, $\mathbf{M}_{\nu}^4 \times \mathbf{N}_{\nu'}$, $\mathbf{N}_{\nu}^4 \times \mathbf{M}_{\nu'}$ and $\mathbf{N}_{\nu}^4 \times \mathbf{N}_{\nu'}$. By inspection of the integrands, in view of the fact that $\mathbf{M} = \mathrm{Re}\,\mathbf{M}^4$ and $\mathbf{N} = \mathrm{Re}\,\mathbf{N}^4$, it is clear that $\mathrm{Re}\,[I]$ and $\mathrm{Re}\,[L]$ are skewsymmetric, whereas $\mathrm{Re}\,[J]$ and $\mathrm{Re}\,[K]$ are symmetric. The surface integrals of eqn. (3.8a) must, in general, be done numerically and are most conveniently performed in spherical coordinates θ, ϕ, for which the appropriate radial coordinate to employ may be given by the parametric specification $r = r(\theta, \phi)$ of the surface. In view of Green's second vector identity

$$\int \mathrm{d}s\hat{n} \cdot [\mathbf{A} \times \nabla \times \mathbf{B} - \mathbf{B} \times \nabla \times \mathbf{A}] = \int \mathrm{d}v [\mathbf{B} \cdot \nabla \times \nabla \times \mathbf{A} - \mathbf{A} \cdot \nabla \times \nabla \times \mathbf{B}]$$

the matrices may be seen to be interrelated by

$$[K] = -[J] - \mathrm{j}[D_+]^{-1},$$

$$[L] = -[I] \qquad (3.8b)$$

where the *diagonal* matrix $[D_+]$ (and $[D_-]$, employed below) has νth elements defined by

$$(D_\pm)_\nu \equiv (\pm 1)^n \frac{\varepsilon_m (2n+1)(n-m)!}{4n(n+1)(n+m)!}. \qquad (3.8c)$$

The Neumann factor ε_m is given by $\varepsilon_0 = 1$, $\varepsilon_m = 2$ otherwise.

It is also desired to compute the scattered field $\mathbf{E}^s$, $\mathbf{H}^s$ given by the surface integrals in eqn. (3.2). Specifically for the electric field, one has

$$\mathbf{E}^s(\mathbf{r}) = 4 \sum_{\sigma mn} [f_{\sigma mn} \mathbf{M}^4_{\sigma mn}(\mathbf{r}) + g_{\sigma mn} \mathbf{N}^4_{\sigma mn}(\mathbf{r})]; \quad r > r'_{\max \text{ on } \sigma}$$

$$\sim \mathbf{F}(\hat{k}_{\text{out}}, \hat{k}_{\text{in}}) \, e^{-jkr}/r; \quad kr \gg 1. \tag{3.9}$$

The vector scattering amplitude $\mathbf{F}$, depending both on direction of incidence $\hat{k}_{\text{in}}$ and observation $\hat{k}_{\text{out}}$, is obtained by introducing asymptotic forms of the outgoing partial waves $\mathbf{M}^4$, $\mathbf{N}^4$ in the preceding expression for $\mathbf{E}^s$ to get

$$\mathbf{F}(\hat{k}_{\text{out}}, \hat{k}_{\text{in}}) = -(4/jk) [\mathbf{C}'(\hat{k}_{\text{out}}) D_- \mathbf{f} - j\mathbf{B}'(\hat{k}_{\text{out}}) D_- \mathbf{g}], \tag{3.10}$$

where $\mathbf{C}'$ is the transpose of $\mathbf{C}$ (and hence a row matrix). The outgoing partial wave expansion coefficients $\mathbf{f}$, $\mathbf{g}$ are expressed in terms of surface currents $\mathbf{a}$, $\mathbf{b}$ by

$$\begin{bmatrix} \mathbf{f} \\ \mathbf{g} \end{bmatrix} = -\text{Re} \begin{bmatrix} [I] & [J] \\ [K] & [L] \end{bmatrix} \begin{bmatrix} \mathbf{a} \\ \mathbf{b} \end{bmatrix}. \tag{3.11}$$

These formulas have been obtained by employing that expansion of the free space Green's dyad valid in the exterior region outside the large dashed sphere of Fig. 3.1.

The scattering cross section σ^{scat} is given by (Saxon, 1955) (the * indicates complex conjugate)

$$\sigma^{\text{scat}} = (16\pi/k^2)(\mathbf{f}'^* D_+ \mathbf{f} + \mathbf{g}'^* D_+ \mathbf{g}). \tag{3.12a}$$

As a numerical check on accuracy, one may also compute the total cross section

$$\sigma^{\text{tot}} = -(4\pi/k) \, \text{Im} [\hat{e}_0 \cdot \mathbf{F}(\hat{k}_{\text{in}}, \hat{k}_{\text{in}})], \tag{3.12b}$$

which must equal σ^{scat} by the forward amplitude theorem (Saxon, 1955). The radar cross section, defined as 4π times the back-scattered power per steradian divided by incident power per unit area, is given by

$$\sigma^{\text{radar}} = (64\pi/k^2) |\hat{e}_0 \cdot \mathbf{C}'(-\hat{k}_{\text{in}}) D_- \mathbf{f} - j\hat{e}_0 \cdot \mathbf{B}'(-\hat{k}_{\text{in}}) D_- \mathbf{g}|^2. \tag{3.12c}$$

If the return signal is regarded as resolved into two orthogonal linearly polarized modes, then this equation gives a measure of the power carried in that mode having polarization aligned with the original incident wave, whereas the *cross-polarized* return is given by replacing $\hat{e}_0$ by $\hat{e}'_0 = \hat{k}_{\text{in}} \times \hat{e}_0$ in eqn. (3.12c).

3.2.2. Evaluation of the Transition Matrix

Instead of first solving eqn. (3.7) for the currents $\mathbf{a}$, $\mathbf{b}$, then substituting in eqn. (3.11) to obtain the scattered wave $\mathbf{f}$, $\mathbf{g}$, the currents may be formally eliminated to obtain the scattered wave directly from the incident wave as

$$\begin{pmatrix} \mathbf{f} \\ \mathbf{g} \end{pmatrix} = -\begin{pmatrix} [D_+]^{-1/2} & 0 \\ 0 & [D_+]^{-1/2} \end{pmatrix} \begin{pmatrix} [T_1] & [T_2] \\ [T_3] & [T_4] \end{pmatrix} \begin{pmatrix} [D_+]^{1/2} & 0 \\ 0 & [D_+]^{1/2} \end{pmatrix} \begin{pmatrix} \hat{e}_0 \cdot \mathbf{C} \\ \hat{e}_0 \cdot j\mathbf{B} \end{pmatrix}. \tag{3.13}$$

The block matrix,

$$[T] \equiv \begin{pmatrix} [T_1] & [T_2] \\ [T_3] & [T_4] \end{pmatrix}, \tag{3.14}$$

is known as the *transition* matrix, and is both symmetric (i.e. $[T_1]' = [T_1]$, $[T_2]' = [T_3]$, $[T_4]' = [T_4]$) and has the property $[T^{*'}][T] = \text{Re}[T]$, i.e.

$$\begin{pmatrix} [T_1]^* & [T_2]^* \\ [T_3]^* & [T_4]^* \end{pmatrix}\begin{pmatrix} [T_1] & [T_2] \\ [T_3] & [T_4] \end{pmatrix} = \begin{pmatrix} [T_1^*T_1 + T_2^*T_3] & [T_1^*T_2 + T_2^*T_4] \\ [T_3^*T_1 + T_4^*T_3] & [T_3^*T_2 + T_4^*T_4] \end{pmatrix} = \text{Re}\begin{pmatrix} [T_1] & [T_2] \\ [T_3] & [T_4] \end{pmatrix}. \tag{3.15}$$

The property eqn. (3.15) is a consequence of unitarity of the *scattering* matrix $[S] = [1] - 2[T]$, as may be verified by substitution in the unitarity condition $[S'^*][S] = 1$.

If one now defines the matrix $[Q]$ as

$$[Q] = \begin{pmatrix} [Q_1] & [Q_2] \\ [Q_3] & [Q_4] \end{pmatrix} \equiv \begin{pmatrix} [D_+]^{1/2} & 0 \\ 0 & [D_+]^{1/2} \end{pmatrix}\begin{pmatrix} [J'] & [L'] \\ [I'] & [K'] \end{pmatrix}\begin{pmatrix} [D_+]^{1/2} & 0 \\ 0 & [D_+]^{1/2} \end{pmatrix}, \tag{3.16}$$

then by comparison with eqns. (3.7) and (3.11) the transition matrix is determined by the matrix equation

$$[Q][T] = \text{Re}[Q], \tag{3.17}$$

which in general must be solved numerically.

Instead of working with the 2 by 2 block form of eqn. (3.17) involving in truncation four $N \times N$ matrices, it is convenient, for the numerical processing, to change over to single $2N \times 2N$ matrices. Thus, define the $2N \times 2N$ matrix $[\hat{Q}]$ by

$$\left.\begin{aligned} \hat{Q}_{(2m-1)(2n-1)} &= [Q_1]_{mn} \\ \hat{Q}_{(2m-1)(2n)} &= [Q_2]_{mn} \\ \hat{Q}_{(2m)(2n-1)} &= [Q_3]_{mn} \\ \hat{Q}_{(2m)(2n)} &= [Q_4]_{mn} \end{aligned}\right\} \; m, n = 1, 2, \ldots, N. \tag{3.18}$$

The matrices $[\hat{T}]$, and $[\hat{S}] = [1] - 2[\hat{T}]$ are defined in exact analogy to this. At this point, eqn. (3.17) may be written in terms of $[\hat{S}]$ as

$$[\hat{Q}][\hat{S}] = -[\hat{Q}]^*. \tag{3.19}$$

Because of the behavior of the radial (Hankel) functions that appear in the matrix elements of $[\hat{Q}]$, the imaginary parts of the elements of $[\hat{Q}]$ will tend to grow very large numerically above the diagonal. In order to avoid loss of precision due to the finite precision arithmetic employed by the digital computer, it is convenient at this stage to reset all the mentioned elements to zero, by Gaussian elimination. This process is straightforward, the net effect being to premultiply $[\hat{Q}]$ by a real upper triangular matrix (all elements zero below the main diagonal). Suppose this conditioning to have been performed on eqn. (3.19), which we continue to employ without change of notation.

To eqn. (3.19) are adjoined the constraints of symmetry and unitarity mentioned above, which are unaffected by the $[S] \to [\hat{S}]$ transformation and thus given by

$$[\hat{S}] = [\hat{S}]' \tag{3.20}$$

and

$$[\hat{S}]'^* [\hat{S}] = [1]. \tag{3.21}$$

Two extremes of view with regard to the system of eqns. (3.19), (3.20) and (3.21) are as follows: first, one might truncate the matrix eqn. (3.19), solve numerically by digital computer, then compare the resulting solution with eqns. (3.20) and (3.21), the latter thus being employed as consistency checks. On the other hand, one might attempt to treat all three equations from a unified point of view from the onset, obtaining a solution in some sense of eqn. (3.19) subject to the constraints of eqns. (3.20) and (3.21). The first approach has been employed in earlier work on the computer for bodies of rotational symmetry, and works quite satisfactorily for a restricted range of body shapes and sizes. The second approach is employed in the present work in order to extend the range of bodies that can be handled, in view of the fact that the constraints essentially determine three-quarters of the solution [i.e. of the $8N^2$ real parameters appearing in the $2N \times 2N$ truncated complex matrix $[\hat{S}]$, it can be shown that only $N(2N + 1)$ are independent, if $[\hat{S}]$ satisfies eqns. (3.20) and (3.21)].

To develop a unified analysis, observe first that if $[\hat{S}]$ could be constructed in the form

$$[\hat{S}] = [U]' [U] \tag{3.22}$$

where $[U]$ is unitary, then both constraints would be satisfied by inspection. This suggests that, rather that inverting $[\hat{Q}]$ directly in eqn. (3.19), it be made unitary. Thus consider the upper triangular matrix $[M]$ (i.e. all elements are zero below the main diagonal) which by premultiplication makes $[\hat{Q}]$ into a unitary $[\hat{Q}_{\text{unit}}]$, viz.

$$[M] [\hat{Q}] = [\hat{Q}_{\text{unit}}]. \tag{3.23}$$

Premultiplying eqn. (3.19) by $[M]$, one can write

$$[\hat{Q}_{\text{unit}}] [\hat{S}] = -[M] [\hat{Q}]^* = -[M] [M]^{*-1} [\hat{Q}_{\text{unit}}]^*.$$

Upon solving for $[\hat{S}]$, there now results

$$[\hat{S}] = -[\hat{Q}_{\text{unit}}]'^* ([M] [M]^{*-1}) [\hat{Q}_{\text{unit}}]^*. \tag{3.24}$$

Substituting this result in eqn. (3.20), the symmetry constraint, it follows without difficulty that the matrix product $[M] [M]^{*-1}$ must be symmetric. But each of the matrices appearing in the product is upper triangular, and their product is again upper triangular. Consequently the product must be a diagonal matrix. Further, the diagonal elements can be written out explicitly, giving

$$[M] [M]^{*-1} = \begin{bmatrix} M_{11}/M_{11}^* & 0 & \\ 0 & M_{22}/M_{22}^* & \cdots \\ 0 & 0 & \\ \vdots & & \end{bmatrix}.$$

If next one can arrange to choose the diagonal elements of $[M]$ to be real, then

$$[M][M]^{*-1} = 1. \tag{3.25}$$

From eqn. (3.24) the $\hat{S}$-matrix is now given by

$$[\hat{S}] = [\hat{Q}_{\text{unit}}]'^* [\hat{Q}_{\text{unit}}]^*, \tag{3.26}$$

which is of the required form eqn. (3.22). Substituting eqn. (3.26), along with the identity $[\hat{Q}'^*_{\text{unit}}]^* [\hat{Q}_{\text{unit}}] = 1$, back in the relation $[\hat{S}] = [1] - 2[\hat{T}]$, the desired transition matrix is given by

$$[\hat{T}] = [\hat{Q}_{\text{unit}}]'^* \,\text{Re}\,[\hat{Q}_{\text{unit}}], \tag{3.27}$$

and the block form of $[T]$ is readily obtained by reversing the transformation of eqn. (3.18).

Returning to $[M]$ for a moment, eqn. (3.25) states simply that $[M]$ is real. Thus the process may be summed up in the (formal) theorem: given the matrix eqn. (3.19), with constraints, eqns. (3.20) and (3.21), on the solution, it follows that the given matrix $[Q]$ cannot be arbitrary, but must be such as to be factorizable into the product of a *real* upper triangular matrix and a unitary matrix, namely

$$[\hat{Q}] = [M]^{-1}[\hat{Q}_{\text{unit}}]. \tag{3.28}$$

The transformation of $[\hat{Q}]$ into a unitary matrix, as required in eqn. (3.23), is done by Schmidt orthogonalization of the $2N$ vectors given by the rows of $[\hat{Q}]$, beginning with the bottom row and working up. The procedure is straightforward, and details are described in a subsequent section.

3.2.3. Application to Special Geometries

In order to apply the equations to bodies having an axis of rotational symmetry, the axis of symmetry is chosen as polar axis for our spherical coordinates and, without loss of generality, the direction of incidence taken in the plane of azimuth $v = 0$, so that $\hat{k}_{\text{in}} = \hat{k}_{\text{in}}(u, 0)$. A reduced index notation may be employed for those matrix elements that do not vanish under the azimuthal integration, writing

$$I_{mnn'} \equiv I_{omnemn'} = -I_{emnomn'},$$

$$J_{mnn'} \equiv J_{emnemn'} = J_{omnomn'},$$

$$K_{mnn'} = -J_{mnn'} - j\delta_{nn'}D_{mnn} - 1,$$

$$L_{mnn'} = I_{mnn'}. \tag{3.29}$$

The independent matrix elements, written out, are

$$I_{mnn'} \equiv m \int_0^\pi d\theta\, \frac{\partial}{\partial\theta}\,(P_n^m P_{n'}^m)\,(kr)^2\, h_n^{(2)}(kr)\, j_{n'}(kr),$$

$$J_{mnn'} \equiv \frac{-2}{\varepsilon_m} \int_0^\pi d\theta \sin\theta \left[\frac{m^2 P_n^m P_{n'}^m}{\sin^2\theta} + \frac{\partial P_{n'}^m}{\partial\theta}\frac{\partial P_{n'}^m}{\partial\theta} \right] krh_n^{(2)}(kr)\, \frac{d}{dkr}\,[krj_{n'}(kr)],$$

$$\frac{-2}{\varepsilon_m}\, n'(n'+1) \int_0^\pi d\theta \sin\theta\, \frac{\partial P_n^m}{\partial\theta}\, P_n^m h_n^{(2)}(kr)\, j_{n'}(kr)\, \frac{\partial}{\partial\theta}\,(kr). \tag{3.30}$$

Observe that the real parts of all these matrices are symmetric. Also, because of the vanishing of all matrix elements with different azimuthal mode indices $(m \neq m')$, there is no coupling and each azimuthal mode $m = 0, 1, 2, \ldots$ may be evaluated separately.

From the defining eqn. (3.16), the *only* non-vanishing elements of the $[Q]$ matrix may now be written in reduced index notation as

$$[Q_1]_{mnn'} \equiv [Q_1]_{emnemn'} = [Q_1]_{omnomn'},$$

$$[Q_2]_{mnn'} \equiv [Q_2]_{omnemn'} = -[Q_2]_{emnomn'},$$

$$[Q_3]_{mnn'} \equiv [Q_3]_{emnomn'} = -[Q_3]_{omnemn'},$$

$$[Q_4]_{mnn'} \equiv -[Q_4]_{emnemn'} = -[Q_4]_{omnomn'}. \qquad (3.31)$$

In addition, the reduced index elements are related by

$$[Q_3]_{mnn'} = [Q_2]_{mnn'},$$

$$[Q_4]_{mnn'} = -[Q_1]_{mnn'} - j\,[1]. \qquad (3.32)$$

Finally, examination of eqn. (3.17) reveals that the non-vanishing elements in the four blocks of the $[T]$ matrix are interrelated exactly as in eqn. (3.31), but not eqn. (3.32), so that the complete solution may be obtained by solving eqn. (3.17) once, using the reduced index quantities.

A further important reduction occurs in the preceding equations for obstacles (e.g. finite cylinder) having a plane of mirror symmetry normal to the axis of rotational symmetry. For this geometry the radius vector $r(\theta)$ specifying the shape of the obstacle will be even about $\theta = \pi/2$, i.e.

$$r(\theta) = r(\pi - \theta). \qquad (3.33)$$

Inspection of the parity of the integrands giving rise to matrix elements in eqn. (3.30) readily reveals that a checkerboard pattern of zeros has emerged, i.e.

$$I_{mnn'} = 0; \quad (n + n') \text{ even},$$

$$J_{mnn'} = 0; \quad (n + n') \text{ odd}. \qquad (3.34)$$

These elements can hence be set to zero without performing the numerical integrations.

Prolate (and oblate) spheroids have a mirror symmetry plane normal to their rotational symmetry axis, so that both mode and parity decompositions may be made, as discussed above. There is another reduction that occurs here, however, which from a theoretical standpoint lays the Rayleigh expansion out in full view, and for numerical purposes yields extremely well-conditioned matrices for inversion.

To see this, let us examine the matrix elements as given by eqns. (3.30). The numerical magnitude of these elements is influenced mainly by the radial functions appearing in the integrand. For $I_{mnn'}$, for example, one has

$$I_{mnn'} \sim (kr)^2\, h_n^{(2)}(kr)\, j_{n'}(kr) \equiv (kr)^2\,[j_n j_{n'} - j n_n j_{n'}].$$

For a given argument x, the Bessel functions $j_n(x)$ decrease rapidly in magnitude, and the Neumann functions $n_n(x)$ increase, roughly as soon as the index n exceeds x. Thus the real part of I, which is obviously symmetric, will eventually decrease rapidly in magnitude as one proceeds along any row or column. The numerical behavior of I is dominated by its imaginary part, for which elements again decrease going out any row, but *increase* going down any column, at such a rate that diagonal elements remain relatively constant. These large numerical values presumably strongly influence the truncated matrix inversion procedure.

One can show, however, that for prolate or oblate spheroids this behavior, specifically the arbitrarily large values by which elements of $[I]$ below the diagonal exceed corresponding elements above, vanishes identically. $[I]$ and $[J]$ become completely symmetric, and dominant terms lie only on the diagonal once either row or column index exceeds kr_{max}, where r_{max} is the radius of the circumscribing sphere.

Based on results given by Watson (1962) one can show that the radial factor for an element below the diagonal in the imaginary part of $I_{mnn'}$ is of the form

$$x^2 n_{n+2s+1} j_n \doteq x^2 n_n j_{n+2s+1} + \frac{1}{x^{2s}} + \frac{1}{x^{2s-2}} + \cdots + 1 \qquad (3.35)$$

where the equivalence symbol ($\doteq$) indicates that the exact coefficients of inverse powers of x^2 have not been included, as they are not required in the present discussion. The first term on the right-hand side corresponds precisely to the symmetrically placed element above the diagonal; we must thus show that the inverse powers of x^2 contribute nothing to the integral

$$\text{Im}\,[I_{m(n+2s+1)n}] = -m \int_0^\pi d\theta\, \frac{\partial}{\partial\theta}\, (P^m_{n+2s+1} P^m_n)\, (kr)^2\, n_{n+2s+1}\,(kr)\, j_n\,(kr). \qquad (3.36)$$

For a prolate (oblate) spheroid, having semi-axes a, b, one has

$$kr = ka\,[\cos^2\theta + (a/b)^2 \sin^2\theta]^{-1/2}, \qquad (3.37)$$

which may be rewritten (identifying x with kr)

$$1/x^2 \doteq P_0 + P_2. \qquad (3.38)$$

Now the product of two Legendre functions may itself be expanded in a series of Legendre polynomials, with indices ranging from the difference to the sum of the original indices (Stein, 1962), i.e.

$$P^m_n P^m_{n'} \doteq \sum_{\substack{p=n-n' \\ (p+n+n'\ \text{even})}}^{n+n'} P_p \qquad (3.39)$$

where again explicit numerical coefficients have been ignored. Substituting eqn. (3.38) in the series of inverse powers of x^2 appearing in eqn. (3.35), then employing eqn. (3.39) repeatedly, one can write

$$x^2 n_{n+2s+1} j_n = x^2 n_n j_{n+2s+1} + \sum_{q=0}^s P_{2q}. \qquad (3.40)$$

This result may be put in eqn. (3.36), recalling also that Re I is symmetric, to get

$$I_{m(n+2s+1)n} - I_{mn(n+2s+1)} \doteq m \int_0^\pi d\theta \, \frac{\partial}{\partial\theta} \, (P_{n+2s+1}^m P_n^m) \sum_{q=0}^s P_{2q}$$

$$\doteq -m \int_0^\pi d\theta \sin\theta \, P_{n+2s+1}^m P_n^m \sum_{q=1}^s P_{2q-1}$$

$$\doteq -m \int_0^\pi d\theta \sin\theta \sum_{p=s}^{s+n} P_{2p+1} \sum_{q=1}^s P_{2q-1}$$

$$\equiv 0, \tag{3.41}$$

where in the second step we have integrated by parts, then employed eqn. (3.39), and finally observed that the highest Legendre polynomial appearing in the second sum is P_{2s-1}, while the first sum begins at P_{2s+1}; because of orthogonality, all the resulting integrals vanish.

To perform the analogous calculation for $J_{mnn'}$, one proceeds by first employing Green's identity to rewrite $J_{mnn'}$ in the more symmetric form

$$J_{mnn'} = -\frac{1}{\varepsilon_m} \int_0^\pi d\theta \sin\theta \, B_{mnn'}(\theta) \, \frac{d}{dx} \, [x^2 h_n^{(2)}(x) j_{n'}(x)]_{x=kr(\theta)}$$

$$+ \frac{1}{2\varepsilon_m} \int_0^\pi d\theta \sin\theta \, C_{mnn'}(\theta) \, [x^3 h_n^{(2)}(x) j_{n'}(x) \, \partial (1/x^2)/\partial\theta]_{x=kr(\theta)} \tag{3.42}$$

valid for $n \neq n'$, with

$$B_{mnn'}(\theta) \equiv \frac{m^2 P_n^m P_{n'}^m}{\sin^2\theta} + \frac{\partial P_n^m}{\partial\theta} \frac{\partial P_{n'}^m}{\partial\theta}, \tag{3.43a}$$

$$C_{mnn'}(\theta) \equiv n'(n'+1) \frac{\partial P_n^m}{\partial\theta} P_{n'}^m + n(n+1) P_n^m \frac{\partial P_{n'}^m}{\partial\theta}. \tag{3.43b}$$

It is convenient this time to write

$$1/x^2 \doteq \text{const} + \sin^2\theta.$$

Using this in conjunction with the inverse polynomial expression

$$x^2 n_{n+2s} j_n \doteq x^2 n_n j_{n+2s} + \frac{1}{x^{2s-1}} + \frac{1}{x^{2s-3}} + \cdots + \frac{1}{x},$$

eqn. (3.42) may be reduced to

$$J_{m(n+2s)n} - J_{mn(n+2s)} \doteq (2s-1)/\varepsilon_m \int_0^\pi d\theta \sin\theta \, B_{m(n+2s)n} \sum_{q=1}^s (\sin\theta)^{2q}$$

$$+ 1/\varepsilon_m \int_0^\pi d\theta \sin^2\theta \cos\theta \, C_{m(n+2s)n} \sum_{q=0}^{s-1} (\sin\theta)^{2q}, \tag{3.44}$$

where in the first term the constant term in the summation has been dropped because of the additional orthogonality relations

$$\int_0^\pi d\theta \sin\theta \, B_{mnn'} = 0, \quad n \neq n'.$$

At this point, using the standard recursion formulas for the Legendre functions one can write

$$\sin^2 \theta \, B_{m(n+2s)n} \doteq P^m_{n+2s-1} P^m_{n+1} + P^m_{n+2s-1} P^m_{n-1}$$

$$+ P^m_{n+2s} P^m_n + P^m_{n+2s+1} P^m_{n-1} + P^m_{n+2s+1} P^m_{n+1}, \qquad (3.45a)$$

$$\sin \theta \cos \theta \, C_{m(n+2s)n} \doteq P^m_{n+2s-1} P^m_{n+1} + P^m_{n+2s-1} P^m_{n-1} + P^m_{n+2s+1} P^m_{n-1} + P^m_{n+2s+1} P^m_{n+1}. \qquad (3.45b)$$

The polynomials in $\sin^2 \theta$ appearing in eqn. (3.44) may be expanded in Legendre polynomials of highest index $2(s-1)$. [Note that a factor $\sin^2 \theta$ has been taken out in the first case to employ in eqn. (3.45a).] By examination of eqn. (3.39) it may be seen because of orthogonality that only the first term on the right-hand side of eqns. (3.45a) and (3.45b) will make a non-zero contribution to their respective integrals. Writing out these non-vanishing terms in eqn. (3.44) explicitly, one finally obtains

$$J_{m(n+2s)n} - J_{mn(n+2s)}$$

$$\doteq -\frac{(2s-1)(n+2s+1)(n+2s+m)(n-m+1)}{\varepsilon_m (2n+4s+1)(2n+1)} \int_0^\pi \mathrm{d}\theta \sin \theta \, P^m_{n+2s-1} P^m_{n+1} (\sin \theta)^{2s-2}$$

$$+ \text{ same expression}$$

$$\equiv 0. \qquad (3.46)$$

Thus $[I]$ and $[J]$ are symmetric, and one need only compute elements on and above the diagonal in eqns. (3.30). The matrices are expected to be well conditioned in the sense that numerical results will converge rapidly to final values versus truncation. From the point of view of the Rayleigh expansion in powers of ka, valid at low frequencies, observe that all matrices may be expanded in powers of ka, e.g. writing $[J^{(m)}]_{nn'} = J_{mnn'}$ one has

$$[J^{(m)}] = [A] + [B](ka) + [C](ka)^2 + \cdots = [A]\{1 + [A]^{-1}\{[J^{(m)}] - [A]\}\} \quad (3.47)$$

where $[A]$ is diagonal, $[B]$ is tridiagonal (all elements zero except on, one above, and one below the diagonal) and so forth. The inverse, expanded in powers of ka, is readily obtainable by the binomial theorem as

$$[J^{(m)}]^{-1} = [1 - [A]^{-1}\{[J^{(m)}] - [A]\} + \cdots][A]^{-1}. \qquad (3.48)$$

3.2.4. Results for Finite Cylinders and a Cone–Sphere

Consider the finite cylinders shown (in section) in Fig. 3.2. Dimensions for the right circular cylinder are shown in Fig. 3.2(i). Keeping the basic dimensions fixed, the shape is then modified to the finite cylinder of Fig. 3.2(ii) by adding spherically bounded ends, with radii of curvature equal to twice the cylinder radius b. Finally, the smooth finite cylinder of Fig. 3.2(iii) is obtained by adding hemispherical ends (radii of curvature equal to cylinder radius).

The cylinders were calculated for sixty aspect angles in the interval $0 \leq u \leq 90°$, using Schmidt orthogonalization to first compute the transition matrix from eqn. (3.28) in terms of $[\hat{Q}_{\text{unit}}]$. Values obtained for radar cross section are shown as small circles in Figs. 3.3 and 3.4 for the two cylinders having edges.

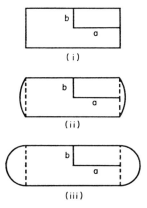

(i)

(ii)

(iii)

FIG. 3.2. A cross-section view of three finite cylinders chosen to test the theory in the presence of edges: (i) right cylinder circular, (ii) finite circular cylinder with spherical end-caps (sphere radius equals twice cylinder radius), (iii) smooth circular cylinder with hemispherical end-caps.

Experimental measurements of radar cross section were also made; resulting values are shown by the solid lines in Figs. 3.3 and 3.4. The models were machined at MITRE from solid aluminum stock, holding a tolerance of about 0.001 in. Microwave scattering measurements were then performed at the RCA laboratories in Moorestown, New Jersey, at a frequency of 9.930 GHz ($\lambda = 3.019$ cm), using for calibration a secondary standard consisting of a finite cylinder of known broadside radar cross section (D. P. Malloy and H. Spiegel, private communication).

Slight inconsistencies were apparent in the measurements themselves (e.g. different experimental values for the two polarizations at end-on incidence, $u = 0$, when theoretically they should be identical by symmetry). Because of this, we have decided for clarity to shift the experimental results so as to match theory and experiment at the peak value of radar cross section, where both should be most accurate. In these instance, the amount of shift, in dB, is noted in the figure captions. The resulting agreement between theory and experiment is seen to be remarkably good, especially when one notes that the scale of the figures in each case encompasses about five orders of magnitude.

The sharp lobe structure in the vicinity of broadside ($u = 90°$) for both cylinders can be fit fairly well by the physical optics approximation (Kirchhoff approximation for surface field), which gives (Mentzer, 1955)

$$\sigma/\pi a^2 \approx b \sin u \sin^2 (2ka \cos u)/\pi k a^2 \cos^2 u. \qquad (3.49)$$

Similarly for near-axial incidence ($u = 0°$), the main lobe exhibited in the radar cross section of the right circular cylinder, Fig. 3.4, is describable by the approximate formula (Mentzer, 1955)

$$\sigma/\pi a^2 \approx (b/a)^2 \cot^2 u J_1^2 (2kb \sin u) \qquad (3.50)$$

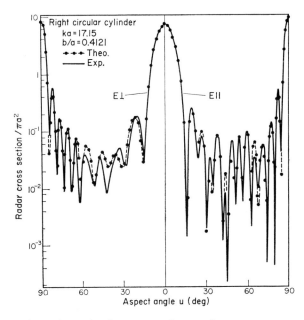

FIG. 3.3. Theoretical and experimental radar cross-section are shown versus aspect angle for the right circular cylinder of Fig. 3.3(i). Lobe structure near broadside ($u = 90°$) and end-on ($u = 0°$) incidence is quite accurately predicted by the physical optics approximation. Experimental $E_{||}$, $E_{\perp}$ shifted up 1.2 dB, 1.9 dB, respectively (see text).

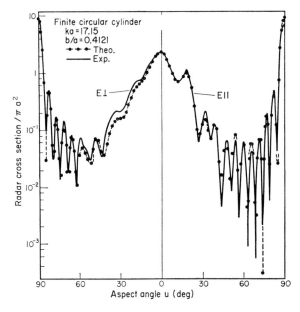

FIG. 3.4. Theoretical and experimental radar cross section are plotted as a function of aspect angle for the finite circular cylinder of Fig. 3.3(ii). Whereas the return near broadside ($u = 90°$) is virtually unchanged from that of the right circular cylinder (Fig. 3.4), the return in the vicinity of end-on incidence ($u = 0°$) is radically different, and strongly dependent on polarization. Experimental measurements have been shifted up 0.2 dB for both polarizations (see text).

(J_1 = Bessel function) for backscattering by circular plates. Such is not the case for near-axial incidence on the finite cylinder of Fig. 3.2(ii), however; a more sophisticated approach would be required, capable of distinguishing between the two incident polarizations.

A similar computation was attempted for the smooth, finite cylinder of Fig. 3.2(iii), after increasing matrix size slightly to allow for the increased overall cylinder length. Rather to our surprise, in view of the fact that this was the only cylinder considered *without* edges, no agreement with experiment was achieved, and we conclude that the computation failed in this instance. Failure is tentatively ascribed to the numerical quadratures used to obtain elements of [Q]; we defer comment until after the next example, where the same situation reoccurs.

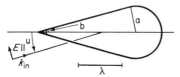

FIG. 3.5. Geometry of a smoothly joined cone-sphere is shown. For the computations, the cone tip was rounded off to a radius $b = 0.1a$, changing the dimensions negligibly in comparison with wavelength, as can be seen.

The other case of interest consists of a 15-degree half-angle cone, joined smoothly to a sphere of radius a. Geometry is shown in Fig. 3.5. For this case the object does not possess mirror symmetry normal to the rotational symmetry axis, and scattered field quantities must be evaluated over the full range of aspects $0 \leq u \leq 180°$.

Measurements for the cone-sphere were made on the microwave scattering range at Avco Corporation, Wilmington, Mass. (N. E. Pedersen, private communication). Again using a target machined out of aluminum, continuous backscattering measurements were made over the full 360° range of aspects for each polarization, at a frequency of 34.25 GHz ($ka = 3.66$). Discrepancies between the two 180° passes, shown by the two light curves in Figs. 3.6 and 3.7 for each of the polarizations, give a measure of experimental error, which is seen to be extremely good, almost without exception in the range $\pm\frac{1}{2}$ dB. The calibration target was an aluminum sphere of known radar cross section.

The first attempt at computation, using Schmidt orthogonalization, again failed. This time, however, the trouble could be traced to the numerical quadratures used to obtain elements of [Q] from eqs. (3.30). Values obtained for many of the elements refused to settle down, with decreasing step size, beyond two or three significant figures (as contrasted with eight or ten significant figures usually readily achievable).

The computation was then modified by rounding off the cone tip to a spherical radius $b = 0.1a$. As can be seen from Fig. 3.5, the resulting dimensional changes are quite small in comparison with wavelength. The coordinate origin was also shifted to the right, so as to remain centered on the long dimension of the (sphere) cone–sphere (see equations of Section 3.3.9). Slightly better convergence was obtained, resulting in the heavy curves shown in the figures. Good correlation is seen between theory and experiment for both number and location of peaks, with numerical agreement generally good to within 3 dB.

Computational difficulties encountered with the cone–sphere, as well as the finite cylinder of Fig. 3.2(iii), can now be explained as follows. In numerically integrating *over the spherical*

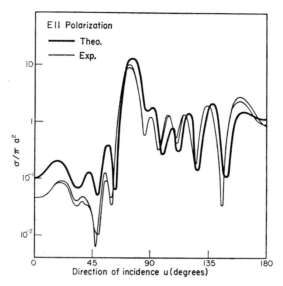

FIG. 3.6. Theoretical (heavy curve) and experimental (light curves) radar cross-section of the cone–sphere is plotted versus aspect angle over the full range $0 \leq u \leq 180°$ for $E_{||}$ polarization. The large peak at $u \simeq 75°$ is due to a specular "glint" from the cone section.

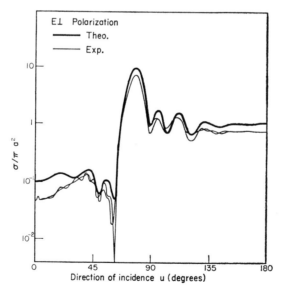

FIG. 3.7. Theoretical (heavy curve) and experimental (light curves) radar cross-section of the cone–sphere is shown as in Fig. 3.7, but for $E_\perp$ polarization. Curves for the two polarizations differ considerably, except for the specular glint at $u \simeq 75°$, which is virtually unchanged.

portion only of the cone–sphere, the function $r(\theta)$ appearing in the integrand becomes singular at an angle slightly beyond the upper end point of integration (that point where the radius vector is tangent to the continuation of the sphere). Consequently the error term in Bode's rule, which is proportional to the sixth derivative of the integrand (Abramowitz and Stegun, 1964), although not infinite can become extremely large. Shifting of the origin, in the course of rounding off the cone tip, served to move the singularity slightly further beyond the range of integration, alleviating the difficulty just enough that results could be obtained. Note that exactly the same situation arises with the smooth cylinder (but not the other two cylinders) of Fig. 3.2. Although we have not attempted to do so, it would appear that these numerical quadrature difficulties could be avoided completely by changing over to integration with respect to arc length in eqns. (2.30).

Some comment on the computer runs is of interest. The cone–sphere results shown in Figs. 3.6 and 3.7 required about $5\frac{1}{2}$ minutes of computer time. The first seven azimuthal modes ($0 \leq m \leq 6$) were employed, in each case truncating at $N = 14$, or a full matrix size of 28×28 complex. (In the absence of numerical quadrature difficulties, we estimate that $N \simeq 10$, and perhaps fifty integration intervals, rather than the abnormally large 500 intervals actually used, would have sufficed. If so, computation time would have been reduced by a factor of about 20.)

For larger bodies computation time increases roughly proportional to $(ka)^4$; of this, one factor $N^2 \simeq (ka)^2$ is due to the number of matrix elements of Q required, another factor proportional to ka arises from the number of points employed in numerical quadrature, a final factor, also proportional to ka, accounts for the number of azimuthal modes which must be included. Experience indicates that the subsequent arithmetic operations involved in matrix processing (inversion or orthogonalization, multiplication), which are also $0 (ka)^4$, represent an insignificant fraction of the total computation time. Mirror symmetry (e.g. the finite cylinders) reduces the computation by a factor of 4; half of the elements of $[Q]$ vanish, the remainder may be evaluated by integrating over the reduced range $0 \leq \theta \leq \pi/2$ in eqns. (3.30). A further reduction of 33 per cent obtains for spheroids, because elements of Im Q above the diagonal need not be evaluated.

3.3. ORGANIZATION OF THE COMPUTER PROGRAM

3.3.1. Introduction

The "EMSCAT" Program has been written in FORTRAN IV language for the IBM 7030 computer to produce solutions to the electromagnetic scattering problems which are outlined above in Section 3.2. Several factors were given consideration in the design of the program:

Efficient coding to reduce computer run time as much as possible. The routine VECMUL for matrix by vector multiplication was coded in machine language to take advantage of specialized coding available at that level. This routine is also available in FORTRAN (though less efficient and accurate) so that the program can be run on machines other than the 7030 computer.

Full single word accuracy of a 7030 register and where necessary double precision accuracy was utilized in the calculation of special functions. Single precision accuracy on the 7030 maintains fifteen digits of accuracy.

Maximum use of core storage. The size of the solution matrices (60×60 complex) was determined so that secondary storage devices such as tapes do not have to be utilized in running the program.

The matrices are stored and manipulated from one of three large blocks of common storage. Each block is dimensioned 120×120. However, through various equivalence statements in the proper routines, these major blocks are resegmented and renamed for ease of programming.

3.3.2. Glossary of the Subroutines

The program operates via a MAIN routine and fifteen auxiliary routines which are briefly described and listed below. Standard I/0 and mathematical routines, e.g. SIN, LOG, etc., are assumed to be available through the FORTRAN operating system.

The *MAIN routine* controls overall run processing and computes the [*I*], [*J*], [*K*] and [*L*] matrices.

Routines called are:

RDDATA

GENLGP

GENKR

GENBSL

PRTMTX

PRCSSM

Subroutine RDDATA reads the user's control parameters and sets up preliminary output heading information.

Routine called is: *CALENP*

Subroutine CALENP computes the sections of θ, the polar angle, and the step size for numerical integration.

Subroutine GENLGP computes the associated Legendre functions over the necessary range.

Subroutine GENBSL controls backward recursion of Bessel functions and forward recursion of Neumann functions.

Subroutine BESSEL computes the Bessel function for a specific argument and order.

Subroutine GENKR computes the parameter "*kr*" and its derivative with respect to the polar angle θ.

Subroutine PRNQOT prints headings and controls printout of the [*Q*] matrix.

Routine called is: *PRINTM*

Subroutine PRINTM prints the elements of a specific matrix of specified rank.

Subroutine PRCSSM generates the [*Q*] matrices from the [*I*], [*J*], [*K*] and [*L*] matrices, and transforms the [*Q*] matrix into the [*T*] matrix.

Routines called are: *NRMQMX*

CNDTNQ

PRTRIT

ADDPRC

Subroutine NRMQMX normalizes the $[I]$, $[J]$, $[K]$ and $[L]$ matrices to obtain the $[Q]$ matrices.

Subroutine CNDTNQ conditions the $[Q]$ matrix before transforming it into the $[T]$ matrix.

Subroutine PRTRIT prints headings and controls printout of the $[T]$ matrix.

Routine used is: *PRINTM*

Subroutine ADDPRC does final processing of the $[T]$ matrix to provide the scattering results.

Routines called are: *GENLGP*

VECMUL

Subroutine VECMUL multiplies a matrix times a vector.

Subroutine DUMP gives a listing of core storage when an error condition occurs.

Subsequent paragraphs detail the above routines where necessary. It should be noted at this point that standard mathematical notation is not necessarily followed, e.g. program notation labels Bessel functions as B instead of j. This was done for ease of relating program mnemonics to mathematical notation. When necessary, parameters have been labeled which have notation different from the earlier text.

3.3.3. The Input Routine

Subroutine *RDDATA* reads the user's control information, prints out headings and obtains information for numerical integration. The input cards and their formats are listed below.

Card 1.	NM, NRANK, NSECT, IBODY, NUANG
	FORMAT (5I12)
NM	No. of values of "*m*". See Card 3.
NRANK	Rank of matrices $[I]$, $[J]$, $[K]$ and $[L]$.
NSECT	No. of sections defining body shape and integration intervals. See Subroutine *CALENP* for fuller description of body shapes.
IBODY	Case no. or body shape identifier
	7: Spheroid
	8: Mirror Symmetry
	9: General Axisymmetric Case
NUANG	No. of aspect angles "*u*". See Card 5.
Card 2.	CONK, BRXT, ALPHA
	FORMAT (3E12.7)
CONK	*ka*, scale factor for *r*, the polar radius, in determining body shape.
BRXT	variable parameter to be used in computing body shapes.
ALPHA	α, or a variable parameter, to be used in calculating body shapes. For a fuller description of its usage see Subroutines *CALENP* and *GENKR* described below.

Card(s) 3.   CMI(I), I = 1, NM
                 FORMAT (6E12.7)
CMI(I)   *I*th value of "*m*" to be used in current solution of scattering problem. As many as
                 thirty values of "*m*", the azimuthal index, may be read in; "*m*" is any integer $\geq$ 0.

Card 4.   NDPS(I), I = 1, NSECT
                 FORMAT (6I12)
NDPS(I)   No. of divisions for integration in *I*th section of the body shape. The body may be
                 divided into as many as six sections. These parameters are used to calculate spacing for
                 numerical integration, and they must be a multiple of 4.

Card(s) 5.   UANG(I), I = 1, NUANG
                 FORMAT (6I12)
UANG(I)   *I*th value of "*u*", a member of a table of aspect angles (in degrees). As many as sixty
                 values of "*u*" may be read in.

3.3.4. Calculation of End Points and Spacing for Integration

Subroutine *CALENP* is one of two special routines that have to be written into the program for specific body shapes. This routine calculates "NSECT" values of the polar angle θ, which provide boundaries for dividing the body into sections for numerical integration. With each boundary point a value of θ is associated. The spacing for integration is then determined by dividing the range of θ by the correct value of "NDPS". Note that the number of divisions does not have to remain constant from one section to the next, but it must be a multiple of 4.

Since the computations for each special version of *CALENP* may vary, the following parameters, "ALPHA", "BRXT", "QB", "SNALPH", and "CSALPH", may be used for communication between routines special values associated with a particular body shape. Note the use of QB below for a variable peculiar to the sphere–cone–sphere shape.

In Appendix I, a listing of the routines *CALENP* and *GENKR* are given for a sphere–cone–sphere body (Fig. 3.8).

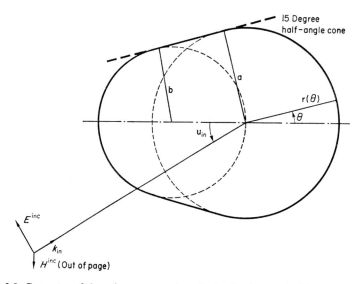

FIG. 3.8. Geometry of the sphere–cone–sphere body showing $E_{\parallel}$ incident polarization.

For the sphere–cone–sphere body, three end points for θ; θ_1, θ_2, θ_3, are computed as follows:

$$\theta_1 = \tan^{-1}\left[\frac{\sin \alpha \cos \alpha}{q - \sin^2 \alpha}\right]; \quad 0 \le \theta_1 \le 105°.$$

α (Fig. 3.8) is an input parameter stored at "ALPHA",

b/a (Fig. 3.8) is an input parameter stored at "BRXT",

$$q = \frac{(1 - b/a)(1 - \sin \alpha)}{2}$$

and is computed and stored in QB.

$$\theta_2 = \tan^{-1}\left[\frac{(b/a)\sin \alpha \cos \alpha}{1 - q - (b/a)\cos^2 \alpha}\right]; \quad \theta_1 < \theta_2 < \pi, \quad \theta_3 = \pi.$$

3.3.5. The First Control Routine

The *MAIN* Routine controls the general flow of the program and computes the real and imaginary parts of the partitioned scattering matrices, $[I]$, $[J]$, $[K]$ and $[L]$. After the user's control data has been read in, a numerical integration system utilizing Bode's third order rule is utilized (Abramowitz and Stegun, 1964). The program computes the $[I]$ and $[J]$ complex matrix elements for the three cases, axisymmetric, mirror-symmetric and spheroidal as follows:

$$I_{ij} = m \int_0^\pi (\sin \theta)(kr)^2 B_j(kr) H_i(kr)$$
$$\times \{(i + j)\cos \theta\, P_i^m P_j^m - (i + m) P_j^m P_{i-1}^m - (j + m) P_i^m P_{j-1}^m\}\, d\theta,$$

$B_j(kr)$: Bessel function of the first kind of order "j" and argument "kr";

$H_i(kr)$: Hankel functions which are defined as

$$B_i(kr) - \sqrt{-1}\, N_i(kr);$$

$N_i(kr)$: Neumann functions of order "i" and argument "kr".

$$P_i^m = \frac{P_i^m(\cos \theta)}{\sin \theta}$$

where $P_i^m(\cos \theta)$ is the associated Legendre function, of rank m and order i.

r: polar radius used in calculating body shape,

i: subscript notation for ith row of the matrix,

j: subscript notation for jth column of the matrix.

$$J_{ij} = \frac{-2}{e_m} \int_0^\pi (\sin \theta) H_i(kr) \{P_i^m P_j^m [kr(kr\, B_{j-1}(kr) - jB_j(kr))(m^2 + ij \cos^2 \theta)$$

$$+ ij(j + 1) \frac{d(kr)}{d\theta} B_j(kr) \sin \theta \cos \theta]$$

$$- (i + m) P_{i-1}^m P_j^m [kr \cos \theta (kr\, B_{j-1}(kr) - jB_j(kr) + (j + 1) \frac{d(kr)}{d\theta} B_j(kr) \sin \theta$$

$$+ (j + m) P_{j-1}^m kr [(kr B_{j-1}(kr) - jB_j(kr))((i + m) P_{i-1}^m - i \cos \theta P_i^m)]\}\, d\theta$$

where

$$e_m = \begin{cases} 1 & \text{for } m = 0, \\ 2 & \text{for } m \geq 1. \end{cases}$$

Within the program each element of the $[I]$ and $[J]$ arrays is used as an accumulator for numerical integration under Bode's rule. Thus, for a specified value of θ, all necessary functions are computed and added to the correct matrix element.

To save computer time, computations which would produce a null contribution to the integration are eliminated, and the following symmetries are taken advantage of in the direct computation of the I and J matrices.

General axisymmetric bodies:

$$\text{Re}\,(I_{ji}) = \text{Re}\,(I_{ij}),$$

$$\text{Re}\,(J_{ji}) = \text{Re}\,(J_{ij}).$$

Mirror-symmetric bodies: use the above plus

$$I_{ij} = 0; \quad \text{if } i \text{ and } j \text{ are } \begin{cases} \text{both odd,} \\ \text{both even,} \end{cases}$$

$$J_{ij} = 0; \quad \text{if } i \text{ and } j \text{ are } \begin{cases} \text{odd, even,} \\ \text{even, odd.} \end{cases}$$

Spheroids: the above, plus

$$\text{Im}\,(I_{ji}) = \text{Im}\,(I_{ij}),$$

$$\text{Im}\,(J_{ji}) = \text{Im}\,(J_{ij}).$$

The $[K]$ and $[L]$ matrices are then calculated from the following relationships with the $[I]$ and $[J]$ matrices:

$$\text{Re}\,(K_{ij}) = -\text{Re}\,(J_{ij}),$$

$$\text{Im}\,(K_{ij}) = -\text{Im}\,(K_{ij}) + bD_{ij}$$

where

$$b = \begin{cases} 1.0 \text{ General Axisymmetric bodies} \\ 0.5 \text{ Mirror-Symmetric or Spheroidal bodies, and body} \end{cases}$$
$$\text{shape } must\ be \text{ inputted for } 0 \leq \theta \leq \pi/2 \text{ for these cases.}$$

$$D_{ij} = \begin{cases} 0.0; \quad i \neq j \\ \left[\dfrac{\varepsilon_m\,(2i + 1)\,(i - m)!}{4i\,(i + 1)\,(i + m)!} \right]^{-1}; \quad i = j \end{cases}$$

$$\text{Re}\,(L_{ij}) = -\text{Re}\,(I_{ij}),$$

$$\text{Im}\,(L_{ij}) = -\text{Im}\,(I_{ij}).$$

The $[I]$, $[J]$, $[K]$ and $[L]$ complex matrices are then printed by Subroutine *PRTMTX* and control passes to Subroutine *PRCSSM* for further processing.

3.3.6. Associated Legendre Functions

Subroutine *GENLGP* generates the associated Legendre functions, $P_i^m(x)$ for a given argument x, a given value of the azimuthal index m, and for all values of degree i from 0 to "NRANK", the input-specified rank of the matrix. The first two values of P are generated by formula, then the remaining values of P are generated by a recursion relationship.

The following formulae are used to generate $P_i^m(x)$. Note that for this particular program, the functions always appear in the context

$$\frac{P_i^m(\cos\theta)}{\sin\theta}.$$

$$\frac{P_i^m(\cos\theta)}{\sin\theta} = 0.0; \qquad\qquad i < m,$$

$$\frac{P_m^m(\cos\theta)}{\sin\theta} = \frac{(2m)!\,\sin^{m-1}\theta}{2^m \cdot m!}; \quad i = m,$$

$$\frac{P_0^0(\cos\theta)}{\sin\theta} = \frac{1.0}{\sin\theta}; \qquad\qquad i = m = 0,$$

$$\frac{P_1^0(\cos\theta)}{\sin\theta} = \frac{\cos\theta}{\sin\theta}.$$

Recursion relationship:

$$\frac{P_n^m(\cos\theta)}{\sin\theta} = \frac{(2n-1)\cos\theta\,[(P_{n-1}^m(\cos\theta))/\sin\theta] - (n+m-1)\,[(P_{n-2}^m(\cos\theta))/\sin\theta]}{n-m}.$$

3.3.7. Bessel Functions

Subroutine *BESSEL* generates a Bessel function of the first kind $B_n(x)$, for a specified argument x, and order n, by means of an infinite series. To preserve accuracy, the computations are performed in double precision arithmetic and truncation error due to neglected terms in the series is $< 10^{-20}$. If the series has not converged to the aforementioned accuracy before the computation of the 100th term, an error indication is given.

The following infinite series is used to compute a Bessel function:

$$B_n(x) = \frac{x^n}{1\cdot 3\cdot 5\cdots(2n+1)}\sum_{i=0}^{\infty}a_i$$

where

$$a_0 = 1.0$$

$$a_i = \frac{-x^2}{2i\,[2n+(2i+1)]}\,a_{i-1}.$$

3.3.8. Recursion Relationships for Bessel and Neumann Functions

Subroutine *GENBSL* calls Subroutine *BESSEL* to obtain two successive Bessel functions for a specified argument, and then uses these first two values to recurse backward over the range of i from *NRANK* to 0. If the two computed functions of order NRANK and NRANK -1 do not satisfy the accuracy requirements mentioned in Section 3.3.7, the routine will increase the order of the computed Bessel function to 4(NRANK). If this fails to produce a satisfactory pair of functions, the run will abort and a dump of core memory is taken.

The recursion relation used for computing Bessel functions is:

$$B_{n-1}(x) = (2n + 1) x^{-1} B_n(x) - B_{n+1}(x).$$

This routine also computes Neumann functions by a forward recursion formula after the first two values are computed by the following formulae:

$$N_0(x) = \frac{-\cos x}{x},$$

$$N_1(x) = \frac{-\cos x}{x^2} - \frac{\sin x}{x}.$$

The recursion relation used for computing the remaining Neumann functions is:

$$N_{n+1}(x) = (2n + 1) x^{-1} N_n(x) - N_{n-1}(x).$$

To test the accuracy of the functions over the range of computed Bessel and Neumann functions for a given argument, two tests are performed in the *MAIN* Routine after the vector of the functions from 0 to *NRANK* is computed. If the following relations are not satisfied to an accuracy of 10^{-10}, an error message indicating such a condition is printed, and the program continues. Though the tests are performed in the *MAIN* Routine after the call to Subroutine *GENBSL*, for convenience they are listed here:

Bessel Test:
$$|x^2 [B_1(x) N_0(x) - B_0(x) N_1(x)] - 1| < 10^{-10}.$$

Neumann Test:

$$|x^2 [B_{\text{NRANK}}(x) N_{\text{NRANK}-1}(x) - B_{\text{NRANK}-1}(x) N_{\text{NRANK}}(x)] - 1| < 10^{-10}.$$

3.3.9. Generating the Body Shape

Subroutine *GENKR* is one of two custom-written routines which are adapted to the particular body shape in question. As noted above in Subroutine *CALENP*, certain parameters are available to the programmer to use as he sees fit to communicate information from one routine to another. The basic function of all versions of *GENKR* is to compute the polar radius r as a function of the polar angle θ, to compute $dr/d\theta$ and to scale these values by the input constant $ka = $ CONK.

To illustrate the use of this routine, a sphere–cone–sphere body shape is used (Fig. 3.8). As a result of subroutine *CALENP* the major divisions of the body as a function of θ have been recorded. This routine, given a value of θ, now computes $(ka)\,r$ and $ka\,(dr/d\theta)$; the scale factor ka is an input to the program.

Section 1 $(0 \leq \theta \leq \theta_1)$:

$$r = \frac{q \cos \theta}{\sin \alpha} + \left[1 - \left(\frac{q \sin \theta}{\sin \alpha}\right)^2\right]^{1/2},$$

$$\frac{dr}{d\theta} = \frac{-q \sin \theta}{\sin \alpha} - \left(\frac{q}{\sin \alpha}\right)^2 \sin \theta \cos \theta \left[1 - \left(\frac{q \sin \theta}{\sin \alpha}\right)^2\right].$$

Note: q was computed in Subroutine *CALENP* and stored in location QB.

Section 2 $(\theta_1 \leq \theta \leq \theta_2)$:

$$r = \frac{1 - q}{\sin (\theta - \alpha)},$$

$$\frac{dr}{d\theta} = \frac{-(1 - q) \cos (\theta - \alpha)}{\sin^2 (\theta - \alpha)}.$$

Section 3 $(\theta_2 \leq \theta \leq \pi)$:

$$r = -\left[\frac{1 - (b/a) - q}{\sin \alpha}\right] \cos \theta + \left[(b/a)^2 - \left(\frac{1 - (b/a) - q}{\sin \alpha}\right)^2 \sin^2 \theta\right]^{1/2},$$

$$\frac{dr}{d\theta} = \left[\frac{1 - (b/a) - q}{\sin \alpha}\right] \sin \theta - \left(\frac{1 - (b/a) - q}{\sin \alpha}\right)^2 \sin \theta \cos \theta$$

$$\times \left[(b/a)^2 - \left(\frac{1 - (b/a) - q}{\sin \alpha}\right)^2 \sin^2 \theta\right]^{1/2}.$$

3.3.10. First Matrix Printout

Subroutine *PRNQOT* controls the printout of the $[Q]$ matrix. Both the real and imaginary arrays are labeled and printed out on the community output tape.

3.3.11. Printout of an Array

Subroutine *PRINTM* will print out a specified square array of given rank.

3.3.12. Generating the $[Q]$ Matrix and the $[T]$ Matrix

Subroutine *PRCSSM* is the second major control routine and it controls the transformation of the $[I]$, $[J]$, $[K]$ and $[L]$ matrices to the $[Q]$ matrices, and the subsequent solution of a matrix equation which provides the $[T]$ matrix.

Subroutine *NRMQMX* (see below) normalizes the $[I]$, $[J]$, $[K]$ and $[L]$ matrices to produce the $[Q]$ matrix.

For notational convenience we define:

$$[Q] = \text{Re}\,[Q] - j\,\text{Im}\,[Q] = \begin{pmatrix} [Q_1]\,[Q_2] \\ [Q_2]\,[Q_4] \end{pmatrix}$$

where

$$j = \sqrt{-1}.$$

The method currently used by the program to transform the $[Q]$ matrix into the $[T]$ matrix involves orthogonalizing the $[Q]$ matrices. After the complex $[Q]$ matrix has been generated by normalizing the $[I]$, $[J]$, $[K]$ and $[L]$ matrices it is in the form noted in Section 3.3.12. From these $[Q]$ matrices, a new complex $[\hat{Q}]$ matrix of rank $2N$ is generated from the following relations:

$$[\hat{Q}]_{(2m-1)(2n-1)} = [Q_1]_{mn},$$

$$[\hat{Q}]_{(2m-1)(2n)} = [Q_2]_{mn}$$

$$m, n = 1, 2, \ldots, N,$$

$$[\hat{Q}]_{(2m)(2n-1)} = [Q_3]_{mn},$$

$$[\hat{Q}]_{(2m)(2n)} = [Q_4]_{mn}.$$

The new $[\hat{Q}]$ matrix is next conditioned as outlined in Subroutine *CNDTNQ* of Section 3.3.14.

Orthogonalization then proceeds as follows:

1. Consider each row of $[\hat{Q}]$ as a vector with $2N$ components, e.g. the components of the first vector $\mathbf{Q}_1$ would be:

$$Q_{11}, Q_{12}, Q_{13}, \ldots, Q_{1(2N)}.$$

Orthogonalization will proceed from the bottom or $2N$th vector upward.

2. Normalize the $2N$th vector as follows:

$$\mathbf{Q}_{2N} = \frac{\mathbf{Q}_{2N}}{(\mathbf{Q}_{2N}^* \cdot \mathbf{Q}_{2N})^{1/2}}$$

where the scalar product of the complex conjugate $\mathbf{Q}_p^*$ by another vector $\mathbf{Q}_q$ is defined as follows:

$$\mathbf{Q}_p^* \cdot \mathbf{Q}_q = \sum_{r=1}^{2N} Q_{pr}^* Q_{qr} = Q_{p1}^* Q_{q1} + Q_{p2}^* Q_{q2} + \cdots + Q_{p(2N)}^* Q_{q(2N)}.$$

3. Orthogonalize $\widehat{\mathbf{Q}}_{(2N-1)}$ to $\widehat{\mathbf{Q}}_{(2N)}$:

$$\widehat{\mathbf{Q}}_{2N-1} = \widehat{\mathbf{Q}}_{2N-1} - [\widehat{\mathbf{Q}}_{2N}^* \cdot \widehat{\mathbf{Q}}_{2N-1}]\,\widehat{\mathbf{Q}}_{2N}.$$

4. Normalize $\widehat{\mathbf{Q}}_{2N-1}$:

$$\widehat{\mathbf{Q}}_{2N-1} = \frac{\widehat{\mathbf{Q}}_{2N-1}}{[\mathbf{Q}_{2N-1}^* \cdot \mathbf{Q}_{2N-1}]^{1/2}}.$$

5. Orthogonalize $\widehat{\mathbf{Q}}_{2N-2}$ to both $\widehat{\mathbf{Q}}_{2N}$ and $\widehat{\mathbf{Q}}_{2N-1}$:

$$\widehat{\mathbf{Q}}_{2N-2} = \widehat{\mathbf{Q}}_{2N-2} - [\widehat{\mathbf{Q}}_{2N-1}^* \cdot \widehat{\mathbf{Q}}_{2N-2}]\,\widehat{\mathbf{Q}}_{2N-1} - [\widehat{\mathbf{Q}}_{2N} \cdot \widehat{\mathbf{Q}}_{2N-2}]\,\mathbf{Q}_{2N}.$$

6. Normalize $\widehat{\mathbf{Q}}_{2N-2}$:

$$\widehat{\mathbf{Q}}_{2N-2} = \frac{\widehat{\mathbf{Q}}_{2N-2}}{[\widehat{\mathbf{Q}}^*_{2N-2} \cdot \widehat{\mathbf{Q}}_{2N-2}]^{1/2}}.$$

7. Continue the orthogonalization and normalization process until $\widehat{\mathbf{Q}}_1$ has been orthogonalized to all subsequent rows.

8. A complex matrix $[\hat{T}]$ is now generated from the complex matrix $[\hat{Q}]$ by the following relation:

$$[\hat{T}] = [\hat{Q}]'^* \, \text{Re} \, [\hat{Q}].$$

9. The $[\hat{T}]$ matrix is then decomposed into the matrices $[T_1]$, $[T_2]$, $[T_3]$ and $[T_4]$ by the reverse of the procedure noted above. The complex $[T]$ matrix is printed by Subroutine *PRTRIT* and then the final processing is performed by Subroutine *ADDPRC*.

3.3.13. Normalizing Matrices

The Subroutine *NRMQMX* normalizes the $[I]$, $[J]$, $[K]$ and $[L]$ matrices to obtain the $[Q]$ matrix. The $[Q]$ matrix is blocked as noted above in Section 3.3.12 and the following procedure is used:

$$[Q_1] = (Z2)^{-1/2} \, [J]' \, (Z2^{-1/2}) \equiv Q_{ij} = \frac{J_{ji}}{\sqrt{Z2_i} \cdot \sqrt{Z_{2j}}},$$

$$[Q_2] = -(Z2)^{-1/2} \, [L]' \, (Z2)^{-1/2},$$

$$[Q_3] = (Z2)^{-1/2} \, [I]' \, (Z2)^{-1/2},$$

$$[Q_4] = (Z2)^{-1/2} \, [K]' \, (Z2)^{-1/2}$$

where

$$Z2_n = \left[\frac{e_m \, (2n+1) \, (n-m)!}{4n \, (n+1) \, (n+m)!} \right]^{-1}.$$

The expression for $Z2_n$ is the same as that used in computing the $[K]$ matrix of Section 3.3.5. The prime on $[J]$, etc., denotes matrix transpose as seen from the second half of the equality statement.

3.3.14. Conditioning Matrices

After the matrix $[\hat{Q}]$ of rank $2N$ has been formed, the matrix is conditioned starting with the last row $\widehat{\mathbf{Q}}_{2N}$ and working towards row $\widehat{\mathbf{Q}}_1$:

$$(\widehat{\mathbf{Q}}_{2N})_i = [1/\text{Im} \, (\widehat{\mathbf{Q}}_{2N})_{2N}] \, (\widehat{\mathbf{Q}}_{2N})_i; \quad i = 1, 2, \ldots, 2N.$$

The notation $(\widehat{\mathbf{Q}}_{2N})_i$ refers to the ith element of the $(2N)$th (last) row vector. Now set

$$\widehat{\mathbf{Q}}_m = \widehat{\mathbf{Q}}_m - [\text{Im} \, (\widehat{\mathbf{Q}}_m)_{2N}] \, \widehat{\mathbf{Q}}_N$$

where the equivalence is performed for each of the $2N$ elements of $\widehat{\mathbf{Q}}_m$, and repeated for all rows $m = 1, 2, , \ldots, 2N - 1$.

Redefine

$$\widehat{\mathbf{Q}}_{2N-1} = [1/\mathrm{Im}\,(\widehat{\mathbf{Q}}_{2N-1})_{2N-1}]\,\widehat{\mathbf{Q}}_{2N-1},$$

then compute

$$\widehat{\mathbf{Q}}_m = \widehat{\mathbf{Q}}_m - [\mathrm{Im}\,(\widehat{\mathbf{Q}}_m)_{2N-1}]\,\widehat{\mathbf{Q}}_{2N-1}$$

for all rows $m = 1, 2, \ldots, 2N-2$.

Continue the above process for all the remaining rows. The final step in the process is to generate

$$\widehat{\mathbf{Q}}_2 = [1/\mathrm{Im}\,(\widehat{\mathbf{Q}}_2)_2]\,\widehat{\mathbf{Q}}_2,$$

$$\widehat{\mathbf{Q}}_1 = \mathbf{Q}_1 - [\mathrm{Im}\,(\widehat{\mathbf{Q}}_1)_2]\,\widehat{\mathbf{Q}}_2,$$

then set $\mathrm{Im}\,(\widehat{\mathbf{Q}}_m)_i = 0.0$; $i = m+1, m+2, \ldots, 2N$; $m = 1, 2, 3, \ldots, 2N-1$.

3.3.15. Printing the [T] Matrix

Subroutine *PRTRIT* controls the printout of the [T] matrix, both real and imaginary elements, in the same manner as Subroutine *PRNQOT* (Section 3.3.10) controls the printout of the [Q] matrix. The community output tape is used. Since this printout is used mainly for checkout, it can be eliminated by removing the "*CALL PRTRIT*" statement following FORTRAN statement 140 in Subroutine *PRCSSM*.

3.3.16. Final Control Routine

Subroutine *ADDPRC* is the third and last control routine which converts the [T] matrix to the final set of results. Two sets of results are generated, a set of answers for the current value of m and an accumulated set of answers for all values of m up to and including the present value of m.

To generate the final results, the following procedure is followed: the [T] matrix is normalized

$$[T(k)]_{ij} = (Z2_i)^{1/2}\,T_{ij}(k)\,(Z2_j)^{-1/2} \quad \text{block}$$

where k indicates one of four blocks.

Note:

$$[T] = \begin{pmatrix} [T_1] & [T_2] \\ [T_3] & [T_4] \end{pmatrix}$$

$Z2_n$ is as defined in Subroutine *NRMQMX* under Section 3.3.13.

Note: For the reader who is relating the mathematics to the program listing in Appendix I, the mapping of COMMON storage in Section 3.3.19 should be consulted.

The associated Legendre functions of form

$$\frac{P_n^m\,(\cos u)}{\sin u}$$

are generated for each value of the aspect angle u, and for $n = 1$ to NRANK. The derivatives of the Legendre functions are computed from

$$\frac{d\,[P_n^m\,(\cos u)]}{du} = n\cos u \left[\frac{P_n^m\,(\cos u)}{\sin u}\right] - (n + m)\left[\frac{P_{n-1}^m\,(\cos u)}{\sin u}\right].$$

Values of the vectors $\mathbf{F}^1$, G^1 and $\mathbf{F}^2$, G^2 are generated by Subroutine *VECMUL*. These vectors are defined as:

$$\begin{pmatrix} \mathbf{F}^1 \\ G^1 \end{pmatrix} = j \begin{pmatrix} [T_1] & [T_2] \\ [T_3] & [T_4] \end{pmatrix} \begin{pmatrix} (-j)^n\, mP_n^m\,(\cos u)/\sin u \\ (-j)^{n+1}\, d\,[P_n^m\,(\cos u)]/du \end{pmatrix}$$

and

$$\begin{pmatrix} \mathbf{F}^2 \\ G^2 \end{pmatrix} = -j \begin{pmatrix} [T^1] & [T_2] \\ [T_3] & [T_4] \end{pmatrix} \begin{pmatrix} (-j)^{n+1}\, d\,[P_n^m\,(\cos u)]/du \\ (-j)^n\, mP_n^m\,(\cos u)/\sin u \end{pmatrix}$$

The final sets of answers are generated from the following equations:

$$\text{SCATT } 1, 2 = \frac{16}{(ka)^2} \sum_{n=1}^{\text{NRANK}} (Z2)^{-1}\,[|F_n^{1,2}|^2 + |G_n^{1,2}|^2],$$

$$\text{TOTAL } 1, 2 = \frac{16}{(ka)^2} \sum_{n=1}^{\text{NRANK}} (Z2)^{-1}\,(j)^n \left[F_n^{1,2}\,\frac{mP_n^m\,(\cos u)}{\sin u} - jG_n^{1,2}\,\frac{d\,(P_n^m\,(\cos u))}{du}\right],$$

$$\text{RTRAD } 1, 2 = \frac{8}{(ka)} \sum_{n=1}^{\text{NRANK}} (Z2)^{-1}\,(-j)^n \left[F_n^{1,2}\,\frac{mP_n^m\,(\cos u)}{\sin u} + jG_n^{1,2}\,\frac{d\,(P_n^m\,(\cos u))}{du}\right].$$

The final results are divided into two classes as noted above by the quantities SCATT 1, 2, etc. The classes are two different incident polarizations. Class 1 is the *E*-parallel incidence; class 2 is the *E*-perpendicular incidence.

3.3.17. Multiplying a Matrix Times a Vector

Subroutine *VECMUL* multiplies a matrix times a vector to compute the vectors $\mathbf{F}^1$, G^1 and $\mathbf{F}^2$, G^2 of Section 3.3.16.

3.3.18. Core Dump

If an abnormal or uncorrectable error condition occurs, Subroutine *DUMP* gives a dump of core memory as an aid in debugging the error condition. The Subroutine *LBPDMP* is a system routine for dumping core between specified limits.

3.3.19. Storage Arrangements

To conserve and fully utilize core storage, three large matrix arrays of dimension 120×120 have been set up in an area of COMMON storage named "MTXCOM". To aid in programming, various routines use EQUIVALENCE statements to resegment these large arrays into manageable blocks.

The FORTRAN array names of the three major blocks are:

$$
\begin{array}{ll}
\text{CMTXRL} & (120, 120) \\
\text{CMTXIM} & (120, 120) \\
\text{SPRMTX} & (120, 120)
\end{array}
$$

Within the *MAIN* Routine the following overlays are made:

$$
\text{CMTXRL}
\begin{cases}
\text{AMXIR} & (60, 60): & \text{RE(I)} \\
\text{AMXJR} & (60, 60): & \text{RE(J)} \\
\text{AMXKR} & (60, 60): & \text{RE(K)} \\
\text{AMXLR} & (60, 60): & \text{RE(L)}
\end{cases}
$$

$$
\text{CMTXIM}
\begin{cases}
\text{AMXII} & (60, 60): & \text{IM(I)} \\
\text{AMXJI} & (60, 60): & \text{IM(J)} \\
\text{AMXKI} & (60, 60): & \text{IM(K)} \\
\text{AMXLI} & (60, 60): & \text{IM(L)}
\end{cases}
$$

The SPRMTX block is unused.

Subroutine *NRMQMX* and Subroutine *PRCSSM*, the second control routine, allocated storage as follows:

$$
\text{CMTXRL}
\begin{cases}
\text{QMTXII} & (60, 60): & \text{QI1} & (60, 60): & \text{IM}(Q_1) \\
\text{QMTXJI} & (60, 60): & \text{QI2} & (60, 60): & \text{IM}(Q_2) \\
\text{QMTXKI} & (60, 60): & \text{QI3} & (60, 60): & \text{IM}(Q_3) \\
\text{QMTXLI} & (60, 60): & \text{QI4} & (60, 60): & \text{IM}(Q_4)
\end{cases}
$$

$$
\text{SPRMTX}
\begin{cases}
\text{QMTXIR} & (60, 60): & \text{QR1} & (60, 60): & \text{RE}(Q_1) \\
\text{QMTXJR} & (60, 60): & \text{QR2} & (60, 60): & \text{RE}(Q_2) \\
\text{QMTXKR} & (60, 60): & \text{QR3} & (60, 60): & \text{RE}(Q_3) \\
\text{QMTXLR} & (60, 60): & \text{QR4} & (60, 60): & \text{RE}(Q_4)
\end{cases}
$$

Note: After Subroutine *NRMQMX* normalizes and moves the [Q] matrix (complex) into the *SPRMTX* and *CMTXRL* areas, the processing which transforms the [Q] to the [T] matrix follows the procedure outlined in Section 3.3.12. The storage allocation is noted above in the eight itemized steps.

Subroutine *INVMBL* always assumes the block matrix which is to be processed is stored in the *CMTXRL* area. The intermediate steps as outlined in Section 3.3.14 are performed in the *CMTXIM* area.

The third and last control routine, Subroutine *ADDPRC* makes the following storage allocations:

$$
\text{CMTXRL}
\begin{cases}
\text{QMTXII} & (60, 60): & \text{FGVECT} & (2, 120, 2) \\
\text{QMTXJI} & (60, 60): & \text{FGMUL} & (120, 2) \\
\text{QMTXKI} & (60, 60): & \text{FGANS} & (60, 10) \\
\text{QMTXLI} & (60, 60): & \text{(unused)}
\end{cases}
$$

$$
\left.
\begin{array}{l}
\text{CMTXIM} \\
\text{SPRMTX}
\end{array}
\right\{
\begin{array}{l}
\text{TCMPLX } (2, 120, 120): \quad \text{real and imaginary} \\
\qquad\qquad\qquad\qquad\quad \text{components of the} \\
\qquad\qquad\qquad\qquad\quad \text{[T] matrix}
\end{array}
$$

Note: That *TCMPLX* overlays both the *CMTXIM* and *SPRMTX* areas. As noted in Section 3.3.16, *FGVECT* contains the $\mathbf{F}^1$, $\mathbf{G}^1$ and $\mathbf{G}^2$, $\mathbf{F}^2$ vectors. The first subscript refers to the real and imaginary components of the vectors, the second subscript refers to the dimension of the vectors which is $2 \cdot \text{NRANK}$ and the last subscript differentiates the two vectors.

FGMUL contains the vectors which post-multiply the [T] matrix to generate *FGVECT*. The first and second subscripts correspond to the second and third subscripts of *FGVECT*.

FGANS contains the final answers. The first subscript corresponds with the value of aspect angle which generated it and the second subscript refers to the answers in the following manner:

1	2	3	4	5
SCATT^1	Re(TOTAL^1)	Im(TOTAL^1)	Re(RTRAD^1)	Im(RTRAD^1)
6	7	8	9	10
SCATT^2	Re(TOTAL^2)	Im(TOTAL^2)	Re(RTRAD^2)	Im(RTRAD^2)

ACKNOWLEDGMENTS

The author is indebted to several colleagues at MITRE for many helpful discussions, and in particular to C. V. McCarthy, who carried out the computer programming and provided the program description. He is also grateful to D. P. Malloy and H. Spiegel of RCA, and N. E. Pedersen, formerly of Avco, for making available certain of their unpublished experimental results. The work was supported by the Advanced Research Projects Agency.

THE FORTRAN IV PROGRAM LISTING

```
T          SUBTYPE,FORTRAN,LMAP,LSTRAP
C          SCATTERING FROM AXISYMMETRIC CONDUCTORS FOR CASES 7, 8 AND 9.
           COMMON DTR,RTD,CPI
           COMMON /CMVCOM/ NM,CMI(30),CMV,KMV,CM2,EM,QEM,TWM,PRODM
           COMMON /FNCCOM/ PNMLLG(61),BSSLSP(61),CNFUMN(61)
           COMMON /THTCOM/ THETA,NTHETA,DLTHTA, SINTH,COSTH,ISMRL,ISWTCH
          1(7),SRMUL,SMULSS(7),CDH(6),DHM,NSECT,NDPS(6),EPPS(6),KSECT
           COMMON /MTXCOM/ NRANK,NRANKI,AMXIR(60,60),AMXJR(60,60),AMXKR(60,60),
          1AMXLR(60,60),AMXII(60,60),AMXJI(60,60),AMXKI(60,60),AMXLI(60,60),SPRMTX(120,
          2120),CMXNRM(60)
           COMMON /BDYCOM/ CKR,DCKR,CKR2,CSKRX,SNKR,CONK,BRXT,ALPHA,
          1IBODY,QB,SNALPH,CSALPH
           DIMENSION CLRMTX(43200)
           EQUIVALENCE (AMXIR,CLRMTX)
C          SET PROGRAM CONSTANTS.
           DTR = 1.7453292519943E—02
           RTD = 57.2957795131
           CPI = 3.1415926535898
           ISWTCH(1) = 2
           ISWTCH(2) = 3
           ISWTCH(3) = 4
           ISWTCH(4) = 1
           SMULSS(1) = 32.0
           SMULSS(2) = 12.0
           SMULSS(3) = 32.0
           SMULSS(4) = 14.0
C          CALL ROUTINE TO READ DATA AND PRINT HEADINGS FOR OUTPUT
    20     CALL RDDATA
           IF(IBODY—9)24,22,24
    22     BDYFCT = 1.0
           GO TO 26
    24     BDYFCT = 0.5
C          SET UP A LOOP FOR M AND SET VARIABLES WHICH ARE A FUNCTION OF M.
    26     DO 900 IM = 1,NM
           KMV = CMI(IM)
           KMV = CMV
           CM2 = CMV*CMV
           PRODM = 1.0
           IF(CMV)40,40,44
    40     EM = 1.0
           GO TO 60
    44     EM = 2.0
           QUANM = CMV
           DO 52 IFCT = 1,KMV
           QUANM = QUANM&1.0
           PRODM = QUANM*PRODM/2.0
    52     CONTINUE
    60     QEM = —2.0/EM
           TWM = CMV&CMV
```

```
C       INITIALIZE ALL MATRIX AREAS TO ZERO
        DO 80 I = 1,28800
        CLRMTX(I) = 0.0
   80   CONTINUE
C       SET UP A LOOP FOR ALL VALUES OF THETA.
        THETA = 0.0
C       SET UP GENERAL LOOP FOR CORRECT NUMBER OF INTEGRATION SECTIONS.
        DO 800 ISECT = 1,NSECT
        KSECT = ISECT
        NTHETA = NDPS(ISECT) &1
        DLTHTA = CDH(ISECT)
        DHM = DLTHTA/22.5
        ISMRL = 4
        DO 700 ITHTA = 1,NTHETA
C       SET SWITCHES AND MULTIPLIERS FOR SIMPSONS INTEGRATION METHOD.
        IF(ITHTA—1)120,120,132
  120   SRMUL = 7.0*DHM
        IF(ISECT—1)700,700,362
  132   IF(ITHTA—NTHETA)200,148,148
  148   SRMUL = 7.0*DHM
        GO TO 340
  200   ISMRL = ISWTCH(ISMRL)
        SRMUL = SMULSS(ISMRL)*DHM
  340   THETA = THETA&DLTHTA
  348   COSTH = COS(THETA)
        SINTH = SIN(THETA)
C       GENERATE THE LEGENDRE POLYNOMIALS.
        CALL GENLGP
C       EVALUATE KR AS A FUNCTION OF THETA. ALSO ITS DERIVATIVE.
        CALL GENKR
        CSKRX = COS(CKR)/CKR
        SNKRX = SIN(CKR)/CKR
        CKR2 = CKR*CKR
C       GENERATE BESSEL FUNCTIONS,THEIR DERIVATIVES AND NEUMANN
       1FUNCTIONS.
        CALL GENBSL
C       PERFORM BESSEL TEST AND NEUMANN TEST
        QUANBT = ABS(CKR2*(BSSLSP(2)*CNEUMN(1)—BSSLSP(1)*CNEUMN(2))—1.0)
        QUANNT = ABS(CKR2*(BSSLSP(NRANKI)*CNEUMN(NRANK)—BSSLSP(NRANK)
       1*CNFUMN(NRANKI))—1.0)
        IF(QUANBT—1.0E—10)360,352,352
  352   THTPRT = RTD*THETA
        PRINT 356,THTPRT,CKR,QUANBT,QUANNT
  356   FORMAT(1HO10X,13H***** THETA =F9.4,6H, KR =F10.4,15H, BESSEL TEST =E12.
       15,16H, NEUMANN TEST =E12.5,6H *****)
        GO TO 362
  360   IF(QUANNT—1.0E—10)362,352,352
  362   CROW = 0.0
        CROWM = CMV
        IMR = 2
        DO 600 IROW = 1,NRANK
        CROW = CROW&1.0
        CROWM = CROWM&1.0
C       SET UP A LOOP FOR EACH COLUMN OF THE MATRICES.
        CCOL = 0.0
        CCOLM = CMV
        GO TO (364,366),IMR
  364   JMR = 1
        IMR = 2
```

```
            GO TO 368
      366   JMR = 2
            IMR = 1
      368   DO 400 ICOL = 1,NRANK
            CCOL = CCOL&1.0
            CRIJ = CROW&CCOL
            CRSSIJ = CROW*CCOL
            CCOLM = CCOLM&1.0
            CCOL1 = CCOL&1.0
            IF(IBODY—7)372,369,372
      369   IF(ICOL—IROW)370,372,372
      370   GO TO (390,398),JMR
      372   BJ 1XP= CCOL1*DCKR*BSSLSP(ICOL&1)*SINTH
            BJBJ1 = CKR*(CKR*BSSLSP(ICOL)—CCOL*BSSLSP(ICOL&1))
            IF(IBODY—9)374,376,374
      374   GO TO (376,392),JMR
C           TEST FOR M = 0.
      376   IF(CMV)388,388,378
C           CALCULATE THE TERM FOR THE CURRENT ELEMENT IN THE I MATRIX.
      378   TERMI = SINTH*CKR2*BSSLSP(ICOL&1)*(COSTH*PNMLLG(IROW&1)*PNMLLG
           1(ICOL&1)*CRIJ—CROWM*PNMLLG(ICOL&1)*PNMLLG(IROW)—CCOLM*PNMLLG
           2(IROW&1)*PNMLLG(ICOL))
            AMXII(IROW,ICOL) = AMXII(IROW,ICOL)&SRMUL*CNEUMN(IROW&1)*TERMI
            IF(ICOL—IROW)388,384,384
      384   AMXIR(IROW,ICOL) = AMXIR(IROW,ICOL)&SRMUL*BSSLSP(IROW&1)*TERMI
      388   IF(IBODY—9)390,392,390
      390   JMR = 2
            GO TO 400
C           CALCULATE TERM FOR CURRENT ELEMENT IN THE J MATRIX.
      392   PTJ1 = PNMLLG(IROW&1)*PNMLLG(ICOL&1)*(BJBJ1*(CM2&CRSSIJ*COSTH**2)
           1&CRSSIJ*COSTH*BJ1XP)
            PTJ2 = CROWM*CCOL*PNMLLG(IROW)*PNMLLG(ICOL&1)*(COSTH*BJBJ1&
           1BJ1XP)
            PTJ3 = CCOLM*PNMLLG(ICOL)*BJBJ1*(CROWM*PNMLLG(IROW)—CROW*
           1*COSTH*PNMLLG(IROW&1))
            AMXJI(IROW,ICOL) = AMXJI(IROW,ICOL)&SRMUL*SINTH*CNEUMN(IROW&1)
           1*(PTJ1—PTJ2&PTJ3)
            IF(ICOL—IROW)398,396,396
      396   AMXJR(IROW,ICOL) = AMXJR(IROW,ICOL)&SRMUL*SINTH*BSSLSP(IROW&1)
           1*(PTJ1—PTJ2&PTJ3)
      398   JMR = 1
      400   CONTINUE
      600   CONTINUE
      700   CONTINUE
      800   CONTINUE
C           SYMMETRIZE REAL MATRICES AND IMAGINARY SPHERICAL MATRICES.
            DO 816 IROW = 2,NRANK
            IENDSY = IROW—1
            DO 812 ICOL = 1,IENDSY
            AMXIR(IROW,ICOL) = AMXIR(ICOL,IROW)
            AMXJR(IROW,ICOL) = AMXJR(ICOL,IROW
C           TEST FOR SPHERICAL BODIES.
            IF(IBODY—7)812,808,812
      808   AMXII(IROW,ICOL) = AMXII(ICOL,IROW)
            AMXJI(IROW,ICOL) = AMXJI(ICOL,IROW)
      812   CONTINUE
      816   CONTINUE
C           SUMMATION FOR ALL MATRIX ELEMENTS COMPLETE. FINISH PROCESSING
           1THEM
```

```
      DO 860 JROW = 1,NRANK
      DO 820 JCOL = 1,NRANK
      AMXIR(JROW,JCOL) = CMV*AMXIR(JROW,JCOL)
      AMXII(JROW,JCOL) = CMV*AMXII(JROW,JCOL)
      AMXJR(JROW,JCOL) = QEM*AMXJR(JROW,JCOL)
      AMXJI(JROW,JCOL) = QEM*AMXJI(JROW,JCOL)
C     COMPUTE K MATRIX AS A FUNCTION OF THE J MATRIX.
      AMXKR(JROW,JCOL) = −AMXJR(JROW,JCOL)
      AMXKI(JROW,JCOL) = −AMXJI(JROW,JCOL)
C     CALCULATE THE L MATRIX AS A FUNCTION OF THE I MATRIX.
      AMXLR(JROW,JCOL) = −AMXIR(JROW,JCOL)
      AMXLI(JROW,JCOL) = −AMXII(JROW,JCOL)
  820 CONTINUE
C     COMPUTE ADDITIONAL TERM FOR THE IMAGINARY PART OF THE K MATRIX.
      CKROW = JROW
      IF(KMV)824,824,826
  824 FCTKI = 1.0
      GO TO 840
  826 IF(JROW−KMV)828,830,830
  828 CMXNRM(JROW) = 1.0
      GO TO 860
  830 IBFCT = JROW−KMV&1
      IEFCT = JROW&KMV
      FPROD = IBFCT
      FCTKI = 1.0
      DO 832 LFCT = IBFCT,IEFCT
      FCTKI = FCTKI*FPROD
      FPROD = FPROD&1.0
  832 CONTINUE
  840 CMXNRM(JROW) = 4.0*CKROW*(CKROW&1.0)*FCTKI/(EM*(CKROW&CKROW
     1&1.0))
      AMXKI(JROW,JROW) = AMXKI(JROW,JROW)&BDYFCT*CMXNRM(JROW)
      CMXNRM(JROW) = SQRT(CMXNRM(JROW))
  860 CONTINUE
C     PROCESS COMPUTED MATRICES
      CALL PRCSSM
  900 CONTINUE
      GO TO 20
      END
```

```
T        SUBTYPE, FORTRAN,LMAP,LSTRAP
C        A PROGRAM TO READ INPUT DATA FOR THE SCATTERING PROGRAM.
         SUBROUTINE RDDATA
         COMMON DTR,RTD,CPI
         COMMON /CMVCOM/ NM,CMI(30),CMV,KMV,CM2,EM,QEM,TWM,PRODM
         COMMON /FNCCOM/ PNMLLG(61),BSSLSP(61),CNEUMN(61)
         COMMON /MTXCOM/ NRANK,NRANKI,CMTXRL(120,120),CMTXIM(120,120),SPRMT
        1X(120,120),CMXNRM(60)
         COMMON /THTCOM/ THETA,NTHETA,DLTHTA,SINTH,COSTH,ISMRL,ISWTCH
        1(7),SRMUL,SMULSS(7),CDH(6),DHM,NSECT,NDPS(6),EPPS(6),KSECT
         COMMON /BDYCOM/ CKR,DCKR,CKR2,CSKRX,SNKRX,CONK,BRXT,ALPHA,IBOD
        1Y,QB,SNALPH,CSALPH
         COMMON /TOTCOM/ ACANS(60,10),STSFCT,RTSFCT
         COMMON /UVCCOM/ UANG(60),NUANG
         DIMENSION CLRTOT(600)
         EQUIVALENCE (ACANS(1,1),CLRTOT)
         DIMENSION EPDEG(10)
C        READ NECESSARY INPUT DATA
         PRINT 40
   40    FORMAT(1H1119X,3HCVM////////////////////1HO39X,40H*************************
        1**************/1HO28X,63HELECTROMAGNETIC SCATTERING FROM GENERAL
        2AXISYMMETRIC CONDUCTORS/1HO39X,40H*************************************
        3*******)
         READ 80,NM,NRANK,NSECT,IBODY,NUANG
   80    FORMAT(6I12)
         NRANKI = NRANK&1
         PRINT 88
   88    FORMAT(1H129X,75H      CASES     MATRIX RANK      SECTIONS
        1BODY SHAPE      U VECTOR)
         PRINT 92,NM,NRANK,NSECT,IBODY,NUANG
   92    FORMAT(1H029X,5I15)
         READ 96,CONK,BRXT,ALPHA
   96    FORMAT(6F12.1)
         RTSFCT = 8.0/CONK
         STSFCT = 2.0*RTSFCT/CONK
         PRINT 100
  100    FORMAT(1H029X,60HBODY PARAMETERS          K(A)      BETA/RHO
        1     ALPHA)
         PRINT 104,CONK,BRXT,ALPHA
  104    FORMAT(1H044X,3F15.3)
         READ 96,(CMI(I),I = 1,NM)
         READ 80,(NDPS(I),I = 1,NSECT)
         PRINT 120,(NDPS(I),I = 1,NSECT)
  120    FORMAT(24H0   INTEGRATIONS/SECTION8I12,/(1H023X,8I12))
         READ 96,(UANG(I),I = 1,NUANG)
C        CLEAR AREA WHICH CONTAINS RUNNING TOTALS.
         DO 136 I = 1,600
         CLRTOT(I) = 0.0
  136    CONTINUE
C        COMPUTE END POINTS FOR THETA.
         ALPHA = DTR*ALPHA
         CALL CALENP
         DO 140 I = 1,NSECT
         EPDEG(I) = RTD*EPPS(I)
  140    CONTINUE
         PRINT 148,(EPDEG(I),I = 1,NSECT)
  148    FORMAT(24H0          END POINTS8F12.4,/(1H023X,8F12.4))
         RETURN
         END
```

```
T         SUBTYPE,FORTRAN,LMAP,LSTRAP
C      A ROUTINE TO COMPUTE A BESSEL FUNCTION OF SET ORDER AND
       1ARGUMENT.
       SUBROUTINE BESSEL (NORDER,ARGMNT,ANSWR,IERROR)
       DOUBLE PRECISION ARGMNT,ANSWR,X,CN,SUM,APR,TOPR,CI,CNI,ACR,PROD,
       1FACT
       IERROR = 0
       N = NORDER
       X = ARGMNT
       CN = N
       SUM = 1.0
       APR = 1.0
       TOPR = —0.5D0*X*X
       CI = 1.0
       CNI = 2*N &3
       DO 60 I = 1,100
       ACR = TOPR*APR/(CI*CNI)
       SUM = SUM &ACR
       IF(DABS(ACR/SUM)—1.0D—20)100,100,40
   40  APR = ACR
       CI = CI &1.0DO
       CNI = CNI &2.0D0
   60  CONTINUE
       IERROR = 1
       GO TO 200
C      THE SERIES HAS CONVERGED.
  100  PROD = 2*N &1
       FACT = 1.0
       IF(N)160,160,120
  120  DO 140 IFCT = 1,N
       FACT = FACT*X/PROD
       PROD = PROD—2.0D0
  140  CONTINUE
  160  ANSWER = FACT*SUM
  200  RETURN
       END
```

```
T          SUBTYPE,FORTRAN,LMAP,LSTRAP
C          A ROUTINE TO GENERATE LEGENDRE POLYNOMIALS.
           SUBROUTINE GENLGP
           COMMON DTR,RTD,CPI
           COMMON /CMVCOM/ NM,CMI(30),CMV,KMV,CM2,EM,QEM,TWM,PRODM
           COMMON /FNCCOM/ PNMLLG(61),BSSLSP(61),CNEUMN(61)
           COMMON /MTXCOM/ NRANK,NRANKI,CMTXRL(120,120),CMTXIM(120,120),SPRMT
     1X(120,120),CMXNRM(60)
           COMMON /THTCOM/ THETA,NTHETA,DLTHTA,SINTH,COSTH,ISMRL,ISWTCH
     1(7),SRMUL,SMULSS(7),CDH(6),DHM,NSECT,NDPS(6),EPPS(6),KSECT
           COMMON /BDYCOM/ CKR,DCKR,CKR2,CSKRX,SNKRX,CONK,BRXT,ALPHA,
     1IBODY,QB,SNALPH,CSALPH
           DTWM = TWM&1.0
           IF(THETA)16,4,16
    4      IF(KMV—1)6,12,6
    6      DO 8 ILG = 1,NRANKI
           PNMLLG(ILG) = 0.0
    8      CONTINUE
           GO TO 88
   12      PNMLLG(1) = 0.0
           PNMLLG(2) = 1.0
           PLA = 1.0
           GO TO 48
   16      IF(KMV)20,20,40
C          THE SPECIAL CASE WHEN M = 0.
   20      PLA = 1.0/SINTH
           PLB = COSTH*PLA
           PNMLLG(1) = PLA
           PNMLLG(2) = PLB
           IBEG = 3
           GO TO 60
C          GENERAL CASE FOR M NOT EQUAL TO 0.
   40      DO 44 ILG = 1,KMV
           PNMLLG(ILG) = 0.0
   44      CONTINUE
           PLA = PRODM*SINTH**(KMV—1)
           PNMLLG(KMV &1) = PLA
   48      PLB = DTWM*COSTH*PLA
           PNMLLG(KMV &2) = PLB
           IBEG = KMV &3
C          DO RECURSION FORMULA FOR ALL REMAINING LEGENDRE POLYNOMIALS.
   60      CNMUL = IBEG &IBEG—3
           CNM = 2.0
           CNMM = DTWM
           DO 80 ILGR = IBEG,NRANKI
           PLG = (CNMUL*COSTH*PLB—CNMM*PLA)/CNM
           PNMLLG(ILGR) = PLC
           PLA = PLB
           PLB = PLC
           CNMUL = CNMUL &2.0
           CNM = CNM &1.0
           CNMM = CNMM &1.0
   80      CONTINUE
   88      RETURN
           END
```

```
T          SUBTYPE,FORTRAN,LMAP,LSTRAP
C          A ROUTINE TO DO FINAL PROCESSING ON THE SCATTERING MATRIX.
           SUBROUTINE ADDPRC
           COMMON DTR,RTD,CPI
           COMMON /CMVCOM/ NM,CMI(30),CMV,KMV,CM2,EM,QEM,TWM,PRODM
           COMMON /FNCCOM/ PNMLLG(61),BSSLSP(61),CNEUMN(61)
           COMMON /MTXCOM/ NRANK,NRANKI,QMTXII(60,60),QMTXJI(60,60),QMTXKI(60,
          160),QMTXLI(60,60),PMX1(60,60),PMX2(60,60),PMX3(60,60),PMX4(60,60),QMTXIR(60,60),
          2QMTXJR(60,60),QMTXKR(60,60),QMTXLR(60,60),CMXNRM(60)
           COMMON /VCMCOM/ ISYBG,JSYBG,KSYBG,NSYMT
           DIMENSION FGVECT(2,120,2),TCMPLX(2,120,120),FGMUL(120,2),FGANS(60,10)
           EQUIVALENCE (QMTXII,FGVECT),(PMX1,TCMPLX),(QMTXJI,FGMUL),(QMTXKI,
          1FGANS)
           COMMON /THTCOM/ THETA,NTHETA,DLTHTA,SINTH,COSTH,ISMRL,ISWTCH
          1(7),SRMUL,SMULSS(7),CDH(6),DHM,NSECT,NDPS(6),EPPS(6),KSECT
           COMMON /TOTCOM/ ACANS(60,10),STSFCT,RTSFCT
           COMMON /UVCCOM/ UANG(60),NUANG
           COMMON /BDYCOM/ CKR,DCKR,CKR2,CSKRX,SNKRX,CONK,BRXT,ALPHA,IBOD
          1Y,QB,SNALPH,CSALPH
C          NORMALIZE AND STORE SECTIONS T1 AND T3 OF THE COMPLEX T MATRIX.
           DO 40 IC = 1,NRANK
           DO 20 IR = 1,NRANK
           JR = IR&NRANK
           QUANNM = CMXNRM(IR)/CMXNRM(IC)
           TCMPLX(1,IR,IC) = QUANNM*QMTXIR(IR,IC)
           TCMPLX(1,JR,IC) = QUANNM*QMTXKR(IR,IC)
           TCMPLX(2,IR,IC) = QUANNM*QMTXII(IR,IC)
           TCMPLX(2,JR,IC) = QUANNM*QMTXKI(IR,IC)
        20 CONTINUE
        40 CONTINUE
C          NORMALIZE AND STORE SECTIONS T2 AND T4 OF THE COMPLEX T MATRIX.
           DO 80 IC = 1,NRANK
           JC = IC&NRANK
           DO 60 IR = 1,NRANK
           JR = IR&NRANK
           QUANNM = CMXNRM(IR)/CMXNRM(IC)
           TCMPLX(1,IR,JC) = QUANNM*QMTXJR(IR,IC)
           TCMPLX(1,JR,JC) = QUANNM*QMTXLR(IR,IC)
           TCMPLX(2,IR,JC) = QUANNM*QMTXJI(IR,IC)
           TCMPLX(2,JR,JC) = QUANNM*QMTXLI(IR,IC)
        60 CONTINUE
        80 CONTINUE
C          SET UP A LOOP FOR ALL VALUES OF THE ANGLE U.
           DO 400 IU = 1,NUANG
C          GENERATE LEGENDRE POLYNOMIALS AND DERIVATIVES. RESET THE LIST.
           IF(UANG(IU))96,88,96
        88 COSTH = 1.0
        92 SINTH = 0.0
           THETA = 0.0
           GO TO 112
        96 IF(UANG(IU)-180.0)104,100,104
       100 COSTH = -1.0
           GO TO 92
       104 THETA = DTR*UANG(IU)
           SINTH = SIN(THETA)
           COSTH = COS(THETA)
       112 CALL GENLGP
           DO 120 IPS = 1,NRANK
           FGMUL(IPS,1) = CMV*PNMLLG(IPS&1)
```

```
        CPS = IPS
        FGMUL(IPS,2) = CPS*COSTH*PNMLLG(IPS&1)-(CPS&CMV)*PNMLLG(IPS)
        JPS = IPS&NRANK
        FGMUL(JPS,1) = FGMUL(IPS,2)
        FGMUL(JPS,2) = FGMUL(IPS,1)
  120   CONTINUE
C       MULTIPLY THE T COMPLEX MATRIX TIMES THE LEGENDRE VECTORS.
        KMVM1 = (KMV-1)/4
        KMVM1 = 4*KMVM1
        IF(KMVM1)132,132,124
  124   DO 128 IZ = 1,KMVM1
        FGVECT(1,IZ,1) = 0.0
        FGVECT(2,IZ,1) = 0.0
        FGVECT(1,IZ,2) = 0.0
        FGVECT(2,IZ,2) = 0.0
        JZ = IZ&NRANK
        FGVECT(1,JZ,1) = 0.0
        FGVECT(2,JZ,1) = 0.0
        FGVECT(1,JZ,2) = 0.0
        FGVECT(2,JZ,2) = 0.0
  128   CONTINUE
        ISYBG = 242*(KMVM1)
        JSYBG = KMVM1
        KSYBG = 2*KMVM1
        NSYMT = NRANK-KMVM1
        GO TO 136
  132   ISYBG = 0
        JSYBG = 0
        KSYBG = 0
        NSYMT = NRANK
  136   CALL VECMUL
C       A LOOP TO ZERO CURRENT SUMS OF SCAT1,2, TOTAL1,2 AND RTRAD1,2.
        DO 140 IZ = 1,10
        FGANS(IU,IZ) = 0.0
  140   CONTINUE
C       SET UP LOOP FOR CURRENT VALUES OF THE SUMS.
        IPTH = 1
        DO 200 ICMS = 1,NRANK
        JCMS = ICMS&NRANK
C       COMPUTE SCATT1 AND SCATT2 SUMS
        FGANS(IU,1) = FGANS(IU,1) &(FGVECT(1,ICMS,1)**2&FGVECT(2,ICMS,1)**2
       1 &FGVECT(1,JCMS,1)**2&FGVECT(2,JCMS,1)**2)/CMXNRM(ICMS)**2
        FGANS(IU,6) = FGANS(IU,6) &(FGVECT(1,JCMS,2)**2&FGVECT(2,JCMS,2)**2
       1 &FGVECT(1,ICMS,2)**2&FGVECT(2,ICMS,2)**2)/CMXNRM(ICMS)**2
C       FORM THE REAL AND IMAGINARY PARTS OF TOTAL1,2 AND RTRAD1,2
        PFR1 = FGVECT(1,ICMS,1)*FGMUL(ICMS,1)
        PFI1 = FGVECT(2,ICMS,1)*FGMUL(ICMS,1)
        PFR2 = -FGVECT(2,JCMS,2)*FGMUL(ICMS,1)
        PFI2 = FGVECT(1,JCMS,2)*FGMUL(ICMS,1)
        PGR1 = FGVECT(1,JCMS,1)*FGMUL(JCMS,1)
        PGI1 = FGVECT(2,JCMS,1)*FGMUL(JCMS,1)
        PGR2 = -FGVECT(2,ICMS,2)*FGMUL(JCMS,1)
        PGI2 = FGVECT(1,ICMS,2)*FGMUL(JCMS,1)
        GO TO (150,154,158,162),IPTH
  150   SGN = &1.0
        IPTH = 2
        GO TO 170
  154   SGN = -1.0
        IPTH = 3
```

```
        GO TO 180
  158   SGN = —1.0
        IPTH = 4
        GO TO 170
  162   SGN = &1.0
        IPTH = 1
        GO TO 180
C       CASE FOR N MOD 4 IS 1 (—I,&I) OR 3 (&I,—I)
  170   FGANS(IU,2) = FGANS(IU,2)&SGN*(PFI1&PGR1)/CMXNRM(ICMS)**2
        FGANS(IU,3) = FGANS(IU,3)—SGN*(PFR1—PGI1)/CMXNRM(ICMS)**2
        FGANS(IU,7) = FGANS(IU,7)&SGN*(PFI2—PGR2)/CMXNRM(ICMS)**2
        FGANS(IU,8) = FGANS(IU,8)—SGN*(PFR2&PGI2)/CMXNRM(ICMS)**2
        FGANS(IU,4) = FGANS(IU,4)—SGN*(PFI1—PGR1)/CMXNRM(ICMS)**2
        FGANS(IU,5) = FGANS(IU,5)&SGN*(PFR1&PGI1)/CMXNRM(ICMS)**2
        FGANS(IU,9) = FGANS(IU,9)—SGN*(PFI2&PGR2)/CMXNRM(ICMS)**2
        FGANS(IU,10) = FGANS(IU,10)&SGN*(PFR2—PGI2)/CMXNRM(ICMS)**2
        GO TO 200
C       CASE FOR N MOD 4 IS 2 (—1,—1) OR 4 (&1,&1)
  180   FGANS(IU,2) = FGANS(IU,2)&SGN*(PFR1—PGI1)/CMXNRM(ICMS)**2
        FGANS(IU,3) = FGANS(IU,3)&SGN*(PFI1&PGR1)/CMXNRM(ICMS)**2
        FGANS(IU,7) = FGANS(IU,7)&SGN*(PFR2&PGI2)/CMXNRM(ICMS)**2
        FGANS(IU,8) = FGANS(IU,8)&SGN*(PFI2—PGR2)/CMXNRM(ICMS)**2
        FGANS(IU,4) = FGANS(IU,4)&SGN*(PFR1&PGI1)/CMXNRM(ICMS)**2
        FGANS(IU,5) = FGANS(IU,5)&SGN*(PFI1—PGR1)/CMXNRM(ICMS)**2
        FGANS(IU,9) = FGANS(IU,9)&SGN*(PFR2—PGI2)/CMXNRM(ICMS)**2
        FGANS(IU,10) = FGANS(IU,10)&SGN*(PFI2&PGR2)/CMXNRM(ICMS)**2
  200   CONTINUE
C       SCALE ACCUMULATIVE SUMS
        FGANS(IU,1) = STSFCT*FGANS(IU,1)
        FGANS(IU,2) = STSFCT*FGANS(IU,2)
        FGANS(IU,3) = STSFCT*FGANS(IU,3)
        FGANS(IU,4) = RTSFCT*FGANS(IU,4)
        FGANS(IU,5) = RTSFCT*FGANS(IU,5)
        FGANS(IU,6) = STSFCT*FGANS(IU,6)
        FGANS(IU,7) = STSFCT*FGANS(IU,7)
        FGANS(IU,8) = STSFCT*FGANS(IU,8)
        FGANS(IU,9) = RTSFCT*FGANS(IU,9)
        FGANS(IU,10) = RTSFCT*FGANS(IU,10)
  400   CONTINUE
C       PRINT PARTIAL SUMS AND ACCUMULATE TOTALS.
        DO 500 IPR = 1,2
        PRINT 420,KMV,IPR
  420   FORMAT(1H137X,31H********** CURRENT SUMS FOR M =I3,11H **********//6H0
       1CLASSI2,82H ANGLE     SCATTERING     TOTAL(REAL)     TOTAL(IMAG)
       2(RTRAD)(REAL)      RTRAD(IMAG)//)
        IBEG = 1&5*(IPR—1)
        IEND = IBEG&4
        DO 460 IUP = 1,NUANG
        DO 432 ICAL = IBEG,IEND
        ACANS(IUP,ICAL) = ACANS(IUP,ICAL)&FGANS(IUP,ICAL)
  432   CONTINUE
        PRINT 440,UANG(IUP),(FGANS(IUP,LP),LP = IBEG,IEND)
  440   FORMAT(1H F14.2,1P7E15.6)
  460   CONTINUE
  500   CONTINUE
C       PRINT THE ACCUMULATE TOTALS.
        DO 600 JPR = 1,2
        PRINT 520,KMV,JPR
  520   FORMAT(1H135X,35H********** ACCUMULATED SUMS FOR M =I3,11H ********
```

```
     1**//6H0CLASSI2,112H  ANGLE     SCATTERING    TOTAL(REAL)    TOTAL
     2(IMAG)    RTRAD(REAL)    RTRAD(IMAG)        RCS    PHASE ANGLE//)
       JBEG = 1 &5  (JPR—1)
       JEMD = JBEG &4
       DO 560 JUP = 1,NUANG
C      COMPUTE PHASE ANGLE AND RCS 1 OR 2.
       PHANG = RTD*ATAN2(ACANS(JUP,JEND),ACANS(JUP,JEND—1))
       RCS12 = ACANS(JUP,JEND—1)**2 &ACANS(JUP,JEND)**2
       PRINT 440,UANG(JUP),(ACANS(JUP,LP),LP = JBEG,JEND),RCS12,PHANG
  540  FORMAT(1H F14.3,1P7E15.6)
  560  CONTINUE
  600  CONTINUE
       RETURN
       END
```

```
T          SUBTYPE,FORTRAN,LMAP,LSTRAP
C          A SUBROUTINE TO PRINT OUT THE T MATRIX.
           SUBROUTINE PRTRIT
           COMMON /MTXCOM/ NRANK,NRANKI,QMTXII(60,60),QMTXJI(60,60),QMTXKI(60,
          160),QMTXLI(60,60),PMX1(60,60),PMX2(60,60),PMX3(60,60),PMX4(60,60),QMTXIR(60,60),
          2QMTXJR(60,60),QMTXKR(60,60),QMTXLR(60,60),CMXNRM(60)
           EQUIVALENCE (QMTXII,CMTXRL),(PMX1,CMTXIM),(QMTXIR,SPRMTX)
           DIMENSION CMTXRL(120,120),CMTXIM(120,120),CMTXIM(120,120),SPRMTX(120,120)
           PRINT 28
     28    FORMAT(1H1///1H052X,16HMATRIX T(1),REAL)
           CALL PRINTM(QMTXIR,NRANK)
           PRINT 128
    128    FORMAT(1H1///1H052X,16HMATRIX T(2),REAL)
           CALL PRINTM(QMTXJR,NRANK)
           PRINT 228
    228    FORMAT(1H1///1H052X,16HMATRIX T(3),REAL)
           CALL PRINTM(QMTXKR,NRANK)
           PRINT 328
    328    FORMAT(1H1///1H05X2,16HMATRIX T(4),REAL)
           CALL PRINTM(QMTXLR,NRANK)
           PRINT 428
    428    FORMAT(1H1///1H049X,21HMATRIX T(1),IMAGINARY)
           CALL PRINTM(QMTXII,NRANK)
           PRINT 528
    528    FORMAT(1H1///1H049X,21HMATRIX T(2),IMAGINARY)
           CALL PRINTM(QMTXJI,NRANK)
           PRINT 628
    628    FORMAT(1H1///1H049X,21HMATRIX T(3),IMAGINARY)
           CALL PRINTM(QMTXKI,NRANK)
           PRINT 728
    728    FORMAT(1H1///1H049X,21HMATRIX T(4),IMAGINARY)
           CALL PRINTM(QMTXLI,NRANK)
           RETURN
           END
```

```
T         SUBTYPE,STRAP
  '       A ROUTINE TO GET THE F1,G1 AND F2,G2 VECTORS FROM T * P(COS U).
          PUNREL
          PUNFPC,LAST,COMMON
VECMUL    ENTER,SVXRS
          PUNCDC
MTXCOM    COMBLOCK,FINAL
VCMCOM    COMBLOCK,FINALV
          XW,0,0,0
SVXRS     SX,$12,XR12                    'SAVE INDEX REGISTERS 12,
          SX,$13,XR13                    '                         13,
          SX,$14,XR14                    '                            14,
          SX,$2,XR2
          SX,$3,XR3
          SX,$10,XR10
          LWF(U),TWERTY                  'COMPUTE ADDRESS FACTOR FOR G1 OR F2.
          D*(U),NRANK
          SHFL,38
          E—I(U),38
          ST(U),G1F2A
          LX,$12,TMXWR                   (RFSET T COMPLEX MATRIX CONTROL.
          V&,$12,ISYBG&0.32
          LCI,$12,2.0
          SX,$12,TMXW
          LX,$13,PMXWR                   'RESET MULTIPLIER VECTOR CONTROL-
          V&,$13,JSYBG&0.32
          LC,$13,NSYMT&0.32
          SX,$13,PMXW
          L(U),NSYMT
          &(U),NSYMT
          LX,$14,FGXWR
          V&,$14,KSYBG&0.32
          LC,$14,$L&0.32
          SX,$14,FGXW
          FZ(BU,1,8),RFGGF&0.20          'SET SIGN FOR ANSWER STORAGE, F1 OR G1
          FZ(BU,1,8),IFGGF&0.20
  '       DO THE REAL PART OF F1 OR G1, G2 OR F2.
BGANLP    LX,$2,$12
          V&,$2,G1F2A&0.32
          LX,$3,$13
          V&,$3,NRANK&0.32
SRLF1R    KC,$14,NSYMT&0.32
          BZXE,NOCMPR
          V&,$12,KSYBG&0.32
          SV,$12,TMXW
          V&,$14,KSYBG&0.32
          LV,$2,$12
          V&,$2,G1F2A&0.32
NOCMPR    LVI,$10,N1F1R
          DL(U),ZERO
SMLF1R    B,0.0($10)
N1F1R     LMR(U),0.0($12)                'N MOD 4 = I OR 1.0
          *&(N),0.0($13)
          LMR(0),1.0($2)
          *&(N),0.0($3)
          LVI,$10,N2F1R
          B,EMLF1R
N2F1R     LMR(U),1.0($12)                'N MOD 4 = —1 OR I
```

```
              *N &(N),0.0($13)
              LMR(U),0.0($2)
              * &(N),0.0($3)
              LVI,$10,N3F1R
              B,EMLF1R
N3F1R         LMR(U),0.0($12)              'N MOD 4 = —I OR —1.0
              *N&(N),0.0($13)
              LMR(U),1.0($2)
              *N &(N),0.0($3)
              LVI,$10,N4F1R
              B,EMLF1R
N4F1R         LMR(U),0.0($12)              'N MOD 4 = 1 OR —I
              * &(N),0.0($13)
              LMR(U),0.0($2)
              *N &(N),0.0($3)
              LVI,$10,N1F1R
EMLF1R        V &I,$12,MTXSZE
              V &I,$2,MTXSZE
              V &I,$13,1.0
              V &I,$3,1.0
              CBR,$13,SMLF1R
RFGGF         SRD(N),0.0($14)              'STORE REAL PART OF F1 OR G1, G2 OR F2
              V &1,$14,1.0
'             DO THE IMAGINARY PART OF F1 OR G1, G2 OR F2.
              LV,$3,$13
              V &,$3,NRANK &0.32
              LV,$12,TMXW
              LV,$2,$12
              V &,$2,G1F2A &0.32
              LVI,$10,N1F1I
              DL(U),ZERO
SMLF1I        B,0.0($10)                   'N MOD 4 = I OR 1.0
N1F1I         LMR(U),1.0($12)
              * &(N),0.0($13)
              LMR(U),0.0($2)
              *N &(N),0.0($3)
              LVI,$10,N2F1I
              B,EMLF 1 I
N2F1I         LMR(U),0.0($12)              'N MOD 4 = —1.0 OR I
              * &(N),0.0($13)
              LMR(U),1.0($2)
              * &(N),0.0($3)
              LVI,$10,N3F1I
              B,EMLF1I
N3F1I         LMR(U),1.0($12)              'N MOD 4 = —I OR —1.0
              *N &(N),0.0($13)
              LMR(U),0.0($2)
              * &(N),0.0($3)
              LVI,$10,N4F1I
              B,EMLF1I
N4F1I         LMR(U),0.0($12)              'N MOD 4 = 1.0 OR —I
              *N &(N),0.0($13)
              LMR(U),1.0($2)
              *N &(N),0.0($3)
              LVI,$10,N1F1I
EMLF1I        V &I,$12,MTXSZE
              V &I,$2,MTXSZE
              V &I,$13,1.0
              V &I,$3,1.0
```

```
            CBR,$13,SMLF1I
  IFGGF     SRD(N),0.0($14)              'STORE IMAGINARY PART OF F1,G1,G2,F2.
            LV,$3,$13                    'SET UP FOR NEXT ITEM.
            V &,$3,NRANK&0.32
            LV,$12,TMXW                  'PREPARE FOR NEXT ROW OF T MATRIX.
            V &I,$12,2.0
            SV,$12,TMXW
            LV,$2,$12
            V &,$2,G1F2A&0.32
            CBR&,$14,SRLF1R
            V &I,$14,MTXSZE              'RESET XR14 FOR G2,F2 VECTOR
            LV,$12,TMXWR                 'RESET TO FIRST ROW IN T MATRIX.
            V &,$12,ISYBG&0.32
            SV,$12,TMXW
            V &I,$13,VCTSZE              'RESET MULTIPLIER VECTOR
            SV,$13,PMXW
            F1(BU,1,8),RFGGF&0.20        'SET SIGN FOR ANSWER STORAGE, F2 OR G2
            F1(BU,1,8),IFGGF&0.20
            CB,$12,BGANLP
            LX,$2,XR2
            LX,$3,XR3
            LX,$10,XR10
            LX,$12,XR12
            LX,$13,XR13
            LX,$14,XR14
            B,0.0($15)
  '         STORAGE REQUIREMENTS FOR THE VECTOR MULTIPLICATION ROUTINE
  XR12      XW,0,0,0                     'SAVE SPACE FOR INDEX REGISTER.
  XR13      XW,0,0,0
  XR14      XW,0,0,0
  XR2
  XR3       XW,0,0,0
  XR10      XW,0,0,0
  TMXW      XW,TCMPLX,0,TMXW             'INDEX CONTROL FOR T COMPLEX MATRIX.
  PMXW      XW,FGMUL,0,PMXW              'INDEX CONTROL FOR POLYNOMIAL VECTOR.
  FGXW      XW,FGVECT,0,FGXW             'INDEX CONTROL FOR VECTOR ANSWERS.
  TMXWR     XW,TCMPLX,0,TMXW
  PMXWR     XW,FGMUL,0,PMXW
  FXGWR     XW,FGVECT,0,FGXW
  G1F2A     DRZ(U),1                     'STORAGE FOR INDEX INCREMENTER G1,F2.
  TWFRTY    (F10)DD(U),240.0X38          'INTEGER = 240
  ZERO      DD(N).0
  MTXSZE    SYN,240.0
  VCTSZE    SYN,120.0
  LAST      SYN,$
            SLCRCOM
  COMMON    SYN,$
            SLCRCOM,MTXCOM
  NRANK     DR(U),1
  NRANKI    DR(U),1
  FGVECT    DR(N),480
  QMIIRM    DR(N),3120
  FGMUL     DR(N),240
  QMJIRM    DR(N),3360
  FGANS     DR(N),600
  QMKIRM    DR(N),3000
  QMLITL    DR(N),3600
  TCMPLX    DR(N),28800
  CMXNRM    DR(N),60
```

```
FINAL      SYN,$
           SLCROM,VCMCOM
ISYBG      DR(U),1
JSYBG      DR(U),1
KSYBG      DR(U),1
NSYMT      DR(U),1
FINALV     SYN,$
           END
```

```
T          SUBTYPE,FORTRAN,LMAP,LSTRAP
C          A ROUTINE TO PRINT OUT A MATRIX ARRAY
           SUBROUTINE PRINTM(P,N)
           DIMENSION P(60,60)
           NR = N
           DO 100 I = 1,NR
           IB = 1
   20      IE = IB&7
           IF(IE—NR)28,28,24
   24      IE = NR
   28      IF(IB—1)36,36,60
   36      PRINT 44,I,(P(I,J),J = IB,IE)
   44      FORMAT(5H0 ROWI3,2X,1P8E15.6)
           GO TO 80
   60      PRINT 68,(P(I,J),J = IB,IE)
   68      FORMAT(1H 9X,1P8E15.6)
   80      IB = IE&1
           IF(IB—NR)20,20,100
  100      CONTINUE
           RETURN
           END
           END
```

```
T         SUBTYPE,FORTRAN,LMAP,LSTRAP
C     A ROUTINE FOR BESSEL FUNCTIONS, DERIVATIVES AND NEUMANN
      1FUNCTIONS.
       SUBROUTINE GENBSL
       COMMON DTR,RTD,CPI
       COMMON /CMVCOM/ NM,CMI(30),CMV,KMV,CM2,EM,QEM,TWM,PRODM
       COMMON /FNCCOM/ PNMLLG(61),BSSLSP(61),CNEUMN(61)
       COMMON /MTXCOM/ NRANK,NRANKI,CMTXRL(120,120),CMTXIM(120,120),SPRMT
      1X(120,120),CMXNRM(60)
       COMMON /THTCOM/ THETA,NTHETA,DLTHTA,SINTH,COSTH,ISMRL,ISWTCH
      1(7),SRMUL,SMULSS(7),CDH(6),DHM,NSECT,NDPS(6),EPPS(6),KSECT
       COMMON /BDYCOM/ CKR,DCKR,CKR2,CSKRX,SNKRX,CONK,BRXT,ALPHA,IBOD
      1Y,QB,SNALPH,CSALPH
       DOUBLE PRECISION PCKR,ANSWR,ANSA,ANSB,ANSC,CONN
C      SET UP A LOOP TO GET 2 SUCCESSIVE BESSEL FUNCTIONS.
       NVAL = NRANK—1
       PCKR = CKR
       DO 40 I = 1,4
       CALL BESSEL(NVAL,PCKR,ANSWR,IERROR)
       IF(IERROR)20,20,32
   20  ANSA=ANSWR
       NVAL = NVAL&1
       CALL BESSEL(NVAL,PCKR,ANSWR,IERROR)
       IF(IERROR)24,24,28
   24  ANSB = ANSWR
       GO TO 60
   28  NVAL = NVAL—1
   32  NVAL = NVAL&NRANK
   40  CONTINUE
C      PROGRAM UNABLE TO GENERATE BESSEL FUNCTION.
       CALL DUMP
C      SET UP FOR PROPER RECURSION OF THE BESSEL FUNCTIONS.
   60  IF(NVAL—NRANK)100,100,64
   64  IEND = NVAL—NRANK
       CONN = 2*(NVAL—1)&1
       DO 72 IP = 1,IEND
       ANSC = CONN*ANSA/PCKR—ANSB
       CONN = CONN—2.0D0
       ANSB = ANSA
       ANSA = ANSC
   72  CONTINUE
C      PROGRAM IS READY TO RECURSE DONWWARD INTO BESSEL FUNCTON
      1VECTOR.
  100  BSSLSP(NRANKI) = ANSB
       BSSLSP(NRANKI—1) = ANSA
       CONN = NRANK&NRANK—1
       IE = NRANKI—2
       JE = IE
       DO 120 JB = 1,JE
       ANSC = CONN*ANSA/PCKR—ANSB
       BSSLSP(IE) = ANSC
       ANSB = ANSA
       ANSA = ANSC
       IE = IE—1
       CONN = CONN—2.0D0
  120  CONTINUE
C      GENERATE THE NEUMANN FUNCTIONS.
       CMULN = 3.0
       SNSA = —CSKRX
```

```
      SNSB = −CSKRX/CKR−SNKRX
      CNEUMN(1) = SNSA
      CNEUMN(2) = SNSB
      DO 280 I = 3,NRANKI
      SNSC = CMULN*SNSB/CKR−SNSA
      CNEUMN(I) = SNSC
      SNSA = SNSB
      SNSB = SNSC
      CMULN = CMULN&2.0
  280 CONTINUE
      RETURN
      END
```

```
T            SUBTYPE,STRAP
             A ROUTINE TO DUMP CORE.
             PUNREL
             PUNFPC,LAST,COMMON
   DUMP      ENTER,START
             XW,0,0,0
   START     B,$MCP
             ,$ABEOJ
             B,0.0($15)                    'RETURN
   LAST      SYN,$
             SLCROM,
   COMMON    SYN,$
             END
```

```
T          SUBTYPE,FORTRAN,LMAP,LSTRAP
C          A ROUTINE TO ORTHOGONILAZE THE Q MATRICES TO PRODUCE T MATRICES.
           SUBROUTINE PRCSSM
           COMMON /MTXCOM/ NR,NRI,QI1(60,60),QI2(60,60),QI3(60,60),QI4(60,60),P1(60,60),P2
          1(60,60),P3(60,60),P4(60,60),QR1(60,60),QR2(60,60),QR3(60,60),QR4(60,60),CMXNRM(60)
           EQUIVALENCE (QI1,RI1),(QR1,RR1),(TMMX,P1)
           DIMENSION RR1(120,120),RI1(120,120),TMMX(120,120)
C          NORMALIZE AND TRANSPOSE THE I,J,K,L MATRICES TO OBTAIN Q MATRICES.
           CALL NRMQMX
C          SET UP REAL AND IMAGINARY MATRICES FOR GENERAL M CASE.
           DO 6 I=1,NR
           MM=I&I
           DO 4 J=1,NR
           NN=J&J
           TMMX(MM−1,NN−1) = QI1(I,J)
           TMMX(MM−1,NN)    = QI2(I,J)
           TMMX(MM,NN−1)    = QI3(I,J)
           TMMX(MM,NN)      = QI4(I,J)
     4     CONTINUE
     6     CONTINUE
           NBGR = NR&NR
           DO 10 I = 1,NBGR
           DO 8 J = 1,NBGR
           RI1(I,J) = TMMX(I,J)
     8     CONTINUE
    10     CONTINUE
           DO 14 I = 1,NR
           MM = I&I
           DO 12 J = 1,NR
           NN = J&J
           TMM(MM−1,NN−1)   = QR1(I,J)
           TMMX(MM−1,NN)    = QR2(I,J)
           TMMX(MM,NN−1)    = QR3(I,J)
           TMMX(MM,NN)      = QR4(I,J)
    12     CONTINUE
    14     CONTINUE
           DO 18 I = 1,NBGR
           DO 16 J = 1,NBGR
           RR1(I,J) = TMMX(I,J)
    16     CONTINUE
    18     CONTINUE
C          CONDITION Q MATRICES BEFORE ORTHOGONALIZING THEM.
           CALL CNDTNQ
C          NORMALIZE THE NTH ROW OF AN N BY N MATRIX
           SUM1 = 0.0
           DO 20 K = 1,NBGR
           SUM1 = RR1(NBGR,K)**2&RI1(NBGR,K)**2&SUM1
    20     CONTINUE
           SUM1 = SQRT(SUM1)
           DO 28 K = 1,NBGR
           RR1(NBGR,K) = RR1(NBGR,K)/SUM1
           RI1(NBGR,K) = RI1(NBGR,K)/SUM1
    28     CONTINUE
C          SET UP A LOOP FOR THE N−1 REMAINING ROWS.
           NMI = NBGR−1
           NROW = NBGR
           DO 100 I = 1,NMI
           NROW = NROW−1
           MROW = NROW
```

```
        DO 36 K = 1,NBGR
        TMMX(1,K) = RR1(NROW,K)
        TMMX(2,K) = RI1(NROW,K)
   36   CONTINUE
        DO 80 J = NROW,NMI
        SR1 = 0.0
        SI1 = 0.0
        MROW = MROW &1
        DO 40 K = 1,NBGR
        SR1 = SR1 &RR1(MROW,K)*RR1(NROW,K) &RI1(MROW,K)*RI1(NROW,K)
        SI1 = SI1 &RR1(MROW,K)*RI1(NROW,K)—RI1(MROW,K)*RR1(NROW,K)
   40   CONTINUE
        DO 48 K = 1,NBGR
        TMMX(1,K) = TMMX(1,K)—SR1*RR1(MROW,K) &SI1*RI1(MROW,K)
        TMMX(2,K) = TMMX(2,K)—SR1*RI1(MROW,K)—SI1*RR1(MROW,K)
   48   CONTINUE
   80   CONTINUE
        SUM1 = 0.0
        DO 84 K = 1,NBGR
        SUM1 = SUM1 &TMMX(1,K)**2&TMMX(2,K)**2
   84   CONTINUE
        SUM1 = SQRT(SUM1)
        DO 88 K = 1,NBGR
        RR1(NROW,K) = TMMX(1,K)/SUM1
        RI1(NROW,K) = TMMX(2,K)/SUM1
   88   CONTINUE
  100   CONTINUE
C       PRINT OUT ORTHOGONALIZED Q MATRICES
        PRINT 120
  120   FORMAT (1H140X,40HREAL SECTION OF ORTHOGONALIZED Q MATRIX.)
        CALL PRNQOT(RR1,NBGR)
        PRINT 128
  128   FORMAT(1H137X,45HIMAGINARY SECTION OF ORTHOGONALIZED Q MATRIX.)
        CALL PRNQOT(RI1,NBGR)
C       PERFORM Q TRANSPOSE * REAL(Q) TO GET T MATRIX.
        DO 160 I = 1,NBGR
        DO 152 J = 1,NBGR
        TMMX(I,J) — 0.0
  152   CONTINUE
  160   CONTINUE
        DO 180 I = 1,NBGR
        DO 176 J = 1,NBGR
        DO 172 K = 1,NBGR
        TMMX(I,J) = TMMX(I,J)—RI1(K,I)*RR1(K,J)
  172   CONTINUE
  176   CONTINUE
  180   CONTINUE
        DO 196 I = 1,NR
        MM =I &I
        DO 192 J = 1,NR
        NN = J &J
        QI1(I,J) = TMMX(MM—1,NN—1)
        QI2(I,J) = TMMX(MM—1,NN)
        QI3(I,J) = TMMX(MM,NN—1)
        QI4(I,J) = TMMX(MM,NN)
  192   CONTINUE
  196   CONTINUE
        DO 208 I = 1,NBGR
        DO 204 J = 1,NBGR
```

```
        TMMX(I,J) = 0.0
204  CONTINUE
208  CONTINUE
        DO 220 I = 1,NBGR
        DO 216 J = 1,NBGR
        DO 212 K = 1,NBGR
        TMMX(I,J) = TMMX(I,J) &RR1(K,I)*RR1(K,J)
212  CONTINUE
216  CONTINUE
220  CONTINUE
        DO 236 I = 1,NR
        MM = I &I
        DO 232 J = 1,NR
        NN = J &J
        QR1(I,J) = TMMX(MM—1,NN—1)
        QR2(I,J) = TMMX(MM—1,NN)
        QR3(I,J) = TMMX(MM,NN—1)
        QR4(I,J) = TMMX(MM,NN)
232  CONTINUE
236  CONTINUE
C       PRINT THE T MATRIX
        CALL PRTRIT
C       DO FINAL PROCESSING
        CALL ADDPRC
        RETURN
        END
```

```
T          SUBTYPE,FORTRAN,LMAP,LSTRAP
C          A ROUTINE TO CONDITION Q MATRICES BEFORE ORTHOGONALIZING THEM.
           SUBROUTINE CNDTNQ
           COMMON /MTXCOM/ NR,NRI,QI1(60,60),QI2(60,60),QI3(60,60),QI4(60,60),P1(60,60),P2
          1(60,60),P3(60,60),P4(60,60),QR1(60,60),QR2(60,60),QR3(60,60),QR4(60,60),CMXNRM(60)
           EQUIVALENCE (QI1,RI1),(QR1,RR1),(TMMX,P1)
           DIMENSION RR1(120,120),RI1(120,120),TMMX(120,120)
C          SET UP LOOPS FOR ALL BUT THE FIRST ROW.
           NBGR = NR&NR
           NROW = NBGR
           DO 60 KR = 2,NBGR
C          RESCALE THE CURRENT ROW.
           SCLE1 = 1.0/RI1(NROW,NROW)
           DO 8 LC = 1,NBGR
           RR1(NROW,LC) = SCLE1*RR1(NROW,LC)
           RI1(NROW,LC) = SCLE1*RI1(NROW,LC)
     8     CONTINUE
C          RESCALE ALL THE ROWS UP TO THE CURRENT ROW.
           MROW = NROW—1
           DO 20 MR = 1,MROW
           RSCL1 = RI1(MR,NROW)
           DO 16 MC = 1,NBGR
           RR1(MR,MC) = RR1(MR,MC)—RSCL1*RR1(NROW,MC)
           RI1(MR,MC) = RI1(MR,MC)—RSCL1*RI1(NROW,MC)
    16     CONTINUE
    20     CONTINUE
           NROW = NROW—1
    60     CONTINUE
C          SET IMAGINARY ELEMENTS ABOVE THE MAIN DIAGONAL = 0.
           NROW = NBGR—1
           DO 80 I = 1,NROW
           IB = I&I
           DO 72 J = IB,NBGR
           RI1(I,J) = 0.0
    72     CONTINUE
    80     CONTINUE
           RETURN
           END
```

```
T          SUBTYPE,FORTRAN,LMAP,LSTRAP
C          A ROUTINE TO NORMALIZE THE I,J,K AND L MATRICES TO GET A Q MATRIX.
           SUBROUTINE NRMQMX
           COMMON /MTXCOM/ NRANK,NRANKI,AMXIR(60,60),AMXJR(60,60),AMXKR(60,60),
          1AMXLR(60,60), AMXII(60,60), AMXJI(60,60), AMXKI(60,60), AMXLI(60,60), QMTXIR(60,
           260),QMTXJR(60,60),QMTXKR(60,60),QMTXLR(60,60),CMXNRM(603)
           EQUIVALENCE (AMXIR,QMTXII),(AMXJR,QMTXJI),(AMXKR,QMTXKI),(AMXLR,
          1QMTXLI)
           DIMENSION QMTXII(60,60),QMTXJI(60,60),QMTXKI(60,60),QMTXLI(60,60)
C          SET UP LOOPS TO PROCESS ALL ROWS AND COLUMNS FOR THE REAL
           1MATRICES
           DO 200 IR = 1,NRANK
           DO 100 IC = 1,NRANK
           QUANNM = CMXNRM(IR)*CXMNRM(IC)
           QMTXIR(IR,IC) = AXMJR(IC,IR)/QUANNM
           QMTXJR(IR,IC) = −AMXLR(IC,IR)/QUANNM
           QMTXKR(IR,IC) = AMXIR(IC,IR)/QUANNM
           QMTXLR(IR,IC) = AMXKR(IC,IR)/QUANNM
  100      CONTINUE
  200      CONTINUE
C          SET UP LOOPS OF ROWS AND COLUMNS FOR THE IMAGINARY MATRICES.
           DO 400 IR = 1,NRANK
           DO 300 IC = 1,NRANK
           QUANNM = CMXNRM(IR)*CMXNRM(IC)
           QMTXII(IR,IC) = AMXJI(IC,IR)/QUANNM
           QMTXJI(IR,IC) = −AMXLI(IC,IR)/QUANNM
           QMTXKI(IR,IC) = AMXII(IC,IR)/QUANNM
           QMTXLI(IR,IC) = AMXKI(IC,IR)/QUANNM
  300      CONTINUE
  400      CONTINUE
C          PRINT OUT NORMALIZED AND TRANSPOSED Q MATRICES
           PRINT 420
  420      FORMAT(1H140X,38HREAL PART OF Q1(NORMALIZED,TRANSPOSED))
           CALL PRINTM(QMTXIR,NRANK)
           PRINT 428
  428      FORMAT(1H140X,38HREAL PART OF Q2(NORMALIZED,TRANSPOSED))
           CALL PRINTM(QMTXJR,NRANK)
           PRINT 436
  436      FORMAT(1H140X,38HREAL PART OF Q3(NORMALIZED,TRANSPOSED))
           CALL PRINTM(QMTXKR,NRANK)
           PRINT 444
  444      FORMAT(1H140 X38HREAL PART OF Q4(NORMALIZED,TRANSPOSED))
           CALL PRINTM(QMTXLR,NRANK)
           PRINT 452
  452      FORMAT(1H138X,43HIMAGINARY PART OF Q1(NORMALIZED,TRANSPOSED))
           CALL PRINTM(QMTXII,NRANK)
           PRINT 460
  460      FORMAT(1H138X,43HIMAGINARY PART OF Q2(NORMALIZED,TRANSPOSED))
           CALL PRINTM(QMTXJI,NRANK)
           PRINT 468
  468      FORMAT(1H138X,43HIMAGINARY PART OF Q3(NORMALIZED,TRANSPOSED))
           CALL PRINTM(QMTXKI,NRANK)
           PRINT 476
  476      FORMAT(1H138X,43HIMAGINARY PART OF Q4(NORMALIZED,TRANSPOSED))
           CALL PRINTM(QMTXLI,NRANK)
           RETURN
           END
```

```
T         SUBTYPE,FORTRAN,LMAP,LSTRAP
C         A ROUTINE TO PRINT OUT A MATRIX ARRAY
          SUBROUTINE PRNQOT(P,N)
          DIMENSION P(120,120)
          NR = N
          DO 100 I = 1,NR
          IB = 1
    20    IE = IB&7
          IF(IE—NR)28,28,24
    24    IE = NR
    28    IF(IB—1)36,36,60
    36    PRINT 44,I,(P(I,J),J = IB,IE)
    44    FORMAT(5H0 ROWI3,2X,1P8E15.6)
          GO TO 80
    60    PRINT 68,(P(I,J),J = IB,IE)
    68    FORMAT(1H 9X,1P8E15.6)
    80    IB = IE&1
          IF(IB—NR)20,20,100
   100    CONTINUE
          RETURN
          END
```

```
T         SUBTYPE,FORTRAN,LMAP,LSTRAP
C         THIS ROUTINE CALCULATES END POINTS AND SPACING FOR INTEGRATION.
          SUBROUTINE CALENP
          COMMON DTR,RTD,CPI
          COMMON /CMVCOM/ NM,CMI(30),CMV,KMV,CM2,EM,QEM,TWM,PRODM
          COMMON /FNCCOM/ PNMLLG(61),BSSLSP(61),CNEUMN(61)
          COMMON /MTXCOM/ NRANK,NRANKI,CMTXRL(120,120),CMTXIM(120,120),SPRMT
         1X(120,120),CMXNRM(60)
          COMMON /THTCOM/ THETA,NTHETA,DLTHTA,SINTH,COSTH,ISMRL,ISWTCH
         1(7),SRMUL,SMULSS(7),CDH(6),DHM,NSECT,NDPS(6),EPPS(6),KSECT
          COMMON/BDYCOM/CKR,DCKR,CKR2,CSKRX,SNKRX,CONK,BRXT,ALPHA,IBOD
         1Y,QB,SNALPH,CSALPH
          SNALPH = SIN(ALPHA)
          CSALPH = COS(ALPHA)
          QB = (1.0−BRXT)*(1.0−SNALPH)/2.0
C         CALCULATE THE FIRST END POINT AND STEP SIZE
          TANGAM = SNALPH*(CSALPH/(QB−SNALPH*SNALPH)
          GAMMA = ATAN(TANGAM)
          IF(GAMMA)20,32,32
   20     GAMMA = GAMMA&CPI
   32     EPPS(1) = GAMMA
          CDVD = NDPS(1)
          CDH(1) = EPPS(1)/CDVD
C         CALCULATE THE SECOND END POINT AND STEP SIZE.
          TANPSI = −BRXT*SNALPH*CSALPH/(1.0−QB−BRXT*CSALPH*CSALPH)
          PSI = ATAN(TANPSI)
          IF(PSI)60,72,72
   60     PSI = PSI&CPI
   72     EPPS(2) = PSI
          CDVD = NDPS(2)
          CDH(2) = (EPPS(2)−EPPS(1))/CDVD
C         COMPUTE THIRD END POINT AND STEP SIZE.
          EPPS(3) = CPI
          CDVD = NDPS(3)
          CDH(3) = (EPPS(3)−EPPS(2))/CDVD
          RETURN
          END
```

```
T          SUBTYPE,FORTRAN,LMAP,LSTRAP
C          THIS ROUTINE COMPUTES KR AND ITS DERIVATIVE AS A FUNCTION OF
           1THETA
           SUBROUTINE GENKR
           COMMON DTR,RTD,CPI
           COMMON /CMVCOM/ NM,CMI(30),CMV,KMV,CM2,EM,QEM,TWM,PRODM
           COMMON /FNCCOM/ PNMLLG(61),BSSLSP(61),CNEUMN(61)
           COMMON /MTXCOM/ NRANK,NRANKI,CMTXRL(120,120),CMTIMX(120,120),SPRMT
           1X(120,120),CMXNRM(60)
           COMMON /THTCOM/ THETA,NTHETA,DLTHTA,SINTH,COSTH,ISMRL,ISWTCH
           1(7),SRMUL,SMULSS(7),CDH(6),DHM,NSECT,NDPS(6),EPPS(6),KSECT
           COMMON /BDYCOM/ CKR,DCKR,CKR2,CSKRX,SNKRX,CONK,BRXT,ALPHA,IBOD
           1Y,QB,SNALPH,CSALPH
           KSECT = KSECT
C          DETERMINE SECTION FOR INTEGRATION
           IF(KSECT—2)40,140,240
C          SECTION 1
      40   QUAN1 = SQRT(1.0—(QB*SINTH/SNALPH)**2)
           CKR = CONK*(QB*COSTH/SNALPH&QUAN1)
           DCKR = —CONK*(QB*SINTH/SNALPH)*(1.0&QB*COSTH/(SNALPH*QUAN1))
           GO TO 300
C          SECTION 2
     140   QUAN2 = THETA—ALPHA
           SNQN2 = SIN(QUAN2)
           CKR = CONK*(1.0—QB)/SNQN2
           DCKR = —CONK*(1.0—QB)*COS(QUAN2)/(SNQN2*SNQN2)
           GO TO 300
C          SECTION 3
     240   QUAN3 = (1.0—BRXT—QB)/SNALPH
           QUNSQ = SQRT(BRXT BRXT—(QUAN3 SINTH)**2)
           CKR = CONK*(QUNSQ—QUAN3*COSTH)
           DCKR = CONK*(QUAN3*SINTH—QUAN3*QUAN3*SINTH*COSTH/QUNSQ)
     300   RETURN
           END
```

```
T          SUBTYPE,FORTRAN,LMAP,LSTRAP
C          A ROUTINE TO COMPUTE THE F1, G1 AND F2, G2 VECTORS.
           SUBROUTINE VECMUL
           COMMON /MTXCOM/ NRANK,NRANKI,QMTXII(60,60),QMTXJI(60,60),QMTXKI(60,60
          1),QMTXLI(60,60),PMX1(60,60),PMX2(60,60),PMX3(60,60),PMX4(60,60),QMTXIR(60,60),Q
          2MTXJR(60,60),QMTXKR(60,60),QMTXLR(60,60),CMXNRM(603)
           COMMON /VCMCOM/ ISYBG,JSYBG,KSYBG,NSYMT
           DIMENSION FGVECT(2,120,2),TCMPLX(2,120,120),FGMUL(120,2),FGANS(60,10)
           EQUIVALENCE (QMTXII,FGVECT),(PMX1,TCMPLX),(QMTXJI,FGMUL),(QMTXKI,F
          1GANS)
           N = NRANK+NRANK
C          THIS LOOP CONTROLS ROW ELEMENTS.
           DO 200 I = 1,N
           SRA = 0.0
           SIA = 0.0
           SRB = 0.0
           SIB = 0.0
           IP = 1
C          THIS LOOP CONTROLS COLUMN ELEMENT MULTIPLICATION.
           DO 100 J = 1,NRANK
           JP = NRANK+J
           GO TO (20,40,60,80), IP
C          N = 1
     20    SRA = SRA+TCMPLX(1,I,J)*FGMUL(J,1)+TCMP(2,I,JP)*FGMUL(JP,1)
           SIA = SIA+TCMPLX(2,I,J)*FGMUL(J,1)−TCMPL(1,I,JP)*FGMUL(JP,1)
           SRB = SRB+TCMPLX(2,I,J)*FGMUL(J,2)−TCMPLX(1,I,JP)*FGMUL(JP,2)
           SIB = SIB−TCMPLX(1,I,J)*FGMUL(J,2)−TCMPLX(2,I,JP)*FGMUL(JP,2)
           IP = 2
           GO TO 100
C          N = 2
     40    SRA = SRA−TCMPLX(2,I,J)*FGMUL(J,1)+TCMPLX(1,I,JP)*FGMUL(JP,1)
           SIA = SIA+TCMPLX(1,I,J)*FGMUL(J,1)+TCMPLX(2,I,JP)*FGMUL(JP,1)
           SRB = SRB+TCMPLX(1,I,J)*FGMUL(J,2)+TCMPLX(1,I,JP)*FGMUL(JP,2)
           SIB = SIB+TCMPLX(2,I,J)*FGMUL(J,2)−TCMPLX(1,I,JP)*FGMUL(JP,2)
           IP = 3
           GO TO 100
C          N = 3
     60    SRA = SRA−TCMPLX(1,I,J)*FGMUL(J,1)−TCMPLX(2,I,JP)*FGMUL(JP,1)
           SIA = SIA−TCMPXL(2,I,J)*FGMUL(J,1)+TCMPLX(1,I,JP)*FGMUL(JP,1)
           SRB = SRB−TCMPLX(2,I,J)*FGMUL(J,2)+TCMPLX(1,I,JP)*FGMUL(JP,2)
           SIB = SIB+TCMPLX(1,I,J)*FGMUL(J,2)+TCMPLX(2,I,JP)*FGMUL(JP,2)
           IP = 4
           GO TO 100
C          N = 4
     80    SRA = SRA+TCMPLX(2,I,J)*FGMUL(J,1)−TCMPLX(1,I,JP)*FGMUL(JP,1)
           SIA = SIA−TCMPLX(1,I,J)*FGMUL(J,1)−TCMPLX(2,I,JP)*FGMUL(JP,1)
           SRB = SRB−TCMPLX(1,I,J)*FGMUL(J,2)−TCMPLX(2,I,JP)*FGMUL(JP,2)
           SIB = SIB−TCMPLX(2,I,J)*FGMUL(J,2)+TCMPLX(1,I,JP)*FGMUL(JP,2)
           IP = 1
    100    CONTINUE
           FGVECT(1,I,1) = SRA
           FGVECT(2,I,1) = SIA
           FGVECT(1,I,2) = SRB
           FGVECT(2,I,2) = SIB
    200    CONTINUE
           RETURN
           END
```

REFERENCES

ABRAMOWITZ, M. and STEGUN, I. A. (1964) *Handbook of Mathematical Functions*, U.S. Government Printing Office, Washington, D.C., p. 886.

HÖNL, H., MAUE, A. W. and WESTPFAHL, K. (1961) *Handbuch der Physik*, vol. 25/1, Berlin, Springer-Verlag, pp. 311 and 354–62.

MENTZER, J. R. (1955) *Scattering and Diffraction of Radio Waves*, Pergamon Press, London, pp. 108 and 131.

MORSE, P. M. and FESHBACH, H. (1953) *Methods of Theoretical Physics*, McGraw-Hill, New York, pp. 1865–1966.

SAXON, D. S. (1955), Tensor scattering matrix for the electromagnetic field, *Phys. Rev. 100*, 1771–5.

STEIN, S. (1961) Addition theorems for spherical wave functions, *Quart. Appl. Math. 19*, 15–24; CRUZAN, O. R., Translational addition theorems for spherical vector wave functions, *Quart. Appl. Math. 20*, 33–40.

WATERMAN, P. C. (1965) Matrix formulation of electromagnetic scattering, *Proc. IEEE 53*, 805–12.

WATSON, G. N. (1962) *Theory of Bessel Functions*, 2nd ed., Cambridge at the University Press, Great Britain, pp. 145 ff.

CHAPTER 4

Integral Equation Solutions
of Three-dimensional Scattering Problems

A. J. POGGIO

Cornell Aeronautical Laboratory, Buffalo, New York

AND

E. K. MILLER

Lawrence Livermore Laboratory, Livermore, Calif.

4.1. INTRODUCTION

The general topic to be considered in this chapter is the solution of a boundary value problem in a three-dimensional domain. The general procedure will be to reduce a three-dimensional problem to two dimensions by casting the solution in terms of unknown surface functions rather than unknown volume functions. Hence, rather than solve the simple appearing wave equation with extremely complicated boundary conditions we choose to formulate the solution in terms of unknown functions over two-dimensional surfaces. This point of view will allow considerable increases in generality over the direct solution of the wave equation although this formulation will lead to integral equations which are, at least in principle, more difficult to solve. The simplifications which arise, namely, the reduction of the number of independent variables from three to two and the avoidance of special coordinate systems, as well as the relaxation of the constraints on the unknown function (it need merely satisfy the integral equation), far overshadow the increased complexity for most problems. No longer will we have to search through all possible solutions of differential equations to determine specific solutions to a given problem. We can now proceed directly to a unique solution for a particular problem (except, of course, in the relatively few cases where the integral equation formulation might not yield unique solutions or where solutions might not exist).

In the text, we will not draw the distinction between integral and integro-differential equations when the differential operation is under the integral sign. We shall refer to integro-differential equations as those integral equations which contain an explicit differential opera-

159

tion on the integral. In a numerical solution sense we are merely distinguishing whether the numerical differentiation procedure is applied to the unknown surface function or to the complete integral.

This chapter is divided in a form which the authors feel is convenient for study of the subject matter. Concisely, we shall proceed from the derivation of integral equations from general integral representations to numerical solution techniques and finally to applications and sample results. Since the chapter is divided in this form, each section can be studied independently.

A list of references is included at the end of this chapter. Many of the works are referred to in the text while others are included as supplementary material. For instance, the reader interested in the history, the development, and the techniques of scattering theory could advantageously study the collection of outstanding papers in the IEEE Special Issue on *Radar Reflectivity* (1965), a work fairly representative of the state of the art in 1965. The serious student would do well to peruse each of the works in order to expand his understanding of the subject matter.

4.2. THE INTEGRAL EQUATIONS OF ELECTROMAGNETIC THEORY

The integral equations used in electromagnetic scattering theory can be written in a general form so that they can be used for either antenna or scattering problems. In this section we will derive the general forms of the magnetic and electric field integral equations in the space–frequency domain and will specialize these to specific problems. Two- and three-dimensional forms will be considered. Also, the space–time domain integral equations will be simply derived from their space–frequency domain counterparts. Finally, a tabulation of the integral equations for both domains will be provided.

4.2.1. The Derivation of Space–Frequency Domain Integral Equations

Two widely used space–frequency domain integral equations, i.e. the electric field (EFIE) and magnetic field (MFIE) integral equations, can be derived using Maxwell's equations as a starting point. A portion of the derivation to be presented is similar to that described in Stratton (1940). However, a technique suggested by N. Bojarski (1969) and Chertock and Grosso (1966) will be used to complete the derivation. This latter technique allows integral equations to be written on surfaces whose tangents may not be differentiable functions of position at all points on the surface. For smooth surfaces the equations reduce to a form similar to those of Maue (1949).

Specialization of these integral equations to cases where a surface may conform with a perfect electric conductor, a dielectric, a body with an impedance boundary condition, or a thin cylindrical conducting wire will be described. Equations which are useful in the evaluation of various field observables will also be derived.

A VECTOR GREEN'S IDENTITY IN TERMS OF ELECTROMAGNETIC FIELDS AND SOURCES

Maxwell's equations in the space–frequency domain are given by (with suppressed time variation $e^{j\omega t}$)

$$\nabla \times \mathbf{E} = -j\omega\mu\mathbf{H} - \mathbf{K} \quad \nabla \cdot \mathbf{E} = \varrho/\varepsilon,$$
$$\nabla \times \mathbf{H} = j\omega\varepsilon\mathbf{E} + \mathbf{J} \quad \nabla \cdot \mathbf{H} = m/\mu,$$

(4.1a)

with the relationships defining the conservation of charge written as

$$\nabla \cdot \mathbf{J} = -j\omega\varrho \quad \nabla \cdot \mathbf{K} = -j\omega m.$$

(4.1b)

$\mathbf{E}$ and $\mathbf{H}$ are the electric and magnetic field vectors, $\mathbf{J}$ and $\mathbf{K}$ the electric and magnetic current densities, and ϱ and m the electric and magnetic charge densities. For a linear, homogeneous, isotropic medium both ε and μ are scalar quantities so that the vector wave equations for $\mathbf{E}$ and $\mathbf{H}$ can be written as

$$\nabla \times \nabla \times \mathbf{E} - k^2\mathbf{E} = -j\omega\mu\mathbf{J} - \nabla \times \mathbf{K},$$
$$\nabla \times \nabla \times \mathbf{H} - k^2\mathbf{H} = -j\omega\varepsilon\mathbf{K} + \nabla \times \mathbf{J}.$$

(4.2)

Let us assume that we desire to solve these equations in a space which contains sources as well as regions where the constitutive parameters differ from those of the medium in the surrounding space. In this endeavor it is convenient to make use of the vector Green's theorem, i.e.

$$\int_V (\mathbf{Q} \cdot \nabla \times \nabla \times \mathbf{P} - \mathbf{P} \cdot \nabla \times \nabla \times \mathbf{Q})\, dv = \int_\Sigma (\mathbf{P} \times \nabla \times \mathbf{Q} - \mathbf{Q} \times \nabla \times \mathbf{P}) \cdot \mathbf{ds} \quad (4.3)$$

where $\mathbf{P}$ and $\mathbf{Q}$ are vector functions of position with continuous first and second derivatives within and on Σ, where Σ is the boundary of V. The element of oriented surface area $\mathbf{ds}$ has an outwardly directed normal $\hat{n}_s$. The pertinent features are illustrated in Fig. 4.1 where Σ has been decomposed into S and S_1 such that Σ is the sum of S and S_1. It will be found convenient in the following to write $\Sigma = S + S_1$ or $\Sigma = \partial V$ as a representation of the boundary of V.

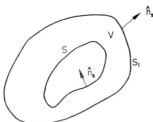

FIG. 4.1. The general representation.

Since the vector function $\mathbf{Q}$ is arbitrary and need merely satisfy the conditions previously specified, it can be written as

$$\mathbf{Q} = \hat{a}\varphi\,(\mathbf{x}, \mathbf{x}') = \hat{a}\,\frac{e^{-jk|\mathbf{x}-\mathbf{x}'|}}{|\mathbf{x} - \mathbf{x}'|}$$

where $\hat{a}$ is a unit vector of arbitrary orientation and $\mathbf{x}$ and $\mathbf{x}'$ are the observation and source point position vectors respectively. Note that the point $\mathbf{x} = \mathbf{x}'$ must be excluded at this stage because of the singularity in φ. If the electric field is substituted for $\mathbf{P}$ one finds after extensive vector manipulations (see Stratton, 1940) that eqn. (4.3) reduces to

$$\int_V \{j\omega\mu\mathbf{J}\varphi + \mathbf{K} \times \nabla\varphi - (\varrho/\varepsilon)\,\nabla\varphi\}\,dv = \int_\Sigma \{j\omega\mu\,(\hat{n}_s \times \mathbf{H})\,\varphi - (\hat{n}_s \times \mathbf{E}) \times \nabla\varphi - (\hat{n}_s \cdot \mathbf{E})\,\nabla\varphi\}\,ds.$$

$$(4.4)$$

The vector operations indicated in eqn. (4.4) are performed in the source coordinates and the relationship between source and observation coordinates enters through the function φ. In the following analysis, primes will be used to indicate vector operations in source coordinates. Also, a prime will be used to indicate a normal defined at a source point.

The choice of the vector functions $\mathbf{P}$ and $\mathbf{Q}$ deserves some comment. In the preceding, $\mathbf{Q}$ has been chosen to be a function directly related to a Green's function representing the magnetic vector potential in a homogeneous space due to a point current source given by $4\pi\hat{a}\delta\,(\mathbf{x} - \mathbf{x}')$. Indeed, any pair of functions $\mathbf{P}$ and $\mathbf{Q}$ satisfying the necessary conditions could have been chosen, and in fact, Harrington (1961) has outlined a number of alternative choices. If we had desired to restrict our attention to a specific geometry with particular boundary conditions, a Green's function for that geometry could have been used with a subsequent reduction in the labor involved in evaluating the surface integral. This technique is often used in the solution of the inhomogeneous wave equation in separable coordinates (Collin, 1960). An example of its use in conjunction with an integral equation specialized to a particular problem will be discussed in a later section. However, in order to allow ourselves the latitude for treating arbitrarily shaped surfaces with general boundary conditions we will, in the following, use the Green's function for an unbounded homogeneous space.

INTEGRAL REPRESENTATIONS OF THE ELECTROMAGNETIC FIELDS

The differentiability and continuity conditions imposed on the field $\mathbf{E}$ and the vector function $\mathbf{Q}$ restrict the applicability of eqn. (4.4). The observation point $\mathbf{x}$ and the source point $\mathbf{x}'$ may not coincide since the singularity in φ at $\mathbf{x} = \mathbf{x}'$ would invalidate the equation. Hence, the observation point may not lie on $S + S_1$ nor may $\mathbf{x} = \mathbf{x}'$ anywhere within V. In order to circumvent this difficulty a sphere of radius r is circumscribed about $\mathbf{x}$ as shown in Fig. 4.2. The liberty has been taken to place $\mathbf{x}$ on S in order to expedite the derivation. The results will be shown to be valid for all $\mathbf{x}$ either in V or on S.

Let the surface S of Fig. 4.1 be separated into two sections. As shown in Fig. 4.2, the surface has been deformed in such a way that there are two distinct portions: S_3 lying outside the intersection of S and S_s, and S_2 which is a deformed portion which would normally lie within S_s. The integrals in (4.4) can then be written as

$$\int_V \left(j\omega\mu\mathbf{J}\varphi + \mathbf{K} \times \nabla'\varphi - \frac{\varrho}{\varepsilon}\,\nabla'\varphi\right)\,dv' = \left[\int_{S_1} + \int_{S_2} + \int_{S_3} + \int_{S_s}\right]$$

$$\times \{j\omega\mu\,(\hat{n}'_s \times \mathbf{H})\,\varphi - (\hat{n}'_s \times \mathbf{E}) \times \nabla'\varphi - (\hat{n}'_s \cdot \mathbf{E})\,\nabla'\varphi\}\,ds' \qquad (4.5)$$

where the normals $\hat{n}'_s$ can take on the representations $\hat{n}_1$, $\hat{n}_2$, $\hat{n}_3$, or $\hat{n}_4$ on the surface of like subscript (except for $\hat{n}_4$ which is the outward normal of S_s).

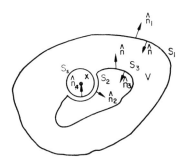

FIG. 4.2. The mathematical surfaces in the derivation of the integral equations.

Let us presently restrict our attention to the sum of the integrals over S_s and S_2 which is taken in the limit of vanishing $r = |\mathbf{x} - \mathbf{x}'|$ and which shall be denoted by I. With $r \to 0$, the phase factors in φ and $\nabla'\varphi$ are negligible, so that with mean values used for the fields at $\mathbf{x}'$ and with

$$\nabla'\varphi = \frac{1 + jkr}{r}\,\frac{e^{-jkr}}{r}\,\frac{\mathbf{x} - \mathbf{x}'}{|\mathbf{x} - \mathbf{x}'|} \tag{4.6}$$

one arrives at

$$I = \lim_{r \to 0}\left\{-\mathbf{E}\int_{S_s}\frac{\hat{n}_4' \cdot \hat{n}_4'}{r^2}\,ds' - \mathbf{E}\int_{S_2}\frac{\hat{n}_2' \cdot \hat{n}_2'}{r^2}\,ds'\right\}.$$

The definition of the solid angle with respect to the point $\mathbf{x}$ $(d\Omega = (\hat{n} \cdot \hat{r}/r^2)\,ds$ with $\hat{n}$ the normal out of the region containing $\mathbf{x}$) allows the integrands to be written as

$$d\Omega_s = \frac{\hat{n}_4' \cdot \hat{n}_4'}{r^2}\,ds' \quad \text{and} \quad d\Omega_2 = -\frac{\hat{n}_2' \cdot \hat{n}_2'}{r^2}\,ds.$$

Hence the limiting value of the integrals with $\mathbf{x}$ within S_s becomes

$$I = -\mathbf{E}(x)\,[4\pi - \Omega_2] \tag{4.7}$$

where Ω_2 represents the absolute value of the solid angle subtended by S_2 at $\mathbf{x}$ in the limit as r vanishes. Although the preceding allows $\mathbf{x}$ to be located on a surface whose tangent is not a differentiable function of position, it nonetheless requires that the fields possess a finite mean value.

The notation in the preceding operations has been simplified by assuming that the observation point was on the surface S. In general, $\mathbf{x}$ may be an element of either S or S_1, i.e. $\mathbf{x} \in \partial V$. In view of this we may drop the subscript notation on the solid angle Ω. One need merely keep in mind that $\Omega = 0$ for $\mathbf{x}$ not on the surface, and $\Omega = 2\pi$ for $\mathbf{x}$ on a smooth portion of ∂V. For $\mathbf{x}$ on ∂V, when ∂V is not smooth, one must determine the subtended solid angle keeping in mind the field behavior conditions. The substitution of (4.7) into (4.5) yields

$$\mathbf{E}(\mathbf{x}) = -\frac{T}{4\pi}\int_V\left(j\omega\mu\mathbf{J}\varphi + \mathbf{K} \times \nabla'\varphi - \frac{\rho}{\varepsilon}\nabla'\varphi\right)dv'$$

$$\qquad -\frac{T}{4\pi}\oint_{S_1+S}\{j\omega\mu\,(\hat{n}' \times \mathbf{H})\,\varphi - (\hat{n}' \times \mathbf{E}) \times \nabla'\varphi - (\hat{n}' \cdot \mathbf{E})\,\nabla'\varphi\}\,ds' \tag{4.8a}$$

where $T = (1 - \Omega/4\pi)^{-1}$ and $\oint_{S_1+S}$ is used to denote the principle value integral over

$S_1 + S$, i.e. the integral over the closed surface excluding an ε neighborhood of the singularity. By the duality of Maxwell's equations, the magnetic field can be written in a similar form, viz.

$$\mathbf{H}(\mathbf{x}) = \frac{T}{4\pi} \int_V \left(-j\omega\varepsilon \mathbf{K}\varphi + \mathbf{J} \times \nabla'\varphi + \frac{m}{\mu} \nabla'\varphi \right) dv'$$

$$+ \frac{T}{4\pi} \oint_{S_1+S} \{ j\omega\varepsilon (\hat{n}' \times \mathbf{E}) \varphi + (\hat{n}' \times \mathbf{H}) \times \nabla'\varphi + (\hat{n}' \cdot \mathbf{H}) \nabla'\varphi \} \, ds'. \quad (4.8b)$$

For discussions on the integrability of the singular integrands and the existence of the principal value integrals, the interested reader is referred to an excellent discussion on similar integrals of potential theory in Kellogg (1953).

EXERCISE: Derive eqn. (4.8) from eqn. (4.3) for $\mathbf{x}$ not on the boundary of V by making explicit use of the vector differential equation for the Green's function

$$\nabla \times \nabla \times \hat{a}\varphi - k^2\hat{a}\varphi - \nabla\nabla \cdot \hat{a}\varphi = 4\pi\delta (\mathbf{x} - \mathbf{x}') \, \hat{a}.$$

Note that the difficulty ordinarily encountered at $\mathbf{x} = \mathbf{x}'$ is circumvented.

A situation of great interest is that which occurs when S_1 recedes to infinity. For sources of bounded extent within V one finds that the radiation condition at infinity requires that the contribution from the integral over S_1 be due entirely from sources outside S_1. We shall refer to this contribution (if it exists) as an incident field and subsequently write eqn. (4.8) as

$$\mathbf{E}(\mathbf{x}) = T\mathbf{E}^{\text{inc}} (\mathbf{x}) - \frac{T}{4\pi} \int_V \left(j\omega\mu\mathbf{J}\varphi + \mathbf{K} \times \nabla'\varphi - \frac{\varrho}{\varepsilon} \nabla'\varphi \right) dv'$$

$$- \frac{T}{4\pi} \oint_S (j\omega\mu (\hat{n}' \times \mathbf{H}) \varphi - (\hat{n}' \times \mathbf{E}) \times \nabla'\varphi - (\hat{n}' \cdot \mathbf{E}) \nabla'\varphi) \, ds' \quad (4.9)$$

and

$$\mathbf{H}(\mathbf{x}) = T\mathbf{H}^{\text{inc}}(\mathbf{x}) + \frac{T}{4\pi} \int_V \left(-j\omega\varepsilon \mathbf{K}\varphi + \mathbf{J} \times \nabla'\varphi + \frac{m}{\mu} \nabla'\varphi \right) dv'$$

$$+ \frac{T}{4\pi} \oint_S (j\omega\varepsilon (\hat{n}' \times \mathbf{E}) \varphi + (\hat{n}' \times \mathbf{H}) \times \nabla'\varphi + (\hat{n}' \cdot \mathbf{H}) \nabla'\varphi) \, ds'.$$

Note that we have tacitly assumed that all inhomogeneities in the space are excluded from V by the surface S. In fact, when the region exterior to S_1 is homogeneous and identical in constitutive parameters to V, the integral over S_1 will always represent a contribution due to sources outside S_1.

EXERCISE: Show that for spatially limited sources in V, the contribution of the integral over S_1 as it recedes to infinity is due to sources outside S_1.

Hint. Decompose the field over S_1 into an outgoing component obeying the radiation condition and another, unspecified portion.

Equations (4.8) and (4.9) are vector integral equations for the field vectors $\mathbf{E}(\mathbf{x})$ and $\mathbf{H}(\mathbf{x})$ when $\mathbf{x} \in S$ and shall be referred to as the electric field integral equation (EFIE) and the magnetic field integral equation (MFIE).

An alternate representation which makes use of only one field variable in a given equation is also possible. For instance, let us represent the integral over the closed surface S in the magnetic field integral equation by $\mathbf{H}^s$ and write it in the form

$$\mathbf{H}^s(\mathbf{x}) = \frac{T}{4\pi} \oint_S \hat{n}' \times (\nabla' \times \mathbf{H}) \, \varphi + (\hat{n}' \times \mathbf{H}) \times \nabla'\varphi + (\hat{n}' \cdot \mathbf{H}) \, \nabla'\varphi) \, ds'.$$

The first step in the reduction is a subtraction of a surface integral of the form

$$\frac{T}{4\pi} \oint_S [(\hat{n}' \cdot \nabla') \, (\varphi\mathbf{H}) + \hat{n}' \times \nabla' \times (\varphi\mathbf{H}) - \hat{n}'\nabla' \cdot (\varphi\mathbf{H})] \, ds'$$

which is identically zero. Then, by making use of the relationships

$$\nabla'\varphi \times (\hat{n}' \times \mathbf{H}) = \hat{n}' \, (\mathbf{H} \cdot \nabla'\varphi) - \mathbf{H} \, (\hat{n}' \cdot \nabla'\varphi),$$

$$\hat{n}' \times (\nabla' \times (\varphi\mathbf{H})) = -\hat{n}' \times (\mathbf{H} \times \nabla'\varphi - \varphi \, (\nabla' \times \mathbf{H})),$$

$$\hat{n}' \times (\mathbf{H} \times \nabla'\varphi) = \mathbf{H} \, (\hat{n}' \cdot \nabla'\varphi) - (\hat{n}' \cdot \mathbf{H}) \, \nabla'\varphi,$$

one can reduce the surface integral in rectangular coordinates to the form

$$\mathbf{H}^s(\mathbf{x}) = \frac{T}{4\pi} \oint_S \left(\mathbf{H} \, \frac{\partial}{\partial n'} \, \varphi - \varphi \, \frac{\partial \mathbf{H}}{\partial n'} + \hat{n}'\varphi \, (\nabla' \cdot \mathbf{H}) \right) ds'. \tag{4.10a}$$

Likewise the surface integral for the electric field becomes

$$\mathbf{E}^s(\mathbf{x}) = \frac{T}{4\pi} \oint_S \left(\mathbf{E} \, \frac{\partial}{\partial n'} \, \varphi - \varphi \, \frac{\partial \mathbf{E}}{\partial n'} + \hat{n}'\varphi \, (\nabla' \cdot \mathbf{E}) \right) ds'. \tag{4.10b}$$

EXERCISE: Show that the steps outlined above do indeed lead to the results given by (4.10a) and (4.10b).

Hence eqns. (4.9), specialized to a source free region, can be written as

$$\mathbf{E}(\mathbf{x}) = T\mathbf{E}^{\text{inc}}(\mathbf{x}) - \frac{T}{4\pi} \oint_S (j\omega\mu \, (\hat{n}' \times \mathbf{H}) \, \varphi - (\hat{n}' \times \mathbf{E}) \times \nabla'\varphi - (\hat{n}' \cdot \mathbf{E}) \, \nabla'\varphi) \, ds',$$

$$\tag{4.11}$$

$$\mathbf{H}(\mathbf{x}) = T\mathbf{H}^{\text{inc}}(\mathbf{x}) + \frac{T}{4\pi} \oint_S (j\omega\varepsilon \, (\hat{n}' \times \mathbf{E}) \, \varphi + (\hat{n}' \times \mathbf{H}) \times \nabla'\varphi + (\hat{n}' \cdot \mathbf{H}) \, \nabla'\varphi) \, ds'$$

or equivalently (but only in rectangular coordinates) as

$$\mathbf{E}(\mathbf{x}) = T\mathbf{E}^{\text{inc}}(\mathbf{x}) + \frac{T}{4\pi} \oint_S \left(\mathbf{E} \, \frac{\partial}{\partial n'} \, \varphi - \varphi \, \frac{\partial}{\partial n'} \, \mathbf{E} + \hat{n}'\varphi \, (\nabla' \cdot \mathbf{E}) \right) ds',$$

$$\tag{4.12}$$

$$\mathbf{H}(\mathbf{x}) = T\mathbf{H}^{\text{inc}}(\mathbf{x}) + \frac{T}{4\pi} \oint_S \left(\mathbf{H} \, \frac{\partial}{\partial n'} \, \varphi - \varphi \, \frac{\partial}{\partial n'} \, \mathbf{H} + \hat{n}'\varphi \, (\nabla' \cdot \mathbf{H}) \right) ds'.$$

The representation in (4.11) is the more commonly used even though it is more complicated in form. Among other reasons, the mathematical representations of boundary conditions on arbitrarily shaped surfaces are more easily implemented in (4.11) than in (4.12). However, eqns. (4.12) do find use in two-dimensional geometries where the separation into TE and TM modes allows for the simple interpretation of the terms in the integral. The use of eqns. (4.12) will be further investigated in conjunction with two-dimensional geometries.

Special cases

In the study of electromagnetic field scattering by various obstacles the integral expressions which have been derived find great usefulness. The special cases to be considered in this section pertain to a class of problems for which the only source is at infinity. Simple modifications need only be performed in order to allow for primary sources within the region.

Although most of our attention will be devoted to surface integral equations, an alternate formulation will be introduced in the case of scattering by a dielectric body. This approach will employ a volume distribution of dependent sources and hence must be solved as a volume integral equation.

Before proceeding, it is advantageous to define the ultimate unknown. We are often interested in the acurate determination of the scattered fields ($E^s(x)$ or $H^s(x)$) outside the volume V_s containing a scatterer where

$$E(x) = E^{inc}(x) + E^s(x)$$

and

$$H(x) = H^{inc}(x) + H^s(x).$$

Clearly then these field quantities can be determined from eqns. (4.9) by considering only the contributions from the integrals over the boundary of V_s with T equal to unity since x is not on ∂V_s. Hence the scattered fields are simply

$$E^s(x) = -\frac{1}{4\pi} \int_{\partial V_s} \{j\omega\mu \, (\hat{n}' \times H) \, \varphi - (\hat{n}' \times E) \times \nabla'\varphi - (\hat{n}' \cdot E) \, \nabla'\varphi\} \, ds',$$

$$\tag{4.13a}$$

$$H^s(x) = \frac{1}{4\pi} \int_{\partial V_s} \{j\omega\varepsilon \, (\hat{n}' \times E) \, \varphi + (\hat{n}' \times H) \times \nabla'\varphi + (\hat{n}' \cdot H) \, \nabla'\varphi\} \, ds'.$$

Equation (4.13) is the integral representation of the scattered field in terms of the fields (or equivalent sources) over the surface of the scatterer. Alternatively the scattered fields could have been determined from a volume distribution of induced sources, i.e.

$$E^s(x) = -\frac{1}{4\pi} \int_{V_s} \left\{ j\omega\mu J\varphi + K \times \nabla'\varphi - \frac{\varrho}{\varepsilon} \nabla'\varphi \right\} dv',$$

$$\tag{4.13b}$$

$$H^s(x) = \frac{1}{4\pi} \int_{V_s} \left\{ -j\omega\varepsilon K\varphi + J \times \nabla'\varphi + \frac{m}{\mu} \nabla'\varphi \right\} dv'.$$

The determination of the field quantities in the integrand of (4.13) requires the solution of integral equations of the type already described. Our attention will now be directed towards the derivation of the integral equations pertaining to specific problems. In the course of examining these examples it will become obvious to the reader that it is often possible to write a number of different integral equations (or sets of equations) for the same problem and that a judicious choice will often simplify the solution process. Also, the authors do not wish to imply that the equations they have derived are the simplest to solve numerically.

(a) *Scattering by a perfect electric conductor.* Let us assume that we are interested in determining the scattering properties of a perfect electric conducting body S when illuminated by a field represented by the complex vector pair $(\mathbf{E}^{inc}, \mathbf{H}^{inc})$. In the classical radar problem the source of these fields is at infinity thereby giving rise to an incident plane wave. Consider then the problem as illustrated in Fig. 4.3.

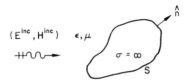

FIG. 4.3. Scattering by a perfect electric conductor.

The boundary conditions on the surface S state that the tangential electric field is zero, i.e. $\hat{n} \times \mathbf{E} = 0$. Furthermore, $\hat{n} \cdot \mathbf{H} = m = 0$, so that one can immediately write the electric and magnetic field integral equations. Since it is sufficient to enforce eqns. (4.9) for the tangential components of the fields on S, the equations become

$$\hat{n} \times \mathbf{E}^{inc}(\mathbf{x}) = \frac{1}{4\pi}\, \hat{n} \times \oint_S \{j\omega\mu\,(\hat{n}' \times \mathbf{H})\,\varphi - (\hat{n}' \cdot \mathbf{E})\,\nabla'\varphi\}\, ds', \quad \mathbf{x} \in S,$$

$$\hat{n} \times \mathbf{H}(\mathbf{x}) = 2\hat{n} \times \mathbf{H}^{inc}(\mathbf{x}) + \frac{1}{2\pi}\, \hat{n} \times \oint_S (\hat{n}' \times \mathbf{H}) \times \nabla'\varphi\, ds', \quad \mathbf{x} \in S.$$

Note that the second equation contains a single unknown whereas the first equation contains two unknowns in the integrand. However, by using Maxwell's equations we can establish that

$$\hat{n}' \cdot \mathbf{E} = \frac{j}{\omega\varepsilon}\, \nabla'_s \cdot (\hat{n}' \times \mathbf{H})$$

where ∇'_s represents the surface divergence operator in source coordinates. If we introduce the equivalent source notation

$$\hat{n} \times \mathbf{H} = \mathbf{J}_s$$

the two integral equations can be written as

$$\hat{n} \times \mathbf{E}^{inc}(\mathbf{x}) = \frac{1}{4\pi j\omega\varepsilon}\, \hat{n} \times \oint_S (-\omega^2\mu\varepsilon\mathbf{J}_s\varphi + \nabla'_s \cdot \mathbf{J}_s\,\nabla'\varphi)\, ds', \quad \mathbf{x} \in S,$$

$$\mathbf{J}_s(\mathbf{x}) = 2\hat{n} \times \mathbf{H}^{inc}(\mathbf{x}) + \frac{1}{2\pi}\, \hat{n} \times \oint_S \mathbf{J}_s \times \nabla'\varphi\, ds', \quad \mathbf{x} \in S.$$

(4.14)

Either of these equations can be used to solve for the equivalent surface current. The particular choice as to whether to use the integral equation of the first kind in electric field or the integral equation of the second kind in magnetic field will in general be dictated by the geometry of the scatterer and the intended solution technique. Although an integral equation of the second kind is generally preferable by virtue of the appearance of the unknown both outside and under the integral sign, the particular one written above becomes useless when S shrinks to an infinitely thin scatterer. The geometrical factors in the integrand are responsible for this behavior. On the other hand, the EFIE is ideally suited for thin cylinders as will be demonstrated shortly. For large, smooth conductors, the MFIE finds its greatest use since the geometrical factors often tend to make the contribution from the integral of only second-order importance. Approximations arising from this feature will be further discussed.

(b) *Scattering by a dielectric body.* In considering scattering from a dielectric body of permittivity ε_2 we allow the surface S to coincide with the surface of the dielectric as shown in Fig. 4.4. Two separate approaches to this problem will be developed. For a more detailed

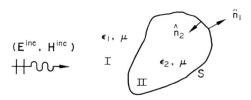

FIG. 4.4. Scattering from a dielectric body.

investigation as well as alternate representation, the reader is referred to Müller (1969). His formulations are mathematically rigorous and may be potentially more useful in numerical solution processes.

(i) *The surface integral equation approach.* The boundary conditions which must be satisfied on S are that the tangential components of the vectors $\mathbf{E}$ and $\mathbf{H}$ be continuous. As a consequence of field equations, the normal component of $\mathbf{D} = \varepsilon\mathbf{E}$ is also continuous. In view of this we can write the integral equations pertinent to regions I and II for the tangential components of the fields on S.

$$\hat{n}_1 \times \mathbf{E}_1(\mathbf{x}) = T\hat{n}_1 \times \mathbf{E}^{\text{inc}}(\mathbf{x})$$

$$-\frac{T}{4\pi} \hat{n}_1 \times \oint_S \{j\omega\mu\, (\hat{n}_1' \times \mathbf{H}_1)\, \varphi_1 - (\hat{n}_1' \times \mathbf{E}_1) \times \nabla'\varphi_1 - (\hat{n}_1' \cdot \mathbf{E})\, \nabla'\varphi_1\}\, ds',$$

$$(4.15)$$

$$\hat{n}_1 \times \mathbf{H}_1(\mathbf{x}) = T\hat{n}_1 \times \mathbf{H}^{\text{inc}}(\mathbf{x})$$

$$+\frac{T}{4\pi} \hat{n}_1 \times \oint_S \{j\omega\varepsilon_1\, (\hat{n}_1' \times \mathbf{E}_1)\, \varphi_1 + (\hat{n}_1' \times \mathbf{H}_1) \times \nabla'\varphi_1 + (\hat{n}_1' \cdot \mathbf{H}_1)\, \nabla'\varphi_1\}\, ds',$$

$$\hat{n}_2 \times \mathbf{E}_2(\mathbf{x}) = -\frac{T}{4\pi} \hat{n}_2 \times \oint_S \{j\omega\mu\, (\hat{n}_2' \times \mathbf{H}_2)\, \varphi_2 - (\hat{n}_2' \times \mathbf{E}_2) \times \nabla'\varphi_2 - (\hat{n}_2' \cdot \mathbf{E}_2)\, \nabla'\varphi_2\}\, ds',$$

$$(4.15)$$

$$\hat{n}_2 \times \mathbf{H}_2(\mathbf{x}) = \frac{T}{4\pi} \hat{n}_2 \times \oint_S \{j\omega\varepsilon_2\, (\hat{n}_2' \times \mathbf{E}_2)\, \varphi_2 + (\hat{n}_2' \times \mathbf{H}_2) \times \nabla'\varphi + (\hat{n}_2' \cdot \mathbf{H}_2)\, \nabla'\varphi^2\}\, ds',$$

where

$$\varphi_i = \frac{e^{-jk_i|\mathbf{x}-\mathbf{x}'|}}{|\mathbf{x}-\mathbf{x}'|}, \quad k_i = \omega\sqrt{(\mu\varepsilon_i)}, \quad \hat{n}_2 = -\hat{n}_1 \quad \text{and} \quad \mathbf{x} \in S.$$

The continuity of the tangential components of the fields requires that

$$\hat{n}_1 \times (\mathbf{E}_1 - \mathbf{E}_2) = 0, \quad \hat{n}_1 \times (\mathbf{H}_1 - \mathbf{H}_2) = 0 \quad \text{on } S_1$$

and continuity of the normal component of $\mathbf{D}$ requires that

$$\hat{n}_1 \cdot (\varepsilon_1 \mathbf{E}_1 - \varepsilon_2 \mathbf{E}_2) = 0.$$

By combining the integral equations, we have

$$\hat{n} \times \mathbf{E}^{\text{inc}}(\mathbf{x}) = \frac{1}{4\pi} \hat{n} \times \oint_S \left\{ j\omega\mu\,(\hat{n}' \times \mathbf{H})\,(\varphi_1 + \varphi_2) - (\hat{n}' \times \mathbf{E}) \times \nabla'(\varphi_1 + \varphi_2) \right.$$

$$\left. - (\hat{n}' \cdot \mathbf{E})\nabla'\left(\varphi_1 + \frac{\varepsilon_1}{\varepsilon_2}\varphi_2\right) \right\} ds', \quad \mathbf{x} \in S,$$

$$\hat{n} \times \mathbf{H}^{\text{inc}}(\mathbf{x}) = -\frac{1}{4\pi} \hat{n} \times \oint_S \left\{ j\omega\varepsilon_1\,(\hat{n}' \times \mathbf{E})\left(\varphi_1 + \frac{\varepsilon_2}{\varepsilon_1}\varphi_2\right) \right.$$

$$\left. + (\hat{n}' \times \mathbf{H}) \times \nabla'(\varphi_1 + \varphi_2) + (\hat{n}' \cdot \mathbf{H})\nabla'(\varphi_1 + \varphi_2) \right\} ds', \quad \mathbf{x} \in S$$

(4.16)

where the subscripts have been dropped for the fields and normals. At this juncture one must consider whether these integral equations, as written, are sufficient to ensure a unique solution. Clearly there exist four scalar equations in six unknowns. However, the normal components of Maxwell's equations on the surface yield relationships of the form

$$\hat{n}' \cdot \mathbf{E} = -\frac{1}{j\omega\varepsilon} \nabla_s' \cdot (\hat{n}_s' \times \mathbf{H})$$

and

$$\hat{n}' \cdot \mathbf{H} = \frac{1}{j\omega\mu} \nabla_s' \cdot (\hat{n}' \times \mathbf{E}).$$

The equivalent surface current representation can be used, namely,

$$\mathbf{J}_s = \hat{n} \times \mathbf{H}$$

and

$$\mathbf{K}_s = -\hat{n} \times \mathbf{E}$$

so that the integral equations can be written as

$$\hat{n} \times \mathbf{E}^{\text{inc}}(\mathbf{x}) = \frac{1}{4\pi} \hat{n} \times \oint_S \left\{ j\omega\mu\mathbf{J}_s(\varphi_1 + \varphi_2) + \mathbf{K}_s \times \nabla'(\varphi_1 + \varphi_2) \right.$$

$$\left. + \frac{1}{j\omega\varepsilon} \nabla_s' \cdot \mathbf{J}_s\nabla'\left(\varphi_1 + \frac{\varepsilon_1}{\varepsilon_2}\varphi_2\right) \right\} ds', \quad \mathbf{x} \in S,$$

$$\hat{n} \times \mathbf{H}^{\text{inc}}(\mathbf{x}) = \frac{1}{4\pi} \hat{n} \times \oint_S \left\{ j\omega\varepsilon\mathbf{K}_s\left(\varphi_1 + \frac{\varepsilon_2}{\varepsilon_1}\varphi_2\right) - \mathbf{J}_s \times \nabla'(\varphi_1 + \varphi_2) \right.$$

$$\left. + \frac{1}{j\omega\mu} \nabla_s' \cdot \mathbf{K}_s\nabla'(\varphi_1 + \varphi_2) \right\} ds', \quad \mathbf{x} \in S.$$

(4.17)

Although we have been able to reduce the number of unknowns such that (4.17) is a properly determined system, a price has been paid in that the integrands now contain surface derivatives of the surface currents.

EXERCISE: Show that this approach can be applied to bodies with finite conductivity σ by allowing the permittivity ε to assume complex values.

(ii) *The volume integral equation approach.* An alternative approach to the problem of scattering by a dielectric body makes use of volume distributions of dependent sources and will be referred to as the polarization current approach. In the derivation of the pertinent integral equations we write Maxwell's equations in both regions as

$$\nabla \times \mathbf{E}_1 = -j\omega\mu\mathbf{H}_1, \quad \nabla \times \mathbf{H}_1 = j\omega\varepsilon_1\mathbf{E}_1 \quad \text{in region I;}$$

$$\nabla \times \mathbf{E}_2 = -j\omega\mu\mathbf{H}_2, \quad \nabla \times \mathbf{H}_2 = j\omega\varepsilon_2\mathbf{E}_2 = j\omega\varepsilon_1\mathbf{E}_2 + j\omega\left(\varepsilon_2 - \varepsilon_i\right)\mathbf{E}_2 \quad \text{in region II.}$$

With the modification made in the last of these equations we note that all fields can now be interpreted as existing in a homogeneous region V (bounded by S) of constitutive parameters ε_1 and μ with a dependent current density given by $\mathbf{J}_e = -j\omega\left(\varepsilon_1 - \varepsilon_2\right)\mathbf{E}_2$. This volume distribution of current sources can be used in the integral equations given by (4.9) keeping in mind that the apparent surface charge due to the discontinuity in dielectric constant leads to a surface integral. The integral equation becomes

$$\mathbf{E}_2(\mathbf{x}) = \mathbf{E}^{\text{inc}}(\mathbf{x}) + \frac{1}{4\pi}\int_V \left(\frac{\varepsilon_2 - \varepsilon_1}{\varepsilon_1}\right)\omega^2\mu\varepsilon_1\mathbf{E}_2\varphi \, dv + \frac{1}{4\pi}\int_S \frac{\varepsilon_2 - \varepsilon_1}{\varepsilon_1}\left(\hat{n}' \cdot \mathbf{E}_2\right)\nabla'\varphi \, ds'. \quad (4.18)$$

The formulation represented by eqn. (4.18) is of a simpler form than that of (4.17) but involves an additional complexity in that the integral equation is written for all $\mathbf{x} \in V$, i.e. the condition implied by the equation must be enforced at all interior points of the volume V. However, some attractive features do arise in the formulation. The first and most significant is that the dielectric inhomogeneity modifies the volume integral in a simple manner. We do not, as a result, have to modify any propagation constants within the dielectric body. Secondly, the limiting form of (4.18) as $\varepsilon_2 \to \varepsilon_1$ is clearly evident and there is no question about redundant or indeterminate equations as arise in the surface integral formulation.

(c) *Scattering by a thin conducting wire.* Let us now direct our attention to scattering by a thin wire. When a scatterer is a perfect electric conductor of circular cross section with a diameter small compared to wavelength, the azimuthal surface current is negligible compared to the axially directed component (Hallen, 1938; King, 1956). Then the surface current density can be written as

$$\mathbf{J}_s(\mathbf{x}) = \frac{I(x)}{2\pi a}\,\hat{l}$$

where $\hat{l}$ is a tangential unit vector pointing in the axial direction as shown in Fig. 4.5 and it has been assumed that the current is azimuthally invariant.

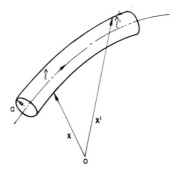

FIG. 4.5. The geometry for scattering by a thin wire.

The boundary condition on the surface of the conductor stipulates that the total electric field is zero. Since we are neglecting azimuthally directed currents and the effects of azimuthally directed incident electric fields, the boundary condition can be readily stated as

$$\hat{l} \cdot \mathbf{E}(\mathbf{x}) = 0.$$

The electric field integral equation for this particular coordinate system therefore becomes

$$\hat{l} \cdot \mathbf{E}^{inc}(\mathbf{x}) = \frac{1}{4\pi j\omega\varepsilon} \hat{l} \cdot \int_L \int_0^{2\pi} \left(-\omega^2\mu\varepsilon I(\mathbf{x}') \varphi \hat{l}' + \frac{\partial}{\partial l'} I(\mathbf{x}') \nabla'\varphi \right) \frac{dl'\, d\theta}{2\pi}$$

where $\int_L dl$ refers to an integral over the entire wire length and θ is the azimuthal variable. A final approximation that the current can be realistically represented by a filament of current on the wire axis while the field is evaluated on the wire surface or vice versa allows this equation to be written as

$$\hat{l} \cdot \mathbf{E}^{inc}(\mathbf{x}) = -\frac{1}{4\pi j\omega\varepsilon} \int_L \left(\hat{l} \cdot \hat{l}' k^2 I(\mathbf{x}') \varphi + \frac{\partial}{\partial l'} I(\mathbf{x}') \frac{\partial}{\partial s} \varphi \right) dl' \qquad (4.19)$$

The scalar distance $|\mathbf{x} - \mathbf{x}'|$ in the quantity φ is now measured from the source point on the axis to the observation point on the surface and thus can never be less than the radius a. Approximations of this type have been widely used in thin wire analyses (King, 1956; Richmond, 1965; Mei, 1965).

By performing an integration by parts on the second term in the integrand in (4.19) and by noting that the current must vanish at the wire ends, an alternate form results, namely,

$$\hat{l} \cdot \mathbf{E}^{inc}(\mathbf{x}) = -\frac{1}{4\pi j\omega\varepsilon} \int_L I(\mathbf{x}') \left[\hat{l} \cdot \hat{l}' k^2 \varphi - \frac{\partial^2}{\partial l' \partial l} \varphi \right] dl'. \qquad (4.20)$$

Equations (4.19) and (4.20) are commonly referred to as thin-wire electric field integral equations. Under the stated assumptions, the term $\varphi(\mathbf{x}, \mathbf{x}')$ is referred to as the thin wire Green's function or the thin wire kernel. For a straight wire φ is written as

$$\varphi = \frac{\exp\{-jk\sqrt{[(l - l')^2 + a^2]}\}}{\sqrt{[(l - l')^2 + a^2]}}$$

which, it will be noted, does not possess the singularity present in the exact representation of the free space Green's function (see Section 4.2.1). Note that (4.20) above is identical to (2.34) in Chapter 2 with slight differences in notation.

One might ask why the magnetic field integral equation was not used in this problem. The reason, which anticipates a numerical solution of the integral equation, is simple. It will be noted that the integrand in the second equation in (4.14) contains a vector cross product between **J** and $\nabla\varphi$. Since the current on the wire is assumed to be axially directed, the use of the thin wire Green's function may lead to computational difficulty by virtue of the small included angle between **J** and $\nabla\varphi$. The electric field integral equation does not suffer from this shortcoming and hence is widely used even though the second derivative of φ can create a theoretical difficulty if one requires that the exact representation of φ (which contains a singularity) be used.

(d) *Scattering by objects with an impedance boundary condition.* It may be possible in many cases of interest to determine a relationship between the tangential components of the electric and magnetic field vectors on a surface. If, for instance, one can establish a relationship such as

$$\mathbf{K} = Z_c \hat{n} \times \mathbf{J} \tag{4.21}$$

where Z_c is the surface impedance and **K** and **J** are the effective surface magnetic and electric currents respectively, then the integral equations in (4.11) can be uncoupled. However, it is not always possible to determine such a simple surface impedance and it is generally necessary to resort to approximate expressions for Z_c.

An example of the use of impedance boundary conditions is found in a paper by K. M. Mitzner (1967) where the problem of scattering from a body of large but finite conductivity is analyzed. The author discusses the Leontovich boundary condition which is of the form of (4.21) above with Z_c given by the wave impedance in the conductor. The validity of this condition is limited in that the radii of curvature of the body must be large with respect to the skin depth (δ). A modified form which allows the treatment of bodies with smaller radii of curvature is also considered and the form (credited to Rytov and Leontovich) is stated as

$$K_u = (1 - p) Z_c J_v, \quad K_v = (1 + p) Z_c J_u \tag{4.22}$$

where

$$p = \tfrac{1}{4} (1 - j) \delta (C_v - C_u),$$

$$Z_c = \tfrac{1}{2} (1 + j) \omega\mu\delta$$

and C_u, C_v are the principal curvatures.

These boundary conditions are derived using asymptotic expansions. Mitzner further generates additional boundary conditions with error estimates. He shows that the Leontovich condition is valid to within errors of $O\,(\delta^2/\omega^2\mu_0\varepsilon_0)$, $O\,(\delta^2/h^2)$ and $O\,(\delta C)$ where h is the distance to the nearest significant source and $C = \max\,(C_u, C_v)$. A further refinement leads to a modification in the last error term and reduces it to $O\,(\delta^2 C^2)$ in the curvature dependent boundary condition

$$(1 + p)\, K_u = -Z_c J_v, \quad (1 - p)\, K_v = Z_c J_u. \tag{4.23}$$

Mitzner also derives a form which involves a surface integral and which is an accurate representation of the actual boundary condition since it does indeed take into account the non-local characteristics of this parameter.

Senior (1960) also discusses the validity of the impedance boundary condition. His treatment proceeds from the wave equations for the fields in the lossy medium, and derives conditions under which the approximations associated with the surface impedance assumption are justified. The physical implications involved in using the surface impedance approximation are also pointed out by Senior.

It should be evident that the accurate representation of the impedance boundary condition is generally difficult. However, this is merely one approach to a problem and in many respects it provides simplifications at the expense of accuracy. The formulation presented for scattering by a dielectric body carries over to this type of scatterer and is another more rigorous approach but it suffers from the necessity of solving coupled integral equations. Clearly a choice must be made when solving such problems which weighs the potential difficulties and errors.

THE INTEGRAL REPRESENTATIONS IN TWO DIMENSIONS

The integral representations in eqns. (4.12) are particularly useful when the surface S is shift invariant along a particular axis, i.e., S possesses axial symmetry. Furthermore, if all field quantities are also invariant along this axis (or possess the same periodic variation) great simplifications can be realized. For instance, in a coordinate system where the cross section of the surface S is independent of the z-axis and t represents the combined transverse coordinates, we might write

$$E(z, t) = E(t)\, e^{\ jk_z z}.$$

Since the surface is independent of coordinate z, we can choose $z = 0$ so that the surface integrals (with $\mathbf{E}(t)$ and $\mathbf{H}(t)$ replaced by $\mathbf{A}(t)$) can be reduced to

$$\oint_C \left(\mathbf{A}\, \frac{\partial G}{\partial n'} - G \left\{ \frac{\partial \mathbf{A}}{\partial n'} - \hat{n}'\, [\nabla_t' \cdot \mathbf{A}_t - jk_z A_z] \right\} \right) \mathrm{d}l$$

where C is the cross-sectional contour of S, $\mathrm{d}l$ is an infinitesimal element on this contour, the subscripts t and z refer to transverse and longitudinal components, and

$$G = \int_{-\infty}^{\infty} e^{-jk_z z'}\, \frac{\exp\left\{ -jk\, \sqrt{(|\mathbf{t} - \mathbf{t}'|^2 + z'^2)} \right\}}{\sqrt{(|\mathbf{t} - \mathbf{t}'|^2 + z'^2)}}\, \mathrm{d}z'.$$

This integral representation for G is well known (Harrington 1961) and is reducible to

$$G = \frac{\pi}{j}\, H_0^{(2)} \left(\sqrt{(k^2 - k_z^2)}\, |\mathbf{t} - \mathbf{t}'| \right)$$

so that its normal derivative becomes

$$\frac{\partial G}{\partial n'} = -\frac{\pi}{j} \sqrt{(k^2 - k_z^2)} H_1^{(2)} (\sqrt{(k^2 - k_z^2)} |t - t'|) \cos(\hat{n}', t - t') \qquad (4.24)$$

where $\cos(\hat{n}, t - t')$ is the cosine of the angle between the normal and the vector from observation to source point in the transverse plane. In view of these relationships, eqns. (4.12) become, under the assumed conditions,

$$\mathbf{E}(t) = T\mathbf{E}^{inc}(t) + T\frac{j}{4}\oint_C \left[\mathbf{E}(t') \sqrt{(k^2 - k_z^2)} H_1^{(2)}(\sqrt{(k^2 - k_z^2)}|t - t'|) \cos(n', t - t') \right.$$

$$+ \left(\frac{\partial \mathbf{E}}{\partial n'} - \hat{n}' [\nabla_t' \cdot \mathbf{E}_t - jk_z E_z] \right) H_0^{(2)} (\sqrt{(k^2 - k_z^2)}|t - t'|)] \, dl,$$

$$\mathbf{H}(t) = T\mathbf{H}^{inc}(t) + T\frac{j}{4}\oint_C \left[\mathbf{H}(t') \sqrt{(k^2 - k_z^2)} H_1^{(2)} (\sqrt{(k^2 - k_z^2)}|t - t'|) \cos(n', t - t') \right.$$

$$+ \left(\frac{\partial \mathbf{H}}{\partial n'} - \hat{n}' [\nabla_t' \cdot \mathbf{H}_t - jk_z H_z] \right) H_0^{(2)} (\sqrt{(k^2 - k_z^2)}|t - t'|) \, dl. \qquad (4.25)$$

These equations are the two-dimensional electric field and magnetic field integral representations respectively. Again, T is defined by $T = (1 - \Omega/4\pi)^{-1}$ with Ω the solid angle subtended by the surface as $t \to t'$. Alternatively, $T = (1 - \Lambda/2\pi)^{-1}$ with Λ the plane angle subtended by the contour C as $t \to t'$.

Special cases

Since two-dimensional problems are of somewhat limited interest and since many of the ideas of special cases, p. 166, carry over into this analysis, only a single problem will be considered in this section.

(a) *Scattering by a perfect conductor illuminated by a plane wave at oblique incidence.* Consider a plane wave incident upon two-dimensional scatterer as shown in Fig. 4.6. For simplicity we shall consider two separate cases, namely,

    1. TM polarization ($\mathbf{H}^{inc}$ perpendicular to the z-axis),
    2. TE polarization ($\mathbf{E}^{inc}$ perpendicular to the z-axis).

For details and examples, the reader is referred to Oshiro (1966) and Andreasen (1965).

    (i) *TM polarization.* For the incident magnetic field perpendicular to the z-axis, we have the incident field in cylindrical coordinates given by

$$E_z^{inc}(t) = E_0 \sin \theta_0 \, e^{jk\varrho \cos(\varphi - \varphi_0) \sin \theta_0}$$

where t represents the transverse observation coordinates (ϱ, φ). From Maxwell's equations it is known that for TM polarization

$$\frac{\partial E_z}{\partial n'} = j\omega\mu H_\varphi = j\omega\mu J_z$$

where use has been made of the relation

$$\mathbf{J} = \hat{n} \times \mathbf{H}.$$

Since $E_z = 0$ on the surface of the conducting cylinder and since $k_z = k \cos \theta_0$ the first equation in (4.25) can be immediately written as

$$E_0 \sin \theta_0 \, e^{jk \varrho \cos (\varphi - \varphi_0) \sin \theta_0} = \frac{\omega \mu}{4} \int_C J_z(\mathbf{t}') \, H_0^{(2)} \, (k \, |\mathbf{t} - \mathbf{t}'| \sin \theta_0) \, dl \qquad (4.26)$$

in which $\mathbf{t}'$ represents the transverse source coordinate (ϱ', φ') and where, due to the convenience of the boundary relations, we have made use of the tangential component of the equations. Equation (4.26) is a Fredholm integral equation of the first kind for the surface current J_z on a cylinder illuminated by a TM polarized plane wave.

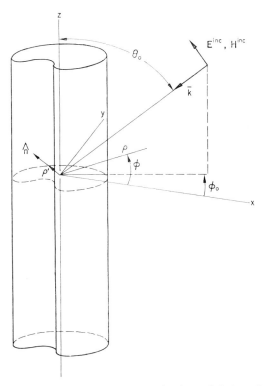

FIG. 4.6. The geometry pertinent to scattering by an infinite cylinder.

(ii) *TE polarization.* When the incident electric field is polarized perpendicular to the z-axis it is convenient to consider the z-directed component of the magnetic field. In this case

$$H_z^{\text{inc}}(\mathbf{t}) = H_0 \sin \theta_0 \, e^{jk \varrho \cos (\varphi - \varphi_0) \sin \theta_0}.$$

Since $\mathbf{J} = \hat{n} \times \mathbf{H}$ prescribes that

$$H_z(\mathbf{t}) = -J_\varphi(\mathbf{t})$$

and since $\partial H_z/\partial n' = -\mathrm{j}\omega\varepsilon E_\varphi = 0$ on a conductor, one finds that the tangential component of the magnetic field equation in (4.25) can be written as

$$2H_0 \sin\theta_0 \, \mathrm{e}^{\mathrm{j}k\varrho\cos(\varphi-\varphi_0)\sin\theta_0} = -J_\varphi(\mathbf{t}) + \frac{\mathrm{j}k\sin\theta_0}{2} \times$$

$$\times \int_c J_\varphi(\mathbf{t}') \, H_1^{(2)}(k\,|\mathbf{t} - \mathbf{t}'|\sin\theta_0)\cos(n',\mathbf{t}-\mathbf{t}')\,\mathrm{d}c. \qquad (4.27)$$

Equation (4.27) is a Fredholm integral equation of the second kind for the φ-directed current on a cylinder illuminated by a TE polarized plane wave.

REPRESENTATION OF OBSERVABLES

In the preceding discussions we have been concerned primarily with the derivation of integral equations relating induced surface or volume currents and specified exciting or incident fields. Since we are generally interested in observable quantities in the far field, the solution of the integral equations is merely an intermediate step. The induced sources must therefore be related to the measurable quantities. Since most far-field measurements are concerned either with the scattered fields or the scattering cross section, we will limit our attention to these quantities.

The far-field limit for the fields scattered by a finite surface denoted by S in terms of induced sources can be easily derived by taking the limit of eqns. (4.13a) as the observation point recedes to infinity. Since $|\mathbf{x} - \mathbf{x}'| \to r - (\mathbf{x}\cdot\mathbf{x}'/r)$ by the binomial expansion for $\mathbf{x} \gg \mathbf{x}'$, with $r = |\mathbf{x}|$ and $\hat{r} = (\mathbf{x}/|\mathbf{x}|)$, one has

$$\varphi = \frac{\mathrm{e}^{-\mathrm{j}k\,|\mathbf{x}-\mathbf{x}'|}}{|\mathbf{x} - \mathbf{x}'|} \to \frac{\mathrm{e}^{-\mathrm{j}kr}}{r}\,\mathrm{e}^{\mathrm{j}k\hat{r}\cdot\mathbf{x}'},$$

$$\nabla'\varphi = \nabla'\frac{\mathrm{e}^{-\mathrm{j}k\,|\mathbf{x}-\mathbf{x}'|}}{|\mathbf{x} - \mathbf{x}'|} \to \hat{r}\mathrm{j}k\,\frac{\mathrm{e}^{-\mathrm{j}kr}}{r}\,\mathrm{e}^{\mathrm{j}k\hat{r}\cdot\mathbf{x}'}.$$

Note that only terms of order $1/|x|$ have been retained. The details for this reduction can be found in Collin and Zucker (1969). The scattered fields can therefore be written as

$$\mathbf{E}^S(\mathbf{x}) = -\frac{\mathrm{e}^{-\mathrm{j}kr}}{4\pi r} \int_S \left[\mathrm{j}\omega\mu\mathbf{J}_s + \mathrm{j}k\mathbf{K}_s \times \hat{r} - \frac{\mathrm{j}k}{\varepsilon}\varrho_s\hat{r} \right] \mathrm{e}^{\mathrm{j}k\hat{r}\cdot\mathbf{x}'}\,\mathrm{d}s',$$

$$\mathbf{H}^S(\mathbf{x}) = \frac{\mathrm{e}^{-\mathrm{j}kr}}{4\pi r} \int_S \left[-\mathrm{j}\omega\varepsilon\mathbf{K}_s + \mathrm{j}k\mathbf{J}_s \times \hat{r} + \frac{\mathrm{j}k}{\mu}m_s\hat{r} \right] \mathrm{e}^{\mathrm{j}k\hat{r}\cdot\mathbf{x}'}\,\mathrm{d}s'.$$

Since $\varrho_s = -(1/\mathrm{j}\omega)\nabla\cdot\mathbf{J}_s$ and $\int_S \mathbf{f}\nabla'\cdot\mathbf{J}_s\,\mathrm{d}s' = -\int_S (\mathbf{J}\cdot\nabla')\,\mathbf{f}\,\mathrm{d}s'$, the integrals can be cast in a more convenient form, namely,

$$\mathbf{E}^S(\mathbf{x}) = \frac{\mathrm{j}\omega\mu\,\mathrm{e}^{-\mathrm{j}kr}}{4\pi r} \int_S \left[(\hat{r}\cdot\mathbf{J}_s)\hat{r} - \mathbf{J}_s - \sqrt{\frac{\varepsilon}{\mu}}\,K_s \times \hat{r} \right] \mathrm{e}^{\mathrm{j}k\hat{r}\cdot\mathbf{x}'}\,\mathrm{d}s',$$

$$\mathbf{H}^S(\mathbf{x}) = \frac{\mathrm{j}\omega\varepsilon\,\mathrm{e}^{-\mathrm{j}kr}}{4\pi r} \int_S \left[(\hat{r}\cdot\mathbf{K}_s)\hat{r} - \mathbf{K}_s + \sqrt{\frac{\mu}{\varepsilon}}\,\mathbf{J}_s \times \hat{r} \right] \mathrm{e}^{\mathrm{j}k\hat{r}\cdot\mathbf{x}'}\,\mathrm{d}s'. \qquad (4.28)$$

Equations (4.28) are the sought after expressions for the scattered far fields in terms of the induced electric and magnetic currents.

Another quantity of interest is the radar cross section (RCS) of a scatterer in a given orientation. It is defined as 4π times the ratio of the radiation intensity (power per unit solid angle) of the far scattered wave in a specified direction to the power per unit area in an incident plane wave of specified polarization from a given direction. Hence the RCS, σ, is given by

$$\sigma = \lim_{r \to \infty} 4\pi r^2 \frac{|E_s|^2}{|E^{inc}|^2} = = \lim_{r \to \infty} 4\pi r^2 \frac{|H_s|^2}{|H^{inc}|^2} \qquad (4.29)$$

where it is understood that the scattered field and σ are functions of angular direction from S. Clearly σ is a scalar quantity defined in terms of power and is independent of the polarization of the scattered field. For certain applications, it might be advantageous to consider an RCS which is dependent upon the receiver polarization, by limiting one's attention to a particular vector component of the scattered field. The polarization state of the receiver then enters explicitly into the evaluation of RCS and allows one to evaluate the depolarization properties of the scatterer.

A discussion of scattering cross sections which includes definitions as well as the implications involved in the measurement of RCS is found in King and Wu (1959). For a comprehensive treatment of depolarization, the reader is referred to Beckmann (1968).

4.2.2. The Derivation of Space–Time Domain Integral Equations

The space–frequency domain integral equations which have been derived for time harmonic excitation will now be used in the derivation of space–time domain integral equations. The specific equations considered pertain to the electric field integral equation (EFIE), the magnetic field integral equation (MFIE), and the magnetic vector potential integral equation for curved and straight wires. The latter is included for the interested reader. The Fourier transform will be used in this analysis and it will be shown that space–time equations can be readily derived from their space–frequency counterparts. The equations derived will be applicable to fields of arbitrary time variation.

THE FOURIER TRANSFORM PAIR

The Fourier transform technique will be used to transform from the space–frequency to the space–time domain. The transform pair which is employed in this derivation is given by

$$\tilde{f}(\omega) = \int_{-\infty}^{\infty} f(t)\, e^{-j\omega t}\, dt,$$

$$\qquad (4.30)$$

$$f(t) = \mathcal{F}[\tilde{f}(\omega)] = \frac{1}{2\pi} \int_{-\infty}^{\infty} f(\omega)\, e^{j\omega t}\, d\omega.$$

One of the pertinent equations which will be extensively called upon is the mathematical representation of the convolution theorem, i.e.

$$\mathscr{F}\left[\hat{f}(\omega)\,\tilde{g}(\omega)\right] = f(t) * g(t) = \int_{-\infty}^{\infty} f(\tau)\,g\,(t-\tau)\,\mathrm{d}\tau. \tag{4.31}$$

Also, the following identity will be employed,

$$\mathscr{F}\left[\mathrm{e}^{-\mathrm{j}\omega\tau}\right] = \delta\,(t-\tau). \tag{4.32}$$

It is convenient at this time to introduce the concept of a vector convolution. For two vector functions of space and frequency, one has, for the conventional Fourier transform of their cross product,

$$\mathscr{F}\left[\hat{\mathbf{f}}(\mathbf{x},\omega) \times \hat{\mathbf{g}}\,(\mathbf{x},\omega)\right] = \mathbf{f}\,(\mathbf{x},t) \overset{*}{\times} \mathbf{g}\,(\mathbf{x},t) = \int_{-\infty}^{\infty} \mathbf{f}\,(\mathbf{x},\tau) \times \mathbf{g}\,(\mathbf{x},t-\tau)\,\mathrm{d}\tau. \tag{4.33}$$

It will be assumed throughout the analyses that the order of time and frequency integration can be interchanged. A sufficient condition for the validity of this interchange is that both $f(t)$ and $g(t)$ are square-integrable, i.e.

$$\int_{-\infty}^{\infty} |f(t)|^2\,\mathrm{d}t \le \infty,$$

$$\int_{-\infty}^{\infty} |g(t)|^2\,\mathrm{d}t \le \infty.$$

This is equivalent to a statement of the "finite energy" condition for $f(t)$ and $g(t)$.

INTEGRAL REPRESENTATIONS OF THE ELECTROMAGNETIC FIELDS

The electric and magnetic field integral representations

The space–time domain integral equations which will be first considered are those which can be derived from eqn. (4.9). For simplicity, only the source-free problem will be considered so that the contribution of the volume integral is zero. Also, only the time-domain representation of the electric field integral equation will be derived in detail since its magnetic field counterpart can be subsequently written down by inspection. The results can be easily extended to include volume distributions of sources within V.

The electric field integral equation in the space–time domain can be derived by taking the Fourier transform of eqn. (4.9). Since the interchange of the order of integration is valid (note that all terms are square integrable), the operations $\mathscr{F}$ (the Fourier transform) and $\oint_s \mathrm{d}s'$ can be interchanged. This leads to

$$\mathbf{E}\,(\mathbf{x},t) = T\mathbf{E}^{\mathrm{inc}}\,(\mathbf{x},t) - \frac{T}{4\pi} \int_s \{\mu\hat{n}' \times \mathscr{F}\,[\mathrm{j}\omega\tilde{\mathbf{H}}\,(\mathbf{x},\omega)\,\tilde{\varphi}]$$

$$- \mathscr{F}\,[(\hat{n}' \times \tilde{\mathbf{E}}\,(\mathbf{x}',\omega)) \times \nabla'\tilde{\varphi}] - \mathscr{F}\,[(\hat{n}' \cdot \tilde{\mathbf{E}}\,(\mathbf{x}',\omega))\,\nabla'\tilde{\varphi}]\} \,\mathrm{d}s'. \tag{4.34}$$

Certain relationships can be used in reducing (4.34) to a more tractable form.

From Fourier transform theory it is known that if $f(t)$ and $(\mathrm{d}/\mathrm{d}t)f(t)$ approach zero as t approaches infinity then

$$\mathscr{F}\left[j\omega\, \hat{f}(\omega)\right] = \frac{\mathrm{d}}{\mathrm{d}t} f(t)$$

Also, one has upon the application of (4.32),

$$\mathscr{F}\left[\varphi\left(\mathbf{x}, \mathbf{x}', \omega\right)\right] = \mathscr{F}\left[\frac{e^{-j(\omega/c)\,|\mathbf{x}-\mathbf{x}'|}}{|\mathbf{x}-\mathbf{x}'|}\right] = \frac{\delta\left[t - \left(|\mathbf{x}-\mathbf{x}'|/c\right)\right]}{|\mathbf{x}-\mathbf{x}'|}$$

and

$$\mathscr{F}\left[\nabla'\varphi\left(\mathbf{x}, \mathbf{x}', \omega\right)\right] = \delta\left(t - \frac{|\mathbf{x}-\mathbf{x}'|}{c}\right)\frac{(\mathbf{x}-\mathbf{x}')}{|\mathbf{x}-\mathbf{x}'|^3} + \frac{1}{c}\frac{\partial}{\partial t}\delta\left(t - \frac{|\mathbf{x}-\mathbf{x}'|}{c}\right)\frac{(\mathbf{x}-\mathbf{x}')}{|\mathbf{x}-\mathbf{x}'|^2}.$$

The substitution of these relationships into eqn. (4.34) will yield an integral containing a number of convolutions of the form of eqn. (4.33). By performing these convolutions and by making use of the defining property of the Dirac delta function one arrives at

$$
\begin{aligned}
\mathbf{E}(\mathbf{x}, t) = T\mathbf{E}^{\mathrm{inc}}(\mathbf{x}, t) - \frac{T}{4\pi}\oint_S \Bigg\{ &\mu\frac{1}{|\mathbf{x}-\mathbf{x}'|}\frac{\partial}{\partial \tau}\left[\hat{n}' \times \mathbf{H}(\mathbf{x}, \tau)\right] \\
&- \left[\hat{n}' \times \mathbf{E}(\mathbf{x}', \tau)\right] \times \frac{(\mathbf{x}-\mathbf{x}')}{|\mathbf{x}-\mathbf{x}'|^3} - \left[\hat{n}' \times \frac{\partial}{\partial \tau}\mathbf{E}(\mathbf{x}', \tau)\right] \times \frac{(\mathbf{x}-\mathbf{x}')}{c\,|\mathbf{x}-\mathbf{x}'|^2} \\
&- \left[\hat{n}' \cdot \mathbf{E}(\mathbf{x}, \tau)\right]\frac{(\mathbf{x}-\mathbf{x}')}{|\mathbf{x}-\mathbf{x}'|^3} - \left[\hat{n}' \cdot \frac{\partial}{\partial \tau}\mathbf{E}(\mathbf{x}, \tau)\right]\frac{(\mathbf{x}-\mathbf{x}')}{c\,|\mathbf{x}-\mathbf{x}'|^2}\Bigg\}_{\tau=t-\frac{|\mathbf{x}-\mathbf{x}'|}{c}}\,ds'.
\end{aligned}
$$

(4.35)

The notation $\partial/\partial\tau \mathbf{E}(\mathbf{x}', \tau)$ is used to represent the time derivative of $\mathbf{E}(\mathbf{x}', t)$ evaluated at the retarded time τ, i.e., $\partial/\partial t\, \mathbf{E}(\mathbf{x}, t)|_{t=\tau}$. Equation (4.35) is the general form of the electric field space–time domain integral equation for a source-free region V bounded by S and the closed surface at infinity. The inclusion of sources in V can be easily implemented by augmenting eqn. (4.35) with the volume integral

$$
\begin{aligned}
-\frac{T}{4\pi}\int_V \Bigg\{ &\mu\frac{1}{|\mathbf{x}-\mathbf{x}'|}\frac{\partial}{\partial\tau}\mathbf{J}(\mathbf{x}', \tau) + \mathbf{K}(\mathbf{x}', \tau) \times \frac{(\mathbf{x}-\mathbf{x}')}{|\mathbf{x}-\mathbf{x}'|^3} + \frac{\partial}{\partial\tau}\mathbf{K}(\mathbf{x}', \tau) \times \frac{(\mathbf{x}-\mathbf{x}')}{c\,|\mathbf{x}-\mathbf{x}'|^2} \\
&- \frac{\varrho(\mathbf{x}', \tau)}{\varepsilon}\frac{(\mathbf{x}-\mathbf{x}')}{|\mathbf{x}-\mathbf{x}'|^3} - \frac{\partial}{\partial\tau}\frac{\varrho(\mathbf{x}', \tau)}{\varepsilon}\frac{(\mathbf{x}-\mathbf{x}')}{c\,|\mathbf{x}-\mathbf{x}'|^2}\Bigg\}_{\tau=t-\frac{|\mathbf{x}-\mathbf{x}'|}{c}}\,dv'.
\end{aligned}
$$

(4.36)

By duality we can immediately write

$$
\begin{aligned}
\mathbf{H}(\mathbf{x}, t) = T\mathbf{H}^{\mathrm{inc}}(\mathbf{x}, t) + \frac{T}{4\pi}\oint_S \Bigg\{ &\varepsilon\frac{1}{|\mathbf{x}-\mathbf{x}'|}\frac{\partial}{\partial\tau}\left[\hat{n}' \times \mathbf{E}(\mathbf{x}, \tau)\right] \\
&+ \left[\hat{n}' \times \mathbf{H}(\mathbf{x}', \tau)\right] \times \frac{(\mathbf{x}-\mathbf{x}')}{|\mathbf{x}-\mathbf{x}'|^3} + \left[\hat{n}' \times \frac{\partial}{\partial\tau}\mathbf{H}(\mathbf{x}', \tau)\right] \times \frac{(\mathbf{x}-\mathbf{x}')}{c\,|\mathbf{x}-\mathbf{x}'|^2} \\
&+ \left[\hat{n}' \cdot \mathbf{H}(\mathbf{x}, \tau)\right]\frac{(\mathbf{x}-\mathbf{x}')}{|\mathbf{x}-\mathbf{x}'|^3} + \left[\hat{n}' \cdot \frac{\partial}{\partial\tau}\mathbf{H}(\mathbf{x}, \tau)\right]\frac{(\mathbf{x}-\mathbf{x}')}{c\,|\mathbf{x}-\mathbf{x}'|^2}\Bigg\}_{\tau=t-\frac{|\mathbf{x}-\mathbf{x}'|}{c}}\,ds'.
\end{aligned}
$$

(4.37)

Equation (4.37) is the magnetic field space–time domain integral equation for a source-free region. The dual of eqn. (4.36) must be added if V contains either electric or magnetic sources.

A special case of great interest is that which arises when the surface S coincides with a perfect electric conductor. The equivalent source representations $\hat{n} \times \mathbf{H}(\mathbf{x}, t) = \mathbf{J}_s(\mathbf{x}, t)$ and $\hat{n} \cdot \mathbf{E}(\mathbf{x}, t) = \{\varrho_s(\mathbf{x}, t)\}/\varepsilon$ will be used. Since the boundary condition requires that $\hat{n} \times \mathbf{E}(\mathbf{x}, t) = 0$ and $\hat{n} \cdot \mathbf{H}(\mathbf{x}, t) = 0$ for $\mathbf{x}$ on S, the space–time domain integral equations for perfect electric conductors can be written as

$$0 = 1\hat{n} \times \mathbf{E}^{\text{inc}}(\mathbf{x}, t) - \frac{1}{4\pi} \hat{n} \times \oint_S \left\{ \mu \frac{1}{|\mathbf{x} - \mathbf{x}'|} \frac{\partial}{\partial \tau} \mathbf{J}_s(\mathbf{x}', \tau) \right.$$

$$\left. - \frac{\varrho_s(\mathbf{x}', \tau)}{\varepsilon} \frac{(\mathbf{x} - \mathbf{x}')}{|\mathbf{x} - \mathbf{x}'|^3} - \frac{\partial}{\partial \tau} \varrho_s(\mathbf{x}', \tau) \frac{(\mathbf{x} - \mathbf{x}')}{\varepsilon c |\mathbf{x} - \mathbf{x}'|^2} \right\}_{\tau = t - \frac{|\mathbf{x} - \mathbf{x}'|}{c}} ds',$$

$$\mathbf{J}_s(\mathbf{x}, t) = 2\hat{n} \times \mathbf{H}^{\text{inc}}(\mathbf{x}, t) + \frac{1}{2\pi} \hat{n} \times \oint_S \left[\frac{1}{c} \frac{\partial}{\partial \tau} \mathbf{J}_s(\mathbf{x}', \tau) + \mathbf{J}_s(\mathbf{x}', \tau) \frac{1}{|\mathbf{x} - \mathbf{x}'|} \right]$$

$$\times \frac{(\mathbf{x} - \mathbf{x}')}{|\mathbf{x} - \mathbf{x}'|^2} \bigg|_{\tau = t - \frac{|\mathbf{x} - \mathbf{x}'|}{c}} ds'. \tag{4.38}$$

The first of these equations is clearly a Fredholm integral equation of the first kind while the second equation is a Fredholm integral equation of the second kind.

The magnetic vector potential integral equation for thin wires

The magnetic vector potential integral equation for arbitrarily shaped wires in the space–frequency domain has been derived by Mei (1965). In order to facilitate the Fourier transformation and the interpretation of the time retarded terms in the integrals, the space–frequency domain integral equation can be written as

$$\int_{h_1}^{h_2} \tilde{I}(l', \omega) \left\{ \tilde{G}(l, l', \omega) \hat{l} \cdot \hat{l}' + \frac{1}{2} \int_{h_1}^{h_2} \theta(\xi - l) \left[\frac{\partial \tilde{G}(\xi, l', \omega)}{\partial l'} + \frac{\partial}{\partial \xi} [(\hat{\xi} \cdot \hat{l}') \tilde{G}(\xi, l', \omega)] \right] \right.$$

$$\times e^{-j(\omega/c)|l - \xi|} d\xi \bigg\} dl'$$

$$= \tilde{C}(\omega) e^{j(\omega/c)l} + \tilde{D}(\omega) e^{-j(\omega/c)l} + \frac{\varepsilon c}{2} \int_{h_1}^{h_2} \tilde{E}_\xi^{\text{inc}}(\xi, \omega) e^{-j(\omega/c)|l - \xi|} d\xi \tag{4.39}$$

where

$$G(l, l', \omega) = \frac{e^{-jkR(l, l')}}{4\pi R(l, l')}$$

$$\theta(\xi - l) = \pm 1 \quad \text{for} \quad \xi \lessgtr l$$

$R(l, l')$ is a distance appropriate to thin wire geometry, and $\tilde{E}_\xi^{\text{inc}}(\xi, \omega) = \hat{\xi} \cdot \tilde{\mathbf{E}}^{\text{inc}}(\xi, \omega)$. The wave number k is given by $k = \omega/c$ where c is the velocity of light. The geometrical parameters pertinent to this equation are described in Fig. 4.7. The only difference between eqn. (4.39) and that derived by Mei is in the exponential term in the integrand, in the presence of the function $\theta(\xi - l)$ and in the limits of the ξ integration (Poggio, 1969). Concisely, the difference arises from the choice of the Green's function for the partial differential equation for the vector potential.

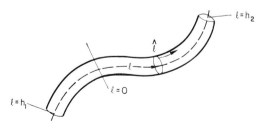

FIG. 4.7. Coordinate system for arbitrary thin wire geometry

The Fourier Transform of (4.39) yields the desired space–time domain integral equation.

$$\int_{h_1}^{h_2} (\hat{l}\cdot\hat{l}')\left.\frac{I(l',\tau)}{4\pi R(l,l')}\right|_{\tau=t-(R(l,l')/c)} dl' - \frac{1}{8\pi}\int_{h_1}^{h_2}\int_{h_1}^{h_2}\theta(\xi-l)$$

$$\times\left\{\frac{(\hat{\xi}\cdot\hat{l}')(\partial R(\xi,l')/\partial\xi)+(\partial R(\xi,l')/\partial l')}{cR(\xi,l')}\frac{\partial}{\partial\tau}I(l',\tau)\right.$$

$$\left.+\left(\frac{\partial R(\xi,l')}{\partial l'}+(\hat{\xi}\cdot\hat{l}')\frac{\partial R(\xi,l')}{\partial\xi}-R(\xi,l')\frac{\partial(\hat{\xi}\cdot\hat{l}')}{\partial\xi}\right)\frac{I(\hat{l}',\tau)}{R(\xi,l')^2}\right\}_{\tau=t-(R(\xi,l')/c)-(|l-\xi|/c)} d\xi\,dl'$$

$$= C\left(t-\frac{l}{c}\right)+D\left(t+\frac{l}{c}\right)+\frac{\varepsilon c}{2}\int_{h_1}^{h_2}E_\xi^{inc}\left(\xi,t-\frac{|l-\xi|}{c}\right)d\xi. \qquad (4.40)$$

Equation (4.40) can be reduced to the special case of the straight wire by merely setting $(\hat{\xi}\cdot l')=1$, $\partial/\partial\xi\,R=-\partial/\partial l'\,R$, so that

$$\int_{h_1}^{h_2}\left.\frac{I(l',\tau)}{4\pi R(l,l')}\right|_{\tau=t-(R(l,l')/c)} dl' = C\left(t-\frac{l}{c}\right)+D\left(t+\frac{l}{c}\right)+\frac{\varepsilon c}{2}\int_{h_1}^{h_2}E_l^{inc}\left(\xi,t-\frac{|l-\xi|}{c}\right)d\xi. \qquad (4.41)$$

THE TRANSIENT FAR FIELDS

A measurable quantity of great interest is the time-dependent scattered fields. These can be derived from eqns. (4.35) and (4.37) for scattering by an arbitrary body by merely removing the incident field term, by setting $T=1$, and by taking the asymptotic limit as $|\mathbf{x}-\mathbf{x}'|\to\infty$. We again assume S is finite. By letting $\mathbf{x}-\mathbf{x}'\to\mathbf{x}=\mathbf{r}$, $|\mathbf{x}-\mathbf{x}'|\to|\mathbf{x}|=r$, and $\mathbf{x}/|\mathbf{x}|=\hat{r}$, while for the retarded time $\tau=t-r/c+\hat{r}\cdot\mathbf{x}'$, one has

$$\mathbf{E}^s(\mathbf{x},t)=-\frac{1}{4\pi rc}\int_S\left\{\sqrt{\frac{\mu}{\varepsilon}}\frac{\partial}{\partial\tau}[\hat{n}'\times\mathbf{H}(\mathbf{x}',\tau)]\right.$$

$$\left.-\frac{\partial}{\partial\tau}[\hat{n}'\times\mathbf{E}(\mathbf{x}',\tau)]\times\hat{r}-\frac{\partial}{\partial\tau}[\hat{n}'\cdot\mathbf{E}(\mathbf{x}',\tau)]\hat{r}\right\}_{\tau=t-r/c+\hat{r}\cdot\mathbf{x}'} dl'$$

and

$$\mathbf{H}^s(\mathbf{x}, t) = \frac{1}{4\pi rc} \int_S \left\{ \sqrt{\frac{\varepsilon}{\mu}} \frac{\partial}{\partial \tau} [\hat{n}' \times \mathbf{E}(\mathbf{x}', \tau)] \right.$$

$$\left. + \frac{\partial}{\partial \tau} [\hat{n}' \times \mathbf{H}(\mathbf{x}', \tau)] \times \hat{r} + \frac{\partial}{\partial \tau} [\hat{n}' \cdot \mathbf{H}(\mathbf{x}', \tau)] \hat{r} \right\}_{\tau = t - r/c + \hat{r} \cdot \mathbf{x}'} \mathrm{d}l'$$

or, by using the equivalent source representation,

$$\mathbf{E}^s(\mathbf{x}, t) = -\frac{1}{4\pi rc} \int_S \left\{ \sqrt{\frac{\mu}{\varepsilon}} \frac{\partial}{\partial \tau} \mathbf{J}_s(\mathbf{x}', \tau) + \frac{\partial}{\partial \tau} \mathbf{K}_s(\mathbf{x}', \tau) \times \hat{r} - \frac{\partial}{\partial \tau} \frac{\varrho_s}{\varepsilon} \hat{r} \right\}_{\tau = t - r/c + \hat{r} \cdot \mathbf{x}'} \mathrm{d}l'$$

and

$$\tag{4.42}$$

$$\mathbf{H}^s(\mathbf{x}, t) = \frac{1}{4\pi rc} \int_S \left\{ -\sqrt{\frac{\varepsilon}{\mu}} \frac{\partial}{\partial \tau} \mathbf{K}_s(\mathbf{x}', \tau) + \frac{\partial}{\partial \tau} \mathbf{J}_s(\mathbf{x}', \tau) \times \hat{r} + \frac{\partial}{\partial \tau} \frac{m_s}{\mu} \hat{r} \right\}_{\tau = t - r/c + \hat{r} \cdot \mathbf{x}'} \mathrm{d}s'.$$

Once the surface current and charges are computed, it is a simple matter to determine the far scattered fields.

4.2.3. Tabulation of Integral Representations and Equations

The space–frequency and space–time domain integral representations and equations are tabulated for convenience in Tables 4.1 and 4.2. For EFIE and MFIE the equations are those pertaining to an externally imposed (outside S_1) source with the interpretation provided in the discussion of eqn. (4.9). In all cases, equivalent sources were used in integrands in order to minimize complexity. These sources are given by

$$\mathbf{J}_s = \hat{n}' \times \mathbf{H}(\mathbf{x}'),$$

$$\mathbf{K}_s = -\hat{n}' \times \mathbf{E}(\mathbf{x}'),$$

$$\varrho_s = \varepsilon \hat{n}' \cdot \mathbf{E}(\mathbf{x}'),$$

$$m_s = \mu \hat{n}' \cdot \mathbf{H}(\mathbf{x}').$$

The following symbols are also defined for convenience:

$$T = \left(1 - \frac{\Omega}{4\pi} \right)^{-1},$$

$$\theta(\xi - s) = 1 \qquad \xi > s$$

$$= -1 \qquad \xi < s,$$

$$\oint_S \mathrm{d}s = \text{principal value integral over } S,$$

$$\varphi = \frac{e^{-jk|\mathbf{x} - \mathbf{x}'|}}{|\mathbf{x} - \mathbf{x}'|}$$

$$G\left(s, s'\right) = \frac{1}{4\pi} \frac{e^{-jkR(s,s')}}{R\left(s, s'\right)}.$$

The notation used to represent retarded time is defined immediately following (4.35).

TABLE 4.1. SPACE–FREQUENCY DOMAIN

E-field integral representation

$$\mathbf{E(x)} = T\mathbf{E}^{\text{inc}}(\mathbf{x}) - \frac{T}{4\pi} \int_V \left\{ j\omega\mu\mathbf{J}\varphi + \mathbf{K} \times \nabla'\varphi - \frac{\varrho}{\varepsilon} \nabla'\varphi \right\} dv'$$

$$- \frac{T}{4\pi} \oint_S \left(j\omega\mu\mathbf{J}_s\varphi + \mathbf{K}_s \times \nabla'\varphi - \frac{\varrho_s}{\varepsilon} \nabla'\varphi \right) ds'$$

H-field integral representation

$$\mathbf{H(x)} = T\mathbf{H}^{\text{inc}}(\mathbf{x}) + \frac{T}{4\pi} \int_V \left\{ -j\omega\varepsilon\mathbf{K}\varphi + \mathbf{J} \times \nabla'\varphi + \frac{m}{\mu} \nabla'\varphi \right\} dv'$$

$$+ \frac{T}{4\pi} \oint_S \left(-j\omega\varepsilon\mathbf{K}_s\varphi + \mathbf{J}_s \times \nabla'\varphi + \frac{m_s}{\mu} \nabla'\varphi \right) ds'$$

Magnetic vector potential integral equation—curved wire

$$\int_{h_1}^{h_2} \tilde{I}(l', \omega) \left\{ \tilde{G}(l, l', \omega)\, \hat{l} \cdot \hat{l}' + \frac{1}{2} \int_{h_1}^{h_2} \theta\,(\xi - l) \left[\frac{\partial G\,(\xi, l', \omega)}{dl'} + \frac{\partial}{\partial \xi} [(\hat{\xi} \cdot \hat{l}')\, \tilde{G}\,(\xi, l', \omega)] \right] e^{-j(\omega/c)\,|l-\xi|}\, d\xi \right\} dl'$$

$$= \tilde{C}(\omega)\, e^{j(\omega/c)l} + \tilde{D}(\omega)\, e^{-j(\omega/c)l} + \frac{\varepsilon c}{2} \int_{h_1}^{h_2} \tilde{E}_\xi^{\text{inc}}\,(\xi, \omega)\, e^{-j(\omega/c)\,|l-\xi|}\, d\xi$$

Magnetic vector potential integral equation—straight wire

$$\int_{h_1}^{h_2} \tilde{I}\,(l', \omega)\, \tilde{G}\,(l, l', \omega)\, dl' = \tilde{A}(\omega)\, e^{-j(\omega/c)\,l} + \tilde{B}(\omega)\, e^{j(\omega/c)\,l} + \frac{\varepsilon c}{2} \int_{h_1}^{h_2} \tilde{E}_\xi^{\text{inc}}\,(\xi, \omega)\, e^{-j(\omega/c)\,|l-\xi'|}\, d\xi'$$

TABLE 4.2. SPACE–TIME DOMAIN

E-field integral representation

$$\mathbf{E\,(x,} t) = T\mathbf{E}^{\text{inc}}\,(\mathbf{x}, t) - \frac{T}{4\pi} \int_V \left\{ \mu\,\frac{\partial}{\partial\tau}\, \mathbf{J}\,(\mathbf{x}', \tau)\, \frac{1}{|\mathbf{x} - \mathbf{x}'|} - \left[\frac{1}{|\mathbf{x} - \mathbf{x}'|} + \frac{1}{c}\,\frac{\partial}{\partial\tau} \right] \frac{\varrho}{\varepsilon}\, \frac{(\mathbf{x} - \mathbf{x}')}{|\mathbf{x} - \mathbf{x}'|^2} \right.$$

$$+ \left[\frac{1}{|\mathbf{x} - \mathbf{x}'|} + \frac{1}{c}\,\frac{\partial}{\partial\tau} \right] \mathbf{K} \times \frac{(\mathbf{x} - \mathbf{x}')}{|\mathbf{x} - \mathbf{x}'|^2} \right\} dv' - \frac{T}{4\pi} \oint_S \left\{ \mu\,\frac{\partial}{\partial\tau}\, \mathbf{J}_s\,(\mathbf{x}', \tau)\, \frac{1}{|\mathbf{x} - \mathbf{x}'|} \right.$$

$$- \left[\frac{1}{|\mathbf{x} - \mathbf{x}'|} + \frac{1}{c}\,\frac{\partial}{\partial\tau} \right] \frac{\varrho_s}{\varepsilon}\, \frac{(\mathbf{x} - \mathbf{x}')}{|\mathbf{x} - \mathbf{x}'|^2} + \left[\frac{1}{|\mathbf{x} - \mathbf{x}'|} + \frac{1}{c}\,\frac{\partial}{\partial\tau} \right] \mathbf{K}_s \times \frac{(\mathbf{x} - \mathbf{x}')}{|\mathbf{x} - \mathbf{x}'|^2} \right\} ds'$$

H-field integral representation

$$\mathbf{H\,(x,} t) = T\mathbf{H}^{\text{inc}}\,(\mathbf{x}, t) + \frac{T}{4\pi} \int_V \left\{ -\varepsilon\,\frac{\partial}{\partial\tau}\, \mathbf{K}\,(\mathbf{x}', t)\, \frac{1}{|\mathbf{x} - \mathbf{x}'|} + \left[\frac{1}{|\mathbf{x} - \mathbf{x}'|} + \frac{1}{c}\,\frac{\partial}{\partial\tau} \right] \frac{m}{\mu}\, \frac{(\mathbf{x} - \mathbf{x}')}{|\mathbf{x} - \mathbf{x}'|^2} \right.$$

$$+ \left[\frac{1}{|\mathbf{x} - \mathbf{x}'|} + \frac{1}{c}\,\frac{\partial}{\partial\tau} \right] \mathbf{J} \times \frac{(\mathbf{x} - \mathbf{x}')}{|\mathbf{x} - \mathbf{x}'|^2} \right\} dv' + \frac{T}{4\pi} \oint_S \left\{ -\varepsilon\,\frac{\partial}{\partial\tau}\, \mathbf{K}_s\,(\mathbf{x}, \tau)\, \frac{1}{|\mathbf{x} - \mathbf{x}'|} \right.$$

$$+ \left[\frac{1}{|\mathbf{x} - \mathbf{x}'|} + \frac{1}{c}\,\frac{\partial}{\partial\tau} \right] \frac{m_s}{\mu}\, \frac{(\mathbf{x} - \mathbf{x}')}{|\mathbf{x} - \mathbf{x}'|^2} + \left[\frac{1}{|\mathbf{x} - \mathbf{x}'|} + \frac{1}{c}\,\frac{\partial}{\partial\tau} \right] \mathbf{J}_s \times \frac{(\mathbf{x} - \mathbf{x}')}{|\mathbf{x} - \mathbf{x}'|^2} \right\} ds'$$

Magnetic vector potential integral equation—curved wire

$$\int_{h_1}^{h_2} (\hat{l} \cdot \hat{l}') \left. \frac{I(l',\tau)}{4\pi R(l,l')} \right|_{\tau = t - \frac{R(l,l')}{c}} \mathrm{d}l' - \frac{1}{8\pi} \int_{h_1}^{h_2} \int_{h_1}^{h_2} \theta \, (\xi - l)$$

$$\times \left\{ \frac{(\hat{\xi} \cdot \hat{l}') \dfrac{\delta R(\xi,l')}{\delta \xi} + \dfrac{\partial R(\xi,l')}{\partial l'}}{cR(\xi,l')} \frac{\partial}{\partial \tau} I(l',\tau) \right.$$

$$+ \left. \left(\frac{\partial R(\xi,l')}{\partial l'} + (\hat{\xi} \cdot \hat{l}') \frac{\delta R(\xi,l')}{\delta \xi} - R(\xi,l') \frac{\partial (\hat{\xi} \cdot \hat{l}')}{\partial \xi} \right) \frac{I(l,\tau)}{R(\xi,l')^2} \right\}_{t = \tau - \frac{R(\xi,l')}{c} - \frac{|l-\xi|}{c}} \mathrm{d}\xi \, \mathrm{d}l'$$

$$= C \left(t - \frac{l}{c} \right) + D \left(t + \frac{l}{c} \right) + \frac{\varepsilon c}{2} \int_{h_1}^{h_2} E_\xi^{\mathrm{inc}} \left(\xi, t - \frac{|l - \xi|}{c} \right) \mathrm{d}\xi$$

Magnetic vector potential integral equation—straight wire

$$\int_{h_1}^{h_2} \left. \frac{I(s',\tau)}{4\pi R(l,l')} \right|_{\tau = t - \frac{R(l,l')}{c}} \mathrm{d}l' = C \left(t - \frac{l}{c} \right) + D \left(t + \frac{l}{c} \right) + \frac{\varepsilon c}{2} \int_{h_1}^{h_2} E_\xi^{\mathrm{inc}} \left(\xi, t - \frac{|l - \xi|}{c} \right) \mathrm{d}\xi$$

4.3. NUMERICAL SOLUTION METHODS

The mathematical formulations which have been presented are of little use unless they can be reduced to forms which can provide a great deal of information concerning a particular problem. The following sections will be devoted to the consideration of numerical solution techniques and to the presentation of typical results.

The procedure of solving a given problem in electromagnetics may be divided into three basic steps. First, it is necessary to express in mathematical form the relationship between the pertinent physical quantities involved. This mathematical description is accomplished through Maxwell's equations, expressed in either integral or differential form, and in a fashion appropriate to the problem (e.g. allowing for spatial dielectric variation in inhomogeneous media problems, etc.). The characterization is physically rigorous in a macroscopic sense, in that we are not concerned with the field of each elementary particle, but only in the "smoothed-out" field and source distributions. It is, in addition, reasonable for most practical problems of the kind we are concerned with here, to consider a linear, time-invariant medium at rest so that relativistic effects may be neglected and superposition is applicable.

A second step in the solution development involves the introduction of the spatial behavior required of the various field and source quantities over appropriate surfaces. This procedure may utilize various simplifying mathematical approximations which may not be physically exact, but which are reasonable representations of the real physical problem. For example, one might assume a metallic body to be a perfect conductor. The application of boundary or continuity conditions then leads to a mathematical formula relating a desired quantity to a particular excitation. In the previously considered problems, the source of the scattered fields (induced sources) were generally related to a specified exciting field through an integral operator.

The final step in the process of solving a problem whose formal solution has been obtained in step two, is that of reducing the mathematical recipe to numerical result. An intermediate step preceding this may involve re-casting the formal solution into a form more amenable to numerical evaluation. In any case, regardless of the theoretical treatment followed in the formulation, it ultimately becomes necessary for all but the most trivial problems to resort to numerical computation. It is this solution step to which this section is directed.

It must be emphasized that the techniques to be discussed are primarily concerned with the integral equation approach. Although several analytical attacks on a given problem may be feasibly pursued, there may be a significant variation in the computational effort required to obtain results of comparable accuracy. It can probably be expected that optimized solution procedures, whatever the formulation employed, will generally lead to a similar amount of effort to obtain the numerical result. Thus the integral equation approach should be at least competitive with alternative methods, and has in addition the advantage of considerable flexibility. We will discuss the numerical approach below first of all for the frequency domain formulation followed by that for the time domain.

4.3.1. Frequency Domain Solutions

While casting the solution for scattering by arbitrarily shaped surfaces in terms of integral equations is rather straightforward, reduction of the equations to numerical results is not at all trivial. There are storage and running times to be considered even with the latest generation digital computers. Thus, from a practical viewpoint, the range of problems that can be considered is somewhat limited, unless resort is made to simplifying approximations in either the formulation and/or the numerical calculations. Therefore, we consider physically oriented approximations such as physical optics and sparse matrix techniques, useful for the large body case as well as the "numerically rigorous" approach required for resonance region scattering. Consideration will also be given to simplifications resulting from special body geometries, and to various types of numerical accuracy checks.

"NUMERICALLY RIGOROUS" SOLUTIONS

In this section we will be concerned primarily with techniques which have evolved from the method of moments and which have found widespread applicability in the area of electromagnetic scattering. An excellent introduction to the application of this method to electromagnetics is found in Harrington (1967, 1968). A recent paper by Fenlon (1969), who has applied this technique in acoustics, is also quite informative. Much of the recent pioneering work in the use of numerical methods in the solution of the integral equations of electromagnetics can be attributed to Richmond (1965, 1966), Andreasen (1964, 1965), Oshiro (1965), and Mei (1965, 1967). The presentation which follows is based on the work of these and innumerable other workers in the field as well as the authors' experience in applying specific integral equation techniques to problems in electromagnetic theory.

(a) *The method of moments.* It is convenient to represent the magnetic field integral equation (MFIE) and the electric field integral equation (EFIE) in operator notation as

$$L_H\left[\mathbf{J}_s(\mathbf{x}'),\ \mathbf{K}_s(\mathbf{x}')\right] = 2\hat{n}\times\mathbf{H}^{\text{inc}}(\mathbf{x}), \tag{4.43}$$

$$L_E\left[\mathbf{J}_s(\mathbf{x}'),\ \mathbf{K}_s(\mathbf{x}')\right] = 2\hat{n}\times\mathbf{E}^{\text{inc}}(\mathbf{x})$$

where

$$L_E[\ ] = -\mathbf{K}_s(\mathbf{x}) + \frac{1}{2\pi}\,\hat{n}\times\oint_S\left(j\omega\mu\mathbf{J}_s\varphi + \mathbf{K}_s\times\nabla'\varphi - \frac{\varrho_s}{\varepsilon}\,\nabla'\varphi\right)\mathrm{d}s',$$

$$L_H[\ ] = \mathbf{J}_s(\mathbf{x}) - \frac{1}{2\pi}\,\hat{n}\times\oint_S\left(-j\omega\varepsilon\mathbf{K}_s\varphi + \mathbf{J}_s\times\nabla'\varphi + \frac{m_s}{\mu}\,\nabla'\varphi\right)\mathrm{d}s'.$$

Note that use has been made of equivalent surface distributions of sources over the surface S and that the tangential components of eqn. (4.9) are used.

A formal solution to the integral equations of the form shown above, which may be represented by

$$L\left[\mathbf{A}(\mathbf{x}')\right] = \mathbf{B}(\mathbf{x}) \tag{4.44}$$

can be undertaken by the method of moments. This is an intuitively logical approach to the solution of (4.44) which, in its simplest form, amounts to enforcing the integral equation in a weighted integral sense over the range of L and thus generating a set of linear equations for sample values of $\mathbf{A}$ in the domain of L. Depending upon the specific functions employed as representative expansions for the unknown $\mathbf{A}$ and the source $\mathbf{B}$, a great variation in the number of calculations required and the resulting solution accuracy can be expected. The general approach is briefly as follows:

The unknown function is represented by an expansion of basis or trial function as

$$\mathbf{A}(\mathbf{x}) \approx \sum_{n=1}^{N} a_n\,\mathbf{f}_n(\mathbf{x}) \tag{4.45}$$

where the a_n are constants to be determined and the functions $\mathbf{f}_n(\mathbf{x})$ are independent and in the domain of the operator. Upon substitution into the integral equation, a residual error $\varepsilon(\mathbf{x})$ is defined as

$$\varepsilon(\mathbf{x}) = \sum_{n=1}^{N} a_n L\left[\mathbf{f}_n(\mathbf{x})\right] - \mathbf{B}(\mathbf{x}) \tag{4.46}$$

where the summation and integration have been interchanged. If at this stage one defines the inner product over S of two tangential vectors $\mathbf{P}$ and $\mathbf{Q}$ as

$$\langle\mathbf{P},\mathbf{Q}\rangle = \iint_S \mathbf{P}\cdot\mathbf{Q}\,\mathrm{d}a \tag{4.47}$$

one can, by taking the inner product of eqn. (4.46) with a set of M weighting or testing functions $\{\mathbf{W}_m\}$ in the range of the operator L, write

$$\langle\mathbf{W}_m\cdot\varepsilon\rangle \equiv \sum_{n=1}^{N} a_n\,\langle\mathbf{W}_m\cdot L\left[\mathbf{f}_n(\mathbf{x})\right]\rangle - \langle\mathbf{W}_m\cdot\mathbf{B}\rangle \quad m = 1, 2, \ldots, M. \tag{4.48}$$

Furthermore, if the projection of the residual error vector on the space of the weight functions is set to zero, i.e. $\langle \mathbf{W}_m \cdot \boldsymbol{\varepsilon} \rangle = 0$, one has an equation which can be cast in the matrix form

$$[Z][A] = [E] \tag{4.49}$$

where the elements of $[Z]$ are given by

$$Z_{mn} = \langle \mathbf{W}_m \cdot L[\mathbf{f}_n(\mathbf{x})] \rangle$$

and those of $[E]$ are given by

$$E_m = \langle \mathbf{W}_m \cdot \mathbf{B} \rangle.$$

The original integral equation has thus been reduced to a deceptively simple appearing linear system of M equations. If the number of equations does not equal the number of unknown constants associated with the expansion for $\mathbf{A}$, the system can be handled by a standard technique (such as the generation of a generalized inverse). The result will in any case lead to a square coefficient matrix. Provided $[Z]$, which we refer to as an impedance matrix, has an inverse, it is possible to solve for the unknown column vector $[A]$ and hence obtain an approximate solution for the function $\mathbf{A}(\mathbf{x})$ as given by eqn. (4.45).

It should be mentioned at this point that each basis function $\mathbf{f}_n(\mathbf{x})$ need not be defined over the entire domain of L. In fact they might be defined over different subdomains of L so that $\mathbf{f}_n(\mathbf{x})$ would exist only over the nth subdomain. In the case of an integral equation where L is in the form of an integral operator, use of this type of basis functions is equivalent to replacing the integration by a finite Riemann sum where the integrands within each interval Δx_n pertain to only one member of the set $\{\mathbf{f}_n\}$. The notation used to depict this definition is simply

$$\mathbf{A}(\mathbf{x}) = a_n \mathbf{f}_n(\mathbf{x}) \qquad \mathbf{x} \in \Delta x_n \tag{4.50}$$

$$= 0 \qquad\qquad \text{elsewhere}$$

or more compactly,

$$\mathbf{A}(\mathbf{x}) = U(x_n) a_n \mathbf{f}_n(\mathbf{x}) \tag{4.51}$$

with

$$U(\mathbf{x}_n) = 1 \quad \mathbf{x} \in \Delta x_n$$

$$= 0 \quad \text{elsewhere.}$$

For a comprehensive discussion of this and other details such as extensions of the range and domain of the operator, the reader is referred to Harrington (1968).

(b) *Basis functions and weight functions.* It can be seen from eqn. (4.49) that the elements of $[Z]$ involve two surface integrations (the integral appearing in the original integral equation $L[\mathbf{f}_n(\mathbf{x}')]$, plus the inner product integration $\langle \mathbf{W}_m \cdot L[\mathbf{f}_n(\mathbf{x}')]\rangle$) which in general cannot be analytically performed. As a result, the computation time required to obtain the Z_{mn} may be considerable. Consequently, it is usually necessary from an economic viewpoint to choose judiciously the $\mathbf{f}_n$ and $\mathbf{W}_m$ functions satisfactorily to meet the conflicting requirements of solution accuracy and computation cost.

Fenlon (1969) has tabulated some of the more usual pairs of functions used for solving an integral equation. These are included with slight modification in Table 4.3. Methods 3, 4 and 5 alleviate the need for a double surface integration by using delta function weights. In addition, method 4 uses Dirac delta basis functions to eliminate the source integration as

TABLE 4.3. REPRESENTATIVE PAIRS OF FUNCTIONS IN THE METHOD OF MOMENTS

Method	nth term of $\mathbf{A}$	Weight function
1. Galerkin	$a_n \mathbf{f}_n(\mathbf{x})$	$\mathbf{f}_m(\mathbf{x})$
2. Least square	$a_n \mathbf{f}_n(\mathbf{x})$	$Q(\mathbf{x}) \dfrac{\partial \epsilon(\mathbf{x})}{\partial a_m}$
3. General collocation	$a_n \mathbf{f}_n(\mathbf{x})$	$\delta(\mathbf{x} - \mathbf{x}_m)$
4. Point matching	$a_n \delta(\mathbf{x} - \mathbf{x}_n)$	$\delta(\mathbf{x} - \mathbf{x}_m)$
5. Subsectional collocation	$U(\mathbf{x}_n) \sum\limits_{p=1}^{P} a_{np}\mathbf{f}_p(\mathbf{x})$	$\delta(\mathbf{x} - \mathbf{x}_m)$

where $Q(\mathbf{x})$ is a positive definite function of position.

well. Method 5 uses expansions as typified by eqns. (4.50) and (4.51). In the notation used in the table we have allowed the unknown function within each subsection to be represented by some series—hence the presence of the double subscript on the coefficients. This allows some latitude in the way one is to approximate the unknown within a particular Δx_n.

As might be expected, there are tradeoffs to be considered between the various possible methods and the type of problem to be solved, as well as the particular choice of $\mathbf{f}_n$. As mentioned by Harrington (1968), there are infinitely many possible sets of basis functions and weight functions; the pairs listed above are just a few of the more commonly used. For any particular problem, it is desirable to choose the $\mathbf{f}_n$ and $\mathbf{W}_m$ which are well suited to its solution with due consideration given to both the economic and physical aspects.

Generally speaking, the $\mathbf{f}_n$ used should closely match the behavior of the unknown function whose solution is sought. As a simple example, consider the scattering from a thin, circular ring for axial incidence of a plane wave. The current in this case is predominantly directed along the ring circumference and varies as $\sin \varphi$, so that use of $\sin \varphi$ for the basis function is particularly suitable since it allows an accurate solution for the induced current to be obtained with a single delta function weight. On the other hand, a solution obtained using a subsectional bases method would require that the number of boundary match points equal the number of constants required to approximate the $\sin \varphi$ current variation for $0 \le \varphi \le 2\pi$. This could result in a less accurately calculated and less efficiently obtained solution. A similar observation holds for representing the current on a two-wire transmission line, where the basis function $\exp(jks)$ would be very well suited. The simplest three-dimensional surface scatterer that can be considered, a perfectly conducting sphere, would be most efficiently treated using a basis function representation of the form $\sin \varphi \sum_l A_l P_l(\cos \theta)$, since the actual current variation is known to be of this form (Jones, 1964).

A practical problem associated with tailoring the basis functions to the expected variation of the unknown is the decreased flexibility afforded by the resulting computer program or algorithm. In addition, the surface integration required when using the more general basis functions leads to generally intolerable computing times to evaluate the impedance matrix elements. Historically, numerical solutions of surface scattering problems have developed using a simple pulse form for the basis function in a subsectional collocation solution. This corresponds to $\mathbf{f}_n(\mathbf{x}) = U(\mathbf{x}_n)$, where $U(\mathbf{x}_n)$ is defined in (4.51). This type of expansion with delta function weights was used by Oshiro (1965) and Andreasen (1964) as well as many others who have done subsequent work in this area. Unless otherwise indicated, most of the results for surface scatterers presented in this chapter were obtained using this type of expansion.

A more sophisticated approach has been subsequently reported on by Mautz and Harrington (1968) who used a combined subsectional-bases Galerkin's method for rotationally symmetric bodies, with triangular shaped functions for $\mathbf{f}_n$ and $\mathbf{W}_m$ over each overlapping subsection on the structure. In one dimension this leads to a piecewise linear approximation to the unknown.

Another interesting basis function which is commonly used in solutions of the integral equations for thin wires makes use of a sinusoidal interpolation procedure (Yeh and Mei, 1967). This simply involves using a subsectional bases method with a current expansion on each wire segment having the form

$$I(l) = a_i + b_i \cos k\,(l - l_i) + c_i \sin k\,(l - l_i) \quad l \in \varDelta L_i$$

where $\varDelta L_i$ denotes the ith segment. The total number of unknowns for a structure having N segments is reduced from $3N$ to N by an extrapolation technique which leads to two of the three constants for each segment being expressed in terms of the center current values on the adjacent segments. This particular expansion has been found to yield more accurate results with a smaller number of segments than the pulse approximation in the straight wire specialization of both the thin wire electric field integral equation [eqn. (4.20)] and the magnetic vector potential integral equation [eqn. (4.37)]. Evidence is provided by Neureuther et al. (1969) and Poggio and Mayes (1969). It is interesting that essentially the same end is achieved by Harrington (1968) using the thin-wire integro-differential EFIE. The reason is that the differential operators in that integral equation are replaced by a finite difference approximation, a process which implicitly involves similar extrapolation in the derivation of the finite difference formula. For further discussion of weight and basis functions the reader is referred to Chapter 2, Sections 3 and 4.

A further comment regarding the choice of a specific basis function is in order here. It may happen that a basis function being considered does not yield a function in the range of the original integral operator. This situation would require that the operator be suitably approximated or that it be appropriately extended by redefining the operator to apply to new functions not in its original domain (Harrington, 1968). An additional restriction may also be encountered in the weight functions allowable for a given combination of operator and basis functions. Generally, problems of this kind are more to be expected in problems involving differential, rather than integral, operators since integration reduces rather than increases the order of the singularities involved in the problem.

(c) *Operator approximation.* In addition to the approximations involved in representing the unknown **A** in implementing a numerical solution to the integral equation, approximations to the operator itself may also be necessary. Since the integrals required for the calculation of the impedance matrix elements cannot usually be analytically performed, resort must be made to numerical integration or quadrature for their evaluation. Efficient methods for accomplishing this have been presented in Chapter 2. Another self-adaptive technique which is finding widespread use has been described in detail in Miller (1970) and Miller and Burke (1969). This procedure is, of course, equivalent to approximating the integral operator by its Riemann sum. A similar situation holds for the inner product of the weight function with the source and integral terms of the integral equation. When differential operators are also involved in the integral equation, a corresponding approximation may be invoked by replacing the analytic differentiation by a finite difference rule. Note that the forms used for any of these numerical operators to approximate such mathematical operations as integration and differentiation are derived by representing the operand as a polynomial and treating it in an exact fashion.

Because the numerical evaluation of these required surface integrations may represent a predominant portion of the total computer time necessary for the integral equation solution, it is usual to resort to rather coarse integration techniques for computing $L[\mathbf{f}_n]$. Thus, for example, in the original work by Oshiro (1965), using the MFIE and the subsectional collocation method, the surface integration was accomplished using a simple rectangular rule. The integration over each subsectional area (patch) was approximated by the value of the integrand at $\mathbf{x}_n$ multiplied by the patch area and the principal value nature of the integral was approximated by excluding the integration over the patch containing the singularity, i.e. $\mathbf{x}_n = \mathbf{x}_m$. In spite of this seemingly crude approximation to the integral equation operator, it is still possible to obtain reasonable results.

Note that for optimum solution efficiency the approximations made in the integral and differential operators should be similar in order to those used to represent the variation of the unknown. For example, the use of a simple pulse approximation for the current may limit the ultimate numerical accuracy obtainable with a given segmentation scheme such that the use of higher order integration methods to represent more accurately the integral operator will not significantly increase the overall solution accuracy. This area has not received much attention largely because of the expense of performing such computer studies. The formulation of general guidelines pertaining to the basis and weight functions and operator approximations which minimize the computer time for a given measure of solution accuracy would be a useful subject for further study.

(d) *Linear system solution.* A solution of the matrix equation $ZA = E$ representing a finite set of simultaneous equations may be accomplished by a number of schemes (Ralston, 1965; Hildebrand, 1956; Fadeeva, 1959; Householder, 1953). Typical of the methods used to find the components of the vector A are direct matrix inversion, factorization and iteration. The matrix inversion scheme which cast the solution in the form $A = Z^{-1}E$ requires on the order of N^3 operations. Similarly the factorization method, which decomposes the coefficient matrix Z into the product of upper and lower triangular matrices, also requires on the order of N^3 operations. Table 4.4 compares the Gauss–Jordan algorithm for matrix inversion and the Gauss–Doolittle algorithm for matrix solution by factorization (Miller and Maxum, 1970).

TABLE 4.4. COMPARISON OF SOLUTION METHODS

Method	No. multiplications and divisions
Gauss–Jordan	
Inversion: Z^{-1}	$N^3 + O(N^2)*$
Multiplication: $Z^{-1}E$	PN^2
Total	$N^3 + PN^2 + O(N^2)$
Gauss–Doolittle	
Factorization: $Z = LU$	$\frac{1}{3}N^3 + O(N^2)$
Solve: $LF_p = -E$	$P \cdot \frac{1}{2}(N^2 + N)$
Solve: $UI_p = F_p$	$P \cdot \frac{1}{2}(N^2 + N)$
Total	$\frac{1}{3}N^3 + P(N^2 + N)$ $+ O(N^2)$

* The symbol $O(N^2)$ means a polynomial of second order in N.

Efficient iteration solutions require only on the order of N^2 computations and provide a useful alternative for large-dimension matrices where the inversion or factorization times may become so prohibitive as to make these methods impractical. However, the iteration procedure must be repeated with each change in the source vector whereas, once the coefficient matrix has been inverted or factored, the unknown vector A can be found by a process where the number of operations varies with N^2. Should the iteration procedure be slowly convergent, it can ultimately become less efficient than the process involving the inverse matrix.

It can be seen from Table 4.4 that factorization is about three times more efficient than inversion in terms of computer time or number of operations. Both cases, however, require about the same amount of computer storage. Hence factorization is generally preferred when iteration is not used. In some cases the generation of an explicit inverse may still be desirable. If, for instance, the coefficient or impedance matrix in an electromagnetics problem is inverted, then the mutual admittance between each of the structure segments is directly available. However, the choice of the particular solution method must eventually be determined by the requirements of the problem under consideration.

It should be emphasized that factorization or inversion of the impedance matrix produces an electromagnetic characterization of the structure which is source independent. Consequently, the admittance matrix which is obtained can be applied to both scattering and antenna problems. Thus the validity of the numerical approach can be established for a given structure by comparison with independent scattering and/or antenna results. The majority of the results to be shown in the application section will be devoted to scattering examples, but in those cases for which only antenna data are available, or where an additional validity check may be useful, some antenna calculations are also included.

SIMPLIFYING APPROXIMATIONS

When resonance region structures are being considered (i.e. $ka \sim \pi$ where a is a characteristic dimension of the structure), the numerical procedure outlined above is economically practical for the solution of the problem. Thus, except for the approximations inherent in using the moment method to reduce the integral equation to a linear system, no other approximations need be resorted to in order to obtain numerical results at acceptable computer costs.

However, for methods using factorization or inversion the computer time depends upon the number of unknowns N as

$$T_c \approx AN^2 + BN^3 \qquad (4.52)$$

where the N^2 term accounts for the impedance matrix calculation and the N^3 term for its solution. Furthermore, since N varies as $(ka)^2$, the computer time in terms of a pertinent dimension to wavelength ratio is given by

$$T_c = A'(ka)^4 + B'(ka)^6.$$

Obviously, there is an upper limit to ka beyond which solutions via factorization or inversion can no longer be seriously considered. Indeed the time required for iteration might even become too large. And we have not even addressed the problem of core storage which certainly limits the applicability of any of the mentioned matrix solution techniques since N (the number of samples) varies as $(ka)^2$. It thus becomes necessary to restrict attention for large ka values to bodies having sufficient symmetry to reduce the computer time to acceptable values (this will be discussed below) or to accept the necessity for approximations which significantly reduce the high-order dependence of T_c on ka. Some commonly used approaches to accomplish the latter are briefly examined below. Since large body scattering and the specialized techniques used to handle it are major subject areas in their own right, the following discussion is necessarily only a brief summary of this important topic.

(a) *Physical optics approximations.* The well-known physical optics (PO) current $\mathbf{J}_s = 2\hat{n} \times \mathbf{H}^{inc}$ has long been used for evaluating the scattering properties of large objects such as reflector antennas. In the context of the MFIE, this solution results from completely neglecting mutual interaction effects, as represented by the integral term, on the illuminated portion of the scatterer, and further implies that in the shadow region the mutual interaction which occurs through the integral term completely cancels the incident field term.

The PO current for the conducting body is thus expressed by

$$\mathbf{J}_{po} = \begin{cases} 2\hat{n} \times \mathbf{H}^{inc} & \text{illuminated region} \\ 0 & \text{shadow region} \end{cases} \qquad (4.53)$$

so that the scattered field due to $\mathbf{J}_{po}$ can be explicitly written in terms of the incident field as

$$\mathbf{H}_{po}^s = \frac{1}{4\pi} \int_I \mathbf{J}_{po} \times \nabla'\varphi \, ds'.$$

P.O. is nothing but the main diagonal

Thus $\mathbf{H}_{po}^{s}$ can be explicitly written in terms of the incident field as

$$\mathbf{H}_{po}^{s} = \frac{1}{2\pi} \int_{I} (\hat{n}' \times \mathbf{H}^{inc}) \times \nabla' \varphi \, ds'$$

where $\int_{I}$ denotes an integral over the illuminated portion of the target. Expression (4.53) is commonly known as the vector Kirchoff approximation and has been widely used in the evaluation of large reflector antennas.

The most time-consuming steps in the solution for the surface current using an integral equation approach have been shown to be the matrix fill and matrix solution procedures. The physical optics approximation entirely eliminates these steps and allows the direct evaluation of $\mathbf{J}$ from a knowledge of the scatterer's geometry and orientation with respect to the incident wave. Both approaches necessitate, however, the integration over the surface current distribution on the scatterer to find the scattered field.

Various degrees of physical optics-type approximations which lie between the two extremes represented by numerically rigorous solution for the induced current and the PO solution may be used in an attempt more accurately to obtain the current. One of the short-comings of the PO approximations is its inability accurately to represent the current near the terminator (the illuminated region—shadow boundary). This can be a source of significant error because of the abrupt discontinuity in current which occurs. A typical way to circumvent this difficulty is to use a "pseudo" PO approximation which employs the standard PO current for the illuminated portion of the scatterer, but uses the integral equation to find the current in the shadow region. Thus

$$\mathbf{J}_{s} = \begin{cases} 2\hat{n} \times \mathbf{H}^{inc}; \quad \text{illuminated region} \\[2ex] 2\hat{n} \times \mathbf{H}^{inc} + \dfrac{1}{2\pi} \hat{n} \times \left[\displaystyle\int_{U} \mathbf{J}_{s} \times \nabla' \varphi \, ds' + \int_{I} (2\hat{n}' \times \mathbf{H}^{inc}) \times \nabla' \varphi \, ds' \right]; \quad \text{shadow region} \end{cases}$$

$$(4.54)$$

where the integral equation for the shadow region currents makes use of the already determined PO currents on the illuminated region to reduce the number of unknowns and $\int_{U}$ denotes an integral over the shadow region. Since, however, the geometry of the shadow region is aspect dependent relative to the incident wave, this method sacrifices the great advantage of the "rigorous" integral equation solution where the matrix representation is source independent.

This modified PO approach allows greater accuracy to be obtained by more careful handling of the current near the terminator. It should be noted that the shadow region solution does not necessarily have to encompass the entire shadow region of the scatterer, but can be restricted to the area near the terminator where the current is largest for large bodies. Thus the order of the linear system for the unknown currents can be further decreased beyond the factor of 2 which is roughly the case when the entire shadow region current distribution is sought.

(b) *Geometrical optics.* Geometrical optics assumes that scattering follows the laws of ray optics, i.e. the incident and reflected rays are coplanar and the local angles of incidence and reflection are equal. This is equivalent to assuming that each point on the scatterer reflects as if it were on an infinite tangent plane at the point of reflection. Thus, in the absence of a specular point for a given scattering direction geometric optics predicts that the field scattered in that direction is zero. The same reasoning can be applied to scatterers which allow multiple reflections. In that case, a given ray must be traced as it undergoes each reflection to determine whether it contributes to the return in a particular direction.

Beckmann (1968) points out that geometric optics approximates the scattered field while physical optics approximates the sources of the scattered field. The former case assumes that the induced sources are locally similar to those excited by a wave impinging on an infinite tangent plane. These sources then radiate in all directions quite unlike the geometric optics prediction. Beckmann also points out that a sufficient condition for the validity of physical optics is that $\lambda^2 \ll \varrho^2$, where ϱ is the surface radius of curvature, while geometric optics requires not only $\sqrt{\lambda} \ll \sqrt{\varrho}$, but also a dominant specular reflection contribution to the scattered wave.

Work has been done in recent years to extend the regions of validity of physical and geometric optics to include edges and terminator effects. The geometrical theory of diffraction as developed by Keller (1962) makes use of knowledge of rigorous solutions for scattering by canonical shapes to establish a connection between the rigorous solution and the approximate solution (physical or geometric optics). Keller's theory allows one to construct the total scattered field from the various fields contributed by the individual canonical forms comprising a body. Ufimtsev (1962), following a similar reasoning procedure, allows calculation of the induced surface currents which are due to various types of discontinuities. This is essentially the primary difference between the approaches due to Keller and Ufimtsev. Beckmann comments that Ufimtsev has "reformed" physical optics while Keller has "reformed" geometric optics.

Geometric optics and the geometrical theory of diffraction have not been used extensively in numerical computations for large scatterers. One of the reasons may be the difficulty involved in following rays and storing the proper information in the computer.

Since a detailed investigation of these types of approximations is beyond the scope of this work, the interested reader is referred to Beckmann (1968), Keller (1962), Ufimtsev (1962), Bechtel (1965), Ross (1966), Ross and Bechtel (1966), and Kouyoumjian (1966).

(c) *Other approximations.* The more familiar approximations used for large ka problems, physical optics and geometrical optics, have been mentioned above. In this section we discuss other approximate methods which may not be as well known. Two of these, the sparse matrix approach and iteration solutions, are natural simplifications of the integral equation approach, whereas the composite simple scatterer method derives from optics region scattering formulae.

(i) *Sparse matrix.* The impedance matrix which is derived from an integral equation accounts for the mutual interaction which occurs between pairs of segments or surface areas on the structure under consideration. As such, the magnitudes of these terms tends to decrease with increasing separation distance between them. It thus seems intuitive that neglect of this mutual interaction between points sufficiently separated on the structure, or the setting to zero of impedance terms small relative to the major (diagonal or self) terms, would not significantly degrade the numerical solution.

The motivation for using this kind of approximation is that the resulting impedance matrix will have a large number of zeros; the larger the structure, the greater the proportion of zeros. As a result, this sparse matrix can be solved by a variety of standard techniques more efficiently than can the original matrix. At the same time, the storage requirements are reduced and, of course, the time required for calculating the impedance matrix can also be substantially decreased. In spite of the advantage offered by the sparse matrix technique, it does not appear to have been applied very extensively to electromagnetic problems, although methods for solving sparse systems have been widely studied in connection with large linear systems, potential equation solutions, etc. (Willoughby, 1969).

(ii) *Iteration solutions.* Strictly speaking, iteration methods need not be considered as approximations, since in principal, the iteration process, if convergent, can be repeated until the solution vector stabilizes to a desired number of significant figures. However, in practical application the iteration technique is repeated only to the point at which the specified solution accuracy is obtained. Consequently, the accuracy achieved may vary considerably from that which would derive from matrix inversion.

The advantage provided by iteration is that a solution is obtained with on the order of N^2 multiplications versus N^3 for inversion or factorization. It may be readily appreciated that the consequent saving in solution time is extremely significant for large structures. This result is not realized without some sacrifice in generality, however, since the solution is obtained for only one specific source. Thus the method is potentially more useful for antenna problems where the bistatic pattern is required for one source distribution, as contrasted with the calculation of the monostatic cross section, where the current distribution is required for each incidence angle. A combination of the iteration solution method with the sparse matrix approach may offer a particularly useful technique for the treatment of large body antenna problems.

In order to demonstrate more clearly the relationship between matrix inversion and iteration, a restatement of the preceding discussion in mathematical terms may be in order. Consider an N-port network such that

$$\sum_{j=1}^{N} Z_{ij} I_j = V_i; \qquad (4.55)$$
$$i = 1, \ldots, N$$
$$\sum_{j=1}^{N} Y_{ij} V_j = I_i; \qquad (4.56)$$

where Z and Y are the impedance and admittance matrices respectively. (Note that these equations are exactly analogous to the linear system representation of the integral equations for the induced current on a perfectly conducting structure.)

A direct solution of (4.55) for I requires that

$$Y = Z^{-1} \qquad (4.57)$$

be obtained. Thus, the N^2 admittance values are obtained, explicitly if the inverse of Z is calculated, implicitly if factorization is used. If iteration is chosen instead, a sequence of source vectors $V^{(1)}, \ldots, V^{(n)}$, will lead to a corresponding sequence of solution vector $I^{(1)}, \ldots, I^{(n)}$ which can be expressed as

$$I_i^{(p)} = \sum_{j=1}^{N} Y_{ij}V_j^{(p)}; \quad i, p = 1, \ldots, N \tag{4.58}$$

or equivalently

$$\mathbf{I}_{ip} = \sum_{j=1}^{N} Y_{ij}\mathbf{V}_{jp}$$

where the N column vectors $I^{(p)}$, $V^{(p)}$ form the $N \times N$ matrices $\mathbf{I}$ and $\mathbf{V}$ respectively.
    Then we formally obtain

$$Y_{ij} = \sum_{p=1}^{N} \mathbf{I}_{ip}(\mathbf{V})_{pj}^{-1} \tag{4.59}$$

where $(\mathbf{V})^{-1}$ is the inverse of V. Clearly, if the $\mathbf{V}^{(n)}$ are chosen such that V is the identity matrix, the corresponding solution current vector provides the N admittances for the driven port. However, for an arbitrary sequence of $\mathbf{V}^{(n)}$, such as a monostatic scattering calculation would produce, the current vectors are not so simply related to the admittances, but are linear combinations thereof, as shown by (4.58). Even in the latter case, however, it is possible as shown by (4.59) to obtain the N^2 admittances from the iteration solution of N current vectors. Thus, iteration allows a generation of the complete admittance matrix, but unless this is accomplished using the identity matrix for $\mathbf{V}$ (i.e. a port at a time), the iteration procedure is less efficient than inversion of Z.

(iii) *Composite simple scatterer.* An approach to predict large, complex body RCS was pioneered by Siegel and his co-workers at the University of Michigan Radiation Laboratory (Siegel *et al.*, 1968). This approach involves the decomposition of the complex body into a number of simple shapes each of which approximates to the degree required that part of the body which it is intended to model. The known scattering characteristics of these basic shapes, usually deduced from geometric optics and/or empirically derived and available in closed form expressions, are then combined to obtain the composite body scattering properties. Note that the interaction of the various portions is neglected. This straightforward approach has been remarkably successful and today still represents a viable alternative for the analysis of large body RCS.

SIMPLIFICATIONS DUE TO STRUCTURE GEOMETRY

    When dealing with an asymmetric structure, the impedance matrix [Z] must be calculated and the entire Nth order linear system solved for the N unknown currents. (The implication of this in terms of the reciprocal nature of Maxwell's equations is discussed in the next section.) Structures having symmetries can be more efficiently handled, however, since the impedance matrix then possesses a known periodicity which allows filling the entire matrix from a subset of its elements. The symmetry can be further exploited when the source has symmetries in common with those of the structure since the number of unknowns can also then be reduced.

Perhaps the most obvious kind of symmetry is that exhibited by a body whose surface is formed by rotating a curved line about some axis. This rotational symmetry allows the current variation in the direction on the surface orthogonal to the rotation axis (azimuthal direction) to be expanded in a Fourier series in the azimuthal angle. Due to the orthogonality of this basis function representation for the various modes in the series expansion, a solution for the modal current amplitudes as a function of surface position along the rotation axis (axial direction) is possible on a mode-by-mode basis. Thus the linear system solution time can be greatly reduced since the matrix order is now determined by the number of sample points required along the axial direction, which is a linear, rather than quadratic, function of body size. In addition, the impedance matrix elements are also required to be calculated along only one axial observation strip on the body, the remainder being derived as permutations of those already obtained. When, in addition, the incident plane wave is along the body axis, only a single current mode is excited, an example of source-body symmetry, further decreasing the computer time involved. Symmetries of the types mentioned have been exploited by Andreasen (1964) and Mautz and Harrington (1968, 1969).

Mirror or plane symmetry, where a structure has one to three perpendicular planes of mirror symmetry, provides a second type of symmetry which can be exploited to reduce the overall computer time required. Consider as an example a metallic, rectangular parallelopiped. This structure has three orthogonal symmetry planes, and it may be shown that the impedance matrix is completely determined by those rows of Z_{mn} for one congruent piece of the structure, thus saving a factor of 2^3 or 8 in matrix fill time. In addition, the subsequent linear system solution time is decreased by a factor on the order of 8^2 since 8 matrices of order $N/8$ replace the original Nth order impedance matrix. Finally, for wave incidence in one of the symmetry planes or along an intersection line of two symmetry planes, the currents also possess a symmetry thus reducing the number of current elements requiring explicit solution to completely determine the surface current distribution. Descriptions of this type of symmetry and its application can be found in Oshiro and Su (1965) and Mitzner (1969).

A third type of symmetry which has characteristics of both rotational and mirror symmetry calculations is that of planar or discrete angular symmetry such as exhibited by a regular polygon. Discrete angular symmetry results in a periodic impedance matrix with the number of periods equal to the number of similar bands or sides which comprise the structure. If the structure has P periods, the matrix fill time is thus reduced by P^{-1}, while the linear solution process can be reduced to the solution of P matrices of order N/P, thereby decreasing this time by P^{-2}. For source-structure configurations which possess common symmetries, resulting in symmetric current distributions, the current calculation is shortened as well. Axial incidence of a plane wave on a discrete angular symmetry structure, for example, requires only one sub-matrix to be solved, a situation analogous to that found for the continuous rotationally symmetric structure for axial incidence. Thus the P sub-matrices in the case of the discrete angular symmetric structure serve a role similar to that of the various Fourier modes for the structure having continuous rotational symmetry. It should be mentioned that discrete angular symmetry perhaps finds its great usefulness in using the thin-wire EFIE for analyzing wire grid models of solid surfaces, and thin-wire structures as well. A description of the process used in the inversion of an impedance matrix with this particular type of symmetry is found in Cheng and Tseng (1969).

ACCURACY CHECKS

The credibility of numerical results for RCS, antenna radiation patterns, etc., which have been obtained from computer solutions of integral equations of the type being considered here must be established before the technique can be confidently used. In this regard it should be emphasized that a demonstration of the numerical accuracy for one scattering structure cannot be relied upon to indicate the validity for arbitrary shapes, so that each class of structure geometries has to be separately considered. Since the complexity and analytic irreducibility of the problem necessitates starting the numerical calculations at a point where relatively little insight is available into the nature of the solution, it is desirable to have recourse to independent validity checks which may be analytical, numerical, or experimental.

Analytic solutions are available for only a few simple shapes, so that they can be used to provide checks for only a few structure geometries. Numerical solutions obtained by independent means, for example using a differential equation approach or a time domain analysis, also can serve as validity checks and are of course not restricted in application to a few geometries. Comparison of independent numerical solutions is less definitive than the analytic solution check, however, since in case of disagreement between the numerical results there is no certainty about which solution, if either, is correct.

Perhaps the most convincing validity check of all, especially to those who are of a more practical bent and not so oriented to computer usage, is a comparison with experimental measurement. It is unfortunately true that precise enough experimental data are not always readily available to validate the calculations, and further, that when there are discrepancies between experiment and calculated data, it is quite often (and also unfortunately often well founded) that the experiment will, whatever its merits, be given more confidence than the numerical result. In many cases, the discrepancies which arise are due to experimental conditions which are not included in the numerical model, such as dielectric model supports, etc. And while the experimental range may be capable of acceptable accuracy, careless or improper measurement procedures can significantly degrade the accuracy of a given piece of data. It consequently behooves the numerical analyst to become acquainted with the experimental procedures and operations if the measured data are to serve as a standard against which the calculated results will be checked.

The validity checks mentioned above are external in nature, that is, independent of the calculation whose results are being evaluated. There also exist various types of internal consistency checks which can be used to ascertain the likely degree of accuracy of the computed results. Among the more easily applied are those pertaining to reciprocity and energy conservation. Reciprocity in the bistatic scattering pattern of a structure or between its transmitting and receiving patterns when operated as an antenna, is required of valid solutions to Maxwell's equations for linear, passive media. Such checks are readily carried out once the admittance matrix has been obtained for the structure. While reciprocity is a necessary property of a valid solution, it alone is not sufficient to establish this fact, because reciprocity is inherently preserved in the numerical solution.

A similar situation holds with regard to energy conservation (Amitay and Galindo, 1969). Thus a Poynting's vector integral over a closed surface surrounding a perfectly conducting scatterer to check that the net power flow is zero is also a necessary but not sufficient condition to verify the solution accuracy. In spite of these limitations, both reciprocity and energy-conservation calculations provide useful indicators of numerical accuracy, and can be employed to estimate the relative validity of solutions.

Another internal program check which can feasibly be used to evaluate solution validity is furnished by the boundary conditions on the fields over the structure's surface. Determination of the actual total tangential electric field on the surface of a perfect conductor from the calculated current distribution and comparison with the exciting field strength serves also to establish the degree of accuracy. The total field, of course, can be expected identically to satisfy the required boundary conditions at observation points. By integrating some measure of this total field at scattered points other than observation points, and comparing the result with the corresponding value for the source field, an indication of the current distribution accuracy is obtainable. Unfortunately, this kind of check calculation would require more computer time to accomplish than that originally needed to compute the impedance matrix. Consequently, its use would necessarily be rather limited, perhaps to establishing guidelines for the modeling of different classes of structures or to examine the boundary condition agreement in the more critical structure areas such as near corners, points, etc.

4.3.2. Time-domain Solutions

The electromagnetic impulse response of a scatterer is one of the most useful results to be obtained from a time-domain analysis. Knowledge of the impulse response allows the computation of the scattering transients produced by an arbitrary time-varying excitation field by use of the convolution integral. In addition, application of a Fourier transform to the impulse response leads to the spectral or frequency domain characteristics. One other practical use of this transient behavior is the analysis of broadband radar returns wherein the impulse response can serve as a "signature" for target identification.

A number of different approaches have been used in efforts to obtain the response of various scatterers to impulse excitation. The physical optics approximation was evidently first employed by Kennaugh and Cosgriff (1958) to calculate the monostatic far-field impulse response of a rectangular plate, a spheroid, and a sphere. Further extensions of the physical optics approach were carried out in a series of papers by Kennaugh and Moffatt (1962, 1965). More recently Rheinstein (1968) has presented a rigorously computed short-pulse response of both conducting and dielectric spheres using the Mie series frequency domain results. Time-domain scattering analyses have also been performed in the area of acoustics. A summary of work up to 1958 is given by Friedlaender (1958). Sound pulse diffraction by infinite length, arbitrary cross-section cylinders has been considered by Friedman and Shaw (1962), while transient scattering by rigid spheres has been studied by Soules and Mitzner (1967).

The work to date in time domain scattering can be separated into a number of classes. In one category are those analyses which proceed from a calculated frequency response of the scatterer to synthesize the time domain response for a specified excitation. Within this category are two separate approaches, one of which uses analytical frequency domain solutions and as such is limited in scope. The other approach makes use of numerically evaluated frequency domain solutions using techniques such as those previously described. Another category includes those analyses which employ approximations to the frequency domain response such as physical and geometrical optics. Naturally this particular approach suffers from the shortcomings described in the previous section but does indeed find great use at high frequencies.

A third method for obtaining the impulse response of scatterers is one which originates from a strictly time domain viewpoint. This method has been applied to acoustics by Soules and Mitzner (1967) and to electromagnetics problems by Bennett and Weeks (1968, 1969) and Sayre and Harrington (1968). It is to this particular approach which uses the time-domain integral equations that we will devote our attention in the remainder of this section. Portions of the discussion below follow Bennett and Weeks (1968, 1969).

"NUMERICALLY RIGOROUS" SOLUTIONS

In the following discussions our attention will be limited to perfectly conducting scatterers. As a result we will be dealing with equations of the form given by (4.38). Furthermore, we will focus our attention on the magnetic field integral equation in the time domain which falls in the class of Fredholm integral equations of the second kind. Hence we will study the numerical solution of

$$\mathbf{J}_s(\mathbf{x},t) = 2\hat{n} \times \mathbf{H}^{\text{inc}}(\mathbf{x},t) + \frac{1}{2\pi} \hat{n} \times \oint_S \left[\frac{1}{c}\frac{\partial}{\partial\tau}\mathbf{J}_s(\mathbf{x}',\tau) + \mathbf{J}_s(\mathbf{x}',\tau)\frac{1}{|\mathbf{x}-\mathbf{x}'|} \right] \times \frac{(\mathbf{x}-\mathbf{x}')}{|\mathbf{x}-\mathbf{x}'|^2}\, ds$$

$$(4.60)$$

where the retarded time τ is given by $\tau = t - |\mathbf{x}-\mathbf{x}'|/c$ and the interpretation of the operator $\partial/\partial\tau$ is provided in the discussion following (4.35).

Before proceeding to a discussion of the method used for solving eqn. (4.60) for $\mathbf{J}_s$, it is worthwhile to comment on some of the features it exhibits. We note first of all that the $2\hat{n} \times \mathbf{H}^{\text{inc}}(\mathbf{x},t)$ term corresponds to the usual physical optics approximation on the illuminated portion of the scatterer. However, the incident field term is also applied to the shadow region where the normal physical optics current is zero. Nevertheless, the presence of a pseudo-physical optics term in eqn. (4.60) is illuminating in suggesting a method for an extension to include the higher frequency components of the incident field without increasing the calculation time.

As a second point we observe that eqn. (4.60) represents a system of three coupled scalar integral equations for the three components of $\mathbf{J}_s$ but since

$$\hat{n} \cdot \mathbf{J}_s(\mathbf{x},t) = 0$$

we are able to reduce the number of independent equations to two. It may be also observed that if the observation point $\mathbf{x}$ lies on the same surface plane as the source $\mathbf{x}'$ then the integral in eqn. (4.60) contributes nothing to the equation. Consequently there is no direct mutual interaction between elements of current flowing on the same planar surface.

Finally, it should be noted that the effect of the source current at $\mathbf{x}'$ is delayed by a time $|\mathbf{x} - \mathbf{x}'|/c$ in affecting the current at the observation point $\mathbf{x}$. This retardation effect is especially important, since it allows solution of the equation for the current without inverting a matrix as is required for the numerical solution of the frequency domain integral equation. Actually, the surface current $\mathbf{J}_s$ may be determined by a "stepping on" procedure in time, since the current at time t is given in terms of the known incident field at that time and the current on other portions of the scatterer at prior times which have already been calculated. This phenomena can perhaps be best visualized by considering the space-time cone in two dimensions as shown in Fig. 4.8. The region of interaction is denoted by the shaded area and is defined by $ct - |\mathbf{x} - \mathbf{x}'| < 0$.

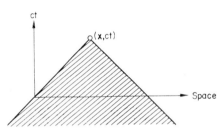

FIG. 4.8. The space–time cone.

The method of moments as described in Section 4.3.1 can be applied to the solution of eqn. (4.60). By choosing Dirac delta functions for weight functions in both the space and time coordinates such that

$$W_{ij} = \delta(\mathbf{x} - \mathbf{x}_i)\,\delta(t - t_j)$$

one can reduce eqn. (4.60) to the form

$$\mathbf{J}_s(\mathbf{x}_i, t_j) = 2\hat{n} \times \mathbf{H}^{\text{inc}}(\mathbf{x}_i, t_j) + \frac{1}{2\pi}\,\hat{n} \times \int_S \left[\frac{1}{c}\frac{\partial}{\partial\tau}\mathbf{J}_s(\mathbf{x}', \tau) + \mathbf{J}_s(\mathbf{x}', \tau)\frac{1}{|\mathbf{x}_i - \mathbf{x}'|}\right]$$

$$\times \frac{(\mathbf{x}_i - \mathbf{x}')}{|\mathbf{x}_i - \mathbf{x}'|^2}\,ds' \tag{4.61}$$

$$\tau = t_j - \frac{|\mathbf{x}_i - \mathbf{x}'|}{c}; \quad i = 1, 2, \ldots, N_s; \quad j = 1, 2, \ldots, N_T.$$

A further simplification arises by replacing the integral over the surface by its finite Riemann sum over N_s surface elements.

If one postulates that the incident field and all surface currents on S are zero for all time less than t_0, then the retarded time τ allows us to start the solution at time t_0 and to view the integral equation as an initial value problem. For instance, let us assume that at time t_1 the incident field has just reached the scatterer. By virtue of the retardation (see the time cone) and the principal value nature of the integral, a current is induced on part of the scatterer which is equal to $2\hat{n} \times \mathbf{H}^{\text{inc}}(\mathbf{x}_1, t_1)$. As the time progresses further to t_2 the current at each point is then given by the known incident field $2\hat{n} \times \mathbf{H}^{inc}(\mathbf{x}, t_2)$ plus a contribution from currents at other points on the scatterer (a contribution represented by the integral) at earlier times which is also known. Thus marching on in time will allow us to build up the current solution from previously known values.

While the solution process as described appears to be relatively straightforward, one must still consider the need for segmentation in both the space and time coordinates. Since an integration is performed in the space coordinate, subsectional collocation with a pulse approximation in space and time can be used as an illustration. The current can therefore be written as

$$\mathbf{J}_s(\mathbf{x}, t) = \sum_{m=1}^{N_s} \sum_{n=1}^{N_T} \mathbf{A}_{mn} V(\mathbf{x}_m) U(t_n) \tag{4.62}$$

where

$$V(\mathbf{x}_m) \begin{matrix} = 1 & \text{for } \mathbf{x} \text{ on the surface segment centered at } \mathbf{x}_m, \\ = 0 & \text{elsewhere;} \end{matrix}$$

$$U(t_n) \begin{matrix} = 1 & \text{for } t \text{ in the time interval centered at } t_n, \\ = 0 & \text{elsewhere.} \end{matrix}$$

The $\mathbf{A}_{mn}$ are the current amplitudes in space-time at (x_m, t_n) which are found by solving the integral equation and N_s and N_T are the total number of space and time samples of current, respectively.

Consideration must be given at this point to the selection of both the appropriate space sample points on the scatterer and to the time sample points. Among the factors which determine the sequence of current samples to be used in the numerical solution are the shape and width of the incident field pulse, the scatterer size relative to the pulse width, and the highest frequency information which is desired in transforming the time response of the scatterer to the frequency domain.

The scatterer sample points are required to be close enough together on the scatterer surface that the spatial variation of the incident pulse is adequately resolved as it propagates past the scatterer. This requirement is closely related to the high frequency constraint mentioned above, in that the more rapidly the incident pulse is changing as a function of time (or, equivalently, as a function of position), the relatively greater portion of its energy which is concentrated at the higher frequencies (or higher ka values). This point will recur in discussing the specific incident pulse shape which has been used in the time domain calculations thus far carried out.

The sample points in time are not independent of the space sample points used. Besides the connection between them which arises from requiring the time samples to resolve the incident field adequately in time as the space sample points must resolve the spatial variation, there is a correlation required because of the equivalence between space and time in the retardation effect. Since it is highly desirable to exploit the property that a current sample on a given part of the scatterer is determined by known currents and fields, we conclude that the time sample spacing ΔT must be related to the space sample spacing ΔR by

$$c \, \Delta T \leq \Delta R. \tag{4.63}$$

If the inequality (4.63) were not satisfied, then it is apparent that the current at one sample point on the scatterer would be dependent upon the adjacent (in space) current sample in the same time interval. This possibility arises solely because of the necessity of finding the current at discrete points in space and time. The inequality is equivalent to requiring that the space sample points be at least as far apart as the distance the electromagnetic field, propagating at the speed of light, travels in the interval between two sample points in time. Note that (4.63) can be relaxed if the current interaction within a time step is properly allowed for in representing the integral equation as a linear system. The advantage of no matrix inversion requirement would be lost, however.

Having considered the general problem of the space–time representation of the current, we can now turn to a specification of the incident field itself. Up to this point we have not restricted the incident field in any way except to require that it has reached the scatterer at some finite time in the past. It has been pointed out in the previous discussion that the incident field of probably greatest usefulness is the plane space-time impulse, since the impulse response of a scatterer allows the determination of the scatterer response to any other plane incident field. Since we are unable from a practical standpoint of computer time, to consider an actual delta function space–time impulse whose frequency spectrum extends from zero to infinity with uniform amplitude, we must instead use an approximate impulse for the incident field. The gaussian impulse, given by

$$\delta_g(t) = \frac{g}{\sqrt{\pi}} \exp\left(-g^2 t^2\right),$$

was chosen for this purpose, since it rapidly decays to zero, and its Fourier transform given by

$$A_g(\omega) = F\{\delta_g(t)\} = \exp\left(-\omega^2/4g^2\right)$$

may be observed to exhibit a rapidly decreasing amplitude with increasing frequency. It may be seen that the high-frequency content of $\delta_g(t)$ is directly proportional to g.

Under the gaussian pulse assumption, incident fields are then conveniently expressed in a cartesian coordinate system and without loss of generality for wave propagation in the z-direction as

$$\mathbf{H}^{inc}(\mathbf{x}, t) = \hat{y}\,(g/\sqrt{\pi}) \exp\left[-g^2\,(t - z/c)^2\right]$$

and

$$\mathbf{E}^{inc}(\mathbf{x}, t) = \hat{x}\,(g/\sqrt{\pi}) \exp\left[-g^2\,(t - z/c)^2\right]$$

where $\hat{x}$ and $\hat{y}$ denote unit vectors in the x and y directions respectively. We note that the incident field has equal derivatives with respect to ct and z. This implies that adjacent space and time current samples should be separated in such a way that

$$c\,\Delta T \sim \Delta z$$

in order to obtain comparable space and time resolution of the incident pulse. This requirement is compatible with eqn. (4.63) since for two adjacent surface sample points,

$$\Delta R \geq \Delta z.$$

The absolute values of the spacings ΔR and ΔT to be used are determined by the parameter g. It may be seen that the $1/e$ points of the incident pulse are separated in time by

$$-(1/g) \le t \le (1/g)$$

and in space are separated by

$$-(c/g) \le z \le (c/g).$$

The pulse widths are then $W_T = 2/g$ and $W_S = 2c/g$ in time and space, respectively. The appropriate sample spacings which result in reasonably accurate numerical results have been found to be on the order of one-fifth the pulse width, so that

$$\Delta T \sim (2/g)/5 = 0.4/g$$

and

$$\Delta R \ge (2/g)\,c/5 = 0.4c/g.$$

The significance of these equations to the practical problem of determining the highest frequency for which useful frequency domain results can be obtained from the approximate impulse response is then readily determined. If we consider the case of the sphere, and recall that the minimum number of sample points per wavelength which can be used for accurate results is approximately four, then we find, where a is the sphere radius, that

$$ka \approx (\pi/2)\,a/\Delta R < \pi g a/c$$

is the largest ka value for which the time domain information will be useful. Alternatively the shortest wavelength for useful information is

$$\lambda \approx \Delta R/4.$$

The relationship between the physical size of the scatterer and the pulse width is thus demonstrated. It may be seen that the most significant parameter is not the scatterer size or the pulse size but the ratio of these two, since,

$$ka \le 2\pi a/W_S.$$

The most straightforward approach to the numerical evaluation of the integral portion of eqn. (4.61) is the use of the rectangular rule. This simply involves replacing the integral by a sum of the sampled current values, each of which is multiplied by the product of the segmental area in which the current sample is located times the kernel of the integrand evaluated at the center of the same segmental area. This rather crude, but acceptably accurate, method was used in obtaining the results to be presented below. Besides the demonstrated accuracy of the numerical results, the use of the rectangular rule is consistent with employment of constant current values on each segmental area of the scatterer. However, more efficient calculations could be obtained by integrating the kernel of the integral within each segmental area of the scatterer while removing the constant current term outside the integral for that segmental area.

A concern of the numerical solution of eqn. (4.61) is the required evaluation of the time derivative of the surface current. This can be conveniently accomplished using the method of finite differences where the differentiation has been performed by analytically differentiating a polynomial approximation to the time variation of the current at the source point. The polynomial coefficients are obtained by fitting the polynomial to the time-sampled current values.

Besides the limitation imposed on the high frequency information obtainable from the time domain results by the current sample spacing on the body, there are several other possible sources of error. First, since the frequency content of the gaussian pulse falls off as $\exp(-\omega^2/4g^2)$, the high frequency current components of the transformed results may be expected to be somewhat less accurate than the low frequency components. The rectangular rule surface integration around the scatterer will not accurately resolve large angular current variations between adjacent surface sample points. Finally, the errors in the time derivative of the current will become more significant with increasing frequency.

APPROXIMATIONS

As the ratio of the size of the object to the pulse width increases, the number of current sample points increases as the square of this ratio. In addition, the increase in number of time steps required for a given observation time period will be inversely proportional to the pulse width. To avoid the excessive computation times inherent in these increases, approximate methods similar to those used in time-harmonic high-frequency scattering analysis can be used. Many of the frequency domain approximations such as physical optics, geometrical optics and composite simple scatterers can be applied as well as to the time domain. Also, structure symmetries and source symmetries can be exploited in a manner similar to the frequency domain. We will not, however, delve into these approximations and simplifications since they are obvious extensions from the frequency domain.

ACCURACY CHECKS

Validity checks on time domain results follow essentially along the same lines as those which may be used for the frequency domain. Because of the different nature of the approach, however, certain types of checks are more suitable in the time domain; the converse also holds of course.

The progress that has been made in short pulse techniques in recent years now makes practical the direct comparison of calculated scattered or radiated pulse shapes with measurements. Some examples of such measurements are given in the following section. Also, comparison of the Fourier transformed time domain results with independent frequency domain data presents another very useful check on the time domain calculation. For those without access to a time domain measurement facility, this method presents perhaps the most useful source for an independent test on the calculation.

Checks of an internal nature analogous to those used in the frequency domain are also applicable to the time domain calculation. Reciprocity between bistatic scattered fields can be examined in terms of the scattered pulse time variation which incidentally is also a direct consequence of the applicability of superposition in the frequency domain. Energy conservation can also be used as a test on the numerical results.

There also exist some additional checks which are particularly appropriate for the time domain. One of these is based on the time delay associated with a creeping current wave which must propagate on the surface of the structure. Consequently, while the incident fields may have already reached regions beyond the shadow boundary, the total fields there must remain zero until the creeping wave, propagating at nearly the speed of light, has time to reach that area. Since the interactions are computed on straight line distances, the fields of the induced currents are required to cancel the incident field in regions that the surface current wave has not as yet reached. This represents a fairly stringent test on the numerical solution accuracy.

Finally, the shape of the scattered pulse, particularly in the backscatter direction, provides an additional indication of the solution accuracy. The time separation of returns from different portions of the scatterer can be examined in order to judge the accuracy of their separate contributions to the scattered field. A knowledge of the transient behavior will further provide an indication of the dominant sources of scattering and serves to locate the scattering centers. Such separation of various sections of a scatterer cannot be so clearly interpreted in the frequency domain return. In addition, the shapes of the returns from the "specular" points can be compared with already validated results for isolated structures similar in shape to the leading edge of such specular points.

4.3.3. Additional Considerations

FREQUENCY VERSUS TIME DOMAIN CALCULATIONS

Integral equations applicable in both the frequency and time domain have been derived and methods for obtaining their numerical solutions have been presented. It is our purpose in this section to delineate more clearly the differences between these two approaches, and thus to identify their relative advantages.

It has been noted that a solution in the frequency domain obtained via matrix factorization or inversion for a given frequency is independent of the exciting source geometry. Thus the induced currents (and the fields which they produce) can be obtained for any illuminating field from the product of the admittance matrix and the source vector. This factor makes the frequency domain approach particularly well suited to calculating monostatic RCS where the currents (and scattered fields) are required for many incidence fields, at one or a few frequencies.

The time-domain formulation is, on the other hand, source-geometry dependent, but can cover a broad frequency range. It is thus well suited, when combined with the Fast Fourier Transform, for obtaining the frequency-dependent backscatter RCS or bistatic radiation pattern for a limited number of different source configurations. The use of a time-domain approach to generate monostatic RCS data for a few frequencies, or the frequency domain approach to derive time dependent scattering results for a few incidence angles can both, on the other hand, be relatively inefficient.

The relative solution efficiencies of the time domain and frequency domain formulations for various types of problems can perhaps be best appreciated by returning again to the characterization of a structure requiring N current samples as an N-port network (see Section 4.3.1). In adopting this viewpoint we see that finding the response of the structure to an arbitrary incident field variation in either the time domain or frequency domain requires determining the currents induced at each of the N ports for as many specific exciting source distributions as are necessary adequately to describe the incident field variation.

Now let us first direct our attention to frequency domain analysis. When the specific incident field is applied at only one port, the N currents induced by it lead as well to the admittance values which relate the driven port to the N ports of the structure. For multiport excitation, as is the case for example when a plane wave incident field is considered, the N currents which result are not so simply related to the specific source distribution but instead involve linear combinations of the N^2 admittance values as shown by (4.58). It is reasonable, however, to view these N currents as equivalent, or pseudo-admittances since it is possible to derive the actual admittances of the N-port network from N linearly independent set of those currents. Thus for general sources and general structures we can represent the numerical solution procedure as one of finding admittance values for the structure approximated as an N-port network. It should be noted that the evaluation of a pseudo or actual admittance value requires approximately the same number of operations. For example, matrix inversion produces N^2 admittances with N^3 operations. An iterative solution on the other hand leads to N pseudo admittances with on the order of N^2 operations. In each case then, on the order of N operations are required per admittance (pseudo or actual) values.

This characterization is quite straightforward in the frequency domain, but may be less clear when the time domain is considered. But having the time variation of the current at one port due to a particular source variation at another is certainly analogous to the frequency domain case. Because of the time variation of the source, however, the N currents which are found are also time dependent. These can be used to derive the corresponding frequency domain values (admittances) over some bandwidth dependent upon the source (and other factors) via a Fourier transform. A similar observation can also be made regarding multiport excitation, in which case time dependent currents are obtained which, when Fourier transformed, lead to pseudo-admittances.

Because the concept of admittances is only valid in the frequency domain, and because in any case a one-to-one correspondence exists between the time and frequency domains, we will perform our comparison of their relative efficiencies in the frequency domain. While more careful consideration of the total number of computer operations required optimally to derive data using either approach may somewhat modify the following results, the overall conclusions remain basically unchanged.

Consider now finding the approximate impulse response of a scatterer. The time domain approach, which as previously noted is source geometry dependent and so bears a resemblance to an iterative frequency domain solution, leads to the frequency variations of pseudo-admittances. On the order of NF total pseudo-admittances are obtained, where F is the number of frequency samples required to synthesize the time variation of the incident wave. (Note that the equivalence of time and frequency via the Fourier transform means that the number of time samples, T, is equal to F.)

For the frequency domain formulation, impedance matrix inversion or factorization yields all N^2 mutual and self-admittances which characterize the N-port structure. Thus, using the frequency domain approach to solve for the structure time domain characteristics for a single source geometry leads to N^2F admittances, and is clearly less efficient than the direct time domain solution.

It can be similarly concluded that the calculation of monostatic scattering information requiring P angles to define the pattern leads to N^2 admittance values in the frequency domain, and NFP pseudo-admittances for the time domain analysis. Thus, assuming the effort necessary for the determination of the admittances (pseudo or actual) is similar using either the time domain or frequency domain approach, the advantage of each derives from the efficiency with which the admittance values it produces are utilized. It is thus primarily a matter of calculating only those admittance values required to determine the information desired about a structure. A tabular comparison of the equivalent number of admittances required for these various cases is presented in Table 4 5

TABLE 4.5. FREQUENCY DOMAIN VERSUS TIME-DOMAIN CALCULATIONS

| | Equivalent admittances for N-port structure | | |
	F.D.	T.D.	F.D./T.D.
Monostatic (P angles)			
Single frequency	N^2	NFP	N/FP
Time response (F-frequencies)	N^2F	NFP	N/P
Bistatic (one angle of incidence)			
Single frequency	N^2	NF	N/F
Time response	N^2F	NF	N

Note that if an iterative solution method is followed for the frequency-domain analysis then the number of admittances obtained from a single source calculation reduces from N^2 to N. In addition, pseudo-admittances rather than actual admittances are obtained for multi-port excitation. Thus, an iteration approach in the frequency domain may have the potential for providing the most flexible analysis. It would allow derivation of frequency domain or time domain information with a minimum of admittance values. At the same time, N iteration solutions for N linearly independent sources would generate the same information as inversion of the impedance matrix since the resulting N^2 pseudo-admittances could thus be transformed to the N^2 actual admittance values which characterize the structure. Thus an upper limit is set on the number of iteration solutions required to handle arbitrary sources. The major factor affecting its use is the efficiency with which a convergent iteration solution can be obtained, since the cost of computing the N admittance values per iteration is linearly dependent upon the number of iterations required.

ALTERNATIVE APPROACHES

The preceding presentation on the numerical solution of scattering problems in the frequency domain has followed a restricted development. In both the derivation of the various integral equations for the induced current and in their subsequent numerical solution it has been assumed, for example, that the observation points on the total field lie on the structure surface. In considering only integral equations we have, as well, neglected alternative approaches (such as that due to P.C. Waterman and discussed elsewhere in this book) which may have significant potential for the numerical solution of scattering problems. We will briefly mention some of these alternative methods in this section. This discussion will be restricted, however, to only a word description, rather than a mathematical formulation of such techniques since a more detailed treatment lies outside the scope of this presentation. Note also that the alternatives considered do not by any means exhaust all present possibilities, and new approaches will no doubt continue to be developed.

(a) *Variation of observation point location.* One of the simplest modifications which can be made to the basic approach considered above is that of allowing field observation points to be located within the structure under investigation. Since the total field inside a perfectly conducting body is zero, clearly then such interior points provide boundary conditions which relate the induced surface current to the incident field. Interior points have been employed in some acoustic scattering problems, but more to avoid the interior resonance problem than to devise an alternative to the surface integral equation (Schenck, 1968).

It may be advantageous to use interior observation points since the surface integration can then be simplified. The resulting impedance matrix may, however, be less stable than the corresponding matrix derived from the surface integral equation. This can occur if the diagonally dominant nature of the impedance matrix is altered as a result of observation points being located a nearly equal distance away from a number of source sample points. Since the use of interior observation points has apparently received little attention, it is difficult to say whether it would offer any real advantage over the surface integral approach.

(b) *Elementary source expansion.* The integral equation approach for the scattering problem is based on integral expression for the fields radiated by a to-be-determined current distribution. It is equally valid to approach this problem from a differential-equation viewpoint where the induced current is represented by a dipole source distribution over the surface. The field of each can be represented by a finite Fourier series expansion in spherical wave functions. Upon summing over the scatterer's surface, an expression is obtained for the radiated field. This sum is reducible to a linear system for the source dipole strengths upon application of the appropriate boundary conditions.

The essential difference between this method and the corresponding integral equation is in the form in which the formal solution for the scatterer is cast; an integral equation in the one case, and a Fourier series in the other. Since a certain discretization of the current distribution is already involved in it, the Fourier series solution is approximate in nature, whereas the integral equation approach is exact. Reduction of the integral equation to a linear system, however, requires introduction of approximations which make it equivalent to the Fourier series form. As discussed by Harrington (1968), either approach permits a flexible computer program to be written involving only the structure geometry, and the choice of one over the other is largely a matter of personal preference.

(c) *Difference equation representation.* If the structure under consideration is enclosed by spherical surface, it is possible to express the external field in terms of a Fourier series of spherical wave function referred to this enclosing surface. This expansion may be viewed as an equivalent source representation for the structure over the spherical surface. The scattered field can then be calculated if the Fourier coefficients in this expansion are known.

These Fourier coefficients can be derived from the differential form of Maxwell's equations. By expressing these differential equations in finite difference form, the space transform between the structure's surface where one set of boundary conditions is applied, and the spherical surface, where continuity of the tangential fields is required, can be established. These finite difference equations generate a sparse linear system from which can be determined the sampled values of the fields on the finite difference net, and consequently the desired Fourier coefficients. This kind of approach can be especially useful for inhomogeneous media problems (Miller, 1968). It reduces of course to the solution of ordinary coupled differential equations if modal decomposition of the fields is allowed by the structure geometry.

(d) *Wire grid modeling.* The preceding variations on the integral-equation approach are mathematically oriented. Wire-grid modeling on the other hand is based on physical reasoning. It is intuitively acceptable, for example, that the difference in electromagnetic properties between a solid, perfectly conducting object and its wire-grid replica can be made to be arbitrarily small as the wire-grid openings are decreased in size. It is thus natural to apply the thin-wire EFIE to the analysis of solid surface structures via wire grid modeling. Richmond (1966) was the first to demonstrate the usefulness of this approach for scattering problems and it has been subsequently used by others (Miller and Maxum, 1970) as well. One advantage of wire-grid modeling is the capability it provides for treating solid objects having sharp corners, edges, and other surface discontinuities as well as thin-wire appendages without special consideration of these features.

(e) *Other methods.* Additional methods, some applicable only to two-dimensional problems, have also been studied. An approach for treating cylinders of arbitrary cross-section, and suited to including inhomogeneous media as well, has been presented by Shafai (1969). Since his method is based on a conformal transformation of the actual geometry to a circular cross section, it is somewhat restricted in its application.

Daniel and Mittra (1970) discuss a technique for solving a linear system (in their case derived from an integral equation, but this is not relevant to the technique's application) based on parameter optimization. Their approach consists of generating a quadratic performance index which provides a measure of the solution accuracy. By minimizing the performance index with respect to an iterated sequence of values for components of the current, an optimal solution to the problem is obtained. This method differs from the usual iteration techniques in that the successive current values are generated by parameter optimization with respect to the current components.

When the structure geometry is such that its various surfaces conform to sections of separable coordinate system, then classical separation of variable techniques can be used. This approach has been investigated by Ruckgaber and Schultz (1969) in the analysis of finned cylinder and spheres. Their results are in good agreement with solutions obtained via other techniques, even for the limiting cases of a flat circular disk and flat strip.

A technique borrowed from structural analysis termed finite elements, somewhat similar to finite differences, has been applied to a problem in geophysical prospecting by Ryu (1970). The problem treated involves the interaction of an electromagnetic field with a finitely conducting half-space having an inclusion of different electrical parameters. The finite element method incorporates analytic solutions to the governing differential equations within each finite element, and connects the resulting expression via the required continuity condition across the element boundaries. Ryu obtained a numerical solution for the finite element formulation by minimizing an energy integral.

4.4. APPLICATIONS

Up to this point our attention has been directed to the formulation of the scattering problem and describing solution methods for the integral equation(s) which give the induced current. Without examples which demonstrate the overall validity of the approach, the preceding discussion may appear to be merely a mathematical exercise. We therefore present in this section a fairly extensive sequence of sample results which are in almost all cases compared with independently obtained analytical or numerical data, or with experimental measurement. The source of the computed data is acknowledged in each figure except when the computations were performed by the authors. Results will first be presented for the frequency domain analysis. Those for the time domain are included in the following section.

4.4.1. Frequency-domain Examples

As has been previously pointed out, three-dimensional conducting bodies can be treated using a solid surface integral equation, or with the use of wire-grid modeling via the thin-wire electric field equation. In addition, many three-dimensional structures of interest consist entirely of interconnected thin wires, and so are naturally amenable to treatment using the thin-wire EFIE. We will consider in order below, solid bodies analyzed using the surface MFIE and EFIE, wire-grid models of solid objects and lastly, thin-wire structures, the latter two following from the EFIE. Unless otherwise indicated the scatterers will be perfect electric conductors.

The E-plane bistatic patterns which follow depict the far-zone scattered electric field parallel to the plane defined by the incident electric field and the incident wave propagation vector as a function of the angular coordinate within that plane. The H-plane bistatic pattern is similarly defined with the magnetic field replacing the electric field.

For the monostatic patterns, E-plane and VV are interchangeably used, as are H-plane and HH. The mutually perpendicular target rotation axis and incident wave propagation vector define the plane of incidence. H-plane monostatic patterns are plots of the scattered electric field component parallel to the incident electric field which is normal to the plane of incidence. The similar definition follows for the E-plane plots by an interchange of electric and magnetic fields.

SOLID SURFACE SCATTERERS

(a) *"Numerically rigorous" solutions.* Historically, the first three-dimensional body to be treated using a numerical integral equation approach was the sphere (Oshiro, 1965), primarily because its cross section is well known, both from measurement and the Mie series solution. An early result for the bistatic *H*-plane RCS of a conducting sphere obtained by Oshiro and Su (1965) for $ka = 1.7$ (*a* is the sphere radius) is compared with the classical solution in Fig. 4.9a. These results were calculated from the MFIE with subsectional collocation (referred to as source distribution technique or SDT) using a numerical model

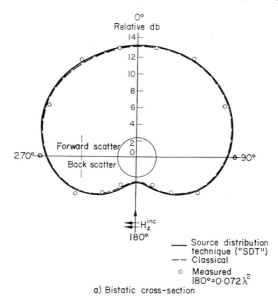

a) Bistatic cross-section

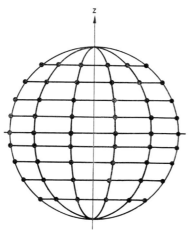

b) Segmentation scheme

FIG. 4.9. Scattering by a sphere ($ka = 1.7$).
(After Oshiro and Su, 1965.)

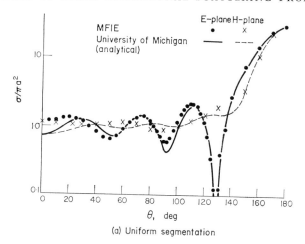

(a) Uniform segmentation

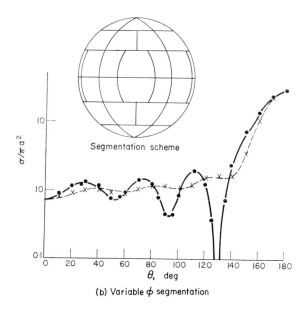

(b) Variable ϕ segmentation

FIG. 4.10. Scattering by a sphere ($ka = 5.3$).

divided into ten equal angular gores in the φ-coordinate and ten equal steps along the sphere's z-axis. This uniform azimuthal segmentation scheme which results in equal area patches is shown in Fig. 4.9b. The numerical integration was accomplished by multiplying the integrand value at the center of a patch by the patch area (rectangular rule). The principal value nature of the integral was realized by excluding the integration over the patch containing the singularity (the self-patch). Excellent agreement between the classical solution and the numerical solution of the integral equation is evident.

Because of the aspect sensitive nature of the numerical model used for the sphere (i.e., its RCS when viewed axially may differ from that when the illuminating wave is incident in the equatorial plane), an additional check on the numerical model is provided by the cal-

8   M.-CTE

culated monostatic RCS of the sphere. The maximum deviation from the classical value of −11.45 db was ±0.3 db as the incident angle is varied 90 degrees from the equatorial to the polar-direction. This result provides some indication of the dependence of the numerical solution accuracy on structure segmentation. A similar check can also be performed for other rotationally symmetric structures.

The data presented in Fig. 4.10 illustrate the effect of the segmentation scheme used for the integral equation solution on the numerical accuracy obtained for the bistatic cross-section of a sphere with $ka = 5.3$. These data were obtained using the author's MFIE program, which fully exploits discrete angular symmetry of the numerical model. In part (a) of Fig. 4.10 uniform azimuthal segmentation as shown in Fig. 4.9b was used. The azimuthal segmentation used to obtain the results of part (b) in the same figure was quadrant symmetric, i.e. the model possessed symmetry through four discrete rotations of 90 degrees about its axis. The sphere was segmented into thirteen bands of equal θ (polar angle) increments and each band starting at the pole divided into patches as follows: 4, 8, 12, 16, 20, 24, 24, 24, 20, 16, 12, 8, 4. The principal value integral was approximated by a sum over all patches with the exception of the patch containing the singularity. A significant improvement in solution accuracy is achieved using the variable segmentation, wherein the surface patches used maintain an aspect ratio (ratio of length to width) closer to unity over the sphere than does the uniform segmentation.

The influence of integration accuracy on numerical solution accuracy is demonstrated in Fig. 4.11 where the bistatic cross-section of a sphere, again for $ka = 5.3$, is compared with analytic results for two surface-integration schemes. The rectangular rule integration previously described is seen to produce less accurate results than those obtained using sub-patch integration with twenty-five sample points. In the latter case, the principal value integral is numerically approximated by omitting the center sample from the integration over the self-patch while in the former case the entire self-patch integration is omitted.

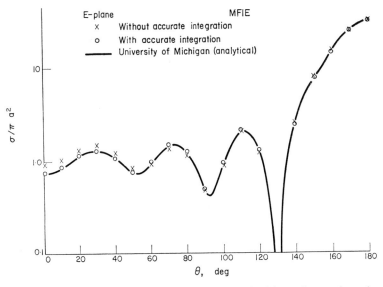

FIG. 4.11. Bistatic E-plane RCS of a sphere ($ka = 5.3$) with two integration schemes.

Note that the use of more current samples on an object may lead to more accurate cross-section values not only because the current variation may be more accurately mapped, but because the numerical integration is at the same time also more accurately carried out as a result of decreased size of the patches.

As our final examples involving the sphere geometry, we include in Fig. 4.12(a) and (b) some data for a monopole antenna driven against a sphere obtained by Tesche and Neureuther (1970). These results, while for an antenna problem, do represent a valid check on the numerical procedures of interest here and, as pointed out previously, the only essential difference between numerically rigorous scattering and radiation calculations is the source terms; in both cases the same admittance matrix is utilized. The integral equation formulation for this problem employed the EFIE and the Green's function for a point current ele-

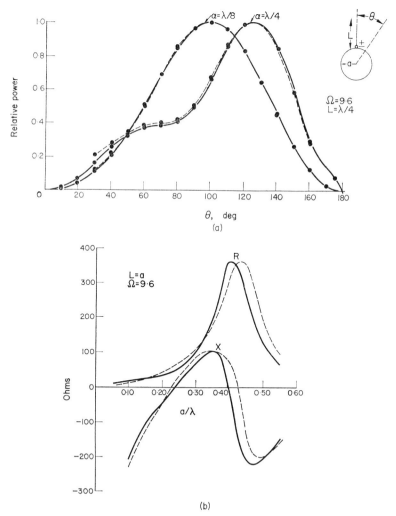

FIG. 4.12. Monopole antenna driven against a sphere; (a) normalized radiation patterns; (b) input impedance (——) (Tesche and Neureuther); (---) (Bolle and Morganstern). (After Tesche and Neureuther, 1970.)

ment in the presence of a perfectly conducting sphere. As a result, the integration over the antenna and sphere, which would be required using the infinite medium Green's function, is reduced to an integration over the antenna only. The results of Tesche and Neureuther obtained in this manner are seen to resemble closely those presented by Bolle and Morganstern (1969) who solved this problem by considering it as a limiting case of a conical antenna mounted on a sphere.

We next consider some sample calculations for body geometries which are generally more demanding tests of the numerical technique than the sphere. Numerous samples for shapes such as disks, finite cylinders, spheroids, cones, etc., have been investigated by Oshiro *et al.* (1966, 1967, 1968, 1969), Andreasen (1965b), Harrington and Mautz (1969), and MBAssociates (1970). Since we are most interested in validity demonstrations of the numerical procedures used, the results presented here are restricted to those cases for which independent corroboration of relative solution accuracy is available. Thus the examples which follow are not necessarily representative results from all those who have made significant contribu-

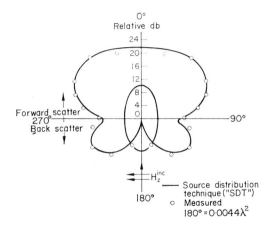

a) Bistatic cross-section (ka = 1·7)

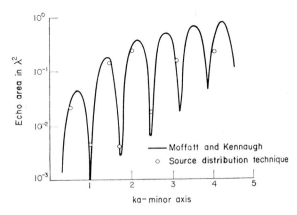

b) Axial echo area

FIG. 4.13. Scattering by a spheroid.
(After Oshiro *et al.*, 1966.)

tions to this area, but rather reflect a sampling of data available to the authors for which independent validity checks can be provided. Since the details of many of the computations are quite involved and lengthy, only major details are included here. For more comprehensive descriptions the reader should consult the indicated references.

In Fig. 4.13 are shown calculated cross-section results obtained from the MFIE for a prolate spheroid (Oshiro *et al.*, 1966). Good agreement is obtained with measurement (Fig. 4.13a) for the bistatic scattering pattern of a spheroid having a *ka* value of 1.7 (*a* = semi minor axis, *b* = semi major axis, *b*/*a* = 2.0). Calculated axial-incidence backscatter cross-section values versus *ka* obtained by Oshiro *et al.* also agree well with the data of Moffatt and Kennaugh (1965) as shown in Fig. 4.13b. Segmentation was realized by ten equal increments along the major axis and ten equal increments in the azimuthal angle about that axis.

The cone–sphere is a basic shape which has received a great deal of attention over the years. A comparison with experiment of an monostatic cross-section calculation using the MFIE for a 30-degree included angle cone–sphere with *ka* = 1.7 is given in Fig. 4.14. The cone–sphere was modeled using uniform azimuthal segmentation and variable-width segments along the cone axis to provide equal area patches on the cone. Note that this segmentation increases the sampling density as the cone–sphere join is approached from the cone; it has been found by experience to provide more accurate results than uniform spacing along the cone axis. Equal area segments were also used on the sphere. The integral-equation results, obtained using sub-patch integration, are within ± 1 db of the experimental curve.

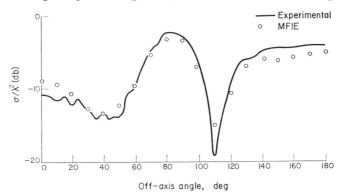

FIG. 4.14. *H*-plane monostatic cross-section of a cone sphere (*ka* = 1.7; included angle = 30°).

A comparison of two calculations for a cone–sphere with a 20 degree included angle and *ka* = 1.26 is shown in Fig. 4.15. The surface current distributions and monostatic scattering patterns for tip-end and sphere-end incidence as obtained using a MFIE program are shown with the corresponding results of Mautz and Harrington (1968) who used an EFIE for rotationally symmetric bodies. As was the case for Fig. 4.14, the MBAssociates cone–sphere model employed equal area segmentation on the cone. The Mautz–Harrington results were obtained from thirty equally spaced samples along the cone–sphere surface. Note that quite good agreement for the tangential current components J_t is achieved between these independent calculations, while the azimuthal current J_φ are significantly different. In spite of the latter, good agreement is observed in the bistatic scattering patterns, demonstrating the stationary property of the scattered field dependence on the current distribution.

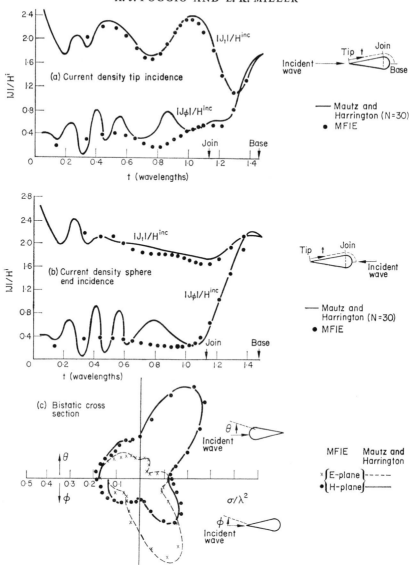

FIG. 4.15. Cone–sphere scattering ($ka = 1.26$; included angle $= 20°$).
(After Mautz and Harrington, 1968.)

Further representative numerical-experimental comparisons for the monostatic RCS of various simple shapes obtained by Oshiro *et al.* (1967) are shown in Figs. 4.16, 4.17 and 4.18. These results were all obtained from the MFIE. In obtaining the numerical data shown, there was no special treatment of the current at surface discontinuities on the structures. The agreement between the calculated and experimental results is very good, generally within ± 2 db.

As a final example of numerically rigorous RCS calculations for perfectly conducting bodies, results are presented in Fig. 4.19b for the monostatic RCS of the stub-cylinder combination shown in Fig. 4.19a. Although the relative agreement between the experimental

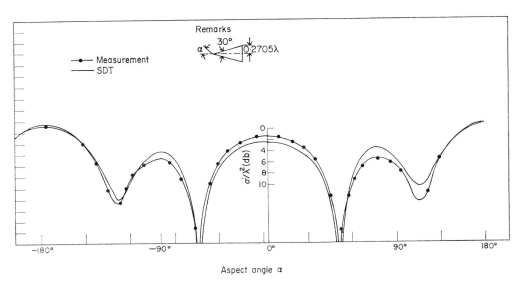

FIG. 4.16. *H*-plane monostatic cross-section of a flat-back cone ($ka = 1.7$). (After Oshiro *et al.*, 1967.)

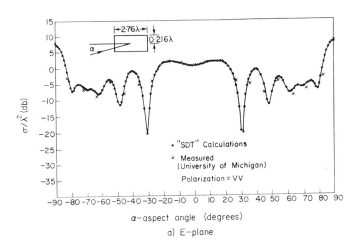

a) E–plane

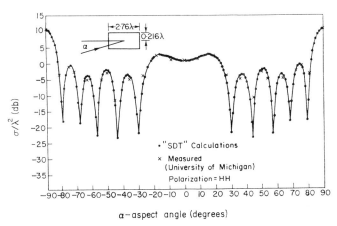

b) H–plane

FIG. 4.17. Monostatic cross-section of a right circular cylinder. *Note:* all dimensions in inches. (After Oshiro *et al.*, 1967.)

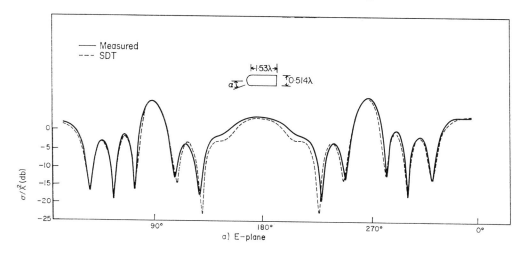

a) E-plane

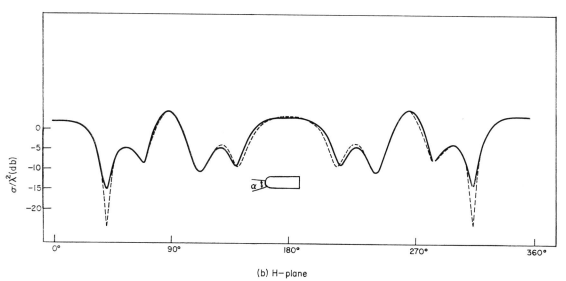

(b) H-plane

FIG. 4.18. Monostatic cross-section of a sphere–cylinder.
(After Oshiro *et al.*, 1961.)

and numerical data (Oshiro *et al.*, 1967) is not quite as good here as for the cases previously shown, the difference is generally less than 4 db in regions away from the deep nulls. In addition, the aspect variation of the calculated data correlates well with the measured curve.

(b) *Approximations and special cases.* Example calculations are included in this section for approximations involving physical optics, and for structures having non-zero surface impedance. The treatment of scatterers at eigenfrequencies of their interior resonance modes will also be examined.

(i) *Physical optics.* The application of physical and geometrical optics to the evaluation of large structure RCS has been discussed in some detail by Siegel *et al.* (1969). Their approach to complex shaped structures is based on decomposing the object into basic shapes, each of which is treated independently, with a subsequent addition of their separate returns to obtain the total cross section. Our consideration of physical optics will here be restricted to two examples, both involving the bistatic cross section of perfectly conducting spheres.

In Fig. 4.20 is a plot of the H-plane bistatic scattering pattern of a sphere ($ka = 10.0$) obtained from physical optics compared with analytic Mie series results. Good agreement is obtained in both the back- and forward-scatter directions, with the only significant departure occurring in the range $\theta = 120$–160 degrees, where deviations on the order of 3 db are observed. The reasons for these deviations have been described in a previous section. The good agreement in the backscatter direction is indicative of the usefulness of physical optics backscatter RCS calculations for simple shapes, but such good results cannot be invariably expected for complex shapes with surface curvature discontinuities.

A demonstration of the compatibility between the integral equation approach and the physical optics approximation is exhibited by the results of Fig. 4.21 (Oshiro *et al.*, 1967).

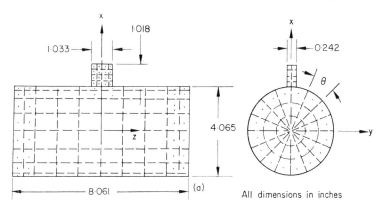

(a) Segmentation

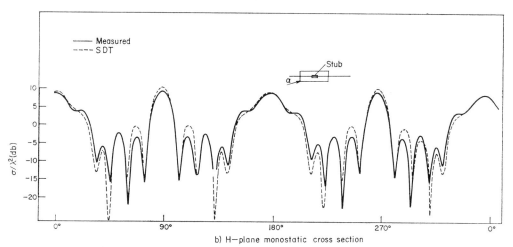

b) H—plane monostatic cross section

Fig. 4.19. Scattering by a stub-cylinder.
(After Oshiro *et al.*, 1967.)

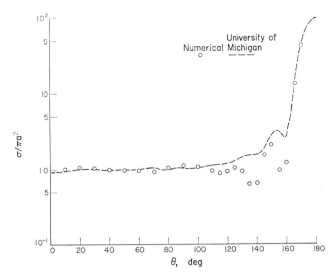

FIG. 4.20. Physical optics *H*-plane bistatic cross-section of a sphere ($ka = 10.0$).

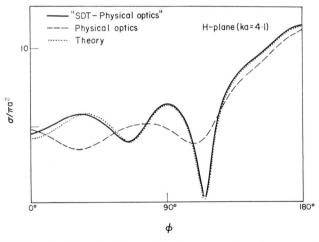

FIG. 4.21. SDT—physical optics *H*-plane bistatic cross-section of a sphere ($ka = 4.1$).
(After Oshiro *et al.*, 1967.)

The bistatic cross section for a sphere with $ka = 4.1$ is shown as obtained from the classical solution and straightforward application of physical optics. Results are also presented for a combined approach wherein the illuminated region current is obtained from physical optics while that in the shadow region is calculated via the integral equation. These results show the improvement which is obtainable by a combination of physical optics with a more rigorous solution method, and also the success with which this modified physical optics approach can be applied to a relatively small scatterer.

(ii) *Interior resonances*. A potential problem which can be encountered in numerically evaluating the scattering properties of a solid conducting body using the MFIE is the excitation of an interior resonance which can lead to a numerically spurious result for the scattered field. This problem can also arise in the use of the EFIE. It results from the numerical imprecision of the calculated currents associated with the interior resonance, which while actually non-radiating, because of their numerical inaccuracy do contribute to the far field to such an extent that the overall cross section results are in error. A discussion of integral equation solutions and the difficulties at eigenfrequencies is found in Copley (1968) for the acoustics regime and in Baker and Copson (1953) and Müller (1969) for the electromagnetics regime.

Since the interior resonances are associated separately with the individual MFIE and EFIE, it is possible to effectively suppress the resonance effect by combining the two integral equations into a single composite equation. This procedure has been discussed by Mitzner (1968) and Oshiro et al. (1970) and shows considerable promise. In essence the approach is ormewhat similar to that required for the solution of problems with finite impedance boundary conditions. By noting the characteristics of the MFIE (the operator is singular at an eigenfrequency) and of the EFIE (the operator does not have a unique inverse and generates

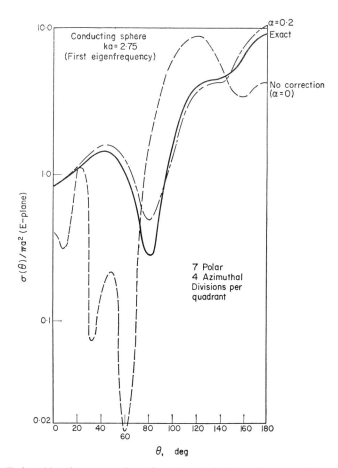

FIG. 4.22. E-plane bistatic cross-section of a sphere at first eigenfrequency (ka = 2.75) for corrected integral equation. (After Oshiro et al., 1970.)

an infinite number of solutions differing by eigenfunctions) as well as the fact that the lossy wall problem has no real eigenfrequencies, Mitzner has constructed an integral equation valid at all frequencies. Referring to the integral operator in MFIE as L and the integral operator in the EFIE as M, he writes

$$(\tfrac{1}{2}I - L + \alpha\hat{n} \times M)\mathbf{J}_s = \hat{n} \times \mathbf{H}^{\text{inc}} + \alpha\,\frac{1}{Z_0}\,\hat{n} \times (\mathbf{E}^{\text{inc}} \times \hat{n})$$

where Z_0 is the wave impedance, I is the unit dyadic, and α is an arbitrary constant $0 < \alpha \leq 1$. This equation provides a unique $\mathbf{J}_s$ at all frequencies except eigenfrequencies where it has an infinite number of solutions differing by eigenfunctions of the interior problem. Since the eigenfunctions of the interior problem do not radiate, the correct exterior fields are found.

The results of Mitzner's approach for the first eigenfrequency of the sphere ($ka \cong 2.75$) are illustrated in Fig. 4.22 in comparison with the analytic bistatic scattering pattern. While the numerical solution obtained from the MFIE alone is completely unacceptable, that obtained from the combined integral equation agrees very well with the correct result. Bistatic results corresponding to those of Fig. 4.22 are shown in Fig. 4.23 for a ka value

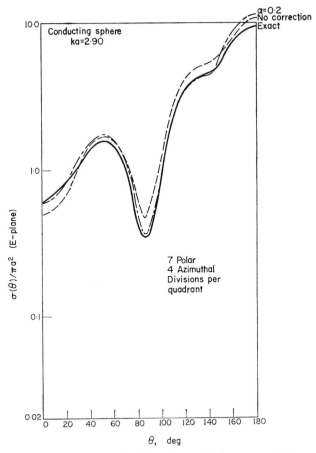

FIG. 4.23. E-plane bistatic cross-section of a sphere ($ka = 2.9$) for corrected integral equation. (After Oshiro *et al.*, 1970.)

of 2.9. This graph demonstrates the validity of the combined integral equation for a non-resonant frequency. In Fig. 4.24 are shown the mean errors in db for three ka values as a function of the parameter α. It may be seen that an α value on the order of 0.2 tends to produce the minimum error for the ka range shown.

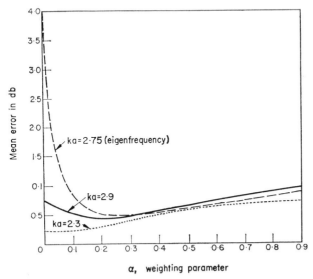

FIG. 4.24. Mean error of corrected integral equation as a function of weighting parameter. (After Oshiro *et al.*, 1970.)

Alternative approaches to the suppression of interior mode resonances in exterior region calculations have also been suggested. A method that has been demonstrated to work in the acoustic scattering problem is that of introducing additional interior sample points in the calculation. As discussed by Schenck (1968) for the acoustic cross section of a rigid sphere, the regularization of the resulting over-determined system for the surface pressure leads to accurate scattered fields for all frequencies including the interior resonances.

(iii) *Impedance loading.* The use of an impedance boundary condition, and the limitations on its use have been previously discussed. Since this approach to treating finitely conducting bodies is an approximation, it is appropriate to compare some results obtained using the impedance boundary condition with exact data. Since it is inconvenient to derive analytically such data for three-dimensional bodies other than the sphere, the comparison presented here will deal with the sphere only.

As presented in Fig. 4.25, where the bistatic scattering patterns of a sphere (with $ka = 0.25$) in the E- and H-planes are shown as calculated from the impedance boundary condition (the zero impedance case is also shown for reference), the results thus obtained agree within 1 db of the exact value. Since the surface impedance differs enough from zero significantly to affect the scattered field, as may be verified by comparison with the perfect conductivity case, this calculation demonstrates the essential validity of the simple Leontovich impedance boundary condition for the spherical case. Note that curvature correction to the Leontovich boundary condition is not required for the sphere, since the principal radii of curvature are

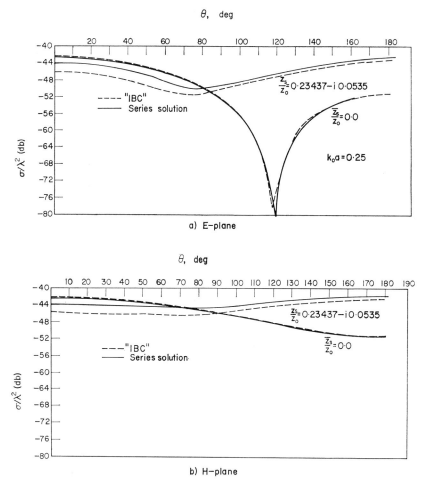

FIG. 4.25. Bistatic cross-section of a sphere ($ka = 0.25$) with impedance boundary condition; (a) E-plan epattern; (b) H-plane pattern. (After Oshiro *et al.*, 1967.)

identical. A more stringent test of the approximation would be provided by non-spherical geometries; Mitzner (1967) presents some examples for the cylinder. It would also be useful to examine the impedance boundary condition as a function of surface impedance and sphere radius to establish the accuracy limitations more conclusively for the sphere geometry.

WIRE-GRID STRUCTURES

The use of wire-grid models for solid surface objects was evidently first explored by Richmond (1966), who applied the technique to a flat and curved surface wire-grid structure. Scattering results obtained by Richmond for wire-grid models of a circular disk and a sphere are presented in Figs. 4.26 and 4.27, where they are compared with experimental and analytic values respectively. The validity of using wire-grid models for these solid surface structures is apparent. These calculations were performed using the method of collocation

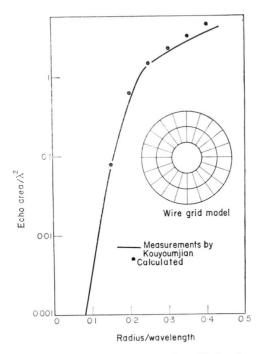

FIG. 4.26. Backscatter echo area of circular wire-grid plate for axial incidence.
(After Richmond, 1966.)

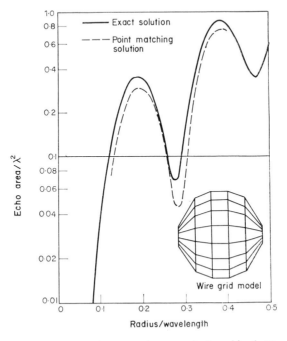

FIG. 4.27. Backscatter echo area of wire-grid sphere.
(After Richmond, 1966.)

with constant current samples and employed a maximum of 300 and 1010 segments respectively for the disk and sphere models. In both cases, the rotational symmetry of the structure was exploited to reduce the computation time.

Wire-grid modeling has also been studied, some results of which are presented in the next several graphs. In Fig. 4.28 is shown a comparison between experiment and calculation for the normal incidence RCS of square wire-grid reflectors. The experimental data obtained

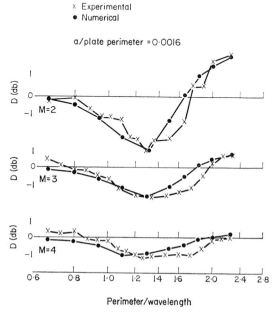

FIG. 4.28. Deviation (D) of the backscatter RCS for normal incidence of an $M \times M$ wire grid from that of a solid plate as a function of frequency. ("Numerical" solid plate uses $M = 6$.)

on a rail line range (Gans, 1965) represents the difference between the RCS of a solid plate compared with a wire grid of the same perimeter and thickness which has M grid openings per side. The numerical curves compare corresponding calculated data, where the solid plate in this case is modeled by the 6×6 wire grid. (The difference between the calculated RCS for the 5×5 and 6×6 wire grids was less than 0.2 db over the perimeter range shown on the graph.) The wire diameter for the calculations is the same as that used for the experimental model. The experimental data of Fig. 4.28 shows that a wire grid with openings less than $\frac{1}{8}\lambda$ per side models within 1 db the normal incidence RCS of a solid plate. In addition the generally close agreement between the experimental and calculated data demonstrates the accuracy of the numerical approach.

In Fig. 4.29(a) is represented a numerical–experimental comparison for the scattering RCS of a wire grid having a slot (Miller and Morton, 1970). The numerical data agree well with the measured results, even in the anti-resonant region where the RCS decreases by more than 20 db. However, as shown by Fig. 4.29(b), where experimental RCS data is shown for a slotted grid and two slotted plates having different thicknesses, the wire-grid anti-resonance is shifted downward in frequency compared with that obtained for the solid plate.

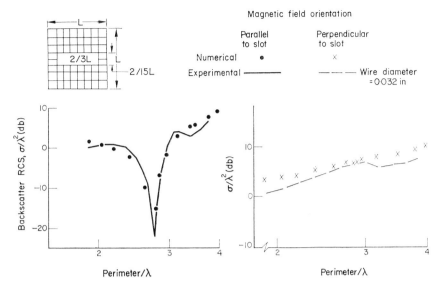

FIG. 4.29. (a) Numerical–experimental comparison of the broadside backscatter RCS of a slotted grid.

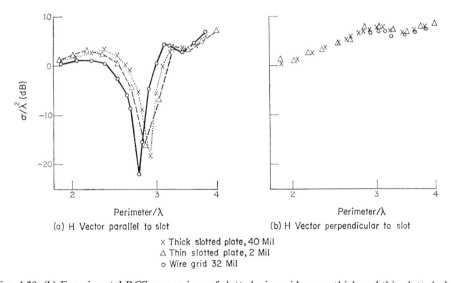

FIG. 4.29. (b) Experimental RCS comparison of slotted wire grid versus thick and thin slotted plate.

Such frequency shifts are frequently observed between the calculated and measured locations of resonant-type scattering responses, and are evidently caused by the effective non-zero impedance loading which results from the discretization associated with the numerical solution technique.

The bistatic scattering cross section of a wire-grid cone sphere with a 30-degree included angle and $ka = 1.0$ is compared in Fig. 4.30 with corresponding data obtained from the solid surface MFIE. The two sets of curves are seen to be within 2 db or so, the greatest discrepancy arising from an angle shift between their respective minima. Such angle shifts appear to be related to the frequency shifts mentioned above, as the position of scattering minima shift with frequency.

A numerical–experimental comparison of the scattering pattern of a wire-grid model of the U.S. Army Light Observation Helicopter, the OH-6A, is shown in Fig. 4.31(a). The data were produced in connection with a study program concerned with numerically predict-

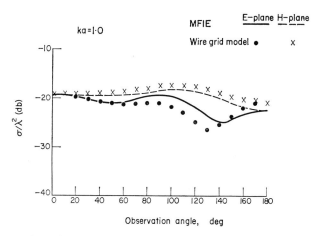

FIG. 4.30. Cone–sphere bistatic scattering pattern for tip incidence (30° included cone angle) as computed using a wire-grid model and MFIE.

ing the performance of homing-type antennas on this aircraft. A sample experimental–numerical antenna pattern result using experimental data obtained from a one-fifth scale model of the OH-6A (Robichaux and Griffee, 1967) is shown in Fig. 4.31(b), since as re-marked previously, there is no essential difference between the numerically rigorous antenna and scatterer analysis other than the source term used. Either calculation may make use of the same admittance matrix.

In concluding this section on the wire-grid modeling of solid surface structures, it is pertinent to comment on the relative efficiency of this approach compared with the solid surface MFIE for the analysis of solid structures. Generally speaking, it has been our experience that more current samples are required for the wire-grid model than for the solid-surface model. For example, sample patches on the order of 0.2λ on a side are found to provide, for the most part, reasonably accurate results when using the MFIE. The thin-wire procedure, however, has been found to require on the order of 0.05λ to 0.1λ grid openings to produce similar accuracy. Then on the order of one-half times $(0.2/0.1)^2$ to $(0.2/0.05)^2$ more current samples may be needed in the wire-grid model to obtain accuracy comparable to the solid surface MFIE.

The reason for this apparently arises from two basic differences between the two integral equations. First of all, the thin-wire EFIE has a kernel which contains a second derivative of the free-space Green's function, compared with the MFIE whose kernel contains only a first derivative. Consequently, the EFIE responds in a more localized manner to the current distribution and may require as a result more closely spaced samples adequately to

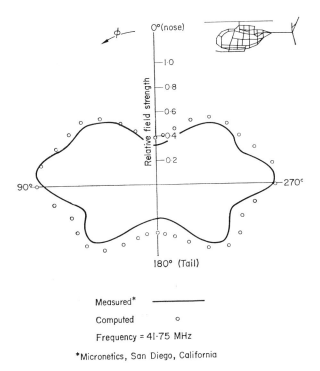

Measured* ————————

Computed o

Frequency = 41·75 MHz

*Micronetics, San Diego, California

FIG. 4.31. (a) Numerical–experimental comparison of the scattered field pattern of an OH-6A helicopter wire-grid model.

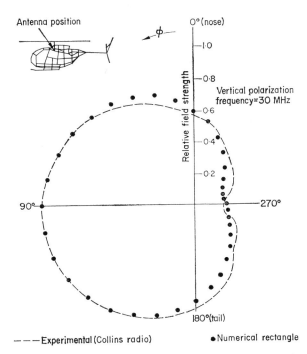

— — —Experimental (Collins radio)   ●Numerical rectangle

FIG. 4.31. (b) Comparison of measured radiation pattern of a towel-bar homing antenna on the OH-6A helicopter with results calculated from thin-wire electric field integral equation.

determine it. As a second point, the self-term in the MFIE is obtained analytically from a limiting process (p. 168). Furthermore, the wire grid modeling is, in itself, an approximation to the solid surface.

THIN-WIRE STRUCTURES

In this section we shall consider scattering by thin-wire structures. The results to be presented were obtained by a subsectional collocation solution of the EFIE for thin wires. The thin wire kernel was used in the mathematical model.

The RCS of two coplanar, concentric rings is shown for axial incidence as a function of the outer ring's circumference in wavelengths, ka_1, in Fig. 4.32. There are two numerical curves on the graph, one obtained using the constant term only for the current expansion and

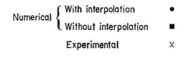

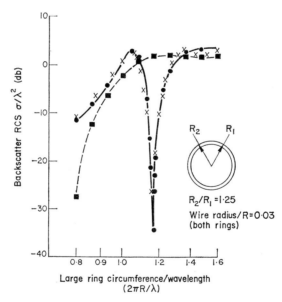

FIG. 4.32. Frequency variation of the axial incidence backscatter RCS of two coaxial, coplanar rings showing the effect of sinusoidal current interpolation.

the other using sinusoidal current interpolation, with eight segments used per ring in each case. The experimental backscatter data, shown by the crosses, were obtained on the rail-line range (Gans, 1965). Clearly demonstrated by these results is the advantage of sinusoidal current interpolation over the constant current expansion. The constant current expansion could also predict the antiresonant dip in RCS, but at the expense of increasing the number of segments and thus the cost of the calculation.

In Fig. 4.33 is shown the RCS as a function of frequency for axial incidence on a planar log-periodic zig-zag array having a cone half-angle α of 6 degrees and a log-periodic expansion parameter τ of 1.15. The computed results may be observed to follow the general trend of the experimental data, also taken on the rail-line range, the major difference being a slight frequency shift between the experimental and numerical results in the resonance peaks.

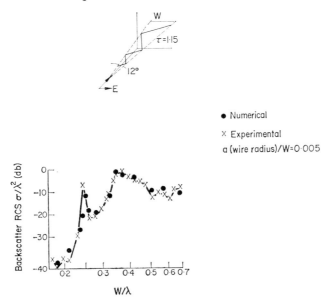

FIG. 4.33. Numerical–experimental comparison of the backscatter RCS frequency variation of a planar, log-periodic zig-zag array for axial incidence with expansion parameter $\tau = 1.15$.

The RCS variation with frequency for a wave incident at angles of 30 and 75 degrees with respect to the axis of a five-element log-periodic array of coaxial circular rings ($\alpha = 8$ degrees, $\tau = 1.2$) having an axial enhancer is shown in Fig. 4.34. Generally, the relative agreement between experiment (again made on a rail-line range) and numerical calculations is within ± 2 db for these results as well as for other incident angles not shown here.

The thin-wire scattering results presented above show the RCS-frequency dependence for several structures. In Figs. 4.35(a)–(i) we present the RCS versus aspect angle variation for various types of thin-wire scatterers. The measured results were obtained on outdoor scattering ranges. For the sake of clarity, a sketch of each scatterer is shown with pertinent dimensions. The measurement frequency is indicated in the caption. The experimental RCS of structures with one plane of symmetry is shown from 0 to 180 degrees for clockwise (CW) and counter-clockwise (CCW) rotation. Structures having two symmetry planes about the rotation axis have their average RCS plotted versus aspect angle with the vertical bars showing the extremes of the four experimental data runs. In all cases, the numerical data is shown by the solid circles.

The agreement obtained between the measured and calculated values ranges from essentially exact in cases such as the straight wire (4.35a) to differences on the order of ± 3 db or so for some of the scatterers such as the tee-pee, if shifts in aspect angle between experimental and numerical maxima and minima are ignored. Some of the differences can be

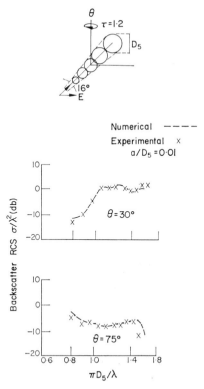

FIG. 4.34. A comparison of the experimental and calculated frequency variation of the backscatter RCS of a five-ring, log-periodic array of circular rings with an axial enhancer for two angles of incidence.

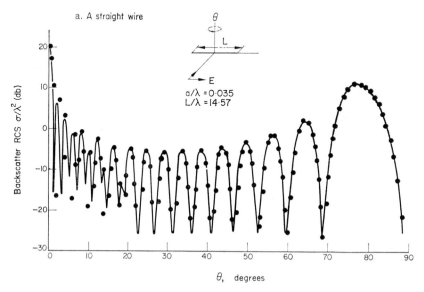

FIG. 4.35. Comparison with experiment (CW, CCW; average of four sweeps—error bar shows extremes) of the calculated (···) RCS versus aspect angle. Diagram inserts show structures for $\theta = 0°$ orientation, with wire radius denoted by a.

b. Straight wire with bow-tie terminations

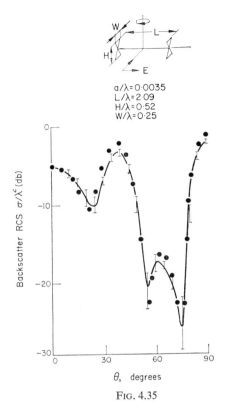

$a/\lambda = 0.0035$
$L/\lambda = 2.09$
$H/\lambda = 0.52$
$W/\lambda = 0.25$

Backscatter RCS σ/λ^2 (db)

θ, degrees

Fig. 4.35

c. Eleven-element array of log–periodically spaced straight dipoles with center strut

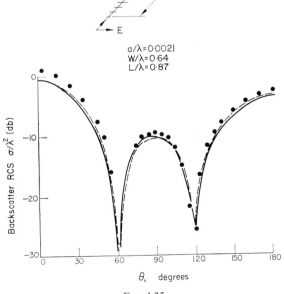

$\tau = 1.25$

$a/\lambda = 0.0021$
$W/\lambda = 0.64$
$L/\lambda = 0.87$

Backscatter RCS σ/λ^2 (db)

θ, degrees

Fig. 4.35

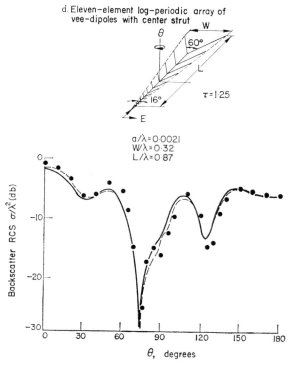

d. Eleven−element log−periodic array of vee−dipoles with center strut

θ

$60°$

W

L

$16°$

E

$\tau = 1.25$

$a/\lambda = 0.0021$
$W/\lambda = 0.32$
$L/\lambda = 0.87$

Fig. 4.35

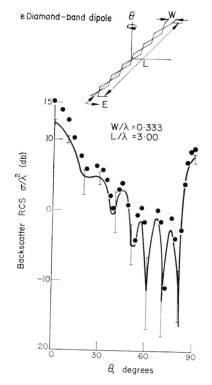

e. Diamond−band dipole

θ

W

L

E

$W/\lambda = 0.333$
$L/\lambda = 3.00$

Fig. 4.35

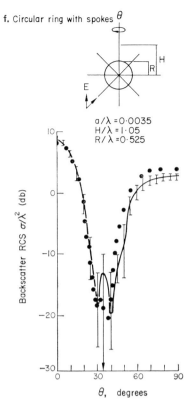

f. Circular ring with spokes

$a/\lambda = 0.0035$
$H/\lambda = 1.05$
$R/\lambda = 0.525$

Fig. 4.35

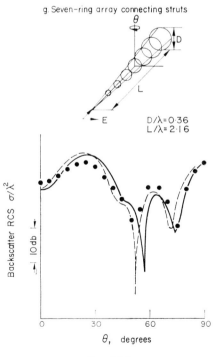

g. Seven-ring array connecting struts

$D/\lambda = 0.36$
$L/\lambda = 2.16$

Fig. 4.35

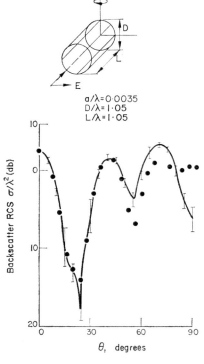

FIG. 4.35

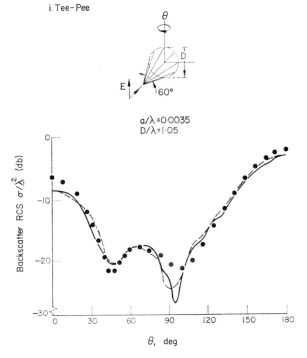

FIG. 4.35

attributed to inaccurately configured models, since substantial variations in the measured results are obtained at some aspect angles, where because of symmetry, identical cross-sections should be obtained. Experimental inaccuracy due to model placement and support structure may also be a contributing factor, as in the case of the tee-pee where the nose-on RCS was found experimentally to differ by about 2.5 db for the two polarizations, where because of symmetry, it should be the same.

4.4.2. Time-domain Examples

As was the situation for the frequency domain examples presented above, the time domain results included here will deal first with solid surface scatterers, followed by the more specialized case of thin-wire structures.

SOLID SURFACE SCATTERERS

The earliest three-dimensional body to be approached via direct solution in the time domain is, not surprisingly, the sphere. Bennett and Weeks (1968) developed the time-dependent MFIE integral equation for the induced surface current, and obtained numerical results for the sphere, as well as a sphere-capped cylinder. Earlier treatments for the sphere as well as other simple shapes had been previously presented by Kennaugh and Cosgriff (1958), Kennaugh (1961), Kennaugh and Moffat (1962, 1965) based on a ramp response physical optics approximation. The sphere was also treated using a Fourier transform of its Mie series solution by Rheinstein (1968). These alternate approaches, while valuable and offering certain advantages over the integral equation analysis, will not be further considered here because our primary interest in this chapter is the integral equation viewpoint.

In Fig. 4.36 is shown the approximate impulse response in the E- and H-planes of a sphere as obtained by Bennett who developed a program for axial incidence on quadrant symmetric bodies. These results were obtained using a variable φ segmentation to satisfy the criterion established on sample point separation in space and time as discussed previously, and employed a total of forty-eight surface patches or area segments. Following what has come to be standard practice, the incident gaussian shaped pulse and reflected pulses are shown to scale together with the scatterer. The outer circle shows the locus of points in space to which the center of the incident pulse would have propagated if it had been reflected from the origin (indicated by the cross at the center of the sphere). The arrow on the incident and reflected pulses is on the positive pulse amplitude axis. The creeping wave return in the backscatter direction is clearly observed as the second positive peak in the scattered pulse. The specular leading pulse is followed by a negative return which may be interpreted as a physical optics type contribution.

A Fourier transform over time of the scattered pulse shapes shown in Fig. 4.36 produces the corresponding frequency domain response. Results obtained in this manner are shown in Fig. 4.37 for the frequency variation versus ka of the backscatter RCS. Bistatic scattered fields are presented in Fig. 4.38 for the two ka values of 1.1 and 2.9. In both cases, the time-domain derived data is compared with analytic Mie series results. Good agreement in the

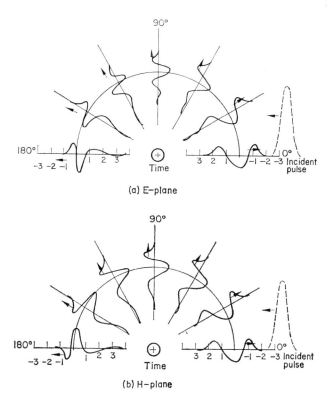

(a) E-plane

(b) H-plane

FIG. 4.36. Bistatic impulse response of a sphere in the E- and H-planes. (After Bennett and Weeks, 1968.)

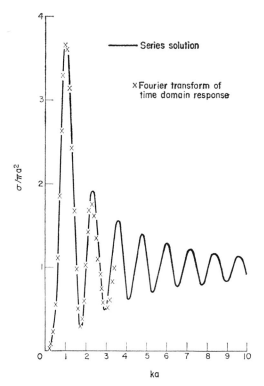

FIG. 4.37. Frequency domain calculations compared with time-domain results for RCS frequency response of a conducting sphere. (After Bennett and Weeks, 1968.)

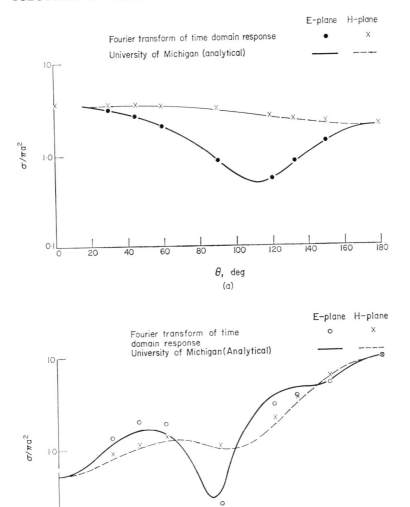

FIG. 4.38. Bistatic RCS of sphere with (a) $ka = 1.1$; (b) $ka = 2.9$.

bistatic patterns may be seen as well as in the backscatter RCS out to a ka value of approximately π, beyond which the time-domain results become progressively worse. This high
frequency cutoff in data derived from the time domain is of course to be expected, due to
the frequency content of the incident pulse and the spatial separation ΔR between current
sample points on the sphere. The latter consideration limits the validity of the results to a
frequency on the order of f_{H}, such that $f_{\mathrm{H}} \gtrsim c/4\Delta R$, i.e. on the order of four sample points
per wavelength are required for accurate data. The incident pulse width W_p relative to the
scatterer size W_s also influences the maximum frequency for accurate results, since the

frequency content of the gaussian pulse falls off as $\exp[-a^2\omega^2]$ where a is on the order of $W_p/4c$. If $W_p/W_s = R$, the frequency spectrum of the incident pulse varies as

$$\exp[-(\omega^2/16c^2)\,R^2].$$

Thus, the wider the pulse, the more rapid the high-frequency falloff. Consequently the upper frequency limit on calculation accuracy will be dependent not only upon ΔR but R as well, because of the necessarily limited accuracy of the numerical computation.

In order to demonstrate the influence of the parameter R upon the scattered pulse shapes, in Fig. 4.39 are shown the E- and H-plane pulses scattered from a sphere such that R is twice that used to obtain the results of Fig. 4.36. A comparison of the data in Fig. 4.36 with

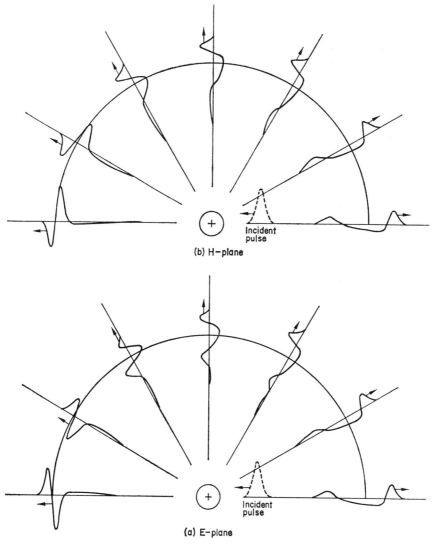

FIG. 4.39. Approximate bistatic impulse response of a sphere.
(After Bennett and Weeks, 1968.)

that of Fig. 4.39 shows that for the latter case the scattered pulse amplitude is increased with respect to the incident pulse and is lengthened as well.

The bistatic scattering patterns for axial incidence of a gaussian pulse on a sphere-capped cylinder, also due to Bennett, are shown in Fig. 4.40. Note that the pulse size relative to the sphere part of the cylinder is the same as that considered for the sphere scattering case shown above in Fig. 4.39, and the cylindrical portion of the structure is two sphere diameters in

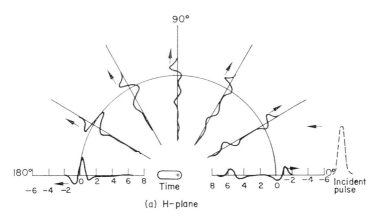

(a) H-plane

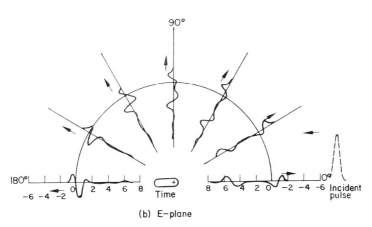

(b) E-plane

FIG. 4.40. Bistatic impulse response of a hemispherically capped cylinder in the *E*- and *H*-planes for axial incidence. (After Bennett and Weeks, 1968.)

length. A comparison of Figs. 4.39 and 4.40 reveals that the leading portions of the pulse scattered from the sphere-capped cylinder (Fig. 4.40) closely resemble the corresponding sphere scattered pulses (Fig. 4.39). A lengthening of the scattered pulse occurs for the cylinder case of course because of its greater size. Of particular interest is the backscatter pulse where the second portion has a leading negative part due to the join, followed by a positive creeping wave contribution.

The frequency response in the backscatter direction for the sphere-capped cylinder is shown in Fig. 4.41. Also presented are experimental data points obtained on the authors' rail-

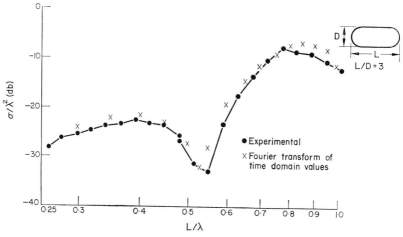

FIG. 4.41. Numerical–experimental comparison of the backscatter RCS frequency response of a hemispherically lagged cylinder for axial incidence.

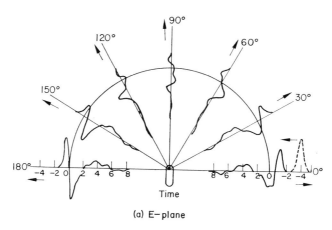

(a) E–plane

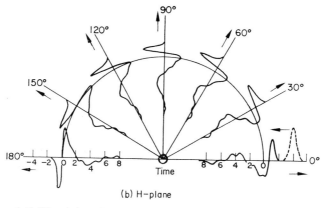

(b) H–plane

FIG. 4.42. Bistatic impulse response of a hemispherically capped cylinder in the E- and H-planes for broadside incidence.

line range (Gans, 1965). Generally good agreement is obtained between the time-domain derived results and the experimental measurement.

Continuing the sphere-capped cylinder example, we present in Fig. 4.42 the *E*- and *H*-plane bistatic scattering patterns for broadside incidence on the cylinder with the incident electric field parallel to the cylinder axis. These results were obtained in early 1969 using a modification of Bennett's program to extend the approach to plane symmetric bodies. A comparison of Figs. 4.40 and 4.42 verifies that the time variation of the bistatic scattered pulses does satisfy the reciprocity requirement of a valid solution to Maxwell's equations.

To conclude the sphere-capped cylinder example, we present in Figs. 4.43 and 4.44 some results for this structure when excited as an antenna by applying a gaussian pulse of azimuthally directed magnetic field across the center band of the cylinder. A Fourier transform of the bistatic radiated fields shown in Fig. 4.43 leads to the radiation patterns presented in Fig. 4.44. Such pattern shapes are compatible with the well-known properties of linear dipole antennas.

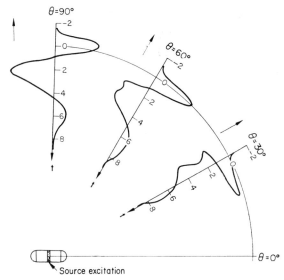

FIG. 4.43. Gaussian impulse response of a cylindrical antenna with hemispherical end caps.

A somewhat more challenging structure for analysis, the cone–sphere, is next considered. The *E*- and *H*-plane bistatic patterns for axial incidence on the tip end and sphere end are presented in Figs. 4.45 and 4.46 respectively as obtained from the authors' time domain program. The cone-tip end may be seen to backscatter much less effectively than the sphere end, but in both cases the join return is substantial. The creeping wave contribution is further observed to be much stronger for the cone-tip incidence case. Note that reciprocity is satisfied for these two angles of incidence which, while not a sufficient test to insure solution accuracy, is a necessary one. A Fourier transform of the tip-end incidence backscatter field leads to the RCS results shown in Fig. 4.47, where they are seen to agree well with experiment. Comparison of the bistatic scattered fields for tip-end incidence obtained from the time domain calculation with the corresponding frequency domain result is presented in Fig. 4.48, where good agreement is also obtained.

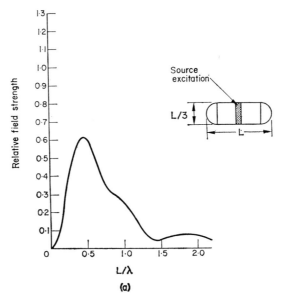

FIG. 4.44. (a) Frequency response of broadside radiation from cylindrical antenna computed from gaussian impulse response.

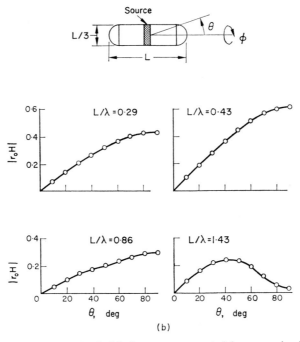

FIG. 4.44. (b) Radiation pattern of cylindrical antenna computed from gaussian impulse response.

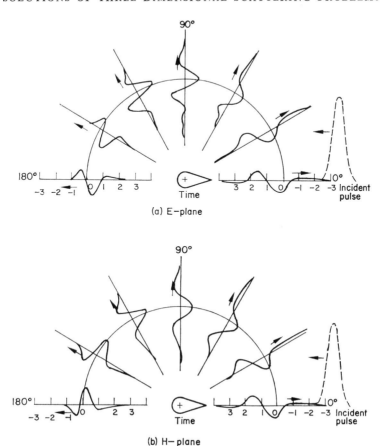

(a) E—plane

(b) H—plane

FIG. 4.45. Approximate bistatic impulse response of a 15-degree half-angle cone–sphere in the *E*- and *H*-planes for cone-tip incidence.

Results for broad-side incidence on the cone–sphere are next shown in Fig. 4.49 for the *E*-field parallel to the cone axis. These results present a further check on the reciprocity of the scattered fields when compared with the data shown in Fig. 4.45 and 4.46.

In addition to observing the time-variation of the scattered fields obtained from this analysis, it is also of interest to examine the induced current variation as the incident pulse propagation past the scatterer. A presentation of the *H*-plane longitudinal surface current at various instants of time on the cone sphere for tip-end incidence is shown in Fig. 4.50. The position of the incident pulse relative to the cone–sphere is depicted for each current plot as a function of arc length along the structure. Propagation of the induced current pulse toward the sphere end is clearly observable, as is its reflection at the sphere end. Note that the current amplitude peaks after the exciting field has already passed beyond the end of the cone–sphere, due to the delay of the creeping wave fields which must propagate around the circumference of the structure. The field computations are based on the geometric distance between source and observation points, whereas the current flow must follow the greater distance along the circumference of the structure. Thus an additional numerical check is

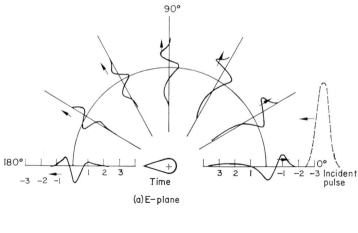

(a) E-plane

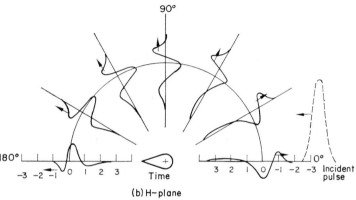

(b) H-plane

FIG. 4.46. Approximate bistatic impulse response of a 15-degree half-angle cone–sphere
in the E- and H-planes for sphere-end incidence.

provided on the solution by the fact that the total field must remain identically zero in the
shadow region until the creeping wave current reaches it.

The validity checks provided thus far have been, apart from the bistatic reciprocity checks,
primarily associated with independent theoretical or experimental results obtained in the
frequency domain. Various facilities now exist for making direct time-domain measurements, so that the intervening Fourier transform need not be resorted to, allowing a more
direct check to be made on the computed results. An example of such a backscatter measurement for a sphere with an incident gaussian pulse width equal to the sphere's diameter is
shown in Fig. 4.51. These data were obtained on the Sperry Rand Research Center ground
plane range (Bennett and De Lorenzo, 1969). The sampling scope display of the incident and
scattered pulse are separately presented, as well as a graph on which are plotted the computed and measured results. This pulse-width to sphere size ratio R reproduces the case already presented in Fig. 4.36. Quite good agreement is obtained between the numerical and
experimental scattered pulse shapes.

A comparison of the measured and computed backscatter pulse shapes for axial incidence
on a right, circular cylinder having a length-to-diameter ratio of 2 is given in Fig. 4.52 (Ben-

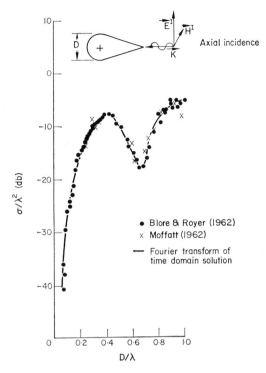

FIG. 4.47. Numerical-experimental comparison of the backscatter RCS frequency response
of a 15-degree half-angle cone–sphere for cone-tip incidence.

nett and De Lorenzo, 1969). The initial return from the flat end of the cylinder closely
approximates a derivative of the incident pulse, as would be expected for a flat surface
[eqn. (4.42)]. A contribution subsequently occurs due to the end discontinuity followed by
the final positive pulse coming from a wave travelling around the rear of the cylinder.

The preceding examples should indicate the potential of the direct time-domain view of
the scattering process. While the examples presented here have been restricted to fairly
simple cases, the method is suitable for analyzing more complex geometries. Though the
discussion has been primarily concerned with scattering problems, the technique is perhaps
even more suitable for antenna analysis. In the latter case, the radiation pattern over a wide
band is obtainable with a single calculation, whereas in order to get the monostatic RCS, the
calculation must be repeated for each angle of incidence required.

THIN-WIRE STRUCTURES

Apparently the first time-domain integral equation solution for the dipole as either a scatterer or antenna is due to Sayre (1969) and Sayre and Harrington (1968), who used the time-
dependent vector and scalar integro-differential equation formulation. Sayre also applied
his analysis to the thin-circular loop. Some of his results are included here.

In Fig. 4.53 are shown the time-dependent driving point currents on a center-fed linear
antenna having a length to diameter ratio, $L/2a$, of 74.2 excited by a unit voltage step. The

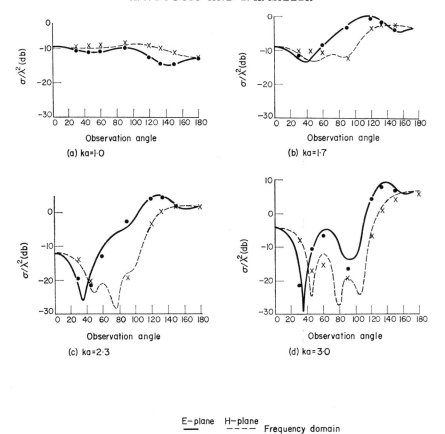

E-plane   H-plane
———   ————   Frequency domain
         •   x   Time domain

FIG. 4.48. Cone–sphere bistatic scattering pattern for tip incidence (30 degree included cone angle) as computed using frequency domain and Fourier transformed time-domain results.

two curves depict results for a zero impedance generator ($R = 0$ ohm) and a 50-ohm generator ($R_g = 50$ ohms) respectively. It may be seen that the only effect of the non-zero generator resistance is to increase the current damping rate, but it has no influence on the current periodicity, compared with the zero impedance case. The period of the oscillation also corresponds closely to the fundamental mode of the center-fed dipole.

The Fourier transform of the driving point current in Fig. 4.53(a) leads to the driving point admittance variation with kL as shown in Fig. 4.54.

Time plots of the induced current and broadside scattered field for broadside incidence of a unit-step in electric field are shown in Fig. 4.55 also for a wire with $L/2a = 74.2$. Both the current and scattered field oscillate with a frequency which closely corresponds to the fundamental mode of the wire. The rounding off of the current waveform with advancing time demonstrates the greater radiation efficiency of the higher frequency current components. This result is similar to that already seen for the antenna case shown in Fig. 4.53.

Some additional results have been obtained by the authors using the time-dependent electric field integral eqn. (4.38) as specialized to thin wire structures (Poggio *et al.*, 1971).

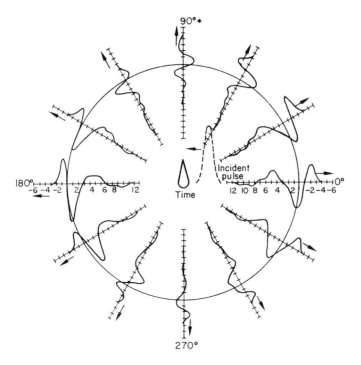

*Reciprocity tests with figures 4.45 and 4.46

FIG. 4.49. Approximate bistatic impulse response of a 15-degree half-angle cone–sphere in the E-plane for broadside incidence.

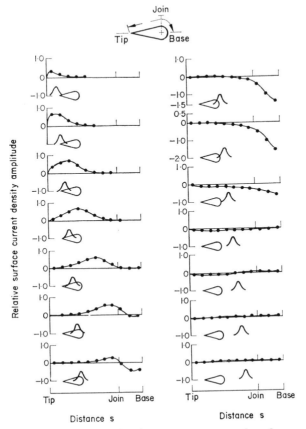

FIG. 4.50. H-plane component of the induced current on a cone–sphere for cone-tip incidence.

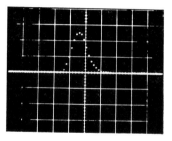

Measured incident pulse
(horiz. scale approx. one sphere radius/div.)

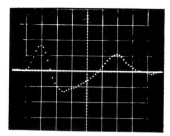

Measured sphere response
(Horizontal scale approximately one sphere radius per div.)

FIG. 4.51. Comparison with experiment of the calculated impulse response of a sphere. (After Bennett and De Lorenzo, 1969.)

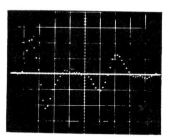

Measured end-on cylinder response
(horiz scale approx. one cylinder diam./div.)

FIG. 4.52. Comparison with experiment of the calculated impulse response for axial incidence of a right circular cylinder. (After Bennett and De Lorenzo, 1969.)

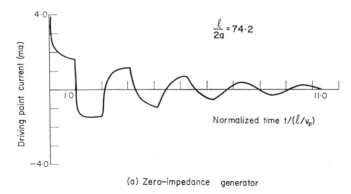

(a) Zero–impedance generator

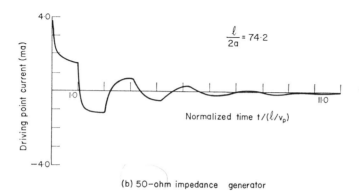

(b) 50–ohm impedance generator

FIG. 4.53. Computed driving point current for unit voltage-step excitation of a linear antenna. (After Sayre and Harrington, 1968.)

By using parabolic interpolation functions in space and time, arbitrary space-time sample point spacing (such that R is not necessarily greater than $c\varDelta T$) became possible. As a result a structure-dependent matrix of order N (but sparse) requires inversion, after which the solution proceeds as previously described by marching on in time. Some examples of time-domain antenna and scattering calculations using this approach for an incident gaussian pulse shape are included here.

Figure 4.56 pertains to a linear, center-fed dipole antenna with a gaussian time-dependent source. The pertinent parameters describing the excitation and segmentation are included on the figure. Part (a) describes the source current and clearly shows the effects of the gaussian-shaped current pulse which is excited on the antenna. Part (b) of the figure illustrates the accuracy of the computations in so far as the input admittance computed by using the quotient of the Fourier transforms of the input current and the excitation voltage agrees with independent data.

The broadside field of the dipole antenna of Fig. 4.56 is shown in Fig. 4.57. Again the Fourier transform is used to obtain the frequency domain data which is compared with frequency domain computed fields over a bandwidth $0 \le L/\lambda \le 3.0$. Hence a single time

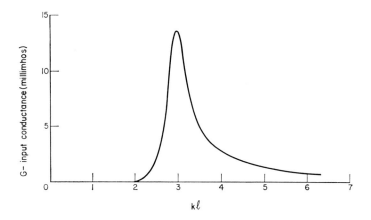

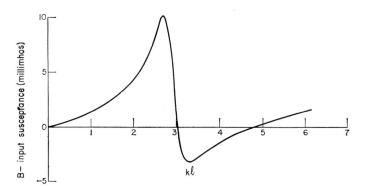

FIG. 4.54. Frequency dependence of driving point admittance for linear antenna derived from step excitation response. (After Sayre and Harrington, 1968.)

domain calculation provides the frequency domain response over a band of frequencies. Figure 4.58 is the time-dependent radiated field at an off-broadside angle of 40 degrees. Here one can locate the effective regions of radiation by noting that the first peak pertains to radiation from the source while subsequent peaks pertain alternatively to radiation from the nearer and further ends of the dipole. The time spacing between the nth peak and the first peak is given by

$$L\{n - (3 + (-1)^{n+1})/2 + (-1)^{n-1}\sin\theta\}/2c$$

with θ the off-broadside angle.

Results for a V-antenna excited by a gaussian time-dependent source is shown in Fig. 4.59. By Fourier transformation-frequency domain results are generated for ready comparison with independent data.

The time-dependent backscattered field for a pulse incident on a V-dipole in a direction normal to its plane and with the electric field perpendicular to the dipole bisector is presented in Fig. 4.60. Also shown is the corresponding frequency dependent cross-section obtained from a Fourier transform of the approximate impulse response, together with values obtained directly in the frequency domain. Note that the backscattered field initially

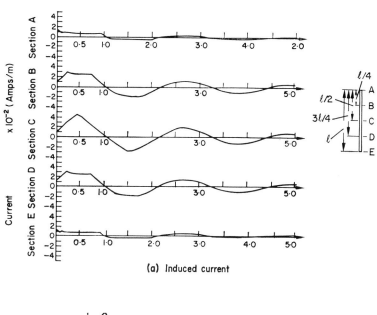

(a) Induced current

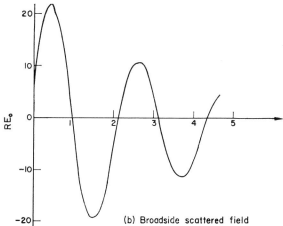

(b) Broadside scattered field

FIG. 4.55. Results for a unit-electric field step at broadside incidence on a straight wire.
(After Sayre and Harrington, 1968.)

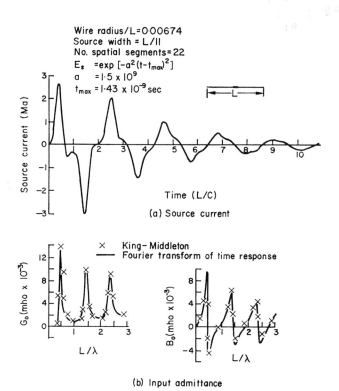

(a) Source current

(b) Input admittance

FIG. 4.56. Linear antenna with gaussian source time dependence.

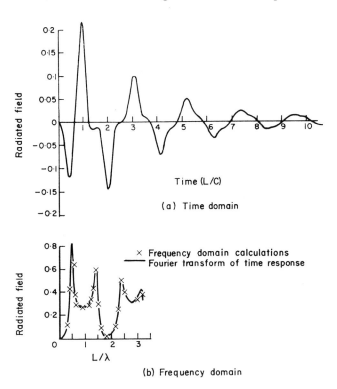

(a) Time domain

(b) Frequency domain

FIG. 4.57. Broadside radiated field of linear antenna with gaussian source time dependence.

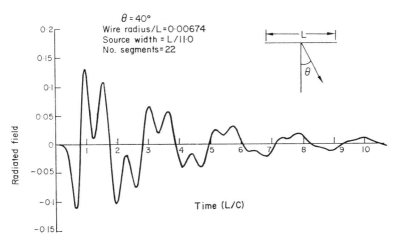

FIG. 4.58. Radiated field of a linear antenna with gaussian source time dependence (off-broadside).

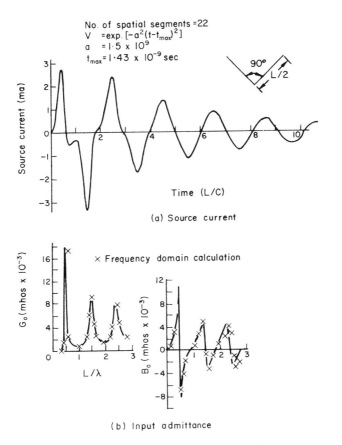

(a) Source current

(b) Input admittance

FIG. 4.59. V-antenna with gaussian source time dependence.

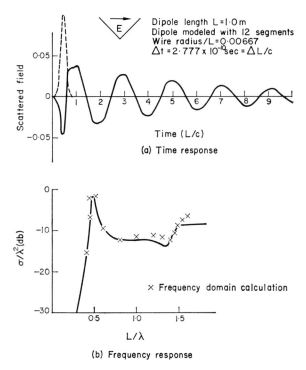

FIG. 4.60. Scattering of a gaussian pulse by a V-dipole.

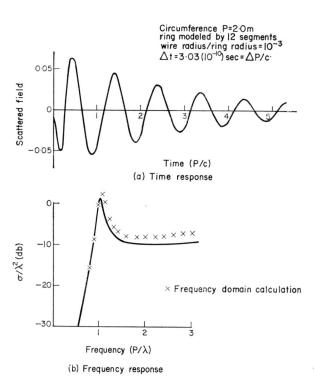

FIG. 4.61. Scattering of a gaussian pulse by a ring.

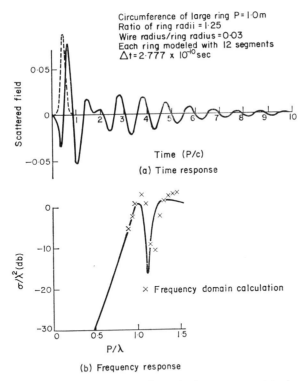

Circumference of large ring P=1·0 m
Ratio of ring radii = 1·25
Wire radius/ring radius =0·03
Each ring modeled with 12 segments
$\Delta t = 2·777 \times 10^{-10}$ sec

Scattered field

0·05

0

−0·05

Time (P/c)

(a) Time response

σ/λ^2(db)

0

−10

−20

−30

× Frequency domain calculation

0   0·5   1·0   1·5

P/λ

(b) Frequency response

FIG. 4.62. Scattering of a gaussian pulse by two concentric rings.

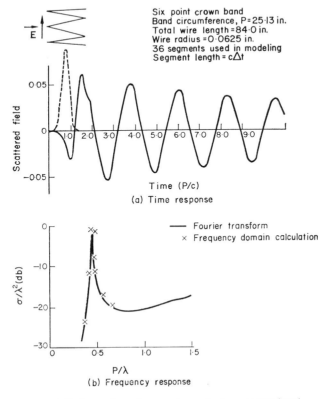

E

Six point crown band
Band circumference, P=25·13 in.
Total wire length =84·0 in.
Wire radius =0·0625 in.
36 segments used in modeling
Segment length = cΔt

Scattered field

0·05

0

−0·05

Time (P/c)

(a) Time response

σ/λ^2(db)

0

−10

−20

−30

—— Fourier transform
× Frequency domain calculation

0   0·5   1·0   1·5

P/λ

(b) Frequency response

FIG. 4.63. Scattering of a gaussian pulse by a crown band.

approximates a derivative of the incident pulse, and that the frequency behavior of the values calculated using these two methods are quite close. A slight frequency shift does occur, possibly due to slight differences in the degree to which the boundary conditions are satisfied.

Results using a similar format are shown in Fig. 4.61 through 4.63 for a circular ring, two concentric coplanar circular rings, and of a zig-zag band (crown) wrapped around a cylinder, all for axial incidence. The time-dependent fields of these various scatterers are very distinctive, indicating the feasibility of target identification using the time-domain approach. In addition, examination of various time dependent phenomena, the near field or current distribution, for example, can offer more insight into the electromagnetic characteristics of a given structure than corresponding frequency domain results.

4.5. CONCLUDING REMARKS

The discussion above has been intended to provide an overview of current numerical methods, capabilities and limitations in the application of integral equation techniques to electromagnetic problems. We have attempted, in the limited space available, to put into perspective the relative value of computer-oriente dapproaches by outlining the theoretical development and numerical treatment of such problems and by presenting sample results. The references quoted and results presented represent of course only a small part of the work performed in the more general subject area of numerical techniques and integral equations. Nevertheless, the material discussed hopefully gives an objective viewpoint on the numerical treatment of electromagnetic problems via integral equations.

In spite of the demonstrated success of the numerical integral equation approach for a fairly wide variety of problems, there are areas where improvements are required for more widespread applicability of such techniques. Foremost among these are the development of modeling and accuracy guidelines for arbitrary structure geometry so that each new geometry does not have to be approached as a new problem. Ideally, this would lead to establishing realistic error bounds in terms of structure size and geometrical peculiarities. Directly related to this is the development of more efficient solution techniques which minimize the overall expense associated with the evaluation of a given problem. This would include the cost and time of developing suitable mathematical models and computer descriptions for the problem and may involve a computer graphics interface with the user.

Extension of the basic techniques to larger structures is also vital. This may include combination solution techniques such as the physical optics-integral equation approach discussed above, and exploiting the advantages of various approximations along the lines of iteration, sparse matrices, etc.

Finally, the capability for the handling of more involved multi-region problems which include dielectric bodies of different permittivity, ground effects, inhomogeneous media, etc., is essential if the treatment of many real-world problems is to be practical. While such problems may appear to be intractable now for other than idealized geometries, it is certain that continued progress both in solution techniques and computer technology, perhaps by expeditious combination of analog and digital machines, will expand the range of practical problems which can be efficiently and accurately treated.

The future of these numerical techniques, based on past developments, appears promising. It is clear, however, that since the ultimate test of a computer-derived result is comparison with experiment, comparable progress is also required in the design and implementation of experimental methods. In the final analysis, theory and experimentation are the complementary tools of electromagnetics.

ACKNOWLEDGMENTS

The authors wish to thank their colleagues, Messrs. G. J. Burke and E. S. Selden of MBAssociates for aid in preparing the material in this chapter. The cooperation of K. M. Mitzner of Northrop Corporation, Aircraft Division, in making available various numerical and experimental data also is appreciated. Above all, the authors are grateful to Miss Cheryl Grauman for her unexcelled efficiency, diligence, and accuracy in the preparation of the manuscript.

REFERENCES

AMITAY, N. and GALINDO, V. (1969) On energy conservation and the method of moments in scattering problems, *IEEE Trans. Ant. & Prop. AP-17*, 747–51.

ANDREASEN, M. G. (1964) Scattering from parallel metallic cylinders with arbitrary cross sections, *IEEE Trans. Ant. & Prop. AP-12*, 746–54.

ANDREASEN, M. G. (1965a) Scattering from cylinders with arbitrary surface impedance, *Proc. IEEE 53*, 812–17.

ANDREASEN, M. G. (1965b) Scattering from bodies of revolution, *IEEE Trans. Ant. & Prop. AP-13*, 303–10.

BAKER, B. B. and COPSON, E. T. (1953) *The Mathematical Theory of Huygens' Principle*, 2nd ed., Oxford University Press, London.

BECHTEL, M. E. (1965) Application of geometric diffraction theory to scattering from cones and discs, *Proc. IEEE 53*, 877–82.

BECHTEL, M. E. and ROSS, R. A. (1966) *Radar Scattering Analysis*, Cornell Aeronautical Laboratory Report No. ER/RIS-10.

BECKMANN, P. (1968) *The Depolarization of Electromagnetic Waves*, The Golem Press, Boulder, Colorado.

BENNETT, C. L. and WEEKS, W. L. (1968) Electromagnetic pulse response of cylindrical scatterers, G-AP Symposium, Boston, Mass. See also *A Technique for Computing Approximate Electromagnetic Impulse Response of Conducting Bodies*, Purdue University Report TR-EE68-11.

BENNETT, C. L. and WEEKS, W. L. (1969) Transient scattering from conducting cylinders, *IEEE Trans. Ant. and Prop. AP-18*, 627–33.

BENNETT, C. L. and DE LORENZO, J. D. (1969), Short pulse response of radar targets, *G-AP International Symposium, Austin, Texas*, pp. 124–30.

BOJARSKI, NORBERT (1969) Private communication.

BOLLE, D. M. and MORGANSTERN, M. D. (1969) Monopole and Conic Antennas on Spherical Vehicles, *IEEE Trans. Ant. & Prop. AP-17*, 477–84.

BOWMAN, J. J., SENIOR, T. B. A. and USLENGHI, P. L. E. (eds.) (1969) *Electromagnetic and Acoustic Scattering by Simple Shapes*, North Holland Publishing, Amsterdam.

CHENG, D. K. and TSENG, F. I. (1969) Pencil-beam synthesis for large circular arrays, *G-AP Int. Symposium, Austin, Texas*, pp. 26–7.

CHERTOCK, G. and GROSSO, M. A. (1960) *Some Numerical Calculations of Sound Radiation from Vibrating Surfaces*, Dept. of the Navy, Acoustics and Vibration Laboratory Research and Development Report 2109.

COLLIN, R. E. and ZUCKER, F. J. (1969) *Antenna Theory*, Part 1, McGraw Hill, New York.

COPLEY, L. G. (1968) Fundamental results concerning integral representations in acoustic radiation, *J. Acoust. Soc. Amer. 44*, No. 1, pp. 28–32.

CRISPIN, J. W. and SIEGEL, K. M. (ed.) (1968) *Methods of Radar Cross-Section Analysis*, Academic Press, New York.

DANIEL, S. M. and MITTRA, R. (1970) An optimal solution to a scattering problem, *Proc. IEEE 58*, 270–1.

FADEEVA, V. N. (1959) *Computational Methods of Linear Algebra*, Dover Publications, Inc., New York.

FENLON, F. H. (1969) Calculation of the acoustic radiation field at the surface of a finite cylinder by the method of weighted residuals, *Proc. IEEE 57*, 291–306.

FRIEDLAENDER, F. J. (1958) *Sound Pulses*, Cambridge University Press London.

FRIEDMAN, M. B. and SHAW, R. (1962) Diffraction of pulses by cylindrical obstacles of arbitrary cross-section, *Trans. ASME*, Ser. E, *29*, 40–47.

GANS, M. J. (1965) The transmission line scattering range, *Proc. IEEE 53*, 1081–2.

GLAUERT, H. (1930) *The Elements of Airfoil and Airscrew Theory*, Cambridge University Press, London.

HALLEN, E. (1938) Theoretical investigation into transmitting and receiving antennae, *Nova Acta Regiae Societatis Scientiarum Upsalienis* (Sweden), Ser. 4, *11*.

HARRINGTON, R. F. (1961) *Time Harmonic Electromagnetic Fields*, McGraw-Hill, New York.

HARRINGTON, R. F. (1967) Straight wires with arbitrary excitation and loading, *IEEE Trans. Ant. & Prop. AP-15*, 502–15.

HARRINGTON, R. F. (1968) *Field Computation by Moment Methods*, Macmillan, New York.

HARRINGTON, R. F. and MAUTZ, J. R. (1969) *Radiation and Scattering from Bodies of Revolution*, Syracuse University, Electrical Engineering Dept., Contract No. F-19628-67-C-0233, Final Report.

HILDEBRAND, F. B. (1956) *Introduction to Numerical Analysis*, McGraw-Hill, New York.

HOUSEHOLDER, A. S. (1953) *Principles of Numerical Analysis*, McGraw-Hill Book Co., New York.

JONES, D. S. (1964) *The Theory of Electromagnetism*, Pergamon Press, New York.

KELLER, JOSEPH B. (1962) Geometrical theory of diffraction, *J. Opt. Soc. Amer. 52*, 116.

KELLOGG, O. D. (1953) *Foundations of Potential Theory*, Dover Publications, New York.

KENNAUGH, E. M. and COSGRIFF, R. L. (1958) The use of impulse response in electromagnetic scattering problems, *IRE Nat'l Conv. Rec.*, pt. 1, pp. 72–7.

KENNAUGH, E. M. and MOFFATT, D. L. (1961) On the axial echo area of the cone sphere shape, *Proc. IRE* (Correspondence) *50*, 199.

KENNAUGH, E. M. and MOFFATT, D. L. (1965) Transient and impulse response approximations, *Proc. IEEE 53*, 893–901.

KING, R. W. P. (1956) *The Theory of Linear Antennas*, Harvard University Press, Cambridge, Massachusetts.

KING, R. W. P. and WU, T. T. (1959) *The Scattering and Diffraction of Waves*, Harvard University Press, Cambridge, Mass.

KOUYOUMJIAN, R. G. (1966) *An Introduction to Geometrical Optics and the Geometrical Theory of Diffraction, Antenna and Scattering Theory: Recent Advances*, Vol. I; Short Courses at Ohio State University.

MAUE, A. W. (1949) The formulation of a general diffraction problem by an integral equation, *Zeitschrift für Physik*, Bd. 126, pp. 601–18.

MAUTZ, J. R. and HARRINGTON, R. F. (1968) *Generalized Network Parameters for Bodies of Revolution*, Syracuse University, Electrical Engineering Department, Contract No. F-19628-67-C-0233, Scientific Report No. 1.

MBASSOCIATES (1970) *Log-Periodic Scattering Array Program*, Final Technical Report under ARPA Order No. 936, Amendment No. 2.

MEI, K. K. (1965) On the integral equation of thin wire antennas, *IEEE Trans. Ant. & Prop. AP-13*, 374–8.

MENTZER, J. R. (1955) *Scattering and Diffraction of Radio Waves*, MacMillan, New York.

MILLER, E. K. (1968) Admittance of an inhomogeneously sheathed infinite cylindrical antenna immersed in an isotropic compressible plasma, *IEEE Trans. Ant. & Prop. AP-16*, 501–2.

MILLER, E. K. (1970) A variable interval with quadrature technique based on Romberg's Method, *J. Comput. Phys. 5*, no. 2 265–79.

MILLER, E. K. BURKE, G. J. MAXUM, B. J. NEUREUTHER, A. R. and PJERROU, G. M. (1969) The radar cross section of a long wire, *IEEE Trans. Ant. & Prop. AP-17*, 381–4.

MILLER, E. K. and BURKE, G. J. (1969) Numerical integration methods, *IEEE Trans. Ant. & Prop. AP-17*, 669–72.

MILLER, E. K. and MAXUM, B. J. (1970) *Mathematical Modeling of Aircraft Antennas and Supporting Structures*, Final Report, ECOM Contract ADDB07-68-C-0456, Report No. ECOM-0456-1.

MILLER, E. K. and MORTON, J. B. (1970) The RCS of a metal plate with a resonant slot, *IEEE Trans. Ant. & Prop.* AP-18, 290–2.

MITZNER, K. M. (1967) An integral equation approach to scattering from a body of finite conductivity, *Radio Science*, 2 (New Series), 1459–70.

MITZNER, K. M. (1968) Numerical solution of the exterior scattering problem at eigenfrequencies of the interior problem, Fall URSI Meeting, Boston, Mass.

MITZNER, K. M. (1969) Electromagnetic scattering from symmetric bodies, Spring URSI Meeting, Washington, D.C.

MOFFATT, D.L. (1962) *Low Radar Cross Sections, the Cone Sphere*, The Ohio State University Antenna Laboratory, Report No. 1223–5.

MOFFATT, D.L. and KENNAUGH, E.M. (1965) The axial echo area of a perfectly conducting prolate spheroid, *IEEE Trans. Ant. & Prop.* AP-*13*, 401–9.

MÜLLER, C. (1969) *Foundations of the Mathematical Theory of Electromagnetic Waves*, Springer-Verlag, New York.

MULLIN, C.R., SANDBURG, R. and VELLINE, C.O. (1965) A numerical technique for the determination of scattering cross sections of infinite cylinders of arbitrary geometrical cross section, *IEEE Trans. Ant. & Prop.* AP-*13*, 141–9.

MUSKHELISHVILI, N.I. (1953) *Singular Integral Equations*, Groningen.

NEUREUTHER, A.R., FULLER, B.D., HAKKE, G.D. and HOHMANN, G. *et al.* (1969) A comparison of numerical methods for thin wire antennas, presented at the 1968 Fall URSI meeting, Department of Electrical Engineering and Computer Sciences, University of California, Berkeley.

OSHIRO, F.K. (1965) Source distribution techniques for the solution of general electromagnetic scattering problems, *Proc. First GISAT Symposium, Mitre Corp.*, vol. I, pp. 83–107.

OSHIRO, F.K. and CROSS, R.G. (1966) *A Source Distribution Technique for Solution of Two-Dimensional Scattering Problems*, Northrop Norair Report NOR 66-74.

OSHIRO, F.K., MITZNER, K.M. and CROSS, R.G. (1967) Scattering from finite cylinders by source distribution technique, *Proc. GISAT II Symposium, Mitre Corp.*, vol. II, pt. I.

OSHIRO, F.K. and MITZNER, K.M. (1967) Digital computer solution of three-dimensional scattering problems, presented at 1967 IEEE International Antennas and Propagation Symposium, Ann Arbor, Michigan, October 1967. Summary published in the *Symposium Digest*, pp. 257–63.

OSHIRO, F.K., MITZNER, K.M., LOCUS, S.S. *et al.* (1969) *Calculation of Radar Cross Section*, Air Force Avionics Laboratory Tech. Rept. AFAL-TR-69-52 (SECRET); also AFAL-TR-69-155 (CONFIDENTIAL).

OSHIRO, F.K., MITZNER, K.M. and LOCUS, S.S. *et al.* (1970) *Calculation of Radar Cross-section*, Air Force Avionics Laboratory Tech. Rept. AFAL-TR-70-21, Part II, April 1970.

OSHIRO, F.K., TORRES, F.P. and HEATH, H.C. (1966) *Numerical Procedures for Calculating Radar Cross-section of Arbitrarily Shaped Three-dimensional Geometries*, Air Force Avionics Lab. Tech. Rept. AFAL-TR-66-162, vol. I (UNCLASSIFIED) and vol. II (SECRET).

OSHIRO, F.K. and SU, C.S. (1965) *A Source Distribution Technique for the Solution of General Electromagnetic Scattering Problems*, Northrop Norair Rept. NOR 65-271.

POGGIO, A.J. (1969) Space-time and space-frequency domain integral equations, MBA Technical Memo MB-TM-69/63.

POGGIO, A.J. and MAYES, P.E. (1969) *Numerical Solution of Integral Equations of Dipole and Slot Antennas Including Active and Passive Loading*, Univ. of Illinois Antenna Lab. Tech. Rept. AFAL-TR-69-180.

POGGIO, A.J., MILLER, E.K. and BURKE, G.J. (1971) Scattering from thin-wire structures in the time domain, presented at 1971 Spring URSI Meeting, Washington, D.C.

RALSTON, A. (1965) *A First Course in Numerical Analysis*, McGraw-Hill, New York.

RHEINSTEIN, J. (1968) Backscatter from sphere: a short pulse view, *IEEE Trans. Ant. & Prop.* AP-*16*, 89–97.

RICHMOND, J.H. (1965) Scattering by a dielectric cylinder of arbitrary cross section shape, *IEEE Trans. Ant. & Prop..* AP-*13*, 334–41.

RICHMOND, J.H. (1965) Digital computer solutions of the rigorous equations for scattering problems, *Proc. IEEE 53*, 796–804.

RICHMOND, J.H. (1966) A wire-grid model for scattering by conducting bodies, *IEEE Trans. Ant. & Prop.* AP-*14*, 782–6.

ROBICHAUX, W.G. and GRIFFEE, L.V. (1967) *Model Studies for Homing Antennas on Army Aircraft*, Contract DA28-043-AMC-02394(E), Tech. Report ECOM-02394-F, Collins Radio Co., Dallas, Texas.

ROSS, R.A. (1966) Radar cross section of rectangular flat plates as a function of aspect angle, *IEEE Trans. Ant. & Prop.* AP-*14*, 329–35.

ROSS, R.A. and BECHTEL, M.E. (1966) Radar cross section prediction using the geometrical theory of diffraction, *IEEE International Antennas and Propagation Symposium Digest*, p. 18.

RUCK, G.T., BARRICK, D.E., STUART, W.D. and KIRCHBAUM, C.K. (1969) *Radar Cross Section Handbook*, Plenum Press, New York.

RYU, J. (1970) *Finite Element Technique to Electromagnetic Modeling*, Preliminary Report, Engineering Geoscience, University of California, Berkeley, California.

RUCKGABER, G.M. and SCHULTZ, F.V. (1968) *Electromagnetic Scattering by Finned Objects*, Purdue Univ., School of Electrical Engineering, Contract No. AF-19(628)-1691, Scientific Rept. No. 4.

SAYRE, E.P. and HARRINGTON, R.F. (1968) Transient response of straight wire scatterers and antennas, *Proc. 1968 Intnl. Ant. Prop. Symposium, Boston, Mass.*, p. 160.

SAYRE, E.P. (1969) *Transient Response of Wire Antennas and Scatterers*, Electrical Engineering Department, Syracuse University, Technical Report TR-69-4.

SCHENCK, H.A. (1968) Improved integral formulation for acoustic radiation problems, *J. Acoust. Soc. Amer. 44*, no. 1, 41–58.

SENIOR, T.B.A. (1960) Impedance boundary conditions for imperfectly conducting surfaces, *Appl. Sci. Res.*, Sec. B, *8*.

SHAFAI, L. (1969) Application of coordinate transformation to two-dimensional scattering and diffraction problems. *Can. J. Phys. 47*, 795.

SILVER, S. (1949) *Microwave Antenna Theory and Design*, McGraw-Hill, New York.

SOULES, G.W. and MITZNER, K.M. (1967) *Pulses in Linear Acoustics*, Northrop Nortronics Rept. ARD 66-60R; see also MITZNER, K.M. (1967) Numerical Solution for Transient Scattering from a Surface of Arbitrary Shape—Retarded Potential Technique, *J. Acoust. Soc. Amer. 42*, 391–7.

Special Issue on Radar Reflectivity (1965) *Proc. IEEE 53*, no. 8.

STRATTON, J.A. (1941) *Electromagnetic Theory*, McGraw-Hill, New York.

TANNER, R.L. and ANDREASEN, M.G. (1967) Numerical solution of electromagnetic problems, *IEEE Spectrum 4*, no. 9, 53–61.

TESCHE, F.M. and NEUREUTHER, A.R. (1970) Radiation patterns for two monopoles on a perfectly conducting sphere, *IEEE Trans. Ant. & Prop. AP-18*, 692–4.

UFIMTSEV, P. (1962) The method of fringe waves in the physical theory of diffraction, *Sovyetskoye Radio*, Moscow.

VANBLADEL, J. (1964) *Electromagnetic Fields*, McGraw-Hill, New York.

VANBLADEL, J. (1961) Some remarks on Green's dyadic for infinite space. *IRE Trans. Ant. & Prop. AP-9*, 563–6.

WATERMAN, P.C. (1965) Matrix formulation of electromagnetic scattering, *Proc. IEEE 53*, 805–12.

WILLOUGHBY, R.A. (Ed.) (1969) *Proceedings of the Symposium on Sparse Matrices and Their Applications*, IBM Watson Research Center, 9–10 Sept. 1968.

YEH, Y.S. and MEI, K.K. (1967) Theory of conical equiangular spiral antennas: Part I. Numerical techniques, *IEEE Trans. Ant. & Prop. AP-15*, 634–9.

CHAPTER 5

Variational and Iterative Methods
for Waveguides and Arrays

C. P. WU

Bell Telephone Laboratories, Inc., Holmdel, N.J.

THE investigation of waveguide arrays has shown that such problems can be most effectively solved by regarding them as interface problems. In this approach, the whole space is viewed as consisting of two, separate, uniform regions; one of them is composed of the aggregate of the waveguides while the other is a half space. The two regions meet at a common interface, i.e. the array face. Since a knowledge of either the tangential electric or tangential magnetic field at the interface will suffice to characterize the fields everywhere, it is desirable to formulate the problem so as to solve for one of these quantities. The integral equation formalism was found to be particularly suitable for this purpose. The kernels of the resulting integral equations, like in many other electromagnetic problems, are complex symmetric in general. This property permits a derivation of variational expressions for the input impedance of the array. The usefulness of the variational principle can be appreciated when one considers that there are really very few problems which are amenable to exact solutions. In using the variational principle to obtain a solution, first the unknown aperture field is approximated by a linear combination of a set of functions. Use is then made of the stationary property of the variational principle to obtain a system of algebraic equations for the determination of the expansion coefficients.

The conversion of the integral equation into a system of algebraic equations may also be effected by a more direct and algebraically simpler procedure, namely, the method of moments. The application of this method to a wide variety of problems has been a subject of extensive research over a long period of time. It has been established that under suitable conditions, using either the variational principle or the method of moments leads to the same results. The implication is that the application of the moments method to the solution of integral equation may in fact be regarded as a variational method. Once the system of algebraic equations is obtained, it can be solved directly by seeking an inverse to the system or by appling an iterative scheme.

The interface viewpoint together with the integral equation formalism has been successfully applied to an extensive investigation of the waveguide arrays. Many different configura-

266 C. P. WU

tions have been analyzed to yield useful information. The results, for the most part, have been presented in various journals. There are many other waveguide type scattering problems which may be advantageously regarded as the interface type and gainfully treated by the integral equation approach. In fact, a simple step discontinuity in waveguides is an obvious example. Our objective here, therefore, is to select some representative examples for consideration.

The specific topics to be covered include scattering from a metallic grating, a step discontinuity for mode conversion in a circular waveguide, transition between a straight and a curved waveguide, radiation from a dielectric covered waveguide, and double discontinuity problems. Possible extension to other related problems will be pointed out as we go along. Emphasis in this discussion will be on the problem formulation and the discussion of specific computational procedures which may be required in the solution of a specific problem.

5.1. SCATTERING FROM AN INFINITE GRATING OF METALLIC STRIPS

Consider a plane wave incident at an infinite grating of perfectly conducting metallic plates. Figure 5.1 illustrates the geometry of the problem. We assume that the incident wave is independent of the y-coordinate, and that it is a TM wave with respect to z. The incident magnetic field then has only an H_y component and the incident electric field lies in the xz plane. We assume further that the metallic strips are infinitesimally thin† and they extend

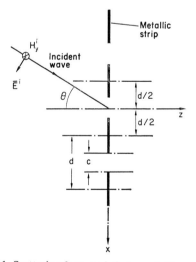

FIG. 5.1. Scattering from an infinite metallic grating.

infinitely in the y direction. These assumptions make the problem a two-dimensional one. As a result, the scattered fields consist of TM waves alone. We shall formulate the problem in terms of integral equations, which may have either the tangential electric field across the aperture, $|x| \leq c/2$, or the induced current on the metallic strip $c/2 \leq |x| \leq d/2$ as the unknown function.

† The case of metallic strips with finite thickness can be treated by the method discussed in Section 5.7.

The incident wave may be described by

$$H_y^i = \sqrt{\frac{1}{d}}\, e^{-jk\,(x\sin\theta + z\cos\theta)},$$

(5.1)

$$\mathbf{E}^i = \frac{k}{\omega\varepsilon_0}\sqrt{\frac{1}{d}}\,(x\cos\theta - z\sin\theta)\, e^{-jk\,(x\sin\theta + z\cos\theta)}.$$

Since the incident wave is a plane wave and the geometry of the scatterer is a periodic function of x with period d, the fields observed at any two points with separation d along a line parallel to the x-axis are identical except for a constant phase shift $\exp(-jkd\sin\theta)$. Mathematically this fact may be stated as follows. Let $f(x)$ denote a field component at x. Then

$$f(x + d) = f(x)\, e^{-jkd\sin\theta}.$$

This means that it is necessary to determine the scattered field only in a basic period $-d/2 \le x \le d/2$. Furthermore, the scattered field may be expanded in terms of the so-called Floquet harmonics or modes. The Floquet harmonics are given by

$$\Psi_m(x)\, e^{\mp j\Gamma_m z} \quad \text{for propagation in } \pm z \text{ directions}$$

(5.2)

where

$$\Psi_m(x) = \sqrt{\frac{1}{d}}\,\exp\left[-j\left(\frac{2m\pi}{d} + k\sin\theta\right)x\right], \quad m = 0, \pm 1, \ldots$$

(5.2a)

gives the transverse variation of the field, and

$$\Gamma_m = \sqrt{\left\{k^2 - \left(\frac{2m\pi}{d} + k\sin\theta\right)^2\right\}}$$

(5.2b)

is the propagation constant. The functions $\{\Psi_m(x)\}$ are orthonormal over $(-d/2, d/2)$ with the following definition of a scalar product:

$$\langle\Psi_m, \Psi_n^*\rangle = \int_{-d/2}^{d/2} \Psi_m(x)\,\Psi_n^*(x)\,dx = \delta_{mn} = \begin{cases} 1 & m = n, \\ 0 & m \ne n, \end{cases}$$

(5.3)

where the asterisk * denotes complex conjugation.

PROBLEM 1. *Verify the expression given in (5.2a) by the method of separation of variables.*

Expanding the scattered fields in terms of Floquet harmonics yields

$$H_y^s(x, z) = \sum_{m=-\infty}^{\infty} I_m\Psi_m(x)\, e^{j\Gamma_m z}$$

(5.4a)

$$\text{for } z \le 0,$$

$$E_x^s(x, z) = -\sum_{m=-\infty}^{\infty} Z_m I_m\Psi_m(x)\, e^{j\Gamma_m z}$$

(5.4b)

and

$$H_y^s(x, z) = \sum_{m=-\infty}^{\infty} I_m'\Psi_m(x)\, e^{-j\Gamma_m z}$$

(5.4c)

$$\text{for } z \ge 0,$$

$$E_x^s(x, z) = \sum_{m=-\infty}^{\infty} Z_m I_m'\Psi_m(x)\, e^{-j\Gamma_m z}$$

(5.4d)

where $\{I_m\}$ and $\{I'_m\}$ are unknown coefficients, and $Z_m = \Gamma_m/\omega\varepsilon_0$ is the impedance relating the transverse electric and magnetic fields of the mth harmonic.

The tangential field components of the incident wave may be expressed in terms of the zeroth Floquet harmonic Ψ_0. The boundary conditions at the interface $z = 0$ require the continuity of the tangential fields across the aperture $|x| \leq c/2$. Thus

$$H_y(x, 0) = (1 + I_0)\Psi_0(x) + \sum_{m=-\infty}^{\infty}{}^{(0)} I_m\Psi_m(x) = \sum_{m=-\infty}^{\infty} I'_m\Psi_m(x), \qquad (5.5a)$$

$$E_x(x, 0) = Z_0(1 - I_0)\Psi_0(x) - \sum_{m=-\infty}^{\infty}{}^{(0)} Z_m I_m\Psi_m(x) = \sum_{m=-\infty}^{\infty} Z_m I'_m\Psi_m(x) \qquad (5.5b)$$

where $\Sigma^{(0)}$ denotes that the zeroth term is to be omitted in the sum. Since the tangential electric field vanishes on the conductor, eqn. (5.5b) may be regarded as valid over the entire period $|x| \leq d/2$. By the orthonormality conditions in (5.3), $\{I_m\}$ and $\{I'_m\}$ may be expressed in terms of the aperture electric field as

$$-Z_m I_m = Z_m I'_m = \int_{-c/2}^{c/2} E_x(x', 0)\Psi_m^*(x')\,\mathrm{d}x' \quad m \neq 0, \qquad (5.6a)$$

$$Z_0(1 - I_0) = Z_0 I'_0 = \int_{-c/2}^{c/2} E_x(x', 0)\Psi_m^*(x')\,\mathrm{d}x'. \qquad (5.6b)$$

Equations (5.6a,b) indicate that excepting the zeroth harmonic, the magnetic fields in $z > 0$ and $z < 0$ are equal to each other but opposite in sign, i.e.

$$I_m = -I'_m \quad m \neq 0, \qquad (5.7)$$

$$1 - I_0 = I'_0.$$

Using these relations, we may write (5.5a) as

$$H_y(x, 0) = 2\Psi_0(x) - (1 - I_0)\Psi_0(x) + \sum_{m=-\infty}^{\infty}{}^{(0)} I_m\Psi_m(x)$$

$$= 2\Psi_0(x) - \sum_{m=-\infty}^{\infty} I'_m\Psi_m(x)$$

$$= \sum_{m=-\infty}^{\infty} I'_m\Psi_m(x), \qquad (5.8)$$

Equation (5.8) implies that

$$\sum_{m=-\infty}^{\infty} I'_m\Psi_m(x) = \Psi_0(x). \qquad (5.9)$$

That is, the tangential magnetic field in the aperture is unperturbed by the grating and is equal to that of the incident wave. This is a well-known result which may be obtained by using a different argument (Born and Wolf, 1959). When (5.6a,b) are substituted in (5.9), we find that

$$\Psi_0(x) = \int_A \left\{ \sum_{m=-\infty}^{\infty} Y_m\Psi_m(x)\Psi_m^*(x') \right\} E_x(x', 0)\,\mathrm{d}x' \qquad (5.10)$$

where A denotes the aperture and $Y_m = 1/Z_m$. This is the integral equation for the aperture electric field.

In obtaining (5.10), the order of integration and summation has been interchanged. This is permissible as the kernel of the integral equation (the expression within the curly bracket) has a singularity which behaves as $e^{-jk(x-x')\sin\theta} \ln [2 \sin (\pi/d) (x - x')]$, so that the integral converges for physically acceptable solution.

PROBLEM 2: Show that the series $\sum_{m=-\infty}^{\infty} Y_m \Psi_m(x) \Psi_m^*(x')$ behaves as $e^{-jk(x-x')\sin\theta}$
$\times \ln [2 \sin (\pi/d) (x-x')]$.

Hint. Make use of the fact $Y_m \sim \omega\varepsilon_0 d/(2|m|)\pi$ for large m and rewrite the series as:

$$Y_0 \Psi_0 (x) \Psi_0^*(x') + \omega\varepsilon_0 \sum_{m=1}^{\infty} \left\{ \left[\frac{jd}{2m\pi} + \left(\frac{1}{\Gamma_m} - \frac{jd}{2m\pi} \right) \right] e^{j((2m\pi/d)-k\sin\theta)(x-x')} \right.$$

$$\left. + \left[\frac{jd}{2m\pi} + \left(\frac{1}{\Gamma_{-m}} - \frac{jd}{2m\pi} \right) \right] e^{-j((2m\pi/d)+k\sin\theta)(x-x')} \right\}. \qquad \text{(Collin, 1960)}$$

We next derive the integral equation in terms of the current on the metallic strip. First, it is observed that the tangential magnetic fields are continuous across the common aperture, but are discontinuous over the conductor by an amount equal to the induced surface current. This fact may be expressed as

$$H_y (x, 0^+) - H_y (x, 0^-) = \begin{cases} 0 \\ -J_x \end{cases} \quad \text{when} \quad \begin{matrix} x \in A, \\ X \in M, \end{matrix} \qquad (5.11)$$

where M denotes the interval $c/2 \le |x| \le d/2$. Substituting the appropriate expressions for tangential magnetic fields and then using (5.7), we find

$$2 \sum_{m=-\infty}^{\infty} I_m \Psi_m (x) = \begin{cases} 0 \\ J_x \end{cases} \quad \text{for} \quad \begin{matrix} x \in A, \\ x \in M. \end{matrix} \qquad (5.12)$$

Again, from the orthonormality condition we have

$$I_m = \tfrac{1}{2} \int_M J_x (x') \Psi_m^*(x') \, dx'. \qquad (5.13)$$

When (5.13) is substituted into (5.4b) and then the total tangential electric field is required to vanish over the metallic strip, the following integral equation is obtained†

$$2Z_0 \Psi_0 (x) = \int_M \left\{ \sum_{m=-\infty}^{\infty} Z_m \Psi_m (x) \Psi_m^*(x') \right\} J_x(x') \, dx'. \qquad (5.14)$$

† The order of integration and summation has been reversed in deriving (5.14). Strictly speaking, this step is not permissible as the integral becomes divergent. The procedure is carried out to obtain a compact integral equation. The difficulty may be circumvented in practice by the choice of bases. It can also be removed by recognizing that

$$\left(\frac{\partial^2}{\partial x^2} + k^2 \right) \Psi_m(x) = \Gamma_m^2 \Psi_m (x)$$

and thus obtaining instead of (5.14) the following integro-differential equation

$$2Z_0 \Psi_0 (x) = \left(\frac{\partial^2}{\partial x^2} + k^2 \right) \int_M \left\{ \sum_{m=-\infty}^{\infty} \frac{Z_m}{\Gamma_m^2} \Psi_m(x) \Psi_m^*(x') \right\} J_x(x') \, dx'.$$

Notice that due to the choice of the coordinate origin as in Fig. 5.1, the limits of integration M extend over two separate intervals: $-d/2 \le x \le -c/2$ and $c/2 \le x \le d/2$. This can be changed to a single interval $-(d-c)/2 \le x \le (d-c)/2$ by a coordinate translation.

Equations (5.10) and (5.14) constitute alternative integral equation formulations of the problem. They belong to the Fredholm integral equation of the first kind. One of the equations has the aperture electric field as the unknown and is valid over the aperture. The other one is expressed in terms of the induced current on the metallic strip and applies over the strip region.

These integral equations are not amenable to analytical solutions except for the special case where the aperture and strip have the same width and the incident wave is incident normally to the strips (Baldwin and Heins, 1954; Weinstein, 1969). It is, therefore, necessary to resort to approximate techniques for a solution.

PROBLEM 3. *Derive the integral equation for scattering from a grating imbedded in a dielectric slab.*

5.2. VARIATIONAL PRINCIPLE, METHOD OF MOMENTS AND ITERATIVE METHODS

5.2.1. Variational Principle

Among the various approximate methods of solving scattering problems, the variational principle is one which has received a very wide use. Variational expressions may be derived from integral equations provided that the kernels are Hermitian[†] or complex symmetric [Schwinger and Saxon, 1968; Lewin, 1951; Collin, 1960 (see chapt. 8)]. The kernels arising in electromagnetic scattering problems usually appear in complex symmetric form, i.e. if $K(x, x')$ denotes the kernel, then it is a complex function of x and x' and possesses the symmetry property $K(x, x') = K(x', x)$ so that $\langle U, KV \rangle = \langle KU, V \rangle$. The kernel in either (5.10) or (5.14) at first glance does not appear to be Hermitian, or complex symmetric. This difficulty may be removed by the following observation. Since

$$\Psi_m(-x) = \{\Psi_m(x)\}^*,$$

eqn. (5.10) may be rewritten as

$$\Psi_0^*(x) = \int_A \left\{ \sum_{m=-\infty}^{\infty} Y_m \Psi_m^*(x) \Psi_m^*(x') \right\} E_x(x', 0)\, dx'. \tag{5.10a}$$

The kernel is now complex symmetric. Multiplying (5.10a) by $E_x(x, 0)$ and then integrating over A, after slight rearrangement, we find by utilizing (5.6b) that

$$Z_0(1 - I_0) = \frac{\langle \Psi_0^*, E_x \rangle^2}{\langle E_x, K' E_x \rangle} \tag{5.15}$$

[†] A kernel $L(x, x')$ is said to be Hermitian if $L^*(x', x) = L(x, x')$. Thus, according to our definition of the scalar product in (5.3), $\langle U, LV \rangle = \langle L^*U, V \rangle$.

where

$$K'(x, x') = \sum_{m=-\infty}^{\infty} Y_m \Psi_m^*(x) \Psi_m^*(x').$$

That this is a stationary expression is readily verified by taking the first variation of $Z_0(1 - I_0)$. Thus,

$$\delta\{Z_0(1 - I_0)\} = \frac{2\langle(K'E_x - \Psi_0^*), \delta E_x\rangle}{\langle E_x, K'E_x\rangle^2} = 0. \tag{5.15a}$$

The stationary property of $Z_0(1 - I_0)$ implies that if E_x is approximated by a function which contains errors up to the first order, the calculation of $Z_0(1 - I_0)$ according to (5.15) will have errors of the second order or higher. In other words, a good approximation of E_x will yield a good estimate of $Z_0(1 - I_0)$. However, if the approximate E_x is far from the true solution, the result can be very poor.

In practical application of the variational principle, the unknown aperture electric field is frequently approximated by that of the incident wave. Such an approximation often but not always yields satisfactory results. In order to improve the accuracy of the variational calculation, one needs a better approximation of the unknown function, which can be obtained by applying the Rayleigh–Ritz procedure (Jones, 1964; Stakgold, 1968). First the unknown function is expanded in terms of a set of linearly independent functions $\{Q_n(x)\}$. Thus,

$$E_x(x) \approx \sum_{n=1}^{N} a_n Q_n(x). \tag{5.16}$$

Substituting the expansion into the variational expression (5.15), and then setting equal to zero all the derivatives of the resulting functional with respect to the expansion coefficients $\{a_n\}$ yield the following system of linear equations for the determination of the expansion coefficients:

$$\sum_{n-1}^{N} K'_{mn} a_n = b_m, \quad m = 1, 2, \ldots, N \tag{5.17}$$

$$K'_{mn} = \langle Q_m, K'Q_n\rangle = \int_A dx\, Q_m(x) \int_A dx'\, K'(x, x')\, Q_n(x')$$

and

$$b_m = \langle Q_m, \Psi_0^*\rangle = \int_A dx\, Q_m(x)\, \Psi_0^*(x).$$

After the solutions to $\{a_n\}$ are obtained, the results are substituted into (5.15) for the evaluation of $Z_0(1 - I_0)$. The same set of algebraic equations as (5.17) may also be derived by the method of moments.

5.2.2. Method of Moments

There have been a number of recent books discussing the application of the moments method to the solution of differential and integral equations. Recall that this method has also been discussed in Chapters 2 and 4 of this book. Thus it will suffice to give only a brief account of the procedure here.

A Fredholm integral equation of the first kind, e.g. (5.10) or (5.14), may be written symbolically as

$$\int_a^b K(x, x') f(x') \, dx = g(x) \tag{5.18}$$

where $K(x, x')$ is the kernel, $g(x)$ is a known function proportional to the excitation and $f(x)$ is the unknown function to be determined. First, the unknown function is expanded, approximately, in terms of a linearly independent set of functions $\{U_p(x), p = 1, 2, ..., N\}$. Thus,

$$f(x') \approx \sum_{p=1}^{N} \alpha_p U_p(x') \tag{5.19}$$

Substituting (5.19) into (5.18), we then take moments (i.e. perform properly defined scalar products) of the resulting functional equation with another linearly independent set of functions $\{V_q(x), q = 1, 2, ..., N\}$. This process reduces the integral equation to a linear system of algebraic equations given by

$$\sum_{p=1}^{N} K_{qp}\alpha_p = \beta_q, \quad q = 1, 2, ..., N \tag{5.20}$$

with

$$K_{qp} = \langle V_q, KU_p \rangle,$$
$$\beta_q = \langle V_q, g \rangle.$$

The set of functions $\{U_p(x)\}$ and $\{V_q(x)\}$ are respectively referred to as the basis (or expansion) and testing (or weighting) functions. The special case wherein $\{U_p(x)\} \equiv \{V_q(x)\}$ is known as the Galerkin or Ritz–Galerkin method.

Applying the above procedure to (5.10a) with $\{U_p(x)\} \equiv \{V_q(x)\} \equiv \{Q_n(x)\}$ readily shows that the same system of equations as (5.17) is obtained. The application of moments method to a pertinent integral equation is therefore equivalent to the Rayleigh–Ritz procedure, provided that appropriate bases are used in both approaches. For this reason, the moments method may be viewed as a variational method. Since the moments method is algebraically simpler, it will be used in the subsequent discussions.

The solution of (5.20) may be obtained by the Cramer's rule, or equivalently by a matrix inversion. Let

$$[K] = \begin{bmatrix} K_{11}, K_{12}, ..., K_{1N} \\ K_{21}, K_{22}, \quad \vdots \\ \vdots \quad\quad \vdots \\ \vdots \quad\quad \vdots \\ K_{N1} \quad\quad K_{NN} \end{bmatrix},$$

$$\alpha = \begin{bmatrix} \alpha_1 \\ \alpha_2 \\ \vdots \\ \alpha_N \end{bmatrix} \quad \text{and} \quad \beta = \begin{bmatrix} \beta_1 \\ \beta_2 \\ \vdots \\ \beta_N \end{bmatrix}.$$

Equation (5.20) may be written in matrix form as

$$[K] \alpha = \beta, \tag{5.20a}$$

Let $[K]^{-1}$ be the inverse of $[K]$. The solution of (5.20a) is then given by

$$\alpha = [K]^{-1} \beta. \tag{5.21}$$

Substitution of $\{\alpha_p\}$ from (5.21) into (5.19) gives an approximate solution to (5.18).

Matrix inversion is very frequently used in solving scattering problems. It is a direct and straightforward method. However, it can be a costly and time-consuming process, especially when very large matrices have to be inverted, or when there is a large number of cases to be treated, such as in the case of doing a parameter study of the problem. In addition, one has to be careful about the conditioning of a matrix. An ill-conditioned matrix (a matrix with a determinant almost zero) is difficult to invert and is easily susceptible to large round-off errors.

5.2.3. Iterative Methods

An alternative approach to solving (5.20) is to apply an iterative procedure. The matrix $[K]$ may be split into the difference of two matrices as

$$[K] = [P] - [Q]. \tag{5.22}$$

Using this decomposition in (5.20a) gives

$$[P] \alpha = [Q] \alpha + \beta, \tag{5.22a}$$

and thus,

$$\alpha = [P]^{-1} [Q] \alpha + [P]^{-1} \beta \tag{5.22b}$$

if $[P]^{-1}$ exists. One can start with an initial solution α_0, obtained by some means, substitute it into (5.22b) and obtain an improved solution α_1. A series solution is generated by continuing the process. A sufficient condition for the series to converge is that the spectral radius (the largest eigenvalue in magnitude) of $[P]^{-1}[Q]$ be less than 1. The advantage of this method is that the decomposition of (5.22) can be made such as to facilitate the determination of $[P]^{-1}$. However, in general, it is rather difficult to evaluate the spectral radius of $[P]^{-1}[Q]$, so that an *a priori* assessment of the convergence of the solution cannot be made. There is an extensive theory on the iterative procedure, which is beyond the scope of the present discussion (Varga, 1962). It should be noted that certain iterative methods have been successfully applied to a few specific problems [Cole *et al.*, 1967; Amitay and Galindo, 1968).

5.3. STEP DISCONTINUITY IN CIRCULAR WAVEGUIDES (MODE CONVERSION APPLICATIONS)

As a first application of the integral equation method, we consider the problem of a step discontinuity joining two circular waveguides of different cross-sections as shown in Fig. 5.2. This problem is of interest as waveguide discontinuities are useful in impedance matching and mode conversion devices (Nagelberg and Shefer, 1965). Several approximate methods have been developed to study the discontinuity problem wherein at most one propagating mode is allowed in each waveguide. In contrast, the integral equation approach can be applied without such a restriction.

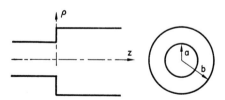

FIG. 5.2. A step discontinuity between circular waveguides.

Consider a TE_{11} mode incident at the junction from the small waveguide. In order to satisfy the boundary conditions, scattered waves will be generated which travel away from the discontinuity. Both TE and TM modes will be excited. Because of the circular symmetry of the geometry, only waves which have the same azimuthal variation as the incident wave will be present in the scattered field.

The normal modes of uniform circular waveguides and the corresponding modal impedances are needed in the integral equation formulation of the problem. They are discussed in detail in many text books on microwave theory. The following results are obtained from the *Waveguide Handbook* (Marcuvitz, 1951).

The 1nth TM mode in a waveguide of radius a is†

$$\mathbf{\Phi}_n^{(1)} = \mathbf{e}'_{1n} = -\sqrt{\frac{2}{\pi}} \frac{J'_1(x_n\varrho/a)}{aJ_2(x_n)} \cos\phi\hat{\varrho} + \sqrt{\frac{2}{\pi}} \frac{J_1(x_n\varrho/a)}{x_n \varrho J_2(x_n)} \sin\phi\hat{\phi} \qquad (5.23a)$$

and the 1nth TE mode is†

$$\mathbf{\Phi}_n^{(2)} = \mathbf{e}''_{1n} = -\sqrt{\frac{2}{\pi}} \frac{1}{\sqrt{(x'^2_n - 1)}} \frac{J_1(x'_n\varrho/a)}{\varrho J_1(x'_n)} \cos\phi\hat{\varrho} + \sqrt{\frac{2}{\pi}} \frac{x'_n}{\sqrt{(x'^2_n - 1)}} \frac{J'_1(x'_n\varrho/a)}{aJ_1(x'_n)} \sin\phi\hat{\phi}.$$
$$(5.23b)$$

In these expressions, x_n, denotes the nth root of the Bessel function $J_1(x)$, and x'_n denotes the nth root of $J'_1(x)$, where the prime indicates derivatives with respect to the argument. These modal functions are orthonormalized as follows:

$$\langle \mathbf{\Phi}_m^{(p)}, \mathbf{\Phi}_s^{(q)} \rangle = \int_0^a \int_0^{2\pi} \mathbf{\Phi}_m^{(p)}(\varrho, \phi) \cdot \mathbf{\Phi}_s^{(q)}(\varrho, \phi) \, ds = \delta_{pq}\delta_{ms} \qquad (5.24)$$

where the Kronecker delta $\delta_{pq} = \begin{cases} 1 & p = q, \\ 0 & p \neq q. \end{cases}$

---

† There are two alternative choices of the φ-dependent functions indicating that there is a mode degeneracy (except for the modes with no azimuthal variation) in the φ variation. Both possibilities have to be included in the formulation of a general discontinuity problem. In the present problem, since the azimuthal dependence of the φ variation of the incident field is preserved owing to the circular symmetry in the geometry, only one of the two choices is needed.

In terms of these orthonormal modes the fields in $z \le 0$ may be described as

$$E_t(\varrho, \phi, z) = (e^{-j\gamma_1^{(2)}z} + Re^{j\gamma_1^{(2)}z}) \, \Phi_1^{(2)}(\varrho, \phi) + \sum_{p=1}^{2} \sum_{n=1}^{\infty}{}' A_n^{(p)} \Phi_n^{(p)}(\varrho, \phi) \, e^{j\gamma_n^{(p)}z}$$

$$(5.25)$$

$$-\hat{z} \times H_t(\varrho, \phi, z) = y_1^{(2)}(e^{-j\gamma_1^{(2)}z} - Re^{j\gamma_1^{(2)}z}) \, \Phi_1^{(2)}(\varrho, \phi) - \sum_{p=1}^{2} \sum_{n=1}^{\infty}{}' y_n^{(p)} A_n^{(p)} \Phi_n^{(p)}(\varrho, \phi) \, e^{j\gamma_n^{(p)}z}$$

where R is the reflection coefficient, $\{A_n^{(p)}\}$ are the unknown modal coefficients, $\gamma_n^{(1)} = \sqrt{\{k^2 - (x_n/a)^2\}}$ and $\gamma_n^{(2)} = \sqrt{\{k^2 - (x_n'/a)^2\}}$ the z-directed propagation constants, and $\{y_n^{(p)}\}$ are the modal admittances. The prime on the summation sign signifies that the term corresponding to the incident mode is to be omitted. The fields in $z \ge 0$ may be described in a similar manner. The orthonormal vector mode functions pertinent to this region may be obtained from (5.23) by replacing a by b. Let $\Psi_n^{(p)}(\varrho, \phi)$ denote the model functions in $z \ge 0$. We may write

$$E_t^+(\varrho, \phi, z) = \sum_{q=1}^{2} \sum_{m=1}^{\infty} B_m^{(q)} \Psi_m^{(q)}(\varrho, \phi) \, e^{-j\Gamma_m^{(q)}z}$$

$$(5.26)$$

$$-\hat{z} \times H_t^+(\varrho, \phi, z) = \sum_{q=1}^{2} \sum_{m=1}^{\infty} Y_m^{(q)} B_m^{(q)} \Psi_m^{(q)}(\varrho, \phi) \, e^{-j\Gamma_m^{(q)}z},$$

where $\{\Gamma_m^{(q)}\}$ and $\{Y_m^{(q)}\}$ are respectively the propagation constants and modal admittances, and $\{B_m^{(q)}\}$ are the unknown modal coefficients. At the aperture $z = 0$, (5.25) and (5.26) become

$$E_t^-(\varrho, \phi) = E_t^-(\varrho, \phi, z = 0) = (1 + R) \, \Phi_1^{(2)}(\varrho, \phi) + \sum_{p=1}^{2} \sum_{n=1}^{\infty}{}' A_n^{(p)} \Phi_n^{(p)}(\varrho, \phi)$$

$$(5.27)$$

$$-\hat{z} \times H_t^-(\varrho, \phi) = -\hat{z} \times H_t^-(\varrho, \phi, z=0) = y_1^{(2)}(1 - R) \, \Phi_1^{(2)}(\varrho, \phi)$$

$$- \sum_{p=1}^{2} \sum_{n=1}^{\infty}{}' y_n^{(p)} A_n^{(p)} \Phi_n^{(p)}(\varrho, \phi)$$

and

$$E_t^+(\varrho, \phi) = E_t^+(\varrho, \phi, z = 0) = \sum_{q=1}^{2} \sum_{m=1}^{\infty} B_m^{(q)} \Psi_m^{(q)}(\varrho, \phi)$$

$$(5.28)$$

$$-\hat{z} \times H_t^+(\varrho, \phi) = -\hat{z} \times H_t^+(\varrho, \phi, z = 0) = \sum_{q=1}^{2} \sum_{m=1}^{\infty} Y_m^{(q)} B_m^{(q)} \Psi_m^{(q)}(\varrho, \phi).$$

By the orthonormality of the modal functions, we may express the $\{A_n^{(p)}\}$ and $\{B_n^{(q)}\}$ in terms of $\mathbf{E}_t$ as

$$(1 + R) = \iint_A \Phi_1^{(2)}(\varrho, \phi) \cdot E_t^-(\varrho, \phi) \, ds \qquad (5.29a)$$

$$A_n^{(p)} = \iint_A \Phi_n^{(p)}(\varrho, \phi) \cdot E_t^-(\varrho, \phi) \, ds, \qquad (5.29b)$$

$$B_m^{(q)} = \iint_A \Psi_m^{(q)}(\varrho, \phi) \cdot E_t^+(\varrho, \phi) \, ds, \qquad (5.29c)$$

where A denotes the aperture at $z = 0$. In (5.29c) the mode orthonormality actually exists over the cross-section of the larger waveguide. However, because $\mathbf{E}_t$ vanishes over the conducting portion of the cross-section, the limits of integration reduces to A as indicated. Equations (5.29b) through (5.29c) may be used to eliminate the unknown modal coefficients, $\{A_n^{(p)}\}$ and $\{B_m^{(q)}\}$ in (5.27) and (5.28). This enables the magnetic fields to be expressed in terms of the electric fields. The fields in the two regions must be continuous at the interface, i.e.

$$\mathbf{E}_t^- (\varrho, \phi) = \mathbf{E}_t^+ (\varrho, \phi) = \mathbf{E}_t (\varrho, \phi) \quad \varrho \le b,$$

$$\hat{z} \times \mathbf{H}_t^- (\varrho, \phi) = \hat{z} \times \mathbf{H}_t^+ (\varrho, \phi) = \hat{z} \times \mathbf{H}_t (\varrho, \phi) \quad \varrho \le a. \tag{5.30}$$

Applying these continuity conditions using (5.27) through (5.29) yields

$$2y_1^{(2)}\mathbf{\Phi}_1^{(2)} (\varrho, \phi) = \sum_{p=1}^{2} \sum_{n=1}^{\infty} y_n^{(p)}\mathbf{\Phi}_n^{(p)} (\varrho, \phi) \int\!\!\int_A \mathbf{\Phi}_n^{(p)} (\varrho', \phi') \cdot \mathbf{E}_t (\varrho', \phi') \, ds'$$

$$+ \sum_{q=1}^{2} \sum_{m=1}^{\infty} Y_m^{(q)}\mathbf{\Psi}_m^{(q)} (\varrho, \phi)\int\!\!\int_A \mathbf{\Psi}_m^{(q)} (\varrho', \phi') \cdot \mathbf{E}_t (\varrho', \phi') \, ds'. \tag{5.31}$$

This is the integral equation for the tangential electric field.[†] Alternatively, one may proceed in a similar manner and derive an integral equation for the tangential magnetic field. The result is

$$2z_1^{(2)}\hat{z} \times \mathbf{\Phi}_1^{(2)} (\varrho, \phi) = \sum_{p=1}^{2} \sum_{n=1}^{\infty} z_n^{(p)}\mathbf{\Phi}_n^{(p)} (\varrho, \phi) \int\!\!\int_{A'} \mathbf{\Phi}_n^{(p)} (\varrho', \phi') \cdot \mathbf{H}_t (\varrho', \phi') \, ds'$$

$$+ \sum_{q=1}^{2} \sum_{m=1}^{\infty} Z_m^{(q)}\mathbf{\Psi}_m^{(q)} (\varrho, \phi)\int\!\!\int_{A'} \mathbf{\Psi}_m^{(q)} (\varrho', \phi') \cdot \mathbf{H}_t (\varrho', \phi') \, ds'. \tag{5.32}$$

where A' denotes the cross-section of the larger waveguide.

PROBLEM 4. *Derive the integral equation using the tangential magnetic field as the unknown.*

Hint. In expressing the unknown modal coefficients in terms of the tangential magnetic field, the limits of integration are different for the two respective regions. This difficulty can be circumvented by defining $\mathbf{\Phi}_n^{(p)}$ to be identically zero in the region $(A' - A)$ and

$$\mathbf{H}_t (\varrho, \phi) = \begin{cases} \mathbf{H}_t^- (\varrho, \phi) = \mathbf{H}_t^+ (\varrho, \phi) & \text{for} \quad (\varrho, \phi) \in A, \\ \mathbf{H}_t^+ (\varrho, \phi) & \text{for} \quad (\varrho, \phi) \in (A' - A). \end{cases}$$

Equations (5.31) and (5.32) form a pair of alternative integral equation formulations of the step discontinuity in circular waveguides. Either one is suitable for a solution by the method of moments.

[†] We have kept the summations out of the integral sign in (5.31) as the interchange of the order of these operations may render the integrals divergent. Also see footnote on page 269.

Let us apply the method of moments to (5.31). We expand $\mathbf{E}_t$ in terms of $\{\mathbf{\Phi}_t^{(s)}(\varrho, \phi)\}$ as

$$\mathbf{E}_t(\varrho, \phi) \approx \sum_{s=1}^{2} \sum_{t=1}^{N_s} a_t^{(s)} \mathbf{\Phi}_t^{(s)}(\varrho, \phi) \tag{5.33}$$

where N_s, $s = 1, 2$ denotes the number of modes to be included in each type.

After substituting (5.33) into (5.31), we take moments of the resulting equation with $\mathbf{\Phi}_v^{(u)}(\varrho, \phi)$ for $u = 1$, $v = 1, 2, ..., N_1$ and $u = 2$, $v = 1, 2, ..., N_2$, and obtain a set of $(N_1 + N_2)$ equations in terms of $(N_1 + N_2)$ unknowns as

$$2y_1^{(2)} \delta_{2u}\delta_{1v} = \sum_{s=1}^{2} \sum_{t=1}^{N_s} a_t^{(s)} \left\{ y_t^{(s)} \delta_{su}\delta_{tv} + \sum_{q=1}^{2} \sum_{m=1}^{\infty} Y_m^{(q)} C_{vm}^{(uq)} C_{tm}^{(sq)} \right\}, \tag{5.34}$$

$$u = 1, v = 1, 2, ..., N_1 \quad \text{and} \quad u = 2, v = 1, 2, ..., N_2,$$

where

$$C_{mn}^{(sq)} = \int_A \int \mathbf{\Phi}_m^{(s)}(\varrho, \phi) \cdot \mathbf{\Psi}_n^{(q)}(\varrho, \phi) \, ds \tag{5.35}$$

are the coupling coefficients between the modes from the two regions. They are given by

$$C_{mn}^{(11)} = 2 \frac{(x_n a/b)^2}{x_n J_2(x_n)} \cdot \frac{J_1(x_n a/b)}{x_m^2 - (x_n a/b)^2}, \tag{5.35a}$$

$$C_{mn}^{(12)} = 0, \tag{5.35b}$$

$$C_{mn}^{(21)} = - \frac{2J_1(x_n a/b)}{x_n J_2(x_n) \sqrt{(x_m'^2 - 1)}}, \tag{5.35c}$$

$$C_{mn}^{(22)} = \frac{2x_m'^2 (x_n' a/b) J_1'(x_n' a/b)}{J_1(x_n') \sqrt{\{(x_m' - 1)(x_n'^2 - 1)\}[(x_m')^2 - (x_n' a/b)^2]}}. \tag{5.35d}$$

PROBLEM 5: *Derive the expression in (5.35a) through (5.35d).*

The set of equations may be solved by either a matrix inversion or an iterative procedure as discussed earlier† (Cole *et al.*, 1967; Masterman and Clarricoats, 1971). The matrix elements of this problem are expressed in terms of the modal admittances and the intermodal coupling coefficients. Both the zeros of $J_1(x)$ and $J_1'(x)$ and values of $J_0(x)$ through $J_2(x)$ are needed to calculate these quantities. Subroutines for Bessel functions are now widely available in many computation libraries. The computation of the coupling coefficients may, therefore, be carried out relatively easily and accurately.

After the solution to the system of eqns. (5.34) is obtained, the reflection and transmission coefficients into the various modes may be calculated by using (5.29). As an illustration, solutions for the mode conversion properties of the discontinuity as a function of the frequency is shown in Fig. 5.3. The mode conversion efficiency is defined as the ratio of the

---

† In order to write (5.34) in matrix form, it is convenient to arrange the system with a single running index. There is no unique way for doing this. One may exhaust numbering one type of modes first and then follow it with the other type. Alternatively, one may arrange the modes according to the increasing magnitude of the propagation constants.

ϱ-components of the electric field of TM$_{11}$ mode to that of the TE$_{11}$ mode evaluated at the walls of the larger waveguide, i.e.

$$\eta = 20 \log_{10} \left| \frac{E_\varrho^{\mathrm{TM}}}{E_\varrho^{\mathrm{TE}}} \right|_{\varrho=b} \mathrm{dB} = 20 \log_{10} \left| \frac{B_1^{(1)} J_1'(x_1)}{B_1^{(2)} J_2(x_1)} \sqrt{(x_1'^2 - 1)} \right| \mathrm{dB}.$$

The computation was made with twenty-five TE and twenty-five TM modes in each region. The results are compared with experimentally obtained data in the figure. They show reasonably good agreement.

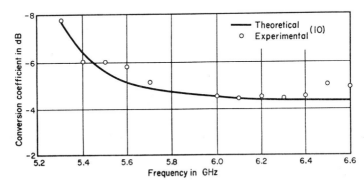

FIG. 5.3. TE$_{11}$ → TM$_{11}$ conversion coefficient of a step discontinuity in a circular waveguide. $a = 1.05$ inches, $b = 1.5$ inches.

It should be noted that mode conversion from TE to TM mode or vice versa may be obtained by other types of discontinuities such as an iris or post. Iris-type discontinuities may be treated by a procedure similar to the one we have discussed. When the irises have thicknesses which are appreciable in terms of the wavelength, the double discontinuities which characterize such a structure may be treated by the procedure to be discussed later.

PROBLEM 6. *Derive the integral equations for a circular waveguide loaded with an infinitesimally thin metallic iris.*

Since the axes of the two waveguides in the above problem coincide, the circular symmetry of the geometry is not perturbed. Consequently, only the scattered waves which have the same azimuthal variation as the incident wave need to be considered. A more general problem allows the axes of the two waveguides to be off-set, as shown in Fig. 5.4(a), or allows a thin iris to be placed at the interface. There are other types of step discontinuity problems. Some examples are shown in Fig. 5.4. The infinite phased arrays form another class of examples belonging to this category. (Amitay *et al.*, 1972). When the cross-section of one of the waveguides cannot be enclosed entirely within the other, one may introduce an "adaptor" section in the middle with such a cross-section that both the original ones are totally enclosed (Piefke, 1968; Knetsch, 1968). The original problem is viewed as the limit when the length of the "adaptor" section is reduced to zero. The modification makes the problem become one of double discontinuities, which will be discussed in Section 5.7.

It is clear from (5.34) that a major task of solving waveguide discontinuity problems lies in an effective evaluation of the matrix elements containing the intermodal coupling coeffi-

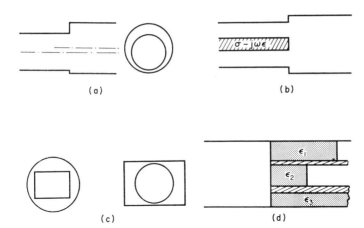

FIG. 5.4. Some examples of Step Discontinuities. (a) Discontinuity between circular waveguides with off-set axes. (b) Discontinuity between a circular waveguide and coaxial ($\sigma \to \infty$) or dielectric loaded waveguide ($\sigma = 0$). (c) Discontinuity between a circular and rectangular waveguide. (d) A waveguide trifurcation.

cients $\{C_{mn}^{(sq)}\}$. When these coefficients can be integrated in closed form, their computation is quite straightforward. In the next section, we consider an example in which these intermodal coupling coefficients have to be calculated numerically. The integral equation technique together with the moments method, in principle, can still be applied even though the waveguide modal functions of the problem are not expressible in analytical form. In such cases, numerical techniques such as the finite difference method must be used first to determine the pertinent modal functions and impedances.

5.4. TRANSITION BETWEEN A STRAIGHT AND A CONTINUOUSLY CURVED WAVEGUIDE

We consider next the scattering from a junction between a straight and a continuously curved waveguide, both of rectangular cross-section (Bates, 1969). The curved section is assumed to form a circular arc in order to facilitate an analysis. Figure 5.5 illustrates the two possible ways of joining a straight waveguide to a curved one. In cylindrical coordinates (ϱ, ϕ, z), the side walls of the curved waveguide are coincident with portion of the coordinate surfaces $\varrho = \varrho_1$ and $\varrho = \varrho_2$. The top and bottom walls are defined by $z = 0$ and $z = a$. (The waveguide is an open section of the structure which sustains an angle ϕ_0.) The direction of propagation is assumed to be in the ϕ direction.

5.4.1. Waveguide Modes in Curved Waveguides

As a preliminary to the formulation of the problem, we have to determine the modes which may exist in the two separate waveguide sections. The modes of a straight section are well known. The modes which propagate in a curved waveguide are less well known, though they have been examined in some detail by numerous researchers (Cochran and Pecina, 1966). Their results have revealed that two types of modes can propagate in such a waveguide. They are called the longitudinal section electric (LSE) modes and longitudinal section magnetic (LSM) modes. The LSE modes refer to the waves which have the electric field lying entirely in the $\varrho\phi$ plane. Similarly, LSM modes refer to the wave modes with the magnetic field distributed in an analogous manner. Normally these two types of modes will be

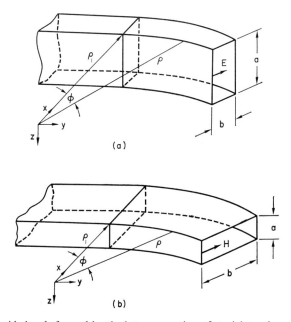

FIG. 5.5. Waveguide bends formed by the interconnection of straight and continuously curved waveguides of rectangular cross-section. (a) E-plane bend. (b) H-plane bend.

coupled at a general junction discontinuity. In the present problem, the uniformity of the geometry in the z direction dictates that the LSE and LSM modes are independent of each other. That is, an LSE mode incident from either side of the discontinuity excites only LSE modes. Similarly, an incident LSM mode excites only LSM modes. We shall, therefore, consider only the LSE case here, as both cases can be treated by a similar procedure.

Since the electric fields of LSE modes are transverse to the z direction, they may be derived from a magnetic Hertzian potential with a single z component

$$\boldsymbol{\pi}_h = \pi_h \hat{z}. \tag{5.36}$$

where π_h must satisfy the Helmholtz equation. In cylindrical coordinates, it is given by

$$\left[\frac{1}{\varrho} \frac{\partial}{\partial\varrho} \left(\varrho \frac{\partial}{\partial\varrho} \right) + \frac{1}{\varrho^2} \frac{\partial^2}{\partial\phi^2} + \frac{\partial^2}{\partial z^2} + k^2 \right] \pi_h = 0. \tag{5.37}$$

The electric and magnetic fields may be calculated from $\boldsymbol{\pi}_h$ by

$$\mathbf{E} = \mathrm{j}\omega\mu_0 \nabla \times \boldsymbol{\pi}_h, \tag{5.38}$$

$$\mathbf{H} = \nabla \times \nabla \times \boldsymbol{\pi}_h.$$

Solutions of the Helmholtz equation may be effected by the technique of separation of variables. First, the propagation factor in the ϕ direction is assumed to be $\exp(\mp \mathrm{j}\nu\phi)$

where v is the propagation constant. Substituting this expression into (5.37) and then proceeding in the usual manner, it is readily seen that to satisfy the boundary conditions, π_h must take the following form:

$$\pi_h = C_v(h_n\varrho) \sin\left(\frac{n\pi}{a} z\right) e^{\mp j v\varphi}, \quad \text{for} \quad n = 1, 2, \ldots \tag{5.39}$$

where $h_n^2 = k^2 - (n\pi/a)^2$, and C_v is given by

$$C_v(h\varrho) = J_v'(h\varrho_2) Y_v(h\varrho) - Y_v'(h\varrho_2) J_v(h\varrho) \tag{5.40}$$

with $J_v(x)$ and $Y_v(x)$ being the Bessel functions of the first and second kind of order v, and the prime denotes differentiation with respect to the argument. The vanishing of tangential electric field at $\varrho = \varrho_2$ is satisfied by the choice of (5.40). Imposing the same condition at the inner radius $\varrho = \varrho_1$ leads to

$$C_v'(h_n\varrho_1) = J_v'(h_n\varrho_2) Y_v'(h_n\varrho_1) - Y_v'(h_n\varrho_2) J_v'(h_n\varrho_1) = 0. \tag{5.41}$$

This is the characteristic equation from which the propagation constants v are to be determined.

PROBLEM 7. *Show that (5.41) is the characteristic equation of the LSE modes in a continuously curved waveguide. Also derive the characteristic equation for the LSM modes.*

The field components of the various modes may be calculated by substituting (5.39) into (5.38). The results will be given shortly. The solutions to the characteristic equation have been carried out by various researchers. Both numerical and analytical techniques are used. The work of Cochran and Pecina (1966) seems to be the most recent one giving detailed numerical results and extensive references.

5.4.2. Formulation of the Integral Equation

Having discussed the modes which may be propagated in a curved waveguide, we are now ready to derive the integral equation for the junction problem. In contrast to the usual practice, we shall describe the field in the straight guide also in terms of LSE and LSM modes for convenience. These modes may be expressed as linear combinations of the ordinary TE and TM modes and vice versa.

PROBLEM 8. *Show that the TE and TM modes in a rectangular waveguide may be combined into LSE and LSM modes and vice versa.*

The (m, n)th LSE modal function of a straight waveguide is given by

$$\mathbf{e}_{mn}^{(s)} = \phi_m^{(s)}(x) \psi_n(z) \hat{x}, \tag{5.42}$$

$$\mathbf{h}_{mn}^{(s)} = -\frac{1}{\omega\mu_0\gamma_{mn}} \frac{d}{dx} \phi_m^{(s)}(x) \frac{d}{dz} \psi_n(z) \hat{x} - \frac{h_n^2}{\omega\mu_0\gamma_{mn}} \phi_m^{(s)}(x) \psi_n(z) \hat{z}$$

where

$$\phi_m^{(s)}(x) = \sqrt{\left(\frac{2 - \delta_{0m}}{b}\right)} \cos \frac{m\pi}{b}(\varrho_2 - x), \quad m = 0, 1, \ldots \tag{5.43a}$$

with

$$\delta_{00} = 1 \quad \text{and} \quad \delta_{0m} = 0, \quad m \geq 1$$

$$\psi_n(z) = \sqrt{\frac{2}{a}} \sin \frac{n\pi}{a} z, \quad n = 1, 2, \ldots \tag{5.43b}$$

and

$$h_n^2 = k^2 - (n\pi/a)^2, \quad \gamma_{mn}^2 = h_n^2 - (m\pi/b)^2.$$

The modal functions are normalized such that

$$\langle \mathbf{e}_{mn}^{(s)}, \mathbf{e}_{pq}^{(s)} \rangle = \iint_A \mathbf{e}_{mn}^{(s)} \cdot \mathbf{e}_{pq}^{(s)} \, ds = \delta_{mp}\delta_{nq} \tag{5.44}$$

where A denotes the cross-section of the waveguide. Notice that the transverse electric field has only one component while the transverse magnetic field has two components. A wave impedance, therefore, cannot be defined in the usual manner.

The modal functions in the curved section are

$$\mathbf{e}_{mn}^{(c)} = \frac{1}{\varrho} \phi_{mn}^{(c)}(h_n\varrho) \, \psi_n(z) \, \hat{\varrho},$$

$$\mathbf{h}_{mn}^{(c)} = -\frac{1}{\omega\mu_0\nu_{mn}} \frac{d}{d\varrho} \phi_{mn}^{(c)}(h_n\varrho) \frac{d}{dz} \psi_n(z) \hat{\varrho} - \frac{h_n^2}{\omega\mu_0\nu_{mn}} \phi_{mn}^{(c)}(h_n\varrho) \psi_n(z) \hat{z} \tag{5.45}$$

where

$$\phi_{mn}^{(c)}(h_n\varrho) = \frac{C_{\nu_{mn}}(h_n\varrho)}{\|C_{\nu_{mn}}(h_n\varrho)\|} \tag{5.45a}$$

with

$$C_{\nu_{mn}}(h_n\varrho) = J'_{\nu_{mn}}(h_n\varrho_2) Y_{\nu_{mn}}(h_n\varrho) - Y'_{\nu_{mn}}(h_n\varrho_2) J_{\nu_{mn}}(h_n\varrho) \tag{5.46a}$$

and

$$\|C_{\nu_{mn}}(h_n\varrho)\| = \left[\int_{\varrho_1}^{\varrho_2} (C_{\nu_{mn}}^2/\varrho) \, d\varrho\right]^{1/2}. \tag{5.46b}$$

The ν_{mn} is the mth solution of the characteristic eqn. (5.41). The functions $\{\phi_{mn}^{(c)}(h_n\varrho)\}$ are orthonormal over the cross-section with a weight function $1/\varrho$ (as can be derived from the differential equation for these functions), i.e.

$$\int_{\varrho_1}^{\varrho_2} \phi_{mn}^{(c)}(h_n\varrho) \phi_{pn}^{(c)}(h_n\varrho) \frac{d\varrho}{\varrho} = \delta_{mp}.$$

As a result, the modal functions for the electric field are orthonormal with a weight function ϱ as

$$\int_0^a \int_{\varrho_1}^{\varrho_2} \mathbf{e}_{mn}^{(c)}(h_n\varrho) \cdot \mathbf{e}_{pq}^{(c)}(h_q\varrho) \varrho \, ds = \delta_{mp}\delta_{nq}. \tag{5.47}$$

To derive the integral equation, we must first introduce appropriate field representations for the two regions. Since there is no change in the z direction in the geometry of the problem, modes with different indices in the z dependence are orthogonal to one another. Namely, if the incident wave has a z dependence of $\psi_n(z)$, the scattered wave will have the same z dependence. Assume that incident waves of $S_p^{(s)} \mathbf{e}_{pn}^{(s)}$ and $S_u^{(c)} \mathbf{e}_{un}^{(c)}$ are originated in the straight and curved sections, respectively. The tangential fields in each region may then be written as

$$\mathbf{E}(x, y, z) = S_p^{(s)} \mathbf{e}_{pn}^{(s)} \, e^{-j\gamma_{pn}y} + \sum_m A_m \, \mathbf{e}_{mn}^{(s)} \, e^{j\gamma_{mn}y},$$

$$\mathbf{H}(x, y, z) = S_p^{(s)} \mathbf{h}_{pn}^{(s)} \, e^{j\gamma_{pn}y} - \sum_m A_m \mathbf{h}_{mn}^{(s)} \, e^{j\gamma_{mn}y}$$

(5.48)

in the straight section, and

$$\mathbf{E}(\varrho, \phi, z) = S_u^{(c)} \mathbf{e}_{un}^{(c)} \, e^{j\nu_{un}\phi} + \sum_m B_m \mathbf{e}_{mn}^{(c)} \, e^{-j\nu_{mn}\phi},$$

$$\mathbf{H}(\varrho, \phi, z) = -S_u^{(c)} \mathbf{h}_{un}^{(c)} \, e^{j\nu_{un}\phi} + \sum_m B_m \mathbf{h}_{mn}^{(c)} \, e^{-j\nu_{mn}\phi}$$

(5.49)

in the curved section.

At the common aperture, the ϱ-axis and the x-axis coincide whereas y- and ϕ-axes point in the same direction. Matching the boundary conditions at the common aperture gives

$$\mathbf{E}_a = S_p^{(s)} \mathbf{e}_{pn}^{(s)} + \sum_m A_m \mathbf{e}_{mn}^{(s)} = S_u^{(c)} \mathbf{e}_{un}^{(c)} + \sum_m B_m \mathbf{e}_{mn}^{(c)},$$

$$\mathbf{H}_a = S_p^{(s)} \mathbf{h}_{pn}^{(s)} - \sum_m A_m \mathbf{h}_{mn}^{(s)} = -S_u^{(c)} \mathbf{h}_{un}^{(c)} + \sum_m B_m \mathbf{h}_{mn}^{(c)}.$$

(5.49)

Using the mode orthogonality as indicated in (5.44) and (5.47), we find

$$S_p^{(s)} \delta_{pm} + A_m = \int_A \int \mathbf{e}_{mn}^{(s)} \cdot \mathbf{E}_a \, ds,$$

$$S_u^{(c)} \delta_{um} + B_m = \int_A \int \varrho' \mathbf{e}_{mn}^{(c)} \cdot \mathbf{E}_a \, ds.$$

(5.50)

Notice that because of the lack of orthogonality between the magnetic modal functions, these unknown coefficients cannot be expressed directly in terms of the aperture magnetic field. Substituting (5.50) into (5.49) yields the desired integral equation

$$2S_p^{(s)} \mathbf{h}_{pn}^{(s)} + 2S_u^{(c)} \mathbf{h}_{un}^{(c)} = \int_A \int \overline{\overline{\mathbf{G}}}(x, z; x', z') \cdot \mathbf{E}_a \, ds$$

(5.51)

where

$$\overline{\overline{\mathbf{G}}}(x, z; x', z') = \sum_m \{ \mathbf{h}_{mn}^{(s)}(x, z) \, \mathbf{e}_{mn}^{(s)}(x', z') + x' \mathbf{h}_{mn}^{(c)}(x, y) \, \mathbf{e}_{mn}^{(c)}(x', z') \}.$$

5.4.3. Application of the Moments Method

In applying the method of moments to (5.51), the unknown aperture electric field may be expanded in terms of either the modes in the curved guide or the modes in the straight guide. Both sets are complete. We use those of the straight section. Let

$$\mathbf{E}_a\,(x, z) = \sum_m a_m \mathbf{e}_{mn}^{(s)}. \tag{5.52}$$

Substituting (5.52) into (5.51) gives

$$2S_p^{(s)}\mathbf{h}_{pn}^{(s)} + 2S_u^{(c)}\mathbf{h}_{un}^{(c)} = \sum_m a_m \left\{ \sum_r (\mathbf{h}_{rn}^{(s)}\delta_{rn} + b_{mrn}\mathbf{h}_{rn}^{(c)}) \right\}$$

where

$$b_{mrn} = \int_{\varrho_1}^{\varrho_2} \phi_m^{(s)}(x)\,\phi_{rn}^{(c)}\,(h_n x)\,\mathrm{d}x. \tag{5.53}$$

We next take the moments with the set of functions $\{\mathbf{h}_{sn}^{(s)}\}$. Evaluating the contribution from the two components in the magnetic field and then combining the results, we find after some algebra and cancellation of common factors that

$$\frac{2S_p^{(s)}}{\gamma_{pn}}\,\delta_{sp} + \frac{2S_u^{(c)}}{\nu_{un}}\,b_{sun} = \sum_m a_m \left\{ \frac{\delta_{sm}}{\gamma_{mn}} + \sum_r \frac{b_{mrn}b_{srn}}{\nu_{rn}} \right\}, \quad \text{for} \quad s = 0, 1, 2, \ldots \tag{5.54}$$

Note that the use of $\{\mathbf{e}_{mn}^{(s)}\}$ and $\{\mathbf{h}_{mn}^{(s)}\}$ has resulted in particularly simple expressions for the matrix elements.

5.4.4. Special Computational Problems

The key to the solution of the problem rests upon the ability to evaluate the modal propagation constants ν_{rn} and the intermodal coupling coefficients b_{mrn}. There are certain computational problems associated with the evaluation of these quantities. As mentioned earlier, the propagation constants in a curved guide are solutions of the transcendental eqn. (5.41). Notice that the order rather than the argument of the Bessel functions is the variable. In fact, the arguments are functions of the frequency and geometry. They are fixed once the frequency and the waveguide dimensions are chosen. When the waveguide is filled with a lossless material, the argument is real. Consequently, the propagation constants are either purely real or purely imaginary, a result which can be expected on physical grounds. Therefore, it is necessary to determine only the real or imaginary ν for given $h_n\varrho_1$ and $h_n\varrho_2$.

Although computer programs for Bessel functions of real integral order are widely available in many computational libraries, programs for noninteger order seem relatively rare. Recently, Cochran and coworkers have developed a set of subroutines using combination of various schemes for computation of Bessel functions of arbitrary real order and real arguments. The techniques include power series expansion of Bessel functions for small order and argument, downward recursion of Goldsmith for moderate values of order and argument, and asymptotic expansion for large order and argument.

No computer program seems available at present for Bessel functions of imaginary order. Fortunately, since imaginary propagation constants are usually large in modulus, unless the modes are very close to cut-off, asymptotic expansion of Bessel function may be employed as an approximation. The uniform asymptotic expansion in terms of Airy functions developed by Olver (1954) are particularly useful for this purpose. The Airy functions may be approximated further by the leading terms of their phase and amplitude expansions. The result is

$$C_v \sim \frac{-2}{\pi\mu \, [(1 + \xi^2 a^2)(1 + z^2)]^{1/4}} \frac{\sqrt{(1 + z^2)}}{z} \cos\left[\mu\left(\omega(z) - \omega\left(\xi z\right)\right)\right] + \frac{z}{2\mu\left(1 + z^2\right)}$$

$$\times \sin\left[\mu\left(\omega(z) - \omega\left(\xi z\right)\right)\right] \tag{5.55}$$

where

$$\omega(z) = \ln\left[\frac{1 + \sqrt{(1 + z^2)}}{z}\right] - \sqrt{(1 + z^2)},$$

$$v = j\mu, \quad z = \frac{h\varrho_2}{\mu} \quad \text{and} \quad \xi = \frac{\varrho}{\varrho_2}.$$

This expression gives results with five to six places of accuracies when $|v| > 5$.

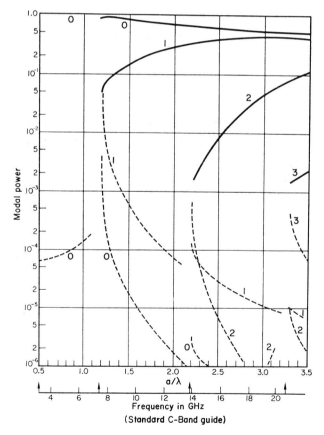

FIG. 5.6. Intermodal coupling at E-plane bend–sharp bend case. (Incident mode = LSE_{01}; incident power = 1.0; $\varrho_1/b = 1.148$; $a/b = 2.15$.) Solid line is for a curved guide; dashed line is for a straight guide.

The above discusses the evaluation of Bessel functions of real argument and arbitrary real or large imaginary orders. The determination of the propagation constants may be proceeded by applying techniques of finding solutions to transcendental equations, such as the bisection method or the Newton–Raphson method (Fröberg, 1965). When the ν's are found, they may be substituted into (5.53) using (5.45 a), (5.46 a) and (5.46 b) to calculate the intermodal coupling coefficients. Since these coefficients cannot be evaluated in closed forms, numerical integration has to be used. Thus, the numerical values of the modal functions needed at a set of points within the interval have to be supplied to the integration routine.

The solution of (5.54) which gives the expansion coefficients of the aperture field may be substituted into (5.50) to determine the various modal coefficients. A calculation using Poynting theorem shows that the power transport in either the straight or curved waveguide is given by the sum of the powers carried by the individual modes. The power carried by the mnth mode is

$$
P_{mn} = \begin{cases} \dfrac{h_n^2}{\omega\mu_0\gamma_{mn}} \, |A_m|^2 & \text{in the straight guide,} \\[3mm] \dfrac{h_n^2}{\omega\mu_0\nu_{mn}} \, |B_m|^2 & \text{in the curved guide.} \end{cases}
$$

An example showing the power coupling into the various modes which propagate in the straight and curved waveguides when an LSE_{01} mode is incident in the straight section is shown in Fig. 5.6.

5.5. DIELECTRIC SLAB-COVERED WAVEGUIDE ANTENNA

Waveguide radiators are useful in a wide variety of applications. They are employed in aircraft as well as spacecraft antennas and are used as the radiating elements in phased arrays. This type of antenna is frequently used in the presence of dielectric slabs. For example, in communications with reentry vehicles, there is a period of time during which the antennas are covered by plasma sheaths. Moreover, antennas are usually protected from the environment by radomes. In the case of waveguide antennas, because they can be flush mounted, the protective radomes can conveniently be made in the form of dielectric slabs. Furthermore, dielectric slabs can also be used for impedance matching in phased arrays (Amitay et al., 1972).

A salient feature associated with the problem of radiation from a waveguide is that we have an infinite region outside the waveguide. As a result, continuous instead of discrete spectral representations have to be used in the field expansions. The Green's function for a half space which contains a dielectric slab above a ground plane is available only in the form of Fourier transform. The kernel of the integral equation, therefore, will consist of Fourier integrals. The objective of this section is to discuss a method of handling this type of kernels in applying the moments method to the pertinent integral equation.

Waveguide antennas can take various shapes such as rectangular waveguides, circular waveguides, elliptical waveguides, etc. For simplicity, the radiation from a parallel plate waveguide will be considered. Figure 5.7 shows the geometry of the problem. Under the assumption of no variation in y, the fields may be decomposed into TE and TM modes with respect to z. We shall consider the TM case below. The TE case may be treated by a similar procedure (Wu, 1969 a, b).

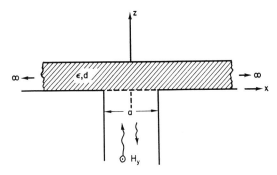

FIG. 5.7. Parallel plate waveguide covered by a dielectric slab.

Although the problem can be formulated with the tangential aperture magnetic field or the tangential aperture electric field as the unknown, it turns out that the latter is more convenient for numerical solution owing to the boundary conditions at $z = 0$. The basic equations governing the TM fields in $z \geq 0$, as can be readily derived from the Maxwell equations, are

$$j\omega\varepsilon_0\varepsilon_p E_x = -\frac{\partial H_y}{\partial z}, \quad j\omega\varepsilon_0\varepsilon_p E_z = \frac{\partial H_y}{\partial x}$$

$$\left(\frac{\partial^2}{\partial x^2} + \frac{\partial^2}{\partial z^2} + k_0^2\varepsilon_p\right) H_y = 0 \tag{5.56}$$

where $\varepsilon_p = \varepsilon$ when $0 \leq z \leq d$, $\varepsilon_p = 1$ when $d < z$.

Let $H(x)$ and $\mathcal{H}(\alpha)$ form a Fourier transform pair defined by

$$\mathcal{H}(\alpha) = \int_{-\infty}^{\infty} H(x)\, e^{-j\alpha x}\, dx, \quad \text{and} \quad H(x) = \frac{1}{2\pi}\int_{-\infty}^{\infty} \mathcal{H}(\alpha)\, e^{j\alpha x}\, d\alpha. \tag{5.57}$$

Taking the Fourier transform of (5.56) with respect to x yields

$$\left[\frac{\partial^2}{\partial z^2} + (k_0^2\varepsilon_p - \alpha^2)\right]\mathcal{H}_y(\alpha, z) = 0. \tag{5.58}$$

Solutions to (5.58) which satisfy the radiation conditions (at $z \to \infty$) may be written as

$$\mathcal{H}_y(\alpha, z) = \begin{cases} B(\alpha)\cos\Gamma_\varepsilon z + C(\alpha)\sin\Gamma_\varepsilon z & 0 \leq z \leq d, \\ D(\alpha)\, e^{-j\Gamma(z-d)} & d \leq z, \end{cases} \tag{5.59}$$

where $B(\alpha)$, $C(\alpha)$ and $D(\alpha)$ are unknown functions to be determined by the boundary conditions at $z = 0$ and d. The branches of the z-directed propagation constants Γ and Γ_ε are chosen such that

$$\Gamma_\varepsilon = \sqrt{(k^2\varepsilon - \alpha^2)} = -j\sqrt{(\alpha^2 - k^2\varepsilon)}, \quad \text{and} \quad \Gamma = \sqrt{(k^2 - \alpha^2)} = -j\sqrt{(\alpha^2 - k^2)}.$$

Using (5.56) and (5.59), we find that the Fourier transform of the tangential electric field is given by

$$
\mathcal{E}_x(\alpha, z) = \begin{cases} -\dfrac{j\Gamma_\varepsilon}{\omega\varepsilon_0\varepsilon}\,[B(\alpha)\sin\Gamma_\varepsilon z - C(\alpha)\cos\Gamma_\varepsilon z] & 0 \le z \le d, \\[3mm] \dfrac{\Gamma}{\omega\varepsilon_0}\,D(\alpha)\,e^{-j\Gamma(z-d)} & d \le z. \end{cases} \tag{5.60}
$$

Setting $z = 0$ in (5.60) shows that $j\Gamma_\varepsilon C(\alpha)/\omega\varepsilon_0\varepsilon$ is the Fourier transform of the aperture electric field, $\mathcal{E}_x(\alpha, 0)$. Application of the continuity conditions at $z = d$ yields

$$
B(\alpha)\cos\Gamma_\varepsilon d + C(\alpha)\sin\Gamma_\varepsilon d = D(\alpha)
$$

$$
-\frac{j\Gamma_\varepsilon}{\omega\varepsilon_0\varepsilon}\,[B(\alpha)\sin\Gamma_\varepsilon d - C(\alpha)\cos\Gamma_\varepsilon d] = \frac{\Gamma}{\omega\varepsilon_0}\,D(\alpha). \tag{5.61}
$$

Equations (5.61) may be solved for two of the three unknowns, say $B(\alpha)$ and $D(\alpha)$, in terms of the third. Thus

$$
B(\alpha) = j\,\frac{\Gamma_\varepsilon + j\varepsilon\Gamma\tan\Gamma_\varepsilon d}{\varepsilon\Gamma + j\Gamma_\varepsilon\tan\Gamma_\varepsilon d}\,C(\alpha),
$$

$$
D(\alpha) = \frac{j\Gamma_\varepsilon}{\varepsilon\Gamma\cos\Gamma_\varepsilon d + j\Gamma_\varepsilon\sin\Gamma_\varepsilon d}\,C(\alpha). \tag{5.62}
$$

After substituting (5.62) into (5.59) and (5.60), we take the inverse transform of $\mathcal{E}_x(\alpha, z)$ and $\mathcal{H}_y(\alpha, z)$ to obtain

$$
E_x(x, z) = \int_A dx'\,\frac{\partial}{\partial z}\,F_\varepsilon(x, z; x', 0)\,E_x(x', 0),
$$

$$
H_y(x, z) = \omega\varepsilon_0\varepsilon\int_A dx'\,F_\varepsilon(x, z; x', 0)\,E_x(x', 0) \tag{5.63}
$$

where

$$
F_\varepsilon(x, z; x', 0) = \frac{1}{2\pi}\int_{-\infty}^{\infty} d\alpha\,e^{-j\alpha(x-x')}\;\times
$$

$$
\times \begin{cases} \dfrac{1}{\Gamma_\varepsilon}\left[\dfrac{\Gamma_\varepsilon\cos\Gamma_\varepsilon(d-z) + j\varepsilon\Gamma\sin\Gamma_\varepsilon(d-z)}{\varepsilon\Gamma\cos\Gamma_\varepsilon d + j\Gamma_\varepsilon\sin\Gamma_\varepsilon d}\right] & 0 \le z \le d, \\[4mm] \dfrac{e^{-j\Gamma(z-d)}}{\varepsilon\Gamma\cos\Gamma_\varepsilon d + j\Gamma_\varepsilon\sin\Gamma_\varepsilon d} & d \le z. \end{cases}
$$

Equation (5.63) gives the field representation for $z \ge 0$ in terms of the tangential electric field at the aperture.

The derivation of the field inside the waveguide may be carried out by a similar procedure as that used in Section 5.3. First the tangential fields are expanded in terms of the normal modes. By applying the orthogonality of the modes, the tangential magnetic field is then expressed in terms of the aperture electric field. When the tangential magnetic field is matched across the aperture, we obtain the desired integral equation as

$$2Y_1\phi_1(x) = \int_A dx' \left\{ \sum_{n=1}^{\infty} Y_n\phi_n(x)\,\phi_n(x') + \omega\varepsilon_0\varepsilon\tilde{F}_\varepsilon(x,x') \right\} E_x(x',0) \qquad (5.64)$$

where

$$\tilde{F}_\varepsilon(x,x') = F_\varepsilon(x,z;x',0)|_{z=0}$$

$$= \frac{1}{2\pi} \int_{-\infty}^{\infty} d\alpha\, \frac{1}{\Gamma_\varepsilon}\, \frac{\Gamma_\varepsilon + j\varepsilon\Gamma\tan\Gamma_\varepsilon d}{\varepsilon\Gamma + j\Gamma_\varepsilon\tan\Gamma_\varepsilon d}\, e^{-jx(x-x')}. \qquad (5.65)$$

The contour of integration (5.65) is along the real axis in the complex α-plane as shown in Fig. 5.8. The integrand has a pair of branch points at the zeros of Γ. (The integrand is an even function of Γ_ε, so that the zeros of Γ_ε need not be considered as branch points.) Branch cuts are introduced to make the integrand single valued. The contour is also shown indented at the pole singularities of the integrand. The poles are solutions to the equation $\varepsilon\Gamma = -j\Gamma_\varepsilon$ $\times \tan\Gamma_\varepsilon d$, which is the characteristic equation of TM surface waves propagating along a dielectric slab above a ground plane.

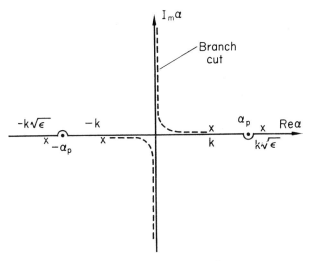

FIG. 5.8. Contour of integration.

The kernel of this integral equation contains contribution of both discrete and continuous spectra. The contribution from the continuous spectrum part seems expressible only in the form of Fourier integrals. When the dielectric constant is set equal to 1, the continuous spectral part may be integrated into a closed form. Thus,

$$\tilde{F}_\varepsilon(x,x')|_{\varepsilon=1} = \frac{1}{2\pi} \int_{-\infty}^{\infty} d\alpha\, \frac{1}{\Gamma}\, e^{-j\alpha(x-x')} = \tfrac{1}{2}H_0^{(2)}(k\,|x-x'|). \qquad (5.65a)$$

Under this condition, the relevant integral equation is simplified accordingly (Wu, 1969a).

PROBLEM 9. *Verify the relation in (5.65a).*

We next consider the application of the moments method to the integral eqn. (5.64). As in the previous cases, we find that the waveguide modal functions are adequate as the basis and weighting functions. Thus, by letting

$$E_x(x, 0) \approx \sum_{p=1}^{N} V'_p \phi_p(x), \quad \phi_p(x) = \sqrt{\left(\frac{2 - \delta_{1p}}{a}\right)} \cos \frac{2(p-1)\pi}{a} x \quad (5.66)$$

and then following the usual procedure, we arrive at a set of N equations in N unknowns

$$\sum_{p=1}^{N} B_{qp} V'_p = 2y_1 \delta_{q1}, \quad q = 1, 2, \ldots, N \quad (5.67)$$

where

$$B_{qp} = y_p \delta_{qp} + \omega \varepsilon_0 \varepsilon \int_A dx \, \phi_q(x) \int_A dx' \, \tilde{F}_\varepsilon(x, x') \phi_p(x'). \quad (5.68)$$

Because of the expression of $\tilde{F}_\varepsilon(x, x')$, the matrix elements B_{qp} as given by (5.68) contain integrals over infinite ranges. The numerical evaluation of such integrals may be difficult as well as time consuming. It is, therefore, desirable to rearrange the integrand in order that the integrals may be significantly simplified. The following physical and mathematical reasoning proves to be useful for this purpose (Wu, 1969b).

The spectral representation of (5.65) indicates that the discontinuity at the antenna aperture excites in the region $z \geq 0$ waves with transverse wave number α ranging from $-\infty$ to ∞. Out of this spectral distribution, only the portion satisfying $|\alpha|^2 \leq k^2$ constitutes the visible spectrum (or propagating) part which contributes to the far field radiation. The range $k^2 < \alpha^2 < k^2\varepsilon$ corresponds to surface wave region. The remaining portion belongs to the spectrum of inhomogeneous (or evanescent) waves which are exponentially attenuated away from the plane of their excitation. It is reasonable to assume that only those waves which are multiply reflected between the antenna aperture and air–dielectric interface can significantly influence the aperture field distribution. The implication is that there exists a number $L > k\sqrt{\varepsilon}$ such that the portion of spectrum which lies beyond L in effect does not "see" the air–dielectric interface because of its exponentially attenuated characteristics.

With this consideration, we examine the integrand of $\tilde{F}_\varepsilon(x, x')$ and note that when $\alpha^2 > k^2\varepsilon$, both Γ and Γ_ε become purely imaginary. Thus, the integrand of $\tilde{F}_\varepsilon(x, x')$ becomes

$$\frac{j}{|\Gamma_\varepsilon|} \cdot \frac{|\Gamma_\varepsilon| + \varepsilon|\Gamma| \tanh|\Gamma_\varepsilon| d}{\varepsilon|\Gamma| + |\Gamma_\varepsilon| \tanh|\Gamma_\varepsilon| d} e^{-j\alpha(x-x')}.$$

Since $\tanh u \approx 1$ for large u, we find a number L sufficiently large such that when $|\Gamma_\varepsilon| d \geq L$,

$$\frac{|\Gamma_\varepsilon| + \varepsilon|\Gamma| \tanh|\Gamma_\varepsilon| d}{\varepsilon|\Gamma| + |\Gamma_\varepsilon| \tanh|\Gamma_\varepsilon| d} \approx 1.$$

This approximation may be made as close as we please by choosing a large enough value for L. This observation then enables us to rewrite (5.65) as

$$\tilde{F}_\varepsilon(x, x') = \frac{1}{2\pi} \int_{-\infty}^{\infty} d\alpha \, \frac{1}{\Gamma_\varepsilon} e^{-j\alpha(x-x')}$$
$$+ \frac{1}{2\pi} \int_{-\infty}^{\infty} d\alpha \, \frac{1}{\Gamma_\varepsilon} \frac{(\Gamma_\varepsilon - \varepsilon\Gamma)(1 - j\tan\Gamma_\varepsilon d)}{\varepsilon\Gamma + j\Gamma_\varepsilon \tan\Gamma_\varepsilon d} e^{-j\alpha(x-x')}. \quad (5.69)$$

The first integral may be evaluated in closed form. See (5.65a). The limits of the second integral may be reduced to L on account of the explanation given above. Thus,

$$\tilde{F}_\varepsilon(x, x') \approx \tfrac{1}{2} H_0^{(2)}(k\sqrt{\varepsilon}\,|x - x'|)$$
$$+ \frac{1}{2\pi} \int_{-L}^{L} d\alpha \left\{ \frac{1}{\Gamma_\varepsilon} \frac{(\Gamma_\varepsilon - \varepsilon\Gamma)(1 - j\tan\Gamma_\varepsilon d)}{\varepsilon\Gamma + j\Gamma_\varepsilon \tan\Gamma_\varepsilon d} \right\} e^{-j\alpha(x-x')}. \qquad (5.69\,a)$$

When (5.69a) instead of (5.65) is used in the evaluation of B_{qp}, the result is

$$B_{qp} \approx y_p\delta_{qp} + D_{qp} + \frac{\omega\varepsilon_0\varepsilon}{2\pi} \int_{-L}^{L} d\alpha \frac{(-1)^{p+q}\sqrt{(2 - \delta_{1p})(2 - \delta_{1q})}}{a}$$
$$\times \left\{ \frac{1}{\Gamma_\varepsilon} \frac{(\Gamma_\varepsilon - \varepsilon\Gamma)(1 - j\tan\Gamma_\varepsilon d)}{\varepsilon\Gamma + j\Gamma_\varepsilon \tan\Gamma_\varepsilon d} \frac{4\alpha^2 \sin^2(\alpha a/2)}{[(2(q - 1)\pi/a)^2 - \alpha^2][(2(p - 1)\pi/a)^2 - \alpha^2]} \right. $$

$$(5.70)$$

where

$$D_{qp} = \frac{\omega\varepsilon_0\varepsilon}{2} \int_A dx\, \phi_q(x) \int_A dx'\, H_0^{(2)}(k\sqrt{\varepsilon}\,|x - x'|)\, \phi_p(x')$$
$$= \frac{\omega\varepsilon_0\varepsilon}{2} \int_0^a ds\, F_{qp}(s)\, H_0^{(2)}(k\sqrt{\varepsilon}\cdot s) \qquad (5.70\,a)$$

with

$$F_{qp}(s) = (-1)^{p-q}\sqrt{[(2 - \delta_{1p})(2 - \delta_{1q})]}$$
$$\times \{(p - 1)\sin[2(p - 1)\pi s/a] - (q - 1)\sin[2(q - 1)\pi s/a]\}$$
$$: \pi[(q - 1)^2 - (p - 1)^2].$$

PROBLEM 10: *Derive the equations in (5.70a).*

SPECIAL COMPUTATION PROBLEMS

The matrix elements of (5.67) consist of two parts. The reduction of the infinite integration limits to finite limits in the part containing contour integrals should make it easier to evaluate these integrals numerically. In practice, the number L does not have to be very large as $\tanh u$ approaches 1 quite rapidly. For example, it can be approximated by 1 with more than five places of accuracy whenever u exceeds 6.5. Therefore, if it is desired to evaluate the integrals up to 5 places of accuracy, a choice of

$$L = \sqrt{\{(6.5/d)^2 + k^2\varepsilon\}}$$

will suffice.

In the practical evaluation of the contour integrals, it is sometimes more convenient to deform the contour away from the real α-axis. This is especially desirable when surface wave poles are present in the integrand. Under such circumstances the integrals have to be taken in the sense of Cauchy principal values (plus the residue contributions from the poles) for which special care has to be exercised in numerically performing the integration.

The evaluation of D_{qp} has to be performed by numerical integration also. Since $H_0^{(2)}(k\sqrt{\varepsilon}\cdot s)$ has a logarithmic singularity at the origin, the integral is best carried out in two stages. Namely, we integrate from 0 to δ and then from δ to a. In the first integral, if δ is chosen sufficiently small, $H_0^{(2)}(k\sqrt{\varepsilon}\cdot s)$ may be replaced by the first few terms of its power series expansion. The result may then be integrated in closed form. The second part can be calculated by regular numerical integration method with values of $H_0^{(2)}(k\sqrt{\varepsilon}\cdot s)$ obtained from a suitable computer program. We find that the Tchebycheff representation of the Hankel function is very convenient for this purpose (Abramowitz and Stegen, 1965).

The solution of (5.67) gives the expansion coefficients of the aperture electric field in terms of the waveguide modes. Various quantities of interest such as the reflection coefficient, the radiation pattern, and surface wave excitation may be calculated from the aperture field. The reflection coefficient is readily available from the solution of the modal coefficients. The radiation pattern and the excitation of surface wave may be computed using the saddle-point method of approximation. Since this method is well discussed in many textbooks, we shall not dwell upon it here in the interest of brevity.

The analysis obviously may be extended to treat the radiation from finite waveguide arrays. The waveguides in the array need not be identical. (For infinite arrays with identical waveguide elements, discrete modal description should be used for the regions both inside and outside the waveguides. The procedure of Section 5.3 may be used for such a case.) The T-junction of rectangular waveguides, both the E-plane and the H-plane, is another example which can be analyzed by a similar method.

5.6. DOUBLE DISCONTINUITY PROBLEMS

So far, we have considered problems involving a single interface. Such problems arise from a wide variety of situations. Frequently, two or more waveguide discontinuities are connected in cascade. Because the evanescent modes generated at a discontinuity are rapidly attenuated, when the junctions are spaced far apart, only the interaction of the propagating modes needs to be taken into account. For closely spaced discontinuities, the interaction between the higher order modes becomes important. Figure 5.9 shows a symmetric and an asymmetric double discontinuity problem. A symmetric double discontinuity problem may be related to two auxiliary single interface problems by applying the bisection theorem. This class of problems is, therefore, not more difficult than the ones which have already been considered. The asymmetric type, in contrast, requires extension of the previously developed techniques. We shall discuss a couple of schemes for treating this latter type.

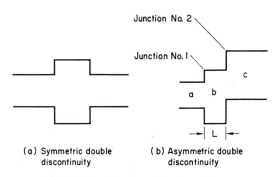

(a) Symmetric double discontinuity   (b) Asymmetric double discontinuity

FIG. 5.9. Double discontinuity problems.

5.6.1. Coupled Integral Equations for Double Discontinuity Problems

Consider the double discontinuity problem as shown in Fig. 5.9b. Let $\{\phi_{an}\}$, $\{\phi_{bn}\}$, and $\{\phi_{cn}\}$ denote the modal functions for the three respective regions a, b, and c. The corresponding modal admittances are given by $\{Y_{an}\}$, $\{Y_{bn}\}$, and $\{Y_{cn}\}$. Assume a wave with a unit modal voltage is incident from region a. The tangential electromagnetic field in each region may be expanded as follows.

In region a,

$$\mathscr{E}_t = (e^{-j\gamma_{a1}z} + Re^{j\gamma_{a1}z})\,\phi_{a1} + \sum_{n=2}^{\infty} V_n e^{j\gamma_{an}z}\,\phi_{an}$$

$$-\hat{z} \times \mathscr{H}_t = Y_{a1}\,(e^{-j\gamma_{a1}z} - Re^{j\gamma_{a1}z})\,\phi_{a1} - \sum_{n=2}^{\infty} Y_{an} V_n e^{j\gamma_{an}z}\,\phi_{an},$$

(5.71a)

in region b,

$$\mathscr{E}_t = \sum_{m=1}^{\infty} (G_m e^{-j\gamma_{bm}z} + F_m e^{j\gamma_{bm}z})\,\phi_{bm}$$

$$-\hat{z} \times \mathscr{H}_t = \sum_{m=1}^{\infty} Y_{bm}\,(G_m e^{-j\gamma_{bm}z} - F_m e^{j\gamma_{bm}z})\,\phi_{bm},$$

(5.71b)

and in region c,

$$\mathscr{E}_t = \sum_{n=1}^{\infty} Q_n e^{-j\gamma_{cn}(z-L)}\,\phi_{cn}$$

$$-\hat{z} \times \mathscr{H}_t = \sum_{n=1}^{\infty} Y_{cn} Q_n e^{-j\gamma_{cn}(z-L)}\,\phi_{cn}.$$

(5.71c)

The tangential fields must be continuous at the interfaces $z = 0$ and $z = L$. Matching the boundary conditions yields

$$\begin{aligned}
\mathbf{E}_t(0) &= \mathscr{E}_t\,(z = 0) \\
&= (1 + R)\,\phi_{a1} + \sum_{n=2}^{\infty} V_n \phi_{an} \\
&= \sum_{m=1}^{\infty} (G_m + F_m)\,\phi_{bm};
\end{aligned}$$

(5.72)

$$\begin{aligned}
-\hat{z} \times \mathbf{H}_t\,(0) &= -\hat{z} \times \mathscr{H}_t\,(z = 0) \\
&= Y_{a1}\,(1 - R)\,\phi_{a1} - \sum_{n=2}^{\infty} Y_{an} V_n \phi_{an} \\
&= \sum_{m=1}^{\infty} Y_{bm}\,(G_m - F_m)\,\phi_{bm};
\end{aligned}$$

(5.73)

$$\begin{aligned}
\mathbf{E}_t\,(L) &= \mathscr{E}_t\,(z = L) \\
&= \sum_{m=1}^{\infty} (G_m e^{-j\gamma_{bm}L} + F_m e^{j\gamma_{bm}L})\,\phi_{bm} \\
&= \sum_{n=1}^{\infty} Q_n \phi_{cn};
\end{aligned}$$

(5.74)

$$\begin{aligned}
-\hat{z} \times \mathbf{H}_t(L) &= -\hat{z} \times \mathscr{H}_t\,(z = L) \\
&= \sum_{m=1}^{\infty} Y_{bm}\,(G_m e^{-j\gamma_{bm}L} - F_m e^{j\gamma_{bm}L})\,\phi_{bm} \\
&= \sum_{n=1}^{\infty} Y_{cn} Q_n \phi_{cn}.
\end{aligned}$$

(5.75)

Using the orthonormality of the modes in each region, we may express the unknown expansion coefficients $\{V_n\}$, $\{F_n\}$, etc., in terms of the aperture electric fields at $z = 0$ and $z = L$. In particular, we find

$$(G_m + F_m) = \int_{A_1} \phi_{bm} \cdot \mathbf{E}_t(0) \, ds, \tag{5.75a}$$

and

$$(G_m \, e^{-j\gamma_{bm}L} + F_m \, e^{j\gamma_{bm}L}) = \int_{A_2} \phi_{bm} \cdot \mathbf{E}_t(L) \, ds \tag{5.75b}$$

where A_1 and A_2 denote the apertures at junctions 1 and 2 respectively. Solving for G_m and F_m yields

$$G_m = \frac{-j}{2 \sin \gamma_{bm}L} \left[e^{j\gamma_{bm}L} \int_{A_1} \phi_{bm} \cdot \mathbf{E}_t(0) \, ds - \int_{A_2} \phi_{bm} \cdot \mathbf{E}_t(L) \, ds \right],$$

$$F_m = \frac{-j}{2 \sin \gamma_{bm}L} \left[\int_{A_1} \phi_{bm} \cdot \mathbf{E}_t(0) \, ds - e^{-j\gamma_{bm}L} \int_{A_2} \phi_{bm} \cdot \mathbf{E}_t(L) \, ds \right]. \tag{5.76}$$

Equations (5.76) may be used to calculate $(G_m - F_m)$ and $(G_m e^{-j\gamma_{bm}L} - F_m e^{j\gamma_{bm}L})$ in terms of $\mathbf{E}_t(0)$ and $\mathbf{E}_t(L)$. We may derive expressions for V_n and Q_n respectively in terms of $\mathbf{E}_t(0)$ and $\mathbf{E}_t(L)$ in the usual manner. Substituting the appropriate expressions for the various expansion coefficients into (5.73) and (5.75), we obtain

$$2Z_{a1}\phi_{a1} = \sum_{n=1}^{\infty} Y_{an}\phi_{an} \int_{A_1} \phi_{an} \cdot \mathbf{E}_t(0) \, ds$$

$$+ \sum_{m=1}^{\infty} \frac{-jY_{bm}}{\sin \gamma_{bm}L} \phi_{bm} \left[\cos \gamma_{bm}L \int_{A_1} \phi_{bm} \cdot \mathbf{E}_t(0) \, ds - \int_{A_2} \phi_{bm} \cdot \mathbf{E}_t(L) \, ds \right] \tag{5.77a}$$

and

$$\sum_{m=1}^{\infty} \frac{-jY_{bm}}{\sin \gamma_{bm}L} \phi_{bm} \left[\int_{A_1} \phi_{bm} \cdot \mathbf{E}_t(0) \, ds - \cos \gamma_{bm}L \int_{A_2} \phi_{bm} \cdot \mathbf{E}_t(L) \, ds \right]$$

$$= \sum_{n=1}^{\infty} Y_{cn}\phi_{cn} \int_{A_2} \phi_{cn} \cdot \mathbf{E}_t(L) \, ds. \tag{5.77b}$$

Equations (5.77a) and (5.77b) form a set of coupled integral equations for the aperture electric fields $\mathbf{E}_t(0)$ and $\mathbf{E}_t(L)$. They have to be solved simultaneously in order to yield meaningful results, especially when L is not large in comparison to the guide wavelength in region b. These equations may be solved by the method of moments. The number of functions which are needed for the expansion of the two unknown fields depends on the geometry. This question has not been fully explored yet.

In the special case of symmetric double discontinuities, the integral equations may be decoupled. The modal functions of regions a and c are identical, $\{\phi_{an}\} \equiv \{\phi_{cn}\}$, and $A_1 = A_2$. Adding (5.77a) to (5.77b) and then simplifying, we have

$$2Y_{a1}\phi_{a1} = \sum_n Y_{an}\phi_{an} \int_A \phi_{an} \cdot [\mathbf{E}_t(0) + \mathbf{E}_t(L)] \, ds + \sum_m \left(j \, Y_{bm} \tan \frac{\gamma_{bm}L}{2} \right) \phi_{bm} \times$$

$$\times \int_A \phi_{bm} \cdot [\mathbf{E}_t(0) + \mathbf{E}_t(L)] \, ds. \tag{5.78a}$$

Smiilarly, subtraction of (5.77b) from (5.77a) gives

$$2Y_{a1}\phi_{a1} = \sum_n Y_{an}\phi_{an} \int_A \phi_{an} \cdot [\mathbf{E}_t(0) - \mathbf{E}_t(L)]\, ds + \sum_m \left(-j\, Y_{bm} \cot \frac{\gamma_{bm}L}{2}\right) \phi_{bm} \times$$

$$\times \int_A \phi_{bm} \cdot [\mathbf{E}_t(0) - \mathbf{E}_t(L)]\, ds. \tag{5.78b}$$

Thus, the sum of the solutions to (5.78a) and (5.78b) gives twice the aperture electric field at $z = 0$, $\mathbf{E}_t(0)$, and their difference is twice the aperture electric field at $z = L$, $\mathbf{E}_t(L)$.

Equations (5.78a) and (5.78b) may be derived alternatively by subjecting the structure to an odd and an even excitation and then sum the results. In the even excitation, waves of equal magnitude and phase (the same as the original incident wave in region a) are assumed incident in regions a and c simultaneously. Since the geometry and the excitation are symmetric with respect to the central plane in region b, $z = L/2$, the total fields will also have the same property. This condition allows an open circuit (a perfect magnetic conductor) to be placed at the plane of symmetry. The problem then becomes a single interface one with the second region terminated in an open circuit. A formulation of this problem gives (5.78a). Next, waves of the same magnitude but with opposite phase are assumed incident in regions a and c. This situation leads to an antisymmetric field distribution. Thus a short circuit (or an electric conductor) may be introduced at the symmetry plane. The formulation of this problem leads to (5.78b). Addition of the two alternative excitations results in twice the original excitation in region a and zero excitation in region c.

The derivation of (5.77a) and (5.77b) requires that the aperture fields at $z = 0$ and $z = L$ be solved simultaneously. The problem may be formulated such that the discontinuities are handled consecutively one at a time. The process is started from the junction closest to the load, and is repeated for each junction toward the excitation. The effects of earlier junctions are incorporated through the scattering matrix formalism (Wexler, 1967).

Alternatively, the scattering property of each junction may be determined independently as if each one were present by itself. The aggregate results of the composite structure may be calculated by using the generalized scattering matrix.

5.6.2. Band Rejection Filter in Coaxial Waveguides

As an example of the symmetric double discontinuity problems, we consider a single coaxial band rejection filter which is formed by changes in the outer or inner radii of the coaxial waveguide to form a cavity (Varon, 1967). A cross-sectional view of the filter is shown in Fig. 5.10. The dimensions of the coaxial waveguide are such that only the TEM mode can propagate. When this wave is incident upon the discontinuities, higher order modes are excited, some of which may be propagating in the cavity region, i.e. in between the two discontinuities. The interaction among the various modes creates a situation in which the cavity appears like a short circuit to the incident wave, thus causing a complete reflection of the incident energy at a single frequency. There are various plausible explanations for the cause of this phenomenon. Since our object is in the method of solution, we shall proceed directly to the formulation of the problem.

Since the incident wave has no ϕ dependence, and the discontinuity is uniform in the ϕ direction, the induced current on the waveguide walls cannot have a ϕ component. Thus, the scattered wave has only TM modes. We apply the bisection theorem to reduce the problem to two related ones of single step discontinuity with either a short or an open circuit termination. The formulation of the latter problems can be carried out by the procedures which have been described.

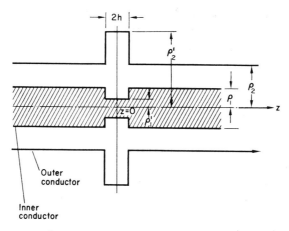

FIG. 5.10. A coaxial band rejection filter.

The TM modal functions of a coaxial waveguide with inner and outer radii ϱ_1 and ϱ_2 are given by

$$\varphi_0(\varrho) = \sqrt{\left(\frac{1}{\ln \varrho_2/\varrho_1}\right)} \cdot \frac{1}{\varrho}$$

$$\varphi_n(\varrho) = \frac{1}{N_n} [J_0\,(\delta_n\varrho_1)\,Y_1\,(\delta_n\varrho) - Y_0\,(\delta_n\varrho_1)\,J_1\,(\delta_n\varrho)] \quad \text{for} \quad n = 1, 2, \ldots \quad (5.79)$$

where $J_p(x)$ and $Y_p(x)$, $p = 0, 1$, are the Bessel and Neumann functions of order p. $\{\delta_n\}$, $n = 1, 2, \ldots, \infty$ are the solutions to the characteristic equation

$$J_0\,(\delta_n\varrho_1)\,Y_0\,(\delta_n\varrho_2) - Y_0\,(\delta_n\varrho_i)\,J_0\,(\delta_n\varrho_\lambda) = 0. \quad (5.80)$$

The propagation constant γ_n of the nth modes is related to δ_n by

$$\gamma_n^2 + \delta_n^2 = k^2$$

and the modal admittances are given by $y_n = \omega\varepsilon_0/\gamma_n$. The normalization constant

$$N_n^2 = \frac{\varrho_2^2}{2}\,\phi_n^2(\varrho_2) - \frac{2}{\pi^2\delta_n^2}.$$

The set of modal functions and the related quantities in the region $-h \le z \le 0$ may be obtained from the above equations by substituting ϱ_1' and ϱ_2' for ϱ_1 and ϱ_2, and σ_n for δ_n. $\{\sigma_n, n = 1, 2, \ldots\}$ are solutions to the characteristic equation (5.80) with $\varrho_{1,2}$ replaced by $\varrho'_{1,2}$. A hat will be used over the modes in $-h \leq z \leq 0$ to distinguish them from those in $z \leq -h$.

By following the usual procedures, we derive the integral equations for the open and short-circuit terminations as follows:

$$2y_0\phi_0(\varrho) = \int_{\varrho_1}^{\varrho_2} \left\{ \sum_{n=0}^{\infty} y_n\phi_n(\varrho)\,\phi_n(\varrho') + \sum_{n=0}^{\infty} \hat{y}_n \frac{T_{s+1}(-\hat{\gamma}_n h)}{T_s(-\hat{\gamma}_n h)}\,\hat{\phi}_n(\varrho)\,\hat{\phi}_n(\varrho') \right\} E_\varrho^{(s)}(\varrho')\,\varrho'\,d\varrho'$$

(5.81)

$s = 1$ for open circuit, $s = 2$ for short circuit

where $T_1(z) = T_3(z) = \cos z$, $T_2(z) = -j \sin z$ are the proper z-dependence functions to insure that the boundary conditions at the bisection plane $z = 0$ are satisfied. The integral equations in (5.81) may be converted into algebraic equations for numerical solutions as the other cases considered earlier.

There are some nice properties of the integral equations, which arise because the second waveguide is terminated in either an open or a short circuit and the step discontinuity excites only TM modes. Transferring the $\phi_0(\varrho)$ mode to the left, we may write (5.81) as

$$(1 - R^{(s)})\,y_0\phi_0(\varrho) = \int_{\varrho_1}^{\varrho_2} \left\{ \sum_{n=1}^{\infty} y_n\phi_n(\varrho)\,\phi_n(\varrho') + \sum_{n=0}^{\infty} \hat{y}_n \frac{T_{s+1}(-\hat{\gamma}_n h)}{T_s(-\hat{\gamma}_n h)}\,\hat{\phi}_n(\varrho)\,\hat{\phi}_n(\varrho') \right\} \times$$
$$\times\, E_\varrho^{(s)}(\varrho')\,\varrho'\,d\varrho'.$$

(5.82)

Under the assumption that only the TEM mode can propagate in $z \leq -h$, $\{y_n, n \geq 1\}$ are all imaginary. The effective modal admittances

$$\left\{ \hat{y}_n \frac{T_{s+1}(-\hat{\gamma}_n h)}{T_s(-\hat{\gamma}_n h)} \right\}$$

are also imaginary for all n. Thus, the kernel function in the right side term is purely imaginary. Since the cavity section is terminated in an open or short circuit, the incident power has to be totally reflected. This means that $|R^{(s)}| = 1$. Let $R^{(s)} = \exp(-j\zeta_s)$. Equation (5.82) may be rewritten as

$$2\,e^{-j\zeta_s/2} \sin(\zeta_s/2)\,y_0\phi_0(\varrho)$$
$$= \int_{\varrho_1}^{\varrho_2} \left\{ \sum_{n=1}^{\infty} (-jy_n)\,\phi_n(\varrho)\,\phi_n(\varrho') + \sum_{n=0}^{\infty} -j\hat{y}_n \frac{T_{s+1}(-\hat{\gamma}_n h)}{T_s(-\hat{\gamma}_n h)}\,\hat{\phi}_n(\varrho)\,\hat{\phi}_n(\varrho') \right\} E_\varrho^{(s)}(\varrho')\,\varrho'\,d\varrho'.$$

(5.83)

If we let $E_\varrho^{(s)}(\varrho) = e^{-j\zeta_s/2}\,\tilde{E}_\varrho^{(s)}(\varrho)$, the exponential factor $\exp(-j\zeta_s/2)$ may be cancelled from both sides of the equation. The result is that we have an entirely real equation. $\tilde{E}^{(s)}$, therefore, may be considered as real also. A real equation, of course, is much easier to handle numerically.

Employing the relation

$$1 + R^{(s)} = \int_{\varrho_1}^{\varrho_2} \phi_0(\varrho)\,E_\varrho^{(s)}(\varrho)\,\varrho\,d\varrho$$

we may also write (5.82) as

$$
\left(\frac{1 - R^{(s)}}{1 + R^{(s)}}\right) \int_{\varrho_1}^{\varrho_2} y_0 \phi_0 \,(y)\, \phi_0(\varrho')\, E_\varrho^{(s)}(\varrho')\, \varrho'\, d\varrho'
$$

$$
= \int_{\varrho_1}^{\varrho_2} \left\{ \sum_{n=1}^{\infty} y_n \phi_n \,(\varrho)\, \phi_n(\varrho') + \sum_{n=0}^{\infty} \hat{y}_n \frac{T_{s+1}\,(-\hat{\gamma}_n h)}{T_s\,(-\hat{\gamma}_n h)}\, \hat{\phi}_n(\varrho)\, \hat{\phi}_n(\varrho') \right\} E_\varrho^{(s)}(\varrho')\, \varrho'\, d\varrho'. \quad (5.84)
$$

Equation (5.84) is an integral equation of the second kind in which the parameter

$$
\left(\frac{1 - R^{(s)}}{1 + R^{(s)}}\right)
$$

serves as the eigenvalue.[†]

Multiplying (5.84) by $\hat{E}^{(s)}(\varrho)\,\varrho$ and integrating from ϱ_1 to ϱ_2, we find that

$$
y_0 \left(\tan \frac{\zeta_s}{2}\right) \int_{\varrho_1}^{\varrho_2} d\varrho\, \varrho \tilde{E}_\varrho^{(s)} \int_{\varrho_1}^{\varrho_2} \phi_0(\varrho)\, \phi_0(\varrho')\, \tilde{E}_\varrho^{(s)}(\varrho')\, \varrho'\, d\varrho'
$$

$$
= \int_{\varrho_1}^{\varrho_2} d\varrho\, \varrho \tilde{E}_\varrho^{(s)} \int_{\varrho_1}^{\varrho_2} \left\{ \sum_{n=1}^{\infty} (-jy_n)\, \phi_n(\varrho)\, \phi_n(\varrho') + \sum_{n=0}^{\infty} (-j\hat{\gamma}_n) \frac{T_{s+1}\,(-\hat{\gamma}_n h)}{T_s\,(-\hat{\gamma}_n h)}\, \hat{\phi}_n(\varrho)\, \hat{\phi}_n(\varrho') \right\} \times
$$

$$
\times\, \tilde{E}_\varrho^{(s)}(\varrho')\, \varrho'\, d\varrho'.
$$

$$(5.85)$$

Under suitable conditions such as in situation where only one type of modes can be excited, this expression gives an upper bound to the approximations (Collin, 1960). A similar equation derived for the magnetic field gives a lower bound. When an upper and a lower bound are obtained, the accuracy of the solution may be estimated.

There are many other double discontinuity problems which occur in practice. Some examples include a thick iris loading of a waveguide, the grating of metallic or dielectric cylinders with rectangular cross-section, waveguide filters of various forms, and double waveguide bends of the type discussed in Section 5.5. There are no doubt many others which may be cited.

5.7. CONCLUDING REMARKS

The above problems which involve only discrete modes could have been formulated by the mode matching method. In this method, modal expansions for the tangential electric and magnetic fields are introduced as we have done. The continuity conditions at the interface are then imposed to relate the expansion coefficients. These relations may be converted into two systems of equations which are subsequently combined into a single one for solution. It turns out that this final equation is identical to the one derivable by applying the moments method to the integral equation, provided that appropriate bases are used. The advantage of employing the integral equation formalism, in addition to its applicability to problems requiring continuous spectrum representations, is that this approach offers considerable flexibility in choosing the bases. For example, in the expansion process the integral may be approximated by various quadrature formulas. Different set of functions may then

---

[†] Obviously, all the integral equations derived previously can be cast into this form. This is an extension of the Fredholm integral equation of the second kind, because operators appear on the both sides of the equation.

be used for testing. Of course, it should be kept in mind that the choice of bases will affect the accuracy of the solutions as well as the economy of obtaining them. Therefore whenever practicable, it is desirable to employ functions which satisfy the Maxwell equations and pertinent boundary conditions. However, for its convenience the point-pulse method wherein a set of pulse functions is used for expansion and a set of delta functions for testing is frequently applied. The method is also very widely employed in exterior type scattering problems.

In the problems discussed above, the two uniform regions can be described by a single coordinate system. As a result, the common boundary is a surface or line of constant coordinate. This is not a necessary requirement. For example, in the junction between cylindrical and conical waveguides shown in Fig. 5.11, the surfaces of constant coordinates (shown dotted) for the coordinate systems suitable for the two respective regions do not coincide. This type of problem is most conveniently treated by modal expansions followed by the point matching procedure.

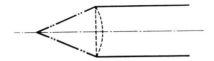

FIG. 5.11. A transition from a conical waveguide to a cylindrical waveguide.

There are certain pitfalls which may arise in problems of this kind. They have to do with the completeness of the set of functions used in the field representations (Lewin, 1970). Due care should be exercised in the consideration of such problems.

Another important point about computer-generated solutions is the verification of its validity and the ascertainment of its relevance to the problem which one tries to solve. Many methods have been suggested for this purpose. They are: (a) reciprocity relations (Jones, 1964), (b) conservation of energy (Amitay and Galindo, 1969), (c) convergence test, (d) use of different bases (Galindo and Wu, 1968), (e) comparison with results obtained by different methods, (f) boundary conditions (Cole *et al.*, 1967), (g) experimental verification, and (h) others. Each method has its advantages and disadvantages. Unfortunately, owing to lack of space, we shall not discuss all of the methods here. Only the convergence test will be discussed in the Appendix because of its special importance in certain problems. The reader is strongly recommended to consult with the original literature for a discussion of the other methods. It should be mentioned, however, that in spite of the numerous methods which have been developed, the checks, with perhaps one exception of experimental verification, can only serve to enhance the degree of confidence in the validity of solution. Techniques for obtaining quantitative measures of ascertaining the validity of computer-generated solutions are therefore very much needed indeed.

Finally, it may be mentioned that the scattering from metallic as well as dielectric obstacles of arbitrary shape inside a waveguide and the excitation of a waveguide by probes or loops may be treated by the integral equation formalism. This class of problems usually requires Green's function representations pertinent to the waveguide regions. Different types of approximation would be more appropriate in applying the moments method to the integral equations of such cases.

Appendix

CONVERGENCE TEST
AND THE RELATIVE CONVERGENCE PROBLEM

In applying the moments method to convert an integral equation into a matrix equation, it is natural to ask how many expansion and testing functions are needed in order to obtain a sufficiently accurate result when the matrix equation is solved. A frequently used criterion is that if the solution remains essentially constant in repeated computations wherein the number of expansion and testing functions are gradually increased, the result is regarded as acceptable. It is implicitly assumed that if the process could be carried out to its limit, an exact solution would be obtained. The constancy of the computed result is taken to imply that it is not far from the true solution. This approach works well for the majority of problems. There are, however, situations in which the process fails to converge or converges to wrong answers unless the limit is taken in a proper fashion. Such phenomena have been found to occur in problems dealing with iris-type discontinuities and in problems involving close-by double discontinuities. The importance of using more than one check procedure to ascertain the validity of numerically obtained solutions therefore cannot be overemphasized.

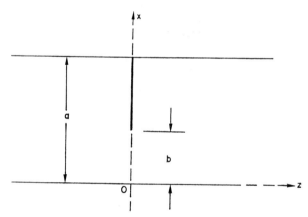

FIG. 5.12. A thin iris in a parallel-plate waveguide.

To illustrate the point, consider the discontinuity due to an infinitesimally thin metallic iris in a parallel-plate waveguide as shown in Fig. 5.12. The formulation of the problem can be carried out readily according to the procedures discussed in the text. Thus, when a TM_s mode is incident, the integral equation for the unknown aperture field E_x is obtained as

$$\int_A K(x, x') E_x(x') \, dx' = g(x) \tag{A.1}$$

where the kernel

$$K(x, x') = \sum_{p=1}^{\infty} Y_p \phi_p(x) \phi_p(x'),$$

300

with

$$Y_p = \omega\varepsilon_0/\gamma_p, \quad \phi_p = \sqrt{\left(\frac{2 - \delta_{0p}}{a}\right)} \cos \frac{(p - 1)\pi x}{a}$$

and

$$g(x) = \phi_s(x).$$

The matrix equation obtained from (A.1) by the moments method using N of $\{Q_n\}$ functions as basis is given by

$$\sum_{m=1}^{N} \langle Q_l, KQ_m \rangle B_m = \langle Q_l, g \rangle \quad l = 1, 2, \ldots, N. \tag{A.2}$$

The evaluation of the matrix elements $\langle Q_l, KQ_m \rangle$ requires summing infinitely many terms as the kernel is an infinite series.† In practical computation, however, the series necessarily have to be truncated, so that another approximation is introduced. Suppose that the summation is terminated at the Pth term.

Since there are now two stages of approximations involved, there arises the question of whether and how the solution will depend on the choice of numbers for N and P. It has been demonstrated by several workers (Masterman *et al.*, 1969, 1971; Lee *et al.*, 1971; Itoh and Mittra, 1971; Mittra *et al.*, 1971) in considering a variety of iris-type discontinuity problems that the correct solutions of such problems are critically dependent on the choice of the relative values for N and P. Specifically, when the matrix equation (A.2) is solved for different values of N with the value of P fixed, it was found that the best approximation to the true solution is obtained for a critical value of N say N_c, which is related to P and the geometry of the problem by

$$N_c = P \, [b/a]$$

where $[b/a]$ denotes the greatest integer value of b/a. A graphical illustration of this fact is given in Fig. 5.13. The variation of the input susceptance‡ presented by the iris as a function of N is shown in the figure. It clearly demonstrates that the computed results quickly deteriorate as soon as N exceeds the critical value. (It is possible to obtain an exact solution by the Wiener–Hopf technique for the special case $a = 2b$.) In particular, when $N = P$, the solution gives zero susceptance implying that there is no discontinuity, an obviously erroneous result.

If, on the other hand, computations are made with varying P while N is held fixed, the results as shown in Fig. 5.14 are obtained. Notice that the computed susceptance first varies rapidly with P, and then remains essentially constant once P exceeds a critical value defined by

$$P_c = N \, [a/b].$$

The graph also shows that better approximations are obtained for larger N with $P \geq P_c$.

The problem also has been investigated by varying N and P simultaneously in such a way

---

† It is possible to closely approximate the kernel as the sum of a singular function and a finite series, the former being extracted by using the quasi-static approximation. This approach makes the evaluation of the matrix elements considerably more complicated. But, it can help avoid the difficulty of relative convergences.

‡ The input susceptance is the imaginary part of the ratio $(1 - R)/(1 + R)$ where R is the reflection coefficient of the incident mode.

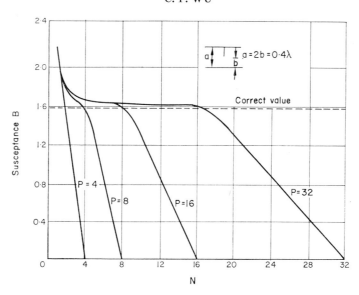

FIG. 5.13. TEM-mode susceptance of an iris discontinuity in a parallel-plate waveguide computed with fixed *P*.

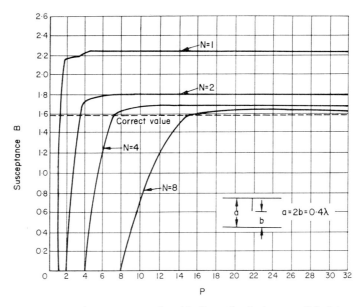

FIG. 5.14. TEM-mode susceptance of an iris discontinuity in a parallel-plate waveguide computed with fixed *N*.

that the ratio P/N is held constant. The results reveal that the susceptance converges most rapidly to the correct answer when the ratio $N/P = b/a$ is used. In fact, Mittra *et al.* (1971) have recently shown by an analytical method that only when the above ratio is chosen will the solution converge to the correct answer, and that only the choice of that ratio will enable the solution to satisfy the edge condition in the limit. It should be noted, however, that in practical computations, it is not imperative to use that particular ratio in order to obtain solutions which are accurate within engineering tolerances. Nevertheless, the use of the proper ratio does provide the advantage of computational efficiency. The phenomenon in which the convergence of a solution depends on the relative numbers of functions used in the approximations is called the relative convergence problem. It was first discovered many years ago (Mittra, 1963) in the solution of the scattering from a bifurcation in a rectangular waveguide.

REFERENCES

ABRAMOVITZ, M. and STEGEN, I.A., Ed. (1965) *Handbook of Mathematical Functions*, Dover, New York, pp. 369–70.

AMITAY, N. and GALINDO, V. (1968) Application of a new method for approximate solutions and error estimates to waveguide discontinuity and phased array problems, *Radio Science 3* (New Series), 830–43.

AMITAY, N. and GALINDO, V. (1969) On energy conservation and the method of moments in scattering problems, *IEEE Trans. on Ant. & Prop. AP-17*, 722–9.

AMITAY, N., GALINDO, V. and WU, C.P. (1972) *The Theory and Analysis of Phased Array Antennas*, Wiley-Interscience, New York.

BALDWIN, G.L. and HEINS, A.E. (1954) On the diffraction of a plane wave by an infinite plane grating, *Math Scand. 2*, 103–18.

BATES, C.P. (1969) Intermodal coupling at the junction between straight and curved waveguides, *B.S.T.J. 48*, 2259–80.

BORN, M. and WOLF, E. (1959) *Principle of Optics*, Pergamon Press, New York.

CLARRICOATS, P.J.B. and SLINN, K.R. (1966) Numerical method for the solution of waveguide discontinuity problems, *Electronics Letters 2* (6), 226–8.

COCHRAN, J., ALAN and PECINA, R.G. (1966) Mode propagation in continuously curved waveguides, *Radio Science 1*, 679–95.

COLE, W.J., NAGELBERG, E.R. and NAGEL, C.M. (1967) Iterative solution of waveguide discontinuity problems, *B.S.T.J. 46*, 649–72.

COLLIN, R.E. (1960) *Field Theory of Guided Waves*, McGraw-Hill, New York, pp. 576–89.

FRÖBERG, C.E. (1965) *Introduction to Numerical Analysis*, Addison-Wesley Publishing Co., Inc., Reading, Mass.

GALINDO, V. and WU, C.P. (1968) Dielectric loaded and covered rectangular waveguide phased arrays, *B.S.T.J. 47*, 93–116.

HARRINGTON, R.F. (1968) *Field Computation by Moment Method*, Macmillan, New York.

ITOH, T. and MITTRA, R. (1971) Relative convergence phenomenon arising in the solution of diffraction from strip grating on a dielectric slab, *Proc. IEEE 59*, 1363–5.

JONES, D.S. (1964) *The Theory of Electromagnetism*, Pergamon Press, Oxford.

KNETSCH, H.D. (1968) Contribution to the theory of abrupt cross-sectional changes in waveguides, *Arch. Elek. Übertr. 22*, 591–600.

LEE, S.W., JONES, W.R. and CAMPBELL, J.J. (1971) Convergence of numerical solutions of iris-type discontinuity problems, *IEEE Trans. on Microwave Theory and Techniques, MTT-19*, 528–36.

LEWIN, L. (1951) *Advanced Theory of Waveguides*, Iliffe & Sons, Ltd., London.

LEWIN, L. (1970) On the inadequacy of discrete mode-matching techniques in some waveguide discontinuity problems, *IEEE Trans. on Microwave Theory and Techniques MTT-18*, 364–72.

MARCUVITZ, N., Ed. (1951) *Microwave Handbook*, McGraw-Hill, New York.

MASTERMAN, P.H., CLARRICOATS, P.J.B. and HANNAFORD, C.D. (1969) Computer method of solving waveguide-iris problems, *Electronics Letters 5*, 23–25.

MASTERMAN, P.H. and CLARRICOATS, P.J.B. (1971) Computer field-matching solution of waveguide transverse discontinuities, *Proc. IEE 118*, 51–63.

MITTRA, R. (1963) Relative convergence of the solution of a doubly infinite set of equations, *J. of Research NBS 67D*, 245–54.

MITTRA, R., ITOH, T. and LI, T.S. (1971) Analytical and numerical studies of the relative convergence phenomenon arising in the solution of an integral equation by the moment method, *IEEE Trons on Microwave Theory and Techniques MTT-20*, 96–104.

NAGELBERG, E.R. and SHEFER, J. (1965) Mode conversion in circular waveguides, *B.S.T.J. 44*, 1321–38.

OLVER, F.W.J. (1954) The asymptotic expansion of Bessel junctions of large order, *Phil. Trans. Roy. Soc., London*, A, *247*, 328–68.

PIEFKE, G. (1968) The application of eigenfunction expansion in diffraction problems in finite regions, *Arch. Elek. Übertr. 22*, 275–81.

SCHWINGER, J. and SAXON, D. (1958) *Discontinuities in Waveguides Notes on Lecture by J. Schwinger*, Gordon & Breach, New York.

STAKGOLD, I. (1968) *Boundary Value Problems of Mathematical Physics*, The Macmillan Co., New York, vol. II, chap. 8.

VARGA, R.S. (1962) *Matrix Iterative Analysis*, Prentice Hall, Inc., New York.

VARON, D. (1967) Radial line band rejection filters in coaxial waveguides, *IEEE Trans. on Microwave Theory and Techniques MTT-15*, 680–7.

WEINSTEIN, L.A. (1969) *The Theory of Diffraction and the Factorization Method*, The Golem Press, Boulder, Colorado.

WEXLER, A. (1967) Solution of waveguide discontinuities by modal analysis, *IEEE Trans. on Microwave Theory and Techniques MTT-15*, 508–17.

WU, C.P. (1969a) Numerical solutions for the coupling between waveguides in finite arrays, *Radio Sciences 4*, 245–54.

WU, C.P. (1969b) Integral equation solutions for the radiation from a waveguide through a dielectric slab, *IEEE Trans. on Ant. & Prop. AP-17*, 733–9.

CHAPTER 6

Some Numerically Efficient Methods

R. MITTRA AND T. ITOH

University of Illinois, Urbana, Illinois

6.1. INTRODUCTION

In recent years detailed solutions to a vast number of problems in the field of scattering and diffraction of electromagnetic waves have been derived via the application of numerical techniques. Typically, the first step in the formulation of the boundary value problem is the derivation of an integral equation for the unknown field at a suitable interface or the current distribution on the surface of a scatterer. Next, this integral equation is converted into an infinite matrix equation by the moment method (see Chapter 5, for instance). Finally, the matrix equation is truncated and solved by the use of a digital computer. The principle of the above approach is relatively straightforward, and, what is equally significant, the range of application of this procedure is very general. Thus, it is not surprising that the method has found widespread application to a diverse array of boundary value problems.

In contrast to the numerical techniques, the analytical methods of solution are usually restricted to limited ranges of application. Exact solutions are possible only for the separable geometries or the so-called Wiener–Hopf geometries, of which there are only a few. There are a number of techniques, such as the low- and high-frequency expansions and ray-optical methods, that extend the scope of the analytical solutions. However, even with these additional tools, the range of application of analytical methods remains considerably limited.

It would appear that the implication of the above discussion is that the numerical methods offer an overwhelming advantage over analytical procedures. While this is true for a class of problems, the numerical route offers no panacea. In principle, of course, one may employ the numerical procedure for solving the problem for an arbitrarily complex geometry. However, the storage requirement on the computer, the execution time of the program, and the numerical error in the solution tend to become excessive and sometimes prohibitive for complicated geometries. On the other hand, the analytical methods, when applicable, offer efficiency of computation, superior accuracy, physical insight into the problem, and so on.

One might suspect that a combination of analytical and numerical techniques may be the desired route to follow for a class of problems that may be identified as modified versions of canonical problems that are tractable by analytical means. The purpose of the discussion to be presented in this chapter is to show that this is, indeed, an efficient way to attack the problems belonging to the above category.

The philosophy of this approach differs from those of "strictly numerical" or "strictly analytical" methods. Instead of getting to the final matrix equation as directly as possible, the hybrid method, to be presented in this chapter, entails a certain amount of analytical preprocessing. This enables one to derive an auxiliary matrix equation that offers a number of distinct numerical advantages. For instance, the size of the matrix that is required to be inverted for a given accuracy is usually much smaller; the routines often have built-in convergence checks that allow one to determine the appropriate truncation size; and the satisfaction of the asymptotic behavior of the fields is guaranteed in the neighborhood of edges and corners when some of the field components are singular and therefore, it is difficult to reproduce this behavior in a conventional formulation.

We demonstrate the application of this "combination approach" by considering a number of different problems such as microstrip lines, gratings, discontinuities in waveguides, radiation from thick-walled phased arrays, etc. Since each of these problems has also been dealt with in the literature using conventional numerical approaches, they offer a convenient comparison.

6.2. ANALYSIS OF MICROSTRIP LINES

6.2.1. Introduction and Description of the Problem

There is much current interest in the study of microstrip transmission lines in connection with the development of microwave integrated circuits. Typically, these lines are characterized by planar geometry, one or more layers of dielectric insulation, and a large ground plane.

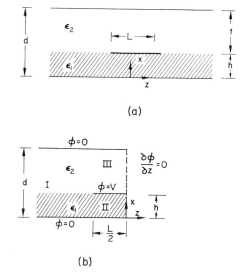

FIG. 6.1. (a) Cross-section of shielded microstrip line.
(b) Equivalent geometry of shielded microstrip line.

The shielded versions of the microstrip lines are supported between a pair of ground planes [see Fig. 6.1(a)].

Although the actual propagating mode in such a structure is not TEM, but a hybrid one (see, for instance, Mittra and Itoh, 1971), it is possible to use the so-called quasi-TEM approximation if the operating wavelength is much larger than the line thickness. In this case, the problem of determining the guide wavelength and the characteristic impedance turns out to be that of deriving the static capacitance of the structure. The principal techniques that have been found useful for the theoretical analysis of the microstrip lines are: (1) modified conformal mapping; (2) relaxation method, and (3) variational or Rayleigh–Ritz method. In what follows, we discuss an alternate approach that entails a combination of analytical and numerical processing. It provides an efficient means of evaluating the charge distribution on the center strip and the potential distribution in the cross-section of the line, the two quantities of primary interest. The capacitance is easily obtainable once these quantities are known.

6.2.2. Formulation of a Boundary Value Problem in Spectral Domain

For simplicity, we will only consider the case where the substrate consists of a single dielectric, although the multilayered case can be analyzed along similar lines.

Assume that the center strip and the ground planes are maintained at V volts and zero volts, respectively. Taking into account that both the structure and the excitation are symmetric with respect to the x-axis, one only needs to consider the half of the structure as shown in Fig. 6.1(b).

The next step is to substitute the potential function $\phi(x, z)$ in each region I, II, or III in a Fourier series as follows:

Region I

$$\phi(x, z) = \begin{cases} \sum_{n=1}^{\infty} A_n \sin(\alpha_n x)\, e^{\alpha_n(z+L/2)} & 0 < x < h, \quad z < -L/2, \\ \sum_{n=1}^{\infty} A_n \frac{\sin(\alpha_n h)}{\sin(\alpha_n t)} \sin[\alpha_n(d-x)]\, e^{\alpha_n(z+L/2)} & h < x < d, \quad z < -L/2. \end{cases}$$ (6.1)

Region II

$$\phi(x, z) = \frac{Vx}{h} + \sum_{n=1}^{\infty} B_n \sin(\beta_n x) \cosh(\beta_n z), \quad h < x < d, \quad -L/2 < z < 0.$$ (6.2)

Region III

$$\phi(x, z) = \frac{V(d-x)}{t} + \sum_{n=1}^{\infty} C_n \sin[\gamma_n(d-x)] \cosh(\gamma_n z), \quad h < x < d, \quad -L/2 < z < 0$$ (6.3)

where α_n is the solution of the transcendental equation

$$\varepsilon_1 \cos(\alpha_n h) \sin(\alpha_n t) + \varepsilon_2 \sin(\alpha_n h) \cos(\alpha_n t) = 0, \quad \alpha_n \neq 0$$ (6.4)

and $\beta_n = n\pi/h$, $\gamma_n = n\pi/t$. The coefficients A_n, B_n, and C_n are yet to be determined. Notice that the potential functions given above satisfy the boundary conditions $\phi = V$ on the center strip, $\phi = 0$ on the ground planes, and $\partial\phi/\partial z = 0$ on the x-axis. The remaining condition to be satisfied is the continuity of the potential ϕ and its normal derivative $\partial\phi/\partial z$ at the interface $z = L/2$. When this is done, the results are

$$\left.\begin{aligned}
\sum_{n=1}^{\infty} A_n \sin(\alpha_n x) &= \frac{Vx}{h} + \sum_{n=1}^{\infty} B_n \cosh\frac{\beta_n L}{2} \sin(\beta_n x) \\
\sum_{n=1}^{\infty} \alpha_n A_n \sin(\alpha_n x) &= -\sum_{n=1}^{\infty} \beta_n B_n \sinh\frac{\beta_n L}{2} \sin(\beta_n x)
\end{aligned}\right\} \quad 0 < x < h \qquad (6.5)$$

and

$$\left.\begin{aligned}
\sum_{n=1}^{\infty} A_n \frac{\sin(\alpha_n h)}{\sin(\alpha_n t)} \sin[\alpha_n(d-x)] &= \frac{V(d-x)}{t} + \sum_{n=1}^{\infty} C_n \cosh\frac{\gamma_n L}{2} \\
&\qquad \times \sin[\gamma_n(d-x)] \\
\sum_{n=1}^{\infty} \alpha_n A_n \frac{\sin(\alpha_n h)}{\sin(\alpha_n t)} \sin[\alpha_n(d-x)] &= -\sum_{n=1}^{\infty} \gamma_n C_n \sinh\frac{\gamma_n L}{2} \sin[\gamma_n(d-x)]
\end{aligned}\right\} \quad h < x < d.$$

$$(6.6)$$

One might attempt to solve these equations after truncating the infinite summation at some finite number. However, this is a rather inefficient way of solving these equations since the truncation size of the matrix required to yield accurate answers is usually quite large and its inversion is time-consuming. Furthermore, convergence checks are not easy to apply when this method of solution is adopted. It turns out that an alternative procedure, that performs its manipulations in the spectral domain, offers the important advantages that the resulting matrix equation can be attacked by the function-theoretic techniques and transformed into an auxiliary set of equations that converges very rapidly. The details of the spectral domain technique appear in the following paragraphs.

As a first step, Fourier analyze (6.5) and (6.6) by first multiplying these with $\sin\beta_m x$ and $\sin\gamma_m(d-x)$, respectively, and subsequently integrating from 0 to h and h to d. Adding and subtracting the resulting equations, we get

$$\left\{\begin{aligned}
\sum_{n=1}^{\infty} \frac{A_n}{\alpha_n - \beta_m} + \frac{1}{\beta_m} &= (-1)^m \frac{h}{2} B_m \exp\left(-\frac{\beta_m L}{2}\right), \qquad (6.7) \\
\sum_{n=1}^{\infty} \frac{A_n}{\alpha_n + \beta_m} - \frac{1}{\beta_m} &= (-1)^{m+1} \frac{h}{2} B_m \exp\left(\frac{\beta_m L}{2}\right), \qquad (6.8)
\end{aligned}\right.$$

$$\left\{\begin{aligned}
\sum_{n=1}^{\infty} \frac{A_n}{\alpha_n - \gamma_m} + \frac{1}{\gamma_m} &= (-1)^m \frac{t}{2} C_m \exp\left(-\frac{\gamma_m L}{2}\right), \qquad (6.9) \\
\sum_{n=1}^{\infty} \frac{A_n}{\alpha_n + \gamma_m} - \frac{1}{\gamma_m} &= (-1)^{m+1} \frac{t}{2} C_m \exp\left(\frac{\gamma_m L}{2}\right), \qquad (6.10)
\end{aligned}\right.$$

$$m = 1, 2, \ldots, \infty$$

where

$$\mathbf{A}_n = A_n \sin (x_n h) \tag{6.11}$$

and we have let $V \equiv 1$, without loss of generality.

Equations (6.7) through (6.11) are the desired equations in the spectral domain. Although the above is still a quadruply infinite set of equations, we will soon show that the auxiliary set of equations derived from them can be effectively truncated to a small size matrix.

The analytical method that is found convenient for attacking (6.7) through (6.11) is referred to as the modified residue calculus technique (MRCT). Since the details of the method may be found in a number of publications, e.g. Mittra *et al.* (1968) and VanBlaricum and Mittra (1969), only the important steps will be given here.

6.2.3. Modified Residue Calculus Technique

As a preparatory step toward the application of MRCT, we eliminate B_m and C_m from (6.7) through (6.10). To do this, multiply (6.8) by $\exp(-\beta_m L)$ and add the resultant to (6.7). A similar procedure is applied next to (6.9) and (6.10). We then have

$$\sum_{n=1}^{\infty} \frac{\mathbf{A}_n}{\alpha_n - \beta_m} + \lambda_m \sum_{n=1}^{\infty} \frac{\mathbf{A}_n}{\alpha_n + \beta_m} = \frac{1}{-\beta_m} + \frac{\lambda_m}{\beta_m}, \tag{6.12}$$

$$\sum_{n=1}^{\infty} \frac{\mathbf{A}_n}{\alpha_n - \gamma_m} + \xi_m \sum_{n=1}^{\infty} \frac{\mathbf{A}_n}{\alpha_n + \gamma_m} = \frac{1}{-\gamma_m} + \frac{\xi_m}{\gamma_m} \tag{6.13}$$

$$m = 1, 2, \ldots$$

where

$$\lambda_m = \exp(-\beta_m L), \quad \xi_m = \exp(-\gamma_m L). \tag{6.14}$$

There is an important feature of (6.12) and (6.13) that is used with advantage by the MRCT method. Note first that the factors λ_m and ξ_m have an exponential decay as $m \to \infty$. The matrix equation obtained by deleting the terms involving λ_m and ξ_m takes a special form called the "double alternant", which can be inverted exactly by the residue calculus technique (Collin, 1960; Mittra and Lee, 1971). This allows one to construct a solution of (6.12) and (6.13) which is a perturbation of the exact solution of the reduced problem ($\lambda_m = 0, \xi_m = 0$).

Some details of the development of this approach will now be given. We will show that the problem of solving the infinite set of equations can be reduced to that of constructing a function $f(\omega)$ of complex variable ω with certain pole-zero characteristics in the complex plane.

Consider a meromorphic function (a function that is regular except for simple poles), $f(\omega)$ of the complex variable ω which has the following properties:

(1) $f(\omega)$ has simple poles at $\omega = \alpha_n$, $n = 1, 2, \ldots, \infty$, and at $\omega = 0$;

(2) $f(\beta_m) + \lambda_m f(-\beta_m) = 0$

$\quad f(\gamma_m) + \xi_m f(-\gamma_m) = 0$; $m = 1, 2, \ldots, \infty$.

(3) $f(\omega)$ has the asymptotic behavior $f(\omega) \sim K_1 |\omega|^{-\nu}$ as $|\omega| \to \infty$, $K_1 = $ constant, $1 < \nu < 2$; and

(4) the residue of $f(\omega)$ at $\omega = 0$, say $R_f(0)$, is -1.

Then, $f(\omega)$ may be represented as

$$f(\omega) = Kg(\omega) P(\omega), \tag{6.15}$$

$$g(\omega) = e^{R\omega} \frac{\pi(\omega, \beta_n) \pi(\omega, \gamma_n)}{\omega \pi(\omega, \alpha_n)}, \tag{6.16}$$

$$R = \frac{1}{\pi} [h \ln(d/h) + t \ln(d/t)] \tag{6.17}$$

where K is a constant to be determined later such that the condition (4) is satisfied, and

$$P(\omega) = 1 + \sum_{m=1}^{\infty} \frac{F_m}{1 - \omega/\beta_m} + \sum_{m=1}^{\infty} \frac{G_m}{1 - \omega/\gamma_m}. \tag{6.18}$$

Also,

$$\pi(\omega, \alpha_n) = \prod_{n=1}^{\infty} \left(1 - \frac{\omega}{\alpha_n}\right) e^{\omega d/n\pi}, \tag{6.19}$$

$$\pi(\omega, \beta_n) = \prod_{n=1}^{\infty} \left(1 - \frac{\omega}{\beta_n}\right) e^{\omega h/n\pi}, \tag{6.20}$$

$$\pi(\omega, \gamma_n) = \prod_{n=1}^{\infty} \left(1 - \frac{\omega}{\gamma_n}\right) e^{\omega t/n\pi}. \tag{6.21}$$

F_m and G_m are constants, as yet undetermined. The factor $e^{R\omega}$ ensures the algebraic nature of $g(\omega)$, viz.

$$g(\omega) \sim |\omega|^{-3/2} \quad \text{as} \quad |\omega| \to \infty. \tag{6.22}$$

Notice that, except for a multiplicative constant, $g(\omega)$ may be identified as the limiting case of $f(\omega)$, for the case of $\lambda_m \equiv \xi_m \equiv 0$ for all m. Physically, this is the solution for the semi-infinite bifurcation problem. It has been discussed in a number of texts, e.g. Collin (1960) and Mittra and Lee (1971). Thus, essentially the only unknown in (6.15) is $P(\omega)$, or, more specifically, F_m and G_m in (6.18). Once $f(\omega)$ has been constructed, the solution to the original equations, i.e. A_n in (6.12), (6.13) is related to $f(\omega)$ as follows. Consider

$$\frac{1}{2\pi j} \oint \left\{ \frac{f(\omega)}{\omega - \beta_m} + \lambda_m \frac{f(\omega)}{\omega + \beta_m} \right\} d\omega = \sum_{n=1}^{\infty} \frac{R_f(\alpha_n)}{\alpha_n - \beta_m} + \lambda_m \sum_{n=1}^{\infty} \frac{R_f(\alpha_n)}{\alpha_n + \beta_m} + \frac{R_f(0)}{-\beta_m}$$

$$+ \lambda_m \frac{R_f(0)}{\beta_m} + f(\beta_m) + \lambda_m f(-\beta_m),$$

$$m = 1, 2, \ldots, \infty. \tag{6.23}$$

$$\frac{1}{2\pi j} \oint \left\{ \frac{f(\omega)}{\omega - \gamma_m} + \xi_m \frac{f(\omega)}{\omega + \gamma_m} \right\} d\omega = \sum_{n=1}^{\infty} \frac{R_f(\alpha_n)}{\alpha_n - \gamma_m} + \xi_m \sum_{n=1}^{\infty} \frac{R_f(\alpha_n)}{\alpha_n + \gamma_m} + \frac{R_f(0)}{-\gamma_m}$$

$$+ \xi_m \frac{R_f(0)}{\gamma_m} + f(\gamma_m) + \xi_m f(-\gamma_m),$$

$$m = 1, 2, \ldots, \infty \tag{6.24}$$

where $R_f(\alpha_n)$ is the residue of $f(\omega)$ at $\omega = \alpha_n$. Because of condition (3), these contour integrals give zero contribution. Making use of conditions (2) and (4), and comparing (6.23), (6.24) with (6.12) and (6.13), we notice that

$$\mathbf{A}_n = R_f(\alpha_n). \tag{6.25}$$

The Fourier series coefficients B_m and C_m appearing in (6.5) and (6.6) may also be related to $f(\omega)$. Consider

$$\frac{1}{2\pi j} \oint \frac{f(\omega)}{\omega + \beta_m}\, d\omega = \sum_{n=1}^{\infty} \frac{R_f(\alpha_n)}{\alpha_n + \beta_m} + \frac{R_f(0)}{\beta_m} + f(-\beta_m). \tag{6.26}$$

Following an argument similar to the one used for deriving (6.25) and comparing (6.26) with (6.8), we have

$$B_m = (-1)^m \frac{2}{h} f(-\beta_m) \exp\left(-\frac{\beta_m L}{2}\right). \tag{6.27}$$

Similarly,

$$C_m = (-1)^m \frac{2}{t} f(-\gamma_m) \exp\left(-\frac{\gamma_m L}{2}\right). \tag{6.28}$$

Using (6.25), (6.27), and (6.28), the potential and charge distributions can be expressed in the following manner. The potential distributions at any point in the microstrip line structure are obtained by substituting (6.25), (6.27), or (6.28) into (6.1), (6.2), or (6.3). For instance, for $x = h$ and $z \leq -L/2$,

$$\phi(h, z) = \sum_{n=1}^{\infty} R_f(\alpha_n)\, e^{\alpha_n(z + L/2)}. \tag{6.29}$$

The charge distribution on the strip is given by

$$\frac{\varrho(z)}{\varepsilon_0} = \varepsilon_1 \frac{\partial \phi}{\partial x}\bigg|_{x = h^-} - \varepsilon_2 \frac{\partial \phi}{\partial x}\bigg|_{x = h^+}$$

$$= \frac{\varepsilon_1}{h} + \frac{\varepsilon_2}{t} + \varepsilon_1 \sum_{m=1}^{\infty} \frac{m\pi}{h^2} f(-\beta_m) \{e^{-\beta_m(L/2 + z)} + e^{-\beta_m(L/2 - z)}\}$$

$$+ \varepsilon_2 \sum_{m=1}^{\infty} \frac{m\pi}{t^2} f(-\gamma_m) \{e^{-\gamma_m(L/2 + z)} + e^{-\gamma_m(L/2 - z)}\}, \quad -\frac{L}{2} < z < 0, \tag{6.30}$$

where ε_0 is the free-space permittivity. Notice that the first two terms in (6.30) correspond to the charge induced on the infinitely long parallel triplate capacitor, while the correction terms correspond to the so-called "fringing effect".

The only remaining step is the construction of $P(\omega)$ given in (6.18), satisfying the condition (2). If the construction of $P(\omega)$ required the solution of an infinite order matrix for the coefficient F_m and G_m, then one would have to concede that little has been gained by the manipulations outlined above. Fortunately, however, the construction of $P(\omega)$ requires the solution of a very small size matrix, typically less than 10. This is due to the fact that it is possible to construct an exact solution to the asymptotic form of condition (2). In the present case, λ_m and ξ_m decay exponentially, as $m \to \infty$, while $f(-\beta_m)$ and $f(-\gamma_m)$ decrease only algebraically for large m. Hence, the asymptotic values of the zeros of $f(\omega)$ are β_m and γ_m. One could determine that, for the above asymptotic behavior of the zeros, v in condition (3) turns out to be $\frac{3}{2}$, so that $f(\omega) \sim |\omega|^{-3/2}$, and the edge condition is satisfied. The edge condition remains unchanged when the semi-infinite bifurcation is truncated. For a thorough discussion of the edge condition, the reader is referred to Mittra and Lee (1971).

It can be shown from the above argument that F_m and G_m decrease exponentially for large m. Thus, it is only necessary to solve for the first few F_m's and G_m's, say M_1 and M_2 of them, after truncating the two infinite series in (6.18) at $m = M_1$ and $m = M_2$, respectively. Before proceeding with the discussion of the numerical aspects of the method of solution, let us briefly summarize the results of the analytical processing elaborated above.

Instead of solving the problem via conventional matrix methods of formulation, we have made advantageous use of the fact that the solution to a related canonical problem, that of a bifurcated guide, is known exactly and the solution to the microstrip problem can be related to it by a perturbational factor in the form of $P(\omega)$. $P(\omega)$ itself can be expressed in a suitable form containing the unknown constants F_m and G_m that have an exponential decay with the index m. Thus, only a few of these need be determined to derive an accurate solution to the problem. In contrast to the exponential decay of F_m and G_m, the original set of coefficients A_n has a slowly decreasing algebraic behavior with n, resulting in slow convergence of the conventional matrix equation for A_n. Of course, the price one pays for working with the auxiliary equations for F_m and G_m is that the matrix elements for this equation have to be derived by evaluating some infinite products. However, in view of the small truncation size of this matrix, the number of such products that have to be evaluated is quite small and the overall efficiency of the method is still quite favorable.

6.2.4. Numerical Computation

Let us now discuss some pertinent aspects of numerical processing in connection with the solution of the microstrip problem by the method detailed in the previous section. These are listed below in the order they appear in the computational procedure.

(i) SOLUTION OF THE ROOTS OF THE TRANSCENDENTAL EQN. (6.4)

For numerical solution of (6.4), it is convenient to rewrite it as

$$F(x) \equiv \left(\frac{\varepsilon_2}{\varepsilon_1} + 1 \right) \sin (xd) + \left(\frac{\varepsilon_2}{\varepsilon_1} - 1 \right) \sin \{x (h - t)\} = 0. \qquad (6.31)$$

This equation has a countably infinite number of roots

$$\alpha_n = \frac{n\pi}{d} + \frac{f_n}{d}, \quad n = 1, 2, \ldots \qquad (6.32)$$

where $\{f_n\}$ are bounded and oscillatory. The roots of the equation $F(x) = 0$ may be determined by any of the iterative methods for solving transcendental equations. For instance, the Newton–Raphson method can be used where the following three steps are involved:

(1) Determination of the distance between the two closest roots. This gives the fastest incrementing value for finding the initial α for the Newton iteration subroutine and specifies a range of α that must not be exceeded in using the Newton method, or roots may be skipped.
(2) Determination of the roots. This is done by the Newton iteration subroutine such as DRTNI available in the IBM 360 Scientific Subroutine Package (SSP), which requires the value and the derivative of $F(x)$.
(3) Determination of a new initial value for the Newton subroutine. The procedure is to increment α and to test the derivative for sign change. As soon as the derivative changes sign, a check is made to see if α is in the range specified in (1).

(ii) EVALUATION OF THE INFINITE PRODUCT (6.19), (6.20), AND (6.21)

In actual computation, the infinite product must be truncated. Therefore, we need to estimate the error in the truncated product

$$P_N = \prod_{n=1}^{N} \left(1 - \frac{\omega}{\beta_n}\right) e^{\omega h/n\pi}. \tag{6.33}$$

Let us define a relative error introduced due to the truncation as

$$\varepsilon_N = \left|\frac{P_\infty - P_N}{P_N}\right| = \left|\prod_{n=N+1}^{\infty} \left(1 - \frac{\omega}{\beta_n}\right) e^{\omega h/n\pi} - 1\right|, \tag{6.34}$$

which, for large N, can be simplified by neglecting terms whose order is smaller than $\omega h/N\pi$,

$$\varepsilon_N \approx \left|\prod_{n=N+1}^{\infty} \left[1 - \tfrac{1}{2}\left(\frac{\omega h}{n\pi}\right)^2\right] - 1\right| \approx \tfrac{1}{2}\left|\frac{\omega h}{\pi}\right|^2 \sum_{n=N+1}^{\infty} \frac{1}{n^2}. \tag{6.35}$$

Note that

$$\sum_{n=N+1}^{\infty} \frac{1}{n^2} < \int_N^\infty \frac{dx}{x^2} = \frac{1}{N}. \tag{6.36}$$

Therefore, we have

$$\varepsilon_N \approx \frac{1}{2N}\left|\frac{\omega h}{\pi}\right|^2 \tag{6.37}$$

if

$$\frac{1}{2N}\left|\frac{\omega h}{\pi}\right|^2 \ll 1,$$

in other words, if $|\omega|$ is not too large.

(iii) SOLUTION OF THE MATRIX EQUATION

The determination of F_m and G_m requires the solution of small-order simultaneous equations derived from the condition (2). Many computer systems furnish subroutines for this purpose. For instance, DGELG in the IBM 360 SSP is designed to solve the simultaneous equations with real coefficients.

(iv) SUMMATION OF SERIES IN (6.29) AND (6.30)

The evaluation of charge and potential distribution in the microstrip line requires the computation of the series in (6.29). We first note that since

$$f(\omega) \sim |\omega|^{-3/2} \quad \text{as } |\omega| \to \infty,$$

$$R_f(\alpha_n) \sim n^{-3/2} \quad \text{as } n \to \infty.$$

As long as the observation point z is not too close to the edge of the center strip (i.e. $|z| \neq L/2$), all of the summations in (6.29) and (6.30) converge very quickly because of the exponentially

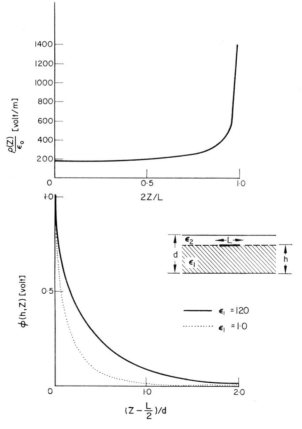

FIG. 6.2. The charge distribution on the strip and the potential distribution at $x = h$, $\varepsilon_1 = 120$, $\varepsilon_2 = 1$, $h = d/\sqrt{1.56}$, $L/d = 1$. (The potential distribution for $\varepsilon_1 = 1$ is plotted with the dotted line.)

decaying factors. The value of (6.29) at the edge is bounded and is unity since the potential at the strip is unity. For calculating the value of the summations in the neighborhood of the edge, we can make use of the asymptotic form of $f(\omega)$ in the manner explained below. Since for large m

$$f(-\beta_m) \sim K_2 m^{-3/2},$$

where K_2 is known, we can make use of the following relation for the calculation of charge distribution as $z \rightarrow -L/2$:

$$\sum_{m=1}^{\infty} m^{-1/2} e^{-m\pi/h(L/2+z)} \sim \left[\frac{1}{h} \left(\frac{L}{2} + z \right) \right]^{-1/2}. \tag{6.38}$$

6.2.5. Numerical Results

Extensive numerical results have been obtained by using the method outlined here and have been published by Mittra and Itoh (1970). Only representative calculations for the charge distribution on the strip and the potential distribution at $x = h$ are shown in Fig. 6.2 for the parameters $\varepsilon_1 = 120$, $\varepsilon_2 = 1$, $h = d/\sqrt{1.56}$, and $L/d = 1$. The charge distribution exhibits the correct singularity at the edge of the strip. The potential distribution for $\varepsilon_1 = 1$ is plotted with the dotted line. The nature of the charge distribution remains the same although the total amount of charge decreases for $\varepsilon_1 = 1$. The computation time on the IBM 360/75 system is about 20 seconds for the entire set of calculations required to generate the data for the curve in Fig. 6.2.

6.3. DIFFRACTION GRATING

6.3.1. Description of the Problem

In this section we illustrate the application of the modified residue calculus technique (MRCT) to an open region problem, that of diffraction by an echelette grating. This type of grating finds extensive application as a frequency-selecting quasi-optical device. In addition, the numerical aspects of the problem of diffraction by such a grating structure are interesting in their own right. This configuration has been analyzed by a number of workers by using the conventional integral equation method or its variants. The method of approach to be presented here will deviate from the conventional approaches and will follow a path somewhat similar to the one in the last section. The discussion in this section is based upon the work of Itoh and Mittra (1969).

Assume that the grating is made of a perfect electric conductor and that it is uniform and infinite in extent in the direction perpendicular to the plane of paper (see Fig. 6.3). Grooves and edges are cut at 90° and lie in planes so that the staggered angle is ψ. We will consider the case of a linearly polarized plane wave incident on the grating with its electric vector parallel to the grooves (TM to y). The object is to compute the complex amplitudes of the scattered waves of various orders reflected by the grating.

The formulation to be presented here will deviate from conventional methods even in the first stages. As illustrated in the previous section, the key step in the MRCT method is to identify the given geometry as a perturbed version of an associated canonical problem that admits an exact solution. The solution to the original problem is then reduced to that of constructing a perturbational factor that modifies the solution to the canonical problem.

In the case of the echelette grating, we observe by reference to Fig. 6.3 that the grating structure in Fig. 6.3(a) is derivable by the process of letting $d = 0$ in the geometry of Fig. 6.3(b). The latter is comprised of an infinite set of staggered parallel plates with perfectly conducting shorting walls which are recessed by the distance d into each opening. It is assumed that the plates are infinitely thin and are perfectly conducting, and that the medium is otherwise homogeneous throughout. Notice that by taking the limit $d = 0$, the physical constraint on the behavior of the electromagnetic fields near the edge (the so-called

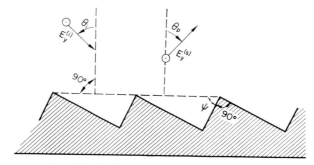

Fig. 6.3. (a) Geometry of the echelette grating.

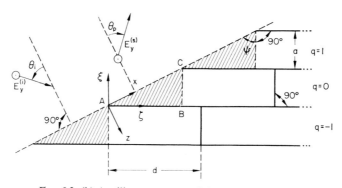

Fig. 6.3. (b) Auxiliary geometry of the echelette grating.

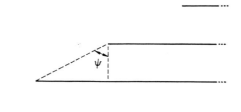

Fig. 6.3. (c) Geometry of the staggered parallel plates.

edge condition, referred to earlier) changes corresponding to the change of edge shape from the original one (edge of thin plate) to the rectangular edge. It will be found that the method of analysis to be followed here will automatically accommodate this change.

If there are no shorting walls in the waveguides, the problem turns out to be that of diffraction by a set of staggered parallel plates. This is the canonical problem for the present geometry (see Fig. 6.3(c)).

6.3.2. Formulation in the Spectral Domain

For convenience of discussion, we will use two systems of rectangular coordinates, viz, (x, y, z) and (ξ, η, ζ). Let the η-axis be chosen to coincide with the y-axis, which is perpendicular to the plane of the paper (see Fig. 6.3(b)). Since the incident electric field has been assumed to have a y-component only, and since the grating structure is uniform in the y-direction, it is sufficient to work with the scalar quantity E_y which satisfies the two-dimensional Helmholtz equation

$$\nabla_t^2 E_y + k_0^2 E_y = 0 \tag{6.39}$$

where k_0 is the free-space wave number, and ∇_t^2 is the Laplacian operator in transverse coordinates.

Let us consider the field in the free space region ($z \leq 0$). Since the structure of the grating is periodic in the x-direction with the period $a \sec \psi$ ($0 < \psi < \pi/2$), the Floquet space harmonic representation is applicable to the total field E_y. Thus, it admits the representation

$$E_y(x, z) = A \exp\left[-\mathrm{j}\,\frac{\phi}{a \sec \psi}\,x - \mathrm{j}\alpha_0 z\right] + \sum_{p=-\infty}^{\infty} A_p \exp\left[-\mathrm{j}\,\frac{\phi + 2p\pi}{a \sec \psi}\,x + \mathrm{j}\alpha_p z\right], \tag{6.40}$$

where A and A_p are the amplitudes of the incident wave and the pth space harmonic, respectively, and

$$\phi = ak_0 \sec \psi \sin \theta_i$$

$$\alpha_p = \sqrt{\left\{k_0^2 - \left(\frac{\phi + 2p\pi}{a \sec \psi}\right)^2\right\}} = -\mathrm{j}\sqrt{\left\{\left(\frac{\phi + 2p\pi}{a \sec \psi}\right)^2 - k_0^2\right\}}. \tag{6.41}$$

The incident angle θ_i is measured in the counterclockwise sense, while the scattered angle θ_p of the pth space harmonic is in the clockwise direction, given by

$$\left\{ \begin{aligned} \sin \theta_p &= \sin \theta_i + \frac{2p\pi}{ak_0 \sec \psi} \\[2mm] \cos \theta_p &= \frac{\alpha_p}{k_0} \end{aligned} \right. \qquad p = 0, \pm 1, \pm 2, \ldots \tag{6.42}$$

Equation (6.42) is known as a grating equation. One of the approaches that has been utilized in connection with this problem is as follows. As a first step, one equates (6.40) to zero on the grating surface (see Fig. 6.3(a)). The formulation results in an infinite order matrix equation, which is solved after truncating the summation on A_p at some large number P and evaluating E_y at $2P + 1$ (x, z) points on the grating surface. This method is numerically inefficient since the coefficients A_p decrease very slowly. In addition, since (6.40) is not valid in the shaded triangular regions in Fig. 6.3(b), this formulation leads to unsatisfactory results due to numerical divergence as P is increased. Although this difficulty can be circumvented by a method developed by Yasuura (1969), the numerical efficiency of the above method leaves much to be desired.

We will now detail the derivation of the equations in the spectral domain that will be found suitable for attack by the MRCT method. To this end, consider the field inside the parallel plate waveguides, i.e. for $qa \leq \xi \leq (q + 1)a$, $\zeta \leq (q + 1)a \tan \psi$; $q = 0, \pm 1, \pm 2, \ldots$ Since the structure is uniform in the y direction, only TE_{n0} modes are allowed. Hence, for the qth guide, we have

$$E_y (\xi, \zeta) = \sum_{n=1}^{\infty} \sin \left(\frac{n\pi}{a} (\xi - qa) \right) [B_n^q \exp \{-j\beta_n (\zeta - qa \tan \psi)\}$$

$$+ C_n^q \exp \{j\beta_n (\zeta - qa \tan \psi)\}], \qquad qa \leq \xi \leq (q + 1) a \qquad (6.43)$$

$$(q + 1) a \tan \psi \leq \zeta \leq (q + 1) a \tan \psi + d$$

where β_n is the wave number of the TE_{n0} mode, given by

$$\beta_n = \sqrt{\left\{ k_0^2 - \left(\frac{n\pi}{a} \right)^2 \right\}} = -j \sqrt{\left\{ \left(\frac{n\pi}{a} \right)^2 - k_0^2 \right\}}, \quad n = 1, 2, \ldots. \qquad (6.44)$$

In view of the periodicity, the amplitude of the TE_{n0} mode in the qth guide, viz. B_n^q and C_n^q, are related to those in the zeroth guide via the equations

$$B_n^q = B_n^0 e^{-jq\phi}, \quad C_n^q = C_n^0 e^{-jq\phi} \qquad (6.45)$$

where ϕ is given by (6.41). Also, B_n^0 and C_n^0, the amplitude of the TE_{n0} mode in the zeroth guide, are related to each other via the boundary condition on the shorting plate at $\zeta = a \tan \psi + d$, i.e.

$$B_n^0 \exp [-j\beta_n (a \tan \psi + d)] + C_n^0 \exp [j\beta_n (a \tan \psi + d)] = 0. \qquad (6.46)$$

Our primary interest is to calculate A_p, the complex amplitudes of the pth scattered wave. As a first step toward this, we will derive a set of equations for these coefficients.

It is pertinent to point out here that the interface matching condition cannot be applied directly to (6.40) and (6.43) because the field expressions given in these equations are not valid in the shaded triangular regions in Fig. 6.3(b). However, as shown below, we can get around this by making use of an artifice that is based on the application of the two-dimensional Green's theorem.

Consider the integral around the boundary of one of the shaded triangular regions,

$$\oint \left(F \frac{\partial E_y}{\partial n} - E_y \frac{\partial F}{\partial n} \right) ds = 0, \qquad (6.47)$$

where n is the outward normal direction and F is an auxiliary function, obeying the two-dimensional homogeneous wave equation.

It may be noted that the periodic nature of the problem allows us to concentrate on a single cell region only, say the zeroth cell. The auxiliary function F can be rather arbitrary. However, the final equations take a convenient form when the following two choices are made for F:

$$F = \sin\left(m\pi \frac{\xi}{a}\right) e^{-j\beta_m\zeta} \quad m = 1, 2, \ldots, \tag{6.48}$$

$$F = \sin\left(m\pi \frac{\xi}{a}\right) e^{+j\beta_m\zeta} \quad m = 1, 2, \ldots. \tag{6.49}$$

Employing (6.48) and (6.49) and performing the integrations in (6.47) results in the following infinite sets of equations:

$$\frac{-A}{\beta_{in} + \beta_m} + \sum_{p=-\infty}^{\infty} \frac{A_p}{\gamma_p - \beta_m} = \frac{a^2\beta_m C_m^0}{m\pi\left[1 - (-1)^m \exp\left\{-j\phi - ja\beta_m \tan\psi\right\}\right]} \quad m = 1, 2, \ldots, \tag{6.50}$$

$$\frac{-A}{\beta_{in} - \beta_m} + \sum_{p=-\infty}^{\infty} \frac{A_p}{\gamma_p + \beta_m} = \frac{-a^2\beta_m B_m^0}{m\pi\left[1 - (-1)^m \exp\left\{-j\phi + ja\beta_m \tan\psi\right\}\right]} \quad m = 1, 2, \ldots, \tag{6.51}$$

where

$$\beta_{in} = k_0 \cos(\theta_i - \psi), \tag{6.52}$$

$$\gamma_p = k_0 \cos(\theta_p + \psi). \tag{6.53}$$

The use of (6.46) reduces (6.50) and (6.51) to the following simultaneous equations:

$$\sum_{p=-\infty}^{\infty} \frac{A_p}{\gamma_p - \beta_m} + \lambda_m \sum_{p=-\infty}^{\infty} \frac{A_p}{\gamma_p + \beta_m} = \frac{A}{\beta_{in} + \beta_m} + \lambda_m \frac{A}{\beta_{in} - \beta_m}, \quad m = 1, 2, \ldots \tag{6.54}$$

where

$$\lambda_m = -\exp\left\{-j2\beta_m(a\tan\psi + d)\right\} \frac{1 - (-1)^m \exp\left\{-j\phi + ja\beta_m \tan\psi\right\}}{1 - (-1)^m \exp\left\{-j\phi - ja\beta_m \tan\psi\right\}}, \quad m = 1, 2, \ldots. \tag{6.55}$$

Recalling that our original problem (Fig. 6.3(a)) corresponds to the limiting case $d = 0$ we let $d = 0$ in (6.54) and (6.55). Also, at this point we set $A = 1$ without loss of generality.

6.3.3. MRCT Method of Solution

By reference to the preceding section, we note that the form of (6.54) suggests the use of the modified residue calculus technique. Instead of solving (6.54) after truncating the infinite matrix, the problem in the MRCT method is transformed to that of constructing an auxiliary function $f(\omega)$. The numerical efficiency in this approach results from the fact that $f(\omega)$

is expressible as a product of $g(\omega)$, the solution to the canonical problem (for $\lambda_m \equiv 0$), times a perturbational factor. Since $g(\omega)$ can be constructed in a closed form, the bulk of the numerical work in constructing $f(\omega)$ is bypassed in the MRCT method.

Let us now consider the construction of $f(\omega)$. Let $f(\omega)$ be a meromorphic function with the following properties:

(1) $f(\omega)$ has simple poles as $\omega = \gamma_p$, $p = 0, \pm 1, \pm 2, \ldots$, and at $\omega = -\beta_{in}$.

(2) $f(\beta_m) + \lambda_m f(-\beta_m) = 0$, $m = 1, 2, \ldots$

(3) $f(\omega) \to 0$ as $|\omega| \to \infty$ and furthermore, $f(\omega) \sim \omega^{-\nu}$, $1 < \nu < 2$ as $|\omega| \to \infty$ in the certain range of arg ω which will be detailed later.

(4) The residue of $f(\omega)$ at $\omega = -\beta_{in}$ is 1.

Next, following a procedure similar to the one given in the preceding section, we consider the contour integrals

$$\frac{1}{2\pi j} \oint \left\{ \frac{f(\omega)}{\omega - \beta_m} + \lambda_m \frac{f(\omega)}{\omega + \beta_m} \right\} d\omega$$

$$\frac{1}{2\pi j} \oint \frac{f(\omega)\, d\omega}{\omega + \beta_m}, \quad \frac{1}{2\pi j} \oint \frac{f(\omega)\, d\omega}{\omega - \beta_m}. \qquad m = 1, 2, \ldots$$

We may readily show that

$$R_f(\gamma_p) = A_p, \quad p = 0, \pm 1, \pm 2, \ldots, \qquad (6.56)$$

where $R_f(x)$ is the residue of $f(\omega)$ at $\omega = x$, and

$$f(-\beta_m) = \frac{a^2 \beta_m B_m^0}{m\pi \left[1 - (-1)^m \exp\{-j\phi + ja\beta_m \tan \psi\}\right]} \quad m = 1, 2, \ldots \qquad (6.57)$$

$$f(\beta_m) = \frac{-a^2 \beta_m C_m^0}{m\pi \left[1 - (-1)^m \exp\{-j\phi - ja\beta_m \tan \psi\}\right]} \quad m = 1, 2, \ldots. \qquad (6.58)$$

Therefore, once $f(\omega)$ is constructed, the problem is considered to be solved.

As a first step toward constructing $f(\omega)$, we define another meromorphic function $g(\omega)$

$$g(\omega) = e^{R\omega} \frac{\pi(\omega, \beta_n)}{(\omega + \beta_{in})(\omega - \gamma_0)\, \pi(\omega, \gamma_n)\, \pi(\omega, \gamma_{-n})} \qquad (6.59)$$

where

$$\pi(\omega, \beta_n) = \prod_{n=1}^{\infty} \left(1 - \frac{\omega}{\beta_n}\right) \exp(ja\omega/n\pi), \qquad (6.60)$$

$$\pi(\omega, \gamma_n) = \prod_{n=1}^{\infty} \left(1 - \frac{\omega}{\gamma_n}\right) \exp(ja\omega\, e^{j\psi} \sec \psi/2n\pi), \qquad (6.61)$$

$$\pi(\omega, \gamma_{-n}) = \prod_{n=1}^{\infty} \left(1 - \frac{\omega}{\gamma_{-n}}\right) \exp(ja\omega\, e^{-j\psi} \sec \psi/2n\pi) \qquad (6.62)$$

and

$$R = -j \frac{a}{\pi} \{\ln(2 \cos \psi) + \psi \tan \psi\}. \qquad (6.63)$$

Except for a normalization factor, $g(\omega)$ can be identified as the function corresponding to the case $\lambda_m \equiv 0$, i.e. the canonical problem (Fig. 6.3(c)). Thus, the only remaining unknowns in constructing $f(\omega)$ are the location of zeros. Therefore, we may write $f(\omega)$ as

$$f(\omega) = K\, e^{R\omega}\, \frac{\pi\,(\omega, \beta_n')}{(\omega + \beta_{in})\,(\omega - \gamma_0)\,\pi\,(\omega, \gamma_n)\,\pi\,(\omega, \gamma_{-n})} \tag{6.64}$$

where

$$\pi\,(\omega, \beta_n') = \prod_{n=1}^{\infty}\left(1 - \frac{\omega}{\beta_n'}\right) \exp\,(ja\omega/n\pi) \tag{6.65}$$

and hence, β_n' is identifiable as the nth zero of $f(\omega)$. The unknown factor K will be determined later in accordance with property (4), viz. $R_f(-\beta_{in}) = 1$. Comparison of $f(\omega)$ with $g(\omega)$ shows that except for a constant factor, $f(\omega)$ is obtained from $g(\omega)$ via a shift of the infinite set of zeros $\{\beta_n\}$ to $\{\beta_n'\}$. Recall that these two sets of zeros coincide in the limit $\lambda_m \equiv 0$. We will now demonstrate that, when the λ_m's are not zero, the difference $\Delta_n = \beta_n' - \beta_n$ between the zeros tends toward a constant, say δ, as $n \to \infty$. Furthermore, what turns out to be an important asset in numerical processing, the limit δ is determinable a priori from the knowledge of the edge condition. Letting $\beta_n' = \beta_n + \delta$ for n large, we arrive at the asymptotic behavior of $f(\omega)$:

$$f(\omega) \sim \omega^{-3/2 + a\delta/j\pi}, \quad 0 \le \arg\omega \le \pi$$

$$\sim (-\omega)^{-3/2 + a\delta/j\pi}\, \frac{\sin\,\{ja\,(\omega - \delta)\}}{\cos\,(a\omega\tan\psi + \phi) - \cos\,(ja\omega)}, \quad \pi \le \arg\omega \le 2\pi. \tag{6.66}$$

It follows from (6.66) that as $|\omega| \to \infty$, $f(\omega)$ decreases algebraically for $-\pi/2 + \psi \le \arg\omega \le 3\pi/2 - \psi$, and has an exponential decay outside of the above range of $\arg\omega$. This behavior is consistent with the required satisfaction of the edge condition. It may be shown that as a consequence of the proper edge condition for the rectangular edge,

$$A_p \sim |p|^{-5/3}, \quad |p| \to \infty,$$

$$\left.\begin{array}{l} B_m^0 \exp\,(-ja\beta_m\tan\psi) \sim m^{-5/3} \\ C_m^0 \exp\,(+ja\beta_m\tan\psi) \sim m^{-5/3} \end{array}\right\}, \quad m \to \infty \tag{6.67}$$

Hence, from (6.57) and (6.58), $f(\beta_m)$ and $f(-\beta_m)$ behave as

$$f(\beta_m) \sim m^{-5/3} \exp\,(-m\pi\tan\psi),$$

$$f(-\beta_m) \sim m^{-5/3} \tag{6.68}$$

where we used the fact that $\beta_m \sim -jm\pi/a$ for $m \to \infty$. Hence, comparing (6.68) with (6.66), we have

$$-\frac{3}{2} + \frac{a\delta}{j\pi} = -\frac{5}{3} \quad \text{or} \quad \delta = -j\,\frac{\pi}{6a}. \tag{6.69}$$

The value of δ can also be derived by directly applying (6.66) to the property (2), i.e. $f(\beta_m) + \lambda_m f(-\beta_m) = 0$, for large m.

It is evident at this point that the only nontrivial step in the construction of $f(\omega)$ for the general case $\lambda_m \neq 0$ is the solution of condition (2). This, in turn, requires the determination of Δ_n and it would appear at first sight that an infinite number of these have to be determined. However, it turns out that numerically it is only necessary to solve for the first few Δ_n's, say for $n = 1, \ldots, M$, and use δ, the asymptotic value of Δ_n, for all $n > M$.

With this background, it is found numerically convenient to work with a form for $f(\omega)$ that reads

$$f(\omega) = Kf_0(\omega) P(\omega), \tag{6.70}$$

where

$$f_0(\omega) = \frac{e^{R\omega}}{(\omega + \beta_{in})(\omega - \gamma_0)} \prod_{n=1}^{M} \frac{\left(1 - \dfrac{\omega}{\beta_n}\right)}{\left(1 - \dfrac{\omega}{\gamma_n}\right)\left(1 - \dfrac{\omega}{\gamma_{-n}}\right)} \prod_{n=M+1}^{\infty} \frac{\left(1 - \dfrac{\omega}{\beta_n + \delta}\right)}{\left(1 - \dfrac{\omega}{\gamma_n}\right)\left(1 - \dfrac{\omega}{\gamma_{-n}}\right)}; \tag{6.71}$$

$$P(\omega) = 1 + \sum_{p=1}^{M} \frac{F_p}{1 - \dfrac{\omega}{\beta_n}}. \tag{6.72}$$

Note that the asymptotic value of the shifted zeros $\beta_n + \delta$ is used in (6.71) for the factors $n \geq M + 1$. Equation (6.72) may be recognized as the Lagrangian interpolation formula. The unknown coefficients F_p are determined by requiring that $f(\omega)$ given by (6.71) satisfy condition (2), viz. $f(\beta_m) + \lambda_m f(-\beta_m) = 0$. The resulting $M \times M$ matrix equation is numerically solved using one of the available subroutines.

At this point, it may be worthwhile to reiterate that even though the MRCT requires the numerical solution of a set of linear equations, the size of the matrix that requires inversion for a given accuracy is much smaller than the one obtained in the process of attempting a direct inversion of (6.54) after truncation.

In addition, the method guarantees the correct asymptotic behavior of A_p for large $|p|$, since the edge condition is incorporated in constructing $f(\omega)$. This is a unique feature of the MRCT as contrasted with the conventional analysis.

6.3.4. Numerical Procedure

Most of the numerical procedures are very similar to those given in the Section 6.2. However, it is convenient to use a computer language which is capable of handling the complex arithmetic. In addition, many subroutines need to be modified to handle complex operations.

6.3.5. Numerical Results

Table 6.1 shows the obtained values of $\{F_p\}$ for a typical case $\psi = 30°$, $a = 0.75\lambda$ and $\theta_i = 45°$. The values of $f(\beta_m)$ and $f(-\beta_m)$ are shown in Table 6.2 for the same parameters. The magnitude of $f(\beta_m)$ decays exponentially, while that of $f(-\beta_m)$ decays only algebraically. Recall that this is in accordance with the prediction in Section 6.3.3.

TABLE 6.1. VALUES OF F_p ($p = 1, 2, \ldots, 10$) FOR $\psi = 30°$, $a = 0.75\lambda$, AND $\theta_i = 45°$

F_1	$0.528 - \text{j}\,1.06$
F_2	$0.430 + \text{j}\,0.267$
F_3	$0.113 + \text{j}\,0.0526$
F_4	$(0.658 + \text{j}\,0.243) \times 10^{-1}$
F_5	$(0.448 + \text{j}\,0.137) \times 10^{-1}$
F_6	$(0.332 + \text{j}\,0.0864) \times 10^{-1}$
F_7	$(0.256 + \text{j}\,0.0579) \times 10^{-1}$
F_8	$(0.202 + \text{j}\,0.0401) \times 10^{-1}$
F_9	$(0.159 + \text{j}\,0.0280) \times 10^{-1}$
F_{10}	$(0.119 + \text{j}\,0.0186 \times 10^{-1})$

TABLE 6.2. VALUES OF $f(\omega)$ AT $\omega = \pm\beta_m$, $m = 1, 2, \ldots, 10$
FOR $\psi = 30°$, $a = 0.75\lambda$, $\theta_i = 45°$

m	$f(\beta_m)$	$f(-\beta_m)$
1	$0.257 + \text{j}\,0.427$	$0.792 - \text{j}\,0.668$
2	$(0.171 - \text{j}\,0.108) \times 10^{-1}$	$0.223 + \text{j}\,0.00775$
3	$(-0.611 + \text{j}\,0.544) \times 10^{-3}$	$(0.911 - \text{j}\,0.00894) \times 10^{-1}$
4	$(0.451 - \text{j}\,0.426) \times 10^{-4}$	$(0.517 - \text{j}\,0.0270) \times 10^{-1}$
5	$(-0.420 + \text{j}\,0.424) \times 10^{-5}$	$(0.340 - \text{j}\,0.0287) \times 10^{-1}$
6	$(0.448 - \text{j}\,0.476) \times 10^{-6}$	$(0.245 - \text{j}\,0.0269) \times 10^{-1}$
7	$(-0.520 + \text{j}\,0.575) \times 10^{-7}$	$(0.187 - \text{j}\,0.0244) \times 10^{-1}$
8	$(0.640 - \text{j}\,0.733) \times 10^{-8}$	$(0.149 - \text{j}\,0.0220) \times 10^{-1}$
9	$(-0.825 + \text{j}\,0.971) \times 10^{-9}$	$(0.123 - \text{j}\,0.0199) \times 10^{-1}$
10	$(0.110 - \text{j}\,0.133) \times 10^{-9}$	$(0.104 - \text{j}\,0.0182) \times 10^{-1}$

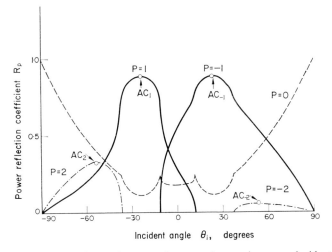

FIG. 6.4. Power reflection coefficients of propagating space harmonics versus incident angle $\psi = 30°$.
$a = 1.0825\lambda$ (AC_p signifies the autocollimation for the pth space harmonic).

Figure 6.4 shows the power reflection coefficient R_p of the pth space harmonic in the visible region, where

$$R_p = |A_p|^2 \frac{\cos \theta_p}{\cos \theta_i}. \tag{6.73}$$

The higher order reflection coefficients R_p ($p \neq 0$) reach their maximum when the autocollimation condition is attained, i.e. at $\theta_p = -\theta_i$. Also, observe the behavior of the reflection coefficients R_0, R_1, R_{-1} in the neighborhood of the angle where one of the space harmonics is diffracted at $\pm 90°$. The abrupt changes occurring at these angles are called Wood anomalies.

6.4. DIELECTRIC STEP IN A WAVEGUIDE

6.4.1. Introduction and Problem Description

Waveguides partially filled with dielectric slabs extending across one of the transverse guide dimensions (Fig. 6.5) find application as matching transformers, phase shifters, slow wave structures, and more recently as models for ferrite devices. The use of such waveguides as circuit components requires a knowledge of the effects of joining a homogeneously filled guide to one which is inhomogeneously filled. Previous techniques for solving such a dielectric step discontinuity problem have emphasized determining an equivalent transmission line circuit. The method given in this section not only provides the information necessary to calculate the components of an equivalent circuit, but also yields an accurate knowledge of the field configuration. It is based on an analysis developed by Royer and Mittra (1972).

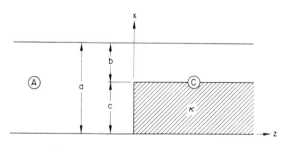

FIG. 6.5. The semi-infinite dielectric step.

Conventional methods of analysis for this problem include the variational or Rayleigh–Ritz procedure and the mode matching method. The accuracy of the variational method is dependent on the correct choice of the trial field and it presents little information about the field configuration, while the modal analysis method becomes unwieldy as the number of modes taken into account increases. In addition, the proper field behavior at the edge of the dielectric is difficult to reproduce in these methods.

A method capable of enforcing the satisfaction of the edge condition has been used by Lewin (1963) to solve the semi-infinite dielectric step. His method uses a quasi-static approximation together with the solution of a singular integral equation. In this method, which is accurate at the low frequency limit, the cases of high relative dielectric constants or high frequencies require the inclusion of a large number of terms that significantly increases the computational labor. The growing use of materials with high permittivities at microwave frequencies leads one to attempt a solution which is not dependent on these parameters.

In this section a two-dimensional parallel-plate waveguide is analyzed to reduce the complexity of the expression, although the results may be easily extended to the rectangular waveguide case. Consider the junction between an empty, semi-infinite parallel-plate waveguide and an identical guide partially filled to a height $x = c$, with a uniform, lossless dielectric slab of relative dielectric constant $\varkappa$ (Fig. 6.5). The parallel plates are taken to be perfectly conducting and infinite in extent in the y-direction which is perpendicular to the plane of the paper. We will consider the case of a TE_{p0} mode incident from the left with amplitude A. The electric vector is parallel to the edge of the dielectric step in the positive y-direction.

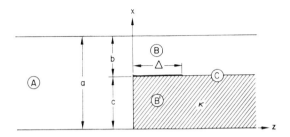

FIG. 6.6. Auxiliary geometry for the dielectric step.

At this point one could proceed with the conventional mode matching technique to formulate the problem. However, the resulting equations would then have to be solved by direct inversion after truncation, or by iteration. To obtain sets of equations suitable for solution by the MRCT, it is convenient first to consider a modified geometry, shown in Fig. 6.6, that is related to the original problem.

The auxiliary geometry shown in Fig. 6.6 is obtained by placing an infinitely thin, perfectly conducting strip on top of the dielectric at $x = c$ in Fig. 6.5. The strip is infinite in extent in the y-direction and extends into the loaded guide a short distance, $z = \varDelta$. Note that as we let $\varDelta$ go to zero the geometry of Fig. 6.6 approaches that of Fig. 6.5. The auxiliary geometry was chosen for its convenience since the normal modes for the region B' ($0 < x < c$, $0 < z < \varDelta$) and B ($c < x < a$, $0 < z < \varDelta$) are known. This choice of an auxiliary geometry is not unique, however. The essential point is that a geometry be chosen such that independent, complete, orthogonal sets of functions are obtained for the region $0 < z < \varDelta$. The choice of an auxiliary geometry is a key step in the MRCT as we have seen in Section 6.3. Having made this choice, we go on to formulate the dielectric step problem via the use of the auxiliary geometry of Fig. 6.6.

6.4.2. Formulation of the Problem

Since the incident electric field has only a y-component and the auxiliary geometry is uniform in the y-direction, Maxwell's equations reduce to a simple form involving the scalar quantity E_y:

$$\left\{ \frac{\partial^2}{\partial x^2} + \frac{\partial^2}{\partial z^2} + k_0^2 \varkappa(x) \right\} E_y = 0 \tag{6.74}$$

where

$$\varkappa(x) = \begin{cases} \varkappa & 0 < x < c, z > 0 \\ 1 & \text{elsewhere} \end{cases} \tag{6.75}$$

and k_0 is the free-space wave number.

The normal modes in regions A, B, and B' are obtained easily. The modes in region C are obtained from the field continuity conditions at $x = c$ together with the boundary conditions at $x = 0$ and $x = a$ (see Collin, 1960 or Harrington, 1961).

The total transverse electric fields in each region are:

Region A

$$E_y = A \sin\left(\frac{p\pi x}{a}\right) e^{-\alpha_p z} + \sum_{n=1}^{\infty} A_n \sin\left(\frac{n\pi x}{a}\right) e^{+\alpha_n z}. \tag{6.76}$$

Region B

$$E_y = \sum_{n=1}^{\infty} \sin\left[\frac{n\pi (x - c)}{b}\right] \{B_n e^{-\beta_n z} + E_n e^{+\beta_n z (z - \varDelta)}\}. \tag{6.77}$$

Region B'

$$E_y = \sum_{n=1}^{\infty} \sin\left(\frac{n\pi x}{c}\right) \{\mathbf{B}_n e^{-\zeta_n z} + \mathbf{E}_n e^{+\zeta_n (z - \varDelta)}\}. \tag{6.78}$$

Region C

$$E_y = \sum_{n=1}^{\infty} C_n \psi_n(x) e^{-\gamma_n (z - \varDelta)} \tag{6.79}$$

where

$$\psi_n(x) = \begin{cases} \sin(h_n x) & 0 < x < c, \\ \dfrac{\sin(h_n c)}{\sin(l_n b)} \sin[l_n (a - x)] & c < x < a \end{cases} \tag{6.80}$$

and

$$\alpha_n = \sqrt{\left\{\left(\frac{n\pi}{a}\right)^2 - k_0^2\right\}}, \tag{6.81}$$

$$\beta_n = \sqrt{\left\{\left(\frac{n\pi}{b}\right)^2 - k_0^2\right\}}, \tag{6.82}$$

$$\zeta_n = \sqrt{\left\{\left(\frac{n\pi}{c}\right)^2 - \varkappa k_0^2\right\}}, \tag{6.83}$$

$$\gamma_n^2 = \begin{cases} h_n^2 - \varkappa k_0^2 & 0 < x < c, \\ l_n^2 - k_0^2 & c < x < a, \end{cases} \tag{6.84}$$

with the square roots interpreted such that the resultant propagation constants are positive real for cut-off modes or positive imaginary for propagating modes. The transcendental equation for γ_n will be given later.

To satisfy the continuity condition, the total tangential components of the electric and magnetic fields are equated at the plane $z = 0$ over the range $0 < x < a$. Again, instead of working in the x domain, we Fourier analyze the resulting equations using the orthogonal properties of the normal modes in the regions B' and B. Multiplying appropriate equations by $\sin(m\pi x/c)$ and $\sin(m\pi(x-c)/b]$, and integrating with respect to x, we obtain:

$$\frac{A}{\alpha_p^2 - \zeta_m^2 - (\varkappa - 1)k_0^2} + \sum_{n=1}^{\infty} \frac{A_n}{\alpha_n^2 - \zeta_m^2 - (\varkappa - 1)k_0^2} = \frac{(-1)^m c^2}{2m\pi}[B_m + E_m e^{-\zeta_m\Delta}],$$
(6.85a)

$$\frac{-\alpha_p A}{\alpha_p^2 - \zeta_m^2 - (\varkappa - 1)k_0^2} + \sum_{n=1}^{\infty} \frac{\alpha_n A_n}{\alpha_n^2 - \zeta_m^2 - (\varkappa - 1)k_0^2} = \frac{\zeta_m(-1)^m c^2}{2m\pi}[-B_m + E_m e^{-\zeta_m\Delta}],$$
(6.85b)

$$\frac{A}{\alpha_p^2 - \beta_m^2} + \sum_{n=1}^{\infty} \frac{A_n}{\alpha_n^2 - \beta_m^2} = \frac{-b^2}{2m\pi}[B_m + E_m e^{-\beta_m\Delta}],$$
(6.86a)

$$\frac{-\alpha_p A}{\alpha_p^2 - \beta_m^2} + \sum_{n=1}^{\infty} \frac{\alpha_n A_n}{\alpha_n^2 - \beta_m^2} = \frac{-\beta_m b^2}{2m\pi}[-B_m + E_m e^{-\beta_m\Delta}],$$
(6.86b)

where

$$A = A \sin\left(\frac{p\pi c}{a}\right),$$
(6.87)

$$A_n = A_n \sin\left(\frac{n\pi c}{a}\right).$$
(6.88)

Using the same procedure at the junction $z = \Delta$ yields the expressions:

$$\sum_{n=1}^{\infty} \frac{C_n}{\gamma_n^2 - \zeta_m^2} = \frac{(-1)^m c^2}{2m\pi}[B_m e^{-\zeta_m\Delta} + E_m],$$
(6.89a)

$$\sum_{n=1}^{\infty} \frac{\gamma_n C_n}{\gamma_n^2 - \zeta_m^2} = \frac{\zeta_m(-1)^m c^2}{2m\pi}[B_m e^{-\zeta_m\Delta} - E_m],$$
(6.89b)

$$\sum_{n=1}^{\infty} \frac{C_n}{\gamma_n^2 - \beta_m^2} = \frac{-b^2}{2m\pi}[B_m e^{-\beta_m\Delta} + E_m],$$
(6.90a)

$$\sum_{n=1}^{\infty} \frac{\gamma_n C_n}{\gamma_n^2 - \beta_m^2} = \frac{-\beta_m b^2}{2m\pi}[B_m e^{-\beta_m\Delta} - E_m],$$
(6.90b)

where
$$C_n = C_n \sin(h_n c).$$
(6.91)

In the expressions (6.85), (6.86), (6.89) and (6.90), m changes from one to infinity, i.e. $m = 1, 2, \ldots, \infty$.

In the limit, as $\varDelta$ approaches zero, the auxiliary geometry (Fig. 6.6) becomes that of the dielectric step (Fig. 6.5). At this stage, letting $\varDelta \to 0$ in the equations (6.85), (6.86), (6.89) and (6.90), then adding and subtracting the equations to eliminate the unwanted coefficients $(B_m, \mathbf{B}_m, E_m, \text{and } \mathbf{E}_m)$, we obtain the following equations for the unknowns $\{\mathbf{A}_n\}$ and $\{\mathbf{C}_n\}$:

$$\sum_{n=1}^{\infty} \left\{ \mathbf{A}_n \left(\frac{1}{\alpha_n - \beta'_m} + \frac{\lambda_m}{\alpha_n + \beta'_m} \right) + \xi_m \frac{\mathbf{C}_n}{\gamma_n + \zeta_m} \right\} = \mathbf{A} \left(\frac{1}{\alpha_p + \beta'_m} + \frac{\lambda_m}{\alpha_p - \beta'_m} \right), \qquad (6.92)$$

$$\sum_{n=1}^{\infty} \left\{ \mathbf{A}_n \left(\frac{1}{\alpha_n + \beta'_m} + \frac{\lambda_m}{\alpha_n - \beta'_m} \right) + \xi_m \frac{\mathbf{C}_n}{\gamma_n - \zeta_m} \right\} = \mathbf{A} \left(\frac{1}{\alpha_p - \beta'_m} + \frac{\lambda_m}{\alpha_p + \beta'_m} \right), \qquad (6.93)$$

$$\sum_{n=1}^{\infty} \left\{ \frac{A_n}{\alpha_n - \beta_m} + \frac{C_n}{\gamma_n + \beta_m} \right\} = \frac{A}{\alpha_p + \beta_m}, \qquad (6.94)$$

$$\sum_{n=1}^{\infty} \left\{ \frac{A_n}{\alpha_n + \beta_m} + \frac{C_n}{\gamma_n - \beta_m} \right\} = \frac{A}{\alpha_p - \beta_m}, \qquad (6.95)$$

where, to simplify the above expressions, the following definitions have been made:

$$\beta'_m = \sqrt{\{\zeta_m^2 + (\varkappa - 1) k_0^2\}} = \sqrt{\left\{ \left(\frac{m\pi}{c}\right)^2 - k_0^2 \right\}}, \qquad (6.96)$$

$$\lambda_m = \frac{\beta'_m - \zeta_m}{\beta'_m + \zeta_m}, \qquad (6.97)$$

$$\xi_m = \frac{2\beta'_m}{\beta'_m + \zeta_m}. \qquad (6.98)$$

The equations are valid for each $m = 1, 2, \ldots, \infty$.

The form of the above infinite sets of linear equations differs somewhat from the equivalent sets of equations which have previously been solved by the MRCT (the preceding two sections). However, by modifying certain steps in the usual procedure, we are able to apply the MRCT to the above equations and obtain a very accurate approximate solution for the unknowns $\{\mathbf{A}_n\}$ and $\{\mathbf{C}_n\}$ very efficiently in numerical calculations.

6.4.3. Method of Solution

In order to apply the extended version of the MRCT, we first consider the following contour integrals in the complex ω-plane:

$$\frac{1}{2\pi j} \oint \left[\frac{f(\omega)}{\omega - \beta'_m} + \lambda_m \frac{f(\omega)}{\omega + \beta'_m} + \xi_m \frac{f(\omega)}{\omega - \zeta_m} \right] d\omega, \quad m = 1, 2, \ldots, \infty, \qquad (6.99)$$

$$\frac{1}{2\pi j} \oint \left[\frac{f(\omega)}{\omega + \beta'_m} + \lambda_m \frac{f(\omega)}{\omega - \beta'_m} + \xi_m \frac{f(\omega)}{\omega + \zeta_m} \right] d\omega, \quad m = 1, 2, \ldots, \infty, \qquad (6.100)$$

$$\frac{1}{2\pi j} \oint \frac{f(\omega) \, d\omega}{\omega - \beta_m}, \qquad\qquad m = 1, 2, \ldots, \infty \qquad (6.101)$$

and

$$\frac{1}{2\pi j} \oint \frac{f(\omega)\, d\omega}{\omega + \beta_m}, \quad m = 1, 2, \ldots, \infty, \tag{6.102}$$

where $f(\omega)$ is the meromorphic function whose properties will be specified shortly, and where the contour is the usual circle of infinite radius enclosing all the poles and zeros of $f(\omega)$. The knowledge of $\{A_n\}$ and $\{C_n\}$ can be efficiently extracted if $f(\omega)$ satisfies the following properties:

(1) $f(\omega)$ has simple poles at $\omega = \alpha_n$ and $\omega = -\gamma_n$, $n = 1, 2, \ldots, \infty$; and at $\omega = -\alpha_p$.

(2) $f(\pm\beta_n) = 0$, $n = 1, 2, \ldots, \infty$.

(3)
$$f(\beta_n') + \lambda_n f(-\beta_n') + \xi_n \left[f(\zeta_n) - \frac{R_f(-\alpha_p)}{\alpha_p + \zeta_n} + \sum_{i=1}^{\infty} \frac{R_f(\alpha_i)}{\alpha_i - \zeta_n} \right],$$

$$- \sum_{i=1}^{\infty} R_f(-\gamma_i) \left(\frac{1}{\gamma_i + \beta_n'} + \frac{\lambda_n}{\gamma_i - \beta_n'} \right) = 0, \quad n = 1, 2, \ldots, \infty.$$

(4)
$$f(-\beta_n') + \lambda_n f(\beta_n') + \xi_n \left[f(-\zeta_n) - \frac{R_f(-\alpha_p)}{\alpha_p - \zeta_n} + \sum_{i=1}^{\infty} \frac{R_f(\alpha_i)}{\alpha_i + \zeta_n} \right.$$

$$- \sum_{i=1}^{\infty} R_f(-\gamma_i) \left(\frac{1}{\gamma_i - \beta_n'} + \frac{\lambda_n}{\gamma_i + \beta_n'} \right) = 0, \quad n = 1, 2, \ldots, \infty.$$

(5) $f(\omega) \sim \omega^{-\nu}$ as $|\omega| \to \infty$ where $\nu > 1$ is given by a physical constraint, the edge condition, specifically
$$\nu = 1 + \frac{2}{\pi} \cos^{-1} \left[\frac{\varkappa - 1}{2(\varkappa + 1)} \right].$$

(6) $R_f(-\alpha_p) = A$,

where again $R_f(x)$ is the residue of $f(\omega)$ at $\omega = x$. Properties (3) and (4) are the significant differences between the present problem and the usual application of the MRCT.

Again the values of the four contour integrals in (6.99) to (6.102) can be shown to be zero by the property (5). Applying the residue theorem to (6.99) to (6.102) with the properties (1) through (4), we obtain

$$\sum_{n=1}^{\infty} R_f(\alpha_n) \left[\frac{1}{\alpha_n - \beta_m'} + \frac{\lambda_m}{\alpha_n + \beta_m'} \right] - \xi_m R_f(-\gamma_n) \left[\frac{1}{\gamma_n + \zeta_m} \right]$$

$$- R_f(-\alpha_p) \left[\frac{1}{\alpha_p + \beta_m'} + \frac{\lambda_m}{\alpha_p - \beta_m'} \right] = 0, \tag{6.103}$$

$$\sum_{n=1}^{\infty} \left\{ R_f(\alpha_n) \left[\frac{1}{\alpha_n + \beta_m'} + \frac{\lambda_m}{\alpha_n - \beta_m'} \right] - \xi_m R_f(-\gamma_m) \left[\frac{1}{\gamma_n - \zeta_m} \right] \right\}$$

$$- R_f(-\alpha_p) \left[\frac{1}{\alpha_p - \beta_m'} + \frac{\lambda_m}{\alpha_p + \beta_m'} \right] = 0, \tag{6.104}$$

$$\sum_{n=1}^{\infty} \left\{ R_f(\alpha_n) \left[\frac{1}{\alpha_n - \beta_m} \right] - R_f(-\gamma_m) \left[\frac{1}{\gamma_n + \beta_m} \right] \right\} - R_f(-\alpha_p) \left[\frac{1}{\alpha_p + \beta_m} \right] = 0, \tag{6.105}$$

$$\sum_{n=1}^{\infty} \left\{ R_f(\alpha_n) \left[\frac{1}{\alpha_n + \beta_m} \right] - R_f(-\gamma_n) \left[\frac{1}{\gamma_n - \beta_m} \right] \right\} - R_f(-\alpha_p) \left[\frac{1}{\alpha_p - \beta_m} \right] = 0, \tag{6.106}$$

for $m = 1, 2, \ldots, \infty$. By comparing (6.103)–(6.106) with (6.92)–(6.95), it is apparent that the solution to the latter sets of equations is given by

$$\mathbf{A}_n = R_f(\alpha_n), \quad n = 1, 2, \ldots, \infty \tag{6.107}$$

and

$$\mathbf{C}_n = -R_f(-\gamma_n), \quad n = 1, 2, \ldots, \infty. \tag{6.108}$$

Thus, once $f(\omega)$ is constructed, the problem is considered solved.

We now consider the construction of $f(\omega)$ which is rather different from the many other applications of the MRCT. This is due to the fact that the properties (3) and (4) are somewhat involved. The infinite summations in the properties (3) and (4) preclude an asymptotic limiting process similar to the one employed in Section 6.3. Thus, we deal directly with the perturbation function as explained below.

From the properties (1) to (4), we may write the function $f(\omega)$ as

$$f(\omega) = K e^{R\omega} \frac{\pi(\omega, \beta_n) \, \pi(\omega, -\beta_n) \, \pi(\omega, \tau_n) \, \pi(\omega, -\eta_n)}{(\omega + \alpha_p) \, \pi(\omega, \alpha_n) \, \pi(\omega, -\gamma_n)} \tag{6.109}$$

where

$$\pi(\omega, \alpha_n) = \prod_{n=1}^{\infty} \left(1 - \frac{\omega}{\alpha_n}\right) \exp(a\omega/n\pi), \tag{6.110}$$

$$\pi(\omega, \pm\beta_n) = \prod_{n=1}^{\infty} \left(1 \mp \frac{\omega}{\beta_n}\right) \exp(\pm b\omega/n\pi), \tag{6.111}$$

$$\pi(\omega, -\gamma_n) = \prod_{n=1}^{\infty} \left(1 + \frac{\omega}{\gamma_n}\right) \exp(-a\omega/n\pi) \tag{6.112}$$

$$\pi(\omega, \tau_n) = \prod_{n=1}^{\infty} \left(1 - \frac{\omega}{\tau_n}\right) \exp(c\omega/n\pi) \tag{6.113}$$

and

$$\pi(\omega, -\eta_n) = \prod_{n=1}^{\infty} \left(1 + \frac{\omega}{\eta_n}\right) \exp(-c\omega/n\pi) \tag{6.114}$$

where $\{\tau_n\}$ and $\{-\eta_n\}$ are the unknown zeros representing perturbations from $\{\beta'_n\}$ and $\{-\beta'_n\}$. To determine the value of R that will assure the algebraic behavior of $f(\omega)$, we proceed as follows. If there were no shift of zeros for large n, i.e. if $\tau_n = \eta_n = \beta'_n$, then

$$f(\omega) \sim k\omega^{-2} e^{R\omega}.$$

An asymptotic shift in the zeros can only introduce an algebraic factor in the asymptotic behavior and hence R must be identically zero if $f(\omega)$ is to have algebraic behavior as $|\omega| \to \infty$.

Now let us write $f(\omega)$ as

$$f(\omega) = K f_0(\omega) \, P(\omega) \tag{6.115}$$

where

$$f_0(\omega) = \frac{\pi\,(\omega,\beta_n)\,\pi\,(\omega,-\beta_n)\,\pi\,(\omega,\beta_n')\,\pi\,(\omega,-\beta_n')}{(\omega+\alpha_p)\,\pi\,(\omega,\alpha_n)\,\pi\,(\omega,-\gamma_n)}, \tag{6.116}$$

$$P(\omega) = 1 + \sum_{n=1}^{\infty} S_n\left(\frac{\omega}{\beta_n'-\omega}\right) + \sum_{n=1}^{\infty} T_n\left(\frac{\omega}{\beta_n'+\omega}\right), \tag{6.117}$$

$$\pi\,(\omega,\pm\beta_n') = \prod_{n=1}^{\infty}\left(1\mp\frac{\omega}{\beta_n'}\right)\exp\left(\pm c\omega/n\pi\right). \tag{6.118}$$

The two summations in (6.117) can be thought of as the perturbational terms in $P(\omega)$.

The only remaining unknowns in $f(\omega)$ are two infinite sets of coefficients $\{S_n\}$ and $\{T_n\}$. We show in the following that we need to find only a finite number of these coefficients.

From the expression (6.115) we have

$$f(\beta_m') \sim S_m m^{-1}, \quad f(-\beta_m') \sim T_m m^{-1}, \quad m \to \infty. \tag{6.119}$$

In order to satisfy the property (5), S_m and T_m must behave as

$$S_m \sim m^{1-\nu}, \quad T_m \sim m^{1-\nu}, \quad m \to \infty. \tag{6.120}$$

If (6.120) is satisfied, then it can be shown that

$$f(\alpha_m) \sim m^{-\nu}, \quad f(-\gamma_m) \sim m^{-\nu}. \tag{6.121}$$

Using this known asymptotic behavior of the perturbation coefficients, it is possible to rewrite $P(\omega)$ as

$$P(\omega) = 1 + \sum_{n=1}^{N_a-1} S_n\left(\frac{\omega}{\beta_n'-\omega}\right) + \mathbf{S}\sum_{n=N_a}^{\infty}\frac{\omega n^{-\mu}}{\beta_n'-\omega} + \sum_{n=1}^{N_b-1} T_n\left(\frac{\omega}{\beta_n'+\omega}\right) + \mathbf{T}\sum_{n=N_b}^{\infty}\frac{\omega n^{-\mu}}{\beta_n'+\omega} \tag{6.122}$$

where $\mu = \nu - 1$ and $\mathbf{S}$ and $\mathbf{T}$ are unknown coefficients which account for all the zeros of order equal to or greater than N_a and N_b, respectively. It is now possible to form a set of simultaneous equations for the $(N_a + N_b)$ unknown perturbation coefficients. The equations take the form

$$f_0(\omega)\,P(\omega)|_{\omega=\omega_m} + \lambda_m f_0(\omega)\,P(\omega)|_{\omega=-\omega_m}$$

$$+\,\xi_m\left[f_0(\varrho_m)\,P(\varrho_m) - R_{f0}(-\alpha_p)\frac{P(-\alpha_p)}{\alpha_p+\varrho_m} + \sum_{i=1}^{\infty} R_{f0}(\alpha_i)\frac{P(\alpha_i)}{\alpha_i-\varrho_m}\right]$$

$$-\sum_{i=1}^{\infty} R_{f0}(-\gamma_i)\left[\frac{1}{\gamma_i+\omega_m} + \frac{\lambda_m}{\gamma_i-\omega_m}\right]P(-\gamma_i) = 0 \quad m = 1, 2, \ldots, N \tag{6.123}$$

where $R_{f0}(x)$ is the residue of $f_0(\omega)$ at $\omega = x$, and

$$\omega_n = \begin{cases} \beta'_n & n = 1, 2, \ldots, N_a, \\ -\beta'_{n-N_a} & n = (N_a + 1), \ldots, N, \end{cases}$$

$$\varrho_n = \begin{cases} \zeta_n, & n = 1, 2, \ldots, N_a, \\ -\zeta_{n-N_a}, & n = (N_a + 1), \ldots, N, \end{cases}$$

$$N = N_a + N_b.$$

As with the previous applications of the MRCT, the number of equations that need to be retained in (6.123) is quite small. (Usually $N = 10$ or even half as many equations are sufficient for good results.) Also, by using the method to be explained shortly, the infinite summations in (6.123) may be carried out very rapidly. Thus, although this method requires a certain amount of advance preparation, this is well compensated for by the increased numerical efficiency gained by the manipulations.

6.4.4. Numerical Considerations

The following important considerations arise in the numerical processing of the problem.

(i) SOLUTION OF THE TRANSCENDENTAL EQUATION

The propagation constant γ_n is obtained by solving the equation

$$\sqrt{(\gamma^2 + k_0^2)} \sin (c \sqrt{[\gamma^2 + \varkappa k_0^2]}) \cos (b \sqrt{[\gamma^2 + k_0^2]})$$
$$+ \sqrt{(\gamma^2 + \varkappa k_0^2)} \cos (c \sqrt{[\gamma^2 + \varkappa k_0^2]}) \sin (b \sqrt{[\gamma^2 + k_0^2]}) = 0. \tag{6.124}$$

for γ. This equation has only real roots for γ^2 and is solved using Newton's iterative procedure. Since we require an ordered set of solutions $\{\gamma_n^2\}$, it is essential to provide as an initial guess a sufficiently accurate approximation for the nth root so that the iteration process converges to the desired root and not to some other one.

One of the techniques for doing this is based on a two-mode approximation for the propagation constant which was obtained by Hord and Rosenbaum (1968) from an analysis related to the variational method. Another method derived by Lewin (1963) is the use of an asymptotic expression for the roots γ_n^2. Though derived for large n, Lewin claimed accurate results down to $n = 1$. This is found to be true for moderate values of the dielectric constant and fill ratio c/a. For a higher dielectric constant and/or fill ratios, the inaccuracy is sufficient to cause the iteration to converge to the wrong root.

A comparison of the above two methods reveals that Lewin's expression consistently give a more accurate approximation, though the inaccuracy of both methods is most pronounced for the lower order roots. For roots of order 20 or greater, Lewin's approximation usually agrees with the exact solution obtained by iteration to six or seven significant digits.

Lewin's expression gives very satisfactory results when used as an initial guess for the iteration procedure. Exceptions are for the cases with high dielectric constants or moderate dielectric constants ($6 \leq \varkappa \leq 10$) combined with high-fill ratio. In these cases, Lewin's method fails to provide sufficiently accurate starting values for the first few roots and cannot be used to start the iterative procedure. Therefore, it is necessary to increment γ^2 until the value of the left-hand side of (6.124) changes sign and then use this value as the initial guess. For the higher order roots, Lewin's approximation gives very good results for all values of the physical parameters. Using either of the above starting methods, the computation of 200 propagation constants to an accuracy exceeding seven significant digits requires less than three seconds on an IBM 360/75 digital computer.

(ii) SUMMATION OF THE INFINITE SERIES

(a) *Infinite series in* (6.122).

To obtain an accurate numerical approximation to the sum of

$$s_1 (\pm \omega, N) = \sum_{n=N}^{\infty} \frac{n^{-\mu}}{\beta_n' \pm \omega}, \tag{6.125}$$

it is convenient to employ the Euler–Maclaurin sum formula and convert the expression in (6.125) to the form

$$s_1 (\pm \omega, N) \approx \sum_{n=N}^{M-1} \frac{n^{-\mu}}{\beta_n' \pm \omega} + \frac{c}{\pi} \left\{ \int_M^{\infty} g(x)\, \mathrm{d}x + \frac{g(M)}{2} - \sum_{k=1}^{\infty} \frac{B_{2k}}{(2k)!} \frac{\mathrm{d}^{(2k-1)}}{\mathrm{d}x^{(2k-1)}} g(M) \right\} \tag{6.126}$$

where

$$g(x) = \frac{x^{-\mu}}{x \pm \alpha}, \tag{6.127}$$

$$\alpha = \frac{c\omega}{\pi}. \tag{6.128}$$

B_{2k} are the Bernoulli numbers, and the asymptotic value of β_n' was used for the Mth and succeeding terms in the series. It is necessary that the value of M be chosen such that $M > |\alpha|$ to assure the convergence of the integral. In addition, M should be large enough to assure $\beta_n' \approx n\pi/c$ for $n \geq M$. The integration was carried out by rewriting $g(x)$ in the form

$$g(x) = \frac{1}{x^{1+\mu} (1 \pm \alpha/x)} \tag{6.129}$$

and expanding the geometric series to obtain

$$\int_M^{\infty} g(x)\, \mathrm{d}x = \int_M^{\infty} \frac{1}{x^{1+\mu}} \sum_{n=0}^{\infty} \left(\pm \frac{\alpha}{x} \right)^n \mathrm{d}x. \tag{6.130}$$

The uniform convergence of the series appearing in the integrand is assured by choosing $M > |\alpha|$.

Termwise integration yields the following rapidly convergent infinite series for the value of the integral:

$$\int_M^\infty g(x)\,dx = M^{-\mu} \sum_{n=0}^\infty \frac{(\mp \alpha/M)^n}{n+\mu}. \tag{6.131}$$

By choosing $M \geq 2|\alpha|$, the initial terms of the series (6.131) and the series in (6.126) containing Bernoulli numbers decrease very rapidly. Sufficient accuracy may be obtained simply by truncating each series at an appropriate number of terms. Note that the derivatives of $g(x)$ evaluated at $x = M$ appearing with the Bernoulli numbers aid the convergence of this series. In practice, the series in (6.131) is truncated at twenty-five terms while only the first four terms of the series containing the Bernoulli numbers are summed. The effect of this truncation is an estimated error in the sum of the original series (6.126) of less than 10^{-8}. The required computation time on an IBM 360/75 is less than 0.01 seconds for $|\omega| \leq 100$.

(b) *Infinite series in* (6.123).

$$s_2 = \sum_{n=1}^\infty \frac{R_{f0}(\alpha_n)\, P(\alpha_n)}{\alpha_n - \varrho_m}, \tag{6.132}$$

$$s_3 = \sum_{n=1}^\infty \frac{R_{f0}(-\gamma_n)\, P(-\gamma_n)}{\gamma_n \pm \omega_m}. \tag{6.133}$$

These series can be summed quite efficiently if we use the asymptotic behavior of $R_{f0}(-\gamma_n)$.

6.4.5. Numerical Results

Since the extensive numerical results are available in the work by Royer and Mittra (1972) only a few of them will be included here for illustration. Table 6.3 shows the comparison of the result given by this method and those by Collin and Brown (1956). Also,

TABLE 6.3. COMPARISON OF PRESENT RESULTS TO THE WORK OF COLLIN AND BROWN
($\lambda_0 = 1.2369a$, $c/a = 0.2756$, $\varkappa = 2.47$)

	Reflection coefficient ($\times 10$)	
	Present study	Collin and Brown
$N = 4$	$-0.6938 + j\,0.7830$	
$N = 8$	$-0.6935 + j\,0.7843$	$(-0.80 \pm 0.17) + j\,(0.87 \pm 0.28)$
$N = 16$	$-0.6936 + j\,0.7841$	

N	Accuracy of present results		
	Energy parameter	Mean square errors	
	ε_p	ε_E	ε_H
4	0.131×10^{-2}	0.989×10^{-5}	0.199×10^{-4}
8	0.175×10^{-3}	0.252×10^{-6}	0.483×10^{-6}
16	0.228×10^{-4}	0.134×10^{-6}	0.247×10^{-6}

three kinds of error criteria are included. The mean square error in the tangential electric field is

$$
\varepsilon_E = \frac{\underset{\text{Aperture}}{\iint} |E_y^+ - E_y^-|^2 \, dA}{\underset{\text{Aperture}}{\iint} |E_y^{\text{inc}}|^2 \, dA}
\tag{6.134}
$$

where E_y^+ is the E_y field at $z = 0^+$ in the C region of the guide (Fig. 6.5), while E_y^- is the E_y field at $z = 0^-$ in the A region. The mean square error in the tangential H field ε_H is defined in a similar manner. The energy parameter is

$$
\varepsilon_p = 1 - \frac{P_r + P_t}{P_i}
\tag{6.135}
$$

where P_i, P_r, and P_t are the incident, reflected, and transmitted powers, respectively.

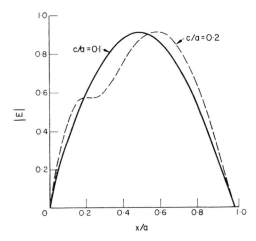

FIG. 6.7. Aperture field ($\lambda_0 = 1.63a$, $\varkappa = 9.91$).

Figure 6.7 shows the electric field at $z = 0$. In contrast to other numerical methods, the difference of the aperture fields for $z = 0^+$ and $z = 0^-$, calculated by the present method, is indistinguishable and hence only one of them is plotted.

6.5. THE GENERALIZED SCATTERING MATRIX METHOD FOR SOLVING DISCONTINUITY PROBLEMS

6.5.1. Introduction

In the preceding sections we have described a number of variants and extensions of the residue calculus technique for formulating boundary value problems. The class of problems to which the above methods apply is typically characterized by a single discontinuity, either in a uniform structure or at the junction of two dissimilar waveguides. A wider class of problems of considerable interest is that involving two or more such junctions that are cascaded to form a composite structure. In this section, we describe a procedure that is suitable for attacking problems in this category when the discontinuity problem associated with the individual junctions can be analyzed, either by using the methods descibed earlier in this chapter or by any of the other available techniques. To illustrate the method, we consider a specific problem, that of a thick-walled waveguide phased array. However, the method itself applies to a diverse range of problems involving both open- and closed-region structures.

6.5.2. Generalized Scattering Matrix Analysis of a Thick-walled Phase Array

Figure 6.8 shows the thick-walled phased array. It is assumed that the waveguides are excited by the TE_{po} mode with uniform amplitude and periodic phasing to scan the beam in the H-plane. The array is infinite in extent in the x-direction. Since the structure of the array and the excitation are both uniform in the y-direction, the problem is a two-dimensional one.

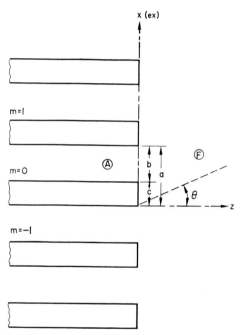

FIG. 6.8. Infinite array of thick parallel plates.

If the waveguide walls are infinitely thin, the problem can be solved exactly by the Wiener–Hopf technique or the residue calculus technique (see Berz, 1951). However, the corresponding problem with walls of nonzero thickness cannot be solved exactly. In the following, it will be shown that this practical problem can be solved efficiently and very accurately by the use of the generalized scattering matrix technique in conjunction with the residue calculus technique and the MRCT.

The concept of the generalized scattering matrix technique is very closely related to the scattering matrix of circuit theory or of microwave network theory. However, it differs from the conventional scattering matrix in that it is extended to consider evanescent as well as propagating modes.

The first step in the method is to identify the individual junctions in the given problem and derive a matrix description of these junctions. The present problem may be viewed as a composite of two junctions—the step discontinuity in a waveguide, Fig. 6.9(a), and the transition of semi-infinite parallel plate waveguides into free space, Fig. 6.9(b). This can be seen

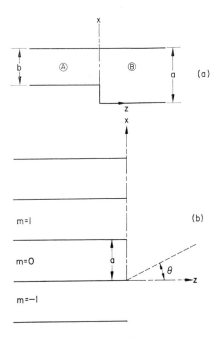

FIG. 6.9. (a) Metal step discontinuity in the waveguide.
(b) Infinite array of thin parallel plates.

in Fig. 6.10, where the two junctions are labeled in the composite structure which reduces to the original one, shown in Fig. 6.8 as $\delta \to 0$.

Following the identification of the junctions, the development of the generalized scattering matrix technique proceeds as follows. We begin with the characterization of the metal step in the parallel plate waveguide, Fig. 6.8(a). Consider the TE_{p0} excitation with unit amplitude from the region A. If the amplitude of the qth mode of the reflected wave into A is A_q, the (q, p) element of the scattering matrix S^{AA} (q, p) is A_q. Similarly, if the amplitude of the mth mode of the transmitted wave into B is B_m, the (m, p) element S^{BA} (m, p) is B_m. The other scattering matrices S^{BB} and S^{AB} may be similarly defined. In conventional scattering matrix formulations, the modes are normalized so that a propagation mode carries unit power. Since the generalized scattering matrix includes evanescent modes, such a normalization is inappropriate. Instead, the scattering coefficients are defined as ratios of the complex amplitude of a scattered mode to that of the incident pth mode whose amplitude is normalized to unity. One consequence is that the scattering matrices are not symmetric, though this does not introduce any difficulties.

6.5.3. Method of Solution for the Thick-walled Phased Array

Let us now consider the auxiliary geometry appropriate for the thick-walled phased array shown in Fig. 6.10. Recall that, if δ is let equal to zero, the auxiliary geometry reduces to the original thick-walled phased array in Fig. 6.8. The junction 1 at $z = -\delta$ in each wave-guide is precisely the step discontinuity described above. Although this problem cannot be solved exactly, it has been found by VanBlaricum and Mittra (1969) that the MRCT de-

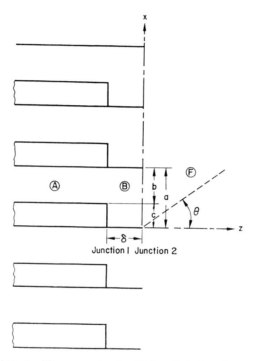

FIG. 6.10. Auxiliary geometry for thick-walled phased array.

scribed in the previous sections can be used to give a very accurate result for the amplitude of the scattered waves, A_q and B_m, and, hence, the generalized scattering matrices S_1^{AA}, S_1^{BA}, etc. The suffix 1 is used to show that the matrices are related to the junction 1. The junction 2 at $z = 0$ is precisely that of the thin-walled array which can be solved exactly (Berz, 1951). Let the scattering for the junction 2 have the subscript 2, i.e. S_2^{BB}, S_2^{BF}, S_2^{FB}, S_2^{FF}.

We will not go into the details of deriving the specific forms for the generalized scattering matrices describing the two junctions, since the result for the step discontinuity problem as well as the thin-walled waveguide radiation problem are found in the literature. Assuming that these scattering matrices are available, we will next proceed with the calculation of the scattering matrices for the composite structure via a multiple-reflection approach outlined below.

Let a general TE wave be incident upon the junction 1 from region A. This wave is completely determined by the coefficients of the modes, and hence can be represented by a mode column vector $\boldsymbol{\phi}^{(i)}$ such that $\phi_n^{(i)}$ is the coefficient of the nth mode in the incident field. At junction 1, fields are reflected back into region A and transmitted into region B. The mode vector for the field reflected back into A is $S_1^{AA}\phi^{(i)}$, while for the field transmitted into B, the vector is $S_1^{BA}\phi^{(i)}$. The transmitted field into B is scattered at junction 2. The part of the field transmitted into region F is $S_2^{FB}S_1^{BA}\phi^{(i)}$ and the part reflected back into region B is $S_2^{BB}S_1^{BA}\phi^{(i)}$. The reflected field progresses toward junction 1 and is scattered there again. This process of multiple scattering continues for an infinite number of times, as depicted symbolically in Fig. 6.11. Notice that the propagation matrices between junctions 1 and 2 have not been included in the above representation, since we have tacitly assumed δ is infinitesimally small.

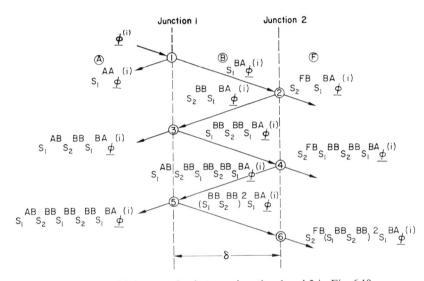

FIG. 6.11. Multiple scattering between junction 1 and 2 in Fig. 6.10.

Summing up all the contributions in region A due to the multiple scattering process gives the reflected field, represented by the column vector $\phi^{(r)}$:

$$\phi^{(r)} = S_1^{AA}\phi^{(i)} + S_1^{AB}S_2^{BB}S_1^{BA}\phi^{(i)} + S_1^{AB}S_2^{BB}S_1^{BB}S_2^{BB}S_1^{BA}\phi^{(i)} + \cdots$$

$$= S_1^{AA}\phi^{(i)} + \sum_{n=0}^{\infty} S_1^{AB}S_2^{BB}(S_1^{BB}S_2^{BB})^n S_1^{BA}\phi^{(i)}. \qquad (6.136)$$

The summation in the expression on the right-hand side of (6.136) is recognized as a Neuman series. It has been shown by Pace and Mittra (1964) that the series is convergent. Thus, we may write the above expression as

$$\phi^{(r)} = S_1^{AA}\phi^{(i)} + S_1^{AB}S_2^{BB}[I - S_1^{BB}S_2^{BB}]^{-1}S_1^{BA}\phi^{(i)} \qquad (6.137)$$

where I is an identity matrix. In an analogous manner, we may obtain an expression for the transmitted field into region F (radiated field).

$$\phi^{(t)} = S_2^{FB}[I - S_1^{BB}S_2^{BB}]^{-1}S_1^{BA}\phi^{(i)}. \qquad (6.138)$$

From (6.137) and (6.138) the scattering matrices for the composite structure are

$$S^{AA} = S_1^{AA} + S_1^{AB}S_2^{BB}[I - S_1^{BB}S_2^{BB}]^{-1}S_1^{BA}, \tag{6.139}$$

$$S^{FA} = S_2^{FB}[I - S_1^{BB}S_2^{BB}]^{-1}S_1^{BA}. \tag{6.140}$$

Similarly, we have two other scattering matrices:

$$S^{AF} = S_1^{AB}[I - S_2^{BB}S_1^{BB}]^{-1}S_2^{BF}, \tag{6.141}$$

$$S^{FF} = S_2^{FF} + S_2^{FB}S_1^{BB}[I - S_2^{BB}S_1^{BB}]^{-1}S_2^{BF}. \tag{6.142}$$

It must be noted that each scattering matrix with subscript 2 is an implicit function of the scan angle. As a result, the composite scattering matrices also are dependent upon the angle.

One particular advantage of formulating the thick-walled array in terms of the scattering matrix equations (6.139) to (6.142) is that when the wall thickness c reduces to zero, the resultant scattering matrices reduce to exactly the thin-walled scattering matrices. This result occurs because when $c = 0$, the scattering matrix description of junction 1 yields

$$S_1^{AA} = S_1^{BB} = 0, \tag{6.143}$$

$$S_1^{BA} = S_1^{AB} = I. \tag{6.144}$$

Substitution of these values into (6.139) to (6.142) reduces the equation to simply the corresponding thin-walled scattering matrices.

6.5.4. Considerations for the Numerical Calculation

The composite scattering matrices (6.139) to (6.142) are formally precise provided the various scattering matrices can be found exactly. For practical computations, it is important to be able to truncate the scattering matrices at the smallest size which yields suitably accurate results, because the matrix inversion must be performed numerically. Since the scattering matrix elements are generated by numerical computation, keeping the truncated matrices as small as possible also reduces computation time of these matrices. Just what constitutes "suitably accurate" has to be decided on the basis of convergence of the individual problem. Fortunately, however, in many practical problems the series in (6.139) to (6.142) converge quite rapidly, permitting accurate evaluation with moderate-size matrices. Numerical results of this section give an indication of the variation of the dominant mode reflection coefficient for matrix sizes of 1×1, 3×3, and 5×5.

The important steps in actual computations are as follows:
   (i) Evaluation of the matrix elements of the scattering matrices related to the junction 1. This can be done by the application of the MRCT to the step discontinuity problems in the parallel-plate waveguide.
   (ii) Evaluation of the matrix elements related to the junction 2. Either the Wiener–Hopf technique or the conventional residue calculus technique gives analytically exact results for this junction problem.
   (iii) Formation of the necessary matrices S_1^{AA}, S_1^{AB}, S_2^{BB}, etc.

(iv) Inversion of the appropriate matrices by the use of one of the matrix inversion sub-routines.

(v) Formation of the composite scattering matrices.

(vi) Obtaining the desired quantity, e.g. the reflection or the transmission coefficient by multiplying one of the resulting matrices by the incident field vector and evaluating the desired element.

6.5.5. Numerical Results

Table 6.4 shows a typical example of the results for the reflection coefficient in the wave-guide for TE_{10} excitation. Physical parameters are chosen to coincide with one of the case given by Galindo and Wu (1966) and to permit comparison of results. Dimensions were chosen to allow only one propagating mode in each waveguide.

Although not tabulated here, several other parameters were chosen for comparison. In each case, the scattering matrix method was found to give numerical results for magnitude and phase of the reflection coefficient versus scan angle which were indistinguishable from the results given graphically by Galindo and Wu. The latter results were obtained via the solution of the integral equation by the Galerkin's method using a 30×30 matrix, followed by a variational correction of the results. It should also be noted that the scattering matrix method requires the solution of two auxiliary problems by elementary means followed by a relatively simple numerical processing in the form of eqns. (6.139) to (6.142). Since the solution to the thin-walled array problem is common to all thick-walled arrays for the same width a, and since the solution of each step width is valid for all scan angles, the number of calculations for many related cases is considerably reduced. However, it should be realized that the Galerkin's procedure is more general and applies to a wider class of problems (see Chapter 5).

In Table 6.4 approximate results for three sizes of truncated matrices are given. The reflection coefficient found by the 5×5 scattering matrix inversion agrees exactly with the values found by Galindo and Wu, and will be considered to be the "correct" value.

TABLE 6.4. REFLECTION COEFFICIENT VS. SCAN ANGLE FOR THICK-WALL PHASED ARRAY
($a/\lambda = 0.6205$, $c/a = 0.063$)

Scan angle	Reflection coefficient (magnitude, angle)		
	1×1 matrix	3×3 matrix	5×5 matrix
0°	(0.3225, 153.3°)	(0.3239, 150.0°)	(0.3240, 148.3°)
10°	(0.3149, 151.0°)	(0.3159, 147.8°)	(0.3156, 146.1°)
20°	(0.2900, 143.4°)	(0.2897, 140.4°)	(0.2884, 138.7°)
30°	(0.2381, 126.4°)	(0.2350, 123.5°)	(0.2317, 121.9°)
40°	(0.0571, 119.6°)	(0.0506, 121.1°)	(0.0463, 123.1°)
50°	(0.0728, 163.0°)	(0.0726, 166.3°)	(0.0725, 168.4°)
60°	(0.0711, 161.2°)	(0.0705, 164.6°)	(0.0703, 166.8°)
70°	(0.0597, 141.8°)	(0.0560, 145.4°)	(0.0538, 148.4°)
80°	(0.0629, 99.1°)	(0.0553, 97.0°)	(0.0500, 96.2°)
90°	(0.1121, 65.0°)	(0.1059, 59.3°)	(0.1009, 55.6°)

It is significant to compare the value obtained from the 1×1 matrix with the correct value. Particularly, for small scan angles, the 1×1 value is very close to the correct value, often well within 1 per cent in magnitude and $5°$ in phase. Since a 1×1 matrix is simply a complex number, the computation of the reflection coefficient is almost trivial.

The mode coefficients for the field reflected back into (A) are the elements of the first column of the scattering matrix S^{AA}. The field at the aperture may be readily computed from the modal expansion at $z = 0$, $c \leq x \leq a$ using these elements of S^{AA}.

As a concluding remark of this section, the following should be mentioned. The principal advantage of the combined technique is that a complex geometry is subdivided into two geometries about which a great deal is known. It uses advantageously the exact solution of the thin-walled array as well as the approximate solution to a well-known waveguide discontinuity problem. The rapidly convergent numerical technique for such a combined geometry may be quite useful for a number of other problems which can be reduced to two or more auxiliary problems solvable by conventional methods or by the MRCT. Examples of such problems are: (1) iris-loaded waveguide phased array for wide angle impedance matching; (ii) double-step discontinuity in a waveguide; (iii) waveguide radiating into a dielectric or plasma layer; and so on.

REFERENCES

BERZ, F. (1951) Reflection and refraction of microwaves at a set of parallel metallic plates, *Proc. IEE (London) 98*, pt. 3, 47–55.

COLLIN, R.E. (1960) *Field Theory of Guided Waves*, McGraw-Hill, New York.

COLLIN, R.E. and BROWN, J. (1956) The calculation of the equivalent circuit of an axially unsymmetrical waveguide junction, *Proc. IEE (London) 103*, pt. C, 121–8.

GALINDO, V. and WU, C.P. (1966) Numerical solutions for an infinite phased array of rectangular waveguides with thick walls, *IEEE Trans. Ant. & Prop. AP-14*, 149–58.

HARRINGTON, R.F. (1961) *Time-Harmonic Electromagnetic Fields*, McGraw-Hill, New York.

HORD, W.E. and ROSENBAUM, F.J. (1968) Approximation technique for dielectric loaded waveguides, *IEEE Trans. Microwave Theory and Techniques MTT-16*, 228–33.

ITOH, T. and MITTRA, R. (1969) An analytical study of the echelette grating with application to open resonators, *IEEE Trans. Microwave Theory and Techniques MTT-17*, 319–27.

LEWIN, L. (1963) Reflection at the junction of an inhomogeneously loaded waveguide, *Proc. Copenhagen URSI Symposium on Electromagnetic Waves*, Pergamon Press, New York.

MITTRA, R. and ITOH, T. (1970) Charge and potential distributions in shielded striplines, *IEEE Trans. Microwave Theory and Techniques MTT-18*, 149–56.

MITTRA, R. and ITOH, T. (1971) A new method for the analysis of the dispersion characteristics of microstrip lines, *IEEE MTT-19*, 47–56.

MITTRA, R. and LEE, S.W. (1971) *Analytical Techniques in the Theory of Guided Waves*, Macmillan, New York.

MITTRA, R., LEE, S.W. and VANBLARICUM, G.F., Jr. (1968) A modified residue calculus technique, *Int. J. Engrg. Sci. 6*, 395–408.

PACE, J. and MITTRA, R. (1964) Generalized scattering matrix analysis of waveguide discontinuity problems, *Quasi-Optics XIV*, 172–97. Polytechnic Institute of Brooklyn Press, New York.

ROYER, E.G. and MITTRA, R. (1972) The diffraction of electromagnetic waves by dielectric steps in waveguides, *IEEE MTT-20*, 273–9.

VANBLARICUM, G.F., Jr. and MITTRA, R. (1969) A modified residue-calculus technique for solving a class of boundary value problems, Part I and II, *IEEE Trans. Microwave Theory and Techniques MTT-17*, 302–19.

YASUURA, K. (1969) A view of numerical methods in diffraction problems, The XVIth General Assembly of the URSI, Ottawa, Canada.

PROBLEMS

1. Consider the partially filled, bifurcated parallel-plate waveguide shown in Fig. P1 (a). This structure is derivable by letting $\delta \to 0$ in the auxiliary geometry shown in Fig. P1 (b). Assume a TE_{po} modal field with amplitude A is incident from the left. Show that the transverse electric fields in the regions A, B, C, and C' may be written as follows:

$$(A) \quad E_y = A \sin \frac{p\pi x}{a} e^{-j\alpha_p z} + \sum_{n=1}^{\infty} A_n \sin \frac{n\pi x}{a} e^{j\alpha_n z},$$

$$(B) \quad E_y = \sum_{n=1}^{\infty} B_n \sin \frac{n\pi (x-c)}{b} e^{-j\beta_n z},$$

$$(C) \quad E_y = \sum_{n=1}^{\infty} \sin \frac{n\pi x}{c} [C_n e^{-j\gamma_n z} + E_n e^{j\gamma_n z}],$$

$$(C') \quad E_y = \sum_{n=1}^{\infty} G_n \sin \frac{n\pi x}{c} e^{-j\bar{\gamma}_n z},$$

where

$$\alpha_n = \sqrt{\left\{ k_0^2 - \left(\frac{n\pi}{a}\right)^2 \right\}}, \quad \beta_n = \sqrt{\left\{ k_0^2 - \left(\frac{n\pi}{b}\right)^2 \right\}},$$

$$\gamma_n = \sqrt{\left\{ k_0^2 - \left(\frac{n\pi}{c}\right)^2 \right\}}, \quad \bar{\gamma}_n = \sqrt{\left\{ \varepsilon_r k_0^2 - \left(\frac{n\pi}{c}\right)^2 \right\}},$$

$$k_0^2 = \omega^2 \mu_0 \varepsilon_0,$$

and A_n, B_n, etc., are the unknown coefficients.

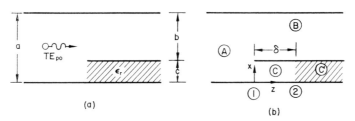

(a) (b)

FIG. P.1

Apply Fourier analysis and the mode matching technique at interfaces 1 and 2 of the auxiliary geometry and derive the following equations for $\mathbf{A}_n$ by letting $\delta \to 0$ in the resulting equations:

$$\sum_{n=1}^{\infty} \frac{\mathbf{A}_n}{\alpha_n - \beta_m} - \frac{\mathbf{A}}{\alpha_p + \beta_m} = 0,$$

$$\sum_{n=1}^{\infty} \frac{\mathbf{A}_n}{\alpha_n + \beta_m} - \frac{\mathbf{A}}{\alpha_p - \beta_m} = \frac{b^2 \beta_m}{m\pi} B_m,$$

$$\sum_{n=1}^{\infty} \mathbf{A}_n \left[\frac{1}{\alpha_n - \gamma_m} + \frac{\lambda_m}{\alpha_n + \gamma_m} \right] - \mathbf{A} \left[\frac{1}{\alpha_p + \gamma_m} + \frac{\lambda_m}{\alpha_p - \gamma_m} \right] = 0,$$

$$\sum_{n=1}^{\infty} \mathbf{A}_n \left[\frac{1}{\alpha_n + \gamma_m} + \frac{\lambda_m}{\alpha_n - \gamma_m} \right] - \mathbf{A} \left[\frac{1}{\alpha_p - \gamma_m} + \frac{\lambda_m}{\alpha_p + \gamma_m} \right] = (-1)^m \frac{c^2 \gamma_m}{m\pi} C_m$$

where

$$\lambda_m = \frac{\gamma_m - \bar{\gamma}_m}{\gamma_m + \bar{\gamma}_m}, \quad \mathbf{A}_n = A_n \sin \frac{n\pi c}{a}, \quad \mathbf{A} = A \sin \frac{p\pi c}{a}, \quad m = 1, 2, \dots$$

Next, construct a meromorphic function $f(\omega)$ such that

$$\mathbf{A}_n = R_f(\alpha_n) = \text{residue of } f(\omega) \text{ at } \omega = \alpha_n.$$

2. (a) Use the generalized scattering matrix approach, to solve the problem in Fig. P1(a). Derive, as first step, the scattering matrices for the individual junctions 1 and 2 [Fig. P1(b)] and subsequently construct the composite scattering matrices as δ goes to zero.

Hint. The scattering matrices for junction 1 may be obtained via the residue calculus technique for the bifurcation problem with $\varepsilon_r = 1$.

(b) Write a computer program for calculating the composite scattering matrices assuming that the elements of the individual scattering matrices for each of the two junctions may be called from subroutines.

3. Figure P2(a) shows the cross-section of a boxed microstrip line. Assume a TEM propagation in the guide. Since the structure is symmetric with respect to the x-axis, it is sufficient to consider an equivalent geometry shown in Fig. P2(b).

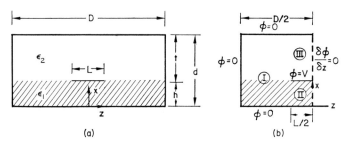

(a)   (b)

FIG. P.2

Using Fourier analysis the mode matching technique and Fourier analyzing, derive the equations:

$$\sum_{n=1}^{\infty} A_n \left[\frac{1}{\alpha_n - \beta_m} + \frac{t_n}{\alpha_n + \beta_m} \right] + \lambda_m \sum_{n=1}^{\infty} A_n \left[\frac{1}{\alpha_n + \beta_m} + \frac{t_n}{\alpha_n - \beta_m} \right] = \left[\frac{1}{-\beta_m} + \frac{\lambda_m}{\beta_m} \right] V$$

$$m = 1, 2, \ldots, \infty$$

$$\sum_{n=1}^{\infty} A_n \left[\frac{1}{\alpha_n - \gamma_m} + \frac{t_n}{\alpha_n + \gamma_m} \right] + \xi_m \sum_{n=1}^{\infty} A_n \left[\frac{1}{\alpha_n + \gamma_m} + \frac{t_n}{\alpha_n - \gamma_m} \right] = \left[\frac{1}{-\gamma_m} + \frac{\xi_m}{\gamma_m} \right] V$$

$$m = 1, 2, \ldots, \infty$$

where $t_n = e^{-\alpha_n(D-L)}$, $\lambda_m = e^{-\beta_m L}$, $\xi_m = e^{-\gamma_m L}$.

Show that the A_n's can be obtained by evaluating the residues of a function $f(\omega)$, i.e. $A_n = R_f(\alpha_n)$, if $f(\omega)$ satisfies the conditions:

(i) $f(\omega)$ has simple poles at $w = \pm \alpha_n$, $n = 1, 2, \ldots, \infty$ and at $\omega = 0$.

(ii) $f(\beta_m) + \lambda_m f(-\beta_m) = 0$, $f(\gamma_m) + \xi_m f(-\gamma_m) = 0$,

$R_f(-\alpha_m) + t_m R_f(\alpha_m) = 0$ $m = 1, 2, \ldots, \infty$.

(iii) $f(\omega) \sim K_1 \omega^{-\nu}$, $1 < \nu < 2$ as $|\omega| \to \infty$.

(iv) $R_f(0) = -1$.

Give a suitable form for such a $f(\omega)$.

Hint. Express the potential function in region I as

$$\phi(x, z) = \sum_{n=1}^{\infty} A_n \phi_n(x) [e^{\alpha_n(z+L/2)} - e^{-\alpha_n(z+D-L/2)}], \quad -\frac{D}{2} < z < -\frac{L}{2}$$

where

$$\phi_n(x) = \begin{cases} \sin(\alpha_n x) & 0 < x < h, \\ \dfrac{\sin(\alpha_n h)}{\sin(\alpha_n t)} \sin[\alpha_n(d-x)] & h < x < d. \end{cases}$$

4. A coupled, shielded, microstrip line is shown in Fig. P3(a). Depending on whether the excitation is odd or even, we obtain two equivalent geometries shown in Fig. P3(b) and (c). For the odd excitation we

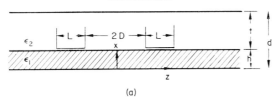

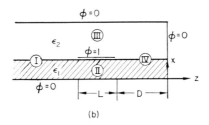

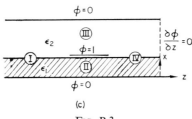

FIG. P.3

may write the potential function in each of the regions I, II, III, and IV as follows:

$$
\phi(x,z) = \begin{cases}
\displaystyle\sum_{n=1}^{\infty} = A_n\, e^{\alpha_n(z+L+D)}\, \phi_n(x) & z < -(D+L), \\[2ex]
\displaystyle\frac{x}{h} + \sum_{n=1}^{\infty} (B_n\, e^{\beta_n z} + D_n\, e^{-\beta_n z}) \sin \beta_n x & 0 < x < h, \quad -(D+L) < z < -D, \\[2ex]
\displaystyle\frac{d-x}{t} + \sum_{n=1}^{\infty} (C_n\, e^{\gamma_n z} + E_n\, e^{-\gamma_n z}) \sin \gamma_n\,(d-x) & h < x < d, \quad -(D+L) < z < -D, \\[2ex]
\displaystyle\sum_{n=1}^{\infty} F_n \sinh \alpha_n z\, \phi_n(x) & -D < z < 0,
\end{cases}
$$

$$
\phi_n(x) = \begin{cases}
\sin \alpha_n x & 0 < x < h, \\[1.5ex]
\dfrac{\sin \alpha_n h}{\sin \alpha_n t} \sin \alpha_n\,(d-x) & h < x < d,
\end{cases}
$$

where α_n are given by (6.4) and $\beta_n = n\pi/h$, $\gamma_n = n\pi/t$.
Derive the following coupled sets of equations for the expansion coefficients:

$$
\sum_{n=1}^{\infty} \frac{A_n}{\alpha_n - \beta_m} - \lambda_m \sum_{n=1}^{\infty} \left(\frac{F_n}{\alpha_n + \beta_m} + \frac{F_n \zeta_n}{\alpha_n - \beta_m} \right) = -\frac{1}{\beta_m} + \frac{\lambda_m}{\beta_m},
$$

$$
\lambda_m \sum_{n=1}^{\infty} \frac{A_n}{\alpha_n + \beta_m} - \sum_{n=1}^{\infty} \left(\frac{F_n}{\alpha_n - \beta_m} + \frac{F_n \zeta_n}{\alpha_n + \beta_m} \right) = -\frac{1}{\beta_m} + \frac{\lambda_m}{\beta_m},
$$

$$
\sum_{n=1}^{\infty} \frac{A_n}{\alpha_n - \gamma_m} - \xi_m \sum_{n=1}^{\infty} \left(\frac{F_n}{\alpha_n + \gamma_m} + \frac{F_n \zeta_n}{\alpha_n - \gamma_m} \right) = -\frac{1}{\gamma_m} + \frac{\xi_m}{\gamma_m},
$$

$$
\xi_m \sum_{n=1}^{\infty} \frac{A_n}{\alpha_n + \gamma_m} - \sum_{n=1}^{\infty} \left(\frac{F_n}{\alpha_n - \gamma_m} + \frac{F_n \zeta_n}{\alpha_n + \gamma_m} \right) = -\frac{1}{\gamma_m} + \frac{\xi_m}{\gamma_m},
$$

where $\mathbf{A}_n = A_n \sin \alpha_n h$, $\mathbf{F}_n = \frac{1}{2} F_n \sin \alpha_n h\, e^{\alpha_n D}$,

$$\lambda_m = e^{-\beta_m L}, \quad \xi_m = e^{-\gamma_m L}, \quad \zeta_n = e^{-2\alpha_n D}.$$

Show that $\mathbf{A}_n$ and $\mathbf{F}_n$ are expressible in terms of the residues of functions $f_1(\omega)$ and $f_2(\omega)$ at $\omega = \alpha_n$, i.e. $R_1(\alpha_n) = \mathbf{A}_n$ and $R_2(\alpha_n) = \mathbf{F}_n$, providing these functions f_1 and f_2 satisfy the properties:

(i) $f_1(\omega)$ has simple poles at $\omega = \alpha_n$, $n = 1, 2, \ldots, \infty$ and at $\omega = 0$.

(ii) $f_2(\omega)$ has simple poles at $\omega = \pm\alpha_n$, $n = 1, 2, \ldots, \infty$ and at $\omega = 0$.

(iii) $R_2(-\alpha_n) = -\zeta_n R_2(\alpha_n)$ where $R_2(x)$ is the residue of $f_2(\omega)$ at $\omega = x$.

(iv) $f_1(\beta_m) + \lambda_m f_2(-\beta_m) = 0$, $\quad \lambda_m f_1(-\beta_m) + f_2(\beta_m) = 0$.

$f_1(\gamma_m) + \xi_m f_2(-\gamma_m) = 0$, $\quad \xi_m f_1(-\gamma_m) + f_2(\gamma_m) = 0$.

(v) $f_1(\omega) \sim \omega^{-\nu}$, $f_2(\omega) \sim \omega^{-\nu}$ as $|\omega| \to \infty$, $1 < \nu < 2$.

(vi) $R_1(0) = R_2(0) = -1$.

Show that an expression for the charge distribution can be constructed in terms of $f_1(\omega)$ and $f_2(\omega)$ evaluated at certain constant values. (See T. Itoh and R. Mittra, "An accurate method for calculating charge and potential distributions in coupled microstrip lines", *Proc. IEEE*, vol. 59, no. 2, pp. 332–4, Feb. 1971.)

5. Consider the problem of radiation from a flanged parallel plate waveguide excited with a TM_{po} modal field from the left, as shown in Fig. P4(a). Assume that the flanges are extended to infinity in the x-direction. The original structure may be recovered from the auxiliary geometry in Fig. P4(b) by letting $\delta \to 0$. Apply

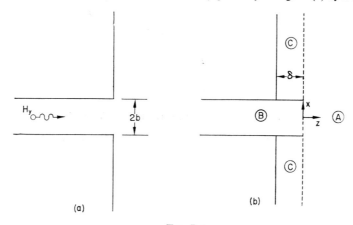

FIG. P.4

the mode matching technique, generalized the accommodate the open regions (A and C) where spectral representations are necessary to express the fields.

Suitable representations for the fields in the various regions are:

$$H_y = \int_0^\infty A(\alpha)\, e^{-\omega z} \cos \alpha x \, d\alpha, \quad z > 0,$$

$$H_y = \cos\frac{p\pi x}{b} e^{-\gamma_{pb} z} + \sum_{n=0}^\infty B_n \cos\frac{n\pi x}{b} e^{\gamma_{nb} z}, \quad z < 0, \ |x| < b,$$

$$H_y = \begin{cases} \int_0^\infty C(\beta)\, [e^{\Gamma z} + e^{-\Gamma(z+2\delta)}] \cos \beta\,(x-b)\, d\beta, & -\delta < z < 0, \ x > b, \\[2mm] \int_0^\infty C(\beta)\, [e^{\Gamma z} + e^{-\Gamma(z+2\delta)}] \cos \beta\,(x+b)\, d\beta, & -\delta < z < 0, \ x < -b, \end{cases}$$

where

$$\omega = \sqrt{(\alpha^2 - k^2)}, \quad \gamma_{nb} = \sqrt{\left\{ \left(\frac{n\pi}{b}\right)^2 - k^2 \right\}}, \quad \Gamma = \sqrt{(\beta^2 - k^2)},$$

$$\gamma_{ob} = jk$$

Match H_y and E_x fields at $z = 0$, and employ Fourier analysis in both the regions $|x| < b$ and $|x| > b$. Then let $\delta \to 0$ to derive

$$(-1)^p \, b\gamma'_{pb} \, (1 + \delta_p^0) \, \delta_m^p = \int_0^\infty \frac{A(x)\,dx}{\omega - \gamma_{mb}},$$

$$\pi \Gamma A\,(\beta)\cos\beta b = PV \int_0^\infty \left\{ \frac{A(x)}{\omega - \Gamma} + \frac{A(x)}{\omega + \Gamma} \right\} dx$$

where PV stands for the principal value integral.

Consider a function $f(\omega)$ in the complex ω-plane with the properties:

(i) $f(\omega)$ has zeros at $\omega = \gamma_{nb}$, $n \neq p$, $n = 1, 2, \ldots, \infty$ and at $\omega = \gamma_{ob}\delta_p^0$.

(ii) $f(\omega)$ has a branch point at $\omega = \gamma_{ob}$.

(iii) $f(\omega) \sim \omega^{-1/2-\nu}$, $\nu = \frac{1}{6}$ as $|\omega| \to \infty$.

(iv) $f(\gamma'_{pb}) = b\gamma'_{pb}\,(-1)^p\,(1 + \delta_p^0)$.

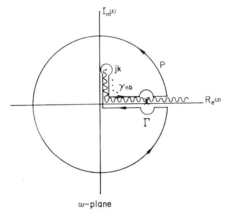

ω-plane

FIG. P.5

Evaluate the contour integrals

$$\frac{1}{2\pi j}\int_P \frac{f(\omega)\,d\omega}{\omega - \gamma_{mb}}, \qquad \frac{1}{2\pi j}\int_P \left\{ \frac{f(\omega)}{\omega - \Gamma} + \frac{f(\omega)}{\omega + \Gamma} \right\} d\omega$$

where the contour P is shown in Fig. P5, and show that unknown coefficient $A(x)$ is expressible as

$$A(x) = \left. \frac{f^+(\omega) - f^-(\omega)}{2\pi j\omega \sin xb} \right|_{\omega \text{ on } L}$$

or

$$A(x) = \left. \frac{1}{2\pi\omega \cos xb}\{2f(-\omega) + f^+(\omega) - f^-(\omega)\} \right|_{\omega \text{ on } L}$$

where $f^+(\omega)$ and $f^-(\omega)$ are the values of $f(\omega)$ on each side of the branch cut L. (See T. Itoh and R. Mittra, "A new method of solution for radiation from a flanged waveguide", *Proc. IEEE*, vol. 59, no. 7, pp. 1131–3, July 1971. Also see R. Mittra and C. P. Bates, "An alternative approach to the solution of a class of Wiener–Hopf and related problems", *Electromagnetic Wave Theory* (Proc. Symp., Delft, The Netherlands), Pergamon Press, New York, 1967, pp. 261–75.)

6. Consider the problem of propagation of a TEM mode in a microstrip line, the cross-section of which is shown in Fig. P6. Suppressing the common factor $\exp(\pm j\beta z)$, where β is the propagation constant, show that the transverse variation of the potential function $\phi(x, y)$ satisfies the Poisson equation

$$\left(\frac{\partial^2}{\partial x^2} + \frac{\partial^2}{\partial y^2} \right) \phi(x, y) = -\frac{\varrho(x, y)}{\varepsilon_0}$$

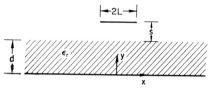

where $\varrho\,(x, z)$ is the charge distribution and is expressed here as

$$\varrho\,(x, y) = \varrho_s(x)\,\delta\,(y - d - s) \quad |x| < L,$$

ϱ_s being the surface charge density.

Apply the boundary conditions:

  (i) $\phi\,(x, 0) = 0$ all x;

  (ii) $\phi\,(x, y) \to 0$ as $y \to +\infty$,   all x;

  (iii) $\left.\dfrac{\partial\phi}{\partial y}\right|_{y=d+s+} - \left.\dfrac{\partial\phi}{\partial y}\right|_{y=d+s-} = -\dfrac{\varrho_s(x)}{\varepsilon_0}$ $|x| < L$;

  (iv) $\phi\,(x, d+s+) = \phi\,(x, d+s-)$ all x,

  $\phi\,(x, d+s) = 1$ $|x| < L$;

  (v) $\phi\,(x, d+) = \phi\,(x, d-)$ all x;

  (vi) $\left.\dfrac{\partial\phi}{\partial y}\right|_{y=d+} = \varepsilon_r\left.\dfrac{\partial\phi}{\partial y}\right|_{y=d-}$ all x;

and derive the following equation after letting $s \to 0$:

$$G(\alpha)\,\tilde{\varrho}_s(\alpha) = \tilde{\phi}\,(\alpha, d)$$

where

$$\tilde{\phi}\,(\alpha, y) = \int_{-\infty}^{\infty} \phi\,(x, y)\,e^{j\alpha x}\,dx,$$

$$\tilde{\varrho}_s(\alpha) = \int_{-L}^{L} \varrho_s(x)\,e^{j\alpha x}\,dx,$$

$$G(\alpha) = \frac{1}{\varepsilon_0\alpha\,[1 + \varepsilon_r\coth\,(\alpha d)]}.$$

Derive a variational expression for the line capacitance C.

Hint. Express the potential function as

$$\tilde{\phi}\,(\alpha, y) = \begin{cases} A(\alpha)\sinh\alpha y, & 0 < y < d, \\ B(\alpha)\sinh\alpha y + C(\alpha)\cosh\alpha y, & d < y < d + s, \\ D(\alpha)\exp\,(-\alpha y) & y > d + s. \end{cases}$$

(See E. Yamashita and R. Mittra, "Variational method for the analysis of microstrip lines", *IEEE Trans. Microwave Theory and Techniques*, vol. *MTT-16*, no. 4, pp. 251–6, April 1968.)

7. Show that $\tilde{\phi}\,(\alpha, d)$ in problem 6 can be written as

$$\tilde{\phi}\,(\alpha, d) = \tilde{\phi}_1(\alpha) + e^{j\alpha L}\,\tilde{\phi}_+(\alpha) + e^{-j\alpha L}\,\tilde{\phi}_+\,(-\alpha),$$

where

$$\tilde{\phi}_1(\alpha) = \int_{-L}^{L} e^{j\alpha x}\,dx = \frac{2\sin\alpha L}{\alpha},$$

$$\tilde{\phi}_+(\alpha) = \int_{L}^{\infty} \tilde{\phi}\,(x, d)\,e^{j\alpha(x-L)}\,dx \quad \text{(unknown)}.$$

Hence the equation

$$G(\alpha)\,\tilde{\varrho}_s(\alpha) = \frac{2\sin\alpha L}{\alpha} + e^{j\alpha L}\,\tilde{\phi}_+\,(\alpha) + e^{-j\alpha L}\,\tilde{\phi}_+\,(-\alpha)$$

contains two unknowns $\tilde{\varrho}_s$ and $\tilde{\phi}_+$. Applying Galerkin's method in the transform domain, derive the matrix equation

$$\sum_{n=1}^{M} G_{mn} A_n = B_m \quad m = 1, 2, \ldots, M,$$

where

$$G_{mn} = \int_{-\infty}^{\infty} \tilde{\xi}_m(\alpha)\, G(\alpha)\, \tilde{\xi}_n(\alpha)\, d\alpha,$$

$$B_m = \int_{-\infty}^{\infty} \tilde{\xi}_m(\alpha)\, \frac{2 \sin \alpha L}{\alpha}\, d\alpha,$$

$\tilde{\xi}_n(\alpha)$ are appropriate basis functions and A_n are the unknown coefficients.

Hint. When expanding $\tilde{\varrho}_s(\alpha)$ in terms of $\tilde{\xi}_n(\alpha)$ with unknown coefficients A_n, choose $\tilde{\xi}_n(\alpha)$ such that $\xi_n(x)$ [inverse Fourier transform of $\tilde{\xi}_n(\alpha)$] is identically zero for $|x| > L$. Then employ Parseval's theorem to evaluate

$$\int_{-\infty}^{\infty} \tilde{\xi}_m(\alpha)\, \tilde{\phi}\,(\alpha, d)\, d\alpha$$

and show that the integrals involving the products of $\tilde{\xi}_m(\alpha)\, \tilde{\phi}_+(\alpha)$ are identically zero.

8. Figure P7 shows the cross-section of the slot line which is a new type of transmission line used in the microwave integrated circuit. One side of the dielectric substrate is coated with two conducting semi-infinite plates separated by the distance $2t$, and the line is assumed to be infinite in the z-direction. The structure

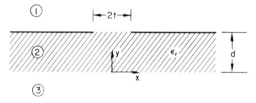

FIG. P.7

supports hybrid modes only and these can be expressed in terms of two scalar potentials $\phi_i^{(e)}(x, y)$ and $\phi_i^{(h)}(x, y)$, $i = 1, 2, 3$ that are proportional to the E_z and H_z fields, respectively, when the common factor $\exp(-j\beta z)$ is suppressed. The boundary and continuity conditions are expressed as

(i) E_z, E_x, H_z and H_x are continuous at $y = 0$.

(ii) $E_{z1} = E_{z2}$, $E_{x1} = E_{x2}$ $-\infty < x < \infty$, $y = d$.

(iii) $E_z = \begin{cases} 0 & |x| \geq t \\ f(x) & |x| \leq t \end{cases}$ $E_x = \begin{cases} 0 & |x| \geq t \\ g(x) & |x| \leq t \end{cases}$ $y = d$.

(iv) $J_x = H_{z1} - H_{z2} = \begin{cases} s(x) & |x| \geq t \\ 0 & |x| \leq t \end{cases}$ $y = d$,

$J_z = H_{x1} - H_{x2} = \begin{cases} \omega(x) & |x| \geq t \\ 0 & |x| \leq t \end{cases}$ $y = d$,

where the subscripts 1, 2, and 3 denote the three regions shown in Fig. P7. The functions f, g, s and ω are as yet unknown functions of x.

Applying the above conditions in the Fourier transform domain, derive the following two equations:

$$\Gamma_1(\alpha, \beta)\, F(\alpha) + \Gamma_2(\alpha, \beta)\, G(\alpha) = e^{j\alpha t} S_+(\alpha) + e^{-j\alpha t} S_+(-\alpha),$$

$$\Gamma_3(\alpha, \beta)\, F(\alpha) + \Gamma_4(\alpha, \beta)\, G(\alpha) = e^{j\alpha t} W_+(\alpha) + e^{-j\alpha t} W_+(-\alpha),$$

where

$$F(\alpha) = \int_{-t}^{t} f(x)\, e^{j\alpha x}\, dx, \quad G(\alpha) = \int_{-t}^{t} g(x)\, e^{j\alpha x}\, dx,$$

$$S_+(\alpha) = \int_{t}^{\infty} s(x)\, e^{j\alpha(x-t)}\, dx, \quad W_+(\alpha) = \int_{t}^{\infty} \omega(x)\, e^{j\alpha(x-t)}\, dx.$$

Also obtain known coefficients $\Gamma_1(\alpha, \beta)$, etc. Solve the above two equations using the Galerkin's method in the transform domain.

Hint. Express the transforms of potentials as

$$\tilde{\phi}_1^{(p)}(\alpha, y) = A^{(p)}(\alpha)\, e^{-\gamma_1(y-d)}, \qquad\qquad y > d$$

$$\tilde{\phi}_2^{(p)}(\alpha, y) = B^{(p)}(\alpha)\sinh\gamma_2 y + C^{(p)}(\alpha)\cosh\gamma_2 y \quad 0 < y < d,$$

$$\tilde{\phi}_3^{(p)}(\alpha, y) = D^{(p)}(\alpha)\, e^{+\gamma_3 y} \qquad\qquad y < 0,$$

$p = e$ or h and

$$\gamma_i^2 = \alpha^2 + \beta^2 - k_i^2, \quad k_1 = k_3 = k_0 = \omega\sqrt{(\varepsilon_0\mu_0)}, \quad k_2 = \sqrt{\varepsilon_r}\cdot k_0.$$

(See T. Itoh and R. Mittra, "Dispersion characteristics of the slot lines", *Electronics Letters*, vol. 7, no. 13, pp. 364–5, July 1, 1971.)

9. The Euler–Maclaurin formula is given by

$$\int_a^b f(x)\,\mathrm{d}x = h\left[\frac{f(a)}{2} + f(a+h) + f(a+2h) + \cdots + f(b-h) + \frac{f(b)}{2}\right]$$

$$- \sum_{k=1}^{\infty}\frac{B_{2k}}{(2k)!}h^{2k}\left[\frac{\mathrm{d}^{(2k-1)}}{\mathrm{d}x^{(2k-1)}}f(b) - \frac{\mathrm{d}^{(2k-1)}}{\mathrm{d}x^{(2k-1)}}f(a)\right]$$

where B_{2k} are the Bernoulli numbers. Using this relation, derive a convenient formula for the numerical calculation of

$$\sum_{n=1}^{\infty}\frac{n^{\nu-1}}{n+\alpha}$$

where $0 < \nu < 1, \alpha > 0$. Write a computer program for this purpose.

Hint. Use the Stieltjes transform formula

$$\int_0^{\infty}\frac{x^{\nu-1}}{x+\alpha}\,\mathrm{d}x = \Gamma(\nu)\,\Gamma(1-\nu)\,\alpha^{\nu-1}$$

where $\Gamma(\nu)$ is the gamma function.

10. Consider a TM surface wave propagating in the z-direction on a dielectric slab of thickness t which is backed by a perfect electric conductor. Derive the characteristic equation which gives the surface wave roots as a function of frequency ω. Write a computer program for obtaining these roots. Choose ω, ε_r and t as the input data.

Hint. TM modes only have a single component of magnetic field, viz. H_y.

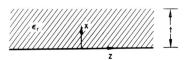

CHAPTER 7

Inverse Scattering and Remote Probing

R. MITTRA

University of Illinois, Urbana, Illinois

7.1. INTRODUCTION

The problem of inverse scattering arises in a wide variety of physical situations. Ground-based as well as satellite-borne remote probing systems are used by meteorologists and ecologists for studying the atmosphere. Magnetotelluric and seismic probing methods are employed by geologists and geophysicists for studying rock formations and mineral deposits within the earth. Inverse scattering techniques find application in plasma diagnostics and in the study of the properties of optical fibers. The problem of target recognition or the so-called identification problem is important in radar technology. An important bioacoustical application of ultrasonic probing is that of finding the location and shape of diseased tissue materials that are embedded in fatty layers. The problems of antenna aperture synthesis and probing also involve the solution of the "inverse problem".

Though there exists a large body of literature dealing with the "forward" scattering problem, the number of works dealing with the inverse problem is relatively few. This is due primarily to the complexities associated with the inverse problem. For one thing, many of the inverse problems do not lend themselves to formulation in terms of linear matrix or integral equations and, consequently, sophisticated techniques are required to resolve them. Even when it is possible to describe the inverse problem in terms of a linear matrix equation, the resulting equation is often ill-conditioned, and its inverse unstable. Special techniques are again necessary to handle these cases.

To introduce some of the computer techniques found useful for solving inverse problems we propose to discuss five illustrative problems in this category. First, we consider the problem of determining the shape of a scatterer from the knowledge of its scatterer far field. Next, we develop an inverse diffraction transformation approach for the problem of locating the defective elements in the aperture of a large phased array by probing its radiated field in the Fresnel region of the aperture. This is followed by a discussion of a method for synthesizing an antenna array to produce a specified far-field magnitude pattern. Then we investigate the problem of determining the profile of a planar, inhomogeneous medium from the knowledge of its scattered field. Finally, we discuss matrix methods for a wavefront reconstruction problem for a planar aperture when the inverse is unstable.

351

7.2. THE TWO-DIMENSIONAL INVERSE SCATTERING PROBLEM

7.2.1. Statement of the Problem and Preliminaries

The problem we propose to investigate may be stated as follows. Given the knowledge of the scattered far field from a perfectly conducting scatterer, find its shape and location in space. Though a general solution of this problem is possible for the general three-dimensional case, for the sake of simplicity we consider the case of one or more cylindrical scatterers of arbitrary cross-section when illuminated by a plane wave with the incident electric

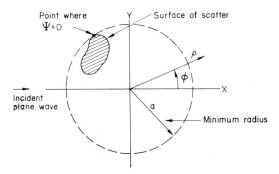

FIG. 7.1. Inverse scattering problem geometry.

field vector parallel to the axis of the cylinder. Figure 7.1 shows the geometry of the problem. The method described herein has been discussed in more detail by Imbriale and Mittra (1970).

The problem at hand may be reduced to an equivalent scalar problem by letting $\Psi(\varrho, \phi) = E_z(x, y)$ and noting that other field quantities may be expressed in terms of Ψ. From Maxwell's equation, one may derive the conventional wave equation

$$(\nabla^2 + k^2)\, \Psi(\varrho, \phi) = 0, \quad \nabla^2 = \frac{\partial^2}{\partial x^2} + \frac{\partial^2}{\partial y^2}, \quad k = 2\pi/h \tag{7.1}$$

subject to the boundary condition that $\Psi \equiv 0$ on all perfectly conducting surfaces and that the scattered Ψ must satisfy the radiation condition at infinity. The total field Ψ is the sum of the incident and scattered field, i.e.

$$\Psi(\varrho, \phi) = \Psi_{\text{inc}}(\varrho, \phi) + u(\varrho, \phi) \tag{7.2}$$

where the incident field $\Psi_{\text{inc}} = \mathrm{e}^{-jk\varrho\cos\phi}$. The associated scattered far field may be written as

$$u(\varrho, \phi) = \mathrm{e}^{-jk\varrho}\,(2j/\pi k\varrho)^{1/2}\, g(\phi), \quad \varrho \to \infty \tag{7.3}$$

where $g(\phi)$ is scattered "pattern function". We assume that $g(\phi)$ is known and our aim is to process $g(\phi)$ to extract the information about the shape of the scatterer.

7.2.2. Numerical Processing of Pattern Function to Derive Object Shape

As a first step, Fourier analyze the far-field pattern $g(\phi)$ and compute the Fourier coefficients a_n such that

$$g(\phi) \simeq \sum_{n=-M}^{M} a_n \, e^{jn\phi}, \quad 0 < \phi < 2\pi. \tag{7.4}$$

Algorithms for Fourier analyzing are well known and standard SSP subroutines may be employed to calculate a_n, if desired. We have assumed that $g(\phi)$ is known for the entire range of ϕ; the extension to the case where information is available only for a partial range of ϕ will be discussed later.

Our immediate task is to express the near field in the neighborhood of the surface of the scatterer in terms of the coefficients a_n. It turns out that this cannot in general be accomplished by a one-step linear algebraic operation for an arbitrary point in space. It is necessary to develop an algorithm for accomplishing the far-field to near-field transformation requirement via a series of manipulations. This is outlined below.

For all points outside the minimum radius enclosing the scatterer, $u(\varrho, \phi)$ may be expressed in terms of a_n as

$$u(\varrho, \phi) = \sum_{n=-M}^{M} a_n j^{-n} H_n^{(2)}(k\varrho) \, e^{jn\phi}, \quad r \geq a \tag{7.5}$$

where $H_n^{(2)}$ is the Hankel function of the second kind.

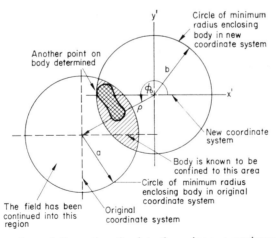

FIG. 7.2. The geometry for analytic continuation into the region $\varrho < a$ using convex body method.

Realize, however, that the minimum radius is not known *a priori* since it is not known where the scatterer is. However, we can find the scatterer by computing the total field using (7.2) and (7.5) for successively decreasing series of radii ϱ, and testing if the total field becomes zero at least at one point on the circumference of the last circular region. When this occurs, we conclude that we have determined at least one point on the surface of the scatterer. We proceed next to determine the location of the rest. If we know *a priori* that there is only a single scatterer and that its shape is convex, we may proceed as follows. We relocate another origin, say at ϱ_0, ϕ_0 (see Fig. 7.2) and repeat the search for a point where the total field is zero. This requires, as a preamble, transformation of the pattern function to the new coordinate system. We write

$$g'(\phi) = g(\phi)\, e^{jk\varrho_0\cos(\phi-\phi_0)} = \sum_{m=-P}^{P} a'_m\, e^{jm\phi} \tag{7.6}$$

where a'_m are the new Fourier coefficients which we have to relate to a_m. This is done by expanding both $g(\phi)$ and $e^{jk\varrho_0\cos(\phi-\phi_0)}$ in the Fourier series and rearranging terms. This gives

$$a'_m = \sum_{n=M}^{M} a_n\, j^{m-n} J_{m-n}\,(k\varrho_0)\, e^{-j(m-n)\phi_0}. \tag{7.7}$$

Equation (7.7) may be regarded as a matrix operation on the vector $\{a_1,\ldots,a_M\}$ and can be easily accomplished on the computer. An important consideration in using (7.6) is the choice of P. Since the coefficients a_n were truncated to $n = M$, it is important to know how large a number one should choose for P. This point will be discussed later in some detail.

Once a'_m have been computed using (7.7), the near field outside and on the minimum radius of the body in the new coordinate system is determined by

$$u\,(\varrho',\phi') = \sum_{m=-P}^{P} a'_m\, j^{-m} H_m^{(2)}\,(k\varrho')\, e^{jn\phi'}. \tag{7.8}$$

Once again, a point on the body located on the minimum radius in the new system can be determined by searching for a zero of the total field. The above process may be repeated as many times as necessary to locate the points on the surface of an arbitrary convex-shaped scatterer. It should be noted that since the minimum radius enclosing the body also provides a bound on its size, very few points would be needed to characterize both size and location of the scatterer.

Let us now turn to the case of a body that is nonconvex. It is necessary to follow a slightly different procedure when the shape is arbitrary or when multiple scatterers are involved.

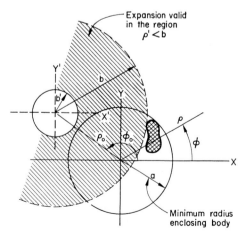

FIG. 7.3. The geometry for analytic continuation into the region $\varrho < a$ using arbitrarily shaped body method.

Refer to Fig. 7.3 where once again we see the pertinent geometry for shifting the origin to a point ϱ_0, ϕ_0. However, this time the so-called inside expansion is used for the representation of fields. The representation for $u(\varrho', \phi')$ in the new system now reads

$$u(\varrho', \phi') = \sum_{n=-Q}^{Q} c_n J_n(k\varrho') e^{jn\phi'} \tag{7.9}$$

which is valid inside and on the circle $\varrho' = b$, shown as the shaded region in Fig. 7.3. As in the previous case, we need to express the coefficients c_n in terms of a_n, the Fourier coefficients of the pattern function $g(\phi)$. The relationship has been derived by Imbriale and Mittra (1970) by using the addition theorem of Bessel functions which reads

$$c_n = \sum_{m=-M}^{M} j^{-m} a_m H_{n-m}^{(2)}(k\varrho_0) e^{-j(n-m)(\phi_0-\pi)}. \tag{7.10}$$

It is observed that (7.10) is very similar to (7.7) and requires similar numerical manipulations. The principal difference between the two is that the former requires the computation of the J_n functions whereas H_n's are required for the latter. Another difference is that for objects of complicated shapes as well as for multiple scatterers, it becomes necessary to use the shifting of the origin more than once to reach all points on the scatterer, or the scatterers, if there are more than one. Such a case is graphically illustrated in Fig. 7.4.

The procedure for finding the scatterer once again entails a search for the location of points where the total field is zero. These points are then interpreted to be located on the surface of the scatterer. The process is continued until the entire shape is determined.

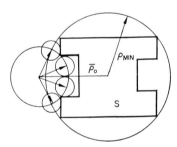

(a) Branching from an auxiliary coordinate system

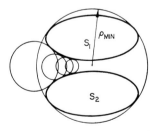

(b) Chains of auxiliary coordinate systems which
are also used for point matching

FIG. 7.4. The use of branches and chains from an auxiliary coordinate system.

In certain situations, the far-field pattern $g(\phi)$ may not be available for all ϕ and the conventional Fourier analysis procedure would not work for determining a_n. One possible way of obtaining the a_n's now is the use of a parameter optimization approach which will be discussed later in Section 7.4 in more detail. Basically, one defines a performance index function F as

$$F(\bar{a}_{-N}, \bar{a}_{-N+1}, \ldots, \bar{a}_0, \ldots, \bar{a}_{N-1}, \bar{a}_N) = \int_{\phi_1}^{\phi_2} |g(\phi) - \Sigma \bar{a}_n \, e^{jn\phi}|^2 \, d\phi.$$

Now if F is minimized, we would obtain a good fit to the pattern function $g(\phi)$ in the range ϕ_1 to ϕ_2 where it is specified (if we can make F small by adjusting the parameter $\bar{a}_n$). Subroutines† for minimizing functions of multiple parameters are available in the SSP package that can be adapted to the present problem.

Once the appropriate coefficients $\bar{a}_n$ have been determined in this manner, we can proceed according to the steps outlined above and search for the location of the scatterer by algebraically manipulating $\bar{a}_n$ to obtain the near field and locating the zero of the total field.

7.2.3. Summary of Computational Procedure for Inverse Scattering

(a) Compute $a_n = \int_0^{2\pi} (g\phi) \, e^{jn\phi}$ from $g(\phi)$ for $n = 1, \ldots, M$, such that

$$\int_0^{2\pi} |g(\phi) - \sum_{n=-M}^{M} a_n \, e^{jn\phi}|^2 \, d\phi < \varepsilon_1$$

where ε_1 depends on the accuracy of the given $g(\phi)$.

b) Determine the circle of minimum radius by minimizing the function

$$E_t(\varrho, \phi) = |\sum_{n=-M}^{M} a_n \, j^n H_n^{(2)}(k\varrho) \, e^{jn\phi} + \Psi_{\text{inc}}(\varrho, \phi)|$$

which represents the magnitude of total electric field. $E_t(\varrho, \phi)$ is minimized with respect to the parameters (ϱ, ϕ) using a suitable minimization technique. If the minimum is less than a small number ε_2, which is stored in the computer, then the corresponding ϱ is the minimum radius a enclosing the body. If no minimum exists, then the given data are not sufficiently accurate.

(c) For a general body, calculate coefficients c_n, using (7.10). The accuracies of the higher order c_n's are very sensitive to the higher order a_n's and it is very important to truncate the computation at an upper limit Q. A suitable numerical criterion‡ is $|c_n| + |c_{-n}| > 5.0$.

(d) Use c_n's to compute the total field via the equation

$$\Psi(\varrho', \phi') = \sum_{n=-Q}^{Q} c_n J_n(k\varrho') \, e^{jn\phi'} + \Psi_{\text{inc}}(\varrho', \phi')$$

† See Appendix A for more details.
‡ A similar criterion applies to the upper limit Q to be used for computing a'_m. (See eqn. (7.7) when the body is convex.)

and find ϱ', ϕ' that minimize the total field. If the minimum is less than ε_2, then this is a point on the body. Increment ϕ_0 by $\varDelta\phi_0$ and repeat the procedure.

(e) If no minimum less than ε_2 is found by the above operation, then choose a new co-ordinate system (ϱ_1, ϕ_1) inside the circle $\varrho = a$. Calculate a new set of c_n'' using

$$c_n'' = \sum_{m=-R}^{R} c_m J_{n-m} (k\varrho_1)\, e^{-j(n-m)(\phi_1-\pi)}$$

and the total field in the (ϱ'', ϕ'') system from

$$\Psi (\varrho'', \phi'') = \sum_{n=-R}^{R} c_n'' J_n (k\varrho'')\, e^{jn\phi''} + \Psi_{\mathrm{inc}} (\varrho'', \phi'')$$

with the criterion for R the same as Q. Search for a minimum of Ψ with respect to (ϱ'', ϕ'') until the minimum is less than ε_2. This corresponds to a point on the body.

(f) Increment ϕ_0 by $\varDelta\phi_0$ and repeat the procedure.

(g) Upon termination, plot the points which are found on the scatterer.

7.2.4. Numerical Results

The numerical processing method elaborated in the previous section has been tested for its practicality. Some typical results will be reported in this section.

The first example is that of a circular cylinder for which exact far fields are available and for which the trivial case of convex body algorithms can be employed. Though not shown here, the reconstruction of the cylindrical surface is almost perfect when the far field is

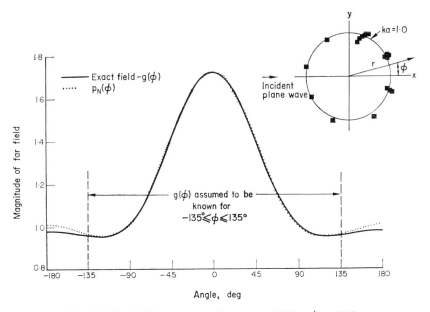

FIG. 7.5. Far field known over the range $-135° \le \phi \le 135°$.

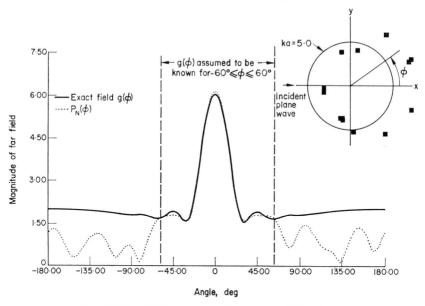

FIG. 7.6. Far field known over the range $-60° \le \phi \le 60°$.

available for all ϕ. Figures 7.5 and 7.6 show the reconstruction obtained when the far field is known in the ranges $-135° < \phi < 135°$ and $-60° < \phi < 60°$, respectively. The extrapolated far-field pattern

$$P_N(\phi) = \sum_{n=-N}^{N} \bar{a}_n e^{jn\phi}$$

is also shown in these diagrams. Considering the smallness of the size of the scatterer and the crudeness of the data provided in the second case ($-60° < \phi < 60°$), the results are considered to be quite good.

The reconstruction of an elliptical scatterer ($ka = 1.0$, $kb = 0.5$), for which the convex body algorithm is again applicable, is shown in Fig. 7.7.

Two examples of the application of the arbitrary body algorithms that require inside expansion (7.10) are shown in Figs. 7.8 and 7.9 for a conducting strip, and a combination of two cylinders, respectively.

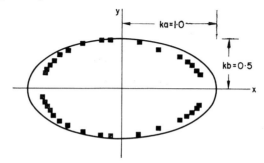

FIG. 7.7. Elliptic cylinder $ka = 1.0$, $kb = 0.5$
– surface of scatterer;   ■ points calculated by computer

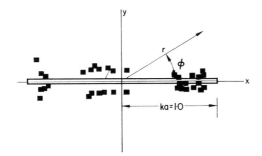

FIG. 7.8. Conducting strip.

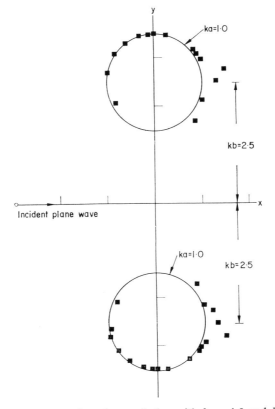

FIG. 7.9. Reconstruction of two cylinders with $ka = 1.0$ and $kb = 2.5$.

The effect of noise in the data has also been investigated and it has been found that fairly good results of inversion are obtained even with noise levels of -20 db in the far-field data.

The computation time for a typical scatterer is of the order of 30 seconds on the IBM 360/75 computer. It should be pointed out that the computation time increases with the size of the scatterer and can become prohibitively large for $ka \gg 1$, i.e. in the geometrical optics region. An alternative approach reported by Lewis (1969) will be found more suitable for dealing with large scatterers.

7.3. REMOTE PROBING OF ANTENNA APERTURES BY HOLOGRAPHIC TECHNIQUES

7.3.1. Description of the Problem

In this section we present some of the analytical and numerical aspects of the problem of determining the aperture field of an antenna by probing the radiated field in the Fresnel region of the aperture. This problem may arise, for instance, when it is desired to locate the defective elements in a large phased array without probing directly into the mouth of each element. The discussion in this section is based on a paper by P. L. Ransom and R. Mittra (1971).

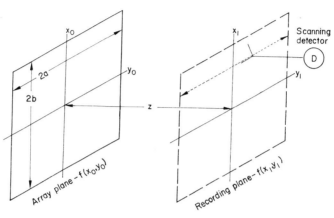

FIG. 7.10. Geometry of the array plane and the recording plane.

The experimental work involves the recording of both the amplitude and phase of the radiator in the Fresnel region over a plane parallel to the array aperture. The geometry of the arrangement is shown in Fig. 7.10. The distance z between the array plane and recording plane may be of the order of the array dimension. The problem is processsling this information to derive certain features of the distribution in the array aperture.

7.3.2. Analytical Development

The field† f in the array plane is related to the field g in the recording plane via the Rayleigh diffraction formula:

$$g(x, y) = \int_{-b}^{b} \int_{-a}^{a} f(x_0, y_0)\, h_z(x_0, y_0, x, y)\, dx_0\, dy_0, \qquad (7.11)$$

where the diffraction transform kernel $h_z(x_0, y_0, x, y)$ is given by

$$h_z = -\frac{1}{2\pi} \frac{\partial}{\partial z}\left(\frac{e^{-jkr}}{r}\right), \quad r = \sqrt{\{(x - x_0)^2 + (y - y_0)^2 + z^2\}}$$

† It is assumed here that the field problem has been reduced to that of an equivalent scalar one. However, the method outlined here can also be extended to the vector case.

and k is the free-space wave number. In view of the difference form of h, eqn. (7.11) may be written as

$$g(x, y) = h(x, y) * f(x, y) \qquad (7.12)$$

where the symbol $*$ implies convolution.

A conventional approach to the inversion problem entails the conversion of (7.11) into a matrix equation, either by a discretization procedure or by the application of the moment method, and subsequent solution of the matrix equation for f by usual procedures. However, this is a very inefficient and time-consuming method when the array aperture is large in terms of wavelength. We describe below a procedure, essentially base on the principle of holography, that performs an approximate inversion of g by using the relationship

$$f(x, y) \simeq h_z^*(x, y) * g(x, y) \qquad (7.13)$$

where the super-asterisk implies conjugation. It is clear that, from the numerical point of view, the use of (7.13) is much to be preferred to the conventional method described above. Admittedly, however, (7.13) is approximate, since it only inverts a portion of the spectrum of f, specifically the visible part† of its spectrum. However, for large apertures, the information contained in this part of the spectrum is usually quite adequate. This will be illustrated in the following by considering the example of a phased-array aperture that is of the order of 30λ square.

In order to study the feasibility of such a method, it is often convenient to simulate the entire procedure, including the experimental data accumulation, on the computer. This will be done here also, i.e. the measured data $g(x, y)$ at z would be generated over a rectangular region in the recording plane for an assumed aperture distribution $f(x, y)$. We will then attempt to recover f by processing g. Rather than assuming that f is entirely arbitrary, it will be assumed instead that a certain percentage of elements are defective in the array aperture due to the presence of random phase errors. The location of these elements also will be assumed to be random. The problem, then, will be to recover the location of these defective elements.

7.3.3. Numerical Procedure

The numerical work comprises the following steps:

1. Simulation of the recorded field g over a rectangular region using (7.11) for an aperture distribution

$$f = f_0 + f_\varepsilon$$

where f_0 is the ideal, cophasal aperture distribution in the absence of any errors and f_ε represents the random phase error in the distribution.

2. Simulate the effect of measurement errors by introducing a bounded random error in g.

† The visible part of the spectrum of a function $p(x, y)$ is defined by the domain of $P(\xi, \eta)$ for $\xi^2 + \eta^2 \leq k^2$, where $P(\xi, n)$ is the Fourier transform of p defined by

$$P(\xi, \eta) = \mathfrak{F}[p(x, y)] = \int_{-\infty}^{\infty} \int_{-\infty}^{\infty} p(x, y) e^{-(j\xi x + j\eta y)} \, dx \, dy.$$

3. Compute the correct field g_0 from the known error-free aperture distribution f_0.
4. Form the error field $g_\varepsilon = g - g_0$.
5. Apply the approximate inversion formula (7.13) to obtain f_ε from g_ε.
6. Predict and plot the location of defective elements by locating regions in the aperture where $f_\varepsilon > T \cdot t(x, y)$, where T is a constant threshold level and $t(x, y)$ is a function that takes into account any amplitude taper present in the aperture distribution.

It is noted that the computation of both the simulated measured data g (step 1) and the inversion (step 5) involves a two-dimensional convolution operation entailing repeated computations of double integrals. Since this is very time-consuming, it is desirable to find a numerically efficient method for computing the convolution integrals. Fortunately, the use of the fast Fourier transform (FFT) algorithm allows one rapidly to evaluate these integrals. To use this technique for the calculation of g, one computes

$$F(\xi, \eta) = \mathscr{I}[f(x, y)], \quad H(\xi, \eta) = \mathscr{I}[h(x, y)],$$

forms the product of the transformed quantities, and finally evaluates the inverse FFT. If f and g are two-dimensional square arrays with N^2 complex values, the direct computation of the convolution integral requires N^4 operations (i.e. a multiplication and an addition). In contrast, the two FFT operations require $4N^2 \ln_2 N$ operation. Hence, the saving in time is proportional to $N^2/4 \ln_2 N$ operations where N^2 is the number of elements in the array. For example, if $N = 60$, the FFT method is approximately 150 times faster than the convolution method. Some details of the use of FFT for computing Fourier transforms of functions are given in Appendix B.

7.3.4. Numerical Results

For computational purposes, a 61×61 element, square $(a/\lambda = b/\lambda = 30.5)$ planar array with uniform $\lambda/2$ spacing was considered. The aperture distribution was assumed to have a gaussian amplitude taper $[t(x, y)]$ with a -20-db edge illumination. It may be useful to note that the effect of phase errors on the performance of an array is much less evident when the amplitude distribution is uniform, rather than tapered in the manner considered in the example here.

The undistorted far-field pattern of the tapered array is shown in Fig. 7.11 for broadside radiation. The main beam which has a width of $2.3°$ is not shown so that the sidelobe pattern which is at least 35 db down can be illustrated clearly. Also, for convenience of comparison, the peaks of all patterns would be normalized with respect to the peak of this error-free pattern. The maximum sidelobe level in decibels down from the peak will be inserted in the legend of each figure.

The random phase error $-\pi \le \phi \le \pi$ was introduced into 5 per cent (186) of the array elements at random locations. This was done by using a simple eight-statement subroutine† which provides a random number between 0 and 1 on each call. For example, the first two calls to the subroutine yield numbers r_1 and r_2 which randomly locate a defective element at

---

† This is the scientific subroutine program, RANDU, which is capable of generating 2^{29} uniform, distributed random numbers, between 0 and 1, before repetition.

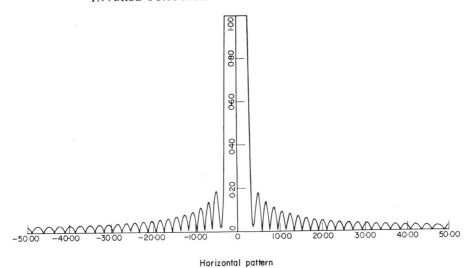

Horizontal pattern

FIG. 7.11. Sidelobe pattern of gaussian tapered array with −20 dB edge illumination.
Maximum sidelobe level −35.4 db down from peak.

row $N_r - r_1$ and column $N_c - r_2$. (N_r and N_c are the number of rows and columns in the array). The third call yields r_3 which affixed the random phase error by the expression $(2 \cdot r_3 - 1) \cdot \pi$. This sequence of calls was repeated 186 times to accomplish the introduction of the random phase errors mentioned above.

The resulting far-field pattern of the phase-spoiled array is shown in Fig. 7.12, where the maximum sidelobe level is seen to have risen to −31.5 db. For some applications, it is necessary to correct this increase in the sidelobe level of the array, and we will now consider the possibility of locating the defective elements in the array aperture.

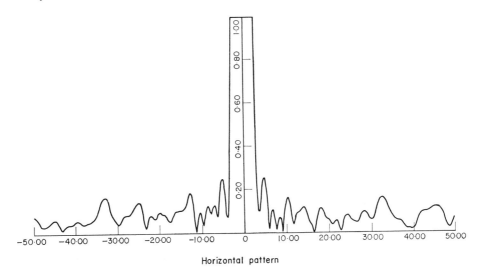

Horizontal pattern

FIG. 7.12. Sidelobe pattern of the array with 5 per cent defective elements.
Maximum sidelobe level −31.5 db.

Next, the distribution in the recording plane was computed for $z/\lambda = 30.5$ and for a square aperture equal in size to the array aperture. The computation was done by the FFT method.

No experimental measurement error was introduced in g for the first example. First g_ε and then f_ε were computed using the method outlined in the previous section. The threshold criterion was applied and the location of the error field where it exceeded $Tt\,(x, y)$ was plotted using a calcomp plotter. The choice of the threshold level T was based on the following equation:

$$T = |f_\varepsilon|_{\text{avg}} + c\,(|f_\varepsilon|_{\max} - |f_\varepsilon|_{\text{avg}}), \tag{7.14}$$

were the constant c, which is somewhat arbitrary, is chosen to vary the threshold level.

Choosing $c = 0.2$ in (7.14), 384 locations were predicted as defective of which 104 actually contained phase errors. The results are shown in Fig. 7.13, where the location of 186 defective elements (denoted by the symbol $\times$) and the 384 predicted locations ($\square$) are plotted in the array aperture. It should be pointed out that more of the correct elements could be predicted by lowering c; however, this procedure would also simultaneously predict more elements that do not actually have any phase errors.

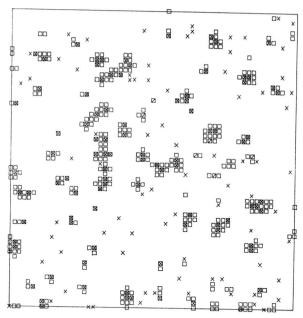

Fig. 7.13. Actual ($\times$) and predicted ($\square$) location of the defective elements with no measurement noise.

It should also be noted that the total number of predicted locations that have to be checked for defective elements is only about 10 per cent of the entire number of elements of which about 28 per cent were actually defective. Furthermore, the predicted locations are not scattered aimlessly over the aperture but are clustered around actual defective elements.

Table 7.1 gives the breakdown of the 104 correct predictions as a function of the four phase error ranges. It is evident that most of the more defective elements were found by the procedure. To evaluate how much the pattern is improved after these 104 elements are cor-

TABLE 7.1. DEFECTIVE ELEMENTS FOUND FOR VARIOUS COMPUTER-SIMULATED CASES

Phase error ranges	0–45°	45–90°	90–135°	135–180°	Total
No. of defective elements	34	58	44	50	186
No. found with 0% noise ($c = 0.2$)	6	21	35	42	104
No. found with 5% noise ($c = 6.2$)	4	24	35	42	105
No. found with 0% noise and two successive applications					
1st application ($c = 0.3$)	2	10	26	35	73
2nd application ($c = 0.4$)	4	29	16	9	58
Total found	6	39	42	44	131

rected, the far-field pattern was recomputed after correcting these elements. The pattern is shown in Fig. 7.14 where the sidelobe levels are down to -34.4 db.

Another example was computed where the computer-simulated measured data g were deteriorated by the presence of a 5 per cent measurement noise. This was done by modifying g by a multiplicative factor $(1 + 0.05r)$, where r is a random number in the range $(-1, 1)$.

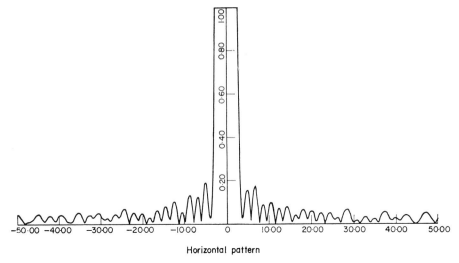

Horizontal pattern

FIG. 7.14. Sidelobe pattern of the array when the predicted defective elements are corrected. Maximum sidelobe level -34.4 db.

The random number r was generated by the subroutine IBM SSP RANDU. Again using the $c = 0.2$ in (7.4), 420 elements were now predicted of which 105 were actually defective, giving a prediction rate of 25 per cent. The phase-error prediction statistics for the noisy case are shown in Table 7.1, where they may be compared with the noise-free case.

The far-field pattern that results after correcting these 105 elements is shown in Fig. 7.15, where the sidelobe level is -34.2 db. So, a 5 per cent noise in the measurement data affects the prediction accuracy only very slightly.

The method could also be successfully applied to find more defective elements by repeating the above procedure.

366 R. MITTRA

While we have chosen to illustrate the aperture remote probing method by considering a specific example, the method itself is quite general. However, it should be reiterated that the holographic procedure for forming a real image by using the scattered field data is only

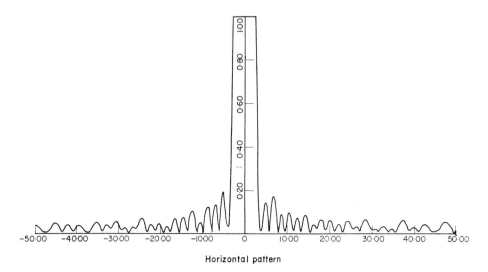

Horizontal pattern

FIG. 7.15. Sidelobe pattern of the array when the predicted defective elements in the 5 per cent noise case are corrected. Maximum sidelobe level −34.2 db from peak.

an approximate one, and the approximation gets poorer as the aperture and recording aperture get smaller in terms of wavelength. A modification of the inverse scattering procedure described in the last section may perhaps be utilized either when the aperture is not large in terms of wavelength or is nonplanar. However, the processing involved would then have to be much more complicated than the one presented in this section.

7.4. ANTENNA POWER PATTERN SYNTHESIS

7.4.1. Introduction and Description of Problem

An important problem in antenna theory is that of synthesizing an aperture distribution that will produce a specified radiation pattern. This problem has been extensively studied by a number of authors for the case where both the phase and amplitude distribution of the far-field pattern are specified. However, such a specification is unrealistic for the practical problem where only the magnitude of the radiation pattern is usually available as a design specification. Conventional methods of synthesis are no longer useful for the latter situation since they are based on linear analysis whereas the "magnitude only" specification calls for a nonlinear approach. The synthesis approach to be outlined in this section has been described by Imbriale *et al.* (1972) and is especially suitable for such nonlinear inverse problems. It is based on a parameter-optimization approach as discussed in Section 7.2; the parameter optimization approach will be discussed again in Section 7.5 along with the problem of remote probing of inhomogeneous media. Although the method outlined below would apply to the problem of synthesizing either discrete or continuous aperture distributions, we will only discuss the discrete case, i.e. that of synthesizing an array of line sources. Other examples of similar procedure may be found in Bojsen *et al.* (1971).

7.4.2. Formulation of Problem

The radiation pattern of a linear array of isotropic sources is given by

$$g(\phi) = \sum_{m=1}^{M} I_m \, e^{jx_m \sin \phi} \qquad (7.15)$$

where I_m is the mth element current distribution, x_m is the distance from the origin to the mth element measured in units of 2π times the number of wavelengths, and ϕ is the angle from broadside. The expression for the power pattern is conveniently derived from (7.15) by expanding $e^{jx_m \sin \phi}$ in a series of Bessel functions and multiplying the resulting expression by a similar representation of $g^*(\phi) = $ conjugate of $g(\phi)$. After some simplification, we arrive at the expression for the power pattern that reads

$$|g(\phi)|^2 = \sum_{n=0}^{\infty} a_n \cos n \left(\frac{\pi}{2} - \phi \right) \qquad (7.16)$$

with

$$a_n = \varepsilon_n j^n \left\{ \mathbf{I}^t A_n \mathbf{I} \right\}, \qquad (7.17)$$

$$\varepsilon_n = 1, \quad n = 0$$

$$= 2, \quad n > 0.$$

$\mathbf{I} = \{I_1, I_2, \ldots, I_n\}$ is the n-element current distribution vector, $J_n(x_i - x_j)$, with J_n the nth order Bessel function. From (7.17) we observe that the problem of synthesizing a given power pattern $|g(\phi)|^2$ is equivalent to synthesizing the coefficients a_n in (7.16) by adjusting the elements of the vector $\mathbf{I}$. It is evident from (7.17) that the relationship between a_n and I_n is nonlinear and hence the conventional matrix or other linear operator techniques are not useful for solving this problem.

An approach that is widely employed in systems theory for attacking such nonlinear problems is the parameter optimization approach.† Let us say that we choose some trial current vector $\mathbf{I}_t$ and a set of spacings x_m represented by the vector $\mathbf{x}_t$; the power pattern of the array for this choice of parameters is P_t. Let P_t be expressed in a representation similar to (7.16) as

$$P_t = \sum_{n=0}^{N} b_n \cos n \, (\pi/2 - \phi). \qquad (7.18)$$

Then we can define a performance index F as

$$F(\mathbf{I}_t, \mathbf{x}_t) = \sum_{n=0}^{N} (a_n - b_v)^2 \qquad (7.19)$$

† For some other applications to e.m. problems, see Sections 7.2 and 7.4.

which, if it can be made equal to zero, would insure that the power pattern P_t for $\mathbf{I} = \mathbf{I}_t$, $\mathbf{x} = \mathbf{x}_t$ agrees with the specified pattern at least to within N Fourier coefficients. Numerically F cannot be made identically equal to zero and its magnitude indicates how well the given pattern function has been synthesized.

Any of the parameter optimization algorithms, e.g. Rosenbrock's, Davidon's or the conjugate gradient method, may be employed for the minimization of F. Some details of these methods may be found in Appendix A.

7.4.3. Numerical Considerations

If array size is not specified, then the choice of N is based on the consideration of the number of the Fourier coefficients of P which are to be approximated. However, if there is a constraint on the maximum size of the array, then, for nonsupergain arrays, N is to be chosen in the following manner. If the maximum allowable array size is $L\ (= x_m - x_1)$, then all the Bessel function arguments in the A_n matrices are less than or equal to L. For n greater than L, the Bessel function asymptotically behaves as $(1/n)^{n+1/2}$ for large n and hence asymptotically approaches zero very rapidly. Thus, as seen from (7.18), to get a reasonable contribution to a_n's for large n, requires large currents $\mathbf{I}$, with accompanying supergain phenomenon. To avoid supergaining, it is necessary to put a bound on the I_n's and then, all the a_n's for some $n > N$ will be approximately zero. The number N is independent of $\mathbf{I}$ and $\mathbf{x}$ but is dependent on the array size L.

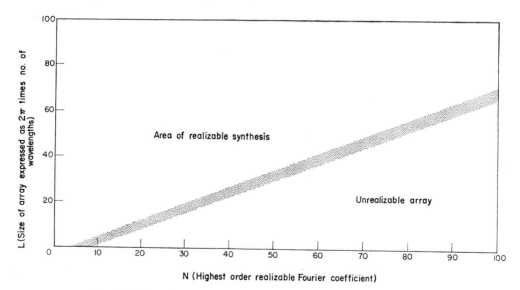

FIG. 7.16. Size of array vs. highest order realizable Fourier coefficient.

This result is graphically illustrated in Fig. 7.16, where the relationship between L, the normalized size of the array, and N, the highest order realizable Fourier coefficient, is shown divided into areas of realizable synthesis. It is noted that the transition region is essentially linear and is approximately given by $N = \alpha L$ with α somewhat greater than unity.

Even if there is no limitation on the number of elements N, it does not follow that the performance index F is continuously minimized by increasing N, provided the array size L remains fixed. Thus, it is not useful to increase N beyond the point after which F reaches a plateau. This is illustrated in Fig. 7.17 for a typical case in which $L = 18$ and it is seen that virtually little is gained by increasing N beyond 7 or so.

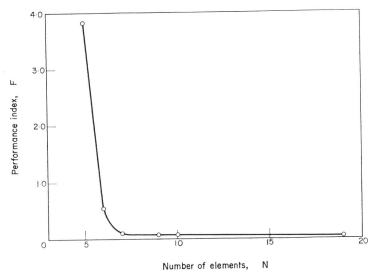

FIG. 7.17. Performance index vs. number of elements.

Another important consideration is the truncation of the summation in (7.16). It is an established fact that the far-field pattern of an antenna is an analytic function of $\sin \phi$, and hence, if the specified pattern does not satisfy the analyticity criterion, e.g. if it has discontinuities, then it cannot be synthesized with these discontinuities present in the pattern. However, in a practical situation, one can approach the desired pattern within a given design tolerance by including increasing number of terms in the Fourier series, which in turn usually requires a larger L.

7.4.4. Numerical Results

The first example to be considered is that of an exponential pattern with a 30° beamwidth between nulls and 15-db sidelobes. The specified pattern was approximated by a twenty-four term Fourier series and this approximate pattern was synthesized by a ten-element array with nonuniform spacing. The results are illustrated in Fig. 7.18. The solution exhibited is for $L = 21$ which falls in the area of realizable synthesis as shown in Fig. 7.16.

A second example considered is that of a discontinuous pattern, $\operatorname{cosec}^2 \phi$, which is non-vanishing for $15° < \phi < 75°$. This pattern was synthesized with a uniformly spaced array of seven elements with a constrained normalized length of 18. According to Fig. 7.16, the highest order Fourier coefficient that can be synthesized is $N = 32$. Figure 7.19 shows the thirty-two term Fourier series approximation and the resulting array pattern. By referring

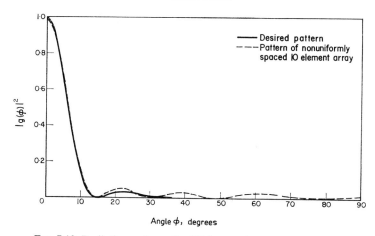

FIG. 7.18. Radiation patterns for 30° beam width and 15-db side lobes.

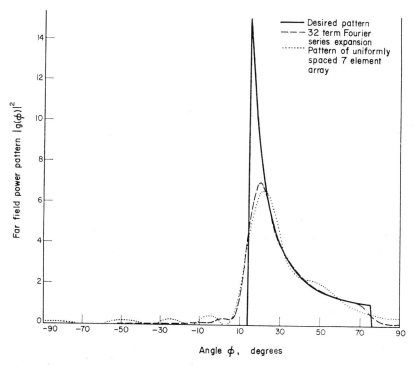

FIG. 7.19. Radiation patterns for CSC$^2(\phi)$ for $15° \leq \phi \leq 75°$.

to Fig. 7.17, which is plotted for this set of parameters, the number of elements was deter-mined to be 7. It is pertinent to mention that beyond a certain point, F is not only independent of the number of elements but it is also relatively invariant to an increase in L.

Finally, it may be useful to mention that the array design could also be broadbanded by allowing the frequency to be one of the parameters. A broadband design is achieved by minimizing with respect to normalized spacing $\mathbf{x}$ and current distribution vector $\mathbf{I}$ the *maximum* value of F with respect to frequency, i.e. minimizing the worst case. This is also referred to in the literature as the "minimax solution" to the problem. Figure 7.20 shows the envelope of the patterns obtained by designing a uniformly spaced seven-element array

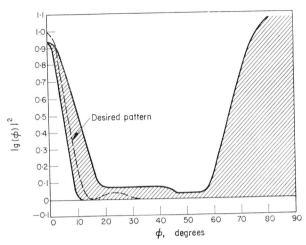

FIG. 7.20. Envelope of radiation patterns obtained by center frequency design.

for operation at the center frequency and then allowing the frequency to carry over a 2 to 1 range. The spacing vector $\mathbf{x}_0$ at the center frequency was chosen as follows: $\mathbf{x}_0^t = [-9.0, -7.0, -5.0, 0.0, 5.0, 7.0, 9.0]$ and the computer was programmed to seek the solution to the minimization problem $\mathbf{I}_{min}[f_{max}(\mathbf{x}_0, \mathbf{I}, f)]$. Figure 7.21 shows the improvement obtained by minimization with respect to frequency in the manner described above.

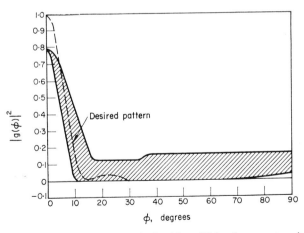

FIG. 7.21. Envelope of radiation patterns obtained by utilizing frequency variation in the design.

7.5. REMOTE PROBING OF INHOMOGENEOUS MEDIA

7.5.1. Introduction

In this section we consider some numerical aspects of the problem† of remote probing and diagnostics of inhomogeneous media whose properties vary as a function of a single dimension only. For an extensive collection of papers on the general topic of "Mathematics of Profile Inversion", the reader is referred to the proceedings of NASA Workshop (ed. Collin, 1972) on the same subject. The methods described below are based on a paper by Mittra and Schaubert (1972) appearing in the publication referenced above.

The problem to be investigated is posed as follows: given the scattering properties of the medium, find the function that describes the nonuniform nature of this medium. We will describe two approaches for attacking the problem, one of which is linear and the other non-linear. This might appear somewhat puzzling at first thought, since one might argue that, given the choice of a linear and a nonlinear approach for solving the same problem, one would obviously choose the former in preference to the latter. What we will demonstrate is that the linear approach described here, though analytically attractive, is not numerically viable. This is because it leads to results that are unstable to the point of what might be described as numerically catastrophic. On the other hand, the nonlinear approach, though perhaps not as elegant, yields rather good numerical solutions for a variety of inversion problems. The latter approach is based on the use of parameter optimization techniques that we have already come across several times in this chapter.

7.5.2. Linear Approach

Consider a plane wave incident on a medium, situated between the planes $z = 0$ and $z = 1$, whose refractive index is a continuous function of z in this range. Let the profile be described by a relative permittivity $\varkappa(z)$, $0 < z < 1$, which is independent of x and y. Let this medium be backed by a perfectly conducting plane located at $z = 1$, as shown in Fig. 7.22.

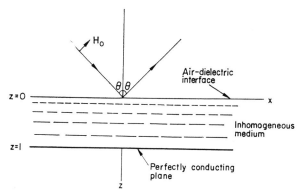

Fig. 7.22. Wave incident at an angle θ on a continuously varying nonuniform medium terminated by a perfect conductor.

† A ray optical approach to the problem has been discussed by Kharadly and Cullen (1967).

Assume that the electric field in the incident wave is polarized in the plane of the paper (y-direction). Then from Maxwell's equation, it is possible to arrive at the scalar wave equation for $\psi = E_y$ that reads

$$\frac{d^2\psi(z,\beta)}{dz^2} + [k^2\varkappa(z) - \beta^2]\,\psi(z,\beta) = 0, \quad 0 < z < 1, \tag{7.20}$$

subject to the boundary condition $\psi = 0$ at $z = 1$. The parameter β in (7.19) given by $k \sin\theta$, θ = angle of incidence of the sensing plane wave† (see Fig. 7.22). We now pose the problem: given the information on the reflection coefficient of the plane wave as a function of the incident angle θ, find $\varkappa(z)$ as a function of z.

A standard procedure of dealing with the partial difference equation of the type (7.20) is to convert it to an integral equation. To this end, define an auxiliary function ϕ via the equation

$$\frac{d^2\phi(z,\beta)}{dz^2} - \beta^2\phi(z,\beta) = 0, \tag{7.21}$$

$$\phi = 0, \quad \text{at} \quad z = 1.$$

Next, multiply (7.20) and (7.21) by ϕ and ψ, respectively, subtract the resulting equations, and integrate with respect to z from 0 to 1. This gives

$$\int_0^1 (\phi\psi'' - \psi\phi'')\,dz_0 + k^2\int_0^1 \varkappa(z_0)\,\psi(z_0,\beta)\,\phi(z_0,\beta)\,dz_0 = 0. \tag{7.22}$$

Integrating the first term on the left-hand side of (7.22) by parts, we get

$$[\phi(z_0,\beta)\,\psi'(z_0,\beta) - \psi(z_0,\beta)\,\phi'(z_0,\beta)]|_0^1 + k^2\int_0^1 \varkappa(z_0)\,\psi(z_0,\beta)\,\phi(z_0,\beta)\,dz = 0. \tag{7.23}$$

Recalling that both ψ and ϕ are zero at $z = 1$, we conclude that the contribution of the first term is zero at the upper limit. Recall also that both the incident plane-wave field and the reflection coefficient due to the plane wave are known for $z \leq 0$. If we now choose

$$\phi(z_0,\beta) = \sinh\beta(z_0 - 1) \tag{7.24}$$

as the solution of (7.21), the contribution of $(\phi\psi' - \psi\phi')$ at $z = 0$ becomes completely known. Let

$$-f(\beta) = (\phi\psi' - \psi\phi')|_{z_0=0} \tag{7.25}$$

be this known function. Then we may rewrite (7.23) as

$$k^2\int_0^1 \varkappa(z_0)\,\psi(z_0,\beta)\,\phi(z_0,\beta)\,dz_0 = f(\beta). \tag{7.26}$$

Equation (7.26) may be regarded as an integral equation for $\varkappa(z_0)$; however, it is different from conventional integral equations. The function that plays the role of the kernel of this

† If a confined source is used for sensing instead of the plane wave, it becomes convenient to interpret β as the wave number of the *spectral* plane wave in the z-direction.

integral equation, viz. $\psi(z_0, \beta)\,\phi(z_0, \beta)$, is not completely known, since, in view of (7.26), $\psi(z_0, \beta)$ is an implicit function of $\varkappa(z_0)$, and both are unknown in the range $0 < z_0 < 1$. To put it another way, (7.26) is a nonlinear equation for $\varkappa(z_0)$. We can, however, extract a linear equation from (7.26) by certain manipulations that are described below.

Regarding β and k as independent parameters in (7.20), we observe by comparison of (7.15) and (7.21) that, in the limit $k \to 0$, ψ tends to ϕ within, at most, a multiplicative factor which is a function of β only. We may choose this multiplicative factor equal to unity providing we suitably normalize the amplitude of the incident field as a function of β. Assuming that this is done, we proceed next to expand both ψ and f in (7.26) as a function of k in the neighborhood of $k = 0$. This procedure leads to the equation

$$k^2 \int_0^1 \varkappa(z_0)\,\phi^2(z_0, \beta)\,\mathrm{d}z_0 + k^3 \int_0^1 \varkappa(z_0)\,\psi^{(1)}(z_0, \beta)\,\phi(z_0, \beta)\,\mathrm{d}z_0 + \cdots$$

$$= f^{(0)}(\beta) + kf^{(1)}(\beta) + \frac{k^2}{2!}f^{(2)}(\beta) + \frac{k^3}{3!}f^{(3)}(\beta) + \cdots, \tag{7.27}$$

where the superscripts indicate orders of derivatives with respect to k, evaluated at $k = 0$.

Equating like powers of k up to k^2, in the two sides of (7.26) we get

$$f^{(0)}(\beta) = f^{(1)}(\beta) = 0 \tag{7.28}$$

and

$$\int_0^1 \varkappa(z_0)\,\phi^2(z_0, \beta) = f^{(2)}(\beta) \tag{7.29}$$

with

$$\phi(z_0, \beta) = \sinh \beta(z_0 - 1).$$

Equation (7.28) yields no new information since it merely expresses a condition satisfied by the known function $f(\beta)$. However, (7.29) is the desired linear integral equation for $\varkappa(z)$ since both the kernel $\phi^2(z_0, \beta)$ and the inhomogeneous terms are known in that equation. Thus, an inversion of (7.29) will lead to us the solution of our problem, the determination of $\varkappa(z_0)$.

However, a numerical study of (7.29) reveals that it is extremely ill-conditioned. It turns out, for instance, that to invert a reasonable profile, the error in the inhomogeneous term $f^{(2)}(\beta)$ must be less than 10^{-10}, which, of course, is absurdly impractical. The above behavior prompts us to ask the obvious question, "What is the cause of this?" The answer to this question is found by studying the behavior of the eigenvalues of the corresponding matrix equation obtained by discretization of (7.29) by the usual moment method. It is found that the eigenvalues have the behavior $\lambda_1 \sim 1$, $\lambda_2 \sim 10^{-2}$, $\lambda_3 \sim 10^{-4}$, $\lambda_4 \sim 10^{-6}$, $\lambda_5 \sim 10^{-10}$ etc. It is well known that the inverse of a matrix with an eigenvalue spectrum as given above is extremely unstable since an expansion of the solution to the matrix equation in terms of its eigenvectors shows that the nth term in such an expansion has a factor proportional to λ_n^{-1}. Thus, for ordinary measured data, which can be expected to have only a few percent accuracy, the use of the particular linearized approach described above leads to answers that are completely meaningless, and one might well describe the situation as a "numerical catastrophe".

However, there is an important property of the linear integral equation that we may exploit to advantage. A study of the linear equation leads to the proof that its solution of the inversion problem is unique, a result that is often difficult, if not impossible, to prove for a nonlinear equation.

For numerical purposes, we are forced to abandon the above linear approach, and seek a method of solution to the original nonlinear problem.

7.5.3. Parameter Optimization Method of Solution

As may be recalled from previous discussions on the use of parameter optimization methods, a first step in the application of the method is the introduction of a suitable performance index F which is a function of the unknown parameters to be determined. The solution to the problem is then obtained by seeking a minimum for F that is as close to zero as possible.

For the inversion problem, a convenient definition of F is given by

$$F = \sum_{m=1}^{M} \sum_{n=1}^{N} |(\psi_g [\beta_m, \omega_n, a_j] - \psi_t [\beta_m, \omega_n, a_{jt}])_{z=0}|^2$$

$$+ \sum_{m=1}^{M} \sum_{n=1}^{N} \left| \frac{\mathrm{d}}{\mathrm{d}z} (\psi_g [\beta_m, \omega_n, a_j] - \psi_t [\beta_m, \omega_n, a_{jt}])_{z=0} \right|^2 \qquad (7.30)$$

where a_j's, $j = 1, \ldots, J$ are the coefficients of the expansion of $\varkappa(z)$ in the range $0 < z < 1$, in terms of a suitable set of known functions. One convenient choice for these functions is z^n, in which event $\varkappa(z)$ is represented by

$$\varkappa(z) = \sum_{j=0}^{J} a_j z^j \qquad (7.31)$$

and the problem reduces to that of determining the a_j's from the knowledge of the incident and the reflected fields at the interface $z = 0$. The terms $\psi_g|_{z=0}$ and $\mathrm{d}\psi_g/\mathrm{d}z|_{z=0}$ in (7.30) are thus considered known from the measured data and our strategy is to adjust the trial parameter a_{jt} such that the square of the difference between the given and trial ψ of the interface added to the square of the difference of $\mathrm{d}\psi_g/\mathrm{d}z|_{z=0}$ and $\mathrm{d}\psi_t/\mathrm{d}z|_{z=0}$ results in a number that is less than a certain small number ε in magnitude. It should be pointed out that in writing (7.30), we have allowed ourselves the liberty of varying the angular frequency ω of the sensing plane wave in addition to its incident spectral angle β.

Once the performance index has been defined as in (7.30), we can attempt to minimize F by one of the parameter optimization schemes. There remains, however, the problem of determining ψ_t for a given choice of the set of a_{jt}'s which in turn characterize the trial profile $\varkappa_t(z)$ via (7.30). Since the fundamental equation satisfied by ψ is (7.20), it is necessary to solve this equation, with $\varkappa(z)$ replaced by $\varkappa_t(a)$, and with the boundary condition $\psi_t(z) = 0$ at $z = 1$. A convenient method of solving for ψ_t is to integrate (7.20) using the Runge–Kutta routine which is available in the IBM SSP package.

7.5.4. Numerical Considerations

The following numerical considerations arise in the parameter optimization method of profile inversion:

(1) GENERATION OF SIMULATED DATA

To test the validity of the method, it is convenient to simulate the measured data $\psi_g|_{z=0}$ and $d\psi/dz|_{z=0}$ by generating them on the computer. This is done by using the Runge–Kutta subroutine. The Runge–Kutta subroutine calls for an accuracy criterion which may be set somewhere in the neighborhood of 10^{-4}, thereby assuring results with good accuracy. Random noise † may then be added to these data to simulate measurement errors. The percentage of random noise may also be varied, say between 2 and 10 per cent.

(2) THE CHOICE OF ε, THE MINIMUM OF R

In the optimization schemes, the program may be terminated either after N iterations, or when the criterion $F \leq \varepsilon$ is reached. Clearly, the closer F gets to zero, the closer the performance of the trial medium is to that of the actual medium. However, it does not necessarily follow that the optimization method will always reach the true minimum if allowed to work sufficiently long. To put it another way, convergence to the true minimum ($F = 0$) is usually not guaranteed by the optimization methods except in special cases—e.g. when the performance index is truly quadratic. For most practical problems, one is at best assured of reaching a local minimum which may be tested for acceptance by checking if F is less than ε. For all of the examples of inversion profiles tested thus far, it has been possible to set $\varepsilon = 10^{-5}$, alth oughfor some profiles it has been possible to achieve values for ε as low asi $\sim 10^{-8}$. It should be reiterated, however, that there is no guarantee in the method that a tral set of iterations will definitely lead to the desired solution, though the experience so far has always been such that a successful termination of the program has been achieved for all of the profiles which have been numerically tested.

(3) ADDITIONAL CRITERION FOR SUCCESS OF INVERSION ALGORITHM

It is also necessary to test the success of the inversion program by comparing the response of the trial medium to the actual experimental (or computer simulated) data for the response of the actual medium. A solution is considered acceptable when these responses at individual values of ω_m and β_n agree to within a certain tolerance figure.

---

† This may be done in a manner similar to the one described in Section 7.3.

(4) CHOICE OF OPTIMIZATION METHOD

Both Rosenbrock's method and the conjugate gradient method have been tried for the minimization problem. As may be seen from the description of the conjugate gradient method (see Appendix A), the algorithm calls for both F as well as grad F. The gradient vector may be explicitly written as

$$(\text{grad } F)^t = \left\{ \frac{\partial F}{\partial a_1}, \frac{\partial F}{\partial a_2}, \ldots, \frac{\partial F}{\partial a_j} \right\},$$

where the superscript t implies transpose. Since, for a trial medium $\varkappa(z)$, ψ is computed only numerically via the Runge–Kutta routine, it is also necessary to compute the gradient vector numerically, using a numerical partial differentiation scheme. Thus, for each iteration step in the conjugate gradient method, the computer has to go through the Runge–Kutta routine n times more than in the Rosenbrock's scheme. For this reason the gradient method is usually more time-consuming in comparison to Rosenbrock's algorithm. However, numerical experience shows that the gradient method is relatively superior in terms of accuracies obtainable.

(5) CHOICE OF J IN (7.31)

In the optimization method, it does not necessarily follow that the increase in the number of terms employed for representing $\varkappa(z)$ in (7.31) will lead to increased accuracy of inversion. A choice of $J = 4$, i.e. a five-term expansion, was found to give answers for the inversion problem that did not change significantly in most cases studied when J was increased to 6. This is not meant to imply that the optimization methods are incapable of handling a larger number of parameters. In fact, for some forward scattering problems that have been studied by the optimal methods, as many as 200 or more variables have been optimized. However, since the minimum in the inversion problem is usually rather shallow, several different profiles may be found to give close-to-identical responses. It is necessary, then, to invoke some smoothness criterion based on some additional knowledge about the physical characterstics of the medium in order to accept one solution instead of the other. One way of enforcing the smoothness criterion is to limit J, the number of terms in the representation of $\varkappa_t(z)$.

(6) CHOICE OF FREQUENCY AND/OR INCIDENT ANGLE VARIATION

It is to be expected that the accuracy of the inversion program will increase with the increase in the number of points in the frequency and incident angle space at which we can match the responses of the actual and the trial media. However, after a good match has been obtained with the angle of incidence as the variable, significant improvement may not result by subsequently varying the frequency, unless the original choice of sensing frequency was outside of the favorable range, i.e. it was either too high or too low. The favorable range of the wave number k for most of the profiles studied was found to be $0.5 < k < 2.5$. However, this range may well be dependent on the nature of the variation in the profile being investigated.

TABLE 7.2. COMPARISON OF THE SCATTERED ψ AND $\partial\psi/\partial z$ FOR THE EXACT AND INVERTED PROFILES. $k = 1$ AND VARYING INCIDENT ANGLE

Incident angle in degrees	Amplitude of scattered ψ			Amplitude of scattered $\partial\psi/\partial z$		
	Exact	Rosenbrock's method	Conjugate gradients method	Exact	Rosenbrock's method	Conjugate gradients method
0	−0.5692	−0.5748	−0.5693	0.1308	0.1293	0.1313
30	−0.5998	−0.6057	−0.5999	0.2108	0.2099	0.2114
60	−0.6637	−0.6699	−0.6638	0.3831	0.3835	0.3837
90	−0.6969	−0.7034	−0.6970	0.4756	0.4766	0.4761

Exact profile $\varkappa(z) = e^{2z}$

	Rosenbrock's method	Conjugate gradients method
Inverted profile	$\varkappa(z) = 1.0 + 2.16z + 2.16z^2 + 0.58z^3 + 0.726z^4$	$\varkappa(z) = 1.0 + 2.07z - 1.64z^2 + 1.42z^3 + 1.3z^4$
Performance index	$F = 0.89 \times 10^{-5}$	$F = 0.136 \times 10^{-8}$
Execution time on FORTRAN compiler	40.11 sec	35.15 sec

TABLE 7.3. COMPARISON OF THE SCATTERED ψ AND $\partial\psi/\partial z$ FOR THE EXACT AND INVERTED PROFILES WITH 2 TO 10 PER CENT ADDED RANDOM NOISE TO SIMULATED DATA, $k = 1$ AND VARYING INCIDENT ANGLE

Incident angle in degrees	Amplitude of scattered ψ field		Amplitude of scattered $\partial\psi/\partial z$	
	Exact	Conjugate gradients method	Exact	Conjugate gradients method
0	−0.5692	−0.5584	0.1307	0.1209
30	−0.5999	−0.5887	0.2108	0.1998
60	−0.6638	−0.6518	0.3832	0.3696
90	−0.6970	−0.6847	0.4757	0.4607

Exact profile $\varkappa(z) = e^{2z}$

	Conjugate gradients method
Inverted profile	$\varkappa(z) = 1.0 + 2.11z + 1.68z^2 + 1.25z^3 + 1.02z^4 + 0.771z^5 + 0.594z^6$
Performance index	$F = 0.234 \times 10^{-1}$
Execution time on FORTRAN compiler	133.71 sec

TABLE 7.4. COMPARISON OF THE SCATTERED ψ AND $\partial\psi/\partial z$ FOR THE EXACT AND INVERTED PROFILES. $k = 1$ AND VARYING INCIDENT ANGLE

Incident angle in degrees	Amplitude of scattered ψ			Amplitude of scattered $\partial\psi/\partial z$		
	Given	Rosenbrock's method	Conjugate gradients method	Given	Rosenbrock's method	Conjugate gradients method
0	−0.7981	−0.7999	−0.7981	0.4654	0.4650	0.4653
30	−0.8351	−0.8370	−0.8351	0.5686	0.5683	0.5686
60	−0.9120	−0.9140	−0.9120	0.7892	0.7893	0.7892
90	−0.9520	−0.9540	−0.9520	0.9069	0.9062	0.9069

Exact profile $\varkappa(z) = e^{+0.5z}$

	Rosenbrock's method	Conjugate gradients method
Inverted profile	$\varkappa(z) = 1.0 + 0.591z$ $- 0.082z^3$	$\varkappa(z) = 1 + 0.495z + 0.134z^2 + 0.337z^3$ $+ 0.557z^4 - 0.162z^5 - 0.163z^6$
Performance index	$F = 0.67 \times 10^{-6}$	$F = 0.271 \times 10^{-9}$
Execution time using FORTRAN compiler	113.93 sec	62.54 sec

TABLE 7.5. COMPARISON OF THE SCATTERED ψ AND $\partial\psi/\partial z$ FOR THE EXACT AND INVERTED PROFILES. $k = 1$ AND VARYING INCIDENT ANGLE

Incident angle in degrees	Amplitude of scattered ψ			Amplitude of scattered $\partial\psi/\partial z$		
	Given	Rosenbrock's method	Conjugate gradients method	Given	Rosenbrock's method	Conjugate gradients method
0	−0.8043	−0.8047	−0.8042	0.4740	0.4736	0.4739
30	−0.8414	−0.8418	−0.8414	0.5778	0.5774	0.5778
60	−0.9187	−0.9191	−0.9187	0.7997	0.7994	0.7997
90	−0.9588	−0.9592	−0.9588	0.9180	0.9178	0.9180

Exact profile $\varkappa(z) = 1.0 + 0.5z$

	Rosenbrock's method	Conjugate gradients method
Inverted profile	$\varkappa(z) = 1.0 + 0.523z$ $- 0.07z^3$	$\varkappa(z) = 1.0 + 0.474z - 0.088z^2 - 0.006z^3$ $- 0.0342z^4 - 0.04z^5 - 0.04z^6$
Performance index	$F = 0.29 \times 10^{-5}$	$F = 0.49 \times 10^{-8}$
Execution time using FORTRAN compiler	31.49 sec	100.12 sec

TABLE 7.6. COMPARISON OF THE SCATTERED ψ AND $\partial\psi/\partial z$ FOR THE EXACT AND INVERTED PROFILES. $k = 1.0$, VARYING INCIDENT ANGLE

Incident angle in degrees	Amplitude of scattered ψ			Amplitude of the scattered $\partial\psi/\partial z$		
	Given	Rosenbrock's method	Conjugate gradients method	Given	Rosenbrock's method	Conjugate gradients method
0	−0.8630	−0.8552	−0.8627	0.5317	0.5382	0.5313
30	−0.9017	−0.8938	−0.9015	0.6410	0.6472	0.6408
60	−0.9822	−0.9741	−0.9823	0.8744	0.8800	0.8746
90	−1.024	−1.016	−1.024	0.9988	1.004	0.9992

Exact profile $\varkappa(z) = 1.0 + z \sin 2\pi z$

	Rosenbrock's method	Conjugate gradients method
Inverted profile	$\varkappa(z) = 1.0 + 0.158z + 0.962z^2$ $- 0.894z^3 - 1.98z^4$	$\varkappa(z) = 1.0 + 1.04z - 1.08z^2$ $- 1.1z^3 - 0.83z^4$
Performance index	$F = 0.99 \times 10^{-3}$	$F = 0.94 \times 10^{-6}$
Execution time using FORTRAN compiler	70.21 sec	85.55 sec

TABLE 7.7. COMPARISON OF THE SCATTERED ELECTRIC AND MAGNETIC FIELD AMPLITUDES FOR THE EXACT AND INVERTED PROFILES. $k = 1.0$, VARYING INCIDENT ANGLE

Incident angle in degrees	Amplitude of scattered ψ		Amplitude of scattered $\partial\psi/\partial z$	
	Given	Conjugate gradients method	Given	Conjugate gradients method
0	−0.7283	−0.7282	0.2864	0.2861
30	−0.7636	−0.7635	0.3821	0.3820
60	−0.8371	−0.8371	0.5874	0.5876
90	−0.8753	−0.8754	0.6971	0.6974

Exact profile $\varkappa(z) = 1 + \sin \pi z$

	Conjugate gradients method
Inverted profile	$\varkappa(z) = 1.0 + 3.06z - 0.823z^2 - 1.51z^3 - 1.47z^4$
Performance index	$F = 0.531 \times 10^{-6}$
Execution time using FORTRAN compiler	98.5 sec

7.5.5. Numerical Results

Computer experiments have been carried out for the following profiles:

(i) $\varkappa(z) = e^{2z}$;
(ii) $\varkappa(z) = e^{0.5z}$;
(iii) $\varkappa(z) = 1 + 0.5z$;
(iv) $\varkappa(z) = 1 + z \sin(2\pi z)$;
(v) $\varkappa(z) = 1 + \sin(\pi z)$.

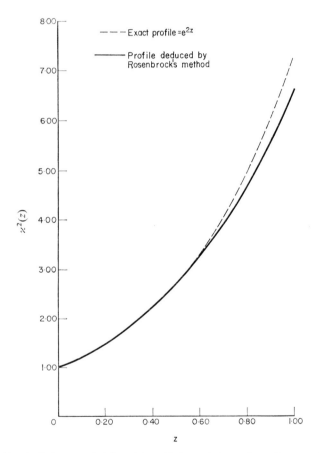

FIG. 7.23. Profile of relative permittivity $\varkappa(z) = e^{2z}$ for a slab terminated by a perfect conductor at $z = 1$. Conjugate gradients method.

The exact and the inverted profiles are shown in Figs. 7.23 through 7.30, and some pertinent data are presented in Tables 7.2 through 7.7. The results bear out the observations made in the previous section regarding the superior accuracy of the conjugate gradient method over Rosenbrock's at the cost of longer processing time for most cases. Comparison of Fig. 7.24 and 7.25 shows the relative insensitivity to the presence of noise in the measured data for a simple profile.

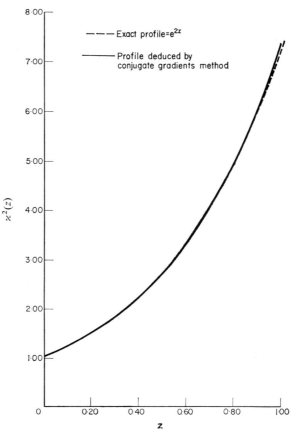

FIG. 7.24. Profile of relative permittivity $\varkappa(z) = e^{2z}$ for a slab terminated by a perfect conductor at $z = 1$. Rosenbrock's method.

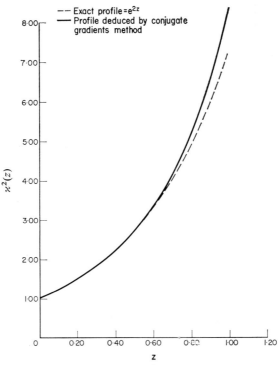

FIG.7.25. Profile of relative permittivity $\varkappa(z) = e^{2z}$ for a slab terminated by a perfect conductor at $z = 1$ with 10 per cent random noise added to the simulated data.

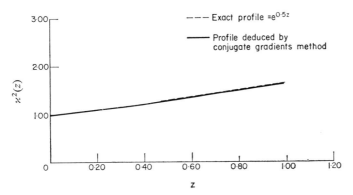

FIG. 7.26. Profile of dielectric constant $\varkappa(z) = e^{0.5z}$ for a slab terminated by a perfect conductor at $z = 1$. Conjugate gradients method.

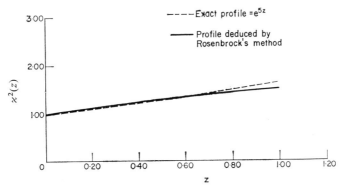

FIG. 7.27. Profile of relative permittivity $\varkappa(z) = e^{0.5z}$ for a slab terminated by a perfect conductor at $z = 1$. Rosenbrock's method.

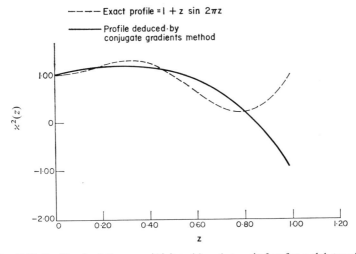

FIG. 7.28. Profile of relative permittivity $\varkappa(z) = 1 + z \sin 2\pi z$ for a slab terminated by a perfect conductor at $z = 1$. Conjugate gradients method.

Figures 7.28 and 7.29 show that a complicated profile which has several slope changes in $\varkappa(z)$ is difficult to invert. However, it is significant that the response of the inverted medium agrees quite closely with that of the actual medium (see Table 7.6). Thus, we conclude that the optimization method accomplished what it was required to do and that it has a tendency to smooth out the gyrations in the profile of the actual medium.

Finally, it should be mentioned that the medium described above is not restricted to continuously varying media but can be readily extended to the case of layered media. It could also be extended to other geometries such as cylindrical or spherical configurations. Useful results for some of these cases have in fact been obtained.

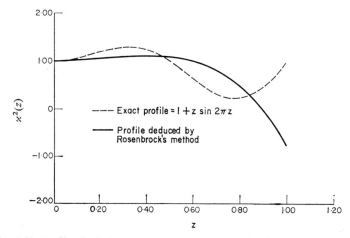

FIG. 7.29. Profile of relative permittivity $\varkappa(z) = 1 + z \sin 2\pi z$ for a slab terminated by a perfect conductor at $z = 1$. Rosenbrock's method.

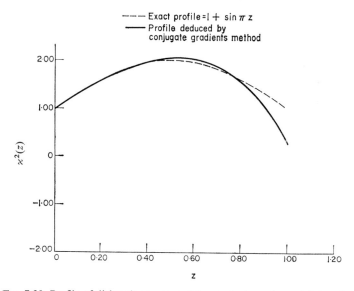

FIG. 7.30. Profile of dielectric constant $\varkappa(z) = 1 + \sin \pi z$ for a slab terminated by a perfect conductor at $z = 1$. Conjugate gradients method.

7.6. NUMERICAL ASPECTS OF WAVEFRONT RECONSTRUCTION USING MATRIX METHODS

7.6.1. Introduction

In Section 7.3 we were introduced to the "inverse problem" of reconstructing the field in the aperture of the antenna from the knowledge of its radiated field. A holographic method of solution was presented for the above problem in which a simple approximation was employed for the inverse of the kernel of the associated integral equation which takes the typical form

$$g(y) = \int_{-a}^{a} K(x, y) f(x) \, dx, \quad -b < y < b. \tag{7.32}$$

However, as pointed out in Section 7.3, such an approximate inversion is justified only when the aperture size and the size of the recording plane are both large compared to the wavelength. One is therefore forced to find a more accurate inverse of the kernel when the above-mentioned criterion on the size of the two planes is no longer satisfied. This is accomplished by converting the integral equation into a matrix equation via conventional methods, e.g. the method of moments. In principle, then, the solution is obtained by numerically inverting the resultant matrix. However, as indicated in the last section, this approach does not always lead to a stable solution; i.e. a slight amount of error in the data produces highly magnified perturbations in the solution when the inverse operator is unbounded.†

Before we proceed with the description of a technique which has been applied by Cabayan and Mittra (1973) for a class of unstable problems, we should remark that this type of problem arises not only in the wavefront reconstruction problem described above but also in connection with the processing of data obtained in a number of other remote probing experiments. It is therefore useful to investigate an equation of a slightly more general form than described by (7.32). Let us consider the equation

$$Tf = g \tag{7.33}$$

where the operator T and function g are known and the problem is to determine f from (7.33) by inverting T. We are particularly interested in the case where the problem is unstable, meaning that even if the difference between the exact field g and the recorded field g_v satisfies the inequality $\|g_v - g\| < v$, with v a small positive number, the inaccuracies in predicting f may be so large as to be unacceptable.

---

† An operator A is said to be bounded if a positive number M exists such that $\|A x\| \leq M \|x\|$ for all x in the domain of A. If such a positive number M does not exist, A is said to be unbounded. The symbol $\|h\|$ is to be interpreted as the norm of the function h defined in the L^2 sense, i.e. where

$$\|h\|^2 = \int_{-a}^{a} h(x) \, h^*(x) \, dx$$

h^* is the complex conjugate of h.

7.6.2. Analytical Background

The method of solution to be followed here is based on the concept of regularization due to Tihonov (1964). Let us introduce a functional

$$M(f, g_v; \alpha) = \|Tf - g_v\|^2 + \alpha W[f] \tag{7.34}$$

$$W[f] = C_0 \|f\|^2 + C_1 \|f'\|^2.$$

In (7.34) α is a positive number, henceforth referred to as the regularization parameter, which will perform a very important role in the discussion that follows. Also, the prime on the function f implies the derivative with respect to its argument and C_0, C_1 are positive constants.

At this point, we refer to a theorem by Tihonov (1964) where it is proven that, for every square integrable g_v, there exists a unique continuous, differentiable function $f_{\alpha v}$ which makes the functional M a minimum for a given choice of α and yields a stable solution for f. Note first that with $\alpha = 0$, and $g_v = g$, the minimum of M is identically equal to zero and is obtained only when f satisfies (7.33). That is, when the recorded g is noise free, the minimization of M as a function of f yields the exact solution to our problem. The motivation for the introduction of the term $\alpha W[f]^2$ in (7.34) is to suppress the highly oscillatory behavior that is present in the direct matrix inversion of f via (7.33) for the practical situation where not the exact g but only $g_v (= g + \text{noise})$ is available. These highly oscillatory solutions are physically unacceptable and hence we wish to enforce some bounds on the growth of f and f' in the process of extracing our solution.

Suppose now that the functional M is minimized for a given α when $f = f_{\alpha v}$ which makes the first variation of M equal to zero. Then, by differentiating the expression of M, we find that $f_{\alpha v}$ satisfies the equation

$$Lf_{\alpha v} = T^\dagger g_v \tag{7.35}$$

$$L = T^\dagger T + \alpha (C_0 I - C_1 D^2) \tag{7.36}$$

and $T^\dagger$ denotes the adjoint[†] operator of T, I the identity operator and D^2 the second derivative operator. We can formally write the solution of (7.35) as

$$f_{\alpha v} = L^{-1} T^\dagger g_v$$

$$= R_{\alpha v} g_v \tag{7.37}$$

[†] For an integral equation of the form (7.32) $T^\dagger$ is explicitly given by

$$T^\dagger g = \int_{-b}^{b} K^*(x, y) g(y) \, dy \tag{7.38}$$

where $K^* = $ complex conjugate of K. Also $T^\dagger T$ operating on a function f is interpreted as

$$T^\dagger T f = \int_{-a}^{a} p(x, x') f(x') \, dx' \tag{7.39}$$

with

$$p(x, x') = \int_{-b}^{b} K^*(x, y) K(x', y) \, dy. \tag{7.40}$$

and use it in place of the direct solution $T^{-1}g_v$ as the desired solution to the problem of inversion of practical data.

It has been shown in Cabayan and Mittra (1973) that for $C_0 = 1$, $C_1 = 0$

$$\|f_{\alpha v} - f_\alpha\| \leq v/(2\sqrt{\alpha}) \tag{7.41}$$

Also if $\|f_\alpha - f\| < \gamma$, then for $C_0 = 1$, $C_1 = 0$ and $v = 0$ (the last implies noise free measurements)

$$\gamma \leq \frac{\alpha}{\alpha + \lambda_N} \|f\| \tag{7.42a}$$

where λ_N is the largest eigenvalue of the operator $T^\dagger T$. For $\gamma \ll \|f\|$

$$\alpha \leq \lambda_N \gamma / \|f\| \tag{7.42b}$$

Equation (7.42) represents an upper bound for α. Note that to use this equation one needs to have an estimate of the norm of the solution $\|f\|$ as well as that of the error introduced by regularization (non-zero γ).

An upper bound on $\|f_{\alpha v} - f\|$ can also be calculated and is given by

$$\|f_{\alpha v} - f\| \leq \frac{v}{2\sqrt{\alpha}} + \frac{\alpha}{\alpha + \lambda_N} \|f\| \tag{7.43}$$

If one wishes to bound this error such that the norm of the difference between the regularized solution in the presence of measurement noise is less than μ then one can show (see Cabayan and Mittra, 1973, *loc. cit.*).

$$\alpha \geq \frac{1}{4} \left(\frac{v}{\mu - \gamma}\right)^2. \tag{7.44}$$

The inequality in (7.43) insures that $\|f_\alpha - f\| \leq v$ while (7.44) assures that $\|f_{\alpha v} - f\| \leq \mu$. These inequalities provide a rough estimate of α when deriving $f_{\alpha v}$.

In order to get a better appreciation of the relative advantage of using (7.37) over the conventional inversion procedure, it will be helpful to describe a numerical experiment carried out to illustrate this point.

7.6.3. Numerical Experiment

The numerical experiment described in this section proceeded as follows. The kernel $K(x, y)$ in (7.32) was assumed to be the Fourier transform kernel $e^{2\pi jxy}$. The object plane was taken to be two wavelengths long (i.e. $a = 1$) and the recording aperture was assumed to cover the whole visible region (i.e. $b = 1$). The uncorrupted recorded field g was numerically computed from (7.32) using a known test function f. The function f was sampled at N equally spaced intervals, and the triangle approximation (see, for instance, Ralston, 1965) was used to set up the quadrature matrix to approximate the integral operator T. The function g was also computed at M equally sampled points. Next, the measurement error was simulated by introducing gaussian random errors independently in the amplitude and the phase of g. Explicitly, the various pertinent quantities were calculated using

$$g = \int_{-1}^{+1} f(x)\, e^{2\pi j x y}\, dx, \quad -1 < y < +1,$$

$$\{\tilde{g}\} = \{g_1, \ldots, g_m, \ldots, g_M\},$$

$$\{\tilde{g}_v\} = \{g_{v1}, \ldots, g_{vm}, \ldots, g_{vM}\},$$

$$g_{vm} = g_m\, (1 + \eta_m)\, e^{j\pi\eta'}\eta'_m,$$

$$E(\eta_m) = \text{expected } \eta_m = 0,$$

$$E(\eta'_m) = 0,$$

$$E(\eta_m^2) = E(\eta_m'^2) = \eta^2.$$

The solution f was next constructed using (7.37) for the uncorrupted as well as the noisy field g and g_μ, respectively. Let these be referred to as f_α and $f_{\alpha v}$, respectively.

Next, the following parameters were defined:

$$\varepsilon_\alpha^2 = \|f_\alpha - f\|^2 / \|f\|^2, \tag{7.45}$$

$$\varepsilon_v^2 = \|f_{\alpha v} - f_\alpha\|^2 / \|f\|^2, \tag{7.46}$$

$$\varepsilon_t^2 = \|f_{\alpha v} - f\|^2 / \|f\|^2. \tag{7.47}$$

The interpretations of various error quantities are as follows. ε_α^2 is the normalized error introduced for the case of noise-free data due to the introduction of the finite regularization parameter. ε_v^2 is the normalized error representing the distance between the inverted f_α for the noise-free data and the actual $f_{\alpha v}$ obtained by inverting the noisy data g_{v1} where both f_α and $f_{\alpha v}$ are computed in the presence of the regularization parameter α. Finally, ε_t^2 represents the normalized error between $f_{\alpha v}$ and the exact f. These error parameters were calculated for each choice of α. The process was repeated for P sets of noise perturbations and the averages ε_v^2 and ε_t^2 were computed. The various quantities f, g, f_α, g_α, etc. and the errors defined above are symbolically displayed in Fig. 7.31.

A study of these errors as functions of α suggests a systematic procedure for choosing the regularization parameter α. This is shown in the next section where some numerical results are presented.

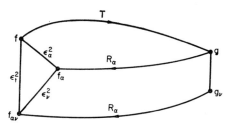

FIG. 7.31. Schematic representation and mathematical formulation of sources and fields, and various error quantities.

7.6.4. Numerical Results

The test function f chosen for this study and the corresponding g computed from (7.32) are shown in Fig. 7.32. N and M were chosen to be 21, i.e. the number of samples of f and g were both 21. The number of trials P for noise perturbation was chosen to be 25, and of these 25 trials, one representative f_{av} was chosen for the constructed field in the presence of measurement noise. To facilitate comparison, the reconstructed f_{av} is displayed in Figs. 7.33, 7.34, and 7.35 for these values of α along with the exact f. Also, the error quantities $\bar{\varepsilon}_{\alpha}^2$, $\bar{\varepsilon}_{v}^2$, $\bar{\varepsilon}_{t}^2$ are plotted in Fig. 7.36 as functions of α.

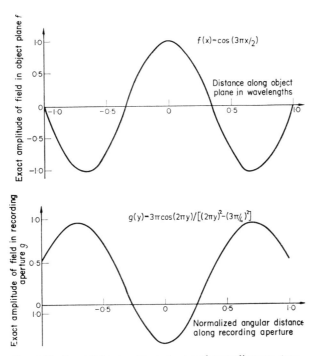

FIG. 7.32. Exact fields in object plane and recording aperture.

From Fig. 7.33 we note that for $\alpha = 0$, the solution is very oscillatory. This indicates that T^{-1} is unbounded and it is necessary to introduce regularization in order to extract meaningful solutions.

It is seen from Fig. 7.36 that the quality of reconstruction begins to improve as α is increased from zero, as evidenced by the reduction of both $\bar{\varepsilon}_{v}^2$ and $\bar{\varepsilon}_{t}^2$ until α reaches a value of the order of 10^{-3}. At the same time ε_{α} increases steadily as α is increased. This is to be expected, since in the absence of noise, the inverted solution f_{α} moves farther away from the exact solution f as α is increased. On the other hand, for the noisy situation we can readily appreciate the usefulness of the regularization procedure by reference to Fig. 7.36 where we see that for the practical noisy situation, the errors in the reconstructed field have precipitous growths with α when α is less than 10^{-4}.

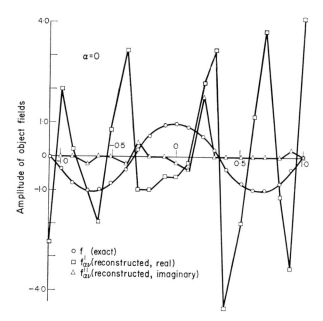

FIG. 7.33. Real and imaginary parts of reconstructed object field in the presence of 5 per cent measurement noise for $\alpha = 0$.

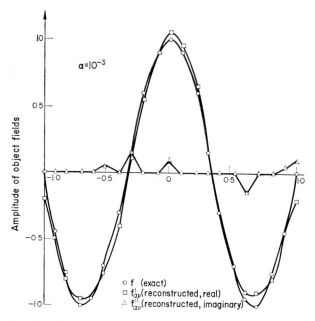

FIG. 7.34. Real and imaginary parts of reconstructed object field in the presence of 5 per cent measurement noise for $\alpha = 10^{-3}$.

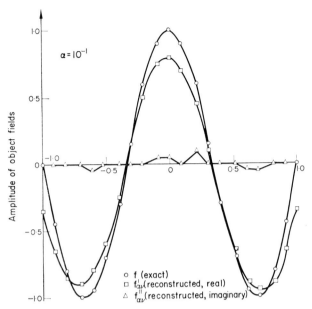

FIG. 7.35. Real and imaginary parts of reconstructed object field in the presence of 5 per cent measurement noise for $\alpha = 10^{-1}$.

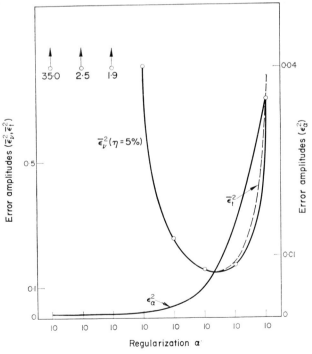

FIG. 7.36. Error parameters ε_α^2, $\bar{\varepsilon}_\nu^2$, and ε_t^2 vs. regularization α.

Note from Figs. 7.34, 7.35, and 7.36 that whereas a "little bit" of α is good, more of it is not necessarily better. A plateau is reached in the errors $\bar{\varepsilon}_v^2$ and $\bar{\varepsilon}_t^2$ somewhere in the neighborhood of $\alpha \simeq 10^{-3}$, beyond which the errors rise again. Correspondingly, the reconstructed f, which is quite close to the exact f for $\alpha = 10^{-3}$, begins to deviate from the exact solution for α above 10^{-2}. It should be noted, however, that whereas the error in $f_{\alpha v}$ is of highly oscillatory nature for very small α, a large value of the regularization parameter accentuates the smoothness in the reconstructed field. This oversmoothing is evidenced by a sharp rise in ε_α^2 which shows that substantial errors are introduced in the inversion even in the noise-free case when α is too large.

On the basis of the above observations, we may arrive at the following procedure for systematically choosing α. To check if the solution is ill-conditioned for a given g_v, we test the behavior of the inverted $f_{\alpha v}$ for a very small value of α. If this is the case, we increase α in small steps until the stable solution first emerges and then "settles down". As we continue to increase α, we find that $f_{\alpha v}$ becomes damped and oversmoothed. If we simultaneously monitor $g_{\alpha v} = Tf_{\alpha v}$, we find that increasing α beyond a certain point makes $g_{\alpha v}$ increasingly deviate from g_v. We know then that we have overregularized the solution and we retrace our steps toward reduced α until we find a value which gives us a good agreement between $g_{\alpha v}$ and g_v consistent with a stable $f_{\alpha v}$. The value of α satisfying the above criterion is then the desired value we are seeking.

Finally, the parameter α can be estimated *a priori* if the noise statistics of the measured data is known, or can be estimated from the data. For further details on this point the, reader is referred to Cabayan and Mittra (1973).

Appendix A

Optimization Methods

A number of different scientific subroutines are available for minimizing a function of several variables. A comprehensive discussion of the various analytical and numerical techniques upon which these subroutines are based may be found in an excellent text by Kowalik and Osborne (1968).

We will only outline very briefly the steps involved in three different optimization algorithms.

(a) ROSENBROCK'S ROTATING COORDINATE SYSTEM METHOD

Given a function $G(\mathbf{x})$, $\tilde{\mathbf{x}} = \{x_1, x_2, \ldots, x_n\}$ to be minimized, the steps are as follows:

1. Start with n orthogonal vectors $\xi_1, \xi_2, \ldots, \xi_n$ originating from an arbitrary point $\mathbf{p}$.
2. Form $\mathbf{p}_{old} = \lambda\xi_k^i = \mathbf{p}_{new}$, λ = arbitrary length, for each ξ_k.
3. If the move is a success, i.e. if $G(\mathbf{p}_{new}) \leq G(\mathbf{p}_{old})$, multiply λ by $\alpha > 1$. If the move is a failure, i.e. $G(\mathbf{p}_{new}) > G(\mathbf{p}_{old})$, multiply λ by $-\beta$, $0 < \beta < 1$.
4. Continue in this manner picking new points until a success is followed by a failure.
5. Repeat the procedure along ξ_{k+1} axis.
6. After all the axis directions are exhausted the search step is complete.
7. Let d_k to be the greatest successful search step size λ in the ξ_k direction. Then form vectors A_k defined by

$$\mathbf{A}_1 = d_1\xi_1 + d_2\xi_2 + d_3\xi_3 + \cdots + d_n\xi_m$$
$$\mathbf{A}_2 = \qquad\quad d_2\xi_2 + d_3\xi_3 + \cdots + d_n\xi_m$$
$$\vdots$$
$$\mathbf{A}_m = \qquad\qquad\qquad\qquad\qquad\quad d_r\xi_m.$$

8. Form new orthogonal unit vectors ξ_k as follows. Define

$$\mathbf{B}_1 = \mathbf{A}_1$$
$$\mathbf{B}_2 = \mathbf{A}_2 - \mathbf{A}_1 \cdot \langle \mathbf{A}_1, \mathbf{A}_2 \rangle / |\mathbf{A}_1|^2$$
$$\vdots$$
$$\mathbf{B}_m = \mathbf{B}_m - \sum_{j=1}^{m-1} \mathbf{A}_j \cdot \langle \mathbf{A}_n, \mathbf{A}_j \rangle / |\mathbf{A}_j|^2$$

then the m orthonormal vectors to be used in the next search step are

$$\xi_i = \mathbf{B}_1 \cdot \frac{1}{|\mathbf{B}_1|}, \quad \xi_2 = \mathbf{B}_2 \cdot \frac{1}{|\mathbf{B}_2|}, \quad \ldots, \quad \xi_m = \mathbf{B}_m \cdot \frac{1}{|\mathbf{B}_m|}$$

9. The search procedure comprising of steps 1 through 5 are repeated using the newly defined basis vectors.
10. Continue the entire procedure until the step distance d_k along the ξ_k is smaller than ε, a number selected *a priori* as a stopping criterion.

394 R. MITTRA

(b) STEEPEST DESCENT

1. Start with an initial assumption for the vector $\mathbf{x}$ say $\mathbf{x}_i$.
2. Compute the gradient vector, either analytically or numerically to find $\nabla G(\mathbf{x}_i) \equiv \mathbf{g}_i$.
3. Form $\mathbf{x}_{i+1} = \mathbf{x}_i - \lambda \mathbf{g}_i$, λ = step size.
4. Find λ_l from $\min_\lambda G(\mathbf{x}_{i+1}(\lambda))$.
5. Obtain new $\mathbf{x}_{i+1} = \mathbf{x}_i - \lambda_i \mathbf{g}_i$.
6. Replace $\mathbf{x}_{i+1}$ by $\mathbf{x}_i$ and return to 2.
7. Repeat process until either $G(\mathbf{x}_i) < \varepsilon_1$, or $\nabla G(\mathbf{x}_i) < \varepsilon_2$ or both. ε_1 and ε_2 are preselected stopping criteria.

(c) CONJUGATE GRADIENTS

1. Start with initial assumption $\mathbf{x}_i$.
2. Compute $\nabla G(\mathbf{x}_i) \equiv \mathbf{g}_i$.
3. Form $\mathbf{s}_i = -\mathbf{g}_i$; for $i = 0$,

$$\mathbf{s}_i = -\mathbf{g}_i + \frac{\tilde{\mathbf{g}}_i \mathbf{g}_i}{\tilde{\mathbf{g}}_{i-1}\mathbf{g}_{i-1}} \mathbf{s}_{i-1}; \quad \text{for } i > 0.$$

4. Form $\mathbf{x}_{i+1} = \mathbf{x}_i + \lambda \mathbf{s}_i$.
5. Find λ_i from $\lambda_{\min} G(\mathbf{x}_{i+1}(\lambda))$.
6. New $\mathbf{x}_{i+1} = \mathbf{x}_i + \lambda_i \mathbf{s}_i$.
7. Replace $\mathbf{x}_{i+1}$ by $\mathbf{x}_i$, return to 2 and repeat until stopping criteria are met by G, ∇G or both.

(d) DAVIDON'S METHOD

1. Start with initial $\mathbf{x}_i$.
2. Compute $\nabla G(\mathbf{x}_i) = \mathbf{g}_i$.
3. Form $\mathbf{s}_i = -\mathbf{g}_i$; for $i = 0$ $(H_{i-1} = I)$
   $= -H_{i-1}\mathbf{g}_i$; for $i > 0$.
4. Form $\mathbf{x}_{i+1} = \mathbf{x}_i + \lambda \mathbf{s}_i$.
5. Find λ_i from $\min_\lambda G(\mathbf{x}_{i+1}(\lambda))$.
6. New $\mathbf{x}_{i+1} = \mathbf{x}_i + \lambda_i \mathbf{s}_i$.
7. Compute $\mathbf{z}_i = \mathbf{g}_{i+1} - \mathbf{g}_i$.
8. Compute

$$H_i = H_{i-1} + \lambda_i \frac{\tilde{\mathbf{s}}\mathbf{s}}{\tilde{\mathbf{g}}_i H_{i-1}\mathbf{g}_i} - \frac{H_{i-1}\mathbf{z}_i\tilde{\mathbf{z}}_i H_{i-1}}{\tilde{\mathbf{z}}_i H_{i-1}\mathbf{z}_i}.$$

9. Replace $\mathbf{x}_{i+1}$ by $\mathbf{x}_i$, return to 2 and repeat until stopping criteria are met by G, ∇G or both.

Appendix B

THE USE OF THE FAST FOURIER TRANSFORM ALGORITHM

(Ransom and Deschamps, 1969; Cochran, 1967)

1. USE OF THE DFT

The continuous Fourier transform integral (CFT) in one dimension is

$$F(\xi) = \int dx \, \varepsilon^{j2\pi\xi x} f(x). \tag{7.48}$$

This integral can be numerically evaluated at N values of ξ by sampling the integrand at N values of x determined by one of the conventional quadrature formulas. All such formulas would require N^2 machine operations. However, due to the unique cyclic behavior of the Fourier transform kernel, the following formula is desirable

$$F_m \simeq \frac{1}{\sqrt{N}} \sum_{n=N/2}^{(N/2)-1} \varepsilon^{j2\pi(mn/N)} f_n; \quad -N/2 \le M < N/2 \tag{7.49}$$

where

$$f_n = f(ns) \quad \text{and} \quad F_m = F(m/T). \tag{7.50}$$

The range of sampling on x, T, and the period of sampling, s, are related by

$$N = T/s. \tag{7.51}$$

Equation (7.49) is known at the discrete Fourier transform (DFT) formula. The primary advantage of the DFT formula over other quadrature formulas is that there exist an algorithm which if $N = 2^p$, p and integer, evaluates the DFT in $2N \ln_2 N$ machine operations rather than the N^2 operations required by direct evaluation. The savings in time can become enormous for even modest values of $N (\sim 10^4)$. The term "fast Fourier transform" (FFT) is used to denote the DFT formula when evaluated by the fast algorithm.

In order for the DFT (right side of (7.49)) closely to approximate sampled values of $F(\xi)$ (left side of (7.49)) requires a judicious choice of values for T and s that is not obvious. Assume the function $f(x)$ has support limited to the range a, and its transform is essentially band limited to the range b. That is

$$f(x) = 0, \quad |x| > a, \quad \text{and} \quad F(\xi) \simeq 0, \quad |\xi| > b.$$

Then to use the DFT;
  (a) Choose $s < 1/b$ to minimize the aliasing error which is due to sampling f (i.e. makes right side of (7.49) $\simeq$ left side).
  (b) Choose $T > a$ to ensure ability to obtain $F(\xi)$ from F_n. According to sampling theorem this can always be accomplished by filtering. But for T sufficiently greater than a, $F(\xi)$ is obtainable from F_n by direct interpolation.
  (c) Set $N = T/s = 2$, p an integer.

395

(d) Sample $f(x)$ at $x = ns$, $-N/2 \le n < N/2$ to get f_n.

(e) Use FFT (7.49) to compute F_m, $-N/2 \le m < N/2$.

(f) Interpolate between F_m to get $F(\xi)$.

2. USE OF THE FFT ALGORITHM

There are numerous versions of the FFT algorithm. One of the shortest and simplest of these is by Ransom and is available from the computer program bank of the Antenna Laboratory of the University of Illinois. The subroutine call parameters are X, N, IFS where X is the name of the complex array (f_n above), N is the number of complex elements in X ($= 2^p$). IFS is set to $+1$ when Fourier analysis (see (7.49)) is desired and -1 when synthesis (inverse of 2) is desired. The algorithm assumes that the real parts of the elements of X are stored in the odd-numbered locations and the imaginary parts in the even numbered ones. For example, if

$$X = \begin{bmatrix} x_1' + jx_1'' \\ x_2' + jx_2'' \\ x_3' + jx_3'' \end{bmatrix}$$

the algorithm require that X be arranged as

$$X = \begin{bmatrix} x_1' \\ x_1'' \\ x_2' \\ x_2'' \\ x_3' \\ x_3'' \end{bmatrix}$$

The original X array (f_n) is overwritten during computation and the Fourier transform (F_m) is returned in X.

3. TWO-DIMENSIONAL FFT

A short companion program (FORT 2D) is also available from the program bank mentioned above. It calls FORT 4 in such a manner as to evaluate the two-dimensional Fourier transform. In particular, the 2D-DFT formula is

$$F_{pq} = \frac{1}{\sqrt{(MN)}} \sum_{n=-N/2}^{N/2-1} \sum_{m=-M/2}^{M/2-1} \varepsilon^{j2\pi(mp/M + nq/N)} f_{mn}, \qquad \begin{array}{l} -M/2 \le p < M/2, \\ -N/2 \le q < N/2, \end{array} \tag{7.52}$$

which can be decomposed into two sequential transforms. First the transform of the columns of f_{mn}.

$$f_{pn} = \frac{1}{\sqrt{M}} \sum_{m=-M/2}^{M/2-1} \varepsilon^{j2\pi(mp/M)} f_{mn}, \qquad \begin{array}{l} -M/2 \le p < M/2, \\ -N/2 < n < N/2. \end{array} \tag{7.53}$$

Secondly the transform of the rows of f_{pn}

$$F_{pq} = \frac{1}{\sqrt{N}} \sum_{n=-N/2}^{N/2-1} \varepsilon^{\mathrm{j}2\pi(np/N)} f_{pn}, \qquad \begin{array}{l} -N/2 \le n < N/2, \\ -M/2 \le p < M/2. \end{array} \tag{7.54}$$

Subroutines FORT 2D is merely a short bookkeeping program which applies subroutine FORT 4 to the proper column or row of the 2D array. The number of machine operations for the 2D-FFT is $4N^2 \ln_2 N$ as opposed to N^4 for DFT.

REFERENCES

BOJSEN, J.H., JACOBSEN, H.S., NILSSON, E. and ANDERSEN, J.B. (1971) Maximum gain of the Yagi–Uda arrays, *Electronics Letters 7*, no. 18, 531–2.

CABAYAN, H.S. and MITTRA, R. (1973) Numerical aspect of wavefront reconstruction (to appear).

COCHRAN, W. (1967) The fast Fourier transform, *Proc. IEEE 55*, 1664–74.

COLLIN, L., Ed. (1972) Mathematics of profile inversion, *NASA Workshop Proceedings* (in press).

IMBRIALE, W.A. and MITTRA, R (1970), The two-dimensional inverse scattering problem, *IEEE AP-18* no. 5, 633-42.

IMBRIALE, W.A., HELLER, J., MITTRA, R. and CRUZ, J.B. (1972) Pattern synthesis of linear arrays using Fourier coefficient matching, *Radio Science*, Vol. 7, No. 7, 757–62.

KHARADLY, M.M.Z. and CULLEN, A.D. (1967) Oblique incidence millimeter wave plasma diagnostics, *Proc. IEE (London) 114*, no 8, 1035–44.

KOWALIK and OSBORNE (1968) *Methods for Unconstrained Optimization Problem*, American Elsevier, New York.

LEWIS, R.M. (1969) Physical optics inverse diffraction, *IEEE T-AP AP-17*, no. 3, 308–14.

MITTRA, R. and SCHAUBERT, D. (1972) Techniques for remote probing of inhomogeneous media, appearing in *Mathematics of Profile Inversion*, L.Collin, ed. *(loc. cit.)*.

RALSTON, A. (1965) *A First Course in Numerical Analysis*, McGraw Hill, New York.

RANSOM, P.L. and DESCHAMPS, G.A. (1969) The diffraction transformation of electromagnetic fields between two parallel planes, Antenna Laboratory, University of Illinois, Tech. Report No. 69-8.

RANSOM, P.L. and MITTRA, R. (1971) A method for locating defective elements in large phased arrays, *Proc. IEEE 59*, No. 6, 1029–30.

TIHONOV, A.N. (1964) Regularization of Incorrectly Posed Problems, *Soviet Math. Dokl.*, **5**, 835.

INDEX

399